Darkening the
Italian Screen

Darkening the Italian Screen

Interviews with Genre and Exploitation Directors Who Debuted in the 1950s and 1960s

EUGENIO ERCOLANI

McFarland & Company, Inc., Publishers
Jefferson, North Carolina

LIBRARY OF CONGRESS CATALOGUING-IN-PUBLICATION DATA

Names: Ercolani, Eugenio, 1984– author.
Title: Darkening the Italian screen : interviews with genre and exploitation directors who debuted in the 1950s and 1960s / Eugenio Ercolani.
Description: Jefferson, North Carolina : McFarland & Company, Inc., publishers, 2019 | Includes bibliographical references and index.
Identifiers: LCCN 2019027210 | ISBN 9781476667386 (paperback: acid free paper) ∞
ISBN 9781476635385 (ebook)
Subjects: LCSH: Motion pictures—Italy—History—20th century. | Motion picture producers and directors—Italy—Interviews.
Classification: LCC PN1993.5.I88 E73 2019 | DDC 791.430945—dc23
LC record available at https://lccn.loc.gov/2019027210

BRITISH LIBRARY CATALOGUING DATA ARE AVAILABLE

ISBN (print) 978-1-4766-6738-6
ISBN (ebook) 978-1-4766-3538-5

© 2019 Eugenio David Ercolani. All rights reserved

No part of this book may be reproduced or transmitted in any form or by any means, electronic or mechanical, including photocopying or recording, or by any information storage and retrieval system, without permission in writing from the publisher.

Front cover: Artwork from the Italian poster of the 1968 film *L'assassino ha le mani pulite (Deadly Inheritance)*

Printed in the United States of America

McFarland & Company, Inc., Publishers
Box 611, Jefferson, North Carolina 28640
www.mcfarlandpub.com

This book is dedicated to my country, a glorious, contradictory, frustrating, addictive hellhole I deeply love. May it one day find a way out of the cultural and political swamp it has plummeted into and may this book be a reminder that we Italians have been, and remain, a nation of good-for-nothings that are capable of anything, even miracles at times.

I also want to dedicate this work to Costanza, always my "zucca," and to my lovely and patient parents that I will forever be indebted to. Finally to Ripley that yawned at, cuddled up and slept through many of the films mentioned in this book.

Table of Contents

Preface		1
1953	A Touch of Class: The Cinema of Giorgio Capitani	7
1958	Armed to the Teeth: The Cinema of Umberto Lenzi	21
	Giovanni Lombardo Radice, a.k.a. John Morghen, on Cannibal Ferox	57
1959	Melancholy and Revolution: The Cinema of Giulio Petroni	65
1961	Jazzing from the Background: The Cinema of Alberto De Martino	89
1961	The Bitter and the Sweet: The Cinema of Romolo Guerrieri	109
1962	Lovable Slobs: The Cinema of Mario Caiano (Interview by Manlio Gomarasca)	126
1967	Call Me François: The Cinema of Franco Rossetti	135
1967	Destruction in Slow Motion: The Cinema of Enzo G. Castellari	155
	From Uruguay with Love: Interview with George Hilton	176
1968	The Serious Caress of Frivolousness: The Cinema of Vittorio Sindoni	188
1968	Real Cannibals: The Cinema of Ruggero Deodato	199
	Italy's Whipping Boy: Interview with Giovanni Lombardo Radice	232
1969	Of Films and Horses: The Cinema of Marcello Avallone	245
1969	Strange Vices in Locked Rooms: The Cinema of Sergio Martino	261
	Designing Mayhem: Interview with Massimo Antonello Geleng	285
	The Origins of EX: Interview with Martine Brochard	292
Chapter Notes		297
Index		305

Preface

One of the first observations I heard on the Italian cinema industry, delivered to me with a smirk of bitter irony by writer-director Franco Rossetti, was a comparison to the hierarchies of Ancient Egypt: "When people talk about how great Italian cinema was, they are usually referring to the magnificence of the pyramids, to the beauty and power of the pharaohs but rarely do we hear words as benevolent for the slaves who made it all possible. Poor devils like myself." We can imagine it as a world of slaves and emperors, or one of "imaginative mercenaries" as Gianni Martucci defines his breed of directors, or even "an industry of proletariats and noblemen" as Marcello Avallone would have it, adding, of course, we "genre directors being part of the first category."

The countless definitions and images chosen by the directors interviewed for this book, whether self-pitying or spoken with the utmost solemnity, all describe a world made up of imbalances and faulty, untrustworthy weights and measures. Descriptions that bring to mind a legend, the one behind the creation of the Arena of Verona. Although many have been the myths surrounding the monument, only one really stands out, dating back to the Middle Ages: A Veronese gentleman sentenced to death for a bloody crime, in the hope of being pardoned, makes a pact with Satan the night before his execution. Satan promises to build the massive structure during the course of that night in exchange for the man's immortal soul; an arena that could contain each and every inhabitant of the city and that could be used as an artistic outlet for everyone. All the devils and demons surfaced from Hell and gathered in Verona to perform this immense feat and all night they worked. But during those hours, the man repents and his prayers for mercy are heard from above; and so the light of day is brought forward two hours ahead of time, forcing the devils to abandon their work. The arena is abandoned at an advanced stage, incomplete, thus saving the man's soul, who will also be forgiven in light of the impressive gift. Ripping away the religious parable of this myth, what remains is a perfect metaphor to describe the feelings of many of the directors included in this book. An enduring monument, solid and majestic, the backbone of an entire country's industry and one of the most crucial vertebrae of the continent's film world, blessed from above but built from the bottom up by generations of filmmakers never helped or pampered by critics.

As much as it has become widely used, it is important to explicate, in this context, the definition of the term "genre cinema." It is a label that groups diverse types of films, all of which have in common an easily accessible filmic language and use of strong narrative and visual elements, whether they be of comic, violent, horrific or sexual derivation. The term is often used as a synonym for "exploitation" or "B movies" and is usually adopted with a derogatory meaning. Films ascribable to this category usually have to follow the rules that administrate and are expected by the genre or sub-genre they are tied to. The expression has often been used in opposition to that of "auteur" or "committed" cinema or even "arthouse," those words referring to a cinema in which a greater attention to content and quality is expected. If this viewpoint may be considered simplistic, it could have been a comprehensible one, if it were not that the term, in Italy, has historically been adopted simply to categorize whatever film does not fit a certain politicized idea of what "high art" should be. Ruggero Deodato: "It is not the 'how' but the 'what' that makes a film a genre one in this country. When a director makes an action film, it is low entertainment but when another director makes a film on a struggling factory worker, it is art. What the director is actually trying to say is secondary. What is important is the perception people have of the film."

If we had to find a straightforward formula that encloses and explains the birth and rise of Italian popular cinema, this would probably be it: making a virtue out of necessity. From the early 1950s, everything that emerged from what has been labeled as genre cinema finds a reason to exist in a simple, wonderfully immediate word: necessity. The incredible amount of genres, sub-genres, currents, crossovers and the way they have overlapped, died out or killed each other off over the decades; the different soils from which production companies germinated—from pirate-like underground markets all the way up to collaborations with huge Hollywood majors; the subsequent fan base that proliferated around this cinema and the blindly obsessive, non-selective nature of the wave of revaluation that came upon us in post–Tarantino years: all this is the fruit of necessity, in post-war years, to contain and control the invasion of U.S. products and at the same time satisfy the new demand that the American industry had created in Italy. The incredibly ambitious aim to snatch a slice of the market from American clutches, especially in the fifties, can be described easily as a silent battle worthy of David and Goliath. Different producers and directors, together with a government interested in restoring a strong Italian industrial and cultural independence, came together to conquer, segment by segment, what seemed to be becoming an exclusively American monopolized market. So necessity and the subsequent struggle for space steered the Italian film world through a rapid Darwinian-like evolution in order to survive. Realizing that they were asked to compensate for the lack of money and substantial investments, camera operators, directors of photography, costume designers, special effects technicians, screenwriters and all the figures that make up the filmic milieu, had to refine and put to use the knowledge, both cultural and practical, accumulated over previous and more prolific decades. Let us not forget that until a few years before the end of the war, Italy had continued to be a cinematically industrious nation also because of Benito Mussolini's belief that cinema was the strongest of all the propaganda machines available, a weapon capable of forging more effectively the minds of the population. So creativeness had to be put to use in the attempt to decode the genres that were being imported, opening them up, dissecting them, understanding what made them work, the elements that were more appealing to the public. In doing so, new narrative interpretations and stylistic elaborations were found that in time revolutionized some genres, unhinging them from the inside. A whole spectrum of colors and flavors reinterpreted and rethought in an ever-growing and chaotic country, one that would live with contrived guilt the success of its most popular and derivative strains. According to the Collins Dictionary, one of the most common definitions of the word "spectrum" is as follows: "a range of different colors which is produced when light passes through a glass prism or through a drop of water. Also a broad range of varied but related ideas or objects, the individual features of which tend to overlap so as to form a continuous series or sequence." What is Italian genre cinema if not this, a rich "sequence" which becomes the logbook not only of a country's political, cultural and social evolution but a blueprint to fully understand the dynamics of Western cinema as a whole and how it shaped the customs, mores and values of its countries.

Reality is the result of multitudes and its truth is never fruit of a single point of view. It is only in the overlapping of perspectives, in the confusion of contradictions, in the ambiguous nature of opinions, in the proliferation of voices that we can hope to find the essence of what we are looking at. Paraphrasing a notable aphorism on the codification of beauty made by Horace, nothing remains true from every single angle. In this simple yet indispensable reasoning, lies the sense and objectives of this book you are holding in your hands. Not everything you will read in these pages is the truth but no lies are contained within. An accumulation of viewpoints, naïve, unilateral or simplistic at times, maybe tainted by personal needs or regrets, by the desire to adjust or cover-up; others more cryptic and complex, perhaps motivated by the wish to mythicize or demonstrate. Nonetheless, what I hope emerges is something close to a truthful and exhaustive portrait of what the world of Italian popular or genre cinema was and how it mutated as the decades passed by, from its first spasms of life in the immediate post–World War II era up to the decadence of the mid- to late-eighties.

Every chapter, personality interviewed, and anecdote told is tied to one another by a long thin thread, like the consequentiality of ever-growing brush strokes on a blank canvas. Various directors are presented in chronological order, on the basis of their debut behind the camera. Some are similar in approach, others diametrically opposed, yet all are branded by fire with the same mark: one that made them distinguishable and recognizable as "genre directors," a term which, when used by many of the film critics of the time, was synonymous with exploitation mongers or with "trash" or "B movies." The list of names that make up this book may appear, at a first and superficial glance, as random choices, selected without strong parameters of judgment, but actually each director fulfills a specific function, both fundamental and complementary in the creation of a huge collage, as far-reaching as it is colorful.

Artistic paths that started out with the boldest of ambitions or on the threshold of the most violent of crisis, so characterized by the most disheartening of compromises; directors from all corners of the film business, ones that had been cinematographers, editors, theater directors, script writers; prolific ones and others with only a couple of titles to their credit; directors that helped forge new currents and others that made them what they are; directors born in the living rooms of the Roman intelligentsia while others matured in the trenches of the most adventurous guerrilla "everything goes" filmmaking. Some were driven by strong political beliefs, others were self-proclaimed mercenaries for hire. Each one, in describing his unique career, helps unhinge those of his colleagues.

This is a collage of recurring techniques and names, of producers' modus operandi and requests, of bandits and martyrs, of the scandals and turmoil which bind and tie them together in a market in which, for some time at least, they could coexist and proliferate. Though probably, having to use a pictorial or figurative metaphor to describe the outcome of this multiplying of perspectives, "psycho-geographic décollage" would be more appropriate. In fact, it is in the current created by Italian artist Mimmo Rotella where we can find the result of the coming together of all these different directors: his is the technique of the layering and ripping of posters, mostly ads. The strategic "vandalizing" by Rotella deforms the chosen image, though never destroying it, while revealing the outlines of what it is hiding underneath, adding and enriching it with new meanings and implications. This is true of the functioning of the industry with its loopholes and trappings as much as for the alternations of the filmic phenomena, the juxtaposition of genres and the metamorphosis they went through over the decades but especially with regards to all those individuals who could not be in this book. In fact, to the personalities interviewed we should add a number of polarizing names that animated the industry: Lucio Fulci, Riccardo Freda, Mario Bava, Sergio and Bruno Corbucci, Walter Chiari, Italo Zingarelli, Barbara Steele, Ferdinando Baldi, Helmut Berger and Antonio Margheriti are among the most talked about. Each personal consideration of the protagonists interviewed for this book, who have intertwined careers with theirs, each slice of gossip and indiscretion, every anecdote slides in adding, sometimes clashing, always enriching the previous one, creating pungent portraits. And somewhere along the road dowels find place in the structure and maybe something not too dissimilar to the truth starts seeping through.

I write all this moreover, in the hope of convincing those who have bought this book to discover it from its first chapter and continue from there. Do not be taken aback by those names that do not resonate in your memory; those are the ones that might surprise you the most. Each chapter is dedicated to a different director and is structured as follows: a quote from one of their films, an introduction, the interview and finally, in some cases, a second interview with an actor or a close collaborator of the chapter's protagonist. All the interviews with the directors are "career interviews," ones that try and include as much as possible, that touch all the turning points and high notes, the beginnings and endings. In the shapes and directions the interviews assume—exactly like the introductions that precede them, and the further supplementary interviews and essays that follow them—nothing fits into a prefixed pattern. There is no repeated set of questions, and just like Rotella's ripping of layers of posters, you never know, and should not know, how big the piece of paper ripped away is going to be and what will end up surfacing. Although a certain harmony and coherence will hopefully be found, in part thanks to the fact that each testimony within this book has been collected by myself, with the exception of Mario Caiano's words, captured instead by Manlio Gomarasca.

Regarding the introductions of the various chapters, some are analyses on specific areas of a director's career, some are more traditionally monographic, while some concentrate on the historical period the filmmaker was born into. This approach was chosen on the basis of what is most known about their body of work and what still lies undiscovered. Most of the introductions are interspersed with quotes and thoughts of directors addressed in other chapters to underline and further the connections and, most importantly, the similar views shared on the faults of the industry, its distinctive elements and finally, its demise.

A stylistic note: The first time an Italian film (or other foreign-language film) gets mentioned in a chapter, its English title is included in parentheses or brackets along with its date of release. The subsequent times the film gets mentioned, within each chapter, the English title is used. Many of the films mentioned in this book were never distributed in English-speaking territories; in those cases, "translation" is used before the English title upon its first mention.

Preface

I would like to thank and acknowledge the assistance, guidance and valuable suggestions of the following people: Camillo Affinita, Ada Lubrano, Giuliano Emanuele, Marica Croce, Carlotta Ercolani, Augusto Caminito, Daniel Zerbini, Domenico Monetti, Gian Giacomo Petrone (who wrote four of the chapter introductions), my lovely parents Silvia Petroni and Giampaolo Ercolani, and then Roberto Girometti, Alessandra Lenzi and Piero Parisi, Caterina Rossetti, Mark Thompson Ashworth, Manlio Gomarasca, Chiara Pani, Roberto Curti, Alessio Di Rocco, Luca Rea, Stefano Lo Parco, Francesco Massaccesi, Simone De Renzo, Marcus Alexander Stieglegger, Alex Wank, Phillip Escott, Simona Tartaglia, Andreas Bethmann, and all the directors who let themselves be interviewed for this book.

1953 A Touch of Class
The Cinema of Giorgio Capitani

"Domitilla! How dare you?! Who taught you these things?!"
"Mom."
"That's wonderful."—Enrico Montesano and Letizia D'Adderio in *Lobster for Breakfast*, 1979

"By 1946 the war had been over for a year. Italian cinema was starting to show the first spasms of life once again and my dream of working in films had not diminished. It never had since, as a small child, my grandmother, in Paris—where I was born—used to take me to the cinema." Giorgio Capitani (29 December 1927, Paris–15 March 2017, Viterbo) took his first steps, artistically speaking, in exciting yet confusing times, in which Italian cinema was going through a frenzied reconstruction. During the last years of World War II, Italy had experienced massive losses and what had previously been one of Europe's leading film industries had dissolved completely, leaving little trace of its past. Amidst this bleak scenario, there was a strong desire for rebirth which, in 1944, led to the creation of ANICA,[1] an association that tried to bring together the interests of producers, distributors and cinema owners, and by 25 April 1945, the National Liberation Committee[2] was trying to restore the democratic freedom that had fallen short during the fascist era. These first fundamental achievements created the possibility to progressively re-establish production and by the end of the year, 28 Italian films were produced. From the birth of the Republic in 1946 to the beginning of the 1950s, Italy's reborn film industry was able to produce 104 films. This growth was facilitated by new assistance policies created by the government and aimed at ensuring industrial stability. During these tumultuous years, Capitani did everything, starting at an incredibly early age: he worked as an AD, a script supervisor, and then as a second unit director but was also active as a writer and from the early fifties became a dubbing director as well. Vittorio Cottafavi, Gianni Franciolini, Giorgio Pastina, Mario Bonnard, Mario Costa but also Vittorio De Sica, Anna Magnani and Mario Soldati: Capitani crossed paths with many of the main players of the time.

"My first recollection of a big screen goes back to the very early thirties. What I believe I saw was Oscar Apfel's *Aida*. When the lights came back on, my grandmother told me that I shouldn't be afraid of what I had just seen because it was all fake, a lie, all make-believe. I only remember being completely exhilarated and captivated, electrified by that wonderful, shining lie." Giorgio Capitani, even after nearly six decades of filmmaking, still speaks about his trade and passion with poetic contemplation and a genuine sense of youthful fascination. Maybe it is this forging purity that has made Capitani the survivor he is, and has been, over the years. In fact, none of the multiple hiccups or crises that have notoriously characterized Italian cinema seems to have affected him in any way. Even the biggest of breakdowns did not stop his career and, even more surprisingly, did not slow down his prolificacy. This is one of the reasons he remains somewhat of an anomaly in Italian cinema and his career, even now, seems to create something close to a short-circuit when the most traditional and institutional spheres of Italian film criticism try to summarize and define his body of work. Capitani is one of a very small number of directors who has tried to make non-politicized, light, sophisticated comedies. To be able to understand what this means exactly, it is important to realize that in Italy a big distinction is made between comedies and "film comici" (literally, comic films). Films that fell into this second category were considered, in their Italian definition, broad and characterized by physical and action-based humor. They were perceived as scatological and not worthy of particular attention, mainly because their only sense of purpose was low-brow laughs. With the exception of a handful of titles in the eighties (between 1981 and 1987), which he directed with complete detachment and little love, Capitani has mostly done comedies but with none of the perceived redeeming elements typically associated with the "commedia all'italiana"[3]: no political or social commentary, very little use of dialects, no strong comedic interpretations of regional habits and clichés (something which is strongly identifiable in Italian cinema as a whole). Nonetheless, Capitani was able to attract and polarize the attention of big producers like Carlo Ponti and Silvio Clementelli and consequentially work with the likes of Vittorio Gassman, Sophia Loren and Marcello Mastroianni. In other words, with the cream of the crop of the "commedia all'italiana"—a branch of Italian comedy that came with a set of "rules" Capitani was not willing to stick to, and the results are quite evident.

Portrait of Giorgio Capitani, early 2000s (courtesy Giorgio Capitani).

Capitani, title after title, compromise after compromise, experiments within the parameters dictated by Italian comedy, looking for something new. A cinema that, while keeping its feet firmly on Italian soil, looks at the sophisticated American approach, in a balance between the stylistic simplicity of a Gene Saks and the elegant buffooneries of Blake Edwards (the best example being *The Party*, 1968). A cinema that has a social conscience but devoid of any class snobbery and is able to appeal to the largest audience possible, without giving in to populist vulgarities. The result being that in reviewing his films, critics over the years have often used words like "innocuous" or "tame." The lack of a political backbone to support his films, plus Capitani's willingness to compromise with the market's needs has ensured that he has never been considered an "auteur," but at the same time the quality of his work has been too above average to be ignored. So, like others, Capitani continues to fluctuate in a limbo. His best work in the genre are the films featuring Enrico Montesano, often produced by Fulvio Lucisano, who was as interested as Capitani in finding a new stylistic approach to comedy. Considering all these aspects it should not be surprising that Hollywood, at one point, took notice of Capitani's work. But that said, what may indeed come as a surprise and add another layer of contradiction to this director, is discovering which of his films he prefers the most, because comedy isn't the only thing Capitani has to offer. Among the roughly 23 films he has directed for the big screen we can find illustrious exceptions to the genre to which he is most associated.

As soon as I enter Giorgio Capitani's house in the historical center of Viterbo, an ancient town an hour from Rome, a small dog and two cats hurry to greet me—during the following hours I will spot another four felines roaming around the impeccably clean and sunny two-story flat—as his wife, Simona Tartaglia, a well-known casting director, holds the door open, smiling. "Giorgio is waiting for you. I was just preparing coffee." I find Capitani sitting in the white living room, his slender legs crossed as he looks out of the huge window a few meters away. He strokes his perfectly trimmed moustache with his thumb as he holds one of those long slim cigarettes between his index and middle fingers while with his other hand he distractedly but slowly plays with a silver lighter. It won't take long for me to discover he is a chain smoker. As soon as he sees me he removes the cigarette from his thin lips and rests it on a heavy-looking crystal-type ashtray in front of him. "Hello. Shall we get started immediately?" he says with smiling, courteous eyes. I haven't even finished sinking into the massive armchair beside his when he starts talking. "You know I only recently had an epiphany. I'm nearly ninety but I still ask myself questions...." He interrupts himself and looks at me, properly for the first time. He takes his pack of cigarettes out of his jacket pocket. "Want one?" he asks.

"No thanks. I have mine. What was the epiphany?"

"Well, I used to ask myself why comedic actors are much more insufferable and irritable than normal ones and only recently have I given myself an answer. The reason is that dramatic actors, if they make a film that doesn't do well or a comedy that doesn't quite work, if they flop at the box office, they are not considered responsible, or at least, they aren't considered the decisive factor, the sole reason for the failure. Justifications tend to be found: 'the script doesn't work,' 'the genre isn't the right one for him,' 'the director wasn't able to value his role,' etc. But when a comic actor's film isn't funny, he is the only one that gets blamed. This is the reason they are always wound-up so tight. They feel the weight of the whole film on their shoulders, even more so than the director. It's a fairly simple deduction but I have only come to realize this in recent times. Maybe, if I had understood this earlier, I wouldn't have fought so much with Enrico Montesano. Comedians are prisoners of their own doing, of their own personas. People expect them to be funny all the time, even off-camera, so they live under the constant pressure of fitting the audience's perception of them and inevitably this pressure becomes intolerable. In a way, comedians are very tragic figures."

Well, it's funny you should say this because your career has been full of such figures. You are one of the quintessential Italian comedy directors.

Well, personally I didn't start off as director wanting or thinking of doing comedies. I wanted to do *La grande illusion* [1937] by Renoir, to direct the kind of films that had convinced me to become a director in the first place. Comedy, the idea of comedy, entered my career when I was given the script for *Ercole, Sansone, Maciste e Ursus gli invincibili* [*Samson and His Mighty Challenge*, 1964]. I was pissed off by the quality of the films I was being offered and this one was no exception. I mean, for goodness sake, they were handing me these God-awful scripts. So I had no intention of doing this film and I was ready to throw it in the bin. "Look what kind of rubbish they have the courage to offer me. I won't do it." I needed the work but, at the time, I was still an idealist. I remember, we were at the beach in Sperlonga, and my wife asked to read the script. When I came out of the water I found her giggling to herself and asked her why. "There is very little to laugh about," I told her. "I disagree," she said. "Try reading it again, as a comedy." I did and realized she was right. It somehow worked, so I called the producer and told him I wanted to rewrite the script. "OK, but it has to be only 25 percent comedy." Don't you love how a producer's mind works? The film turned out to be a massive success and in the early nineties the Australians used it for a film of theirs. Do you know this story? There is this Australian film [*Hercules Returns* by David Parker, 1993] about a small cinema owner who buys a European B-movie because it's the only one he can afford, only to discover that it's not dubbed or subtitled so they have to do it quickly before the premiere. The cheap film he buys is mine, *Samson*. When I was contacted by the Australian producers they were worried I would be angry or offended but I was more than happy to know they had chosen my film. It was a comedy in the first place, I told them. So this is how I got into comedies. I guess that after the success of the film I was perceived as a comedy director, so those were the films I was offered.

Going back to your origins, according to many sources your first experience as a 1st AD was on **Guglielmo Tell** *[William Tell, 1949]. Is this true?*

My first film was *Lo sconosciuto di San Marino* [*The Unknown Men of San Marino*, 1948]. I was hired, initially, as a script supervisor but, truth be told, I wasn't any good at it. It's a hard job, you must always be concentrating and I just didn't have it in me. We were in San Marino, it was just after the war and there was very little public transport. The country was still in shambles and the 1st AD of the film fell sick so I was picked in a hurry to take his place. Vittorio Cottafavi took me under his wing. I learned a lot from him. Actually, the two directors that I owe the most to are Cottafavi and Gianni Franciolini.

There has been some speculation about who directed **The Unknown Men of San Marino.** *Officially the film was directed by Michał Waszyński and Cottafavi was the second unit director.*

I never felt that I was Waszyński's AD. I would get my directions only from Cottafavi. Waszyński was kind of the … how can I put it … the artistic director. He would oversee things but didn't really deal with the nuts and bolts of the film. He suffered from a very severe case of diabetes and some days wouldn't even come on the set. The same goes for *William Tell*, which you mentioned before. The real director on that was Giorgio Pastina, who, if I remember correctly, is credited as a unit director. Anyway, Waszyński's general health was not good. I don't recall much else about him except that he was very open about his homosexuality and always kept an eye out for handsome young men.

What kind of person was Cottafavi?

He was a true director but an unlucky one. He didn't enjoy the films he did. All those peplums,[4] he would direct them with rage in his eyes. Even if the "Cahier du

Cinéma" was always very generous with him, he wasn't happy but nonetheless, he was a real director. He is the one who gave me my first shot as a writer with *La fiamma che non si spegne* [translation: *The Flame That Can't Be Extinguished*, 1949] together with Siro Angeli, who was a very well-respected writer of that period. Angeli and I became a writing duo in the following years, working mostly for Cottafavi.

What do you remember of Teseo contro il Minotauro [The Minotaur, the Wild Beast of Crete, 1960]?

I was the second unit director on *The Minotaur*. The script required some underwater scenes and before being hired, the production asked me if I had any diving experience. I answered that of course I had, which naturally wasn't true. I immediately rushed over to see the brother-in-law of a girl I was going out with. He was a diving instructor and in a week I learned as much as I could. Plus, I had a fake underwater photographer always by my side. He was a friend of this instructor and his job was to keep an eye out for me and make sure I stayed alive. One of the scenes I directed was with a bunch of nymphs swimming around and they were wearing these thin golden bras that wouldn't stay in place. So at one point, one of the girls, an American, got fed up. She took hers off and threw it away so I shot the scene without bras. That was one of the very first times, in Italian cinema, you got a quick glance at a pair of bare tits. Not many people know this but the film was started by Mario Bonnard and then picked up by Silvio Amadio. I think it was one of Amadio's first films, if not his very first.

Bonnard was an important figure in Italian cinema, especially before the war. What kind of person was he?

Mario Bonnard, an old man at that point, was convinced he was very talented. According to others he wasn't that great, but he was sure of being very, very good. He was the quintessential 1930s director who grew up in the silent film era. He didn't talk much with the actors, if at all, and would usually concentrate more on the geography and composition of the scene. He was always impeccably dressed with these big hats and long, white coats. He was a homosexual and a bit of dandy, a funny man but I wasn't interested in his approach and the kind of director he represented. I perceived him as a surpassed figure.

You said Bonnard didn't really pay much attention to the acting. Would you say this was a common trait among Italian directors?

A film is based on two elements: one is the script, the story, and the other one is the acting. The biggest defect of Italian directors was—and things haven't changed—a lack of care for the actors and their portrayals. Most directors have never acted, never put themselves in front of the camera. I, on the other hand, started out as a theater actor. I studied at the C.U.T, the Centro Universitario di Teatro [University Drama Center] with Marcello Mastroianni and Gabriele Ferzetti, among others, and that's where my passion for acting started. For example, when I was working with Cottafavi, I would go to him and tell him my impressions and he would accept them. I mean, he accepted the fact I would make suggestions. He might not have always followed them but he would listen and most of what I had to say was related to the acting. "I think he is trying too hard." "Maybe she should try to deliver the line looking over there..." etc. One episode I can mention that came as a big surprise to Cottafavi and was kind of a revelation for me was on the set of *The Flame That Can't Be Extinguished*. There was a scene in which Maria Denis finds out that Leonardo Cortese had died in the war. I said that it couldn't be done with her acting all desperate and crying. You know, with a close-up. Maria Denis was a lovely woman, very attractive and sweet, but she wasn't exactly a great actress and I felt that a big, melodramatic scene with her wouldn't have turned out well. I went to Cottafavi and said: "How about this: she gets the news of his death, she turns around, slowly walks down the corridor towards the bedroom. The camera stays on her back. She enters the room, closes the door and the camera stops and stays on the closed door." These sort of things mean taking care of the acting, knowing when it's better to suggest rather than show. By the way, thinking back, I believe that was the moment my collaboration with Cottafavi really began.

La notte è fatta per ... rubare *[translation:* The Night Is Made for ... Stealing, *1967]* is the first comedy to really have the Capitani touch.

It was my first real attempt at making the comedic elements more sophisticated. The director I love the most is Billy Wilder. Wilder and Frank Capra. Theirs is the approach I was looking for. Stories told with sophistication, charm and elegance. I did my best. That said, one of the biggest regrets of my career is connected with this film. Previously, I had made for Silvio Clementelli—an arrogant but intelligent man—the comedy *Che notte, ragazzi!* [translation: *What a Night!* 1966], an Italian-Spanish co-production with Marisa Mell and Philippe Leroy that did very well. So together with *The Night Is Made for ... Stealing* I had two big successes under my belt. I had even more decision-making clout and I was attracting attention. Carol Levi, the Italian manager of the William Morris agency, had sent my film to Max Setton, who was the managing director of Columbia Pictures at the time, in an attempt to get work for a couple of actors in the film. Setton didn't care for them but was very interested in the director. So I went to the States, met with him and signed a contract for three films in three years. The first script I was given was called "Once Upon a Crime," a lovely comedy written by Ronald Harwood. Fred Astaire, who was going to play the villain, and Paula Prentiss were already on board. So we started looking for a lead who was supposed to play this British lord type. I had set my mind on James Fox, whom I had seen in *The Servant* [1963] by Joseph Losey and thought would've been perfect. Setton wasn't convinced and wanted an American to play the part. He called me up one morning and said: "I got an appointment for you tomorrow for breakfast with an actor I'm sure you'll like." I went to the meeting at this restaurant, with the executive producer and as soon as I saw this guy, I had a heart attack. I thought to myself, "How can Setton see this guy playing a sophisticated and elegant gentleman?" He was blond, his cheeks were severely pockmarked and he had a kind of a smug grin on his

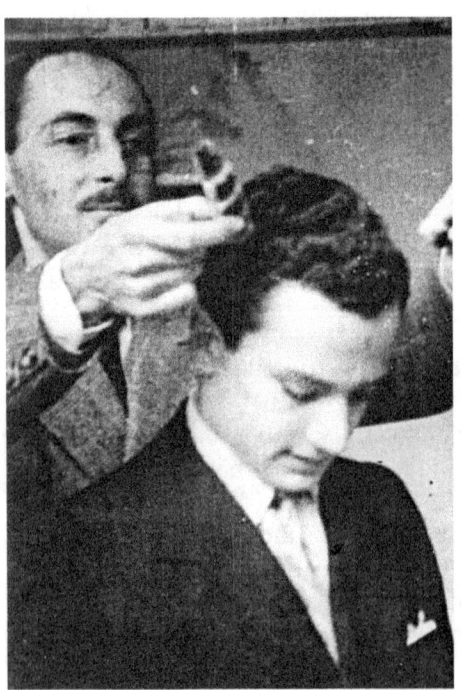

Capitani in front of director and mentor Vittorio Cottafavi. "It's funny how directors would be so elegant on set. Blazers and ties, while now it's T-shirts and shorts" (courtesy Giorgio Capitani).

face. I told him the story in the worst possible way because I wanted him to say no and, in fact, he was not impressed and just said he would think about it. When I called Setton to tell him how it went I said, "Max, we are looking for a baronet not a cowboy." He answered that it was a shame. "He has only done commercials and one film as a protagonist but I feel this Robert Redford will have a future." The only film he had done, the one Setton referred to, was *Barefoot in the Park* [1967].

What happened after? Why wasn't the film made?
When Setton was fired from Columbia Pictures, all the projects which he had greenlit were chucked and that meant all the films I was working on. There was even a Fred Zinnemann film that didn't get made because of Setton being sacked. I still got paid until the end of my contract but was never able to shoot anything.

Had you started working also on one of the other two films you were supposed to direct?
Yes. The second script I was handed was called "The Man from Medicis." We already had a cast: George Segal, Eli Wallach, Curd Jurgens, Claudia Cardinale and a young girl my script supervisor had pointed out to me, Goldie Hawn.

So even in the States you were going to direct comedies...
Yes, in a way the genre ended up trapping me. It's very difficult to get rid of labels. This is usually said about actors but it happens to directors just as much. I've done some comedies I'm very happy about, though. One being *Aragosta a colazione* [*Lobster for Breakfast*, 1979], which I like very much, also *Pane, burro e marmellata* [*Bread, Butter and Marmalade*, 1977] is not bad. But the best film I've done, the one I'm proudest of, is the one I did for the Americans, the Western *Ognuno per sé* [*The Ruthless Four*, 1968] with Van Heflin and Gilbert Roland. That was a film I wanted to do before even knowing I was going to do it. It was the kind of film that I had in mind.

Written by Fernando Di Leo.
Yes, but I changed the script substantially. I wasn't interested in making a pure Western. I liked to call the film "The Treasure of the Sierra Daughter." Even *The Treasure of the Sierra Madre* [1948] isn't a Western in the traditional sense. Di Leo and I met once or twice but he didn't approve the changes I had made to the script, which, for me, were fundamental. He had written a Western-Western when I wanted something that was completely rooted in the psychology of the characters. He spoke very badly about me and the film in later years, saying that I wasn't capable of understanding the genre. I couldn't care less. If these criticisms had come, for example, from Sergio Corbucci, who was one of those directors who was able to be quite refined in the genre, then I would have taken, maybe, more notice but from Fernando Di Leo...

Did you choose to sign the film as George Holloway?
I didn't want to use a pseudonym. I had told the producer I was going to sign it with my real name and he agreed but at the time, to get films sold abroad, the foreign distributors wanted American-sounding names, especially the Germans. The name George Holloway, however, was only used on publicity materials and never put on the actual film.

Did you choose the cast?
No, most of the actors had been decided by the production in agreement with the Americans so the cast was practically chosen and ready when I was offered the job. I did have to struggle to keep Klaus Kinski in the film though, because they didn't want him

anymore. You know that thing Herzog said after Kinski passed away—"I'm sorry he's dead because I would have wanted to kill him"? I can understand him, he was frustrating, but with me things went fine, after a rough beginning. Anyway, it wasn't a simple cast to handle. There were a lot of egos involved and I had to put my foot down more than once. I remember that Van Heflin came to me complaining about a scene once. "You can't change the script without consulting me first." I knew exactly what his problem was but I played along. I had added some lines to Gilbert Roland's character for a scene in which Heflin was supposed to be the only one speaking. "The scene is identical. Nothing has changed." "There are more lines." "Yes, but they are not yours and they don't modify…" "I don't like them and they weren't in the script that was given to me." "OK," I said. "True, they weren't … but neither were all the changes we agreed on, all the things we modified from the Di Leo script. You want the film you signed up for? Fine! Then we are going back to the original version." He thought about it for a second and then said, "The lines can stay," and went off. You have to sometimes show actors that you're in control. If not, it's over, it's chaos. Heflin ended up being better than I could have ever hoped. He was perfect. There is the scene in which he reaches this water pump, dehydrated and exhausted, only to find that it's full of sand. I asked him to repeat the scene but this time sobbing. Initially he was adamant about it. "Crying? C'mon it's a Western. I can't do it." But he did and he was fantastic. When tears started rolling down his cheeks all the crew was captivated by his performance. He was a very talented actor and exceeded my expectations.

What else can you tell me about your relationship with Kinski?

When I first met him he seemed fine but I knew that there were going to be problems. I felt it in the air and in fact, one day, during pre-production, I received a call from my assistant urging me to go down to the costume department. I found Kinski having a fit. He was ripping his clothes off, trampling and spitting on his costume, shouting like a maniac. I went up to him and said I was going to call the William Morris agency and ask if Corrado Pani was free and willing to play one of the leads in the film. I asked my assistant to go up to the office and call immediately. Kinski fell silent and just stared at me. My assistant came back. Pani was available and waiting for a definitive answer by evening. "OK, it's over. You may go home," I told Kinski. "What do you mean it's over?! I'm going to break your fucking skull!" I tried to stay calm. "It's useless. We haven't even begun shooting and look at us. I have no intention of going on like this throughout the making of the film. So you either calm down and accept what we ask of you or, as I said, you are free and can leave immediately. This is what your character wears. If it doesn't fit properly, we will make all the necessary adjustments." "Look at this fucking hat! I can't wear this…" "You're right. This hat is ugly and we will find another one that suits you better but you will be wearing a hat. As we speak Pani is waiting for an answer. So what shall it be? Shall we shake hands here and call it a day or shall we get back to trying on costumes?" He nodded and from that moment on things between Kinski and me went smoothly. That was the film I had the most fun on. Three wonderful months.

What about Gilbert Roland?

He was an adorable dickhead. A flamboyant, over-the-top show-off. He liked being handsome, he liked women, he liked attention. Every time somebody would go, "Look,

Opposite: American poster of Capitani's only western, *The Ruthless Four*.

that's Gilbert Roland," he would start strutting around like a spiked hen. In Spain we went to see the Corrida and Roland paid the torero to get him to dedicate his victory to him. So he got up and saluted everybody, winking at the girls…. He was nice, he was a very nice man to work with. An irresistible poser…

After such a positive experience, why didn't you return to Westerns?
I don't know … I don't know. [He stares for a moment at the nth cigarette he is rolling between his fingers.] It didn't do particularly well in Italy. It did much better in France and Germany but in Italy it passed a little under the radar so maybe producers didn't feel that the combination of Westerns and myself was a winning one. Maybe, I should have insisted a little bit more.

One of your most well-known comedies, especially abroad, is La pupa del gangster [Sex Pot, a.k.a. Poopsie & Co., a.k.a. Get Rita, a.k.a. Gun Moll, 1975].
That was put together by Carlo Ponti. I had just finished *La schiava io ce l'ho e tu no* [*My Darling Slave*, a.k.a. *The Slave*, 1973] with Lando Buzzanca, produced by Ponti, when he called me and told me roughly what the idea of the film was. Not a great idea, to be honest. "Who is going to be in it?" I asked. "My wife and Marcello Mastroianni." "I'll do it!"

So this is another film that was offered to you with a cast that had already been put together and was ready to go?
Yes, but … I had just begun pre-production when I received a phone call from Monica Vitti. We had never met but I recognized her voice instantly. "I know you are going to direct this film. I read the script and I would be perfect for it. Sophia Loren isn't suitable for this sort of thing. Choose me and you won't regret it. You know I would be wonderful for the role." I knew she would, so I said I'd talk it over with Ponti. I found the courage to do so and made my case with him. "Vitti wants the part. I know you have your mind set on Sophia but she won't have much time to prepare for the role…." As we were in pre-production she was finishing *Il viaggio* [*The Voyage*, 1974] by Vittorio De Sica with Richard Burton. "I'll think about it," answered Ponti but I could tell he wasn't happy. A week later he called me, didn't say anything except "OK, get that other one." When I told Monica, she was ecstatic and invited me over to her place for dinner. The screenwriters, Age and Scarpelli, started working on the script again to readapt it for her and that is when things went south. She would drop by the production offices when I wasn't there, to read the new changes to the script. When Scarpelli told me, I was furious and called her immediately. "You don't read anything! Don't do that anymore! You don't get anything until I approve it and then and only then, you get to read it." She started crying, and I was heartbroken. Only later did I discover that this, crying and playing the victim, was a hallmark of hers. After this episode she disappeared and I mean disappeared into thin air. We tried calling everybody. We sent her the new script. No answer. Nothing, even her agent didn't know what had happened to her. The costume department needed her for fittings, Ponti wanted her to sign the contract, which she hadn't done yet, I wanted to talk to her about the character, and we also wanted to do some lighting tests on location … nothing. Vanished. Then we received a call from her agent telling us that she would not even look at the contract unless she got the script again but this time with each page signed by myself and Ponti with a written agreement that nothing, not even one line, would be changed. Ponti took action: "OK, that's it. Don't even answer her. We are using my wife!" Another few days passed before Vitti calls again. I was on the soundstage talking to Enrico Sabbatini

In 1975, all the men of *Sex Pot* (left to right): Aldo Maccione, Giorgio Capitani, Pierre Brice and Marcello Mastroianni (courtesy Giorgio Capitani).

about the set design when they told me that she was on the phone. Now, something happened that had never happened to me before and has never happened since. I was having a fling, at the time, with a girl whose name happened to be Sophia. I hadn't even met Loren yet; she was still in London wrapping things up with De Sica. I don't know how it was possible. Perhaps I was tired or absent-minded. I picked up the phone and: "Hello, Sophia...." It took me a split second to realize my mistake. Sabbatini was at the door, frozen as I was, looking at me with wide, incredulous eyes. I started tapping on the receiver. "Hello? Who is this? Is anybody there?" With a weak, almost whispered voice, she asked me why she received no reply to her last request. I explained that she had pushed Ponti too far, that she should have trusted us more, that it was too late, that I was sorry ... but I don't know how much of all this she actually heard. Somewhere through my explanation she had hung up. I never got a chance to meet or talk to her again since.

This might seem like a strange observation but has anybody told you that many of your comedies have a certain melancholy to them?

No, but I can see what you mean. I think it has to do with the fact that my protagonists tend to be losers, but real losers. They are weak, needy, unlucky, depressed but they are never caricatures. That's why I liked working with Montesano, he would never fall into that trap.

What exactly happened between you and Enrico Montesano? You spoke of a break-up, fights...

At one point he decided that comedy in some way was beneath him, that being a comic wasn't dignified. "What will I tell my son? That his father makes a living being a buffoon?" That's what he told me once and I was quite hard with my response. Maybe my mistake was that I didn't really understand what he was going through at that moment in his life. I'm sorry about how things went. He was very talented and had a presence and a persona that was congenial to me.

You also directed Lando Buzzanca. A very different kind of comedian.

With him everything is externalized, it's all on the outside. The exact opposite of Montesano. Buzzanca knew how to choose his films very well, he knew how to use his physical presence and in what kind of stories it would work best. He went through a period of enormous success and was box-office gold, but afterwards he went through an equally long period in which nobody wanted him, even for small or minor roles. Years ago I wanted to do an experiment with him; I wanted to direct a stage production of *Richard III* with him as the lead. I think that in the role of this vile, cowardly, manipulative character he would have been perfect. Even from this point of view Montesano is the direct opposite of Buzzanca. Montesano is perfect in comedies because he brings out the drama whereas Buzzanca is a perfect dramatic actor because he injects comedy into his roles. I had a good time when I did *The Slave*. That is also one of my favorite comedies.

You have worked with most of the big comedians and comedic actors of the seventies and eighties. What do you remember, for example, about Paolo Villaggio[5]?

We were next-door neighbors for some time, years ago. Well … Villaggio is not an actor, he is more of a character, a caricature and I wasn't interested in his world. Plus, there wasn't much communication…. We never clicked. I wasn't interested in him or his comedic style or approach. He wasn't an actor, he was a comic and not easy to direct. I mean even Vittorio Gassman didn't like getting directions, let alone being asked not to ham things up, but he was Gassman…

If I may say so, Odio le bionde [I Hate Blondes, 1980] is the last of your "golden era" comedies…

Probably, though I felt the story was weak. I still do, very weak. I had just come from the experience of *Lobster for Breakfast*, which is a very well calibrated comedy and *I Hate Blondes* was an attempt to make a light but elegant comedy in that same vein. I wasn't able to replicate the style. But working with Jean Rochefort was a real pleasure.

The presence of French actors is a fil rouge of the Montesano films you made.

Those were all Italian-French co-productions so naturally I had to cast French actors but I would have chosen them anyway because they were marvelous. Working with both Claude Brasseur and Rochefort was wonderful. More recently, for a TV movie, I also worked with Philippe Noiret and he was a pleasure to talk to. He played this old man who was in a hospital bed most of the time, practically a vegetable. On the first day, Noiret came to me and said: "I see you have added some dialogue but I chose to do this film because I was supposed to be silent. I really need the rest."

Did you switch to television because you didn't like what was being offered to you?

Yes, and in fact in television I was able to do things I could never have done in cinema. So yes, you could say that I turned to television to get away from what cinema had become by the late eighties, the decadency. All the films I did prior to this new life with television, the comedies of the eighties, were done professionally but not with the same

Enrico Montesano (left) and Giorgio Capitani on the set of *Lobster for Breakfast*, 1979. "This photo I think encapsulates perfectly our relationship" (courtesy Giorgio Capitani).

care I had previously and after a while I realized I had done enough of them. Incredibly, in television I had more liberty than in cinema.

You have only recently retired.
  Now Italian television, public television, has become completely politicized. It's polarized by politics and clientelism. Managers dictate the rules and it's all white-collar maneuvers. I'm not interested in working in that kind of climate. The producers I grew up with loved the films they were working on 80 percent of the time. Nowadays they don't give a damn. On one of the last films I did, the producer took his wife and went for a month's vacation to Mexico while I was shooting. I was furious. For me, producer and director are a team. People like Ponti, Emo Bistolfi, Clementelli were real producers. You fought with them, discussed ferociously sometimes, but you felt it was for the good of the film in most cases. Now, television directors in Italy are simple employees, like the ones of a bank or post office, just following orders, that are given creative power with an eye-dropper. There is no more space for people like myself or Vittorio Sindoni. We are not cinema or television directors, only directors. So, now I'd rather stay home and watch *House of Cards*, even though, speaking of American television, I get a feeling they are copying each other too much. A lot of series that look and feel the same, plus they are too long. *House of Cards*, for example, was absolutely perfect for the first few seasons, now they just talk and talk. It's getting boring. Americans never know when to stop.

What would you say is the biggest defect in the new generation of filmmakers?

My feeling is that the new generation thinks that by acquiring technical abilities you are able to become a good director. This is not true at all and in fact technical expertise is becoming something of a burden. What I mean is that it's preferable to have imagination and ideas rather than know everything about a camera. Plus, young directors now are heavily influenced by a new American approach where everything is quick and chop-chop, especially when it comes to editing. There is an enormous search to find things that are new, from a technical standpoint, but new doesn't mean good. Personally, I find this quick-paced editing and general flashiness boring. I want to hear and see what I'm being told. You can't resolve all your problems with post-production, with editing tricks, Photoshop and color correction. So the general feeling that technique can resolve everything is one of the illusions plaguing newcomers. What is important is the story and the acting. Nowadays there is too much acting though, actors try too hard. Billy Wilder, on the set of *Some Like It Hot* [1959], made Jack Lemmon repeat a scene four times, and each time asking him to do less. By the third take Lemmon said, "If I keep doing less it's not even acting anymore." And Wilder answered, "Exactly!" Actors should think more and act less, they should trust what their eyes communicate.

Viterbo, 2016

1958 Armed to the Teeth
The Cinema of Umberto Lenzi

"Life's a hole: we are born from a hole, eat from a hole, shit from a hole, and end up in a hole."—Tomas Milian in *Syndicate Sadists*, 1975

"Their idea of lunch is fresh, hot entrails soaked in blood."—Ivan Rassimov in *Eaten Alive!*, 1980

Introduction by Gian Giacomo Petrone

Umberto Lenzi (6 August 1931, Massa Marittima–19 October 2017, Rome) approaches the world of cinema at the end of the forties. He sets up, together with Guido Aristarco and Callisto Cosulich,[1] a film club in his native city and begins working as a film critic, collaborating with the prestigious magazine *Bianco e Nero*. As an intuitive and passionate cinephile, Lenzi devours American, Soviet and European films, though his reference point is primarily American cinema: Raoul Walsh, Michael Curtiz and John Ford among the masters of classical narration; younger subversive innovators like Don Siegel and Samuel Fuller; equally important to mention is William Friedkin, who, with *The French Connection* (1971), creates one of the polar stars, not only for Lenzi but for many of those Italian directors active in police thrillers, and last but not least, the most important of his European-based masters, Henri-Georges Clouzot. The period between 1961 and 1968 is one of "settling" for Lenzi, with twenty films including various period adventures, some spy movies, a couple of negligible Westerns and two war epics. While none of these titles stand out for thematic depth or stylistic consideration, it is also true that quite a few can be configured as well-made entertainment products, where the absence of jolts in style somehow becomes a distinctive balancing feature, representative of the director's linear approach. Lenzi, especially in this early stage of his career, presents himself as a classic storyteller, a lover of directorial transparency who rarely likes his presence to be felt behind the camera. In the period in question, Lenzi best exemplifies this with his adventure films of "salgarian" derivation, *Sandokan—La tigre di Mompracem* (*Sandokan the Great*, 1963), *I pirati della Malesia* (*Sandokan: Pirate of Malaysia*, a.k.a. *The Pirates of the Seven Seas*, 1964) and *La montagna di luce* (*Temple of a Thousand Lights*, a.k.a. *Sandokan*, a.k.a. *Jungle Adventurer*, 1965), not to mention the more than worthy *Duello nella sila* (*Duel of Fire*, 1962), a curious example of a proto-spaghetti Western set in the Risorgimento period, which is far better than the two "orthodox" Westerns he directed, in 1968: *Tutto per tutto* (*Go for Broke*, a.k.a. *Copperface*, a.k.a. *All Out*) and *Una pistola per cento*

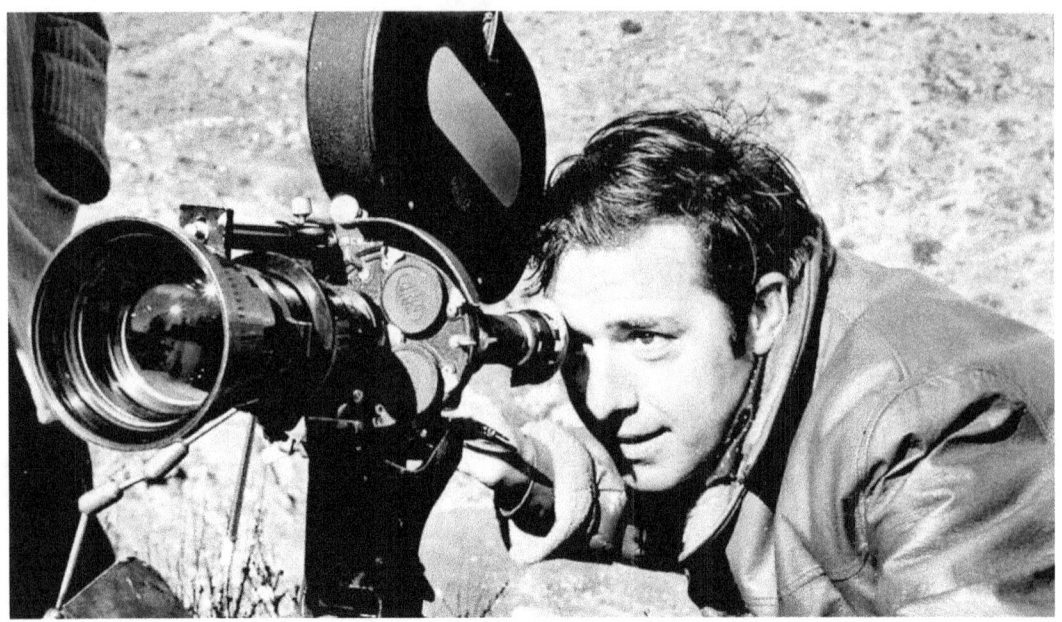

Umberto Lenzi (courtesy Umberto Lenzi).

bare (*Pistol for a Hundred Coffins*, a.k.a. *A Gun for One Hundred Graves*). What shines through in these early works, at least in the most successful examples, is an authentic taste for the poetic and romantic novel-like dimension of adventure. Characters, locations, costumes and colors are effectively utilized without any form of intellectualized superstructures. In 1968, Romolo Guerrieri, with *Il dolce corpo di Deborah* (*The Sweet Body of Deborah*, a.k.a. *The Body*, a.k.a. *Married to Kill*), slightly anticipates the tones and themes which will be prominent in Lenzi's first gialli and is responsible for involving for the first time in the genre, and generally speaking in popular Italian cinema, the American diva Carroll Baker, who shortly after becomes what Lenzi defines as his "muse."

Umberto Lenzi's giallo period can be ideally divided into two thematically distinct sections: in the first one we find the unraveling of a plot in the context of upper bourgeois/aristocratic families and nucleuses, often portrayed with sardonic wit and vaguely Bunuelian overtones; the second is the construction of a narrative closer to the Italian sensitivity, with a whodunit/giallo structure following mysterious serial killings spiced with expressionistic color schemes and surreal visual stylings. Within the first section we find titles such as *Orgasmo* (*Paranoia*, a.k.a. *Orgasm*, 1969), *Così dolce ... così perversa* (*So Sweet ... So Perverse*, 1969), *Paranoia* (*A Quiet Place to Kill*, 1970) and marginally *Un posto ideale per uccidere* (*Oasis of Fear*, a.k.a. *Dirty Pictures*, a.k.a. *An Ideal Place to Kill*, 1971). In all four films mentioned, the development of an archetypal sexual triangle is a recurring element (in *So Sweet ... So Perverse* or *A Quiet Place to Kill*, for example, the entrance of unexpected characters transforms the triangle into more complex geometrical shapes) with implications of perverse physical control of the designated victim and with a continuous change in perspective, both in the exposition of information and regarding characters, which often find their role/function radically changed. The first title of this quartet is probably the best, since it is staged in the form of a Kammerspiel, a sadomasochistic ritual. It begins as the carnal instinct of a rich widow (Baker) in relation to two mysterious individuals (Lou Castel and Colette Descombes), with all the oscillations between manifest and latent obsessions. These turn into a game of death between perpetrators and victims, where the carnal tones slowly fade, reaching the psychological dimension of hallucination and addiction.

Paranoia is better structured than his subsequent efforts in the genre, thanks to a more compact narrative, the unity of the place in which the story unfolds, and the presence of a perfectly cast Lou Castel, very effective in portraying the ambiguity of his character. Carroll Baker works in her role although the acting style and the type of character she will continue playing in the Tuscan director's films tend, in the long run, to be repetitive and monotonous. What should also be noted is the presence of a punctuated and manifest eroticism, a true trademark of the genre, which will distinguish it from the classic archetypes and that only in the most successful cases will find a functional context in the narrative rather than be a mere accessory to attract audiences. *Paranoia* is a film indebted to *Les Diaboliques* (1955) by Clouzot, forger and guiding star of practically all of Lenzi's attempts in the genre between 1969 and 1970, however, without forgetting the influence of other classics, with marked gothic atmospheres: *Gaslight* (1944) by George Cukor, *The Spiral Staircase* (1945) by Robert Siodmak, *Dragonwyck* (1946) by Joseph L. Mankiewicz, *Secret Beyond the Door* (1947) by Fritz Lang, and the more recent *Games* (1967) by Curtis Harrington. This whole rigmarole of titles is to emphasize how, as a cinephile, Lenzi looked at the great European and American strongholds to create films in which the most important things are the plot, the development of drama and a meaningful concatenation of the various segments of the narrative, without overwhelming linguistic digressions or authorial imprints, which characterize the style of other Italian masters and contemporaries such as Bava, Fulci and Argento. Moreover, *Paranoia* would not suffer, in a hypothetical comparison, with the cruelest works of Rainer W. Fassbinder, a master at exploiting closed spaces to sketch the bondage and servility of the psychosexual addiction characterizing some of his greatest character-victims (mostly female), even if in stories with a more pronounced political accent.

Starting with his second thriller, Lenzi will tend to multiply the elements of the plot, not always managing to firmly keep hold of the reins of the story. *So Sweet ... So Perverse* appears more ragged and less compact, while taking advantage of a cast that in addition to Carroll Baker, also vaunts the presence of Jean-Louis Trintignant; Lenzi doesn't seem to find the right amalgam of ingredients of its predecessor, rendering it at times sometimes slow and unnecessarily bizarre. *A Quiet Place to Kill* is a far better effort, where harmony and balance is achieved between the natural scenic elements, the cast (Baker once more, Jean Sorel, Anna Proclemer and the beautiful Marina Coffa, very serviceable in the role of the perverse Lolita) and the dramaturgical development, with excellent calibration between the progression of the story and judiciously placed, impactful plot twists—despite some bland functional theoretical digressions—and with an ending that brings to mind Fritz Lang's *House by the River* (1950).

The next three Lenzi gialli appear at times derivative and less inspired. *Oasis of Fear* is the negative of *Paranoia*. It repeats the basic situation by reversing the polarity of the elements: two young dropouts are housed in the luxurious mansion of a wealthy widow, who has murdered her husband; they unknowingly get exploited by the woman who uses them to distract the police in their investigation. The tragic ending is the same as in *Paranoia*, even if, reversing the roles of the characters and their function, it loses a lot of the satirical vein of the previous title. In addition, the two young protagonists, Ray

Lovelock and an underage Ornella Muti, seem out of place, miles away from Castel and Descombes. Furthermore, the depiction of the counterculture hippie youth movement of the late sixties is implausible and at times too naive. With *Sette orchidee macchiate di rosso* (*Seven Blood-Stained Orchids*) and *Il coltello di ghiaccio* (*Knife of Ice*), both dated 1972, we enter the "argentian" orbit (and inevitably "bavian," given the historical importance of the master, always ahead of his time): serial murders, "whodunit" structure, violence which originates from old, unresolved traumas, psychoses and neuroses not necessarily of a sexual nature. The comparison—lost, in this case—with Argento and with the best of his rivals and contemporaries, is located fundamentally in what, in other contexts, is an indisputable merit of Lenzi's: the love for progressive narrative organization and linear stories that don't require a frenzied aestheticism and avid technicalities, the prevalence of a linear content and its dominance on the form. All elements, these, which can benefit a classically structured giallo, a film story in which the elements of the plot must engage to allow fragments of the narrative puzzle to come together forming a single panoramic image, but wind up being lumbered in a film where the visual aspect should predominate. Argento has often been criticized for concocting improbable plots but at the same time he has often been referred to, in a conceptual vicious circle, as a "horror director." The fact is that all his best films—both those, few indeed, openly horror and the gialli—are conceived and filmed as horror films, a genre in which narrative coherence, the perfect and geometric correspondence of the narrative elements, can be functional to the outcome, but are not expressly required. That is why, to find worthy opponents to Argento's visual styling, we have to turn to Fulci, but also, for example, to a Luigi Bazzoni or a Francesco Barilli, visionary image-based directors who are able to transcend the linearity of classical narrative to uncover the unconscious dimension and to make it flow out in the images, so that they become distorted mirrors of human interiority. It is here where Lenzi is lacking, in the ability to deconstruct the real, making him certainly much more suited to action rather than visionary composition. Reasons, these, that make his gialli, from 1971 onwards—with the exception of the notable *Spasmo* (1974)—certainly enjoyable but lacking that pictorial aura which is supposed to disturb and fascinate in equal measure.

The years between 1973 and 1979 embrace the most relevant portion of Lenzi's career, being the golden age of Italian crime films, his preferred genre. Although the official birth of this phenomenon is dated 1972, with *La polizia ringrazia* (*Execution Squad*) by Stefano Vanzina, it has to be pointed out that a rich and varied filmography exists from the fifties and sixties, and anticipates many themes and trademarks. It is necessary to mention the names of such directors as Pietro Germi, Francesco Rosi, Carlo Lizzani, Damiano Damiani and of course Elio Petri who directs a fundamental title in the evolution of the genre with *Indagine su un cittadino al di sopra di ogni sospetto* (*Investigation of a Citizen Above Suspicion*, 1970). All the names in this brief list anticipated issues, atmospheres and stylistic elements, but have a common trait that separates them from what they will help create: their cinema has almost always a marked political and civil connotation and, although not infrequently containing spectacular visuals, their priority is a sociopolitical analysis. Lenzi's debut in the urban criminal universe takes place in 1973 with *Milano rovente* (*Gang War in Milan*), though the film has more to do with French polar and gangster movies, with its attention directed towards secondary characters, dialogue and plot development. The two antagonist gangsters, Toto Cangemi and Roger Daverty (played respectively by Antonio Sabato and Philippe Leroy), come face to face for territorial issues, "moral" ones (the old with prostitution and the new with drug trafficking), and even sexual issues (the masculine Sicilian gangster antithetical to the sexually ambiguous French criminal). With the appearance of a femme fatale (Marisa Mell), the overall tone shifts even more towards French noir, helped also by the music composed by Carlo Rustichelli. The next metropolitan detour by Lenzi, *Milano odia: la polizia non può sparare* (*Almost Human*, 1974), is still far from the dynamics that will trigger off in Lenzi's films from the mid-seventies right to the end of the decade and can be seen as a kind of counterpoint to *Gang War in Milan* in the dimension of the stateless person. If in the first film the figure of the "southerner" Toto is rebalanced thanks to his prominent role in the Milanese underworld, making him an organic element of the urban fabric, in the case of Giulio Sacchi in *Almost Human* (superbly played by Tomas Milian), his statelessness (given the specific nature of his accent marked by the unmistakable voice, at least for the Italian public, of Ferruccio Amendola, whose inflection, in this, as in all the Lenzi films in which he was called to dub Milian, is markedly Roman) is not configured only as regional, but it becomes, so to speak, a spiritual dimension. A restless soul, predatory, vicious, biting, sarcastic, cynical, cowardly, intensified by the eloquence of a great orator, a histrionic storyteller, and especially with the inexhaustible will to be abysmally evil. Statelessness, in his case, cannot be institutionalized, because he has no friends, home, family, roots: he is a wild animal that will not be stopped, will not be torn down. Comparisons between Henry Silva and Milian would be unfair, seeing the monumental interpretation of the latter. Though Silva, who plays commissioner Grandi, will find a consistency, with his granite face and monotonous look, in the end when, tired, wounded and disillusioned, he becomes a ruthless automaton of death for Giulio Sacchi. The formal elegance of *Gang War in Milan* melts, leaving space to opaque and contrasted colors, the indefinable shades of the environments in which the characters of *Almost Human* move in. The outskirts of Milan, the gloomy sidewalks and, above all, the squalid abandoned barge, in which some of the pivotal action takes place, become symbols of an exterior degradation and a reflection of an interior one: a world of waste, scraps and leftovers for losers, for the rejects and discarded members of society. The finale, with Sacchi dying among heaps of garbage, makes the metaphor even clearer, without turning it into a simple caption of the concept, but keeping alive a certain ambiguity.

After the unmemorable *Il giustiziere sfida la città* (*Syndicate Sadists*, 1975), the big meeting with Maurizio Merli finally comes about. When *Rome Armed to the Teeth* is released in theaters on 25 February 1976, Lenzi and Merli, along with Milian, will be permanently enshrined as icons of the genre. This and the subsequent *Napoli violenta* (*Violent Naples*, 1976)—in which Merli becomes the only protagonist—can be considered a sort of metropolitan diptych, where the real protagonists are the two Italian cities. Lenzi, together only with Fernando Di Leo, had a flair and an unmatched ability in "feeling" the size of the big city; in communicating to the viewer the taste and smell of the asphalt and the degradation of the suburbs; in exploiting natural resources with insights invented on the spot that enable fictional drama to mix with the surrounding reality; in building greatly spectacular sequences of impact thanks to the ingenious—and only seemingly simple—technical stratagems of experienced and first-rate technicians. Both *Rome Armed to the Teeth* and *Violent Naples* are based on a very fragmented diegetic, mosaic-like narratives and although there is a basic storyline, the strong core of the two films is located where the action reaches its climax: in robberies, in pursuits, in shootouts to the death behind mountains of multicolored rags; in the motorcycle ride at breakneck speed through Neapolitan alleys; in the ascent of a padded funicular full of hostages and a crazy cop glued to the roof; in duels between cars, guns and moving bodies. Lenzi is not afraid to act on the form, thus proving of being able to break out of the canons of classical narrative, to experiment, innovate and enhance the outcome of a genre he is perfectly in control of. The beautiful and "surgically" perfect music by Franco Micalizzi makes the overall mechanism of the two films even more frantic and addictive.

Il trucido e lo sbirro (*Free Hand for a Tough Cop*, 1976) opens a new phase for Lenzi and, more generally, for the Italian genre as a whole. The genus has already given many of its most prized fruits and is on the verge of a decline, which similarly to what had happened with peplums and especially with Westerns, meant an increasing amount of parody-like derivations. In 1976, from the sagacious pen of Dardano Sacchetti, comes a new character, tailored to the histrionic traits of Tomas Milian: Sergio Marazzi, known as "Er Monnezza," a figure that echoes some aspects of the hunchback previously played by the actor in *Rome Armed to the Teeth*, the difference being that basically, Monnezza is a pure soul, a less angelic and smarter Ninetto Davoli if you will; in other words a positive character, whereas the hunchback was the embodiment of the ugliest and dirtiest shadowing of the proletariat. The figure of Monnezza, introduced in an epic context, sometimes as violent as that of previous films, changes some fundamental characteristics at the root, smoothing the rawness with continuous jokes, gags and one-liners. The odd couple formed by ex-convict Monnezza and the cop played by Claudio Cassinelli, in the fight against time to free a kidnapped child who is likely to die from a serious illness, often becomes a comical one. The hybridization between comedy and action inserts works pretty well, although you may notice a certain discontinuity between the lighter and more violent moments, so much so that the former can ideally be expunged from the movie and shown independently, without losing its sardonic charge. Nevertheless, there is a certain awareness in the film, which Lenzi begins with a full screen sequence of a Western: wide open spaces and men on horseback; the camera moves back to show that it is actually a film within a film: convicts are watching a Western inside the projection room of a prison; in a single, brilliant sequence, Lenzi shows sardonically the historic passing of the baton from one genre to the next. This concept is perfectly embodied also in the choice of title for *Il cinico, l'infame, il violento* (*The Cynic, the Rat & the Fist*, 1978), a clear reference to Sergio Leone's *Il buono, il brutto, il cattivo* (*The Good, the Bad and the Ugly*, 1966). Lenzi seems, with this film, to have returned partially to where he had started, with Milian proposing a more "traditional" character closer to his most repulsive villains in a much more serious context than *Free Hand for a Tough Cop*. However, at times you begin to feel a certain déjà vu: the cliché of repetition and the overuse of well-established stereotypes. The film has its moments but not as many as one would expect from Lenzi; the formula is now familiar and is inexorably becoming obsolete. Something partly innovative, the crossing of the new path with the old, is represented by *La banda del gobbo* (*Brothers Till We Die*, 1978), in which Milian symbolically "doubles," playing the twins Vincenzo Marazzi, the hunchback, and Sergio Marazzi, known as "Er Monnezza." The "serious" and the "parodic" are confronted in a film that entrenches the actor's farewell to traditional interpretations of the genre.

The final chapter of Lenzi's crime filmography takes place emblematically in 1979, the twilight of a rich and unique decade for Italian genre cinema. He goes out with a bang: *Da Corleone a Brooklyn* (*From Corleone to Brooklyn*, a.k.a. *The Sicilian Boss*, 1979). This is an unusual film, given its structure as a road movie and the setting of the final act in New York. Even the plot is detached from the recurring themes of the "poliziottesco": an Italian cop (Merli) must escort from Palermo to New York a turncoat mobster (Biagio Pelligra, who steals the show) to testify against the Sicilian boss Michele Barresi (Mario Merola). Not only do two actor-icons of distant genres like police thrillers (Merli) and Neapolitan melodrama (Merola) confront one another, but two distant sidereal worlds do too, as the first embodies the whole of Italy and is easily exportable, while the second is connected exclusively to the reality of Naples. The psychological depth of Merli's cop and Pelligra's mafia witness is unfurled in an "on the road" context; the raw melancholy of a New York frozen by the harsh winter; the use of atypical locations of the American city, together with the rigorous realism in the employment of faces and bodies recruited amongst street people and authentic American police agents, make this the ideal swan song of the genre and a little gem within it, mournful and melancholic, culminating symbolically with the freeze frame of Merli's close-up, an image of an era that had inexorably ended.

Umberto Lenzi will place any person visiting his house on the same sofa, in the same room, always in the same spot. A small studio, which looks and feels very much like a shrine: photos, flyers, film posters (a huge Thai one of *Eaten Alive!* overshadows all of them, and reveals itself as soon as the door is shut, being firmly pinned behind it), books, books on cinema, books written by Lenzi, books on Lenzi—a pile of copies of his newly released biography are placed at the center of the small table in front of the faded yellow couch. A room full of dregs and artifacts, surviving pieces of a career spanning decades. You are placed at the center of what only apparently might seem like a chaotically fascinating miniature warehouse of stacked and overlapping memorabilia, but looking closely, photos, dusty VHSs and DVDs are placed strategically on the swollen shelves with museum-like criteria. But there is something reassuring in looking at all this, a sort of perfectly closed circle. Everything one has learned to associate to Umberto Lenzi and his cinema is present in those few square meters and unravels itself before your eyes: the history books on the Spanish Civil War, of which Lenzi is a scholar and self-proclaimed expert, and a whole floor-to-ceiling bookcase suffocated by double rows of the best that Hollywood produced from its birth right up to the late sixties. You are immersed in his world, or should I say, you are sitting in the front row of his chosen stage and, like a veteran actor, Lenzi picks his spot, queries what you will be asking, what "tone" he should use during the interview, "what kind of person," in my opinion, "will get to read this interview," and as he turns off the main light, preferring the small lamp on his desk, carpeted with documents and more film-related books, I realize he was directing our meeting, lighting it, preparing it, as if it were a scene from one his films.

You are part of a rare breed, one of the only truly cinephile directors of your generation.
When I was in high school I had a teacher called Angelo Paoli who, prior to teaching literature, had attended the CSC—Italy's most prestigious and selective film school—with the likes of Pietro Ingrao, Gianni Puccini and Giuseppe De Santis and instead of talking about Manzoni and Leopardi he would tell us about René Clair, Renoir and Sergei Eisenstein. He was a film maniac and I remember on one particular occasion he took us to a screening of *The Lodger*, not the Hitchcock version but the 1944 one directed by John Brahm. The film hadn't been very successful, at least not in Italy, but it was wonderful, you know, with that expressionistic kind of photography. The director was a German who had immigrated to the States and despite the very distinctive kind of style, it

A young Umberto Lenzi (on the right) as he shoots the documentary *Dalle tenebre al mare* (*From the Darkness to the Sea*) in 1955 (courtesy Umberto Lenzi).

had a linear, simple narrative, following the classic thesis that Jack the Ripper was in fact a doctor ... anyway, where was I? Yes, what was fascinating for me was that he would explain to us the meaning and importance of a shot and the power of editing using poetry and literature! If you change the order of a poem's words, even without modifying the meaning, you end up radically changing the emotional impact and the same goes for cinema. He would show us how a certain kind of editing could change the way an audience reacts and how the juxtaposition of certain moments can revolutionize the rhythm and with it the interest of who's watching. The actors count for nothing! It's all editing and directing. Hitchcock would get angry when people talked about good acting. For example, Kim Novak ... I like to jump from one thing to another, I know ... Novak, when she was picked for *Vertigo* (1958), was all excited about working with a master like Hitchcock and when she was on set, on the first day, she went like [Lenzi clutches his hands firmly together as he proceeds to imitate a female voice, his bushy eyebrows raised in an expression of gleeful anticipation as his head slightly tilts to one side as if to recreate a certain teenage ingenuity], "please ... please ... Mr. Hitchcock, please tell me, should I say these lines with a passion that rises uncontrollably from the heart or with cerebral consciousness?" "Baby," [Lenzi's voice changes abruptly, contaminated inexplicably by a Dean Martin quality], "it's only a film. Only a movie, baby." Understand? It's all the director doing the magic.

Going back to your story...

Yes, with this teacher of mine I ended up opening a film club. Always in Massa Marittima, where I was born and raised. We are talking roughly around 1949. Then, later on, I opened another one in Grosseto. This was the beginning of the golden age of film clubs. All over Italy they began to proliferate, creating a generation of cinephiles. This activity pushed me to try and do something more. You know, in this world of conferences and retrospectives I would get to meet people, create a network of friends and collaborators, talk to directors. It was a catalyzing force. So, I managed to get into the CSC with a scholarship in 1954, after having gotten a law degree the previous year at the University of Pisa. I did brilliantly there, in fact I was Alessandro Blasetti's favorite student. He even asked me to participate, as a volunteer-assistant, on a couple of his films and made me act as well … unfortunately. After, I started working and it didn't take me long to make my debut as a director. I was really young, about 26, when I went to Greece with my first wife. It was a completely Greek production.

We are talking about **Mia Italida stin Ellada [An Italian in Greece, 1958].** *The film was never distributed in Italy.*
No, but an Italian edition was made. I followed the dubbing process, an Italian title had been chosen and even the posters had been printed. Everything was ready and done when the distributor, a young man, a Sicilian—I don't remember the name—died in a strange car accident. There were rumors that he was involved in illicit traffickings, mafia connections. The film got blocked and it never saw an Italian cinema but in Greece it did very well. It's considered like a classic there. It was also distributed in South America and in all those places filled with Greek immigrants. The protagonist was Wandisa Guida, Luciano Martino's wife with whom I had gone to the CSC.

A few years pass by before you are able to direct a second feature.
Of course, because when I came back to Italy it was as if I had been on vacation. None of the producers were able to see what I had done. Nobody in Italy even knew I had made a film and so, for the time being, I had to abandon the idea of being a director. I started writing and I managed to sell a few scripts but what changed things was being the first assistant director on *Costantino il grande* [*Constantine and the Cross*, 1961] by Lionello De Felice with Cornel Wilde. That was the biggest thing I had done, up until that moment. The scale was huge: massive sets, scenes with 600 extras, 400 horses galloping through the countryside … it was a spectacular film to work on. All shot in Yugoslavia, during most of the second half of 1960. Anyway, that film really started me off. I was called shortly after, again as a 1st AD, to work on *Il terrore dei mari* [*Guns of the Black Witch*, 1961] by Domenico Paolella.

Franco Rossetti told me that he mentioned your name to the producers of **Constantine and the Cross.**
Yes, I had met Franco during my years at the CSC and we had become friends. I knew his wife very well, Gaia Romanini, who was a very active costume designer throughout the sixties. She pushed him to become a director. She was very ambitious and wanted him to be more like her, but he should have stuck to screenwriting. He worked on the script of *Constantine* and pointed me out to the production. A nice man, Franco, but not a very good director. Another future director I met, but earlier during my film club years, was Giulio Petroni. He was in Tuscany shooting a documentary and was looking for people who knew the territory. He directed one of the greatest Italian Westerns, *Tepepa* [a.k.a. *Blood and Guns*, 1968], but then used my first muse, Lisa Gastoni, for a terrible film, *Labbra di lurido blu* [*Lips of Lurid Blue*, 1975].

After Constantine and the Cross *you worked with Paolella who was one of the most well-respected directors of his generation. What do you remember about him?*

He trusted me a lot and I owe him. When I did *Guns of the Black Witch* he had just had his appendix removed and couldn't shout and move around too much because of the stitches. So he would stay seated and explain, quietly, what kind of shot he wanted. This said, you must understand that the film was shot mute, no live recording, and this was a swashbuckling adventure with pirates leaping around, people throwing themselves from boats and so on. It was all shot on a lake, the Lago di Garda, where two galleons had been transported piece by piece. When the rough footage was screened for the producers, they couldn't hear anything except a mad person shouting, "You, throw yourself now!" "Run faster and you ... you've just been shot!" So, they asked, "Who is this guy giving orders?" "That is the 1st AD, Umberto Lenzi." "Ah! He's good. OK, he can do the next pirate movie."

How did the previous generations of directors perceive newcomers like yourself? People like Mario Costa, Paolella, Carmine Gallone...

Well, maybe generally with a little hostility, not in my case though. But I didn't really work with many of them because I started as a director almost immediately. Blasetti for example, who had been my teacher, was always very kind. He helped me get in touch with people who could help me and would often write up references. I met many directors, yes, but during the film club years. I'll tell you this story.... The first short film I directed, my diploma project, was *Ragazzi di Trastevere* [translation: *The Boys of Trastevere*] which was inspired by the world of Pasolini. The script was perfect, original and written by me but I got inspiration and the use of a certain kind of lexicon from the novel *Ragazzi di vita* [literally translated as "Boys of Life," idiomatically as "hustlers"]. Pasolini was nobody at the time—he would become famous in the following two or three years—and I met up with him to get his permission to use some names and lines from his book. He read the script and thought it was wonderful and said that once I got out of the CSC I should give him a call because he was working on something I might be interested in. We did meet but twenty years later at Ouarzazate in Marocco where he was shooting *Edipo Re* [*Oedipus Rex*, 1967] and I was doing *Attentato ai tre grandi* [*Desert Commandos*, a.k.a. *Attack on the Big Three*, 1967]. Going back to your question, I only had a few experiences on other directors' sets: De Felice, Paolella and of course Piero Vivarelli who was a good friend. I worked on his musicarelli [literally: small musicals]. But those were intellectual musicarelli! *San Remo—La grande sfida* [translation: *San Remo—The Big Challenge*, 1960] and *Io bacio ... tu baci* [translation: *I Kiss ... You Kiss*, 1961]. You know, of course, that Vivarelli wrote the song *24 mila baci* with Lucio Fulci. I was present the day they came up with the song!

Ah! Wait! [Lenzi raises both his arms in the air and freezes.] I forgot the most important thing! [He points towards one of the cramped shelves behind me.] See that?! There, there! [Lenzi's immediate impatience and excitement pushes me to lie. "Yes, there it is. I see it." My eyes frantically continue to jump from one book spine to the other, scanning the numerous black-and-white photos, most of them polaroids, that cover the titles.] That is the certificate Universal Studios gave me. Because I didn't start with just anybody! I entered cinema from the main door, called by Hollywood! [Now I see it, a tattered, yellowish diploma-like document, tainted by age, its corners wrinkled. In the center a colorized version of one of the old Universal logos. The best and most minimal, the last black and white logo used by the studio, between 1946 and 1964 with Lenzi's name elegantly written in cursive.] They gave me that for a film I did with them. It was all set on a desert island and directed by Richard Wilson. Wilson was one of Orson Welles's closest and most valued collaborators. He produced and edited many of his films and also acted in *Citizen Kane* [1941]. It had Jeff Chandler, Esther Williams, Rossana Podestà, Edoardo De Filippo, Rik Battaglia ... and that's practically it. A very small cast. The title at the time was *The Islander* then changed to *Raw Wind in Eden*. Did you know that Chandler died a couple of years later because they made a mistake during surgery? I think they cut his aorta. Not a great actor but he did work with one of my masters and mentors, Samuel Fuller. Anyway, initially they wanted to shoot in Sardinia but they also wanted to be able to see the dailies and that region had no structures that would permit the production to print and screen the footage, so they ended up choosing a part of the Maremma coast, close to where I grew up. This is one of the reasons I was chosen and, by the way, I got to do that Greek film also thanks to having worked with the Americans. We shot it in the summer of 1957 and the whole crew and cast was made up of 120 people! Roughly seventy Americans and fifty Italians. The film didn't do well, it virtually ended Esther Williams' career.

***Before, you were explaining that you got your chance of really starting your career as a director thanks to Paolella's film,* Guns of the Black Witch.**

Yes, because after the Paolella film, the producers asked me to make their next pirate movie, *Le avventure di Mary Read* [*Queen of the Seas*, 1961] with Lisa Gastoni. I discovered Lisa Gastoni! She was beautiful, elegant and spoke English fluently. Her mother was Irish and she began her career in Britain but I was the one to make her a leading actress. Quite authoritarian though, a tough girl and very confrontational but I liked her a lot. I mean I fell in love with her ... well, maybe infatuated is more correct. We had a love affair, though it didn't last long. I was married and she was engaged.... So, anyway I began immediately with straight-up genre films. In fact, after, I did *Duello nella Sila* [*Duel of Fire*, 1962], which was an attempt to make a Western in the Sicily of the 19th century but it didn't do well because Italian Westerns just didn't click with audiences at that time. It's a shame, the film was very well made and there are some good scenes for which I got inspiration from *Stagecoach* [1939] by John Ford. The first really big-budgeted film I was given was *Caterina di Russia* [*Catherine of Russia*, 1963]. Initially Anita Ekberg was supposed to be the protagonist but she asked too much money so I mentioned Hildegard Knef's name to the producers. She was a great actress and singer who became popular just after the war thanks to a bunch of songs and then went to Hollywood where she did, among other things, *The Snows of Kilimanjaro* [1952] with Gregory Peck. A survivor, she lived through seven cancer-related surgeries, continued working and lived until ten years ago.

These, and other films you did in the early sixties, are imitations of typically American products. There is also a Robin Hood film in this initial phase.

Yes, *Il trionfo di Robin Hood* [*The Triumph of Robin Hood*, 1962]. I remember choosing Gia Scala, who was not an American like most people thought. Her real name was Giovanna Scoglio and she ended up in the States as a child after becoming an orphan. At the time she was famous mostly for having worked in *The Guns of Navarone* [1961]. She had a lovely face and I was happy to have her, but the producer had the bad idea of signing on both her and her husband Don Burnett, who just didn't work. If you're going to make a film about Robin Hood you need a charismatic figure, an Errol Flynn–like hero. This Burnett guy was completely insipid. Good looking but anonymous. On the first day we mounted him on a horse and after three meters he collapsed to the ground. We had to postpone production for a week. Plus, the story wasn't very good. The final result is quite mediocre.

When it came to casting, did you have the final word?
Sometimes yes and sometimes no. It depended on the film and the producer. In the case of *Catherine of Russia* what I asked, I got. But then, there are often unforeseeable problems. For example, on *Duel of Fire* I had picked the cast myself and the protagonist was supposed to be Edmund Purdom, but during the first week of shooting he also fell from his horse and we had to find a substitute in less than a day. We got Fernando Lamas through an American agency working in Italy called Kaufman & Lerner.[2] These big American agencies were a force to be reckoned with. Lamas ended up marrying Esther Williams and when she came to Italy to accompany him, there was a moment of embarrassment for both of us. I remember catching her, more than once, fucking with Jeff Chandler on the set of *Raw Wind of Eden* and I think she remembered that. By the way, she had really beautiful, juicy-looking tits.

Right at the beginning of this interview you manifested a certain dislike for actors but on set what was your approach and relationship with them. Hitchcockian, as you mentioned…?
Worse! Much worse! [A wide grin of satisfaction crosses his face.] I was a South American dictator! I would fight fiercely with any actor who wouldn't obey my orders … but they would always obey in the end. I had a few problems with George Peppard because of his drinking. I also had some disagreements with Tomas Milian…. [He interrupts himself and his smile, together with any kind of irony in his expression, disappears instantly. His eyes, fixed on the faded orange rug at his feet betray him. I can tell he is weighing his words, picking them carefully for what he is going to say next.] Milian was a great actor, is a great actor … but … but he was full of problems at the time. He was bisexual and living with the weight of what had happened to his father in prison, the tortures and then the strict military-like education he would impose on his kids and finally his suicide. Tomas was present when his father shot himself. At the time he wouldn't talk about it. I discovered all this through other people in more recent years. Now he tells anybody willing to listen but then nobody would have imagined it. [His eyes are animated once again by that child-like enthusiasm and maliciousness that had, for a moment, disappeared.] Plus, he would fuck anything that moved. Did you know how many times I would go to his dressing room and find someone kneeling down giving him a blow job? Man, woman, ugly, old, anybody. He was a very difficult character to deal with and our relationship has always been one of love and hate. Speaking of finding people in compromising positions, on one of the few comedies I made—it's a genre I just don't like making—I had a flaming homosexual as the producer. He filled the film with his friends and loads of transsexuals, who mind you, were supposed to play normal women. I went along with the whole thing because, by the time I discovered what I had gotten into, I had already signed the contract. Well, I caught him, near the set, getting fucked in the ass by a trans woman…

You and Milian made six films together, between 1974 and 1978. How did your paths cross?
Truth be told, I pulled him out of a tomb when I called him to be in *Milano Odia: La polizia non può sparare* [*Almost Human*, 1974]. He had just made a film with Alberto

De Martino, *Il consigliori* [*The Counsellor*, a.k.a. *Counsellor at Crime*, 1973], which was terrible and had bombed at the box office. After having contacted his agent, Milian asked to meet me. When we were together I was always tense because his state was, for one reason or another, altered. He would often work completely drunk. On set he would finish a whole bottle of vodka and would take three/four tablets of Optalidon.[3] A lethal combination with doses high enough to kill somebody. But I was one of the only directors who could tolerate him, in fact I directed him six times. Most of my colleagues abandoned him after one or two experiences. The only exception being myself and Bruno Corbucci. Though after six films, I let him go as well. I chose to direct my war film *Il grande attacco* [*The Great Battle*, a.k.a. *The Greatest Battle*, a.k.a. *Battle Force*, 1978] instead of another cop thriller with him. He asked me to give him a role and I answered "no way!" He never forgave me for that but I had reached the limit, I was just too fed up with him. On the last film we did he was always, and I mean always, stinking drunk. On the first day we were shooting in a restaurant and we had to repeat the scene 23 times. It was *La banda del gobbo* [*Brothers Till We Die*, 1978] and in the scene he was supposed to explain to the other members of the gang, the hit he was putting together. He arrived laughing with a rose between his teeth and started throwing petals around the set. Actors always have panderers and boot-lickers among crew members, usually in the hair and make-up department, and I would notice when and where they would hide the booze and drugs for him. Anyway, going back to the original question. I was never interested in actors or their suggestions. They had to do what they were told and that was all.

Let's jump back to the first half of the sixties. Needless to say, you passed through peplums as well. One of the biggest and most prolific genres of that decade.

L'ultimo gladiatore [*The Last Gladiator*, 1964] with Richard Harrison. Now that is a good film! I saw it again recently and it's very well done. Harrison was good, always professional. When I watch the films we did together I find him better now than how I found him then. Later, when we parted ways, he wasn't able to choose his projects wisely and ended up working on terrible Z-movies. Lisa Gastoni is in it as well, our third film together. She plays Messalina and for her death scene I elaborated a monologue similar to the one Lady Macbeth gives in Shakespeare's play when she dies. Gastoni, I remember, was very happy with her role. I had a good relationship with her, and still do. We sometimes call each other on the phone. But you see ... let me just go back to what we were saying about actors. If I went back to directing now I would have serious difficulties because nowadays the director is the guy behind the monitor. He sits there, watches the scene and goes "OK." Once the scene is done, the actors want to watch it. "Oh, let's do it again. My hair was out of place." "I don't like my expression. I want another take." Actors only see themselves, and now directors have become their hostages. When Tomas Milian asked to repeat a shot, it was easier to convince him that it wasn't necessary. I would ask the operator or the DOP to be my accomplices and tell them that he looked wonderful.

Did you have similar problems with Maurizio Merli?

Merli had a morbid fixation with his hair. He was always combing it, calling the hairdresser on set, checking himself in the mirror. On the last film we did together, *Da Corleone a Brooklyn* [*From Corleone to Brooklyn*, a.k.a. *The Sicilian Boss*, 1979], he was particularly upset about his hair because, I don't remember, they had made a mistake when dying it ... the wrong color or something like that. We were shooting in New York at one point, it was February, we were out in the snow, freezing and we were waiting for

Merli to get his hair done for the scene when Van Johnson came up to me and said, "Umberto, tell him he's a son-of-a-bitch." Films, for actors, are like photo albums, things in which to admire their reflection. Real actors do theater. Cinema is just for faces. In America it's different because, there, the script is sacred and you can't touch or modify anything once production has begun. You choose the actors, you read the script with them and talk in detail about every aspect and once everything is approved, there is no going back.

You mentioned having had a bad experience with George Peppard on the set of Contro quattro bandiere [From Hell to Victory, 1979].

Yes, because he was always drunk, possibly more so than Milian would be. At one point, when we were in Paris, he beat his wife to a pulp. He was arrested and the Italian and French producers had to intervene to save the film because we just couldn't continue without him. I don't remember exactly how things were resolved but I think it was officially claimed that she had fallen from the stairs when instead he had smacked her around fiercely. All this went to my advantage in a way, because Peppard had still two scenes to shoot and the producer took him aside and said, "If you keep drinking and breaking Umberto's balls, I swear you're going back to jail." In fact, the last few days he was a lamb. He was the only American I had problems with. All the rest were wonderful: George Hamilton, who was one of Peppard's co-stars on that film, Henry Fonda, John Huston…

I get a feeling that the films you made in the early sixties, the adventure films, were done with professional detachment. What was the film that you consider the turning point in your career?

Without a shadow of a doubt, *Orgasmo* [*Paranoia*, a.k.a. *Orgasm*, 1969] with the wonderful Carroll Baker, with whom I did other three films. We had a wonderful relationship … but, yes, that is my turning point. I directed it particularly well, with inspiration. Initially the title was supposed to be *Paranoia* and not *Orgasmo*. It remained *Paranoia* for the American market but got changed for the Italian one. That was a decision made by the distributors while I was in Spain doing a film with Jack Palance, another crazy person, but a talented one … kind of an American Tomas Milian.

Two versions were made of the film.

Yes, two. One for the Italian market which was softer, with less nudity and sex scenes. Remember that in the late sixties censorship, especially when it came to sexual matters, was still very strong and catholic-oriented. The film was still quite sexual and strong from that point of view but nothing compared to the American version we made, in which there is full-frontal nudity. Often, our films got changed and modified when they got picked up for foreign distribution. Anyway, when the film was screened at the Venice Film Festival in 2004 during the retrospective organized by Quentin Tarantino, I was sitting next to him and Joe Dante and I turned to my wife and said, "Let's see if five minutes before the end the public's reaction will be the same as when it was first screened in Rome." *Paranoia* had had its premiere at the Fiamma, an important cinema in the historical center, and after the final dramatic turn of events there was a standing ovation. Even the Devil himself couldn't have guessed that ending. So, I told Olga, my wife, that if nobody reacted during this scene we would leave because it meant that the film had aged badly and I didn't want to be present and watch people silently leave the theater. Needless to say, every single person stood up and cheered as the credits rolled. That said, that was an important film because my filmic language changed radically. I started using more details, many more close-ups than I had previously. I began playing around with colors as well, in a more expressionistic manner. I think the quality of my work changed after that film. It's not that the things I made before were worse but simply more classical. I had the formal approach, coherent with the cinematic grammar of that period. My first gialli, however, are ahead of their time, I feel.

Correct me if I'm mistaken, but wasn't Eleanor Powell supposed to star in the film instead of Carroll Baker? And secondly, isn't Bertrand Tavernier credited as an assistant director?

Yes, in the very first stages of pre-production we did talk about Powell being in the film but the problem with her was that she was too old, she wouldn't have been credible. The role needed a woman who wasn't young anymore but who was still sexually appealing. As far as Tavernier is concerned, yes, he is credited as one of my assistants but he didn't actually work on the film. As you probably know, in co-productions it's all about percentages. That was an Italian-French co-production so there had to be a certain percentage of French technicians and actors and another percentage of Italian crew and cast. So once the film was done, you had to sometimes add names here and there to actually get the doses right. The actual assistants on that film were Italian. Anyway, after the massive success the film had in the States, the Italian producers and distributors said: "Wait, if the Americans used the title *Paranoia*, that means it works! Let's make another giallo directed by Lenzi, with Carroll Baker again and use this title." A producer's reasoning is just that simple!

So that is how Paranoia *[A Quiet Place to Kill, 1970] got under way?*

Exactly. It was a very good film as well, with a good cast: Baker, Jean Sorel, Anna Proclemer. A co-production, but with Spain this time, and it was entirely shot in Palma di Majorca, but a lesser title, compared to *Orgasmo/Paranoia* which is my favorite film together with *Almost Human* and *From Corleone to Brooklyn*, as far as cop thrillers are concerned. And of a course all my war films are masterpieces. But let's keep those aside for the moment … those are a whole different story because my real nature, you should know, is one of a historian. If I hadn't become a director, I would've been a professor of contemporary history. You see this wall?! [He slowly turns around, remaining seated on his wooden chair, and points towards the massive bookcase behind him.] All these books are about the Spanish Civil War. All of them! More than 200 volumes … and documentaries I have on the subject. Look! [Before turning back towards me, he stares at his collection, silently contemplating, his arm still raised towards the epicenter of his great passion.] In the next few days they're going to come and take everything away. I've decided to donate all of this to a historical archive. I don't have many more years to live and I don't want it to go to waste. This was just to explain my predilection for war films. I'm an expert on history and thrillers and noir literature. I even wrote a series of detective stories that were published.[4] Next week I'm going to present my last masterpiece that closes the saga. They are all about a man investigating strange murders in the film world, and specifically Cinecittà, during the fascist era. I tried to propose the project for a television series but it would cost too much, that kind of period reconstruction… That reminds me, speaking of war movies, when we shot *La legione dei dannati* [*Legion of the Damned*, a.k.a. *Battle of the Commandos*, 1969] with Jack Palance, there was a scene in the script which took place, during the war, in a devastated, bombed London. I went there with five crew members and a couple of actors without knowing how the hell we were going to pull it off. On the second day, we found a whole area that was going to be demolished, two or three blocks full of crumbling, run-down houses, which were also perfect architecturally and historically speaking, for the film. We found a few extras, put them in costumes and you can see the scene during the opening credits! We Italians were truly full of resources. But those were different times and long gone…

You used the term "crazy" to describe Palance. Why?
Because he would light up in a second, shout, act crazy… You got the impression he could do anything at any moment. Before, I compared him to Milian, but this is not correct because Tomas was more contorted, subtler and, more importantly, he was confrontational only with me whereas Palance was the same with everybody. Even with his fellow actors, particularly so with his co-star Thomas Hunter, who was terrified of him. But Palance knew when to stop and never slowed down production. Not like Peppard…

Kriminal [1966] is one of those titles that stands out from the other films you made in that decade as a bit of an anomaly. Though it kind of prepared you for the gialli than would come later on…
I met a certain Giancarlo Marchetti, who had worked a little as a production manager but was very good at everything and ended his career as the assistant of Pasquale Squitieri, when Squitieri became a senator. Anyhow, he was trying to become a producer and was looking for a project to launch his new career. He approached me, he was Tuscan like myself, and asked me if I had any ideas for a film. I said, "Yes, since comics are selling well, let's try Satanik." So we went to Milan and met with Magnus, the creator of Satanik, at the offices of Corno Comics.[5] They had already sold the rights but they were willing to give us Kriminal. Initially they wanted to write the script, Magnus himself was supposed to, but I put my foot down because I didn't want that amount of violent sex that was present on paper. I made Kriminal more docile than he was in the comics. He was still a chiseler but a funny, more ironic one. *Kriminal* got produced by Marchetti but I asked Venturini, who had produced some of my adventure films, to assist him. The film was shot in Turkey, mostly Istanbul, London and Rome. The result was a very pleasurable film, so much so that Venturini wanted to make a sequel, but I was given the chance of directing *Desert Commandos* and I abandoned the project.

You are one of the few directors who would watch the films of your colleagues. Did you get a chance to see the sequel Il marchio di Kriminal [The Return of Kriminal, 1968] or Satanik directed by Piero Vivarelli?
It's true that I tried to see the films that were being made, at least the successful ones, but I never got a chance to watch these. I've been told that Satanik isn't very good, but it doesn't surprise me. Piero was an intelligent man, cultured and with good ideas but not a very good director. He was never incisive … but a good journalist. I talked to him the day before he died…

One of the few genres you didn't really sink your teeth into is Westerns. How come?
Because I loathe Westerns! Hate them! Plus, I don't like horses. I enjoy the great classics by Ford and Hawks and Leone's films as well but as a whole the genre doesn't interest me. In fact, the few Westerns I did are mostly hybrids, like *Zorro contro Maciste* [*Samson and the Slave Queen*, 1963] which fused Western and peplum elements together. The initial, idiotic, concept of putting Zorro and Samson in the same film was the pro-

ducer Fortunato Misiano's idea. Guido Malatesta, who had been a director, but was unemployed most of the time and working for me as a writer, suggested turning it into a comedy and in so doing reverse the roles: to turn Zorro, who is usually depicted as an astute hero, into a moron and have Samson as the clever one. This was Malatesta's idea. But anyway, this is stuff I'm not interested in. Let's talk about the gialli I made...

Well, we only fleetingly mentioned her, but I would like your personal portrait of Carroll Baker.

If I had ever had a muse, she would have been it. Before working with me she had acted for John Ford, Henry Hathaway, Elia Kazan, William Wyler, George Stevens. She was a high-class actress. I knew and admired her work long before meeting her in person. She was good at everything she did, even the lighter stuff like *The Carpetbaggers* [1964] by Edward Dmytryk. Always professional, punctual and prepared. But despite all this she was extremely reserved and polite, in an almost old-fashioned way. Very sweet and tactful. I liked her from every point of view imaginable. You got the feeling that she was intelligent but not clever, as in sly. She seemed quite naïve. She found herself in Italy because of her naivety, in a way. She had married one of her teachers at the Actor's Studio, Jack Garfein, a Jew, who was Strasberg's assistant. She even converted to Judaism for him. Anyway, they get married, he directs her in a film which, if I'm not mistaken, didn't do very well but nonetheless her career builds up steam and she gets to work with all the wonderful directors we mentioned before. Garfein began intervening more and more, as a manager or an agent would. At one point she signed a contract with Paramount for seven years. After the success of *The Carpetbaggers,* Garfein demanded that her monthly, or weekly, salary be doubled. At the time, before the Hollywood revolution, actors had fixed salaries. The Paramount management answered that they would consider it but only after another film. That other film was *Harlow* [1965], the story of Jean Harlow, by

Lenzi (left) directs Carroll Baker and Jean-Louis Trintignant on the set of *So Sweet ... So Perverse,* in 1969 (courtesy Umberto Lenzi).

Gordon Douglas. The film bombed, a complete disaster and Paramount basically told her, "We will continue to pay you until your contract expires but feel free to look for work outside our studio." Soon after, she found herself at the Venice Film Festival where she had been invited and there she met Marco Ferreri who offered her the leading role in *L'harem* [*Her Harem*, 1967], a film of no importance and few qualities. But Marco Ferreri is an extremely overrated director. Anyway, after that she did Romolo Guerrieri's film *Il dolce corpo di Deborah* [*The Sweet Body of Deborah*, 1968] and then mine. But every time she got paid, the Italian producers wouldn't give her the money but would send it to Paramount because throughout all this period she continued to receive a salary from them on a weekly basis. Working with her was always easy. Consider one thing, we are the same age, me and her, so in 1968 when we did our first film together she was 36, not exactly a kid anymore, but she did all the completely naked scenes without ever using a double. The producers and the crew were sure she would change her mind about some scenes once on the set ... you know, a big Hollywood actress ... but she arrived covered only by a nightgown and as soon as I said action, it would come off. The only thing she would demand was that her pubic hair be covered or dyed. She had problems with that area, but tits and ass ... no problem and she had a truly beautiful ass.

Why didn't you continue working with her after, in the subsequent gialli of the seventies?

As I said before, Carroll Baker was naïve and very trustful of people. She fell into the hands of this pseudo-agent, who was nobody, a charlatan, whose family was in the cultivation of tomatoes, if I recall correctly. I won't say his name but I will tell you that he used to work for Kaufman & Lerner. He spoke English, had a few contacts and slowly gained her trust. After having met him, the quality of her films degenerated and she started doing things with Marino Girolami and then Andrea Bianchi. A truly painful thing to watch. When this started happening, I began looking elsewhere. For example, in the case of *Spasmo* [1974], I chose a British actress, Suzy Kendall, and had the brilliant idea of coupling her with Robert Hoffmann. Hoffmann was lovely and a good actor. He understood the character deeply and really managed to give his role a certain mental ambiguity in a very subtle way.

In the varied and multi-layered world of Italian gialli, where do you fit in exactly? What is your importance in the genre?

Well, I invented what is vulgarly defined as the "sexy thriller" but I find this term to be a little undermining and belittling. My gialli had a dose of morbidity and eroticism that had never been seen in Italian cinema, or any other cinema for that matter. Plus, more so than my colleagues active in the genre, my films depicted a specific world, a very elitist social layer with no moral values, no ethical principles and that followed only the call of money and with it came the sex and the bored decadent perversions. So my films were morbid in the way they fleshed out the intrinsic characteristics of a high-class social layer. My protagonists are lawyers, entrepreneurs, high finance businessmen. All protagonists of a crumbling capitalist world in which there is no space for the pure emotions of love and compassion. In fact, when I wrote these films I would often get inspiration from real events. For example, the main idea of *A Quiet Place to Kill* is taken from a true story. The Duke D'Acquarone, an important aristocrat in the forties, had a villa in Acapulco and was married to a beautiful younger woman. But according to some sources, he was fucking his mother-in-law as well. The wife found them together and shot him several times. His body was found floating in their pool. After a long investigation, the mother accused herself and ended up in a Mexican prison. All these elements, the pool, the villa, the incestuous atmosphere ... I took all these things and used them in my story. Probably the film that perfectly exemplifies what I'm talking about is *Cosi dolce ... cosi perversa* [*So Sweet ... So Perverse*, 1969] in which Jean-Louis Trintignant plays this corrupt industrialist who ends up being the victim of his wife and her lesbian lover. The only giallo I made, that slightly distances itself from this jet-set world, is *Il coltello di ghiaccio* [*Knife of Ice*, 1972], the last of my Carroll Baker thrillers. That was a remake of *The Spiral Staircase* [1946] by Robert Siodmak. The only real difference between my version and Siodmak's is the twist at the end, because I reveal that the mute girl, tormented by this ominous presence, is in reality a dangerous psychopath!

When you part ways with Baker, your style radically changes. Your gialli become much more pop, psychedelic and surreal. We mentioned Spasmo **before, but** Gatti rossi in un labirinto di vetro *[Eyeball,* **a.k.a.** The Devil's Eye, *1975]* **would also be a good example of this new stylistic course.**

Yes, some people have referred to this period as "argentiano" [in the style of Dario Argento]. One critic even wrote that *Sette orchidee macchiate di rosso* [*Seven Blood-Stained Orchids*, 1972] was a bad copy of an Argento film. Argento had been one of my writers on *Legion of the Damned* and is a friend of mine but my films have nothing to do with his. Yes, of course you might find some similar elements, mainly one: the fact that the killer is dressed in black and his face and identity aren't revealed until the end. But in my film there is a reason he is all in black. He's a priest! It's justified, understand? In my film everything has an explanation, a justification whereas in Dario's films the killer goes around with black gloves, a black trench coat, a hat and a dagger ... but why? It makes no sense. This film and maybe *Eyeball*, which you mentioned, may have certain little things that are connected to Argento's world, but that's it. *Spasmo*, for example, is a film of unsurpassed originality! I told the producer I wasn't sure people were going to be captivated because I knew I was going to create a very surrealistic, even confused narrative and over-excited camera style. But I was rewarded, because now, in the States, *Spasmo* is considered one of my best works and speaking of Italian films distributed in America, I want to say something important. The films by the Taviani brothers, Antonioni but even Pasolini and all the so-called auteurs, were shown in theaters bought by the government or screened in the Italian consulates. My films, and the ones of other genre directors, got distributed all over the place. Don't get me wrong, as a film lover and cultured person which I am, I liked auteurs' films when they still worked. Let's take Fellini for example: *I vitelloni* [1953] is a masterpiece and one of my favorite films of all time, *La dolce vita* [1960] is fantastic but *8½* [1963] is a ball-buster. Antonioni, for one of his films, colored the houses of a whole town green and red and then, as Monica Vitti stares at them she whispers, "my hair hurts." What a pretentious pile of shit! If your hair hurts, call a mental clinic immediately! The lines that are spoken in Antonioni's films are often ridiculous. The first films of these directors were very good. Some I didn't like much, like *La strada* [1954] which was too Catholic and I'm not, but they're good, well-conceived films but then, because they were given an unlimited power, they started getting crazy ideas. They never had to confront themselves with the market, something that directors like myself had to do. We were not allowed to exempt ourselves from the logics of the market's needs and demands. Antonioni after two/three really good films, came up with the "incommunicability of the human soul"! [He pronounces the term with visible repulsion made even stronger by placing his hand at the center of his checkered shirt, in a theatrical manner.] Oh, fuck off! Yesterday afternoon, on television I came across *Dodsworth* [1936] by William Wyler, with a wonderful Walter Huston. A complex film that analyzes the balance between love and fame. A timeless, intelligent film which opens itself to a wide audience. Those are the films I'm interested in making. That is cinema! In fact, when the Americans invested money in Italian films, they didn't contact them, the auteurs, but us. My *Sandokan* with Steve Reeves [*Sandokan, the Great*, 1963] was co-produced by MGM! All the *Sandokan* films Sergio Sollima directed later, were copied from mine, let's not forget this.

We missed a sub-genre you had a crucial role in creating in the giallo period of your career. I'm talking about Il paese del sesso selvaggio [Deep River Savages, a.k.a. The Man from the Deep River, 1972] and the cannibal films that followed it.

I had a feeling we were getting to this. *Deep River Savages* was a strange project: the story was written by Emmanuelle Arsan, a lady who had an incredible success with the creation of Emmanuelle, a kind of soft-core porn. She was Thai, and she wrote this brief story about some primitive tribes set on the border between Burma and Thailand. The producer, fascinated by this subject matter, commissioned two professional writers to come up with a script, and then approached me to direct it. But I thought it was a little too much of a documentary, and so I participated in the revision of the script and based the narration on this character, which was copied entirely from *A Man Called Horse* [1970]. We shot the film in real locations, in an area between Burma and Thailand that was completely wild, with natives that didn't speak any language at all. I would communicate using an invented language that would sound sometimes firm to them, sometimes jovial, other times approving. I remember the scene of the amputation of the tongue, or the one with the cannibals, which is terrible though very brief, with them all sitting down eating human flesh, and this girl who has been killed and who is missing an arm, a hand... No Thai actress or extra would do the scene so I had to get a prostitute from a brothel who did it and did it well. We used special tricks invented by me at the moment: we dug a hole and buried her arm up to her elbow, then covered it with pieces of bloody meat, and the result was credible ... it seemed as if she was missing an arm. And we did the same with her leg, burying it up to her knee. We also created two fake breasts that we applied over her own—they, like in the case of most Oriental girls, were very small. This single scene gave rise to the whole Italian cannibal genre. Still, the whole story branched from that of *A Man Called Horse*, which in our case was more like "A Man Called Photography," because the lead was a photographer who undergoes all these humiliations and challenges. The film was amazingly successful in Germany as well as in many other countries, but in Germany it was released with an Italian title invented by them: *Mondo Cannibale*.

Why didn't you direct a follow-up?

The Italian producer asked me to make a sequel, because the Germans wanted another film with Umberto Lenzi as the director and Ivan Rassimov and Me Me Lay as the protagonists. I asked for a fee which I considered fair after the success of the first film, which was released in Italy with a stupid title [literal translation: The Country of Wild Sex], chosen by the Italian distributors; the original title was *The Man from the Deep River*. But then the producer disappeared and only much later did I discover that

Lenzi offering a canteen to Me Me Lai, as he unknowingly creates the "cannibal genre" with his *Deep River Savages*, 1972 (courtesy Nocturno Cinema).

the project had been passed on to Ruggero Deodato. The film was called *Ultimo mondo cannibale* [*Last Cannibal World*, a.k.a. *The Last Survivor*, a.k.a. *Jungle Holocaust*, 1977].

We are getting closer to the genre you are most associated to, crime thrillers and action films.

I'm a person, even before becoming a director, who was heavily inspired by American noir cinema of the forties, which was the best period for Hollywood noirs. Films like *Laura* [1944] by Otto Preminger for example, then all the films by Jules Dassin, Edgar Ulmer and all those directors of European origin. Also Raoul Walsh, a master and a director very dear to me, because he directed a lot of films, like I did. Just think that he started in the silent era as Griffith's 1st AD. He directed Humphrey Bogart's first important film, *High Sierra* [1941], and numerous films of great visual impact throughout the forties. This is just to say that I was very happy to make a noir, which many consider my first police thriller. A pure noir, like the ones of Di Leo, such as *Milano rovente* [*Gang War in Milan*, 1973], produced by Milanese industrialists who were trying to enter the film world. The protagonist is a kind of mafia boss who controls the drug and prostitution racket. It was strongly influenced by *The Godfather* [1972], but it doesn't really have the structure and look of a gangster movie. It was all shot in Milan in some very nice locations. It came out well and even now it is often released on DVD and Blu-ray. It is considered the only noir I made but one of the best of that period also because I describe this bleak city populated by thieves, assassins, pimps and drug dealers very well. I had Antonio Sabato as a protagonist. He wasn't a great actor but worked well also because he is a Sicilian who made his way to the North where he worked as a laborer, before becoming an actor, so he was familiar with this kind of world. Then I had a wonderful actor like Phillipe Leroy who had a great stage presence. With this film, I opened and closed my relationship with noirs. Then came the most glorious period of my career, the one of police thrillers...

You acknowledged that Almost Human *is one of your best films. How did it come to be?*

Initially the director was supposed to be Sergio Martino, who was the obvious choice because he had just made *Milano trema: La polizia vuole giustizia* [*The Violent Professionals*, 1973]. But he chose to make *La bellissima estate* [*Summer to Remember*, 1974] instead, which was a mistake. A bullshit melodrama inspired by an American film that didn't do well. So anyway, Luciano Martino asked me to step in. I met with Milian, who as I told you wanted to get to know me before accepting and I started working on the script.

What did you change in Ernesto Gastaldi's original script?

Not much. I added some scenes. But when Gastaldi praises himself for his work, he always omits to say that all the dialogue was rewritten completely by Tomas and that many moments were improvised on the set. When Giulio Sacchi and his gang are in the villa and he orders the man to give him a blow job, that was improvised by Tomas on the spot. All the film is filled with things he invented. I let him do anything he wanted on that film because I could tell he knew what he was doing, he had a real grip of that character's psyche. This is one of the reasons he wanted to work with me so much from that moment onwards. Sergio Martino was hated by Milian for example, after they had worked on *40 gradi all'ombra del lenzuolo* [*Sex with a Smile*, 1976] because he didn't like a scene that Martino insisted he should do. Don't misunderstand me, Martino is a great director. Maybe even better than me when it comes to gialli but Milian was like a kid, you had to know when to praise him and when to scold him. Going back to Gastaldi, he recently wrote, on Facebook, that Martino is a great director and I'm nobody. Of course! The Martino brothers were his employers. He was under contract with Dania Productions[6] so it's obvious he loves him. If he worked at all it's thanks to Sergio and his brother. Now, I can accept somebody saying they prefer Martino as a director to Lenzi, but to say I'm a nobody is preposterous! I worked with him twice. Well, actually once, because with *Almost Human* the script was given me done and ready, I didn't even have a meeting with him. The first time was on *So Sweet ... So Perverse* and if there is something that doesn't work, it's the script!

Let's talk about the other screenwriters you worked with. Let's start with Vincenzo Mannino, with whom you made Il giustiziere sfida la città [Syndicate Sadists, 1975].

Poor thing, he died young. Well, Mannino was always brown-nosing Milian. Anything Tomas asked he would do. The script was heavily derivative of Leone's film *Per un pugno di dollari* [*A Fistful of Dollars*, 1964] with the story of two rival crime families and the lone stranger who gets in between them. The story changed though, just before starting production when Tomas came back from Miami, where he had gone to visit his mother. When he was there, he had picked up a book called *First Blood* ... So the character was renamed Rambo and Mannino changed the script to include references and connections to the book. The main structure remained intact, but this idea Milian had pervaded the whole story of the film. The clothes he wears are inspired by *First Blood*. If you watch the Stallone film, at the beginning, he is dressed almost identically to Milian.

The writer who is most associated to your cinema is Dardano Sacchetti.

Yes, because he wrote some of my most popular films. We started working together with *L'uomo della strada fa giustizia* [*Man Hunt*, a.k.a. *Man Hunt in the City*, 1975] but the best thing he wrote for me was *Roma a mano armata* [*Rome Armed to the Teeth*, a.k.a. *Brutal Justice*, 1976], our second collaboration. He wasn't a great writer but he had one quality, which always seemed to save him; he was quick, very quick. He would listen to what was needed, go home, steal here and there from various films and in a week you would have a finished script. Sacchetti had some great qualities but also some big defects. He created solid stories but when he developed them, they were often too brief or approximate, rough round the edges because he wrote ten a year. So, I would find myself having to rethink or rewrite huge portions of his scripts, which always contained some interesting aspects because he was very imaginative. The narrative development though, was always lacking. Mannino was the exact opposite. He was an ex-prefect who started working in cinema thanks to his friendship with director Alberto De Martino. He was very bureaucratic in his approach: he would document himself, work on the dialogue... He wrote *Napoli violenta* [*Violent Naples*, 1976], which had a very good script. He went a month to Naples where he infiltrated a mob family to research for the film. All the episodes in the story are true, told by these mobsters. So they are two very different writers: one creative with the story but limited in developing it; the other with fewer ideas but much more structure.

You once stated in an interview that cinema is the prosecution of a limited amount of narrative structures.

Yes, I stick by that statement. Cinema is an interdependent activity, where nobody has really done anything new, except for the Russian and American directors of the silent

Lenzi (left) and Tomas Milian on the set of their first film together, *Almost Human,* **in 1974 (courtesy Nocturno Cinema).**

era. After Murnau, Von Sternberg, the first Howard Hawks, the first John Ford, cinema has always remained the same. Experiences were passed on without many variations, and if there was a turning point on a linguistic level, it belonged to Roberto Rossellini with *Roma città aperta* [*Rome Open City*, 1945] and especially *Paisà* [*Paisan*, 1946] in which, through various episodes, he tells the story of the liberation of Italy by American troops and the Italian Resistance. Apart from this, everything is tied together.

In Syndicate Sadists **you work with a legend like Joseph Cotten.**
   I've worked with some of the greatest Hollywood actors. One being the underrated Arthur Kennedy, who worked with me in *Rome Armed to the Teeth*. He was a great actor who co-starred with Humphrey Bogart and appeared in numerous other films. We didn't have much of a relationship, though. He would do his scenes and leave. Joseph Cotten … for my wife and I he was a legend, for films such as *Duel in the Sun* (1946).… He had made his debut with Orson Welles, with whom he began working in the theater and then they made a lot of films together, being also united by a deep friendship. He worked on some of Hollywood's biggest classics: *Portrait of Jeannie* [1948] and *Shadow of a Doubt* [1943]. He was a giant. But in life you change. He was very cold; he didn't talk much. Professional yes, but he didn't promote or try to have a dialogue. I would have liked to have told him, "I was inspired by many of your films. I've seen them all." I would have asked him about his rapport with Alfred Hitchcock and Orson Welles, but there was no dialogue. These were actors who would complete their role in a week, so either you had established a feeling right away or there wasn't going to be any time. On the contrary,

with Mel Ferrer, with whom I worked a couple of times, I had a good relationship, especially on *Incubo sulla città contaminata* [*Nightmare City,* a.k.a. *City of the Walking Dead,* 1980] where he had a bigger role. He worked a lot in Italy, especially while married to Audrey Hepburn and with him, I must say, there was friendship. With Arthur Kennedy we had a civil relationship throughout production. But I've worked with many greats: George Hamilton and Henry Fonda for example. But with them it was different because they had important roles so I had a chance to be with them for weeks and we got along fantastically. With John Huston I shot a scene between him and Ray Lovelock, on the beach at sunset, with that so-called "in-between" light. He had to recite this poem to comfort Lovelock on his brother's death. A poem by John Donne: "No man is an island … if Europe…" We roughly had 30 minutes to shoot the scene because time was running out. I had studied the shots in every detail with the DOP. When we finally started shooting, with the right light, he started his poem … but he would interrupt himself, "keep rolling Umberto." He would say a line, stop, think, start again. The camera operator told me that we had to hurry, because we had nearly finished the film in camera. Finally I managed to solve everything by doing a longshot. Lovelock is on the left and Huston, in profile, on the right. Within this shot he only says the first two lines of the poem, then I did a quick close-up and all the rest of the poem I shot at the zoo in Rome where there were some palm trees. This whole sequence began in a tavern, then we shot 100 kilometers from Los Angeles, where we found a structure similar to the ones you could find during the war. Huston coming out of the tavern and going towards Lovelock on the beach was shot on various locations, using a small tank, which we also took to Santa Monica, as a linking device for each part of the scene. He told my wife: "Olga, if I had directed this sequence I would've taken a week. Umberto is great. Technically outstanding."

With Milian you would make exceptions, when it came to leaving decisions to actors.

I never gave anybody any liberty except for Tomas, because he was a genius when it came to dialogue. He was able to find some lines that managed to stick in the public's imagination and get quoted every day on Facebook. The one on the hole: you eat from a hole, you are born from a hole, you die and end up in a hole. It was fantastic. That was his first great invention. One day I nearly had an argument with him but I realized he was right. We were shooting *Rome Armed to the Teeth*, a scene in which he was being chased by the police and needed to stop at a gas station because of a flat tire. This kid, after having changed the tire, asked him for 500 liras. Milian asked, "What's your name?" "La Pira Galeazzo." "La Pira Galeazzo, I don't have a dime and you can grab my cazzo (cock)." I was directing the scene and I immediately shouted, "Cut!" He was supposed to give the kid the money and go off. "Are you crazy?!" I asked him. "Umberto, I'm begging you, leave this line in the film." When it premiered, in February 1976 at the Adriano cinema in Rome, with 2,000 people present—I went to see it with my wife and Maurizio Merli—and that moment came, people went nuts, shouting and laughing. From that moment, inventing these kind of absurd lines became his trademark.

Another figure which is crucial to the creation of your imagery is Franco Micalizzi. It's not a Lenzi cop thriller without Micalizzi's funky tunes.

Ah! I forgot … he's coming over for dinner tomorrow. I had forgotten. Well, yes … Franco is a friend. For the past few years now, I've stopped because I'm just too old, but for quite a few years he would tour around Italy and Europe with his jazz band playing the soundtracks of my films and I would go with him. The collaboration between us has always been very good. His style just adapted perfectly to the rhythm I wanted to give the films. I wrote some of the songs with him. In *The Great Battle* there is a song called "Winter in Berlin," which was sung by an award winning singer called Maggie MacNeal. After twenty years she sang the song again at San Remo, with my lyrics. The same goes for "Man Before His Time," the main song of *Violent Naples*. Franco still works, because most musicians managed to survive the crises in the eighties….

We haven't mentioned Ennio Morricone.

My first police thriller had the music of Morricone. He had done something wonderful! After *Almost Human* I asked him to work on another film but he refused, saying that his wife had been shocked by the violence of my films and had told him not work on such brutal projects. I had to find a new composer, but at that time there weren't any that really had a sense of urban violence, that could accompany such rhythmic dialogue. I found myself desperately seeking a musician until a man from RCA told me: "Lenzi, try to use Franco Micalizzi, he hasn't worked much for films but I consider him a great talent." He had composed the music for *L'ultima neve di primavera* [*The Last Snows of Spring*, 1973], which had been a hit. I called him and the first film he did for me was *Syndicate Sadists*, then came *Rome Armed to the Teeth*, then *Violent Naples*. Subsequent to the success of my films, various producers started contacting him. A very sweet person and as far as film music is concerned, amazing, because he managed to create, especially in *Violent Naples*, a really obsessively cumulative music but touched by small melodies that would give a sense of context. You can hear a quick tarantella in the middle of this jazz orchestration. Like in *From Corleone to Brooklyn* where I wrote a song with him, which is very nostalgic and was conceived for a sequence in New York, when the two protagonists enter a house of immigrants and see all these old photos of their ancestors. He composed a marvelous piece for which I wrote the lyrics. Then he composed the music for my war films. We never parted ways. I never had other composers. I only did two films with Stelvio Cipriani but for the most part Micalizzi was my composer.

You and Milian part ways in a moment in which the "poliziesco all'italiana" had started to be heavily contaminated by comedy and was losing its appeal.

Yes, this in hindsight is true, but the reason we stopped working together was simply that I was fed up with dealing with his craziness, his mood swings and probably I was eager to pass on to something different. You could say that *The Great Battle* and *From Hell to Victory* were films I made to decontaminate myself from all those films with Milian. I was unlucky though, because shortly after, he went to Asia to purify his soul with a famous Indian guru and when he came back he had stopped doing drugs, he had stopped drinking. In fact, with Bruno Corbucci he made sixteen films. Corbucci got the calm, spiritual Milian, I got the out-of-control, ball-busting, pain-in-the-ass Milian. Though I will tell you something … all those films they did together, all the series of Nico Giraldi, were actually directed by Tomas. Corbucci was not well, he had to undergo dialysis treatment every day and would let him do whatever he wanted and you can tell, technically they are all over the place. Corbucci made a lot of money but you can't really consider them his films. Tomas would even choose the cast and throw in all his friends. Those, however, were the tired wheezings of a dying genre.

What about the relationship between Milian and Maurizio Merli?

There wasn't one. They beat each other up on the set of *Rome Armed to the Teeth* and never shared a scene together since. But Merli was right on that occasion. In the last

Again Lenzi (front) and Milian, this time on the set of *Syndicate Sadists*, 1975 (courtesy Nocturno Cinema).

scene of the film, during the big face-off, Merli ended up on the floor and Milian had to kick him but he was supposed to fake it ... but he did it for real, and kicked hard several times. Merli got up and wanted to strangle him. Two stage technicians had to hold him down. On the next film I did with them *Il cinico, l'infame, il violento* [*The Cynic, the Rat & the Fist*, 1978] I had to use doubles for wide shots and do the reverse shots of them speaking to each other separately.

I imagine the atmosphere on the set of **The Cynic, the Rat & the Fist** *was quite tense.*
They didn't want to work together, very similar to *Heat* [1995], the film with Robert De Niro and Al Pacino where they meet once at a bar and have a dialogue, all done with tricks: shot and counter-shot using a double. I had to re-think the film in such a way that the two characters never met. Their two stories run parallel to each other: with Milian who is looking for him and Merli who pretends to be dead so as to be able to move around freely. These two stories then tie in the ending, when they finally meet. In the scene Milian had to get into a jeep and try to run down Maurizio Merli. I directed it with a specific technique. For the longshot, we used doubles and then the close-ups of their reactions. They did that scene, each one on different days. They never met for it.

The Cynic *is a film that was conceived with different intentions to what we see on screen.*
The film script had a mistake in it. The producer initially wanted it to be about a robbery, a heist in a James Bond kind of style. I told him: "I don't think this approach you want to impose on me is the best choice. It's not the genre that works in Italy. What works are films like *Rome Armed to the Teeth* or *Violent Naples*. But we ended-up shooting the

whole film with the title "Together for a Great Heist." A really idiotic title even because the heist in the film is reduced to a scene of little importance. If you watch the trailer you won't find *The Cynic, the Rat & the Fist* but "Together for a Great Heist." The problem is that for a film to be successful, the director has to be put in the condition to choose the title. They asked: "Why don't you want this one?" "Because who the hell goes and watches, at the height of urban violence, 'Together for a Great Heist,' when moreover the heist is very modest? It sounds like a Village People song!" "What do you suggest?" "I would copy Sergio Leone: *The Cynic, the Rat & the Fist*." It was an amazing success, superior to the quality of the film, because it's not one of the best of my cop films. The best are *Almost Human*, *Rome Armed to the Teeth* and, the one I love the most, *From Corleone to Brooklyn*. Though *The Cynic* has some elements I'm proud of. Tomas played a very interesting character. He was called "the Chinese" because he had gotten inspiration from a fruit vendor in some Roman working-class suburb that was called that way for his oriental-looking eyes. He created some situations that without being too similar to "Monnezza" and without being too serious, nonetheless managed to be a compromise between the cruelty of previous police thrillers and a new grotesque cynicism. There are two scenes that have become cults and that people often upload on YouTube. One is when he goes and visits Gianni Musy in hospital, because he's been beaten up by Merli, and is completely immobilized. Milian goes to talk to him to understand what had happened. At the end Tomas pulls nearer and asks: "What do the doctors say?" "That in twenty days I should be out of here." "Unless there are complications," and shoots him in the forehead. And then there is another scene which helped make the film so successful. When the great actor Riccardo Garrone, who hasn't paid the protection tax, is taken into this car. He sees one of Milian's men with a jack in his hand. He asks why and Milian answers, "Seeing you have paid a part of what you owe me I will only break one of your legs. If you hadn't I would've broken both of them." You see the actor becoming scared but with an almost incredulous expression as they stretch out his leg and break it. That was a fun scene to shoot but what made it work was the dialogue, which was amusing but aggressive. Anyway the film was a success despite having begun with a wrong title and a story about a heist that didn't work.

Though brief, the heist sequence is quite impressive.
That scene was shot with real danger for the actor. It was done on the top floor of a German insurance company building which was in front of the headquarters of AGIS, the association of cinema owners, that gave me permission to shoot there. We put a pole that went from one of the windows to the roof of the other building using those tubes that extend like a telescopes. We tried to shoot the scene only once because the actor had to sit on this chair in a pulley, suspended in mid-air, at 12 or 13 meters from the ground. Anything could have gone wrong, plus we had to shoot at night and had to light the road and the buildings. It wasn't a simple task. You have to be careful not to underexpose the film and you have be resourceful. The scene came very well. We shot from the windows, at street level and I must say that Merli was truly fearless. He was an actor that was remarkable from a physical standpoint, like when he did that long sequence on the cable car in *Violent Naples*. He ran and jumped when the cable-car was at a 90-degree angle, having to move and shoot. Even in this case he showed great courage, and was able to dose his physicality fantastically. In fact, when he died of a heart attack as he was trying to serve during a friendly tennis match, I was shocked because it would have made more sense if he had died during one of the stunts he did for my films.

What do you remember about John Saxon who acts alongside Merli and Milian in the film?

John Saxon was a delightful person. He began his Hollywood career with Universal Studios where he would usually play the romantic lead. He was a very sweet and composed, he wouldn't behave like a diva. His roots are Italian, I don't remember his real surname but his parents were immigrants. He spoke Italian fluently and we would understand each other well. In fact, I did various films with him, one also in the States. But he had his limits. Not being a kid anymore, the Universal years were long gone, he was more of a supporting actor. At least with me he was never the lead but a support to the protagonist. I have good memories of him. Very good.

You mentioned the criminal played by Milian in The Cynic, the Rat & the Fist—***you seem to have a very favorable, non-condeming attitude towards the villains in your films.***

In the case of *Almost Human*, the script by Ernesto Gastaldi was almost perfect. Tomas, fueled by drugs, would invent lines that hadn't been written but were very strong and spot-on. As much as the character was cynical, cruel and violent, he had some aspects that made him likeable. He is an outcast, a social misfit: without a job, always at a local bar.... Then in *La banda del gobbo* [*Brothers Till We Die*, 1978] and in *Rome Armed to the Teeth* I would root for him completely, for this proletarian hunchback ... particularly in *Bothers Till We Die*, where I describe his moving relationship with this prostitute. The film critics at that time were very black-and-white. They would see fascist overtones in these films, especially because the police would use brutal force and put justice in their own hands but it's a mistake to analyze things in this manner. If one goes and watches the American gangster classics, like *Scarface* [1932] by Hawks or Wellman's *The Public Enemy* [1931], there is always a shootout in which the villain, or should I say antagonist, gets killed. In *Scarface*, Paul Muni gets riddled by bullets, for example, and this continued throughout the years. Just think of *Bonnie & Clyde* [1967] where they end up gunned down as soon as they exit their car. A film has to be judged on its aesthetical merits, with a Benedetto Croce approach, and not like Stanow, the head of the Stalinist intelligentsia who would shoot you if you didn't like the artwork of the regime. Films should be judged for their artistic and narrative merits. An approach that is used by people like Tarantino, Joe Dante, Tim Burton—thanks to whom we've been revitalized. This way of labeling our films according to their political message really penalized us. I remember newspapers, like *Paese Sera*, would call me fascist, an assassin, a reactionary, when I'm exactly the opposite. I'm an anarchist and I demonstrated this in the ending of *Brothers Till We Die*.

The war films you direct in the late seventies separate two very distinct periods of your career. In the eighties you plunge into a genre you hadn't really dealt with before. Let's start by talking about your reconcilement to the cannibal genre.

Mino Loy called to tell me that there were a couple of films that had to be done for the Germans, who admired my work on *Deep River Savages*, or *Mondo Cannibale* like they called it, and who would give me carte blanche. I wanted to do something a little different. I didn't want to make a pure cannibal movie, so I did *Mangiati vivi* [*Eaten Alive!*, 1980]. The story was inspired by true events. This infamous sect, led by the Reverend Jim Jones who, in Guyana, led more than 200 followers to commit suicide when the authorities were closing in on him. Production took place in Sri Lanka, where we shot for about six weeks. I had, many years before, in 1963–65, already directed *Sandokan* and other adventure movies in this area. When I went there the first time, it was still Ceylon, a British colony, and by the early 1980s it was a Republic animated by a wind of civil war that would explode soon after we left, between the Tamils, who were in favor of a unification with India, and the Sinhalese, who were Buddhists. It was an interesting experience and, having already been to these places, finding the right spot to shoot was easy. We shot a considerable amount of the film in the National Park of Kandy, a place in which you can find everything, from huge spiders to all sorts of snakes, but what impressed me the most were all these huge vampires hanging from the trees, bats … this big [he stretches his arms exaggeratedly as he smiles] … and you just needed a rifle shot to see this massive black cloud which I put in the film. The locals had learnt about cinema from the Italians, and you could find some technical equipment, like dollies and lights, which were imported from Rome in the hopes of creating an independent Sri Lankan film industry. Sergio Martino filmed *Il fiume del grande caimano* [*The Great Alligator*, 1979] there. My film went well, especially because of these gruesome cannibal scenes towards the end. Having been struck by the whole Jim Jones affair, I liked the idea of putting together the cannibal element with a macabre true event. Paola Senatore is the one that gets devoured, her breasts cut and then eaten in front of the camera. I took a bunch of young Thais and Filipinos in difficulty, and forced them with severity and sadism to eat this fake flesh made out of bloody rubber foam. [His choice of words and the gleeful expression on his face makes me wonder, like it has numerous times before, how much his over-the-top mannerisms are fruit of the precise will of creating a character and persona for himself.] There was first the cutting of the breast, then a reaction shot, and then a prosthetic was placed strategically and put in the same way you would put on a wig.

Did you know who Robert Kerman really was when you cast him?
I had no idea that Kerman was a fake name and that he was a porn actor called Richard Bolla. If I had known I probably wouldn't have chosen him, but they had spoken well of him and he ended up in the film. A mediocre actor, without a great physique … maybe he had some sexual secret, but anyway he wasn't worth much. The actress instead,

Lenzi, in white, on the set of *Eaten Alive!*, in 1980 (courtesy Nocturno Cinema).

Janet Agren, was very fascinating from a physical standpoint; she was beautiful and had a Nordic charisma. She was Swedish and was fairly cold in her acting but she had a great screen presence. She holds the film on her own two shoulders, more than Kerman, more than Senatore, who was a minor character but fundamental because of her cannibal scene. Senatore had no problems stripping, and in fact ended her career in porn.

We've mentioned a number of films of yours he's acted in but we haven't talked about Ivan Rassimov.

I'm very sorry Ivan died so young, we were good friends and we would often meet up with our families. With me he had done *Spasmo* but our first film together was *Deep River Savages*. I had trouble finding an actor with the right face for that film. They had suggested Gianni Garko and I auditioned him but he refused the role because he didn't want to do the film half naked. He told me he didn't look good in the nude, so I thought of Ivan, whom I had seen somewhere and who had this very Slavic face. My wife is Slavic too so I don't mean it in a bad way. He had very hardened somatic traits which were perfect for the role of a photographer who undergoes and overcomes terrible tortures. In *Eaten Alive!* he plays the cinematic equivalent of the fanatical Jim Jones, the head of this multiracial sect in the middle of the jungle, that ends up in a mass suicide when the police helicopters arrive and find practically only corpses. The fundamental defect of the film is that I should have had 300 extras, but putting together some American, Canadian and Belgian tourists, I only managed to round up ten, the rest were indigenous, so I wasn't able to give the suicide scene the epic feel I would have wanted.

Cannibal Ferox [a.k.a. Make Them Die Slowly! 1981] is your most violent and infamous film...

It's a completely different kind of film. It was always the distributors of *Deep River Savages* who wanted more cannibal movies, and what they wanted was a cannibal movie that would beat any kind of record as far as violence and blood were concerned. Even here I was given complete freedom. They offered little money but a big percentage on international sales and I wrote the script. In fact, the idea, the script and the dialogues are mine; this regards both *Eaten Alive!* and *Cannibal Ferox*. With *Ferox* I tried to give a logic to the film, meaning I envisioned the story of a New York university student who is working on her thesis on the colonial slavery of the whites against Amazon tribes in Latin America, which is a historical fact. Pizarro, Cortes, the Spanish and the Portuguese colonials had slaughtered hundreds of poor natives in Brazil, Argentina and Colombia, creating a spiral of violence which caused the near extinction of these tribes. The few that are left are hidden in the most remote corners of the Amazon forest. So it was fundamental that a film with such a story should be shot in the proper locations. We got a plane from Bogotá to Leticia, a flight that was only available twice a week, travelling over massive portions of jungle between Brazil and Colombia, where there was nothing, not even a village, just a sea of green. Not only were we scared, but in this place, drug lords, mercenaries, adventurers ran free. There wasn't even a hospital, and there wasn't the possibility of calling Europe. The only way to communicate with the outside world was through some acquaintances with the Colombian border line presidio, who would let us use their radio. I recall that at that time there had been the Irpinia earthquake,[7] and there was panic among the crew because they were anxious to have news of their loved ones but the thing that most worried me was that if anybody got hurt or fell sick, they would have died for lack of any kind of first-aid station. There were no roads, and in an emergency you had to wait for one of the two weekly flights. Leticia is located at the mouth of the Amazon River, and you could see these huge merchant ships sailing up and down the river. I can't tell you how much we suffered. We only had pasta ... we didn't know what else to eat. The protagonists of *Cannibal Ferox* are all indigenous locals and very few real actors make up the cast: two women, Danilo Mattei who plays the young one of the group and Giovanni Lombardo Radice who plays this terrible and bloodthirsty villain who is wanted by the police. In fact, the film begins with detectives looking for him in New York. I was lucky enough to have two actresses who were willing to shoot terrible scenes: one was Zora Kerowa, a Czech actress, and the other was Lorraine De Selle, who has now become an important TV producer and who comes from a noble family. Her father was the French ambassador in Australia. Both of them consented to act in awful scenes, surrounded by mud and animals.

Let's talk gore. The head being sliced open is one of the scenes that is most remembered.
Ah yes! The head-cutting scene was a stroke of directorial genius, because I created this table with a hole in it, so that a piece of the actor's head stuck out and when they thrust the machete, the actor's head is no longer there, and in its place there's half a coconut with fake hair on it. I lowered the camera to show the actor's face covered in blood, you know? These are small tricks one invents on the spot, but even a slight mistake will ruin the final result. The table was three/four centimeters thick, so it could hide the real actor's head underneath, and if you watch the scene it seems real.

It's said that you and Giovanni Lombardo Radice didn't exactly have an idyllic relationship during the making of the film.
No, on the contrary. On set, my relationship with him was excellent, I had no problems. The problems came years later, because he is a loser who owes his success all over the world to two films: *Cannibal Ferox*, and a small role in Lucio Fulci's *Paura nella città dei morti viventi* [*City of the Living Dead*, a.k.a. *The Gates of Hell*, 1980] where he gets his cranium drilled with a machine. Apart from this, he's a complete loser, and started talking badly about me on the Internet, saying things that are absurd. Why would you talk crap about a film that has given you so much visibility? I don't understand. On the set—I repeat—there was never a single problem between the actors and myself and he specifically responded perfectly to all the scenes, even the most repugnant ones, like the castration. His grudge began years later, when his career came to an end and he remained famous—but really famous—all over the world because of my film and a small part in the one directed by Fulci. I can't understand all this anger and malevolence, and this cynical refusal of a film that has given him fame and success.

Needless to say a lot of the attention the cannibal sub-genre got was due to the amount of violence but also, and perhaps mainly, because of the actual animal killings. What do you have to say about that?
It all began with an article written by a famous Neapolitan writer, a novelist, she's dead now ... I can't remember her name but she was very well known. She wrote an article for *L'Europeo*[8] accusing me of cruelty to animals, and she had every reason to do so. Sure, in my film you can see natives catch a tortoise and cut its head off with a machete, but have you ever seen how Tuscan farmers kill pigs? Watching a scene like that is much more desecrating, cruel and incredible than what I did. From the dawn of time, man has

killed, tortured and eaten animals; the cruelest thing a person can do is kill a pig. It starts squealing in pain as they drag it and cut it in half ... terrible. It's something I experienced when I lived in Massa Marittima. I used to go to the slaughterhouse because my father had connections in that field. The cruelty used to put meat on our tables is the same cruelty used in our cannibal movies. We killed snakes, evil snakes, some tortoises, and for the rest we invented things. For example, in *Eaten Alive!* there is a giant boa devouring a big rodent ... you can see it entering the snake's mouth, but it wasn't true because I stopped the scene and had someone pull it out. Still, I have to say that these accusations towards my colleagues and myself are legitimate. But they forget that these things happen in our civilized world, in Rome, in Milan, in Naples. And there's nothing worse than how animals are butchered.

Considering the little love you have for these films, how did you react when they achieved a cult status over the years?

When in the nineties they called me for interviews about these films, I hung up. I mean, in the context of my filmography these two films are terrible, based on violence and perversity and when I realized that the films I love the most and that are important in my career like *The Great Battle* are completely ignored.... I mean, I did films with George Peppard, George Hamilton, Annie Duperey, Jean-Pierre Cassel, Capucine and then I have to see that the films that are most recognized worldwide are the ones with Zora Kerowa and Lombardo Radice! You can imagine the pleasure I had in having to talk about them! Nearly all my war films are masterpieces, and when Tarantino was asked to make a list of the ten best "spaghetti war movies," he said that the first one was *The Legion of the Damned* because it's not true that he got inspiration for *Inglorious Basterds* from Castellari's film ... from Castellari he only got the title, but the whole idea of a group of criminal soldiers was taken from my film! So, out of the best spaghetti war movies, he placed *The Legion of the Damned*, *The Great Battle*, *Desert Commandos*, *From Hell to Victory*, all films with huge budgets, this last one was shot in Almeria one month, in Paris one month, and in Rome one month, with an incredible cast. Nobody watches these films. *Eaten Alive!* and *Cannibal Ferox* for example were shown on TV last night and for the hundredth time they had a number of "likes" on Facebook. The only reason I talk about these films is because they've given me great financial success. So now I do it out of recognition.

If you had to pinpoint the moment in which you realized these films had become cults which would it be?

In 1996, when I got a call from Cinecittà telling me that there was an American asking about me: it was Sage Stallone, the son of Sylvester Stallone. He was a 22-year-old man who had come to Italy to buy *Cannibal Ferox* to release it in cinemas and distribute it on laser disc through a company called Grindhouse founded by himself and Bob Murawski, who won an Oscar for *Spiderman 2* [2004]. They restored the whole film at Cinecittà. They redid the music with a big orchestra and it cost them a lot of money. If they had asked me before, I could have helped them out somehow ... you know, Stallone's son arrives with another American, and of course they took them for everything they had. When they came to my house to interview me, they brought a bunch of posters they wanted autographed for a certain Quentin, and that was the first time I heard of Tarantino, whom I later met in Venice. My fundamental successes are my two cannibal movies and *Nightmare City*, at least as far as the foreign market is concerned.

Nightmare City *is your only—I know this is going to irritate you—zombie film...*

It is not a zombie film!! Those are not zombies! They are contaminated people! [I realize I'd hit an even more sensitive spot to what I initially thought. Lenzi looks completely distraught about the improper term I incautiously used. I apologize.] Do not call them that anymore, please! Oh…

Are your feelings for **Nightmare City** *similar to those you have for your cannibal movies?*

Yes. The problem was the script. It was horrible! It was a script I totally hated but more importantly it was incomplete. The script they gave me couldn't have been longer than 50 or 60 minutes of screen time. The producer wanted a movie with different looking zombies. When you're only the director, you are mainly just the executor of a project which has been decided before. It was one of those rare cases where I wasn't involved with the original concept. But I managed to change the script, if not the premise, quite substantially. I thought, and still do, that the biggest threat to society was the contamination from radiation and chemicals that cause sickness and death. So I introduced the idea that these were not living dead but contaminated people, mutated by a nuclear meltdown. I wasn't interested in making a zombie film because that is Romero's territory plus Fulci had added everything that could be added to it. I didn't want to try and surpass them. This producer came to me with the script, he specialized in co-productions … and in fact *Nightmare City* involved Italy, Spain and Mexico. The lead is Mexican and was imposed on me. A fucking terrible actor … what was his name … Hugo Stiglitz! He was a star in his country but one of the worst actors I've worked with. A nice man but a lousy actor. And then I had an actress who was a disgrace, a whore … she was Mario Cecchi Gori's lover and then she became the wife of a well-known politician. You know, most whores are very clever! Anyway Cecchi Gori calls me up and tells me he has this talented actress under contract, Laura Trotter, and asks me the favor of putting her in my film. She had just finished shooting something with Damiano Damiani.[9] In exchange for this favor he would find a distribution for us, because we still didn't have one. All the rest of the cast was strategic in order to get the film bought in various countries: Mel Ferrer for the States, Francisco Rabal

Lenzi's wife and script supervisor Olga Pehar (8 February 1938, Zagreb, Croatia-20 November 2015, Rome), legend John Huston and Lenzi on the set of *The Great Battle*, 1978. The bearded man is unidentified (courtesy Umberto Lenzi).

for Spain, Maria Rosaria Omaggio for Italy and so on. Speaking of the pleasure of working with American actors, Mel Ferrer was one of those individuals I could have done a thousand films with. He came, did what had to be done and left. I think he didn't even read the scripts, but just his dialogue. A very reserved man. Anyway, *Nightmare City* was done on a tight budget. Consider that the military plane you see at the beginning of the film is actually four different planes. We were at the military airport of Zaragoza but they only gave us one plane to work with, which could not be flown so we had to wait around and film these huge planes as they arrived and edit everything together in such a way that it seemed like a single plane landing. In fact, if you watch the film carefully, you'll notice that the serial number on the plane changes in the various shots.

These films coincide with the massive crises that struck Italian genre cinema. What happened, exactly?
In the early eighties, genre cinema was practically dead or was mortally wounded, let's say, and this is due to the sudden birth of hundreds of private TV stations and, later on, to the creation of Mediaset.[10] Every station would show at least two films a day. They would get them from God knows where, often illegally, without authorizations or else they would buy complete catalogues from dying production companies. The masses, who were the ones that saw our films, would be content and we found ourselves in serious difficulty. Everything started collapsing between 1977 and 1980. In the nineties another problem came along: modern TV series. Popular cinema was channeled on television, trying to copy the American approach … badly, of course! From that moment on, we have been invaded by awful, dumb products that all pensioners watch because they don't have to move from their sofa.

What can you tell me about **Nightmare Beach—La spiaggia del terrore** *[Welcome to Spring Break, 1989]?*
Let's begin by saying that to participate in a specific film current you have to love it. It's like what I said about my Westerns. I didn't like them and they didn't turn out well. My Westerns, anyway, were produced all by Salvatore Alabiso. A man that came from nothing and did very well for himself. Initially he worked with Grimaldi at P.E.A. then he founded Tritone Cinematografica, with which he produced various co-productions with Spain. After some hits, among which a couple of Sergio Corbucci Westerns, he transferred to the States. He later became a millionaire producing Bud Spencer and Terence Hill movies over there. We were very close for a while and then just lost track of each other until he called me for *Welcome to Spring Break*. This is what happened with that film. They wanted to make two films. I had read both scripts. One was fucking awful and one wasn't bad. I took the one I liked the most and rewrote it. It was about a female scientist that has an accident in her lab and becomes genetically mutated, transforming into a tiger. I was very eager to do it. But once I arrived to the States I discovered they had flipped things over and wanted me to do the other, which was a generic slasher film. The other film, which was a homage to *Cat People* [1942] by Jacques Tourneur, became *Rage—Furia primitiva* [*Primal Rage*, 1988] and was directed by Carlo Rambaldi's son, Vittorio. What most people don't know is that I shot my film but left as soon as production wrapped up. I never participated in post-production. The producer was an asshole. I tried telling him that the whole premise of a killer priest was old, and I had already used it for *Seven Blood-Stained Orchids* but he wouldn't listen. The film is signed as Harry Kirkpatrick, who is an existing person, a writer. I had met him a few times to go over

the script. I only shot the film because I was in Miami and they paid me well but I consider that film a vacation. Working with John Saxon again was nice but Michael Parks was a fucking snob. The whole thing was a mess.

In the second half of the eighties you direct, for the most part, horror films.

Yes, one of the best being *La casa 3* [*Ghosthouse*, 1988]. That film was written keeping in mind documented paranormal phenomena. Some people can see strange events happening on the other side of the world. The genius idea of my film is that the murders that occur are not picked up by humans but by a radio! As if evil travelled in sound waves. After the massive success of my film I proposed a second horror. Something along the lines of *Psycho* [1960], with a woman who gets out of prison and goes back to a villa where some terrible, bloody murders had taken place. I was told that these stories were out and that there was no space for them on the market. In reality, the cheap bastards wanted to spend as little as possible and in fact they made *La casa 4* [*Witchery*, a.k.a. *Witchcraft*, 1988] by Laurenti and then later *La casa 5* [*Beyond Darkness*, 1990], because Claudio Fragasso was even cheaper than Laurenti. This business is made of cutthroats.

How was your relationship with Massaccesi, Joe D'Amato?

Good. He knew his trade very well and was genuinely funny. I would enjoy every time he came on the set. I would have liked to become friends with him but those were difficult times. Initially he wasn't the producer. I had written *Ghosthouse* for Di Girolamo. Though, one day, he calls me and says that he has personal issues and can't see the film through. That is when Aristide stepped in.

You direct two films for Massaccesi's company, Filmirage.

Ghosthouse, you see, was released without my name. They used a stupid pseudonym, Humphrey Humpert. I called my lawyer but before things got really nasty we found an agreement and that is how I made *Paura nel buio* [*Hitcher in the Dark*, 1989]. The title is horrendous but what was worse is that they made me change the ending. In the original script, the kid asks his father, "What will you do with the camper?" Zoom on a girl hitchhiking. "I think I will go for a ride." Ending. Credits. They forced me to direct a happy ending with the serial killer dying. It's a shame, it could have been a masterpiece. By this time I didn't have the same contractual power I used to have, during previous decades. Same thing goes for *Demoni 3* [*Black Demons*, 1991]. It wasn't my idea to try and connect the film with Bava's films, which I don't even like. All these films were made on shoestring budgets. Don't forget this. *Black Demons* was made back to back with *Caccia allo scorpione d'oro* [*Hunt for the Golden Scorpion*, 1991] with Andy J. Forrest as the lead and was an attempt to cash in on the success of *Romancing the Stone* [1984]. It was all shot in Brazil, with the help of Michele Massimo Tarantini, who had moved there and had various connections. Me and the producer decided to stay on an extra few weeks and with extra stock we had brought we made *Black Demons*. I had a big fight with my DOP on that. He fucked up the lights and when we printed it, the whole sequence in the cemetery was too dark … plus the actors I used were all black so you couldn't see a thing.

You ended your career doing films exclusively for the international market. Films like **Cop Target** *[1990] or* **Hornsby e Rodriguez—Sfida criminale** *[Mean Tricks, 1992], which is also your last film.*

Yes, those were all done for the North but mostly South American markets. Some haven't even been released in Italy or if they have, the distribution was very limited. They would have an American cast, shot in English and in my case usually shot in Santo Domingo or in some parts of the States, like Miami. Castellari was there during that same period working on the same kind of products I was. I directed six or seven films in the space of roughly five years. It's a mixed bag. *Cop Target* is a decent enough film though Robert Ginty broke my balls, behaving like a big star. A year after having wrapped production he wrote a bleeding heart letter asking my forgiveness for having behaved so badly. I didn't even answer. That said, *Cop Target* is OK but *Mean Tricks* is a pile of shit, for example, mainly because Italo Zingarelli, after the success of the *Trinity*[11] films, was fixated on creating new couples, but he chose two actors that weren't worth the clothes they wore. I just did these films so as to work. The scripts were painful to read and the budgets were getting smaller and smaller. At that time, in Italy, they would tax you according to what they presumed you were going to earn, on the basis of how much money you had earned in previous years. Things had changed and I needed to work to keep up with the taxes. Then keeping up became harder and harder to do and I had to let go. In more recent times I received a few propositions, mostly for horror films and specifically cannibal films but I'm too old now and it wouldn't make any sense.

I imagine, if you were able and could choose, you wouldn't pick the cannibal genre as your return to cinema.
Maybe not, but I would think about it carefully. I did some excellent films in that genre.

I thought you said you didn't like those films.
Oh no, I don't, but they are masterpieces. Just masterpieces I don't like.

Ostia, Rome, 2015, 2016

Giovanni Lombardo Radice, a.k.a. John Morghen, on *Cannibal Ferox*

If Ruggero Deodato represents the heart of the most savage and brutal current of Italian cinema, opening it up, giving it rules and extracting all of its potential, Umberto Lenzi represents the two opposite ends of it. Lenzi, after having directed *Mangiati vivi* (*Eaten Alive!*, 1980), in which the "booster" sequences for the public are for the most part recycled from *Ultimo mondo cannibale* (*Last Cannibal World*, a.k.a. *The Last Survivor*, a.k.a. *Jungle Holocaust*, 1977) and Sergio Martino's *La montagna del Dio cannibale* (*The Mountain of the Cannibal God*, 1978), tries to raise the bar of gore and directs, in 1981, *Cannibal Ferox*, the last pure example of the genre worthy of mention. It seems like Lenzi's way of saying, "I started all this, I will end it." A thin and flimsy plot leads the customary heterogeneous group to seek, in the thick jungle of the Amazon, traces of primitive communities devoted to cannibalism: all the more extreme fears of the characters, as they become aware of their recklessness, and the most atrocious expectations of the viewer will come true, with a succession of atrocities among the most heinous seen on screen until that point. What is left of *Cannibal Ferox* is the inevitable and repulsive power of the most extreme violence, an embodiment of freedom that contemporary Italian cinema—and not only Italian—has long lost. The genre, for all these reasons, for its rage, its cynical attitude towards society, its violence and the mechanisms of the film market itself, is the perfect last cry of a dying industry. The rest of the eighties is characterized by more than just a few successful films: Fulci and Argento still have to finish draining their inspiration, Michele Soavi and Lamberto Bava still have to show off some of their best work, Aristide Massaccesi will direct some of his better known and most outrageous films, but all these are the successes of single directors and not of an industry, films and hits ascribable to an ever diminishing number of survivors; no currents or new subgenres will be created, no new paths or generational cycles put in motion. Italian genre didn't start fizzling out, gasping silently but died, drowned in the desperate jungle cries of victims, beaten and raped, stripped and ready to be devoured. For a cinema famous for imploding its genres, for self-cannibalizing itself, this couldn't be a more perversely metaphoric ending.

So, with Lenzi's 1981 offering, we have the most cynical film of the genre and, at the same time, we have a perfect example of the strange upturning of which only a specific kind of B-movie is capable of. In fact, with *Ferox* we can observe the magic of exploitation cinema, where defects, limits, general campiness and bad taste become strong points. The rapid zooms, the poorly conceived costumes, the implicitly racist growls and hisses of the tribesmen and the minimal photography give it that rough, icky and sticky porntheater vibe which makes out the appeal of the film. Over the years, what has added to its reputation has been Lenzi's difficulty in accepting the film's cult status and more importantly the conflict between him and his lead actor. Many fans of the film are aware of the harsh words both Lenzi and Giovanni Lombardo Radice (born 23 September 1954, Rome) have been using, in interviews, to describe each other. Lombardo Radice, who is credited in the film as John Morghen, has stated that he knew, from the start, what he was getting into. "To be honest, I didn't want to do it, I mean, there's a limit to everything. When I read the script I said to myself, 'No, no no…' It

Radice is castrated in one of the cruelest scenes of *Cannibal Ferox*, 1981 (courtesy Nocturno Cinema).

was a steaming pile of shit. Keep in mind that initially I was offered the role of the wounded friend. I had just come from a series of films in which I played weak characters, often dependent on the protagonist, and I was fed up with that sort of thing. But I had a desperate need for money, which is a nice recurrent feature of my existence, so I said to my agent, 'Tell them I'm only willing to play the protagonist, and I want three times what they offered.' I had played important parts but had never been a lead, the actual protagonist, and this prospect was quite appealing, despite the project was shit. Anyway, unfortunately they answered yes to all my requests and that's how I found myself on a plane headed for the Amazon."

Ironically you had worked with Ruggero Deodato not long before.
Yes, the first film I did was *La casa sperduta nel parco* [*The House on the Edge of the Park*, 1980] by Ruggero which was neither a horror nor a cannibal movie, but a genre film nonetheless. That was a very small world, everybody knew each other and Italian cinema has never shined for originality, meaning that if you play a priest once, then you'll play bishops and cardinals all your life. So I found myself stuck in this mechanism, they called me for these kind of films and these are the kind of films I did. But I have to underline the fact that I've never liked these genres or had any passion as a spectator for them. But I've always tried to do them to the best of my capability.

Going back to Ferox, *what is your recollection working on that film?*
It was an incredibly stressful film. Leticia, which is a pimple on the Amazon's ass, is the last outpost before the unknown, and to reach it—because the production wanted to save money—we had this endless 36-hour journey from one airport to the other. First of all, the Amazon is a place God created in a moment in which he was really pissed off. It's absolutely terrible for humans … the nature there is incredibly aggressive from all points of view: the vegetation, the animals, the climate. Plus, that's the golden triangle of cocaine, so they would shoot each other on the streets. Leticia you could only reach by plane. It's a bunch of huts by the river, but they're also very rich because of the drug dealing, so in this kind of shantytown, you can see big cars, motorcycles, a small casino … an absurd place. We had to wake up at the crack of dawn and travel 3 to 4 hours from Leticia to get to the set and I really don't get why.… I mean, apart from some animals and plants, it's basically bushes and shrubbery … those who went and shot similar films in their backyard or in botanical gardens were perfectly right! You don't need to go and spend months in a place forgotten by man and God when the result will anyway be the same … just more moving leaves.

Were you aware of the animal killings when you accepted the role?
No, I naively thought that all the things in the script regarding animals were going to be fake. Only after did I discover what was going to happen. One day Lenzi says to me, "Tomorrow you're killing the piglet." "What am I gonna do tomorrow?!" "Why, didn't you read the script?" "Listen, I'm not gonna kill any pig, forget about it," and this started, if not a fight, a very fiery debate. "Consider yourself lucky that we're in the middle of the jungle, or else I would have reported you to animal protection services, I'm not killing anything" … and he goes, "De Niro would have done it!" "No, De Niro would have kicked your ass all the way back to Rome." Anyway, this poor piglet ended up being killed by Bombardone[12]—the special effects supervisor—with a machete, but they needed the reverse shot of my face and Bombardone, who's a nice guy but not the sharpest knife in

the drawer, was holding a bowl of fake blood keeping his hands underneath it. I had this massive machete and I had to sadistically dip it in the bowl so it would seem that I had just killed the pig. I wasn't looking where Bombardone was keeping his hand, so I forcefully dipped the machete breaking the bowl and slicing through Bombardone's hand ... so hospital, doctors, et cetera, but at least I vindicated the poor piglet.

Did you have any other problems with certain scenes? Did the violence disturb you?

Apart from the animal parts, I did everything that was in the script. I think we did two versions, one which was more splatter and violent, for the Japanese or German market, and a version which was slightly softer for other countries. By that time I was used to blood-filled films. As always these special-effects based scenes are very long and tedious to do, uncomfortable and unpleasant for actors, but this wasn't the aspect of the film I was most disturbed by. What repelled me was the implicit racism, "savages are savages after all," and this titillation of the most violent instincts, and there was even something slightly pedophiliac ... there was a scene in which I molest some barely teenage girls.... I mean, the film is full of filth, come on, let's be honest here.

Your relationship with Lenzi on the set?

Lenzi was odious, I'm too Anglo-Saxon and a lover of the understated to like someone like Lenzi, but that said, our relationship was nonexistent; he tried to be friendly but was a kind of person, and still is, who is very self-centered, always complimenting himself. "I'm like John Ford!" So I was well-mannered, smiled and didn't pay attention. The relationship was "go here, do this, do that." Apart from the piglet episode, there weren't any fights on the set. It was a civil and professional relationship. Like most Italian directors, he didn't understand much about actors so he just let us be. He would say "a little less, a little more," but he really didn't direct actors. From this point of view, he was in good company. I found myself alone to deal with a character that was very difficult to bring to life. I'm absolutely awful in that film ... I've said it many times and I'll say it again, I think I'm horrendous. That character was inexistent: he was bad because he was bad, full stop. There wasn't much to work on. Even Shakespeare created characters that were bad because they were bad, but the dialogue was written by Shakespeare, not Lenzi! So the only thing I could do was shout a lot. The sole element that helped me a bit was that he snorted cocaine like a madman, and at the time I was doing the same so I knew the effects of cocaine, and that's it ... therefore I find myself dreadful. Mike Logan was a character without any life, we know nothing about him. He's there and he's evil. End of story. In fact, Lorraine De Selle would jokingly call me "Naughty Mike." So he did a series of atrocious acts, he was pissed off because of the coke, which makes people go round the bend, but there was nothing else to explore about this character, he was as flat as a sheet of paper.

I take it that your relationship with De Selle, with whom you had already worked on Deodato's film, was a positive one.

Lorraine was my only salvation of that set. As long as she was an actress we met often and always got along. If I was a female I would be Lorraine, we were very similar, luxury gypsies with large families behind us. She was also trilingual. On the set of *Cannibal Ferox* we would speak in French, so nobody understood us and we could speak about everybody. She was the best thing about working on that film even though she broke my balls for the insects but that was understandable. She was always screaming. I could only tell her: "Put insecticide around the bed and pray."

Radice, face to face with the rage of his director Umberto Lenzi on the set of the infamous cannibal shocker (courtesy Nocturno Cinema).

What do you remember of Zora Kerowa?

She was fucking with Danilo Mattei so it's not that I saw a lot of her. [He laughs.] A nice girl, Zora. But I must say that I got along with all the actors. Apart from Mattei, who was a bit of a prick, because he was one of those macho types, a bit of a bully. But Zora was nice. Some time ago I played a joke on her. An American journalist came here to interview me and he gave me her phone number. I called her: "Hi, this is Mike Logan. I'm back from hell to get you!" I hadn't heard from her in ages.

You have worked with both Lenzi and Deodato. In what way do they differ?

In many ways. They are very different. The only thing they have in common is that they both shout a lot, but with a fundamental difference: Lenzi is really unpleasant, he insults, says personal things ... Deodato instead, has a great sense of humor, something that Lenzi doesn't even know how to spell, so yes, Deodato would shout, but then after, he would add a funny comment, in fact the crew loved him, whereas Lenzi was hated by everybody. A grotesque episode I can tell you about is the following: to cut costs, part of the crew was made up of locals, and when I say locals, I don't mean New Yorkers, but semi-uncivilized people that had never even seen a film in their lives. So the assistant sound technician was an Indio, and the first day, not hearing him say "Partido," Lenzi made a scene, and the poor guy, who didn't even understand the language, understood only one thing: that he was supposed to say "Partido!" So throughout he film he kept repeating, "Partido! Partido! Partido!" When we got back to Rome, I get a phone call from the producer, Mino Loy, saying, "It's a complete disaster, please save me!" "What happened?" "The film has no audio track!" You see, this guy kept on saying, "Partido!" but then didn't do anything. So there was no dialogue … nothing! So, for Mino Loy's sake, I readapted the whole dialogue and sat in the editing room redubbing the film, not with a computer, but using reels … a nightmare!

But for Lenzi you will write the script of **Incontro nell'ultimo paradiso** *[Daughter of the Jungle, a.k.a.* **Adventures in Last Paradise***, 1982].*

That film was born because of Mino Loy, who was the producer of *Cannibal Ferox* and a delightful person. Mino called me and Marina Garroni, who was my writing partner, for this thing, a comedy that had to be done by Lenzi. Loy decided everything. I remember these meetings in his office where he took notes, and it was a continuous taking away. "Guy enters with two elephants." "No, one elephant. Actually no, no elephant, no elephant." But, believe me, I never met Lenzi as I worked on that, not once. I knew he was going to direct the film but he never came to the meetings.

Not many people know you have been active as writer as well.

I am one of the founding fathers of modern Italian television series. This is because I was part of the group that created the first experiment, which was *Aereoporto internazionale* [translation: *International Airport*, 1987], produced by Paolo Di Valmarana, who I knew very well having been a close friend of his daughters. Paolo comes to see a small musical, which I had written with Marina Garroni, in which she starred alongside Saverio Marconi, called *Happy End*. He took both me and Marina for this new experiment, which started my writing career. Enzo Tarquini was the director, but soon after became a television executive and the main delegate for Raidue for TV series. After that I did many other things, among which was *I ragazzi del muretto* [translation: *The Kids from the Block*, 1991] directed by Deodato.

But with what intentions was **Daughter of the Jungle** *born with? The result is a weird blending of genres.*

Well, it might seem hard to believe but originally it was a comedy adventure in the vein of the Bud Spencer and Terence Hill movies, that sort of stuff. As they were shooting in South America, *The Blue Lagoon* [1980] came out and was going crazy at the box office. Loy calls me and says we have to insert a scene under the waterfall between the girl and … so, there were two possible guys, one was Rodolfo Bigotti, who was good looking and credible but narratively it didn't work, he couldn't be the one that finished under the waterfall and then there was Renato Miracco, with whom I had already worked with in the theater, who is as witty as he is ugly. So in the end we had to invent this scene which is pathetically false.

This was, like **Ferox***, a Dania production. How did you find yourself with the Martino brothers?*

So, I worked twice with Sergio Martino. First something about Etruscans, *Assassinio al cimitero etrusco* [*The Scorpion with Two Tails*, 1982] and then later on a TV series with Giuliano Gemma on copyright theft, *Caccia al ladro d'autore* [translation: *Hunt for the Art Thief*, 1985–1986]. Martino, empathy minus seven, but he's one who knows what he's talking about. He tells you those three things that help you. I have always given the best with Martino. I respect him. Luciano, the producer, I've almost never seen. My main contact within Dania was Mino Loy.

Tell me about when Sage Stallone came to visit you in Rome.

One day I listen to my answering machine and I find a message from an American with a Donald Duck voice. At that time, I used to hang out a lot with Luca Barbareschi, with whom I've been friends since we were very young, and he's famous for impressions and for doing pranks and I was sure it was him. Then the phone rings again and it's the same weird voice, but something told me it wasn't Barbareschi, so I stopped before saying, "Fuck off, Luca!" It was Sage Stallone. He tells me that he's preparing a laser disc, which I had never heard about, and that he wants an audio commentary. I asked, "Is there any money?" "No, we are so poor..." which, said by the son of Stallone.... Anyway, mostly to get rid of him, I accepted. He and his partner Bob Murawski arrived on a limousine which took three blocks. Sooo poor my ass! They take me to a dubbing studio, show me the film, and I have to comment it as it played. This audio commentary has become legendary, and they made a lot of money out of it, because then it passed onto DVDs ... and I never saw a dime. Anyhow, the result was pretty funny because they had also taped Lenzi's commentary, so he would go, "What a masterpiece!" I would go, "What a pile of shit!" plus my reactions were very spontaneous because I hadn't seen the film in ages. Once we finished he asks me, "Could you sign a few things for me?" These few things ended up being a suitcase of everything imaginable: posters, T-shirts, anything, and I sat there patiently signing "To Mary," "To Christian" ... at one point he says, "To Quentin" and I go, "Tarantino?" "Yes," "To Quentin with love..."

Why are we still talking about this film after nearly forty years?

I have asked myself this, numerous times. I swear I don't know. The success of *Cannibal Ferox* resides in the fact that people are sick. I mean, I had no good memories of that film, then I had a 20-year blackout, ended that chapter of my career, and continued doing a lot of other things for television and theater. For me all those films were done and forgotten. With the advent of internet, I found out there were hundreds of pages about these films and about me, and a huge cult following. Sometimes I had been called from an American or British magazine, but I thought it was a niche, like the adorers of Stalin's moustache. Specifically, on *Cannibal Ferox*, when I started navigating on the web, I was shocked to read comments of people saying that they would love to do to women what we did in the film. So there is a titillation of the most primitive human instincts, I'm not saying it's only this, but definitely people like violence and brutal scenes. It's probably a way of projecting out of oneself a series of feelings ... I don't know.

What are your thoughts about the cannibal phenomenon as a whole?

My aversion towards cannibal movies resides in the fact ... OK, let's start off by saying that I don't like blood and guts, but that's my problem. This said, the horror genre, which comprises a massive number of different films, can be dealt with in three different ways: the first is the one of realism, which is the path many films take, like *The House on the Edge of the Park*, there is a mystery, investigations, and it's a story that could happen in real life and that's fine. Another option is the world of imagination, with zombies, monsters, Freddy Krueger, etc. ... which is the realm of fantasy, and that's OK by me, because these films are a modern version of fairy tales. The third option is to sell as truth something that is completely preposterous, and this is the cannibal genre, which tries to expose a pile of violent shit as reality. In fact, cannibal films derive from the work of that revolting fascist, Gualtiero Jacopetti, who tried to convince us that the shit he directed were documentaries. This I find disgusting, it's a kind of filmmaking which I find immoral.

Rome, 2015

1959 Melancholy and Revolution
The Cinema of Giulio Petroni

"With peyote you will feel close to God."
"How can you feel close to something that doesn't exist?"—Magda Konopka and Luke Askew in Nest of Vipers, 1969

When you've waited fifteen years to find a man ... it's a shame you can only kill him once!—American tagline for Death Rides a Horse, 1967

Not a harbor, a station, an airport or any of the numerous railroads that crossed the country had been left intact. After the end of World War II, with the exception of a large part of Rome, which had been declared an "open city," Italy was in shambles, reduced by bombs to rubble. In addition to this tragic aftermath, the occupation by foreign armies created a condition that widened the chronic development gap with the more advanced European economies. When Giulio Petroni (21 September 1917, Rome–31 January 2010, Rome) left Italy, in 1945, with his wife and limited resources, he left behind him a broken country. "I had lost weight and was unrecognizable, going, as I was, towards possibly nothing more than a glimmer of hope." This is how he described his state while crossing the ocean towards what was then called Ceylon, now Sri Lanka: "I didn't know how and when I was going to return to Italy." However, the new geopolitical logic of the Cold War made it possible for Italy to be perceived as a hinge country between Western Europe and the Mediterranean, and from a fragile democracy, threatened by the proximity of the Soviet-controlled Iron Curtain, Italy became, from an American prospective, a potential ally for the Free World. Therefore, its past as an enemy was put aside and the country was admitted to the financial help provided by the Marshall Plan. Specifically, the European Recovery Plan was an economic reconstruction program that the United States would fund, placing itself in continuity with aid provided since 1943 to war-affected populations. Some opposition was made against this by left-wing political and trade union movements, the main accusation being that the U.S. was trying to colonize Europe. Beyond any ideological conviction, it is impossible to deny that the humanitarian motivation hid an anti–Soviet political agenda. However, just two years after the approval of the plan, Europe showed signs of a rapid economic revival. The completion of the plan, in 1952, that might have stopped this recovery, coincided neatly with the culmination of the Korean War (1950–1953), creating a strong demand for metal and other manufactured products. This, combined with a large and cheap labor force, laid the foundations for a spectacular economic growth. Petroni, with new contacts and a new reputation, would move back to

Giulio Petroni on the set of *The Usual Thieves from Milan*, in 1963. A comedy caper starring Peter Baldwin, Dominque Boschero and Maurizio Arena and written, among others, by Bruno Corbucci (author's collection).

Italy, in the fifties, right in the midst of this slow but unstoppable evolution in the financial and social life of the country. He found a stronger Italy and a film industry that could not have been imagined before his departure. By the time Petroni directed his first film, the industry had blossomed. However, during his years in exotic lands, he had never completely lost touch with his country. After having conquered the trust of local politicians, he started to forge what would become the foundation of Sri Lanka's Government Film Unit. Petroni sent for technicians and experts from Italy to teach locals the grammar of filmmaking. In the space of a few years he had become a relevant figure in the country who had let him in and was an appreciated documentarian back in his homeland.

Similarly to Giorgio Capitani, but even more so, Petroni entered the milieu of Italy's film world from the living rooms of Rome's intelligentsia. Although he had acquired a more than adequate technical knowledge directing, photographing and editing short documentaries, his cardinal activity remained that of a writer. Though his first novel will be published in 1961, after his debut as a director, Petroni's past was filled with short stories and essays published in various magazines. This aspect of his artistic path, together with his political beliefs, his outspoken atheism, his reputation and body of work as a socially conscious documentary filmmaker, opened the doors to a certain intellectual environment. He meets, mingles and creates friendships with many important personalities of that period, some of whom will become recurring figures in his cinema: Ugo Pirro, Pasquale Festa Campanile, Massimo Franciosa, Pier Paolo Pasolini and Gillo Pontecorvo. Unlike other directors who will emerge in the late fifties or early sixties, like Umberto Lenzi or Alberto De Martino, who are completely at the disposal of the industry and needs of the market, Petroni's approach to the film world is guided by his left-wing beliefs and a personal code regarding content. Petroni is of course, as he defined himself, a genre director but at the same time he refused to touch any type of film of which he disapproved: police thrillers, horrors and sex comedies were not appropriate containers for his personal set of beliefs, be it for the fascist overtones of the first genre mentioned or the crude vulgarity of the last. Westerns, on the other hand, like the comedies he had previously directed which stemmed from the "commedia all'italiana," was a genre loose and innocuous enough to fit the symbolisms and narrative metaphors Petroni was interested in, but more importantly it was a genre that he believed would enable him to gain enough visibility to start directing what he was really interested in. Like Campanile, Capitani, Pirri, Samperi but also Di Leo or Squitieri, Giulio Petroni was an "in-between figure." Despite never managing to conquer the contractual and decisional power of some of the above-mentioned directors, Petroni can be considered an "auteur," in the broadest sense of the word, in genre cinema.

Putting aside his excursus as a journalist, his prolific activity as a documentarian and as an assistant director, and dwelling exclusively on his activities as a film director, it is fairly easy to identify very distinct phases in the career of Giulio Petroni. The first is represented by comedy, which officially begins in 1959 with *La cento chilometri* (*The One Hundred Kilometers*) and is made up of four films. Petroni's debut, though dated, has acquired over the years somewhat of a historical value, a photograph of a specific cultural and social atmosphere, also thanks to a cast populated by familiar faces: the famed singer Fred Buscaglione, the star Massimo Girotti and a long list of popular character actors and TV personalities such as Carlo Giuffré, Gigi Reder, Gianrico Tedeschi, Riccardo Garrone, Marisa Merlini, Mario Carotenuto (who will appear in other two times films by Petroni) and many others. The film is a success partly due to a much discussed censorious intervention regarding the shapely legs of a teenage Paola Pitagora. Petroni then directs, chronologically: *I piaceri dello scapolo* (*The Pleasures of a Bachelor*, 1960), *Una domenica d'estate* (*Always on Sunday*, 1962) and *I soliti rapinatori a Milano* (*The Usual Thieves from Milan*, 1963). This last film marks the end of this first chapter. The following one will give fame and prestige to Petroni's career, inextricably combining his name to the Italian West.

Petroni's Western filmography unravels itself in five titles: *Da uomo a uomo* (*Death Rides a Horse*, 1967), *...e per tetto un cielo di stelle* (*A Sky Full of Stars for a Roof*, a.k.a. *And for a Roof a Sky Full of Stars*, 1968), *Tepepa* (a.k.a. *Blood and Guns*, 1968), *La notte dei serpenti* (*Nest of Vipers*, a.k.a. *Night of the Serpent*, 1969) and finally *La vita a volte è molto dura vero Provvidenza?* (*Life Is Tough, Eh Providence?*, a.k.a. *Sometimes Life Is Hard—Right, Providence?* 1972). On *Death Rides a Horse* much has been said. It was praised and paid homage to by Quentin Tarantino, who uses various stylistic and narrative elements from it to shape the structure of his *Kill Bill* (2003–2004) saga. It was one of Italy's most successful Westerns worldwide, including in the States, where it was picked up by United Artists. Lee Van Cleef, who gives one of his best performances, is placed at the center of a rich cast that includes John Philip Law, Luigi Pistilli, Josè Torres, Anthony Dawson and Mario Brega. It also marks the long collaboration between the Roman director and Ennio Morricone, who for the occasion, composes a vibrant and dark soundtrack that perfectly fits what many consider the quintessential Italian "vengeance Western."

A theme, that of vengeance, that returns in another extremely successful film directed by Petroni, *Tepepa*, which together with Damiano Damiani's *Quien sabe?* (*A Bullet for the General*, 1967) is the purest and most representative example of so-called "revolutionary Westerns."[1] Tomas Milian, in a role clearly inspired by the figure of Ernesto "Che" de la Serna Guevara, leads his fellow peons through the violence and disappointments of a revolutionary uprising at the start of 20th century Mexico. Like Damiani before him, Petroni too had difficulties considering his film a Western, as he himself explained:

> *Tepepa* is much more of a historical film. It has none of the iconography of Italian Westerns, or American ones for that matter: no gunfights, no saloons and no Americans or cowboys. John Steiner's character is called "Yankee" but simply because the Mexicans in the film don't make any distinction between Americans and British. There is dust and there are horses but that's it. Attention was paid to infuse the film with the right scenography and costumes. Contrary to my previous Westerns, here I tried to make sure the film was visually realistic and as close as possible to historical reality, something that was not normally necessary in Westerns, Italian ones I mean, because our West was not an actual historical period. It's a parallel dimension which has more to do with literature, comic books and cinema itself. It's an abstract West not a realistic one. Mind you, this is what made Italian Westerns successful. So, *Tepepa* in this sense, cannot be labeled as a Western, though on the other hand it is too metaphorical and symbolic, too over-stylized and bigger than life to be considered a historical film. So I guess it lives in an in-between territory. Though I don't mind people calling it a Western. I understand why they do, but it's incomplete as a definition.

The film stirs up much attention upon its release, starting from the cast which, besides Milian—at a peak in his popularity—also features Orson Welles as the antagonist.

Between these two columns of his filmography, Petroni directs another Western, a strange and atypical one graced by a poetic, nearly bucolic title: *A Sky Full of Stars for a Roof* with Giuliano Gemma and Mario Adorf. The relationship between the two protagonists anticipates many of the elements that will be utilized in subsequent Giuseppe Colizzi Westerns, that ultimately will help create the Bud Spencer and Terence Hill couple. If Gemma plays a character not dissimilar to the ones of his previous films—the romantic scoundrel, the irresponsible but loveable troublemaker—it is Adorf's character that represents a new input, and more importantly, the contraposition of the two opposite but compatible personalities. It is difficult not to observe and analyze Adorf's behavior without comparing it to what Bud Spencer was just on the brink of becoming: strong though naïve, capable of violence but ultimately childlike and idealistic, prone to simple pleasures, Adorf is the barely controllable arm of Gemma's brain. What makes Petroni's second effort in the genre such a peculiar one is not solely tied to the comedy within it, but to the contradictory results these comedic elements create when put together with the sudden peaks of drama and violence the film encompasses. In fact, the film has one of the more spectacular and violent beginnings in Petroni's West. However, the podium for the most cynical and violent film has to be left free for what has yet to come after this successful triptych.

Fierce and tense, *Nest of Vipers* is a forgotten Western. Petroni has always considered it a minor effort within his body of work and has often refused to talk about it. But the film, over the years, has found a niche of admirers, such as Spanish critic Carlos Aguilar who, for example, considers it one of his favorite Westerns, comparing the redemptive parable within it to *Lord Jim*. Not dissimilar in tone to other darker themed Westerns of the late sixties, such as the subsequent *E Dio disse a Caino* (*And God Said to Cain*, 1970), *Nest of Vipers* feels the influence of the new and growing giallo genre. So it shouldn't come as a surprise to discover that someone like Lorenzo Gicca Palli helped Petroni write the script. Gicca Palli in fact, must have firmly believed in the combination of these two genres, so much so that soon after he will direct *Il venditore di morte* (*Price of Death*, a.k.a. *Last Gunfight*, 1971), a film which is as much a Western as it is a giallo. This is confirmed by Petroni himself: "Definitely Palli was the one more interested in developing the mystery part of the film, which I would tone down. I was interested in making a different kind of Western, visually speaking, but concentrating more on the characters and in the redemption factor, the arc the character has to live through. Before dying out or before becoming innocuous and purely comedic, there were attempts to find new interpretations to the genre. Probably the fusion with giallo was one of those attempts. It was certainly something Palli had in mind."

To conclude the cycle, we find *Life Is Tough, Eh Providence?* with Milian, Gregg Palmer and Janet Agren, which Petroni directs with great detachment.

> By the early seventies it was blatant to me that Westerns were dying. I was not the creator of the genre, of course, but I had helped it become what it was and I didn't want to participate in the inevitable vulgarization that had begun. I refused many projects around that time. Westerns need money but most importantly they need space and faces. Producers are not forward-looking, they only see what is happening in the present and what was happening was that people would go and see any Western that was thrown at them. So all of a sudden, a fleet of improvised actors, usually stuntmen, with unlikely faces, were upgraded to leading men as the budgets got slimmer and slimmer. For all my Westerns I was fortunate enough to have big producers and the right amount of time to be able to give the epic breath the films required. I wasn't willing to help destroy the genre that, I can't say I loved, but that had given me a lot. *Providence* is a film I did for financial reasons. I needed the money, but it was still dignified enough. I mean, it had a good cast and a reasonable budget.

The huge success of the film, which spawned a 1973 sequel directed by Alberto De Martino, also anticipates the current of over-the-top, grotesque Western comedies derivative of Enzo Barboni's *Trinity* movies: *Il bianco, il giallo, il nero* (*The White, the Yellow, and the Black*, a.k.a. *Shoot First … Ask Questions Later*, a.k.a. *Ring Around the Horse's Tail*, 1975) by Sergio Corbucci and *Cipolla Colt* (*Cry, Onion!* a.k.a. *The Smell of Onion*, 1975) by Enzo G. Castellari. In five films Petroni looks at Westerns from five completely different points of view, creating what he called a short circuit: "I intentionally looked for different projects, mainly because I wanted to try new things and explore the genre as much as I could, but actually this didn't pay in terms of visibility because people thought they were all made by different directors." Despite the fact that his Westerns are so different from each other, there is a very strong thematic unity: the torque as the polarizing element around which the story rotates, revenge and stolen innocence. Interesting, in this respect, is the role of children: the opening sequence of *Death Rides a Horse*, in which the child, who will later become John Philip Law, witnesses the cruel extermination of his family or *Nest of Vipers*, in which Askew is forced to live with the remorse of having killed his own son while drunk and then of course *Tepepa* where the last one to dirty his hands with blood is little Paquito. Even Adorf and Palmer, in their respective films, are, perhaps, nothing more than children too grown up for their context. The figure of the child is always surrounded by violence or contaminated by it. Trauma and the emotional aftermath is also a recurrent theme within Petroni's later films, in the seventies.

In the immediate post-war period you leave for Ceylon.

Yes, between 1945 and the following year. I had nothing to lose. The war had taken its toll on me. When I look at the few photos of that period, I realize how hard life had been. I was so thin and looked so much older than my age. Remember I had participated actively in the resistance. I had killed and seen many of my fellow partisans die. I had nothing to lose. What my life had been before the war seemed like a distant memory, somebody else's life and one that had no importance anymore. I was married at the time, Italy was in ruins and the world seemed much bigger then than it does now.

Talk to me about the war. You received a Silver Medal for valor…

I don't like talking about that period but, anyway … where can I start from? Well, one moment is as good as another. I guess things really changed with … Manlio, my brother. I was in Rome training as a pilot when I stopped getting news from him. Communications were interrupted. I fled to Naples without saying anything to anyone. I had to know what had happened to him. When I reached Naples, it was chaos. What went down in history as "The 4 Days of Naples" had just begun. There was a huge insurrection against the German occupation. There were bodies in the streets. I contributed and helped out as well as I could. It was only when the Americans arrived from the south of Italy that I discovered what had happened to my brother. He was a captain in the navy, and the last time I talked to him he had told me that he'd received orders to take the battleship *Roma* to an Allied-controlled port. This was after Italy had declared the armistice with the Allies. But things were done badly and in a hurry. The details of the armistice were fuzzy, to say the least. All the Italian top brass fled from Rome together with the monarchy leaving Italian armies scattered around Europe with no precise orders. Do you know what Operation Achse is? It's what the Germans put into action when they discovered about the armistice. History books define the operation as an attempt to invade and occupy Italy but the orders really were to kill, destroy, annihilate as many Italians as possible. From 1943, Italian was a dangerous thing to be. Everything began with the bombardment of the battleship *Roma*. Manlio was on that ship, in the middle of the Mediterranean Sea, going to surrender to the Allies when Luftwaffe planes attacked, but because of the nebulous orders regarding the armistice, the ship was late in responding to the attack. Many men died, 1,352 to be precise. Manlio died a few days later in Majorca. He had severe burns on his face and body and died slowly and painfully. I was distraught and determined to do something, so I went to the Americans. They trained me as a paratrooper and dropped me behind enemy lines, in Piedmont which was controlled by German forces. My mission was to take dispatches to members of the resistance and then find my way back to Rome and repeat. Three times I was dropped. After my last mission I stayed with the partisans till the end of the war. But all this means nothing. Italy has forgotten the names and faces of the fallen.

Why did you choose Ceylon, after the war?

My other brother Attilio, also a high-ranking officer of the Navy, after having been in China for some time became consul in Ceylon. He asked me to join him there so I embarked on this adventure with Lidia, who was my wife at the time. As I said, I had no reason to say no. Attilio described the place as a land of opportunity.

Still, I guess it wasn't easy at first.

Absolutely not. It was a very long trip, days. No planes of course. Days and days on a ship. When I arrived there I had limited economic resources and, though I had picked up some English working for the American Secret Service, it was by no means sufficient. Anyway, my brother had made friends in the diplomatic and political spheres and introduced me to a few people. You must keep in mind that at that time the government was trying to gain independence, which it did soon after thanks to Prime Minister Don Stephen Senanayake. The political atmosphere was very left wing and I was still a member of the Communist Party and had been the head of one of the movement's most important headquarters in Rome. So, I managed to convince the local government to put me in charge of what was to become the Government Film Unit. Ceylon had no cinema, everything that was screened there was imported from India. You can say I invented cinema for them. Once things got rolling I brought technicians and equipment from Italy to teach a team of locals I had put together the grammar of cinema. We made them independent.

Over these years, under your direction, the Film Unit produces an incredible number of works.
Yes, newsreels, documentaries, some of which had positive feedbacks here in Europe, like *Capitol Hill* [1951], that was selected for the Edinburgh Festival. Plus we would give technical and logistical support to foreign productions that would come to shoot there. For example, in the case of *Outcasts of the Islands* [1952] by Carol Reed, based on Conrad's novel, I provided assistance through my Film Unit. Those were great years. I remember long dinners with Arthur C. Clarke who had a house there…

Had you already been in contact with the world of cinema previously?
Right before my departure I worked as 1st AD on Marcello Pagliero's film *Desiderio* [*Desire*, 1946]. A film that had to be suspended because of the war and which Roberto Rossellini had begun.

Who was the director when you started working on it?
Pagliero. The film was started in 1943 and had a different title ["Scalo merci," meaning Goods Yard]. The director was Rossellini but after just a few weeks of shooting the production closed down as all cinema did in the last years of the war. I had nothing to do with this initial phase. I stepped in when I was called to help Pagliero—who, mind you, is not remembered but was an important figure at the time—who picked up where Rossellini left off. However the script got substantially changed and turned into something closer to a melodrama. That was my first, big introduction to cinema. I had already worked as an editor or advisor on a number of scripts—I had a way with words—and I had been on several sets but *Desire* was my first official film. Before then, right to the end of the thirties, my main activity had been writing for newspapers. Mainly as an art and literary critic but then shortly after I started writing short stories for a number of weekly publications.

Would you write about cinema too?
Not much. Sometimes, maybe. I would mostly write about literature. There's something you need to know, but don't take it badly … I've never loved cinema that much. I had other interests. I know this may seem strange to some but I've never been a cinephile. I entered the world of cinema through a natural process, a spontaneous germination you could say. Things were different back then, I followed the flow. Cinema was the biggest thing after the war. People wanted to see films. It seemed like the thing they wanted the most and I was truly interested by the medium. I wanted to learn the grammar of cinema. I felt, like all young people, that I had things to say and cinema seemed like the best means of saying them. I was well respected by my peers and I was very resourceful so I was sought after. But having said this, my first love is literature, and has been ever since I was a child.

Before leaving for Ceylon you also direct your first short film. How did the transition from critic to director take place?

Wait, when I directed my first short film I wasn't a critic, I was a writer of short stories and poems and thanks to those publications, INCOM[2] called me and asked me to work for them, and I said yes. My first short-documentary was *Goethe a Roma* [*Goethe in Rome*, 1945].

Let's take a step forward. You continue making documentaries even after you leave Sri Lanka. This is your main activity throughout the fifties.

I would make producers happy, because mine was a one-man show. I would take care of everything, even the music. I don't know how many documentaries I directed during that decade. Dozens. I've lost count. I travelled all over the world ... Ireland, Israel, Morocco, the Aran Islands ... and I was extremely happy with some of these works. *Lembi di Albania in Calabria* [translation: *Pieces of Albania in Calabria*, 1956], just to name one, got the Premio San Giorgio at the Venice Film Festival.

You also work in feature films, don't you?

Yes, one of the first things I did once I moved back to Italy was contribute to the making of the film *Un marito per Anna Zaccheo* [*A Husband for Anna*, 1953] by Giuseppe De Santis.

We are getting closer to your debut as director of feature films.

By 1959 I had a solid reputation as a documentarian. What I had done in Sri Lanka was pretty well known and had been covered by the media, so it only made sense that I should direct my first film. *La cento chilometri* [*The One Hundred Kilometers*] was written by Pasquale Festa Campanile, Massimo Franciosa and myself. With Franciosa I had a long-lasting friendship. Many years later, my company Dalia published one of his novels. He was a reserved and sensitive man. We also wrote a screenplay together, that remained locked up in a drawer, based on one of my novels [*La strega di Colombraro*, translation: "The Witch of Colombraro"]. My relationship with Campanile was more of a carefree nature, he loved a good joke. This is definitely not the film I would have chosen, given the chance, but making it was good fun and I was still learning.

The film had problems with censorship.

Yes, unexplainably so. Things were very different then and censorship was still extremely strict. In the film there is a shot of a girl's legs on a stage, nothing much, but the Public Prosecutor's Office decided to confiscate it. By the way, those legs belonged to Paola Pitagora, who was still a young girl and had never appeared in anything.

Your first films follow the trend of the "commedia all'italiana." Directors like yourself but also Romolo Guerrieri and Lucio Fulci, just to mention a couple of names, emerged from that world.

Yes, but my films were much lighter compared to the so-called masters of the "commedia all'italiana" and were conceived for a broader audience. Political and social issues were always present but in a very grotesque and accessible way.

Fulci once called you the "oldest young director of Italian cinema."

I will just say one thing about Fulci, not as a director—I don't think I've ever seen a film of his—but as a man. When he left a room the window would be opened immediately. Wherever he stopped the air would become unbreathable. I think this says enough about who Lucio Fulci was.

Petroni and Swedish beauty Ulla Jacobsson on the set of *Always on Sunday*, 1962 (author's collection).

The early sixties are extremely prolific years for you. In quick succession, you direct **I piaceri dello scapolo [The Pleasures of a Bachelor, 1960], Una domenica d'estate [Always on Sunday, 1962] *and* I soliti rapinatori a Milano [The Usual Thieves from Milan, 1963]. *What do you recall about these films?***

These were films I made, how can I put it, in a detached way. Definitely not films I would have chosen but they would do very well at the box office. When I re-watch them I'm surprised by how well they stand the test of time. I mean, thematically, of course, they are dated. The narrative elements are all surpassed by today's standards but they are really well made. My favorite of the bunch is *The Pleasures of a Bachelor*.

Anyway, they all had great casts. Who do you remember the most?

Nobody in particular. At the time you could have these great actors quite easily. Just think of *Always on Sunday*: Jean-Pierre Aumont, Jacques Bergerac, Daniela Bianchi, Francoise Fabian, Ugo Tognazzi, Ulla Jacobsson, Karin Baal, Eddie Bracken. The same goes for the other films I did in that period. You could have these glorious international casts because the industry was booming. Films were shot on every street corner.

The first Western by Sergio Leone was released in 1964. What was your relationship with that genre before **Da Uomo a Uomo [Death Rides a Horse, 1967]?**

The only Westerns I loved were the American ones. Like Orson Welles said when he was asked who his mentors were: "John Ford, John Ford, John Ford." *Stagecoach* [1939], for example, is one title I've seen numerous times. But also *Fort Apache* [1948], *The Searchers* [1956] and *Viva Zapata!* [1952] by Kazan. In other words, the classics.

Yet, if I can say so, among the great American directors, your films are more similar to those by Howard Hawks.

Maybe you're right ... I haven't seen all of Hawks' films but he was a great director, no doubt about it. *Rio Bravo* [1959] is a masterpiece. Leone's films were very captivating too, but of all those products that came out in Italy later on, only a few are really worthy. Leone was a true Western lover, an expert in the field. Can't say the same about myself but I believe I managed to get in tune with the genre. Most of those who tried to do the same only created pathetic, shameful products. Just think of *Requiescant* [a.k.a. *Kill and Pray*, 1967] by Carlo Lizzani, a director who can't even spell the word Western.

There has often been talk about the similarities between Death Rides a Horse *and* Pursued *[1947] by Raoul Walsh.*

Yes, I know, and I keep repeating the same thing: I haven't even seen Walsh's film, and the screenplay for *Death Rides a Horse* was created in an extremely natural way, with a number of elements that gradually started to fit together. And much of this happened while already on the set.

Film critic Marco Giusti, in his dictionary on Italian Westerns,[3] states that Antonio Margheriti may have contributed to the screenplay. Anything to say about this?

What am I supposed to say? It's not true. The only people to have worked on the screenplay were Luciano Vincenzoni and myself.

How was your relationship with Vincenzoni?

I believe he thought that the genre wasn't worthy of his amazing intellect. Still, the film benefited from his contribution. Many, not all, but a lot of the screenwriters, directors and actors who worked in genre films and who are now dancing in front of the camera saying how wonderful making those films was, at the time were bitching and moaning, lying about having worked on them, hiding behind pseudonyms—and don't believe the story that they all had to because the market required it. Many gladly hid behind those ridiculous names. I directed five Westerns, all of which were distributed all over the world, so why wasn't I asked to use an Anglo-Saxon-sounding name? Lizzani and Vincenzoni were among those people, though in the case of Luciano, he, at least, was talented and a very competent writer.

Who chose Lee Van Cleef?

When Alfonso Sansone and Enrico Chroscicki came to me with the idea of making a Western, they already had his name in mind. I don't think they had a contract ready but they definitely wanted him in the film. He was a great horse rider and a high-level professional. One of the many amazing things Leone did was to bring back old actors whose careers were going downhill. Van Cleef, however, still had a few issues with alcohol. I remember that on New Year's Eve we made a toast, on set, and his glass was full of Coca-Cola.

This film marks the beginning of your collaboration with Ennio Morricone.

Yes, a long-lasting one. I always had good relationships with composers. Before Ennio all the music for my films had been composed by Armando Trovajoli. So four films with him, six films with Morricone, two with Riz Ortolani. They liked working with me because I did not have the presumption to think I knew what they were supposed to do. I liked

Petroni (left) and John Phillip Law on the set of *Death Rides a Horse,* **1967 (author's collection).**

Morricone in particular because his approach was very cerebral. I wouldn't make him listen to music, perhaps a classical piece sometimes, but for the most part I would describe the scene using straightforward, simple adjectives. *Death Rides a Horse* has a great soundtrack but, believe it or not, it was the simplest of all the films we did together. We would meet on a regular basis, discuss things and he got it right at the first attempt, while on other films the process was much longer and made of more attempts and failures.

Death Rides a Horse *is somewhat of a classic in the U.S., especially following Tarantino's statements.*

It doesn't surprise me that these Westerns of mine stood the test of time, because I was quite involved. I was interested in doing something different. With the comedies I had directed earlier, I had a professional but extremely detached approach, as I said before. They were a good opportunity to work, improve, make my name known. Westerns—despite many who would act somewhat snobbishly towards this genre—were a chance to do something more important. I was fascinated by their adventurous, wild nature; I liked the idea of making films that would remind me of the novels I'd loved as a boy. In fact, my inspiration came more from books than cinema. All five of my Westerns are very different one from the other and this depended on the fact that my priority was finding a different approach and interpretation to the genre each time. This is why my films are more famous than I am, because people don't connect the films together, if you know what I mean. Going back to *Death Rides a Horse* I knew from the word go that the film had what it took to be successful. Alfonso Sansone and Henryk Chroscicki had good contacts with foreign production companies and I already knew it would have been distributed by United Artists and in Italy by Titanus. As far as Tarantino is concerned, I know he has often spoken highly of me…

He did more than that: the two Kill Bill movies contain clear homages to your film.

The beginning, the violence at the beginning, yes. Morricone's music also, but not much else. To be honest I found his films a bit boring. There's too much of everything, a bit of a cartoon-like jumble. But, hey, maybe I'm just out of touch with today's tastes to really understand.

Let's go back to the cast. What about John Philip Law?

When I was approached to direct the film, the only name that was being bounced around was Van Cleef's. Law was one of the various options we discussed. I remember Antonio De Teffè [Anthony Steffen] was one actor that was mentioned a couple of times. Terence Hill was another—remember that at that time he was doing serious, straight-up Westerns. There were quite a few in the mix. I ended up choosing Law because he was getting a lot of attention in the States but I don't think he had done any Italian films before he was cast for mine. I remember an article, maybe in *Variety*, that kind of pointed him out as a newcomer to keep an eye on. But more importantly he had a certain quality I was looking for. De Teffè, Hill, Law … they all had a common trait. They had a childish look, a certain purity. Clean faced, baby-eyed men. The story was about a traumatized child who grows up into a man thirsty for revenge, living in the past, reliving in his mind, in a continuous loop, those terrible moments of his past—watching his family being killed, his mother and sister raped. I wanted him to maintain the innocence of a child at least in his face, to contrast the violence of his adult sentiments and actions. That said, Law isn't a great actor by any means but I think he works well in the film. Sansone believed he had a new Clint Eastwood on his hands.

Let's talk about Luigi Pistilli. This is the first of the two films you directed him in.

He is the best actor of the film. Very, very easy to work with. Professional, punctual and always spot-on. I would have liked to have had him in other films as well. In *Death Rides a Horse* he was proposed to me and I thought he fit the role but the second time around I specifically asked for him. Work-wise there is nothing much to add. As a person he was very well-mannered and was a nice person to have around but you could tell he was in a dark place. Broody, melancholic, with a self-destructive streak you could notice pulsating under the surface. When I discovered how he died, I can't say I was surprised.[4] Don't get me wrong, I'm not saying it was in any way foreseeable but it made sense. I don't think anybody who really knew him can say that it took them by surprise. There

At work on *A Sky Full of Stars for a Roof* (1968). Mario Adorf is far right, as Petroni (white arrow), observes the scene (author's collection).

was a time-bomb ticking away in some shadowy place of his psyche. Anyway, he was an actor who deserved better treatment and bigger roles.

Let's talk about ...e per tetto un cielo di stelle *[A Sky Full of Stars for a Roof, a.k.a. And for a Roof a Sky Full of Stars, 1968]*.

I liked working on that. It was much more easy-going than *Death Rides a Horse*. Firstly, because on that film everybody had their eyes on me. It was like a second debut in many ways. They knew I could direct and I came from a string of box-office successes but was that success only limited to comedies? This is what people were asking themselves. After the massive success of *Death Rides a Horse*—and I'm using the word lightly, you can check, it was one of that year's biggest grossing films in several countries—I was highly regarded. In a way, I had nothing to prove anymore.

Another solid cast.

Yes, on this film I had a greater decisional power in the casting process. You know that saying, casting is half the work? It's true. Plus, one of the qualities I think I had as a director was managing to create positive, trust-based relationships with the actors on set. I've always had great respect for their craft. I think one of the most important aspects of directing is understanding what an actor needs so as to work in the best possible way.

This doesn't mean pampering and spoiling them or doing whatever they ask. A director needs to understand each actor's personality and fears in order to be able to circumnavigate problems and create an exclusive and personal dialogue with them. You have to become a little bit of a psychiatrist. Speaking of which, I want to tell you an anecdote that has Gillo Pontecorvo—one of the greatest bluffs of Italian cinema—as a protagonist. I was the camera operator on a few of his documentaries and we also directed one together. Anyway, I knew a few people who were working on *Queimada* [1969], and I even went on set myself once when they were shooting at Cinecittà. Gillo would make Brando re-do the scenes dozens of times. On one specific occasion he reached forty takes, so Brando got up and went: "OK. I agree, let's do another one. Let me know how it goes."

Going back to your second Western, it's unclear who is responsible for the script. Many names have been thrown in the mix over the years: Alberto Areal, Mariano Laurenti, Bernardino Zapponi and even Gemma himself is said to have participated.

Let's put some order in this mess. Gemma did not work on the script in any way. He, of course, helped shape his character and would discuss with me about dialogue changes but he never helped construct the story. Giuliano was on board right from the start, even because often, the idea for these films would be triggered by an actor: "Let's do a film with Gemma, or Milian, or whoever. What would be suitable for him?" So, yes, from this point of view, he did participate, but that's it. As far as Mariano Laurenti is concerned, I have no idea why people think he might have helped write this film. It's a bit like the *Death Rides a Horse*–Antonio Margheriti theory. Completely unfounded. I have never even met Laurenti in my life. I know of him, he is the one that used to do all those sex comedies, right? Alberto Areal I don't think even exists. Could he be somebody's pseudonym? The film was written by Bernardino Zapponi, I wrote the first treatment using as a starting point Gianni Hecht Lucari's idea of making a Western version of Steinbeck's novel *Of Mice and Men*. Zapponi chose not to sign the film because he was afraid of associating his name to a genre product. At the time he was one of Fellini's closest collaborators…

What do you recall about Mario Adorf?

His character is the heart and soul of the film and I think he steals the show. Acting-wise he does an excellent job, but from a more personal point of view, Adorf was definitely less approachable than Gemma, more of a loner, but I had no problems with him either.

The two female leads, Magda Konopka and Julie Menard, are an interesting pair.

Magda Konopka, I chose her. We had met previously and I liked her. She was a natural choice. During production we had a relationship. I usually don't like talking about these things but at the time it was a known fact and we ended up having our photo in a magazine. I cast her again on *La notte dei serpenti* [*Nest of Vipers*, a.k.a. *Night of the Serpent*, 1969]. As for Julie Menard, I honestly don't remember. I think she was Gianni Lucari's choice.

Wait, I was told you also had a relationship with Julie Menard?

Let's proceed with the questions…

How did you come up with the idea of this bitter-sweet mix? The film has moments that are quite violent and others which are comedic, almost farcical. But the film, as a whole, is somewhat melancholic.

This mix you talk about is due to various factors. First of all, consider that by the time we got to this film, the genre was still going strong, very strong, but at the same time it was beginning to be overloaded with insignificant, improvised films. Purely imitational products that didn't change or add but just tried to replicate with less money and talent. The need to find new interpretations and points of view became important. And, before *Trinity* came out, we thought of the brains-and-brawn combination. My films often have a duo at the core: Milian-Steiner, Gemma-Adorf, Milian-Palmer. The beginning of a friendship, the so-called male bonding, is always interesting in the context of a film and Westerns are perfect for this kind of relationship. Secondly, the initial concept of the film, the one of adapting, or better still, rethinking Steinbeck's novel and the subsequent creation of Adorf's character, allowed the lighter elements to be introduced very spontaneously. I simply hope that the comedic aspect doesn't overpower the rest. For me this is still a pure Western and I wanted to make it clear from the beginning. I wanted a very strong opening. A violent one. I think it's the best thing in the film, also thanks to Carlo Carlini, a great director of photography, that I expressively asked for after the previous Western. Going back to Morricone, by the way, I think his music for this film is better than the music for *Death Rides a Horse*. Everybody raves about that soundtrack but I find this one more complex and suggestive. I also think *A Sky Full of Stars for a Roof* has some of the best action scenes I've directed. *Death* is more atmospheric, nearly gothic at times, but the idea was that both the violence and action should be quick and sudden. For this film I wanted much more dynamism. I had a great team of stuntmen: Riccardo Pizzuti, Alberto Dell'Acqua, Benito Stefanelli...

Speaking of screenwriters, Franco Solinas often said that his contribution was minimal, and that Tepepa [a.k.a. Blood and Guns, 1968], your third Western, was actually written by Ivan Della Mea.

This is a colossal lie. I met this Mr. Della Mea no more than a couple of times, almost accidentally, I may say. That screenplay is by Solinas. Period. The reason he didn't like to talk about the film or to be associated too much with it, is because he is not responsible for the story. Not many people know this, but the original story was written by Adriano Bolzoni and myself.

Some versions have a different ending, where they cut Tepepa riding with Morricone's music in the background.

Yes, the final scene underwent some changes. Initially I had removed the final allegory with Tomas Milian riding, just before the credits start rolling because Solinas didn't like it—again, simply because it wasn't his idea. Then I realized it was perfect, and put it back where it belonged. But you're referring to censor cuts. I later came to know that—for the American distribution—Paramount had cut Tepepa riding in the finale. This probably was due to the ambiguity of the character. He is a rapist and murderer and that sequence makes the character kind of mythical. Anyway, there are two versions of the film: the real one, which was released on DVD not long ago in Italy, that has a duration of about 130 minutes, and a much shorter version wanted by Alfredo Cuomo, the producer. He thought, I don't know on what basis, that my cut was too long, so I had to shorten it. In Italy, the film was released in its integral, original version and then, shortly after, the Cuomo-cut version was distributed.

Let's talk about Orson Welles.

Cuomo managed to get in touch with him through some agencies. When I met Welles I told him that the idea of directing *Citizen Kane* was quite intimidating, but, with a grin on his face, he just said, "Don't be silly." When I made *Tepepa* I was no longer that

Mounted on a ladder, Tomas Milian gives José Torres and Luciano Casamonica (on horseback) the eye line, while script supervisor Silvia Petroni and director Giulio Petroni (in plaid shirt, hand on hip) watch over things (author's collection).

young, and this was a relief for him because he couldn't stand newbies. Needless to say, he was preceded by his reputation as an unmanageable, grouchy man—which he actually was, but not with me. Welles and I spent many nights talking over a bottle of whiskey. He liked drinking. He would often talk about Rita Hayworth … I suppose he never got over her. He never interfered with my work or role on set; maybe a suggestion once or twice … and he was always perfectly right. Unfortunately Tomas Milian became his target. He would call him "the tiny Cuban."

What can you tell me about Tomas Milian?

A good actor but sometimes a bit hard to manage. He was a powerhouse of ideas, therefore he had this tendency of going a bit overboard. When we were working on *La vita, a volte, è molto dura, vero Provvidenza?* [*Life Is Tough, Eh Providence?* a.k.a. *Sometimes Life Is Hard—Right, Providence?*, 1972], he would come to me with these odd suggestions and I had to contain him. For example, in that film, the yoga thing was his idea. He was very self-doubting as well. On the one hand he would be a very dominant presence on set but on the other he was very self-conscious and insecure. Welles was after him and I think he felt very much under pressure. He especially had problems with his physical appearance. He felt ugly and would constantly be comparing himself to other men. This is one of the reasons he felt the need to seduce everybody. Tomas hated, in a pathological way, the idea of being unnoticed or unappreciated.

Tepepa is the second so-called "Western rivoluzionario" after **Quien Sabe [A Bullet for the General, 1966]** *and together with Damiano Damiani's film, it is the most important film of this subgenre.*

Yes, I've seen Damiani's film, though I don't remember much about it. There are quite a few analogies between my film and his but these are due to Solinas, who would often end up writing the same film. *Tepepa* has a primate that none of the other films of this genre can boast. It's the only film that the Mexican government considered worthy of being distributed in their country. I was invited, but wasn't able to go, to the big premiere they held. I think it tapped on feelings that animated that period but at the same time my film is the most cynical, definitely more than Damiani's previous one and even more so if compared to future efforts, like Corbucci's stuff. At the end of *Tepepa* everybody loses. Welles, Steiner and Milian all finish in the dust. Ideals end up corrupting each one of them.

Your fourth Western is the least known of the lot and one of the strangest Italian Westerns ever made. What do you recall of **Nest of Vipers**?

That film is a bit of a disappointment for me. First of all it interrupted the flow of hits. All three of my Westerns had done extremely well. Not that *Nest of Vipers* was a flop but nothing compared to the others. After *Tepepa,* producers were all over me and I could have chosen any project I wanted ... I mean in the Western genre. Those were the only films they were asking me to do. I don't think I chose wisely.

How did the story take shape?

Gianni Minervini had been the production manager both on *Death Rides a Horse* and *Tepepa* and he came to me with this story written by Gicca Palli. Not a script, just a plot outline. I liked the idea of a mystery story set in the West, mainly because it was a completely different concept compared to what I had done previously. I don't remember meeting Gicca Palli but he wrote the first version, of that I'm sure—the idea was his— but I changed the story substantially. I created the character of the prostitute played by Chelo Alonso, for example, which was not present in the first treatment. Also the town priest is my doing...

Speaking of priests, all of your Westerns are strongly anti-clerical but in the case of **Nest of Vipers** *this aspect is taken to the extreme. It could be defined as the first openly atheist Western ever made.*

In all my films my social and political consciousness can be found looming in some corner. I'm an atheist and have always been one. It's in my blood. My great-grandfather was the last person to be condemned to death by the Church. He spent nearly twenty years in the Vatican prisons. I remember during the premiere of the film, a man got up from his seat and started repeatedly making the sign of the cross, shaking his head like an epileptic, in the scene when Luke Askew says, "I don't have imaginary friends" after he'd been asked if he believed in God. If it hadn't been a Western, so unworthy of attention, that scene would have probably been cut.

Luke Askew was a peculiar choice.

I was the one who chose him as I chose everybody in the film. The production company sent me to Los Angeles asking me to come back with someone new. I picked him through a big casting agency in the heart of Hollywood. He'd had a role in *Easy Rider* [1969] and before that he had been in *Cool Hand Luke* [1967]. I chose him mainly because I thought he would be credible in a Western context, but also because of his modern face.

AVISOS	HABITACION ROOM
Para D. / TO M. JULIO PETRONI	N.°

DIA - DAY	HORA - HOUR	HABITACION ROOM
19·10·68	19.—	N.° 807

☐ Ha llamado D. ....

☐ Ha venido de MADRID
from   ciudad   pais

OBJETO DEL AVISO / NOTICE

TELEGRAMA

I VERY MUCH ENJOYED WORKING WITH YOU PLEASE THINK OF ME AGAIN. WARMEST REGARDS

ORSON

RECIBIDO POR

Original telegram sent by Orson Welles to Giulio Petroni, after his work was finished on the set of Petroni's seminal "tortilla western" *Tepepa*, in 1968 (author's collection).

I wanted somebody that would have been credible as a hippy. And I didn't regret it: just like all American actors, he was punctual and meticulous. They all were, regardless of their artistic abilities. I had no problems with Askew. He smoked a lot of weed but, after Milian on *Tepepa*, I was used to that sort of thing. Milian had just discovered cocaine. I had a good relationship with everybody on that film. Chelo Alonso was a bit of a diva but nothing I couldn't handle. *Nest of Vipers* was my seventh film so I had built a trustworthy team. Divo Cavicchioli came back after *Tepepa* as a set photographer. Pistilli, Minervini, Luciano Casamonica, Magda Konopka … I had good people on that film.

Your first and only Western without music by Morricone.

Yes, and I think the film suffered because of his absence. Riz Ortolani did a good job, the main theme is lovely, but it's a little too classical. I'm sure Morricone would have tapped into the undercurrent themes of the film better.

In your Westerns, children are always at the center of violence. In Death Rides a Horse a child watches his family being brutally slaughtered; in Tepepa the child ends up becoming part of a spiral of violence and in Nest of Vipers we have a protagonist that is guilty of the most heinous of crimes, having killed his own son. Coincidence?

The loss of innocence is a theme I'm very attached to. I guess, on a subconscious level, it has to do with the war. I had to grow up very quickly and I think this transpires in my films. There is very little space for innocent things in the world we live in.

Petroni (center) directs Luke Askew (right) on the set of *Nest of Vipers*, as DOP Mario Vulpiani sets the scene (author's collection).

Let's talk about Life Is Tough, Eh Providence?

First of all, I didn't like this title. Too long, too much punctuation. But the producers insisted, and I eventually gave up. We came up with the name Providence to follow a trend there was back then of giving characters ... evangelical names. After what we've just said, I think this is enough to understand how detached I was when directing this film.

Did you have the opportunity of seeing the sequel Ci risiamo vero, provvidenza? *[Here We Go Again, Eh Providence?, 1973] by De Martino? What did you think of it?*

Yes, I saw it once, and I thought it was quite bad. Milian is left adrift, which is wrong with any actor but especially with someone like him. As I already said, Tomas needs a director who's able to stop him when he goes too far. No, it's simply a dull film—and sure enough—it ended up being a flop, contrary to mine, which made good money, for the producers, of course. I never got rich through my films. My fault.

What do you mean?

Well, considering that most of my films were reasonably successful, and a couple of them even strikingly so, one wouldn't expect me to be living in a basement. But I've always been a terrible businessman, really bad at managing money.

Were you asked to direct the sequel?

Yes, initially I was but I immediately made it clear that I wasn't interested. You can't make more than one film of that kind, plus I felt the need to move on to something new. Westerns were dead.

Indeed, Providence *is your last Western...*

Apart from my personal aspirations, it must be said that the genre had started to decline and I didn't want to find myself involved in the vulgarization that was taking place. I felt guilty enough, having directed *Providence*.

Probably not many people know that Mario Bava collaborated on the film.

Yes, he did. We all knew from the start that some sequences were going to be particularly complex. One scene, especially, stood out: the pool table moment, when Providence makes the balls go all over the place. I knew who Bava was and that he had become a director, but to me he was still a cinematographer. That was his reputation, for me at least. I don't think I had seen anything he had directed. He worked on the special effects for a couple of days. He was quick and very respectful.

How were you offered the film?

Milian proposed me to Papi and Colombo, the producers. I needed the money, mainly because I had just founded my production company, with which I had already directed and produced a film. I needed to cover a lot of expenses. Milian believed in the film a lot. He was looking to create a franchise that could compete with the Spencer-Hill films that were doing so well in that period. This was the first Western of mine that was not shot in Almeria, in Spain. I tried my best to choose the locations carefully but you can tell ... it just isn't the same thing. The script was terrible. Castellano and Pipolo had written a script that was unreadable, just awful. The first thing I told the producers was: "OK, I'll do it but I want to rewrite it." I brought Piero Regnoli into the film.

What do you remember of Janet Agren?

I had seen her photo in a magazine and thought she would be suitable. She hadn't done much, if anything, in Italy. She was not a very good actress, kind of cold, but I had no particular problem with her. Tomas didn't like her because she would forget her lines and he would call her "bambolina" [little doll]: "Get the dolly out of her box!" I have good memories of Greg Palmer though, very professional and Gabriella Giorgelli, who was a fun and loose girl to have around.

So, in the early seventies you also start producing your own films. Where does this need come from?

Well, I'd actually begun to think of working as a producer many years earlier. My relationship with producers has always been difficult, quite contentious, even back when I worked with Emo Bistolfi, who produced *Always on Sunday* and *The Usual Thieves from Milan*. A boorish, small-minded man, with no sense of humor or wit whatsoever. With *Non commettere atti impuri* [translation: *Do Not Commit Impure Acts*, 1971] I finally managed to fulfill this dream. As I said, Westerns as a genre was experiencing a decline and I began to feel the need to explore new territories and take more control over my films. Not that I hadn't had it until then but—naive as this may sound—I wanted as few compromises as possible.

What's the story behind **Do Not Commit Impure Acts***?*

A few years earlier, at the end of the sixties, I had written a short story—then published in the magazine *Athos*—called "La crisi mistica" [translation: "The Mystical Crises"]. That's how the screenplay came into being. Originally, it was to be set in Turin, then I chose Assisi to increase its desecrating atmosphere. I used to own a house there, in the vicinity of Assisi, with a pig-breeding farm.

Again we have a rich cast. What do you remember about Barbara Bouchet?

I chose her mainly because she was doing very well at the box office. All her films had done well, plus she hadn't worked much in comedies. Keep in mind that in 1971, sex comedies weren't the thing yet. Though it's debatable that my film is definable as a comedy.

What kind of person was Luciano Salce,[5] who plays an important role?

In a sense, very similar to the character he plays in the film. He definitely wasn't an attractive man, but he was aware of it and had a great sense of humor, so much so that you could easily call him a *tombeur de femmes*, with a thing for young girls. On set, he was accurate and professional, always refined and gentle. I don't think that role was hard for him—it was custom-made.

Similar contents and locations make one think of this film together with **Crescete e moltiplicatevi** *[Grow and Multiply, 1973] and* **Labbra di lurido blu** *[Lips of Lurid Blue, 1975] as a trilogy.*

True, it makes sense, but I never wanted to make a trilogy. Still, these three films share some themes, such as my repulsion for the moralistic ignorance that surrounds Catholicism. Plus, I tried to cast these films, especially the first two which have more comedic elements—the third is a full-blown drama—using names that were atypical for the genre. I didn't want actors that were associated with the various types of comedy that were being made. I'm happy with my choices though they were quite unpopular and risky. The trio Hugh Griffith, Lionel Stander and Raymond Pellegrin is a crazy choice for an Italian farce.

As for nude scenes, how would you handle your actresses? Was it hard to convince them or negotiate with them?

It really depended on the actress. There were times when nudity wasn't a problem at all, like with Barbara Bouchet; other times, it was harder. Simonetta Stefanelli was definitely more shy and adamant about taking her clothes off. She has a scene in which she is fully nude but I was clear from the start, before anybody signed anything, about what would be shown and that there wouldn't be any surprises.

Lips of Lurid Blue *is undoubtedly your most controversial film, one might say "damned."*

Well … I don't think I deserved the lynching I got after that film was released. I wanted to shed light on a theme that was felt pretty strongly in the mid-seventies. A part of society wasn't able to analyze itself and lived a profound conflict: desires, on one side, and taboos, on the other. The film was quite successful, the audience chose not to give credit to those critics who were destroying me. I might have failed to convey my message, but I would have accepted this criticism had it originated from an analysis of the contents of the film; instead, the attack was totally uncalled for, unjustified.

Petroni and Rosalba Neri during a break on the set of *Grow and Multiply,* 1973 (author's collection).

What happened after **Lips?**

Long trips around the world and a return to Sri Lanka. I wanted to distance myself from this country, after being publicly mocked by mediocracy. The resentment and rancor I felt were so intense that I believe the film had accidentally touched a raw nerve. As a matter of fact, when I saw it again, I realized it rummages through the garbage of Italian self-righteousness.

It has a very interesting cast.

I produced, directed, wrote it, did the editing … and picked the cast. I got everybody I wanted. Initially I had picked Giorgio Strehler for the role that eventually went to Silvano Tranquilli but apart from that, I had the cast I wanted right from the beginning. Lisa Gastoni was a natural choice for that part. She was the perfect actress to play the morbidity behind the façade of bourgeoisie. Corrado Pani

Lisa Gastoni is taunted by latex punk demons in *Lips of Lurid Blue*, 1975 (author's collection).

and Jeremy Kemp are choices I'm very happy about because they were the exact opposite of the stereotype homosexual perpetrated in Italian cinema.

The last part of your career is very hazy and unclear. Shall we talk about* L'osceno desiderio—Le pene nel ventre *[Obscene Desire, 1978]? For many years you have denied directing this film. The only horror of your filmography.

Yes, this is true. I still don't consider it mine. I want nothing to do with the film. Basically what happened is this: as I said before, *Lips of Lurid Blue* had gone fairly well but not for me. The bank took everything away, including my farm in Umbria. I had indebted myself too much and had to close down Azalea, my production company. I needed money. I was offered this film and I did it but in my contract I had a clause that stated that my name would not be used. I only discovered once it was released, that Giulio Petroni was all over the place, big on the poster: a film by Giulio Petroni. Initially it wasn't supposed to be a horror but an erotic film but halfway through pre-production everything was changed. In that period films on the devil were the big thing and the producer decided to ride that wave. The script is mainly Piero Regnoli's.

You have never talked about this film. Just tell me a little more about the genesis of it. You say Regnoli is the person most responsible for the story, though the context in which the film takes place is very similar to the one present in your previous efforts with Azalea.

In the mid-seventies I had written a script, I think called "Onirica" [translation: "Dream-Like"]. It was a strange film, sort of an erotic, metaphysical mystery about a killer who turns his victims into statues. Luigi Mondello commissioned it to me and I wrote in collaboration with Vittorio Vighi, who was the main writer of his films. Mondello wanted to make it at all costs. This was a year or so before *Lips of Lurid Blue*. Mondello also asked me to involve Tomas Milian, seeing I knew and had worked with him. In that same period Tomas was looking for a story to make his debut as a director. Crazy as he was, he was paying all sorts of people to write ideas and scripts for him. At one point he even involved me in a project about Christ ... a modern reimagining of the biblical parable of Jesus Christ, but that's another story.... Anyway he was hunting for ideas and fell in love with my script which he bought off me straight away and, believe me, I didn't give it away cheap. When Mondello discovered this he was furious but I calmed him down and reassured him I would give him something new that would have been equally good. I didn't. By this time I was completely involved in the making of *Lips* and just wanted Mondello off my back. I wrote for him what will later become the basis for *Obscene Desire*. He got the script and changed it radically. Mine was more of an erotic thriller, with some slight giallo overtones. After the financial crisis I had to confront following *Lips*, I accepted Mondello's proposition to direct it. Not straight away, the project stayed in a drawer for a couple of years. After *Lips* I tried to make another film with my Azalea, something I had written with Massimo Franciosa but the times had changed and money was lacking, genres had changed. I decided to make the film for Mondello on the condition, as I said before, that my name would not appear anywhere.

Who is Joaquín Domìnquez, who is credited as one of the writers?
A name put simply for matters of quotas possibly the guy who translated the script. Sometimes the translator or adaptor would be credited.

Where was the film shot?
In Spain, it was an Italian-Spanish co-production.

Though despite having a considerably lower budget than your previous films, it has a solid enough cast...
Maybe compared to similar products but certainly not compared to what I was used to. Lou Castel was the producer's choice and he was a nightmare. He was arrogant and completely unprofessional, always drunk and speaking shit. One day I went nuts, I was fed up with his shit and literally threw him off the set. I shot his scene using a double. Chris Avram was fine, so was Laura Trotter ... but it was all very depressing and shoddy.

In past interviews you stated that you only directed a few scenes and then left, leaving everything in the hands of your Spanish 1st AD.
Well, some scenes were not shot by me but most of the film was, though I participated marginally to the editing process. I had to for contractual reasons. I would have been accused of breach of contract if I hadn't participated at all.

Over the years there has been speculation that Jésus Franco participated, in some form or another, in the post-production of Obscene Desire.
The Spanish midget with the pointy beard? Yes, I remember his name being bounced around but as I said, my participation after principal photography was very minimal.

Which is the film you prefer among the ones you made?
I think *Tepepa*, *Lips of Lurid Blue* and *Death Rides a Horse* are my best films. And there are things I like in *Grow and Multiply* and *Don't Commit Impure Acts*. But overall the film I love the most is the one I wasn't able to make.... They stopped me from making it....

Rome, 2007–2009

1961 Jazzing from the Background
The Cinema of Alberto De Martino

"This time I'm going to win. You're all afraid, you stinking pots of shit!"—Carla Gravina in The Antichrist, 1974

He will destroy the world. No man can stop him. No man will even try. He is The Chosen.—American tagline of *Holocaust 2000* a.k.a. *The Chosen*, 1977

As written in the preface of this book, creativity and imagination had to be put to use by the Italian film industry, in an attempt to decode the genres that were being imported. If there is a director most representative of this modus operandi—the study, elaboration and recalibration of American product—that is Alberto De Martino (12 June 1929, Rome–2 June 2015, Rome). Son of the well-known makeup artist Romolo De Martino, Alberto starts as an assistant director on small films, mostly melodramas, followed, during the "Hollywood on the Tiber" years, by adventure films and period pieces. During this time he will meet Sergio Leone for whom he wrote, in 1953, *Taxi ... signore?* (translation: *Taxi ... Mister?*), a short film that to date cannot be found and can be considered lost, and for whom he would later direct the second unit of *Giù la testa* (*For a Fistful of Dynamite*, a.k.a. *Duck, You Sucker*, 1971). Like Leone, Mario Caiano and most directors of his generation, De Martino makes his debut with a mythological epic: *Il gladiatore invincibile* (*The Invincible Gladiator*, 1961), which also has the merit of bringing to Italy Richard Harrison, who will be a recurring protagonist of many Italian films throughout the sixties and will be at the center of another fundamental turning point for the Roman director: *100.000 dollari per Ringo* (*$100,000 for Ringo*, 1965).

De Martino has never been a trendsetter, he has never been a director who wanted or was capable of revolutionizing a genre, of giving birth to a new current but he has always distinguished himself in each one he got close to and right from the start of his directorial career, dedicated himself to the most popular genres. In fact, he is at the center of each big phenomenon, at the forefront of each major switch in cinematic tastes and fashions, though his tendency to have a so-called Anglo-Saxon touch, to infuse his films with an American feel, is the aspect most emphasized in his stylistic approach and has followed him around all his life, as he himself has often stated. "Now I don't read stuff about myself anymore. I leave this sort of thing to other people, even because now, with internet, it would become a full-time job. But at the time I would always read what the major newspapers would write about my films and it didn't matter if they spoke well, or at least with a benevolent tone, or if they would rip me apart ... they would always mention this thing about being American. I would look out for it." This ambiguous definition, "the most American of Italian genre directors," has the bitter taste of a backhanded compliment, but is, to a certain point, a justified one, particularly when the description was used in reviews of the period. It is partially due to the fact that all of De Martino's films have been rich with American presence. In fact, nearly every one of the almost 30 films he directed contains at least one (fading) Hollywood star or well-known character actor. If this is common to most Italian genre directors, with De Martino the list is exceptionally long: Kirk Douglas, John Cassavetes, Martin Balsam, Michael Moriarty, Anthony Quayle, Arthur Kennedy, Mel Ferrer, Donald Pleasence, Greg Palmer, Telly Savalas, Stuart Whitman, Simon Ward, Martin Landau, Frederick Strafford, John Ireland, John Saxon and more. Another aspect that is important to underline to further comprehend this specific viewpoint on De Martino's body of work is the choice of genres and the criteria and prospective used by him when tackling them. For starters his is one of the few filmographies not to contain within it a single comedy, the only exception being the Western parody—of the American genre, we are in pre–Leone years—*Due contro tutti* (*Terrible Sheriff*, a.k.a. *Two Against All*, 1962) with Raimondo Vianello and Walter Chiari, but like all Western comedies, they are firstly Westerns and then secondly comedies, seeing that even the most irreverent of them is obligated to follow a series of linguistic rules and iconography. De Martino has always made films that could be easily exportable, especially in Anglo-Saxon territories or films that could satisfy the thirst for a second helping of big American successes: peplums, Westerns, war, gangster and actions films, horrors and he even tried to tap into the neo-superhero subgenre.

De Martino (left) with Sergio Leone: "Here we were in his office. It was huge, full of colonial furniture and big history books. It was taken shortly after I had helped him on *Duck, You Sucker,* around 1972/73" (courtesy Alberto De Martino).

This last point brings us to a further, and possibly more important and exhaustive consideration: De Martino's take on genres is one completely dominated by the American market, and especially from the late sixties onwards he concentrates on American culture. Whereas, for example, Castellari's and especially Lenzi's fascination with the States originates from the cinematic collective imagery and their elaborations and portraits of American trademarks stem nearly exclusively from cinema and their film knowledge,

Alberto De Martino seems more interested by the culture itself—by the ways of thinking and the places more than by cinephile fascinations.

> I have always preferred making films than watching them. I love cinema eh ... I mean I grew up on sets, tripping over cables and talking to grips and teamsters. It's the only place you can find the smells and the electricity a set is filled with. It's a stench that once you get used to it, becomes addictive ... you always want more. That said, I never was, in my youth, one of those kids always shut inside a cinema auditorium watching one film after the other. I would go to see films but as most of the kids would, to meet up with friends, to have fun, to socialize. The cinema auditorium was a meeting point, maybe a place to start off the evening ... then we would go out for a pizza or hang out somewhere else. I did study films and what made them work, but from the inside, watching other directors work especially when I was 1st AD, observing their decisions and mistakes. As for America ... I'm Italian and wouldn't move from Italy but I was interested in their way of thinking. I mean, they are crazy ... it's a big place filled with everything, they have all sorts of contradictions. I was definitely interested in what was happening there. I kept an eye on what they were up to. It's a fact that they controlled the market, not only with regards to cinema but generally, and when you're there you feel at the center of things. You couldn't ignore what Hollywood was doing, or at least I couldn't.

Hollywood "intromission" is a long and complex aspect of Italy's popular cinema. Italian police action films, for example, definitely feel the presence of big American hits such as *Dirty Harry* and *The French Connection* (both 1971), trying to reproduce the most spectacular aspects of them, but like with horrors and especially Westerns, the American influence is one of a number of layers and inputs. We have, with genres such as "poliziotteschi" and gialli, the logistic and geographic connotations that take over and forge the look and structure of a film; cities like Rome, Naples and Milan are pivotal visual and narrative elements. We have the extremely strong influence of so-called "auteur cinema"—using police thrillers again as an example, let's think how fundamental certain films by Elio Petri, Pietro Germi and Luigi Zampa are in pinpointing the evolution of the genre, films that have little, if anything to do with the American viewpoint and style— which infuses popular cinema with new themes which get used, elaborated or exploited in the most diverse ways. And then there is the country's rich literary and pictorial heritage, its historic predisposition to the visual art forms and an interest in cinema that germinated very early on in the history of the medium; not to mention, of course, each individual director's interests, background and personal views. The mixture of all these elements, when the dosages and timings are right, create very unique results: films that work as commercially exportable products capable of being understood and appreciated in the most varied of cultural contexts, remaining not only profoundly Italian, both in technique and in content, but also manage to be (sometimes un)conscious snapshots of the social, urbanistic, cultural and political turning points of the country's life. So, in the best examples of Italian genre cinema the "American element" ends up representing sometimes the most superficial visual input of products that are pervaded by an Italian, or European, sensitivity. Though, looking at De Martino's most representative titles one can notice how he chooses to ignore the narrative structures of his colleagues' successes. De Martino re-elaborates, paying attention exclusively to American interpretations, and so most of his films from the seventies and eighties can be ascribable to one major hit (*The Godfather, Dirty Harry, The Exorcist, The Omen*). We can see this in his horrors and Westerns but by sticking to police thrillers, what is being illustrated really takes form. De Martino's so-called contributions to the genre have very little to do with the major Italian strongholds. At the birth of the genre he prefers concentrating on the new wave of gangster movies that Francis Ford Coppola's *The Godfather* (1972) had given birth to, with *I familiari delle vittime non saranno avvertiti* (*Crime Boss*, 1972)—despite a confusing original title (translated as The Relatives of the Victims Will Not Be Informed)—aimed to lead audiences into believing they were about to watch a pseudo-giallo with police thriller overtones, and more importantly with the superior *Il consigliori* (*The Counsellor*, a.k.a. *Counsellor at Crime*, 1973). Though it has to be said that this continuous, to use the words of De Martino, "figuring out what the next big thing from the States was going to be," resulted in some drab and flatly composed imitations (*Crime Boss*) or true disasters like *L'uomo puma* (*The Puma Man*, 1980), for which De Martino had probably bit off more than he could chew. Though, despite De Martino's attempts to ignore Italian trends, when he hits the spot it's usually with films streaked with an undoubtedly Latin touch. *L'anticristo* (*The Antichrist*, a.k.a. *The Tempter*, 1974) with the mixture of a comic book strain (the blue-tinted sequence of the invocation of Ippolita's ancestor, during the orgiastic Sabbath); a documentary feel with the use of real faces and locations from Southern Italy (the procession of the "Madonna dei Sette Dolori" filled with cripples and crazed figures); and a taste for the over the top exploitation of sexual innuendo and gore, all wrapped up with the most American packaging possible, make it the perfect example of what Alberto De Martino was capable of.

One of the first things I noticed when I entered his office, the biggest room of his apartment, was a small black-and-white photo hanging at the entrance. I recognized both the figures standing behind a black polished piano: De Martino and on his right Lucio Fulci. "We wanted to start a jazz band together," says Alberto, as he notices me studying the photo. "Look! When I was young they mistook me for Johnny Dorelli all the time. It's true though, I look like Dorelli's disgraced brother!" He laughs. Laughing is what he will do throughout the interview: with me and to himself, rummaging through memories, some of which I can tell he will not share. More than what, it is how De Martino tells his story and describes his career that I find fascinating, with a satisfied smile and a twinkle in his eye, a twinkle of somebody who had fun, who enjoyed every moment of the ride. I didn't even care that at one point or another I would have to gulp down half a glass of Amaro Petrus he insisted I accept, a tonic liquor you could use to kill cockroaches or drain the kitchen sink with because his office—with its walls covered, as they were, with posters of each and every one of his films and furniture just delivered straight from the mid-seventies—was like a time capsule.

How and when did you first approach the world of cinema?

I was introduced to the film industry thanks to my father, who was a makeup artist. Romolo De Martino. I began with *Scipione l'africano* [*Scipio Africanus*, a.k.a. *Scipio the African*, a.k.a. *The Defeat of Hannibal*, 1937] by Carmine Gallone, with Annibale Ninchi as the leading actor, where I made a brief appearance as Scipio himself. Yes, because the film tells the story of Scipio in three different stages of his life if I'm not mistaken, and I played him as a child. But I don't know if I'm actually in the film or if they cut my part out. I never actually saw it. Anyway, I started off as an actor, doing some small roles especially in films starring Lilia Silvi,[1] who was a big celebrity at the time, and my father was her regular makeup artist. I made a lot of appearances, with lines, without lines, long or short ones, but the only film where I am credited is *Elisir d'amore* [translation: *The Love Potion*, 1941] by Amleto Palermi, with Armando Falconi, Margherita Carosio, Roberto Villa. Names that are unknown today, but that were rather popular back then. However, you were asking how the idea of becoming a director came about… So, I was asked to play the role of a shepherd boy in an adaptation of *I promessi sposi* [*The Betrothed*],[2] I was supposed to witness Lucia's abduction from afar. The director shouted: "You are scared!" and so I acted scared. "More scared! More! More! You are petrified! Show me!" Nothing. "Stop!" I get labeled unsuitable, fired and kicked out. The following day they call another boy, another background actor, and here they go again: "More scared! More scared! More!" Unsuitable, fired, kicked out. When the film was released, I went to see it. I mean, I wanted to see who they ended up choosing. There were two shepherd boys, not one, the director clearly needed some camera movement, I don't remember, or maybe an intercut. Anyway, Lucia screams, the two shepherd boys look at each other. Cut. End of the scene. So I told myself that being a director was easier than being an actor. But I have to say that I would have never dreamed of becoming a director if I hadn't met, during my high school years, my Latin and Greek teacher who became my spiritual father. In my time, directors were unreachable, almighty gods. Blasetti, Mario Soldati, they … huh … they were giants, semi-gods! So, back then, aspiring to become a director meant dreaming big, really big, but I was lucky enough to meet this teacher, Filippo Maria Pontani. He gave me my first books on film editing, he would encourage me, he knew I worked as an actor and he was happy about it. He was a great Hellenist, you know, an incredibly intelligent man. He watched all my films, until *Horror* [1963]. So, I owe everything to these two fathers of mine. My real father, mainly, and this teacher who gave me a good push in the right direction.

There's another fundamental step in your path towards becoming a director, your years as a 1st AD.

Of course! I worked on more than twenty films as 1st AD, with Mario Costa, Masini, Giorgio Simonelli … I learned a lot from Simonelli. He was always sitting there with a whistle in his mouth, and he would use it to go "Action!" to make sure everybody would hear him. Working with these directors was important but I think I learned the most from editing, something I did while working as an assistant director. Timing, rhythm, the right duration of the scenes, and so on. Also, I was a jazz pianist, so they would often call me to take care of the music. For example, I would do a lot of sound editing.

So, let's recap: actor, 1st AD, editor … anything else?

Yes, dubbing, dialogue adaptation, which I did for a long time. Actually, there was a moment when I thought I would never become a director. It seemed I couldn't manage to make my first film. They would call me "the Campari Soda guy" because, every time I was about to make a film, the producer would go: "OK, let's make it." We would make a toast with Campari and I would never hear about the project or from the producer again. I was "the Campari Soda guy"…

How did you turn things around for yourself?

Well, I worked as 1st AD on *Teseo contro il Minotauro*[3] [*The Minotaur, the Wild Beast of Crete*, 1960] by Silvio Amadio, who had replaced another director.[4] I ended up as second unit director, something I had already done, but this time the word had spread that I knew what I was doing and so they really started calling me. They actually called me this time to direct my first film! So that is how I got the script for *Il gladiatore invincibile* [*The Invincible Gladiator*, 1961]. When I talk about this film, I can't but recall this story: I was handed the script as I was working as a dubbing director on *La dolce vita* [1960]. I had started as Franco Rossi's assistant but then, after two weeks, Rossi left to go make his film *L'Odissea* [*The Odyssey*]⁵ and Federico made me take his place. So, I went up to him and we talked. As a 1st AD, I was working on very commercial stuff, but in the dubbing field I was working on films by Zampa, Monicelli and De Santis. This is what I asked Federico: "What should I to do with this film, make it or not?" and he replied with something I will never forget. "If you have strings to your bow, it will show, even if you make films on invincible gladiators." I thought OK, let's do it. I rewrote the screenplay and directed it. The film was a success, and twenty-eight more followed.

As far as I know, at that time, right before your directorial debut, you worked with Sergio Sollima. On what exactly?

Oh, sure! With Sergio I co-directed two documentaries, at the end of the fifties. They were called *Intervista con il cervello* [translation: *Interview with the Brain*] and *Turista con il pollice* [translation: *Hitchhiking Tourists*]. Two really good documentaries. You know, Sergio and I had this idea of creating an artistic duo, like Steno and Monicelli. We had met while working as assistants on a film by Mario Costa, and we got along pretty well. We became friends, we thought highly of each other … let's give it a go! Then, over time, we changed our minds and went our separate ways. We remained good friends as the decades rolled by. We don't talk anymore though, because Sergio is awfully sick and he can't speak.⁶ I don't know the details, I just know he's sick. I talked to his daughter, he's conscious but he can't speak. So I can't even call him on the phone. Becoming old is a terrible thing.

Which one of Costa's films were you working on when you two met?

Trieste mia! [translation: *My Trieste*, 1951]. I have a funny anecdote about that film. One of the actors was Ermanno Randi, who was homosexual. Unbelievable … women loved him, no one would have ever thought he was gay. The leading actor was Luciano Tajoli, but Ermanno had a major role … anyway, he was killed during the making of the film. We had three more days of work when his South American lover shot him. The following day Sergio and I were on the set discussing who was supposed to inform Costa about what happened. "You go." "No way, you go." "Nope, you go." I was the one who ended up having to tell him. Costa arrives, I walk up to him. "Ermanno Randi was killed." He stands there, petrified. But his eyes gaze into space, moving quickly from left to right. Silence. He's calculating if he has got everything he needs to edit the film. More silence, then he goes: "Okay, fine. It can be done! So tell me, how did it happen?"

At the beginning of the sixties, when you made your directorial debut, the Italian film industry was going through radical changes. The international market was becoming increasingly important.

Yes, absolutely. So much so that *The Invincible Gladiator* was conceived for the American market. Well, I must admit that all of my films were export films. All but the second one: *Due contro tutti* [*Terrible Sheriff*, a.k.a. *Two Against All*, 1962] with Raimondo Vianello and Walter Chiari, which was a Western comedy. This is why I was labeled in the industry as "the most American Italian director."

You anticipated my question. Is this the only reason you are defined as an "American director"?

Apart from the reason I just gave, the genres I did, I can't tell … it might be because I've always chosen American actors, or because of my shooting style. I mean, stylistically I follow my instinct, my momentary impetus. What I'm sure of, is that I give priority to composing the background. I always start from what's in the background, never from what happens in the foreground. Aside from all this, I can say that I try to use static shots as much as possible, just like Americans do. Just like Charlie Chaplin used to do, I don't believe he ever moved the camera more than an inch in his entire life. I don't know, I can't think of anything else…

Well, you were also known as a director who yielded sure results.
My films were rather successful. If they weren't successful in Italy, or at least not as much as we hoped, they would do better abroad. I remember being in Montreal shooting a film when I came to know that during its first week in theaters, my *L'anticristo* [*The Antichrist*, a.k.a. *The Tempter*, 1974] had been doing better than Spielberg's *Jaws* [1975].

According to some European prints, both your first and second film were co-directed by Antonio Momplet.
I guess it must be a random name thrown in by the Spanish share, seeing they were both Italian-Spanish co-productions but he didn't do anything at all. I have no idea who he is.

How did you choose Richard Harrison for The Invincible Gladiator?
At that time, Richard Harrison was working as a stuntman in the States. The talent agent Filippo Fortini, who had also found Steve Reeves for Pietro Francisci, noticed him. He showed us some pictures: he was handsome, had a great physique, so we decided we'd bring him to Italy for a screen test. The producer, Italo Zingarelli, wanted to audition him with and without a beard.

What do you recall about Two Against All?
I wasn't the first choice, but the director—I don't remember who he was—left the film and the producer, Emo Bistolfi, asked me to replace him. The challenge was to gain Walter Chiari's[7] trust, which was a hard task for a new director. So I came up with a stratagem together with Damiano Damiani, with whom I had already worked as a sound editor on some of his films. In order to win Chiari over, we agreed that while I was talking to him, Damiano would stop by and put in a good word for me. We were outside a café, Chiari and I, and Damiani stops by and goes: "Excellent director, Alberto. You are working with him? Good choice! He is going to go far!" You had to be a bit of a smartass in this business.

You mentioned the producer Italo Zingarelli before. A name of great significance, with whom you created a real partnership.
Yes, I made three or four films with him. Then he made the *Trinity* films, which we didn't do together for a number of reasons. But I was one of the candidates. There were many, but I was high on the list. Then Enzo Barboni came along with the right story and he ended up making the film, but I was working on a script … go figure! … with Renato Izzo and we had even worked out the first act. However, Zingarelli wasn't totally convinced, so… Let me explain better. Italo wanted to make his debut as a director. He had chosen this project, which ended up starring Giovanna Ralli and Giancarlo Giannini, *Una prostituta al servizio del pubblico e in regola con le leggi dello stato* [*Prostitution Italian Style*, 1971]. But he was having difficulties coming up with the amount of money he needed. So he thought that a Western would be a quick and easy way of doing just that. His film ended up being a massive flop and it's funny to think that *Lo chiamavano Trinità*

[*They Call Me Trinity*, a.k.a. *My Name Is Trinity*, 1970] was made to finance a film nobody remembers. In fact, he was never on the set of *Trinity*; the one who worked on the actual making, was his associate's brother. Zingarelli only took care of the screenplay, of choosing the director and the actors, because he was busy on the pre-production of his own film. But he was the one who chose the Terence Hill/Bud Spencer duo, based on the success of Giuseppe Colizzi's films. My stunt coordinator Giorgio Ubaldi, who was great, created all the most popular gags and the action scenes, like the one with the gun and the slap. That was his idea. No one ever mentions him or gives him credit for that.

Since we're talking about important collaborations in your career, what can you tell me about your relationship with Sergio Leone?

Oh, I had a wonderful relationship with Sergio, we were close friends ... really close. I worked on *Giù la testa* [*For a Fistful of Dynamite*, a.k.a. *Duck You Sucker*, 1971]. I directed the long train sequence, towards the end, and the attack of the peons, of the Mexicans. The film has at least ten minutes directed by me. Not consecutively, of course. Anyway, I strictly followed Sergio's instructions. But our relationship was amazing. He was a great man. Every now and then I watch parts of his films on YouTube and they're awesome, even Morricone has never written music as beautifully as he did for Sergio. I was going to be the executive producer for the film he was supposed to make in Russia in the eighties, "L'assedio di Leningrado" ["The Siege of Leningrad"], and for the TV series about the Colt revolver based on Sergio Donati's script, that he was to shoot in the U.S. The whole Russian project was ready; can you imagine, Sergio had managed— just with a brief synopsis—to receive from Gorbačëv the equivalent of twenty billions in tanks and locations. The night before his departure to the States, where he was supposed to sign the contract with the American production company, we talked over the phone, and the next morning he was dead. He had this heart disease and knew he might die any day.

Going back to the sixties, we can say that—with a few exceptions—your three main genres, the ones where you left a significant mark, the ones you devoted yourself the most to, are mythological films, Westerns and spy films. Which of the three are you fonder of?

Look, genre to me is secondary. My approach towards a new film was trying to share with the audience the emotions that I felt, or those that I'd want to feel if I were one of them. I tried to give them what they wanted, but I always started with the plot and the characters. In this sense, I used to pay less attention to genre. As for your question, well, maybe Westerns, but I don't know for sure. I wrote a film called *I sette gladiatori* [*Gladiators 7*, a.k.a. *The Seven Gladiators*, 1962], which eventually was directed by someone else, that was inspired—as the title suggests—by *The Magnificent Seven* [1960]. So I can say I was among the first to try to attempt a crossover between peplum and Western. Someone would have ended up doing it anyway, but I was among the first, maybe even the absolute first, to try and actually do it. I ended up not making the film because there was something going on with the Spanish quota, maybe a debt ... I don't remember, but I'm sure that in the end it was directed by a Spaniard.[8]

Opposite: **Italian poster of *Perseus the Invincible*, 1963.**

How many peplums did you make with Richard Harrison after **The Invincible Gladiator?**

After the first one, I was to make *Perseo l'invincibile* [*Perseus the Invincible*, a.k.a. *Valley of the Stone Men*, a.k.a. *Perseus Against the Monsters*, a.k.a. *Medusa Against the Son of Hercules*, 1963]. That was supposed to be my second film but then, as I've already told you, the director of *Two Against All* had to leave and I replaced him. I didn't do anything else with Harrison in this genre but they are the best peplums I made. Ironically, the last one I directed was a sequel of that Western-peplum crossover I mentioned, *La rivolta dei sette* [*The Spartan Gladiator*, a.k.a. *The Revolt of the Seven*, 1964]. Then the genre came to an end but in the meantime Sergio Leone had launched a new way of conceiving Westerns.

The first Western you made was **Gli eroi di Fort Worth** *[Assault on Fort Texan, a.k.a. Charge of the Seventh Cavalry, a.k.a. Heroes of Fort Worth, 1965].*

That's not a film I'm very fond of. The leading actor was Edmund Purdom. A good guy who was also a good sound man and mixer, a kind of hobby of his, but the film I'm not particularly proud of. Probably the problem was that I was still anchored to an old way of perceiving Westerns, with a style that tried to mimic the classic American style. *100.000 dollari per Ringo* [*$100,000 for Ringo*, 1965] is a whole different story.

What do you recall about that film?

I recall the box office figures! I still get emotional when I think about it. We were sitting on that sofa [from the table he's sitting at, he points to the opposite side of the room, towards a liberty-style sofa with an old-fashioned floral print] when we got a call from the producer's son, Marco, who began reading us the figures. [He stops, his voice charged with emotion.] Unbelievable. My wife answered the phone, listened in silence, hung up and burst into tears and I did the same.

It's probably your most iconic film from that decade.

Look, very few people really got the subtext of that film and its origin. The kid in my film is called Shane. He is the protagonist of *Shane* [1953], the George Stevens classic. What I had in mind was to tell the story of that character's childhood. My film was what allowed him to live the experiences in the film with Alan Ladd. By the way, since we're talking about names, Ringo isn't a reference to Tessari's films starring Giuliano Gemma, but to John Wayne's character in *Stagecoach* [1939]. A few years ago, in Venice, during that event on Italian Westerns,[9] they screened the film and the audience clapped for five minutes straight. Absolutely crazy! People clapping and getting emotional over the final scene. My films are a bit melodramatic, I always want there to be some watery eyes. [He laughs.]

If I'm not mistaken, this film marks the beginning of your long-lasting collaboration with Ennio Morricone.

Yes, with Ennio—and with Bruno Nicolai—I made eight films.

What can you tell me about your three spy movies?

Missione Lady Chaplin [*Special Mission Lady Chaplin*, 1966] and *Upperseven—L'uomo da uccidere* [*The Spy with Ten Faces*, 1966] are the best ones, in my opinion. I made the former with Amati, but the latter has become a cult, especially in Germany.

Ok Connery *[Operation Kid Brother, 1967] is the weirdest one.*

Oh, sure. Let's say that is was a bit of a fraud. We took Sean Connery's brother and

De Martino (looking directly at the camera) with his team on the set of *Operation Kid Brother*, 1967 (courtesy Nocturno Cinema).

surrounded him by all the actors who had starred in James Bond films. There was Anthony Dawson, great professional, Bernard Lee, Lois Maxwell, Adolfo Celi and Daniela Bianchi. Daniela made three or four films with me, she's one of the most beautiful actresses I've ever worked with.

How was Neil Connery?

He wasn't an actor and he didn't look much like his brother either. When I saw him for the first time, a good guy, very nice, I even met him again recently ... but as soon as I saw him I realized we had to transform him a bit. So I gave him to my dad who changed his teeth and widened his eyes with two hidden rubber bands. He actually couldn't work for more than a few hours with that stuff on his face. Since ... how can I put this ... he wasn't as good an actor as his brother, we decided to make him speak as little as possible. That's why in the film he hypnotizes people. This way he had to only stare all the time and that was it.

Let's talk about one of the exceptions to the genres we mentioned earlier. Right after your last Western, **Django spara per primo *[Django Shoots First, 1966]* you made Dalle Ardenne all'inferno *[Dirty Heroes, 1967]*. What do you recall about this war film?**

They had just released a film starring Omar Sharif, I don't remember its title, but it had been really successful; it was about the murder of a prostitute and the investigation that followed. It was set during World War II, but it wasn't strictly a war film.[10] So the idea behind *Dirty Heroes* was that of making a war film without the military aspect, if you know what I mean. Just think that I got the idea when a friend of mine called me on the phone and told me he'd read on *La settimana enigmistica* [a famous magazine of word games and crosswords] about this group of German and American soldiers, deserters, who wanted to rob a bank together. This is where the idea came from. But then Edmondo Amati, the producer, said: "I pre-sold the film all over the world, but they expect it to be a war film. We need at least one battle." So we arranged everything, tanks, paratroopers, and we shot the final scene. It's a good battle, and it goes on for a while. Even in this film there is a little tear-jerking scene. When, at the end, she says: "I never told you, but I'm a Jew." "I know, I've always known, and I've always loved you."

How did Frederick Stafford land the leading role?
   We couldn't find anything better.

Generally, what was the process as far as casting was concerned?
   Each film was different, though normally we would choose the cast through agencies. Then, in the case of huge American stars, I mean really big ones, such as John Cassavetes or Kirk Douglas, things were more complicated. As for Kirk, it was a real adventure. Right after *Holocaust 2000* [a.k.a. *The Chosen*, 1977] was released, a critic wrote, "Douglas must be in need of money." I called him and asked him to take back that sentence, because that is not how things work. This is how it's done: you send the script to the actor's agency in America, and if they like it they ask for a "film off," that is to say the production starting date, the duration of the shooting and so on, but without giving the actor the script. Because if the film is an American production and it doesn't do well, the fault falls upon the production company, but if the film is European, then it's the agency that gets blamed. This being the situation, you had to get the actor you wanted to read the script in alternative ways: through a friend, at a party… At the time, nobody was giving Douglas our script. We managed to get Carol Levi, the Italian representative for William Morris, to call him and say: "You have to read this, and it's under my responsibility." In other words, you needed someone who was willing to take the responsibility on behalf of the actor. He eventually read it, liked it, and did it. Things are always more complicated than one might think.

You mentioned John Cassavetes, with whom you did Roma come Chicago *[Bandits in Rome, a.k.a.* Rome Like Chicago, *1968]. He was known to be a difficult actor to work with. How did your relationship develop?*
   One day John would love everybody and the next day he would hate everybody. I mean, I'm talking really violent mood swings. When Gena Rowlands came to Rome, we hadn't started shooting yet and he introduced me: "Gena, this is Alberto, the most intelligent native I've met in Europe." She leaned forward and whispered in my ear, "Give him time." She was right … by the end of the first week we had fought a thousand times. After we wrapped production he said, "Alberto, it has been nice working with you … these last two days."

Specifically, how did he behave? What did he do to disrupt things?
   He was crazy. I mean, he never interfered with the directing aspect, he was simply crazy and unpredictable. For instance, I was explaining a scene to him when he interrupts me … "I don't do this." "What do you mean 'I don't do this'?" "No, I don't do this." "Fine, we're not shooting today, you can all leave!" When he heard this, he realized he might be losing money and putting the film in danger, so he did the scene and said, "OK. I follow orders." From that day on, though, if you asked him a question or wanted an opin-

ion—"What do you think of…?" or "Would you rather shoot this scene in this way?"—he would say, "I follow orders." A ballbuster. Did you know that when he was working with Giuliano Montaldo[11] he didn't let him shoot a close-up of his death, for the final scene?

Let's back up a second and talk about some of your previous films we left behind. In the sixties, probably your most interesting film, outside of the genres you were most active in, is Horror [The Blancheville Monster, 1963].

I only found out a few years ago that it has become a cult movie. To tell you the truth, I was never fond of it, but recently I got to see it again and actually, it isn't bad. There are some cute things in it.

In scale and budget it's quite small compared to your other films of that period. How much did it cost?

Six million lira. It was a co-production with Spain. In fact, nearly the whole cast is Spanish, though there were some actors I'd already worked with, like Leo Anchoriz, who appeared in some of my mythological films. I would like to add something: the film was made because gothic horror was going well, but if you watch it attentively, it's not like the ones by Margheriti or Bava. It is easily associated with the gothic current because it's in black and white, a choice made not for stylistic purposes but simply to cut costs. I took inspiration much more from Hitchcock than anything else. As I've already said, genre to me is secondary.

Edgar Allan Poe's name dominates many versions of the poster but the film has nothing to do with Poe's work.

A lot of silliness and not my idea. That was all the distributor's doing. At the time, Poe was a box office draw, thanks to the huge success of *The Pit and the Pendulum* [1961] by Roger Corman. The title, on the other hand, is Zingarelli's creation. He always wanted to be the one choosing the titles.

What can you tell me about Femmine insaziabili *[Carnal Circuit, 1969]?*

That film was very complicated. The project started off with the title "L'uomo Palmolive" ["The Palmolive Man"], from a script written by Ennio De Concini and myself. It was a good idea, and it would have given me the possibility of doing something different, but then Goffredo Lombardo—the producer—twisted the whole thing.

This is the only film you've made which one might consider erotic. How was your approach to the more risqué scenes?

I wasn't comfortable directing those moments, plus my concept of eroticism is based more on atmosphere and context than nudity. On that film I had trouble with Romina Power. Her mother wanted to destroy me. [He giggles.] During an underwater scene the camera operator unexpectedly and without her knowing, pulled down the bottom part of her swimsuit. For a moment you can see her bum. Afterwards, Romina's mother went to Lombardo shouting and complaining about me. She would've cut my head off.

What was the film originally about?

It was supposed to be about a man who gets chosen as the new face for Palmolive,[12] signs a contract, goes to the U.S., becomes famous and ends up destroying everything. Money, women, and fame get to his head. It was going to be, forgive the term, more of an auteur film.

In 1973, with Ci risiamo, vero Provvidenza? *[Here We Go Again, Eh Providence?], you say goodbye to Westerns. What's the story behind this film and how was your relationship with Tomas Milian, with whom you had already worked on* Il consigliori *[The Counsellor, a.k.a.* Counsellor at Crime, *1972]?*

My relationship with Tomas was really good, we were very fond of each other. Before *The Counsellor* we didn't know each other at all. We'd never even met. Then, working on that film, we built a good relationship based on a strong mutual respect. We never had any problems on either of the two films we made together.

Many of the directors who have worked with him describe him as an insecure, egocentric person.

In a way, they're right. You know what? John Cassavetes was one of those actors who always needed to be high, totally pumped, in order to work, maybe because he was afraid that otherwise he might have … disappeared. Tomas was a real natural, a true cinema actor. He never missed a beat. Sure, he was insecure, but all actors are. Though he had an obsession with disguising himself. He always insisted on wearing make-up, wigs … I got a feeling that on some level he wanted to hide away. I mean, just look at him as Providence! But not like Connery's brother that looked like a Dutch cyclist. [He laughs.] Anyway, we made *The Counsellor*, that did really well, and then *Providence*. He was the one who called me to make that film, I don't know if I was the first choice, but Milian recommended me to the producers. The first film had been quite successful [*La vita a volte è molto dura, vero Provvidenza?* a.k.a. *Life Is Tough, Eh Providence?* by Giulio Petroni, 1972], and mine didn't do badly either. It had some positive reviews as well. I had a little adventure with Gianluigi Rondi[13] around that film. [He smiles behind his hand.] He wrote a review saying wonders of the film. So I told my press agent: "Call him and thank him." Rondi replied, inviting me to take part in a radio program he hosted. "Great!" I thought. "Finally a critic who speaks highly of me." I go on air: "De Martino, this is your first film…!" "But I've already made twenty…." "Doesn't matter! This is the first one!" "Okay, whatever." He interviewed me and we said goodbye. My next film was *L'anticristo* [*The Antichrist*, a.k.a. *The Tempter*, 1974]. I told my press agent again: "Tell Rondi we made this film and we want to arrange a private screening for him." He left during the third reel and wrote the worst review ever. He didn't even criticize the direction, but the contents themselves: the Devil, God, the Pope … and since, he has been hell-bent in ruining me. Seriously.

De Martino (right) going over a scene with the two leads of *Here We Go Again, Eh Providence?* (1973): Gregg Palmer and Tomas Milian (courtesy Nocturno Cinema).

In that period your director of photography was Aristide Massaccesi, who would later become famous as Joe D'Amato.

Exactly! Our first film together was *I familiari delle vittime non saranno avvertiti* [*Crime Boss*, 1972]. He was great. With three lightbulbs he could create wonders. He was excellent with hand-held cameras. He could do it all. But I've always had amazing operators. The one before Aristide … huh … I don't remember his name…. This must be some form of pre–Alzheimer kicking in … whatever … he would do beautiful things as well. You know how you work hand-held cameras going backwards? Synchronizing the steps. It's an easy trick, but not many know how to do it.

Talking of directors of photography, you also worked with the great Gabor Pagony on L'uomo dagli occhi di ghiaccio *[*The Man with Icy Eyes*, 1971].*

Yes, that film we shot in Albuquerque, working with a reduced crew. Fourteen people in total, we didn't even have a camera dolly. One of his electricians would climb up the street lights to get power. A screwdriver and bam! we were ready to shoot.

While we're talking about your major collaborations, let's go back to your relationship with Ennio Morricone. How did things work between you?

He would watch the film and immediately understand what he had to do. He watched and started composing, sometimes on the spot. But after making a few films together, I arranged a tiny orchestra for rehearsing. I remember once that a piece of music he had given me wasn't suitable. How do you complain to Ennio Morricone? The guy, who in my book, is the best living composer! So I had my own small orchestra we could experiment with. I have a fond memory of the first film we made together, *$100,000 for Ringo*. I went to his house, or it might have been Bruno Nicolai's place … anyway they had to play something for me on the piano. Morricone: "You do it." Nicolai: "No. You go." So I sat down and started playing! [He laughs gleefully.] They didn't see that coming!

Since you're also a pianist, a musician, have you ever wanted to write some music for your films?

Only once. *Ringo* has a slow ballad written by me, but I didn't even want to play it. Preziosi played it. Do you know who he is? The one who killed his wife…

We mentioned many actors, Milian, Stafford, Connery, but what about…

Rossella Falk! You were about to ask who my favorite actress was, right? Rossella Falk with whom I worked on *L'assassino è al telefono* [*Scenes from a Murder*, a.k.a. *The Killer Is on the Phone*, 1972]. She was really good, and stylish, too. She would always put very expensive dresses on the production's tab. Besides our great stars, let's say that amongst the least famous ones, she was the best. Always perfect on stage.

Back to your films, what can you tell me about **The Counsellor?**

I've already told this anecdote more than once, but it's always worth repeating. I gave the script to Amati, the producer, he liked it, but he wanted it to be revised by an American, a contact of his. Michael Gazzo, the one who wrote the play *A Hatful of Rain*. "Great!" I thought. Gazzo was also a member of the Actors Studio. I got the script back. Scene one: Martin Balsam's character talks to a coat stand. Oh well, I must have read it wrong…. So I got the script translated and we found out that he had entirely rewritten it, making a terrible mess. We chased him out, but Amati had already paid him.

You once said that you weren't happy with Dagmar Lassander either.
Eeeh. [He takes a deep breath.] When we chose her and she signed the contract she had just given birth. "Dagmar, you need to lose at least six pounds over the next month." "No problem, Alberto." When I saw her again, she hadn't lost a single ounce. Had we been in Rome, I would have immediately sent her away, but being in America, that would have meant interrupting production for too much time.

How long did it normally take to shoot your films?
It depended on the film. Five, six weeks, even nine sometimes.

The film you made that took the smallest amount of time?
Probably *Il trionfo di Ercole* [*The Triumph of Hercules*, a.k.a. *Hercules vs. the Giant Warriors*, 1964]. Have I told you about the little monkey with the dagger?

No.
So ... there was this little monkey that was supposed to pull out this magic dagger that made incredible things happen, like the appearance of the Seven Golden Men who would beat everybody up. And as soon as it put the dagger back in its place, they would disappear. Making the monkey pull it out was easy, we had tied one of its paws with a nylon string and we would pull it at the right moment. But making it put it down was a whole different story, so I came up with a simple solution: reversing the footage. I'm very proud of this idea.

Let's go back to the seventies.** Una Magnum special per Tony Saitta [Blazing Magnum, a.k.a. Strange Shadows in a Dark Room, 1976] **made during that decade is very popular among your aficionados.
I got a chance to see it again recently, and I didn't mind it at all. I shot it in Montreal, Canada, which is the reason why Stuart Whitman accepted to make the film. He needed to get away from Hollywood because some husband was tracking him down to kill him. [He laughs.] A great womanizer ... and he drank a lot, as many of these actors did.

The film has long action sequences and a very long car chase. Did you use storyboards?
No, because I can't draw and I hate those who can. It's stronger than me, I'm a pianist. Plus, I direct like I play jazz. I begin from the background and improvise from there, just like a jazz player.

It's probably your most violent film. What's your relationship with violence in cinema?
My theory has always been that the less you see, the more you imagine. And this is very much a pillar of my visual style. I like audiences to imagine the violence, this is why I can't make these films with worms coming out of heads and animals ripping people apart. It just isn't in me. Actually this is the only rule I have maintained throughout my career: less is more.

But you are more comfortable with violence than you are with eroticism.
Yes, absolutely. For example, something I didn't mention when we were talking about *Carnal Circuit* is that a short while after I'd made it, the phenomenon of sex farces and erotic comedies exploded. All of a sudden you could show a lot more as far as nudity and sex were concerned. The producer asked me to shoot some extra scenes, nudity and hotter situations, for the Japanese market. I did it, mind you, but unwillingly. It's just not my sort of thing. It's stuff I like doing as a protagonist rather than watch as a spectator

or director! Actually ... once upon a time ... now they're only memories.

It's time to talk about what is probably your most famous film: **The Antichrist.** *Had you already seen* **The Exorcist** *[1973]?*

Yes, I had seen it in New York. Edmondo Amati called me and told me the film was making a lot of money. "Let's go see why. Bring a screenwriter." I brought with me Vincenzo Mannino, with whom—among other things—I had gone to high school. We realized the devil was back in fashion. I wasn't interested in making a film entirely based on religious elements, though. In fact, in my film the possession originates from a deep sexual frustration. But she isn't really possessed! I mean, the same things happened, but in my film it was all in the head. I've always sustained something that I try to fit in all the interviews I give, and that I'll repeat again now, before Alzheimer kicks in: I believe all phenomena, even the ones involving extra-terrestrial sightings, the devil, God ... are manifestations of the unexplored regions of our brain and one day science will understand why we see and believe we see certain things. Why we invent God. I don't know if I've made myself understood.

Perfectly clear. But what can you tell me about after it was released? Were there any legal actions or accusations of plagiarism?

Yes, there was a lawsuit. They argued I could not have the

American publicity material for one of De Martino's most popular films: *The Antichrist*, 1974.

exorcism sequence, but the judge ruled on my side. Monsignor Balducci made a technical appraisal where he illustrated exactly how you make an exorcism, and he said that not only a director has the right to show and describe it, but also that what I had shown was correct under the official criteria and rules. *The Exorcist* is, may I add, a bedroom and a kitchen, a film of make-up and tricks. *The Antichrist* has a broader vision, there's the Vatican, churches, masses, cardinals … there's a lot more in it, no? It's more like cinema should be!

How did you get along with Carla Gravina and Arthur Kennedy?

Gravina was wonderful, and steals the show from everybody. She had difficulties with English, so I decided to make her speak only in the first two scenes I shot, so the foreign distributors would be convinced when watching the first ten minutes we screened for them. The Americans are oversensitive about proper sync. Kennedy was a very good actor, and did everything he was told. In one scene, he was supposed to violently fall to the ground. I asked if he wanted a double. He answered: "Don't worry, I've been falling all my life." A true professional.

Mel Ferrer?

Sometimes he would act a little strange and be kind of inappropriate. One day we were late with our schedule because of a malfunction with a special effect; he came up to me and shaking his head theatrically said: "What a shame! What a shame!" He was taking the piss.

How was your relationship with Kirk Douglas during the making of Holocaust 2000?

I first met Kirk when he called me and Sergio Donati after reading the script. There were a few things he didn't like about it, some dialogues. We went to his house. He somehow managed to improve the lines by simply removing a couple of words. He would go, "Stronger. Simpler. Shorter. Stronger." [He laughs.] He was right about everything. So much so, that when we got up and left, I told Donati: "Whatever he says next, even if he's right, let's say we disagree. I mean, we can't go 'yes, yes' to everything he says. We look like shmucks." I never had problems with Kirk, we got along perfectly well and I'm glad we worked together. He thought pretty highly of me. He would always tell Amati, the producer: "You have a good director!" Or while I was explaining a scene to an actor, he would come near and say: "He's right." [He laughs.] He would complain a bit, from time to time, but he trusted me.

What do you recall about Agostina Belli?

Remember that scene in *Bandits in Rome*, the one of the robbery in Piazza Navona? She's the girl screaming from the window! She started off as Carlo Lizzani's protégée … and lover. During the making of *Holocaust 2000*, there were some minor problems between her and Kirk. He wanted the whole film to be shot in English, rightly so, also because he had a percentage on international sales. But sometimes she wouldn't study, and that would create some friction. Anyway, nothing serious. All in all, a good girl.

L'uomo puma [The Puma Man, 1980] marks the beginning of a new phase in your career, and of a new decade too.

Puma Man kind of destroyed me. I remember nobody went to the cinema to see it. The modern era of television had begun. Previously on RAI they used to show one film a day but, by the late seventies, people could watch a huge number of films sitting comfortably in front of their TV sets. With the flop of *Puma Man*, I couldn't help but ask myself some questions. I reached the conclusion that I had lost the pulse of my public. But then ... it did well abroad and it managed to reach the minimum guaranteed, otherwise I would have ended up having to sell my house. In Italy it didn't even reach half a billion lira, but abroad the minimum guaranteed was a clean billion. People are still talking about this film, it's become sort of a cult film. In America they looked for the protagonist all over the place. He wasn't a real actor, I don't think he did anything after my film.

From **Puma Man** *onwards you sign your films as Martin Herbert. Why?*
Well these were films, the ones I did in the eighties ... they were completely conceived for the foreign markets so having an American sounding name helped, but to be honest, I didn't feel those films are mine. They were not films I would have chosen and they don't satisfy me. You are the first person I say this to ... maybe I was happy in a way, that I had a chance to hide behind a pseudonym because I felt a little ashamed. There, I said it!

What do you recall about Michael Moriarty, the leading actor in **Extrasensorial** *[*Blood Link, *a.k.a.* The Link, *1982]?*
A ballbuster. At first he was all nice and happy, but then, right before the beginning of production, he changed. He was another one who took a lot of drugs. He wanted to change the script, he made unreasonable requests. I don't even know how we managed to finish the film. He created a lot of problems on the set. Not a particularly brilliant cast ... even Penelope Milford was a small actress, nothing special.

*7, Hyden Park—*La casa maledetta *[*Formula for a Murder, *1985]?*
I don't remember much about that film. I remember directing Rossano Brazzi. I believe that was his last film. I don't have a terrible recollection of that film, however. It was nothing like the hell of *Miami Golem* [*Miami Horror,* a.k.a. *Cosmos Killer,* 1986]. I shouldn't have put my name on that film. I left before completion. What you see in the film is shot by me, but nothing of the editing process and post-production is mine. As for all my films, I had a contract in which it was specifically said that I had final word and had to approve all the technicians. The producer didn't want to give me my editor, probably to save money, and I left without hesitation. I didn't even get paid for the last couple of weeks. I have never seen it and I don't even want to see it. I couldn't care less ... yeah, I should never have put my name on that.

For some time now there has been word about a project called "The Book—The Italian Masters Return" involving a number of genre directors, among which is yourself.
Yes, I wrote this little script called "Efebus." It was supposed to last twenty minutes. A curious little story, quite amusing. My episode begins when a medium touches a cursed mask from Brazil. There is a cross-dresser who wants to take revenge upon those who killed his girlfriend, who died in a car accident. Who was driving and run her down, though, is innocent. Crazy stuff happens. He takes his vengeance using this mask. The villain is a transvestite, I think it's the first time that ... ah, no, wait a second ... there are transvestites also in *Blazing Magnum*. I wonder what that means. My son asked me: "Why an evil transvestite?" Why not? That's where the title comes from, "Efebus," because at the beginning we think that the mask is of Efebo, protector of love and youth, and instead it's Ermafroditus! There's also an exorcism in it.

Isn't Dardano Sacchetti the screenwriter of these episodes?

Who? No, I don't even know who this Dardano Sacchetti is. Ah, yes, maybe once I might have met him. Is he the guy who wrote the film about the evil midget produced by Fabrizio De Angelis?

Quella villa in fondo al parco [The Rat Man, 1986] by Giuliano Carnimeo.

Yes, he wrote that, right? The one about the midget. OK, then I did meet him. At that time I was supervising projects on behalf of Fabrizio De Angelis' production company, in the mid-eighties. I often ended up changing scripts and helping put together projects. This also happened in post-production, and I sometimes changed stories completely. I crossed paths with this film about an evil midget and said: "Everybody stop!" I mean, there was a mistake there, not so much in the script but in the story's premise. So I got this Sacchetti fellow to come and see me, and I explained to him a few things. I'll use an example to simplify.... If you see a shark fin in the water, you are afraid because you know there's a shark underneath that fin. The problem here, was that there was only a fin. And why should this dirty midget be scary? I mean, you see him coming and you just squish him. So I came up with the idea that he was infected, or that he could infect people, or something along these lines. In fact, that was the only thing that critics seemed to save from the film. [He laughs.] They asked me to direct the sequel, but I said no and I don't believe they made it in the end. Anyway, De Angelis was a good friend and I helped him as much as I could.

How do you feel about the possibility of going back on a set after so many years?

I don't know, it's not that I feel ecstatic by the idea. You know what it is, it's that I'm out of touch. I don't know what people like, what people watch, what they go and see. I mean, once I had the public's pulse in my hands. Plus, when I was directing films, I was always on my feet. I moved continuously, giving indications to the actors. Now I see directors always in front of a monitor ... I don't know ... we'll see. My son is worried that I might have a heart attack on set. My answer is, could there be a better death?

Rome, 2013

1961 The Bitter and the Sweet
The Cinema of Romolo Guerrieri

"If all honest people had a little courage, things would change."—Enrico Maria Salerno in *The Police Serve the Citizens?*, 1973

Introduction by Gian Giacomo Petrone

Romolo Girolami (born 5 December 1931, Rome) is an important member of a small family dynasty, which has left a deep and lasting mark in the history of popular Italian cinema: brother of director and *pater familias* Marino Girolami (1 February 1914, Rome–20 February 1994, Rome), uncle of Enzo Girolami (Enzo G. Castellari), possibly the most well known member of the clan, and actor Enio Girolami (14 January 1935, Rome–16 February 2013, Rome), both sons of Marino. Too many Girolamis around, between the sets of Cinecittà: changing one's surname became a necessity. Romolo will adopt (as will, in turn, his nephew Enzo), his mother's maiden name, rather than choosing a pseudonym: a sign of continuity and proximity to his roots, that will also mark—perhaps by chance, perhaps by fate—a clear break from his older brother and, most of all, from his nephew Enzo in his approach to cinema. Apart from thematic divergences, both moral and political, that separate the films of Guerrieri and Castellari, what should be highlighted are the differences in style: in the former we see the development of a violence the director builds from a neutral point of observation, close but detached; whereas in the latter, the violence is insistent, physical, paroxysmal, sometimes rather solemn and hieratic like an archaic ritual, and the eye of the director participates in the action from the inside: the filming, often baroque and hyperbolic, is not descriptive, but "acts" alongside the characters.

A seagull, waves, a beach, two men lying on the sand, one visibly relaxed, one dead; it is only from their clothing that one can vaguely sense the Western context; the dead man's eyes are wide open and turned towards the blue sky, while the live one speaks, contemplating the vastness of the sea: "Oh the sea, my friend, what a wonderful thing.... But you don't care, do you? You're only interested in the sky." Right from the beginning, *10.000 dollari per un massacro* (*10,000 Dollars for a Massacre*, a.k.a. *Guns of Violence*, a.k.a. *$10,000 Blood Money*, 1967), the third and last of Guerrieri's Westerns, shows a certain sharp ironic detachment in his approach, one that is scarcely present in contemporary products—generally less subtle—and infused with a dreamer's melancholy. It is not easy to run into cinematic gunslingers who lingeringly scrutinize the horizon, because who-

Romolo Guerrieri and Ewa Aulin: director and star of *La controfigura* (*The Double*), made in 1971 (courtesy Nocturno Cinema).

ever carries a weapon, in the Western universe, is a man of action and few words, an observer only when it comes to investigating the environs, looking for threats or identifying favorable opportunities, certainly not a man given to the bucolic pleasure of contemplation. Later in the film, the gunslinger-dreamer (Gianni Garko, in the guise of one of the many Djangos brought to the screen following the success of Sergio Corbucci's 1966 classic) will find himself crying—another element of decisive withdrawal from the cliché of the cynical hero—before the corpse of the beloved Mijanou (Loredana Nusciak), killed by the bandit Manuel Vasquez (Claudio Camaso).[1] In this conclusive experience with Westerns, Guerrieri, while adhering to many of the narrative and stylistic trademarks of the genre, as he had also done with his two previous efforts, manages to impose at times a personal style that already shows a strong expressive personality, often alien to the approach of the majority of his colleagues; a personality that will emphasize, especially in future films, a look often different in nature compared to the established canons of Italian productions, while hardly ever overstepping the boundaries of Italian genre cinema. In his Western phase, Guerrieri still expresses an attitude altogether gregarious in respect to the general trends but displays, notwithstanding, a solid level of craftsmanship and professionalism—due to the many years spent cutting his teeth as an assistant director on dozens of films—hence providing the means for handling stories with insight and expertise, but allowing himself some interesting stylistic digressions that manage to innervate imperceptible under-the-skin feelings, tracing the basis that will later become an uncommon directorial style.

It is from 1969 onwards that Guerrieri really manages to release himself in a more accentuated way from the dictates of the predictable realms of popular Italian cinema, managing, nonetheless, to continue working within it as a sort of foreign body, neither completely organic to it nor becoming refractory to compromise, even if unwilling to be placed behind a camera just for the sake of working. Evidence of this selective attitude is also represented by the limited number of titles that make up his filmography as a director. It has been said that 1969 is the crucial year in which Guerrieri reaches a more personal creativity, leading him to bring to fruition the most important titles of his career. However, an important junction has been left behind: the year before, in fact, Guerrieri directs a germinal film for Italian genre cinema: *Il dolce corpo di Deborah* (*The Sweet Body of Deborah*, a.k.a. *The Body*, a.k.a. *Married to Kill*, 1968), which will open the way for the "pre–Argento giallo" that will become highly popular in the last two years of the sixties, and that will find in Umberto Lenzi its biggest and most important exponent. This work by Guerrieri, besides the obvious debt to the French scene (especially *Les Diaboliques*, 1955, by Clouzot), has some merit: it officially begins Carroll Baker's long stint in popular Italian cinema and most of all, it contains one of the great narrative templates that encompasses almost all the possible solutions and narrative outlets that will then be squeezed to the bone in subsequent giallo films.

Un detective (*Ring of Death*, a.k.a. *Detective Belli*, 1969) moves its axis around a normal man who finds himself at the center of an intrigue bigger than himself, a chief of police who, acting alone, turns into an ordinary private detective. If the characters of the previous film are all classically evil figures, perverse, as well as having joint criminal minds in a game of chess and mirrors, in the turbid unraveling of a tangled skein like a spider's web though marked by an internal geometry, those of *Ring of Death* seem puppets in the hands of a master—the director himself, in this case—who moves them around at will for his personal entertainment. A game that does not spare anybody or take any prisoners, that deftly moves on the side of social criticism, showing a degradation that not only touches the upper echelons of society, the institutions, but also the criminal underworld, in which big and small fish swim and feed, but are never totally satisfied, in this large, muggy swamp. Guerrieri manages to build an elliptical, spiraling tale of Chandlerian derivation. Chief of police Belli (Franco Nero) is already showing traits that will characterize other protagonists of Guerrieri's film world: more observers than men of action. In a conception that visibly draws from Michelangelo Antonioni's *Blow-Up* (1966), in which looking does not mean understanding, the use of cognitive abilities does not clarify the roughness of reality, because the latter is marked by its own unreadable opacity and strength. Proof of this is the way Guerrieri outlines the places, often dispossessed of their topographical dimension, to become mental spaces where time is suspended and where actions and situations are landlocked and repeated circularly. The danger for the protagonist is not only represented by the antagonist (Florinda Bolkan) but by the elusiveness of truth that will lead inevitably to a tragic and mocking finale, more bitter than epic, in which we find the spirit of certain films by Jean-Pierre Melville. Though, it is with police thrillers—and his own personal reinterpretation—that Guerrieri manages to reach the pinnacle of his poetic, turning out a bunch of solid and evocative films. Three titles, produced between 1973 and 1976, with only one worthy though decidedly less personal, exception, *Salvo D'Acquisto* (1974).

La polizia è al servizio del cittadino? (*The Police Serve the Citizens?*, 1973) is the first of the duo, and right from its title we perceive a detachment from the coordinates of the genre, managing to overturn a slogan with a question mark and with it, reversing an ideology that permeates many contemporary films attributable to the same genre. The element that distinguishes this film from many other similar products is to be found in the different relationships between the police force, the law and society. If in many of the police thrillers of the seventies the gap between the police and the social structure is identified in the legal weakness of the legislation, which prevents effective action of deterrence and repression of crime, in *The Police Serve the Citizens?* the problem is no longer legal but social and existential. Guerrieri tells us that it is not so much the law that "protects" criminals but rather the social structure as a whole and the acceptance of a servile status quo on the part of the lower classes; the few who try to be authentic citizens, not subjects or serfs, will be crushed. On the basis of these considerations, the protagonist chief of police Sironi (Enrico Maria Salerno, fresh from the success of *La polizia ringrazia* [*Execution Squad*] by Stefano Vanzina, released the previous year) will not be moved by ideological instances or the myth of a new order to be established by force, he will not become an executioner, but simply a man who, defeated in his private life, looks for personal and existential redemption in chasing criminals. Even in the case of Sironi, and previously of Belli in *Ring of Death*, we are faced with an observer who wants to see clearly by first dominating the environment in which he finds himself; his ultimate goal, though, is not so much finding some sort of truth but more importantly, understanding. When the circumstances dictate that he must come to blows, he will do so but, mind you, only to keep faith to his personal ethics and not to realize an ideology mistaken for morality, even though he is a deeply moral character. However, also in this case the action will not actually manifest itself since there will not be any physical contact with his opponent, the corrupt engineer Breda (Daniel Gélin). Sironi imprisons him with no chance of escape inside his car which he then parks on a railroad track, after which he places himself a short distance away, silently observing, with cynical detachment, the violent demise of the criminal. Guerrieri, with this effort, continued his act of deconstruction from within the genres of popular Italian cinema by inverting, in the case of police thrillers, the structural assumption that underlies it. In the general coordinates of the lodging, it is the action that determines the personality of the central characters; in the case of Guerrieri, on the contrary, it is the multi-faceted and contradictory dimensions of the characters that guide their behavior, which is often clumsy and realistically inadequate, as is the norm in everyday life.

If Guerrieri's previous films concentrate on the sins of the fathers *Liberi, armati, pericolosi* (*Young, Violent, Dangerous*, a.k.a. *Young, Violent and Desperate*, 1976) looks beyond and focuses on their symbolic heirs. Story and screenplay are by Fernando Di Leo, who is the ideal cantor of the bleakness of "Milano nera." The story develops from the pages of writer Giorgio Scerbanenco from which, specifically for this film, Di Leo selects the story "Bravi ragazzi bang bang" (translation: "Good Kids Bang Bang"), but it is used only as a starting point for a new vision that is completely and fully attributable to Di Leo and Guerrieri. After the metropolitan opening, which introduces the three protagonists—Luigi Morandi, known as "Luis" (Max Delys); Mario Farra, known as "The Blond" (Stefano Patrizi); and Giovanni Etruschi, called "Gio" (Benjamin Lev), in other words the three "good kids"—the middle section and ending of the film develop as a road movie, with the three youngsters chased and hunted by the police. This film is presented as one of the best constructed, from the point of view of the narrative progression, among those of the Roman director.[2] Three young men of the "Milanese bourgeoisie" seem, at first, to be only looking for crazy but harmless fun, in order to kill the boredom of wealth and well-being; then comes the robbery and the serial murders, as in a furious "shoot 'em all" avant la lettre; the meeting with another gang of bored, rich youths armed to the teeth, an assault in a supermarket, the extermination of a rival/ally band, the escape. In a matter of minutes, Guerrieri and Di Leo perfectly depict the transition from city to countryside, symbolically implying the movement of the protagonists from the civilized dimension—though still aberrant, passive, dull—to the feral, primal jungle. Despite acting as a small tribe, the members of this improvised gang are anything but united. Gio is a sort of jester, who mocks the events with continuous quips, which largely deform well-known Italian or American police thrillers and that seem to entertain only him. The link between Luis and "The Blond" is complex and layered, made of mutual dependence—Luis is mesmerized by Mario's charisma, although his love is all for the seductive Lea (Eleonora Giorgi), while Mario, despite his position as a leader, seems preoccupied only by gaining Luis's attention, to whom he is morbidly attracted—using blackmail to retain his friendship, the only value that seems to harbor in his arid and icy mind. If the three are thoroughly wicked, the commissioner on the other hand, interpreted with intensity by Tomas Milian, appears to be fragile, unable to grasp the complexity of the situation. Milian is probably a figure entirely or in large part created by Guerrieri, given that he has the same hypo-perceptual and hypo-cognitive traits of the director's previous members of law enforcement; even though endowed with sensitivity and intelligence, he is never able to anticipate or prevent the moves of this small but ferocious "wild bunch." His moral monologue to the powerful parents of the three criminals, while motivated by good reasons and a strong case, sounds like the howling of a dog at the moon: once again the man of action is inexistent, because in his place there is a man simply articulated by psychology, by problematics, and for that reason not equipped to react when faced with the actions of others, especially if triggered by purely primal instincts of destruction and oppression. The tragic ending shows the silent commissioner observing from afar and in this sequence you can read the epitaph of Romolo Guerrieri: man can only observe from a distance the flow of events, with no power of intervention, without any ability to stop the inexorable march of destiny, without any ability to react.

Your real name is Girolami. Why did you choose Guerrieri?
   My father's name is Girolami, which is also my surname of course, but I chose to use my mother's maiden name, Guerrieri. The reason is my brother. By the time I made my first film as a director, my brother Marino[3] had already been working for some time. Between Marino and myself there was a huge age gap, nearly twenty years. Actually my first film was a Western and like all the directors who did Westerns I was asked to use an alias. I chose Rod Gilbert. For my second film the producer said I could use my own name but suggested I found an alternative. Romolo Guerrieri sounded good.

You anticipated my next question which is on your family. You are part of cinematic dynasty…
   There are the three directors: Marino Girolami, my brother, his son Enzo G. Castellari and myself. Then there's Enio Girolami, Marino's first son and Enzo's brother and finally the newest generation, Enzo's children: Stefania and Andrea.

Let's talk a little about your brother.
   Everything started for Marino when he wrote the script for *Campo de' fiori* [*The Peddler and the Lady*, 1943] with Aldo Fabrizi and Anna Magnani. But he came from the

world of sport, he was a boxer. I never saw him fight on the ring because I was too young, as I said there were eighteen years between us. He would also work as a masseuse and gave Magnani therapeutic rubdowns as he would, I believe, also to the son she had with Massimo Serrato, who suffered from polio. I hope I'm getting all this right because if not I will be receiving a telephone call from Enzo scolding me. Anyway, it was through her that he got a chance to start working in films. Then he became Mario Soldati's assistant and not only his. Marino knew three languages—Italian, French and Spanish—so he was able to work on many co-productions.

When did you start working on one of your brother's sets?

In 1952. The film was *Noi due soli* [*We Two Alone*] with Walter Chiari and Hélène Remy. The story is set in a dream-like, post-apocalyptic Rome and we shot it in August when, in those days, the capital would empty itself completely. Now it wouldn't be possible. I was a volunteer assistant on that film. I did five films without seeing a dime before finally getting paid. Something even more impossible for today's standards. Then I let go of my brother. I learned the most when I worked as a 1st AD. I would absorb everything I could from the directors I worked for. I learned a lot also from my brother Marino and he will forgive me, wherever he is, but with him I learned what NOT to do. Every time he did things I didn't like or thought weren't professional, I would take notice and later on made sure not to repeat those mistakes: the out-of-place camaraderie on set, the superficiality he would show when talking to actors, the rudeness. Technically he was fantastic, he could pull off things I would never have managed to do, like shooting two or three films at the same time.

You are very prolific as a 1st AD between 1958 and 1962 and you work with some very interesting directors. Mario Bonnard for example…

With him I did *Afrodite, dea dell'amore* [*Slave Women of Corinth*, a.k.a. *Aphrodite, Goddess of Love*, 1958]. There were two assistants on that film. I was one and Alberto De Martino was the other. I remember Bonnard took a subtle pleasure in seeing me struggle. On one occasion he asked me to find a specific sword he wanted. Believe me when I tell you that I didn't sleep for days trying to look for this sword in antique shops and secondhand dealers. Only later did I discover that he had given the same assignment to De Martino, and needless to say, that sword wasn't needed. Bonnard was an old baron of cinema, who came from the silent era. Once we were shooting and all of sudden he went, "Stop!" and started shouting at the actress. I don't remember if it was Isabelle Corey or someone else: "What are you doing?! You walk like a duck!" She started crying and I thought to myself, "how can you destroy and mortify an actress like that?" I'm ashamed to say that I did something similar on one of my films. A film I don't like talking about. I reacted in the same way and I'm still very sorry for having done so.

Do you remember anything about Carlo Campogalliani, another big director of the silent era?

Ah Carlo! He was another character that was larger than life. On one of the films I did with him, *Rosmunda e Alboino* [*Sword of the Conqueror*, 1961] I had a surreal time because halfway through production Campogalliani and Jack Palance, who was the lead, stopped talking. They would pretend not to hear each other so I had to repeat everything they said. Though, these American actors, even in difficult situations, always ended up doing everything they were supposed to and did it well. On one film I did for television, one of the last, *Due vite, un destino* [*The Final Contract*, 1992] the protagonist was Michael Nouri. We were shooting a night scene, an important one, in which Nouri had to drive around. The camera car was ready, the camera was placed but we had to put a small generator in the back seat for the lights, right next his head. He said: "But how can I act like this, with this noise in my ears." I told him, "We're going to dub everything anyway." A terrible thing to tell an actor. So, these Americans who came here had to get used to a very different way of working. It can't have been easy for some of them.

As far as I know, you never had big problems with actors.
 With one ... David Janssen on *Sono stato un agente C.I.A.* [*Covert Action*, 1978]. He drank a lot, more than you can ever imagine, and in fact he died a few years later of cirrhosis of the liver. A lot of American actors were heavy drinkers. Arthur Kennedy, who liked to drink as well, once told me that the biggest drinker he had ever met was Errol Flynn. He would drink vodka as if it were water. Anyway with Janssen I had to really struggle. When I got fed up, he would come up to me like a child and apologize. Literally like a child would ... his head dangling and without managing to look me in the eye.

Going back to your years as a 1st AD, you worked on Goliath contro i giganti [Goliath Against the Giants, a.k.a. Goliath and the Giants, 1961].
 Actually I didn't work on that. I know it's in some filmographies of mine, especially on the web, but I didn't do that film.

Though you did work with Sergio Corbucci, an important and much-loved director. Give me your personal portrait of Corbucci. Who was he according to Romolo Guerrieri?
 Well, you must know that Sergio loved what he called "the French schedule." In other words he liked working from two o'clock in the afternoon onwards. In the morning he didn't exist, you couldn't even speak to him. We were shooting in Spain and we were waiting for him to arrive on set. I had the production manager following me around everywhere. "Romulus, ¿qué ocurre? Pero ¿dónde está el director? Tenemos que empezar a trabajar." "He's coming, he's coming! We sent a car to pick him up." There was a tense atmosphere ... when all of sudden we see in the distance his car coming towards us and as soon as he gets out with a big smile on his face, all that tension just evaporated. The head grip goes: "Where shall we put the camera?" "Prepare everything for a dolly shot." "How long?" He thinks for a few seconds. "Uhm ... eight meters. From here..." he starts walking as he counts his steps, "...to here!" All the grips start working and Sergio calls me to his side: "I needed to rest a little longer." "Don't worry Sergio, go and sit down. It will be at least another twenty minutes before we are ready to shoot." "I know," he answers, "but what the hell are we going to do with this dolly shot?"

What was the film?
 Minnesota Clay [1964] with Cameron Mitchell. Sergio was incredibly funny, a pleasure to have around and very, very well prepared. Technically he was phenomenal. He could overcome any problem and he knew how to treat the actors.

Which is your proudest moment in those years as an AD?
 The film I gave my biggest contribution to is *Italiani brava gente* [a.k.a. *Attack and Retreat*, 1964] by Giuseppe De Santis.[4] In fact, on that film I appear on the credits as an

"associate director." I directed a lot of the battle sequences, from the moment in which De Santis had to leave Moscow to go back to Rome to rewrite and add some scenes with Ennio De Concini. Do you know this story? Well, *Italiani brava gente* was a co-production between Italy, Russia and the U.S. The Russian quota put locations, a massive amount of extras, tanks and the American side provided some of the leading actors like Arthur Kennedy and Peter Falk. Both of them were chosen through the William Morris Agency. Kennedy was a veteran but Falk was not a big star yet and at the time was more of a character actor specialized in petty Italian-American gangsters. We were shooting an important scene in Ukraine when the Russian PR, Anya Popova, went to the airport to pick Falk up. When she returned to the set again, after having left Falk at his hotel, she came up to me and asked me if I had ever seen an actor with a glass eye. "No. Why do you ask?" "There is something strange about this American." Anyway, we just laughed about the matter and it ended there but I told De Santis about it. "Why would she say something so stupid?" That evening we were back at the hotel when Giuseppe knocked on my door. "She's right, he has a glass eye." So he went back to Rome to write, with De Concini, a backstory for Falk's character. When he left, he gave me a short little sequence to direct. When he saw the dailies I had shot, he liked them so much that he told me to shoot the battle scenes I mentioned before. Peter Falk, by the way, is one of the sweetest people I've met. Like most Americans, a true professional and very much in love with his wife.[5]

I think I'm touching a raw nerve here but the first film you undertake as director is Bellezze sulla spiaggia [Beauty on the Beach, 1961] ...
I want to clear the air on this matter. I did not direct that film, and if I had I would be very ashamed about it. I just want to make a premise: I loved my brother Marino very much and so I want to clarify that if I say certain things about him, is out of affection. That film is all his doing. He put together various stuff he had done previously, got outtakes and bits and pieces of different films and tied them together with some new material which he shot with my nephew Enio. I was asked to sign it for fiscal motives. I don't remember the exact reason, something to do with tax deductions.... The film, which is pretty awful, has nothing to do with me. In fact, on that film they used my real name, Romolo Girolami.

Your real debut then was in 1966, with 7 magnifiche pistole [Seven Magnificent Guns, a.k.a. Seven Guns for Timothy]. Correct me if I'm wrong, but I remember reading somewhere that you are not really fond of this film. Is this true?
Despite what many say, when you pass from being an AD to directing a film it's a big jump ... it's a leap. Before this film I had never really directed actors. My mistake was probably that I continued thinking like an AD. I would worry more about cuts and getting all the shots I needed rather than concentrating on the actors and the story. When you direct your first film you have to learn to work with producers' nails always under your skin. I enjoyed doing the film, even because we shot all the exterior scenes in Spain, which is a country I'm very fond of, but I did feel the pressure of having to deliver. The cast was good, though. Not great, but good. I had Sean Flynn, Errol's son, who died in Vietnam, and he was a nice guy, clean-cut, very well-mannered. Then there was the pretty Evelyn Stewart, whose real name was Ida Galli. But I think who really shines in the film are the host of Spanish character actors. That said, my subsequent two Westerns are much better and both of them have stronger stories.

In this period you also begin your career as a screenwriter and not only of your own films. Vado … l'ammazzo e torno [Any Gun Can Play, 1967] by Castellari is one of the first.

Something quite unpleasant happened on that film. At the time one of my closest collaborators was Sauro Scavolini. We had the idea of using Leone's dialogue from *Il buono, il brutto, il cattivo* [*The Good, The Bad and The Ugly*, 1966] as a title for a film … when Eli Wallach goes "vado, l'ammazzo e torno" [translated as "I'll go, kill him and be back"]. We both thought it would make a really cool title. We wrote a script and I gave it to Edmondo Amati, the producer. Enzo had built a relationship with Amati and … I don't want to get into the details but Enzo ended up doing the film. I was put aside…

What do you think of your nephew as a director?

He's good, especially when directing action scenes. I've never had a strong inclination towards them. I mean, you can find some big action sequences in my films but I would direct them with detachment. Not Enzo, he would identify himself with those moments, he would think up elaborate ways of shooting, he loved discussing them with the stunt coordinators. In those scenes he would excel.

Johnny Yuma [1966] is your second Western: bigger scale, bigger budget and starring an increasingly popular actor like Mark Damon. What sort of a person was Damon?

Very vain and conceited. He was good-looking and would worry about how he would appear in shots. He would spend a lot of time doing his hair. He was adamant about not growing a beard. I think he was the only Western star not to have a beard, not even stubble. But he was nice. Vain but not lazy. When we had to get things done he would pull his sleeves up and dig in.

You've often stated that you consider 10.000 dollari per un massacro *[10,000 Dollars for a Massacre, a.k.a.* Guns of Violence, *a.k.a.* $10,000 Blood Money, *1967] your best Western. How come?*

I recently watched *Johnny Yuma* again. I think there is an obsessive search for detail that gets out of hand and the scenes are too dilated and slow. These elements would work perfectly in the hands of Leone but I guess I was still finding my personal style. Plus in that film, the nemesis is not strong enough. Luigi Vannucchi, who played the villain, was an important theater actor but he was too over-the-top, sneering and laughing all the time. A little too theatrical. Furthermore on *Yuma*, Italo Zingarelli, the producer, wanted to press the accelerator on violence. I remember we had to get a fake limb made for a scene in which Vannucchi breaks a kid's arm. Those sort of scenes are not really my thing. I consider *10,000 Dollars for a Massacre* a more personal film. Plus it had a little irony I enjoyed. Like the beginning with the protagonist, a bounty killer, lying on the beach, contemplating the sea. "Ah the sea is a lovely thing. But what do you care about the sea?" He turns around and a corpse is revealed, dumped next to him. Plus, I think Gianni Garko was the strongest lead I had until that moment. He would work meticulously on his character, he would study the time period, the costumes. He would bring a lot of ideas, like the one of having his character wear a white silk scarf. The music by Nora Orlandi is very good as well.

You used the word irony to describe your film but it's not really the word you would use to describe your cinema. Bittersweet would seem more appropriate.

Absolutely. You can tell even from the kind of actors I would choose, Enrico Maria Salerno, for example, with whom I made three films. I was able to get him to express a certain melancholy, which was something he probably felt in real life. The characters he played were very introspective, closed towards society. Salerno was a difficult actor, though, who also came from the theater. I never managed to get him to not use a wig. He looked wonderful bald, but he wouldn't even consider it. I think his interpretation in *Un uomo, una città* [*City Under Siege*, 1974] is fantastic, as is Luciano Salce's, in the same film. The ending is probably the most melancholic and bitter moment in the whole of my cinema.

After the Westerns, we have your only giallo: **Il dolce corpo di Deborah *[The Sweet Body of Deborah, a.k.a. The Body, a.k.a. Married to Kill, 1968]*. *You direct Carroll Baker in her first big Italian hit, and together with Umberto Lenzi you are one of the most important directors of the first generation of gialli.***

At the time it was labeled as a "sexy-giallo" and I got slapped with an R rating. There was nothing really sexy about the film, except a scene in which Carroll Baker takes a shower, and you can see her naked. Baker was perfect, you couldn't wish for a better actress. She was never impatient, never complained, never a gesture of intolerance. A great professional. Anyway, the idea of the film came from Luciano Martino, who had produced my last Western. He made me read a first treatment and asked my opinion. I didn't like it. The plot was Luciano's doing, then later developed by Ernesto Gastaldi. Initially I had envisioned Giancarlo Giannini in the part that later went to Jean Sorel. I met Giannini and discussed the film with him. He was willing to do it but Martino intervened and said no. He believed it wouldn't have been sellable internationally with Giannini. "I can get you Sorel and Baker." Sorel had just made a film with Visconti and another one with Bunuel. Carroll Baker, for me, was *Baby Doll*, Elia Kazan's muse. So I said yes. The first actor I met was Jean, in Rome, at Piazza del Popolo. The conversation was quick: "Jean, did you like the script?" "No. Did you?" "No. Do you want to do the film?" "Oh absolutely." Then there were Luigi Pistilli and George Hilton. A strong cast that I think compensated for the problems concerning the script.

At what stage was the script when you read it and how was your relationship with Gastaldi?

When I was called by Martino, the script was complete, finished. I changed and tweaked it here and there but I didn't do anything radical. I just, as you say in the business, "me lo sono cucito addosso" [I sewed it to fit me]. As far as Gastaldi is concerned we met once or twice, and fleetingly for that matter. He was not interested in knowing if I liked it or not, or in any changes I might have wanted to make. We didn't have any kind of relationship.

Let's talk a little more about the sexual aspect of the film.

Well, I find Jean Sorel to be, yes, handsome but not an erotic presence. There are some actors, who are much less dashing let's say, than he is and yet are able to infuse the scene with much more eroticism that is more naturally carnal. If the film can be defined erotic, it is not for the scenes that made it get an R rating. For instance, there is a sequence set in a strip club in Nice, and there is this moment in which Carroll Baker is watching out of the corner of her eye, her husband looking at the show, and you can tell she is aroused by the situation. That is erotic, not a bit of skin in a shower scene.

Your filmography embraces a number of genres but the one that you are associated the most with, or at least you seem to have particularly excelled in, is the police thriller.

But this isn't really accurate because your films didn't follow the Italian trend. Films like Un detective *[Ring of Death, a.k.a.* Detective Belli, *1969] or* City Under Siege *are more noirs than action films. Noirs that seemed to look more towards the French approach rather than the American one.*

Yes, this is absolutely true. I think it's due to the fact that I would focus primarily on the characters, especially in my police stories, much more than I would on the dynamism of the story. In my films the main character IS the story ... better still if he is a loser. If this wasn't present in the scripts I was given, it would be the thing I would work on the most, extracting from the plot the fragilities and tragic humanity of the protagonists. In fact, my policemen and detectives aren't men of action, they don't jump from cars or start shooting in the streets. As far as inspiration is concerned, I can just say that I was definitely not interested in American cinema, at least not on a stylistic level. Of course some of my films were conceived for the American market but that was tied more to the genre in itself, or the choice of actors, but when it came to directing, I think my feet stayed glued to European soil, and definitely, as you said, with an eye on what was being done in France.

Among the films you made, Ring of Death *is your favorite. The film was released in 1969 and I find it is a perfect bridge between the decades, both stylistically and narratively. It incorporates so many elements of what had been done until then, conveyed with a taste which is closer to the seventies.*

The film is an adaption of a novel by Ludovico Dentice called *Macchie di belletto* [translation: *Stains of Rouge*]. A wonderful title I thought, but Mario Cecchi Gori believed it was too cryptic. I remember that to draw inspiration, the writers Alberto Silvestri and Franco Verucci and myself, screened a series of old Italian and French noirs. Cecchi Gori discovered this and got mad. "I don't want one of those films! Don't get any strange ideas!" He wanted to Americanize the story as much as possible, when I wanted something much more European. It's a miracle the film turned out the way it did. It's also the first film in which I think, I expressed my potential and ability ... I don't want to use the word talent, but ability yes. By that time I had managed to shrug off the technical rigidities and formalisms of the previous films and really focus on the story and on finding my voice as a director.

Franco Nero?

He was chosen because, if I'm not mistaken, he was under contract with Cecchi Gori. He was an international star who had made a lot of films elsewhere, even in the States, so I was happy enough with the idea of having him in the film. For some time, after the making, he did not speak to me because I had decided to dub him. He is from Parma and I felt his accent was still too strong.

Then came the biggest anomaly in your career: Il divorzio *[The Divorce, 1970], which is the continuance of the classic "commedia all'italiana." At one point it seemed like big producers would pick genre directors to helm films starring these barons of comedy. Completely star-driven films like this one. Giorgio Capitani, for example directed Vittorio Gassman in the same period you did[6] and stated that he felt he had no power over the film. What was your experience?*

The Divorce is not my film, it's Vittorio Gassman's. What you say is true. They would choose more commercial directors instead of the usual names that would normally direct those kind of films, more well-respected people like Mario Monicelli or Dino Risi.... This was because they knew we were technically competent and that we could deliver what was needed, and at the same time they thought we were easily controllable. I had just finished *Ring of Death* and Cecchi Gori was very happy with the results. He proposed this project to me. "If Gassman approves, you can do the film." I met with Vittorio and had a long conversation with him. Evidently he liked me because I was chosen. I'm very detached from the film, though. It's not a good film. It's well made and people seemed to appreciate it but it's not really that good. I didn't have much fun directing it either because my job was preparing the scene and going "action!" letting Gassman be Gassman. There wasn't much to direct. Minimal camera work and you couldn't really give Vittorio any indications or pointers. I watched it again, a few years ago, and it's really boring. I found it utterly boring.

Generally speaking comedy wasn't a genre you felt very comfortable directing, was it?
   For the most part, I was a director lucky enough to have had medium-high budgets. I was never able to shoot films in three/four weeks like some of my colleagues. *City Under Siege* took ten weeks to make, *Salvo D'Acquisto* [1974] eleven weeks, *Ring of Death* eight weeks. I needed time. So I was one of those directors who got hurt the most by the crisis. Those who survived were people who were able to direct films with increasingly smaller budgets and in less time. Plus, I had the possibility of choosing the films I wanted to work on. Of course always with a margin of compromise but generally I had the luxury of being selective. Something you just can't be during a crisis so I attempted to make a few films for … money. I'm not proud of this but it's the truth. I only managed to do a few and then had to stop. I thought retiring was more dignified.

We've mentioned him already but I would like to talk a bit more about Enrico Maria Salerno.
   When I first had the idea of signing him up for a film, many colleagues told me not to. "He is a pain in the ass. A real ball-buster." He had already made his debut as a director by then, making him even more untouchable for many. Personally, I never had any trouble with him. It's true that he would create problems but more for the production than for me. He would never accept working overtime, he would make the budget get bigger because he wanted to eat well and have his choice of foods, stuff like that. But with me there was maximum respect. Salerno was the perfect actor for the thinking man's police thriller and he was an actor who could work in those films without being labeled as reactionary or fascist because he was politicized … an intellectual actor. They did accuse you but let's say they were a little softer, a little more lenient. In fact, I wanted him for my most political film which was *La polizia è al servizio del Cittadino?* [*The Police Serve the Citizens?*, 1973].

What about Maurizio Merli, was he the exact opposite of Salerno? You worked with him on Covert Action.
   I didn't have a good relationship with him. He was more an actor for my brother. Marino directed him in more than a film. We didn't get along. He did do a good scene, when we were shooting in Athens, in a huge amphitheater which would have filled my nephew Enzo with joy. A scene in which Merli has a punch-up with two stuntmen and he did it well. He had a natural inclination for those kind of scenes but we were a bit coldish with each other. He was extremely egocentric. Plus *Covert Action* was a film in

which he was not the lead—you know, he was in a declining phase—and he struggled to get as much screen time and attention as possible. On that film I had, on the one side, a sobbing David Janssen who was drunk most of the time and on the other a macho like Merli, always worried about his hair.

**Let's talk about Liberi, armati, pericolosi *[Young, Violent, Dangerous, a.k.a.* Young, Violent and Desperate, *1976]. Where did this film stem from?*

It began with a script written by Fernando Di Leo, a director we all know and appreciate, and an excellent writer. I don't remember if he was supposed to direct it initially but I'm pretty sure he was the one who mentioned my name. "Romolo would be perfect for a story like this." I never got to know if he appreciated how I used his script but I enjoyed making the film. I don't know if this was what Di Leo was thinking about while writing the script but definitely while directing I was thinking about "i ragazzi del Circeo"[7]: the city of Milan, the upper-class context and the consumerist, money-oriented cynicism of a certain youth of the time. There are many elements that tie the film to that incident. Ah … before I forget … this film marks the debut of Diego Abatantuono.[8] It's the first time Diego appears on screen. He plays this young, wealthy fascist, the son of a gun trafficker, who ends up killed by these three kids who are at the center of the story.

Let's talk a little bit about the casting. Tomas Milian, by this time, was making a different kind of film. Although in the same genre, his were films contaminated by comedic elements. In the late seventies police thrillers were slowly dying out in a similar way Westerns had vanished. Was it difficult to convince Milian to go back and take part in a more rigorous and serious film?

Yes, very difficult at first. I went to his house. I will always remember his sitting room, surrounded by mirrors. There wasn't a single corner you could stand in without seeing your reflection staring back at you. Anyway, initially he would be very defensive with me. He was so used to hiding himself behind the wigs and make-up of Monnezza[9] that he couldn't envision himself as anything else. I got up and pulled his hair back and said: "Isn't it time to come out from under that wig, if not for just one film?" I told him I thought he could be a fantastic police commissioner, different from what was being done at that moment. A few days passed by when I received a call from him: "I've decided to trust you." He is very good in the film, he works perfectly. On set he was always very professional, prepared. I never had a single problem with him.

What do you remember of Eleonora Giorgi?

I feel a little guilty in regards to Eleonora. She didn't end up being what I had hoped for in the film. Maybe she was going through a strange or difficult time or maybe I wasn't able to communicate as I should have. It is only in certain moments of the film that I can say I'm satisfied with her acting, in others … not as much, but perhaps, as I said, it's my fault. I wasn't able to make a connection with her.

The three real protagonists of the film are Stefano Patrizi, Max Delys and Benjamin Lev. The script supervisor of Young, Violent, Dangerous, Silvia Petroni,[10] remembers that they would get into trouble a lot during the making of the film. She also recalls there being a drug problem on set.

Yes, they would arrive late on set, often in terrible condition and we'd have to wait for them to sober up before shooting. Lev was particularly bad. I can tell you one episode which is exemplary. We were shooting somewhere in Milan and Benjamin came up to me and asked to leave early that day. He said he had an appointment with a producer at the Hilton, in the evening. When an actor asks you something like that you do your best to help him out. So that's what I did. The next day he doesn't show up ... vanished. We started looking for him, calling up anybody we thought might know his whereabouts. Nothing. Many hours later we discovered that he had been arrested. Apparently the police was after him and had been for a while. I don't remember if he was charged with detention or drug trafficking. Anyway, we had to stop production for three days, go over our work plan. Nobody noticed, but for many scenes we used a double. Thank goodness we had already shot his big death sequence. I hope Benjamin has overcome his problems. I never knew what happened to him.

Going back to Fernando Di Leo, did you work on the script together and if not how much did it change once in your hands?

I only met Di Leo once, maybe twice, and in none of those occasions did we ever discuss changes to the script. I did, however, modify the story a little bit with the help of Mino Roli, who was a very well respected playwright. Nothing really substantial was changed. All the work and imagery of Di Leo is still there and can be noticed quite easily. Actually, we haven't mentioned that Di Leo wrote also, or at least participated in writing, the script of *Johnny Yuma*, but on that particular occasion we never met. I hadn't even heard of him. The script was given to me with his name on it. I did what I pleased and that was the end of it.

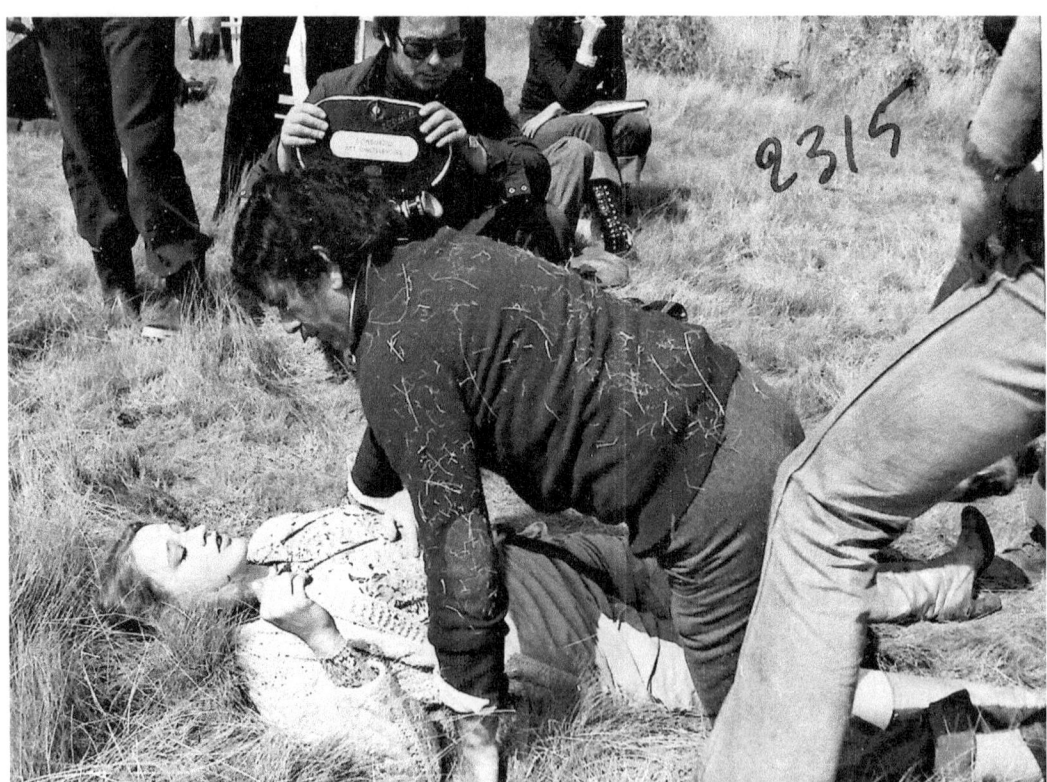

Eleonora Giorgi rehearses one of the most crucial scenes of *Young, Violent, Dangerous* (1976) with director Romolo Guerrieri (on top of her) (courtesy Sylvia Petroni).

Young, Violent, Dangerous *is one of the very last great Italian police thrillers. Soon after, before dying out, the genre will end its inevitable mutation. The farcical and comedic interpretation will finish cannibalizing the genre completely. The few serious films that get made are hardly worth mentioning. What happened?*

The same thing happened with Westerns. Basically, the modus operandi is the following: a few directors, sometimes one is enough, manage to emphasize, reanimate or invent a genre. The first generation of directors tied to the genre manage to make it successful, structure it and give it its rules. But then we don't know when to stop and the market gets inflated by a huge number of films that are derivative, cheaply made and quench the public's thirst for that genre too quickly. The market gets desaturated and new elements have to be introduced to be able to keep the genre alive. And then the same thing happens again. Somebody directs the first Western comedy, for example. A good film, solid but then everybody starts doing Western comedies. The whole game gets repeated over and over in an endless loop. Sometimes the same directors who made the genre successful in the first place end up being corrupted by what they helped create. Of course you have to add to this the confusion that journalists and film critics would generate. They made no distinction. They didn't help the public understand what was worthy and what wasn't. We were all the same in their eyes. All genre directors were unworthy of any kind of analysis. At one point I stopped reading the reviews because they would systematically accuse me of being a reactionary. Especially left-wing newspapers, which were the ones I read, because my political beliefs—well political is maybe a big word—hang more towards the left. One of the only films that got some decent reviews was my purest noir, *Ring of Death*.

Guerrieri on the set of *Due vite, un destino* (*The Final Contract*), 1992 (courtesy Nocturno Cinema).

By the late seventies you started accepting films that were beneath you. You mentioned this earlier.

Yes, I did two films, one after the other, that perhaps I wouldn't have made if I could turn back time. *L'importante è non farsi notare* [translation: *The Important Thing Is Not Being Noticed*, 1979] and *La gorilla* [*The Female Bodyguard*, 1982]. The best things I did in comedy were the ones I wrote for the Martino brothers. Me and Franco Verucci, who was my closest collaborator, participated in the scripts for films like *Cornetti alla crema* [*Cream Horns*, a.k.a. *Cream Puffs*, 1981]. Even if they were populist and a little lowbrow, they were in good taste. Especially thanks to Sergio Martino with whom I shared a certain approach.

Of the two you directed, the one you seem to hate the most is the second one. To my knowledge, you've always refused to speak about the film in any interview.

When they gave me the script for *The Female Bodyguard*, I hadn't been working for a few years. Not only was the script terrible but they told me that it had to be done with Lory Del Santo. No discussion about it, a complete imposition. It was a publicity stunt because she had appeared on some tabloids for some high-profile flirts or love affairs. "OK, fine ... but has she ever acted? I mean she's been in a few TV shows as a starlet but..." "No, no, no! It will be a hit!" I tried for a short period to push another actress's name forward but I found a wall in front of me. "If Lory Del Santo is not in it, the distributors are not interested. The film won't get made." I met her, one summer morning. She was wearing a miniskirt, a sleeveless T-shirt and high heels. You couldn't walk two meters with her without somebody whistling, shouting, starring at her and for one fleeting moment I thought to myself: "Maybe they're right, maybe we can pull this off." Alas ... things went differently.

What do you mean?

She simply wasn't an actress. When I was speaking before about Bonnard and I mentioned having had a similar reaction with an actress, I was referring to Lory Del Santo. We were shooting in a bar and I stopped the scene. We had been repeating it for an hour. She couldn't remember her lines and would be laughing and goofing around ... wasting everybody's time. I went up to her, in front of the whole crew: "Please tell me and everybody why you want to be an actress! You are utterly hopeless!" As much as she had pushed me to the limit, I should not have reacted that way. I was no better than Bonnard. For that, I'm sorry.

Your last film for the big screen is* L'ultimo guerriero *[The Last Warrior, a.k.a.* The Final Executioner, *1984]. A post-apocalyptic action film. Something tells me you are not very fond of this either.

Ah, damn! Yes, I forgot about that. My God, I did make so many mediocre films when I look back at my career in perspective. Anyway, one of the best things about working on that film was Woody Strode. He was very good, a solid man. We shot the entire film somewhere not far from Rome. It wasn't a film that touched my sensibility. I didn't feel it was mine though maybe by the way the protagonist is characterized, you can perhaps tell that I'm behind the camera ... the solemnity and melancholic resignation of the protagonist.

Do you consider yourself a melancholic person?

I think it's a sentiment, a sweet sentiment, that doesn't have to be neglected or ignored. It can keep you company. Often melancholy is confused or thought of as sadness. Sometimes it can instill itself with nostalgia and it happens to me at times but mostly, when I'm pervaded by melancholy, a smile appears somewhere inside of me. Though when I think of my career, perhaps there is a tinge of sadness as well, for all the lost opportunities.

Rome, 2016

1962 Lovable Slobs
The Cinema of Mario Caiano

"You had your revenge. Why don't you kill me? Kill both of us."
"You, I will kill you, you tart, you. You and your filthy friend. But death, my dear, must come to you only after I've torn from your bodies all the suffering and pain a human being can stand, and you don't know yet how long it takes to die of pain."
"You're a monster."—Barbara Steele and Paul Muller in Nightmare Castle, 1965

What rose from the ashes of an aching, fragmented country is so vast and complex that it is imperative to understand, to go back and look at the years following the war and the Marshall Plan. Already in the late forties, the demand for the spectacle of cinema was incredibly high, so much so that cinemas were among the first buildings to be restored or constructed. The pulsating need to exorcize the years of dictatorship and war was evident, and in a matter of a couple of years, every borough, suburb and town had its cinema. Structures built, for the first time thinking big: modern, comfortable spaces able to accommodate a conspicuous number of spectators. Alongside this capillary phenomenon, as elsewhere mentioned, came the dominant presence of American films, a flow that had ceased completely during the fascist era. Initially, Neorealism was partly trying to satisfy this demand with stories of anguish and sorrow, set in the dusty streets and impoverished city outskirts, describing the poetry of the human drama hidden behind ruins and shantytowns and at the same time trying to metabolize and understand what the country was going through. Neorealism, which was initiated by Rossellini's *Roma città aperta* (*Rome Open City*) in 1945, immediately became a political creature as well as an ideological manifesto, that deconstructed the filmic language of fascist cinema thus becoming a starting point for debate and discussion. But as fundamental as Neorealism was, it didn't quench the thirst that many had for a cinema that was mainly recreational, that was able to be pure entertainment. In fact, at the peak of the neorealist movement, some of the highest grossing films were the first post-war adventure stories that had nothing to do with the country's economic and social life: *Aquila nera* (translation: *Black Eagle*, Riccardo Freda, 1946) and *Genoveffa di Brabante* (Primo Zeglio, 1947).

Then, in 1948, 20th Century–Fox decided to shoot *The Prince of Foxes* by Henry King in the studios of Cinecittà, anticipating what, a few years later, would become a habit that gave rise to a unique period in Italian history: "Hollywood on the Tiber." The films in production were adventurous spectacles and romantic films, set among Roman ruins and narrow sunlit alleys, but most of all, they were what the industry called "sandaloni" (translated as "big sandals"), peplums, over-the-top, lavish and opulent mythological fantasies set in Ancient Rome. The Neorealist manifesto that forged or gave birth to the careers of auteurs like Rossellini, Vittorio De Sica, Pietro Germi, Giuseppe De Santis and Alberto Lattuada, started fading, dying out completely in the mid-fifties. But by this time the success and invasion of American productions had introduced, to the provincial and simple Italian and Roman society, a new social phenomenon made up of an Olympus of divas and stars, parties, nightclubs, "paparazzi" and a jet-set lifestyle. The relationship between demand and offer whirls into unprecedented frenzy and in 1954, 700 million tickets were sold to a public in need of candy-flavored Hollywood dreams and neon lit stars. Italian cinema started building up again, stronger and faster than ever: comedies, musical plays, cape-and-dagger and period dramas were among the genres which producers were drawn to at the start of the fifties. But all this began attracting many people not only to the darkness of a film theater but also to the industry itself, now that the doors were wide open and the demand was high. What can be described as a decade-long training period began for a great number of future directors. The possibility of creating a career in cinema was a difficult but concrete one and many took their first steps as ADs, like in the case of most of the directors mentioned until now—Giulio Petroni (1953), Romolo Guerrieri (1952) and Alberto De Martino (1952) to which we now have to add the name of Mario Caiano (13 February 1933, Rome–20 September 2015, Rome).

Mario Caiano directed nearly thirty films, including peplums, Westerns, gialli, horror, comedies and even a nazisploitation and is, among all the directors analyzed previously, together with Alberto De Martino, the most representative of the decade he was artistically born in. Son of producer Carlo Caiano, Mario starts young, at the bottom of the hierarchical pyramid, rising through the ranks, film after film, passing from little comedies, melodramas and reaching big adventure epics. A genre in which, like Giorgio Capitani, he started directing second units. In this fructuous period, he would work with many important figures of the previous generation: Sergio Grieco, Fernando Cerchio, Camillo Mastrocinque and even Edgar G. Ulmer. Prolific was something Caiano would continue to be even after his debut as a director in 1962 with what could have only been a peplum: *Ulisse contro Ercole* (*Ulysses Against Hercules*, a.k.a. *Ulysses Against the Son of Hercules*, 1962). However, Caiano has, for a long time, been remembered exclusively as the director who went up against Sergio Leone's first Western … and lost. His *Le pistole non discutono* (*Bullets Don't Argue*, a.k.a. *Pistols Don't Argue*) was produced by the same company, shot practically simultaneously and in the same locations as Leone's *Per un pugno di dollari* (*A Fistful of Dollars*). Caiano already had six films under his belt and was one of the most important and representative directors of the early sixties Spanish co-produced proto-Westerns, such as *Il segno del coyote* (*The Sign of the Coyote*, 1963) and *Il segno di Zorro* (*Duel at Rio Grande*, a.k.a. *Sign of Zorro*, 1963), films that, if not groundbreaking, were successful at the box office. It is in Spain that Caiano starts learning the rules of Westerns, in a period that he describes as one of the most adventurous of his career, alongside American producer Harry Joe Brown who was attempting to recreate the great classics of the thirties, reimagining characters like Captain Blood and Zorro. "Westerns are the genre I have given myself most to. I like all types of films but maybe Westerns have a slightly bigger portion of my heart."

Sirpa Lane and Mario Caiano talk things over as they shoot *Nazi Love Camp 27*, in 1977 (courtesy Nocturno Cinema).

Whereas Caiano was very much appreciated by his peers, Leone on the contrary, was not well looked upon by producers. He was held unsuitable for the genre with too many expensive ideas that were regarded as pointlessly eccentric. *Bullets Don't Argue* was the second Western produced by Arrigo Colombo and Giorgio Papi's Jolly Films after *Duello nel Texas* (*Gunfight at Red Sands*, a.k.a. *Gunfight in the Red Sands*, 1963) which, despite being directed by Ricardo Blasco, was actually "saved" by Caiano who was rushed in to direct most of the duels and action scenes. This event would be decisive in Papi and Colombo's decision to hire him for *Bullets Don't Argue*. It has come to be a well-known fact that Leone's film originated at the same time as Caiano's: both Italian-Spanish-German co-productions; the screenplay and set designs were conceived simultaneously and both films have music composed by Ennio Morricone and are both photographed by Massimo Dallamano. Although they were "twin" projects, they were not treated or perceived as equal by their producers. Caiano was given a "real" actor, Rod Cameron, while Leone got the unknown Clint Eastwood. When it was screened on 21 August 1964, Caiano's film found the public's approval, but it was destined to be a short-lived success. What built up from the 12th day of the following month when Leone's film hit theaters, was going to overshadow anything done in the genre previously. The thunder conjured up by *A Fistful of Dollars* created a storm that blew away Caiano's effort—too old-style and anchored to American traditions—and changed film history forever. Though important, this specific junction in Mario Caiano's career was one of many in a filmography that spreads itself over nearly four decades. Westerns would continue to accompany Caiano throughout his career. He managed to separate himself from previous clichés with successful crossovers, the biggest being *Il mio nome è Shanghai Joe* (*My Name Is Shanghai Joe*, a.k.a. *The Fighting Fists of Shanghai Joe*, a.k.a. *To Kill or Die*, a.k.a. *The Dragon Strikes Back*, 1973) which decontextualizes Kung Fu, transferring it to the Far West.

Interview by Manlio Gomarasca

Let's start by talking about that great decade for Italian cinema which was the sixties. What is the first thing that comes to mind when you think about that period?

Well, the first thing I remember when thinking back, is the fun. I had a lot of fun and realized, even then, that I had chosen the best job in the world. Though in hindsight, I also find it all quite pathetic. We were all scurrying around trying to work, trying to get something made. When you were not on a set you were obsessed with finding something to do, a project. You would constantly think of yourself as a loser. "I'm no good. I will never work in cinema again." So you would be willing to direct anything that came along, with the weirdest concepts and scripts, begging producers to make you work. When you finally did get a film off the ground, your only worry was money. Money and time. The producers would manage to find some money through distributors, then, with some of it they would pay off debts, some they would put in their pockets and with what was left they would finance the film. It has happened to me to have producers give me a check, halfway through production, and go, "We have to finish the film with this." But I had a lot of fun. I did what I always dreamed of doing. I would always be travelling and meeting new people. I loved history as a child and I have always been attracted by the classical world. In fact, I began as an archaeologist and then moved towards cinema. So when they offered me to direct *Ulisse contro Ercole* [*Ulysses Against Hercules*, a.k.a. *Ulysses Against the Son of Hercules*, 1962], it was like going back to my first love. It was a dream to write a story about these mythological figures ... even if Hercules was a dazed boxer called Mike Lane, who walked around like a Golem with clay feet. It didn't matter that Ulysses was a mediocre French actor called Georges Marchal. What was important was the adventure of making the film. We shot that on the Island of Tenerife. You know, I was 25 years old, doing whatever I wanted, inventing and playing around with "the bird men" and "the troglodytes," having Dominique Boschero as the Queen of the Bird People, prancing around half naked with this wonderful multi-colored mask, with long feathers.... It was the best job in the world. It was a buffoonish industry, the one we were working in, often populated by squalid and irresponsible people, but it was glorious nonetheless and we were all lovable slobs.

How exactly did you start working in films?

How I got to cinema is pretty banal and simply said. My father [Carlo Caiano] was a distributor, who later on started producing as well, when he hooked up with this stateless swindler who drew money from God knows where.[1] They would go, as many did at that time, to that mecca, which was Spain. The country had just come out, or let's say they were still recovering from a civil war, cars were a huge luxury, and everything was dirt cheap. Italian productions would find a Spanish one who would cover certain expenses and, more importantly, help logistically.

One of the genres you are most associated with is Westerns.

This connects perfectly with what I was saying about Spanish-Italian relations. There was this strange writer called Josè Mallorquì, who would go around dressed like a vaquero, with a huge gun belt, big boots and a sombrero and was specialized in Westernish, Zorro-type stories. With him I did one of the first Italian Westerns, *Il segno del coyote* [*The Sign of the Coyote*, 1963]. It wasn't a pure Western but it had all the elements that characterizes the genre: the village and gunfights, horses and villains. The lead was a torero who called himself Fernando Casanova, completely ridiculous and so wrong for the role. The actress, I don't remember her name [Marìa Luz Galicia] was the producer's lover. It was all a little improvised, but that was my introduction to the genre. You could say I was born with Westerns seeing it was only my second film. My relationship with the West started in 1963 and continued right up to the early seventies ... 1972 I think. By that time they had started looking for new variations and possible crossovers to keep the genre alive and even then I made one of the weirdest examples of the time. Seeing Kung Fu movies were big, we decided to fuse Westerns with martial arts. I'm talking about *Il mio nome è Shanghai Joe* [*My Name Is Shanghai Joe*, a.k.a. *The Fighting Fists of Shanghai Joe*, a.k.a. *To Kill or Die*, a.k.a. *The Dragon Strikes Back*, 1973], which was a big success. Klaus Kinski was in that as well. He would accuse me of wanting him dead. There was a scene in which his character was supposed to fall from a cliff. I did the master shot using a stuntman of course and I only needed a close-up of him just about to throw himself. It was a one, maybe two, meter fall onto a pile of cushions and he started screaming: "He's a maniac! He wants to see me die! He wants me dead!" That was Kinksi and after two days I would have thrown him off a 50-meter cliff. Anyway, I did about fifteen Westerns. One of the titles I'm most happy about is *Un treno per Durango* [*Train for Durango*, 1968] with Anthony Steffen and Enrico Maria Salerno, which was also my first real attempt to infuse a Western with comedy.

But you left a strong mark on the horror genre as well.

I definitely would have wanted to direct more of them. The only real one I directed is *Amanti d'oltretomba* [*Nightmare Castle*, a.k.a. *Lovers from Beyond the Tomb*, 1965]. I had been flirting with the idea of doing a horror for some time. My dream was to do an adaptation of the novel "The Pit and the Pendulum" and some elements I think survived in the film I managed to make. Well, Barbara Steele is in it but she was a must-have if you intended to shoot a gothic horror film in the sixties. I wrote the story and then developed the script with Fabio De Agostini. Initially the film was supposed to be shot in black, white and red. It would have been really stylish and avant-garde but my father, who was the producer, after having checked out the development and printing costs, rejected this possibility. The film went well but I was never offered others. In later years I did cop thrillers, dramas, adventure films but no horrors. Speaking of the various genres, I want to point out the names and definitions that critics would use to describe the films we would make: starting from "spaghetti Westerns" but also "musicarelli" [literally, tiny musicals] and "poliziotteschi" [deformation of the word "poliziesco," police thrillers]. All these labels were aimed at dismissing and mocking our films. We managed to work, despite the media that would, in the best of cases, ignore us.

Well, you did do another horror after that,* Ombre roventi *[Shadow of Illusion, 1970].

I think that film was made only to sell a crane to the Egyptians! I was in Indonesia shooting documentaries when I receive a call from an Italian producer who was setting things up. "What do you think of shooting a film in Egypt?" "I think it would be nice. Who is producing it?" "A building speculator who is packed with money. Don't worry about a thing." "Who are the actors?" "Aaaahh ... big, big stars. American ... Hollywood names. John Wayne!" He didn't say John Wayne but somebody along those lines. We wrote this script, me and Fabio Piccioni, and I went to Egypt, but this big American star was nowhere to be seen. When we got to what was supposed to be the first day of shooting, he never showed up, so I received a call from this pseudo-producer who was organizing everything, an excellent poker player, and he goes: "He changed his mind. He isn't coming." Luckily I had come to know that another Italian film was being shot there, right behind my hotel, so I go and find William Berger, who was big in Westerns at the time. "William, do you want to be the lead in my next film?" "Sure. I wrap up on this one in two days." So, that's how I got my protagonist. The actress was a certain Paola ... bah ... I don't remember and maybe that's best, because we replaced her after three, four days and got Daniela Giordano instead. I didn't finish the film because all of a sudden they tell me that there is a crises in current assets which is another way of saying we hadn't a dime anymore. So I just shot a huge chunk of the film and forgot about it. Many years later, twenty, thirty years later, a British film lover sends me an English-dubbed copy of the film. It was in a pale black and white, with scenes that weren't even in the script and had become even a little pornographic. I'm not so sure it's supposed to be in my filmography.

Didn't something similar happen with La svastica nel ventre *[*Nazi Love Camp 27, *a.k.a.* Living Nightmare, 1977*]*?

Yes, though *Nazi Love Camp 27* was done with a serious production and a good budget and everything went smoothly until the distributors saw it and complained that it wasn't strong enough and needed more sex scenes. Without my knowledge, they called a director, specialized in these sort of additions ... he actually might have been a real pornographer. They shot some extra stuff. But justice exists because years later, the film was sold to Mediaset. They called and asked me to recut the film. So at least on television, my version was shown. Maybe a little softer than my version but definitely close to it.

Do you like the film?

The whole operation was dreadful. I tried to nobilitate it as much as possible but it was a lost cause. When you have a Finnish actress who used to work in a brothel…

Sirpa Lane?

Yes, she was a high-class prostitute from, let's say, a noble brothel in Paris. What can you expect? The story is about Aryan soldiers copulating with Aryan-looking prisoners in concentration camps…

What seemed like your main skill was being able to adjust yourself to small budgets and managing to do the best with very little. Would you say this was the common trait of Italian cinema in the sixties and seventies?

Well, one of them. Italian cinema was very complex. The system was very much multi-layered. You had Luchino Visconti and people like him, who would have all the time and money in the world to shoot whatever they wanted and then there was the endless, dark pit of genre cinema in which there was a bit of everything. Directors and producers who would shoot entire films in a villa owned by a cousin, a brother, or running around the city without any permits. It was a reality in which all sorts of approaches and scales were able to coexist.

Let's talk about your police thrillers: ...a tutte le auto della polizia... [Calling All Police Cars, a.k.a. Without Trace, a.k.a. The Maniac Responsible, 1975] is the first and possibly the best. It's also a hybrid, partly a crime thriller and partly a giallo.

All the merit of this contamination goes to Massimo Felisatti and Fabio Pittorru who were a pair of brilliant writers, specialized in gialli. They wrote for films and were very prolific in this activity but they were mainly novelists that had created a whole series of books on the life and work of a specific detective. My film is the adaptation of one of these books, which had a different title, probably. Initially it was supposed to be a pure giallo, then in time the investigative aspect of the story contaminated the film more and more. Personally I don't consider it a police thriller though, but an atypical giallo. Later on I did straightforward action films. In *Calling All Police Cars* the nucleus of the story is who is committing this string of murders ... suspense more than the action itself, plus there is also a tinge of eroticism which is an element traceable more to gialli than police thrillers, in which violence was the big appeal.

Speaking of action films, you direct two perfect examples of what the genre was able to do: Milano violenta [Bloody Payroll, 1976] and Napoli spara! [Weapons of Death, a.k.a. Naples Shoots, 1977]. Anything you are particularly proud of ... a sequence, an invention?

There is a long sequence towards the end of the film, a high-speed pursuit race on the highway. The villain is driving this huge petrol tanker chased by the hero, Leonard Mann. First the tanker pushes a car full of poor souls that rumbles down a hill but then the protagonist manages to get onto the tanker and overpower the driver. All this big scene was object of an in-depth analysis in a French magazine. They studied the shots and use of space to point out what we Italians were capable of doing. I didn't invent anything. What I can say about my technical approach is that I would favor wide shots and use few details, especially in action scenes. Plus I would try and look for some kind of realism. For example, in Westerns there was this ridiculous habit of having the stuntmen jump backwards five meters when hit by the bullet of a Colt. I would look for more credible solutions. But that said, I didn't invent anything, at least not on a formal level. My creativity came out mostly in the narrative. Especially in the peplums I made, I would pump them with as much color and fantasy elements as possible. In Westerns I had more classical approach. As most people know, my film *Le pistole non discutono* [*Pistols Don't Argue*, a.k.a. *Bullets Don't Argue*, 1964] was made simultaneously to Sergio Leone's *Per un pugno di dollari* [*A Fistful of Dollars*, 1964]; same production company, same locations, but his ended up being the success everybody knows and mine simply went well, had a normal, average box-office result. He created a new language with long, extremely dilated scenes, everlasting silences, extreme close-ups of details and faces. My film wanted to imitate the American approach ... Leone chose an unknown actor who had mostly done television and I picked a star of the golden era of American Westerns, Rod Cameron. Basically, a piece of beef with legs.

Why do you think all this productive system died out?

Well, I think television is mainly responsible for the death of our industry. All of a sudden people could watch commercial films staying comfortably at home and would

Opposite: **Italian poster of *Weapons of Death*, 1977.**

have a choice of two, three titles a day. They could choose from a whole array of titles: both American films and Italian, the films we had been making until that moment.

You are one of the few directors who, in the eighties, managed to transition to television.

I've never calculated this, but in the end I think I worked more for television than I did for cinema. I started working as a 1st AD in 1952 and I continued being one until roughly 1961 and from that moment I became a director. My very first film for television was in 1975 and for a while I worked for both the small and big screens. But they started calling me less and less to direct films for cinema until, in the space of about five or six years, they stopped completely. I worked for television for nearly thirty years.

What is the main difference between cinema and television from a directorial and technical point of view?

Personally, I didn't feel I was switching medium, at least from a stylistic standpoint. I would behave in the same identical way. Well of course, censorship is and was, much stronger for television so what I had been able to show previously in films, violence and sex-wise, I could never have pulled off for television. Also things are quicker when you are working for a TV network but even there, I didn't feel the difference that much because in cinema I always had to work with small budgets and tight schedules. Evidently, though, there must be a difference because my films for cinema are remembered much more so than anything I ever did for television. Quentin Tarantino doesn't speak highly of my TV series but he does of my Westerns and action films and this is something that still amazes me. I don't know about my colleagues but I would have never imagined, even remotely, that these genres and films would have been celebrated thirty, forty, fifty years later. I saw myself as sort of a journeyman, a little bit of a slob at times, who would manage to get things done, with a little luck and con-man inventiveness. I mean that in a good way but still I would have never believed it possible to be here giving interviews about the things I directed in those years. I remember, before the advent of internet, I received a telephone call from two brothers—two carpenters, and I had no idea who they were—and they just wanted to tell me how much they loved what I had done. "We found a copy of *A Train for Durango* ... the Japanese VHS and we got hold of *Nightmare Castle* in Italian with Spanish subtitles...." I was really moved. I would never have imagined it.

Rome, 2013

1967 Call Me François
The Cinema of Franco Rossetti

"If you're a coffin maker ... sure did pick a good town to settle, sure did."
—Ángel Álvarez in *Django*, 1966

They dealt in violence and death!—American tagline for *The Dirty Outlaws*, 1967

Neither beauty nor perfection, but the possibility of things: "In chaos, there is fertility." The apparently random alignment of events and suggestions within disarray create not art but the potentiality of it, the inception of creativity and fruitfulness. When French-born novelist and passionate eroticist Anaïs Nin put pen to paper and wrote this simple yet profoundly truthful intuition, the last possible thing she might have had in mind was the Italian film industry of the fifties and sixties. Yet it works perfectly in describing this multi-layered world made up of ever-mutating rules, and moved by abstract and arbitrary parameters. A world that had the silhouette of an industry—churning out a great number of internationally competitive films, directors and adaptable genres—but not the somatic traits of one. The arrival of the American Hollywood machine on Italian soil, and the parallel economic revival that accompanied it, had created a number of overlapping productions and new realities. A garden with impeccably kept rows of flowers and firmly rooted plants but in which nothing is ripped out, and weeds, unpredictable herbs and all plant life are allowed to grow freely. Films of any and every kind: pale imitations; low-budget products filled with a rainbow of pseudonyms strategically placed to cozen and mislead spectators; films financed by improvised producers; retailers, small-businessmen and merchants of every shape and size attracted by the honey-glazed promises of cinema: money, sex and the possibility of mingling with stars and sexually available comets. Each one of them with an idea and a lover or girlfriend to launch into stardom. The contradictions and competiveness were many and fierce. Rome, in the space of less than a decade, had become one big film studio and Cinecittà the pulsating heart of it, with tentacles that radiated and touched the whole country. Films, production companies and projects were born and died out in a continuous loop. When asked about the atmosphere in the late fifties, Giulio Petroni gave one of the most lucid answers: "You could enter one of the bars in the center of Rome for an espresso and come out with a signed contract for a film and sometimes you would have an appointment with a producer at some bar and leave having only sipped an espresso." Offices became cafes and restaurants or wherever business was taking place and not only in the golden caves that animated Via Veneto and the other roads and alleys of the dolce vita, but everywhere and anywhere. As the words of Alberto De Martino perfectly summarize: "Once your foot was in, you were bombarded with promises and offers. Everybody had a plan and every plan included you, somehow. Cinema was a complex world to move in because it was so full of crooks and artists. Sometimes crooked artists."

In 1959 *Ben-Hur* by William Wyler is released, becoming the majestic epitome of the previously American-dominated years and a marvelous swan song that sanctions the end of "Hollywood on the Tiber." It is accompanied by other period adventure films and peplums animated by varied ambitions and budgets, such as *La battaglia di Maratona* (*The Giant of Marathon*) by Jacques Tourneur (and Mario Bava, who steps in to reshoot some sequences) and *Gli ultimi giorni di Pompei* (*The Last Days of Pompeii*) by Mario Bonnard (and Sergio Leone, who finishes the film due to Bonnard's deteriorating health), both films with Steve Reeves and followed by big distributions helmed by MGM and United Artists respectively. But that same year, comedian Totò impressively makes five films, among which is Lucio Fulci's debut, *I ladri* (*The Thieves*); Roberto Bianchi Montero directs four films between comedies and soap-opera melodramas, while Marino Girolami directs three; Roberto Rossellini and Mario Monicelli make film history, the first by directing Vittorio De Sica in *Il generale Della Rovere* (*General Della Rovere*) while the second conquers the Academy Awards with *La grande guerra* (*The Great War*); Mario Bava helps Riccardo Freda, giving a sense of direction to the blob-like creature of *Caltiki—il mostro immortale* (*Caltiki—The Immortal Monster*). This is just part of a pinnacle, seeing that in 1959 more than 110 Italian films are made, each stemming from different soils, from dry and dusty to fresh and rich, all belonging to the same wondrous garden—a jungle-like garden in which surviving meant having a series of tools and capabilities that had little or nothing to do with talent. Struggle and squeeze, chase and climb, hunt down, accept compromise and seduce. "Producers considered us ... not all of course but many, interchangeable, and so timing was an issue. You had to convince them in the least amount of time possible that you were the right person for the job, the only person that really understood what the film was about." These are the words of Romolo Guerrieri, who adds, "This goes for all those people perceived as genre directors, of course." A concept which perfectly matches and is made even more complete by what Giorgio Capitani says about the surviving skills necessary: "The most important thing was being liked. People had to like you. It didn't matter how good your ideas were, if you couldn't impose your charisma and persona it was all useless and I'm not talking about the set but at parties, during meetings with producers, at premieres…"

"Have you ever fallen in love with a woman who didn't reciprocate your feelings for her? That mixture of hope and fear ... that is me and cinema. With the difference that cinema wasn't straight with me, she didn't refuse me but kept me hanging on, flirting and playing with my feelings." This is one of the very first things Franco Rossetti (1 October 1930, Siena–11 June 2018, Rome) told me as soon as I sat down on one of the chairs placed around a wooden table, full of bottles of water and medicines neatly clustered together in their boxes, in his small, modest living room. I knew straight away that Rossetti wasn't like any of the people I had interviewed previously.

All the names mentioned up to this point—Petroni possibly being the only exception, having had a prolific parallel career as a writer and journalist—owe their first opportunity of directing to their activities as ADs or documentary makers, regardless of having all participated, at one point or another, credited or mostly uncredited, to scripts often of films they would later end up working on as assistant directors. This makes Franco Rossetti the first figure, and one of the only ones present in this book, to have built a solid reputation as a screenwriter before helming a film. His work as a screenwriter had been so solid that it has always overshadowed his career as a director, which is made up of seven films for the big screen and one for television and begins in 1967 with the genre he has dedicated himself the most to, Westerns.

Like De Martino and Mario Caiano, Rossetti's career begins with the classic trend for newcomers which he ironically defines as "a bit of serving in paradise and some more serving in hell." Rossetti works on a handful of films as second assistant director—lowbrow comedies on the one side and films with big institutional names like Monicelli and Steno on the other. This, immediately after having gotten his degree at the CSC the same year of fellow alumnus Umberto Lenzi, and then passes on to historical and mythological adventure films but not as a

Franco Rossetti observes his leading lady, Barbara Bouchet, on the set of *A Completely Naked Female Horse*, 1972 (courtesy Franco Rossetti).

second unit director, like most of his colleagues, but as a screenwriter. His natural predisposition to words, together with a reserved and sensitive character, don't make him an ideal AD, as he himself admits: "I would do my job and sometimes do it well but I didn't, perhaps, have the necessary resilience that ADs should have." He tells me this with a tranquility that is only apparent. Talking about his career moves and shifts things within him as he reflects before answering each one of my questions. He often turns towards my direction and asks me what I think of these films of his I am referring to, but he is not searching for compliments, certainly not looking for approval or appraisal but simply trying to understand who he is talking to and to test my sense of analysis and objectivity. I can tell he doesn't care about the impression people might have of him. His image is not something he is concerned about. It doesn't take him long to turn the interview into an intimate conversation in which what I have to say is as important as what he is telling me. All this as his caregiver moves around in the kitchen preparing what I gather will be his lunch. "I can smell cigarettes. Do you smoke?" "Yes. Camels." "Ah I used to smoke those as well. Light one up and let me have a puff, but hurry before she comes back."

"Franco didn't have the temperament of a director" were the words Lenzi had used talking about Rossetti when I had met with him and in a way I can see what he meant.

Rossetti is a man of thought and caution, a man of dialogue. "I judge people for their ideas and opinions. Working with people I don't feel esteem for, intellectual esteem, is something very hard for me." I open the living room window that looks out onto a stretch of white, severe-looking buildings, typical of the fascist architecture of EUR, in the south of Rome. I slip the lighted cigarette between his smooth, slim fingers. "Am I holding it right?" I knew he was blind before going to meet him and despite his whitened eyes and his perennial "staring into darkness" as he puts it, he has a mental vivacity that is palpable. "I listen to films now." He tilts his head back and says: "God I miss smoking so much…"

After having entered the realm of cinema, after a number of scripts, he will work extensively without being credited (films by Freda, Vittorio Cottafavi and Franco Rossi), and having proven himself a valid pen, he chooses to abandon the mythological context and dedicates himself entirely to the new genre that was rapidly conquering the market. "I preferred Westerns because you could inject them with more imagination, more metaphors. Peplums had more rules and were a more restrictive genre. It was all too traditional, tied too much to the American perspective: the hero and the fights, good against evil. Westerns were more modern." Throughout the sixties, Rossetti associates his name mainly to that of Ferdinando Baldi and more importantly to Sergio Corbucci. The two meet for *Romolo e Remo* (*Duel of the Titans*, 1961) and Rossetti will write four more films for him. Despite having to adapt to numerous currents and, more importantly, to completely opposite approaches within the Western genre—the most representative example would be the musical Western with Rita Pavone and Terence Hill *Little Rita nel West* (*Rita of the West*, a.k.a. *Crazy Westerners*, 1967) by Baldi—Rossetti manages to create a recognizable touch and imagery. It is now a historically given fact that he is the writer who is principally responsible for *Django* (1966), which represents not only Rossetti's most successful film but also the epicenter of his specific vision of the West.

"I've always liked throwing my characters in the mud." I can't help but interpret this statement as something actual as well as metaphorical. Rossetti's protagonists are losers, both in the idiomatic way of intending the word and more literally because they can't "keep hold of the things they love." Melancholy is what punctuates all of Rossetti's career both as a writer and as a director. When I tell him this, he turns towards my voice quite suddenly: "I've always thought that a certain melancholic view of the world seeps through my films." His debut as director launches the career of Andrea Giordana, a promising new star who had emerged from television and his story is completely based on the injustices faced by the protagonist—like with Nero in *Django*, Terence Hill in *Preparati la bara* (*Django Prepare a Coffin*, 1968) or Leonard Mann (Leonardo Manzella) in *Ciakmull—L'uomo della vendetta* (*Chuck Moll*, a.k.a. *The Unholy Four*, 1970), Enzo Barboni's first and only straight Western as a director.

Many were surprised when Rossetti chose to jump into the director's chair and gossip at the time wanted it to be a decision he was pressured into by his wife, a well-known costume designer, Gaia Romanini. "She was ambitious and would try and push Franco to be more like her," says Lenzi. What is certain is that thanks to her prolific career, Rossetti would meet with all the top players of the time. "Our home would be constantly visited by directors and producers. Seventy percent came to see my wife and the other thirty percent came for me." He laughs while saying this, which is something he does frequently, though often his smiles culminate in frozen sighs. In everything Rossetti says, his culture comes through, followed by a strong intellectual independency that has no gods or divinities, no forces from above, no moral pre-established codes. After his first Western and a giallo worth fishing out from the oblivion it has fallen into, *Delitto al circolo del tennis* (*The Rage Within*, 1969), Rossetti broaches the seventies. Comedy is what he directs the most, films often dismissed by critics and which received good, but never great returns at the box office, labeled as rustic, nudie picks. Undoubtedly they are films completely dictated by the market but if taken separately, each one is an example of the comedic subgenre it is a part of, but put together they paint a very different picture. "I will tell you something that I've come to understand only in more recent times. All of us did films at the time, for the women ... not to have sex but to be with them.... I don't know, maybe I'm just talking nonsense. I have always been fascinated and frightened by women and I have a feeling you can tell from my films." Women in his films are on the highest pedestals, not only as objects of sexual desires but as the only possible redeeming factor in the life of a man.

Before becoming a director you were known as a prolific screenwriter, but let's start right from the beginning. Tell me about your first steps towards cinema.

Everything started with the CSC. I'm not from Rome so I came here to attend the school and after that, I went hunting for work. Unfortunately, the year I got my degree was not a good period for cinema ... there was a bit of a halt, so I took a while to get things going.

Well, Italian cinema has always been fluctuating.

Always ... always ... for pity's sake. Anyway, the good thing was, that the short film I directed at the CSC had been very much appreciated and was considered one of the best works of that year, especially story-wise. It was called *Il ritorno* [translation: *The Return*, 1956] and it helped me get my first job as a writer. You know who one of the actors in it was? Umberto Lenzi. I think it's the only thing he's ever acted in. Is he in your book?

He is.

He was a megalomaniac then as he is now and don't think for a single moment that he was any different when he was younger. I met him for the first time when he began his film club because I was immersed in that world as well. I had a club in Siena, where I was born. Tonino Valerii was also at the CSC at the time and I had initially involved him in the writing of my short, on which I was working with my Dutch girlfriend, but when he started hitting on her, I told him that his expertise was no longer needed.

Which is your first film as a writer?

I had collaborated on a few scripts previously but my first real film was *Costantino il grande* [*Constantine and the Cross*, a.k.a. *Constantine the Great*, 1961)]by Lionello De Felice. It was a film made following the Hollywood criteria but all in all it's not a bad film.

You've mentioned elsewhere that the first person connected to cinema, you meet in Rome is Ennio De Concini.[1]

Yes, knowing somebody in Rome was fundamental at the time. Moving was much more expensive but more importantly entering a new world, like the Roman one, was complicated if you knew nobody. A relative of mine recommended me to De Concini, but if I could've I would have done without this meeting. Ennio was not a person I had sympathy for. He was a "baron" of cinema, undoubtedly full of talents but on a personal level he was one of the worst people I've met. He was very competitive and would only help you if he could gain something from it. I realized, early on, that I would have never managed to get noticed or get my career going thanks to him. He made me work but always making sure I didn't get away from his shadow. I have a very frustrating anecdote regarding him. I have never told anybody and maybe it is best I continue being silent … naah, I don't care anymore, what's the point! If you want it to hear I will tell you. This pitiful chapter of my career occurred in the mid-to-late eighties. I was not working anymore in cinema, I hadn't for quite a few years but I still kept in touch with many people I had met or worked with over the years. De Concini was among these people. At the time he was still working and once, while visiting him at his house, he casually told me that Alberto Sordi wanted to do a film entitled "Il portaborse" [translated as "The Lackey"]. "What is it about?" "He just has a title. He likes the title. Why don't you write something down?" I went back home—that was a period in which I didn't have much to do—and started writing a story. The more I wrote the more I liked what was taking shape. Though, as I was conceiving this story I would not have Sordi in mind. By the late eighties he was too old to play a brown-nosing administrative consultant, plus I wasn't giving the script—well actually more of a first treatment—any ironic or comical overtones. It was all quite serious. Anyway, I give this fifty-page treatment back to De Concini, and forgot about it. I was used to these sort of things … not as much as other screenwriters, most of what I wrote got made, but still when you turn in a script you never know how things develop. In fact, years pass and I forget about the whole thing until I read in a newspaper that Nanni Moretti was working on a film, directed by Daniele Lucchetti, called *Il portaborse* [*The Factotum*, 1991], as an actor and producer. I call De Concini and he tells me that he had given my script to a couple of writers that gravitated around Moretti, one was a certain Franco Bernini. "But they probably just used the title. It's going to be released next week, go and check it out." I did and it was my film, of course it had been adapted for Moretti's persona and many elements had been modified but the main story and plot twists were identical. The only thing Ennio had to say was, "I think it's too late to do anything." That was the last script I wrote. Lucchetti's film was very successful and was nominated for the Palme d'Or at the Cannes Film Festival.

You mentioned that there were other scripts that never developed into films. Any example?

In the early sixties I was good friends with Walter Chiari and he fell in love with a story I had written and asked me to develop it. I would often be at his house brainstorming and talking about this film. He firmly felt it could become an important film. The story was about a writer, novelist, who goes to Venice for a few days to pick up a literary prize he is being awarded. While there he meets a woman for which he loses his mind, falling in love. They pass those days in Venice always together in a passionate embrace. Then they part ways and he goes back to his wife, a woman that doesn't have his intellect but is nonetheless a woman of many qualities, intelligent and understanding. He, though, feels the artistic urge to write about those Venetian days and in his mind the story for his next novel develops. His wife becomes increasingly suspicious and he cannot hide the romantic enthusiasm he feels while writing this book of his but he has to do something, because as much as his creativity is fueled by the memory of this woman, he doesn't want to leave his wife. So he has an idea. He decides, before starting each chapter to relive those days with his wife, to reenact everything, so making her believe his novel is about her, about them. They leave for Venice and he leads his wife through each pivotal moment of those three days. In doing so, he discovers aspects of his wife he had never realized existed and what begins as a mechanical reenactment becomes something independent. I don't remember how it ends, if he tells her the truth or she discovers it on her own. Chiari loved it, though he wanted to develop the lighter tone of the story. We passed many hours fleshing out every aspect of the script.

Why wasn't it ever made?

Actors, big actors like he was at the time, fell in love with ideas and projects all the time, more than one at a time. The majority get abandoned. He was all over the place in that period, doing films, having affairs, travelling all over the world. It just disappeared after a while, but I liked Chiari, he was a sweet man, very hyper and energizing but kind and very warm with those he liked, and I think he liked me. His house was full of people, intellectuals, directors and writers. Specifically, in the years in question—because this project took some time to evaporate—a person who was always visiting his house was Lucio Fulci.

What kind of person was Fulci?

Intelligent, quite cultured though less cultured than how he is depicted nowadays. People speak of him like he was some sort of messiah. He was undoubtedly very smart and pungent. Though he would smell, he had a terrible personal hygiene. His shirts and trousers were full of grease stains. That said, I can speak well of him. He was very sexualized, he would always look out for the possibility of hooking up with some woman. He probably felt he had to compensate for an appearance which wasn't exactly appealing. Though he did nothing to help himself.

I imagine this "hyper-sexuality," as you defined it, was common to many people in that environment.

Actors aside, most producers and directors if they hadn't chosen this particular profession they would have never seen a woman, not even with binoculars in their dreams. Many people I met had a reverence towards women due to the fact that they felt their social stature was one of the main reasons they could be desirable. I'm not only talking about financial power but also creative and artistic merits. De Concini would have women that were fascinated with his way with words and he was kind of sweet because despite his age and reputation he would fall in love as soon as a woman talked to him.

You were, for many years, the closest collaborator of director Ferdinando Baldi. You wrote a number of scripts for him. What kind of person was he?

A very good, decent person but as a director he never had any strokes of genius. He played it safe and would just do what was strictly necessary, but his films would have big names, like Terence Hill and Franco Nero. We drifted apart in later years ... he's dead, isn't he?

Yes, he died quite some time ago.

Anyway, I can only speak well of Ferdinando. He was a sure-handed director, in the typical Italian tradition. He needed good scripts though, in the sense that he wasn't the kind of director who could save a film through sheer technical inventiveness and creativity. I recently found myself thinking back to a film I had written, with a certain amount of enthusiasm, for him, *Preparati la bara* [*Django, Prepare a Coffin*, 1968]. I remember

The Italian poster of the cult western *Django Prepare a Coffin*, written by Rossetti in 1968.

thinking at the time that he had directed it appropriately. Do you know what I mean by that? He followed the rules, competently. He was one of the few directors who would stick religiously to the text, so if he had a solid script, the film would turn out all right but he wasn't able to take it to the next level. The title isn't mine, that was the idea of producer Manolo Bolognini, who was from Tuscany like myself and had a passion for playwright Sem Benelli, so he got the title from a play of his.

Prepare a Coffin *is, from an iconographic point of view, indissolubly tied to* **Django** *[1966], which you wrote.*

Yes, in the way the character is presented, aesthetically speaking, and of course by the fact that the protagonist has the same name. But I can tell you that while I was writing it, I wasn't thinking of Corbucci's film and if I'd had a choice, I wouldn't have put any references in the script to link the two films together. From the moment I was hired, that was the deal and the producer's wishes.

Django *has become a bona fide classic.*

Even too much so. It irritates me, all this talking about *Django*.

Why?

Well, maybe it's due to old memories. That wasn't an easy film to work on, even because … I will tell you something that I haven't told anybody … Sergio Corbucci didn't want to make the film. He didn't like going to Spain to shoot, he preferred staying in Italy much more. He hated getting planes and having to move around and he didn't like the script I had written with Piero Vivarelli, but most of all he didn't like the concept, the whole premise of the film. *Django* was something he struggled a lot with—Corbucci I mean—before deciding to do it. He was unenthusiastic throughout the whole writing process and would find excuses to procrastinate. In fact, at one point he called in his brother Bruno to have a look at the script. I mean, scripts were always passed around, but in that case it was surreal. It even ended up in Fernando Di Leo's hands at one point. It was a circus that was very depressing for a writer to observe. Something that could never happen in the United States. In Hollywood the writers are the only ones that have rights on their work. But we have never really been an industry. It looked like one, from the outside, but really we weren't part of an industry.

From where, exactly, did **Django** *germinate? When interviewed, Vivarelli stated that the initial idea was his.*

That's funny. Well, I guess he would say something like that. Now, this is how the story goes. In the mid-sixties I would hang out at Piero's house quite often. We were both born in Siena and knew each other fairly well. At the time he was married to a woman who was very wifely and his place was a seaport: people coming and going at every hour of the day, though Vivarelli, as they say in my region, "didn't have a coin to make a blind man dance." Completely broke. I had just begun my collaboration with Corbucci, shortly before. So, when Corbucci called me up to help him with an idea for a Western he was trying to put together, I decided to involve Piero. I had already written *L'uomo che ride* [*The Man Who Laughs*, 1966] for Corbucci, among other things, so he trusted me, but when he gave me fifteen days to write this Western of his, I told him I would need some kind of collaborator, someone who could help me. Fifteen days to write a script from scratch is too short a time. "Get whoever you want but I will be speaking only to you. I consider you the person responsible."

What exactly was Corbucci's idea? You said you had to write from scratch so I guess he had nothing really written down. No synopsis or outline.

Oh no, nothing of the sort. But it was fairly common for a director or producer to give a writer just a few elements to work from: a context, sometimes a title, a gimmick of some kind, a name. It could be anything. I don't remember what Corbucci's indications were but I remember them being muddled and vague. However, in spite of my attempt at involving Vivarelli, I ended up writing the script practically by myself. Vivarelli became disinterested in the film at a very early stage. But he did come back into the picture once I had left. Because when I gave Corbucci the script and realized what his attitude was towards the film, I went my own way and stopped participating in it anymore. At that point I know that Vivarelli kind of returned, though I have no idea how deep his involvement ended up being.

How different is the film compared to your script?

The story changed quite a bit but a lot of the details and elements survived and I think also a certain simplicity. My story was very essential, minimalist. Not to mention the violence, that was present from the start. I consider *Django* one of mine, but not as mine as other films, like Baldi's film we mentioned before. I have to confess I'm a bit fed up of talking about, and listening to people discussing about *Django*. I think better things have been made in the genre in that same period by others, by Corbucci and by me. Plus, all this business with Tarantino and his film… I'm a little bored by the whole thing. Bored and irritated.

You wrote some of Corbucci's most famous films of the sixties but **Bersaglio mobile** *[Death on the Run, a.k.a.* **Moving Target***, 1967] is a big exception.*

Was that film even finished? I remember being flanked by a certain Massimo Patrizi, who was the son of Luigi Comencini. The film was hurried and I think it was interrupted and picked up again at a later stage. Those were prolific and confused times. Before I said that prior to *Constantine and the Cross,* I had worked on a few scripts but that was a superficial way of putting it because, even if uncredited, I did some things I'm very happy about. I think nobody knows that I helped out on *I giganti della Tessaglia—Gli Argonauti* [*The Giants of Thessaly*, 1960] by Riccardo Freda. He liked me, and I thought highly of him … he was a cultured and intelligent man. In that same period, I wrote a film for Vittorio Cottafavi, with Duccio Tessari: *Messalina, Venere imperatrice* [*Messalina*, 1960]. I should have been credited for that film because I worked on it for a long time. I didn't get along with Cottafavi as much as I did with Freda. He was cordial but a bit stuck-up and didn't have much of a sense of humor.

What are your feelings in relation to **Ciakmull—L'uomo della vendetta** *[Chuck Moll, a.k.a.* **The Unholy Four***, 1970]?*

It's a film that was a little mistreated upon its release. I'm responsible for both story and script. I was happy with my work but I realized immediately, because I would go and visit the set, that Enzo Barboni had no idea what he was doing. It just wasn't in his style but the film has a certain charm and I feel a kind of benevolence towards it.

Let's talk about your debut. It had to be a Western: **El desperado** *[The Dirty Outlaws, a.k.a.* **Big Ripoff***, a.k.a.* **King of the West***, a.k.a.* **The Desperado***, 1967]. How was the transition from writer to director?*

When I got a chance to direct my first film, I was going strong as a screenwriter. If

I remember correctly, one of the last films I wrote before making my debut was *Little Rita nel west* [*Rita of the West*, a.k.a. *Crazy Westerners*, 1967] again by Baldi and that also went well. A nice film, by the way. The idea of making a musical Western was not mine but I must say a gracious little thing came out of it. Anyhow, I had been trying to make the transition from writer to director for some time but things never seemed to line up properly. Everything changed thanks to Ugo Guerra, who had been a prolific and successful writer himself and by that time was trying to become a producer. I think he had already produced a few films before but nothing really worthy of attention. So you can say that we unified our ambitions.

What do you think of the film?
I like it. I made it enthusiastically and believed in it. I think the only real, objective problem with it was the actor, Andrea Giordana. He looked too much like a kid and had trouble even holding a gun properly. That kind of role needed more of an actor like Gemma, clean-cut but manly. The film is still appreciated now so I guess it works despite Giordana. You know I made *The Dirty Outlaws* against the opinion of my whole family including my wife, who was a well-known costume designer. The fact of making my debut in that genre, they said, was beneath me and it would have trapped me as a genre director forever. The very first review I read of *The Dirty Outlaws* was written by a certain Dario Argento and he gave a very good analysis of the film.

The film made money and you were considered a specialist of the genre having written at least half a dozen films. So, why did you only direct one Western?
Shortly after wrapping up my film I was offered another Western. A reinterpretation of Hamlet, written by Sergio Corbucci. *Johnny Hamlet* I think it was called. Then the title was changed to *Quella sporca storia nel west* [translation: *That Dirty Story in the West*, 1967]. Initially Sergio had to direct it but after my refusal, it ended up in the hands of Castellari. I chose not to direct it because I thought the concept was absurd and, I don't know, I just believed that Shakespeare and Westerns was not a winning combination. I'm told that the final result is not exactly a masterpiece.

In nearly every filmography of yours, you appear as one of the writers responsible for Michelangelo Antonioni's Zabriskie Point *[1970].*
I know, but I never worked on that film. I would have loved to but I just didn't. You know, for some time I even received money from the SIAE[2] and I had to call and tell them that I had nothing to do with *Zabriskie Point*. I don't know where this misunderstanding originated from.[3]

Your second film is a giallo, an atypical and unlucky film, Delitto al circolo del tennis **[The Rage Within, 1969]. All the subsequent films you direct in the seventies are tied together by characteristics not present in your first two films. Desecrating stories, often decadent, in which the satirized elements are punctuated by an eroticism that often gives rise to an abundant dose of morbidity.**
Yes, the switch from one decade to the other is quite radical. I would have wanted to direct other Westerns but consider that, in addition to not liking what was being offered, the genre was beginning to die out. It continued to go strong for some more years but its death was in the air. *The Rage Within* seemed like an interesting diversion from the genre I had worked on for so many years but it was unlucky, as you said, as far as the box office was concerned. Then again it was appreciated among insiders, professionals

and colleagues. Did you know the photography of the film is by Vittorio Storaro? The first color film he made. It's a film that was too big a flop to put me in the position of choosing whatever I wanted for my next film, but it was favorably looked upon by my peers, which enabled me to continue my career. From then on, though, I had to succumb even more to the demands of the market.

The Rage Within *is a giallo that is very difficult to place in the Italian panorama of the time. It has no connection with what will be done in the genre the following decade and it doesn't seem to be inspired, unlike Lenzi's and Guerrieri's gialli, by French cinema.*

This is because my film originates from television ... that's where the idea came from. There had been a few very popular mystery stories made for television that took place in the world of sports and in fact, my film is set in a tennis club. I wrote the story with Ugo Guerra—well actually he wrote very little—who had produced *The Dirty Outlaws* and who produced this film as well. Goffredo Lombardo was the distributor. At one point, between the two, there was a big diatribe concerning the title. Guerra stuck by the one he had chosen during pre-production [which translates as "Murder at the Tennis Club"] which he had bought the rights from Alberto Moravia, who had written a novel by the same title. Lombardo instead insisted that it was too tame and that the risk of people confusing it with a TV movie leftover, was very high. I strongly believe the fiasco of the film was due to the weak title but I'm to blame as well. Lombardo and Guerra came to me and asked me to take sides and seeing I'm an honest asshole, I took Guerra's side. He had helped me direct my first film and felt I had to remain loyal to him. Of course, I was the one who paid the biggest consequences because Lombardo, who mind you, loved the film, changed his initial plan and distributed the film terribly.

So your next film is not one you would have chosen?

Una cavalla tutta nuda [translation: *A Completely Naked Female Horse*, 1972] is a film I chose once I realized that a comedy was the only film they wanted me to direct. I have something curious to tell you about the film. At the time, I was a regular at Manolo Bolognini's office. I had been for a long time, but during that period I was writing *Naked Female Horse* and another person who would often be there was Pier Paolo Pasolini. I don't remember if they were working together on *Teorema* [1968] or something else; anyway Manolo asks me if he can show my script to Pasolini. Keep in mind that in the late sixties, early seventies "decamerotici"[4] didn't exist. There was nothing of the sort. Some time goes by and I forget about this small episode until halfway through the production of *Female Horse,* Pasolini's *Il decameron* [*The Decameron*, 1971] is released. It's a strange coincidence, don't you think? I knew Pasolini and I liked him. We had met many years before through Ennio De Concini. My story was based on a specific and lesser-known novella by Boccaccio, "Il decamerone," which is also present in Pasolini's film. Plus, I had added a lot of dialogue because, in the typical style of Boccaccio, his novella was very bare and lacking in it. When I went to the cinema to see Pasolini's film, I noticed that some of the lines were extremely similar to the ones I had written. Now, I'm not saying that he stole from me ... but maybe, after reading my script, some parts of it lingered in his mind and ended up, subconsciously, in his film....

Was Barbara Bouchet your choice?

Well, yes ... I mean she was chosen in accordance with the producers. Even if I was the real producer of that film.

Franco Rossetti (on the ladder) and DOP Roberto Girometti (peering over Rossetti's shoulder) on the set of *A Completely Naked Female Horse* (courtesy Roberto Girometti).

What do you mean?

Initially Bolognini wanted to do it but then he backed away so I decided to produce it with an American friend of mine called Jack Lauder. He was supposed to be the main producer and I was more of an executive let's say, but money ran out and we had to involve a third person, whose name we had better not mention. Someone who had nothing to do with the world of cinema. I was the only person who knew what he was doing, so I became the one who had to deal with everything and ended up putting in a lot more of my money than what I had initially planned.

It did quite well at the box office.

In Tuscany and Naples, for example, yes, it made good money but in the north of Italy the film was invisible. Let's start by saying that it was badly distributed. At the time, films were distributed either by national companies, like *The Dirty Outlaws* which was distributed by Interfilms, or by regional distributors, which were, for the most part, delinquents. Usually, for comedies or low-budget films, you would entrust the distribution to these pirates who, in some cases, would change the titles, add scenes, sell the film without your permission... Stuff like that. Plus, *Naked Female Horse* has a very specific geographical collocation: it's all spoken in Tuscan dialect, which might have made it a little harder to sell. The dubbing director of the film was Duccio Tessari, who accepted to do it out of friendship and did a good job.

It's very raunchy. Barbara Bouchet is naked throughout the whole film. Did you have any problems with her, from this point of view?

With Bouchet?! No, she was very comfortable in those scenes. She liked being watched, being admired. For some obscure reason she has always been dismissive of the

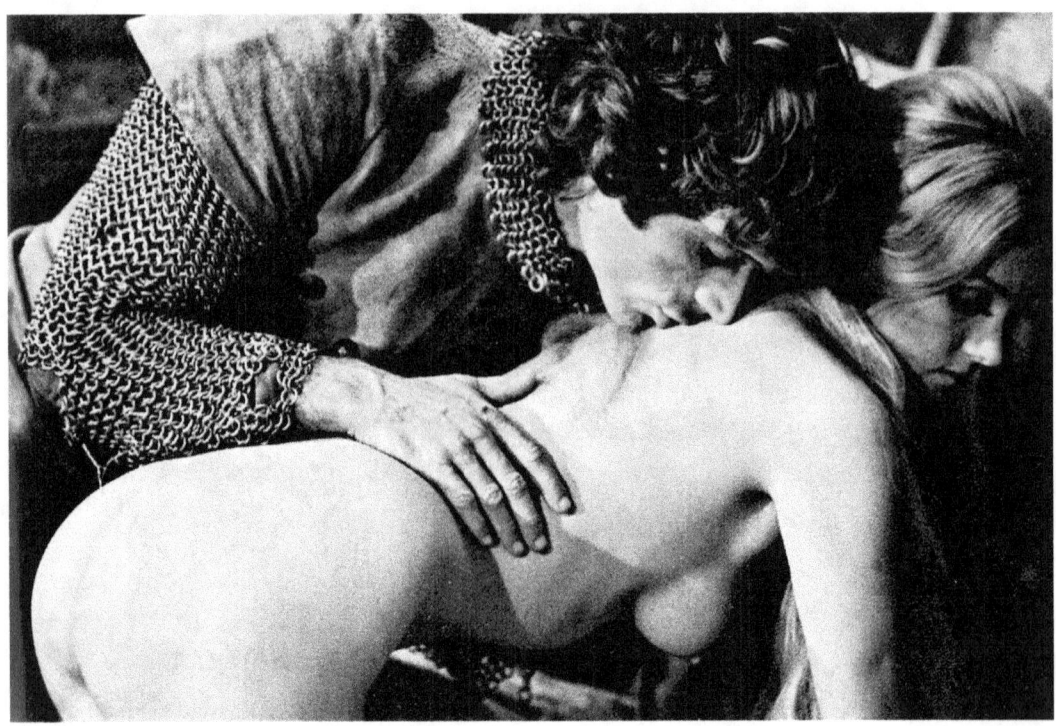

Don Backy and Barbara Bouchet in one of the most audacious examples of the "decamerotic" subgenre: *A Completely Naked Female Horse* (courtesy Nocturno Cinema).

film. "Oh, but that's nothing. A film of no importance." Once I met her husband, producer Luigi Borghese, and he complimented me on the film, defining it a delicate fairy-tale for adults. I thanked him and went: "What's your wife's problem?" He just smiled. Even because ... as I speak, things come to mind ... shortly after I'd made the film, I went to the theater with my wife, since she had to speak with Pasquale Festa Campanile, who was the director of the play, and we met Bouchet. She was enthusiastic and continued repeating that if I had another film in the making, to please give her a role.

Speaking about sex, tell me about one of your most mysterious films, Il mondo porno di due sorelle *[translation:* **The Pornographic World of Two Sisters,** *a.k.a.* **Emanuelle and Joanna,** *1979].*

Technically it's a porn film but I don't consider it so. Porn films, real ones, are gynecological. Sexual organs and blowjobs all shown in extreme close-ups. I shot those scenes for what they were ... in an anthropological way, if you know what I mean. I have to say that I like this film very much. I don't want to seem like a victim, because I realize I've been complaining a lot during this interview, but you can't imagine how difficult it was to get this film made. No money and no help whatsoever. Both story and script are mine. I got inspiration from the short story by a Spanish writer, born in the nineteenth century, called Ramón Gómez de la Serna. I wrote the first version of the script in the early seventies and it took me nearly a decade to get the film made.

What can you tell me about the actresses, Sherry Buchanan and Paola Montenero?

Sherry Buchanan was a starlet, who had mostly done publicity. Paola Montenero I don't remember where I fished her out from. I don't think she did much afterwards. I have to confess something... While making this film, I fell madly in love with Sherry. It made things even harder for me on set because directing somebody you are falling in love with is not an easy task. Anyway, I chose both of them through agencies, terrible second-class agencies.

The hardcore scenes were all directed by yourself?

Yes, using doubles, of course. Even there, everything was surreal. I had asked for a double for Sherry, who was very delicate, with a small nose and big eyes. One of the most beautiful faces I have ever seen. They sent me a woman, taller than I am with a huge nose, big bones... Once they sent a black woman to double a white actress. It was all pretty grotesque.

These scenes were conceived for which market?

This is how things went. The film was produced by Anaconda Films and their only condition was that the film should include some porn scenes. So I knew from the start that these scenes had to be shot and in fact, we used the same sets, costumes and locations. As a matter of fact, part of the cast was made up of porn actors. The explicit version was used for the foreign market, mainly French, and the softer version for the Italian one. But those were decisions made by the distributors. The scenes were directed by me with the help of a 1st AD I had chosen, who had experience in the field of porn.

Did you ever direct anything else, maybe using a pseudonym, in a similar vein? And secondly, did the actors know that a hardcore montage would have been made? Buchanan has said that she didn't know about this.

It's possible she wasn't fully aware. She was very naïve and confused at the time. She could hardly understand any Italian. However, she can't really go around saying she had no idea what was going on because even though she was never in any explicit scenes, she did mime a blowjob, for example. I can say that I'm pretty sure Paola Montenero knew about everything. As far as having directed anything else, with pornographic inserts, the answer is no. I simply wasn't offered anything like that. I might have accepted.

Montenero knew about everything. What do you remember of her?

That she was coked up at every hour of the day. She would arrive on set literally with her nose white with cocaine. She wasn't even discreet about it. The producers were worried she would overdose on set. Once I had to interrupt the shoot because she was losing blood from her nose for having snorted too much.

You signed the film as Fred Gardner. Why? You said you liked the film, so why did you feel the necessity of an alias?

Because Italy is a bigoted and ignorant country and hiding behind a fake name was necessary. There was a high risk of being labeled as a pornographer and I didn't want that.

You said that some members of the cast were professional porn actors. Who were you referring to, exactly?

Marina Frajese[5] has a role in the film, a small one, for example. She was a real nymphomaniac. I'm not exaggerating, believe me. I would go "cut" and she would continue fucking. Her life was basically one long orgy and once in a while a director would shoot a bit of it for his film.... I was once told that on a film she started sucking an actor's dick, I believe Aldo Sambrell, and he couldn't get away. They had to pull her off, in front of all the crew.

Shortly before Emanuelle and Joanna, *you had directed a completely different film. I'm talking about* Quel movimento che mi piace tanto *[translation:* That Movement That I Like So Much, *1976].*

I officially disown that film. There, I said it. I refuse and disavow that film! But we can talk about it.

What is the first thing that comes to mind when you think about the film and why all this hatred?

The choice of the city was wrong. Siena is a closed city, too cryptic. Arezzo, which is not very far away, would have been much better. It's more provincial but at the same time it's younger and sunnier. I should have shot it there. Plus, in Siena we couldn't find extras. I had two assistants on that film who were both completely incompetent. One of the two was Carlo Verdone[6] who was on the first, or maybe second, set of his life and didn't know what he was doing. I sent them looking for people for bit parts but it was a massacre. All these things though, were minor aspects compared to the actor, the protagonist, Carlo Giuffrè. He was a mediocre actor, very presumptuous and too old for the role and to be flanked by an actress like Cinzia Monreale.

You and Vittorio Sindoni are the two directors who launched Monreale's career, years before the horror films of Lucio Fulci and Joe D'Amato. What do you remember about her?

I liked Cinzia. She had a fresh, modern face. She was different to the other actresses active in the so-called "commedia sexy." There were big fights between the two during production, between her and Giuffrè. Oh, yes… He was intolerable … a drama queen. Aldo, his brother, was much better and had a more interesting face. Anyway, the best cast of my directing career was the one I had for *Nipoti miei diletti* [translation: *My Dear Nephews*, 1974]: Romolo Valli, Adriana Asti, Luciano Salce…

…and Marc Porel and Renzo Palmer. Was that a film made thanks to the massive success of Malizia *[Malice, a.k.a.* Malicious, *1973] by Salvatore Samperi?*

Yes, light, incest-themed erotic comedies were a thing, a new taboo to break, if you like. Formally, it's probably my best film. We were poor devils but we managed to do some things that weren't bad.

The director of photography for most of your career was Roberto Girometti.

Girometti was a very good DOP and I don't think he has received the attention and recognition he deserves. I have had people come up and congratulate me on the photography of some of the films we made together. "It's not my doing," I have to tell them, unless we take for granted the paradox that the operator and DOP direct the film and the director is responsible for the photography. It's a paradox Gianni Minervini used to draw attention to and it makes sense, if you think about it.

By the late seventies did you sense that things were changing for Italian cinema?

Maybe yes, but if I did, I probably underestimated whatever it was I felt. Italian cinema has always been inconsistent and impossible. Maybe I was unlucky but I don't have fond memories of the cinema world. The films I managed to make, I made despite everything: often sloppy actors, producers ... let's not even talk about them! I will just say that the producer of *That Movement* was called "er sola" [a term that in Roman dialect means an unreliable scoundrel]. I had to struggle during my entire career, for everything. I didn't abandon cinema, cinema abandoned me. By the early eighties I couldn't find work and the few things I was offered were indecent stuff I wouldn't even consider.

**But you did direct one film during the eighties. Al limite cioè ... non glielo dico *[translation:* Well Then, I Mean ... I Won't Tell Her, *1984].*

Yes, that was a film produced by Istituto Luce thanks to Article 28, so mostly done with government funding. I love it like I'd love a son but it was released in Rome and Bari for two days and then vanished. Granted, the film didn't have a great cast. Massimo Wertmuller, who is the protagonist, and Carlo Taranto are the biggest names, but the problem was that the producer was a crook. I know, I know, I'm being a victim again.... Nicolò Pomilia did the film knowing he wouldn't distribute it, and ran away with the money secured through Article 28. I had met this Pomilia in the sixties, through my wife, because he had been a production manager on *Tepepa* [a.k.a. *Blood and Guns*, 1968], and my wife was responsible for the costumes of that film. You know, she worked with all the directors of that period. I remember she liked Alberto De Martino a lot. He died recently ... how?

A cardiac arrest, if I'm not mistaken.

Ah, yes ... now that is a way to die.... Anyhow, this is my most Roman film and the last chapter of a sad love affair.

Let's close the circle. At the start of this interview I said that you became well-known as a writer, but that wasn't your only activity in the initial part of your career. You worked as an AD as well, especially between 1957 and 1959.

I began working as an AD thanks to an uncle of mine who was an official at the National Bank of Agriculture and he put in a good word for me with a producer called Felice Felicioni. Most of the films of that period, I did with him. I worked on *Il medico e lo stregone* [*Doctor and the Healer*, 1957] by Mario Monicelli and Steno. The former is a little overrated and the latter is seriously underrated. Steno was much nicer to work with and was much more fun. But I can't say I learned much from either. The director I absorbed the most from is Franco Rossi. Rossi wasn't an auteur, he was a director and a very good one. But my first film was *La canzone del destino* [translation: *The Song of Destiny*, 1957] with Claudio Villa. Romolo Guerrieri was Marino Girolami's 1st AD and I was Guerrieri's assistant. Girolami began his career only because he was fortunate enough to have Mario Soldati as a next-door neighbor, and a very noisy neighbor too ... and after the last of numerous arguments with Girolami, he gave him his first job. Soldati knew that he wanted to be in the business and had been working as an extra. Girolami was really a boxer and remained one even after he had retired from sports. He was a super-competitive, macho type and very stingy and narrow-minded. He would shout a lot, especially at the costume department. His brother Guerrieri was a whole different matter. A nice person, more reflective and well-mannered, without the arrogance of Marino, who was, thinking back, also a hypocrite. He was very patriotic and moralistic but he ended up doing porn films. I sort of did one too, but I believed in what I was doing and I'm definitely not patriotic.... In fact, I should tell you, that I've decided to change my name. I would appreciate it if you called me François.

Adriana Asti and Marc Porel in *My Dear Nephews*, 1974 (courtesy Nocturno Cinema).

Why François?

For an old love of mine for France and French cinema. I like the idea of being French. It's an appreciation, the one for this culture, that had ancient roots in me.

You don't feel Italian?

Very little Italian. There is very little of this country in me.

Who is François Rossetti?

A director not worse than many others. I can't say much more.

We have been talking about all your career, but at the end of the day what do you consider yourself: a director or a writer?

I consider myself a cinema employee. I guess I'm both but I often had to write other people's films because I wasn't being given the chance to direct. The film industry didn't give me the possibility to unload, to vent my creativity.

What is the nature, the disposition of François Rossetti?

One that isn't exactly enviable. I'm closed, shy, fundamentally timid, fundamentally … closed. Without great sympathy for the human race. I guess I'm what some people would define a loser.

Describe to me the prototype of the Rossetti hero.

It doesn't exist because what I like is not my character, my personality. I'm everything but a narcissist. I'm naturally brought to envy those with strong characters and more incisive personalities than mine.

Let's go through some people you have worked with, some we might have already mentioned. Just give me a quick portrait or definition. The first thing that comes to mind: Sergio Corbucci.

On one side affection, a feeling of affection and friendship while on the other a self-imposed need to criticize him. To be very critical of him, with myself.

Ferdinando Baldi.

A competent director, with less charisma than Corbucci. But I must say, one of the most honest and proper people I met in the business. If I was asked to describe someone proper it would probably be him.

Riccardo Freda.

I was called by Freda to work on the script of *The Giants of Thessaly*. This is the only occasion we worked together. The script was practically finished when I stepped in but Freda wasn't convinced about some aspects of it. He struck me right away as a person that knew what he was doing, and had an undeniable creative eye. To be precise he wanted, or needed me, to be able to justify the cut of a portion of the script written by Giuseppe Masini. Masini, like most neophytes, had written too much and had handed in a massive script. Among the scenes that went on for too long there was also the construction of the ship, Jason's ship, which wasn't as interesting as he probably thought. Freda asked me to decapitate Masini's script, which I did happily. Giuseppe was an intelligent man and he didn't hold a grudge. Though at the time cinema was full of improvising figures that didn't really know what they were doing.

Piero Vivarelli.

This is a rough spot … why are you asking me again about him? I'd rather skip him.

Well he's a figure you crossed…

…more than once! Me and Piero were next-door neighbors. Where my house finished, his began. It was an obligational relationship in many ways, more than a friendship. His brother would pass me films from the Museum of Cinema of Milan, sometimes precious finds like *The Freshman* [1925] with Harold Lloyd. He sent me a copy of this, and other films, for my cine-club. At the end of the day I probably had more of a relationship with his brother than with Piero himself. His brother and I had this thing going made of films and small favors. Piero, on the other hand … when I met him he was married to a very beautiful woman and his prime activity was making her jealous. For example, an actress that was going strong at the time was Cosetta Greco, who Piero would seduce and court in the way that was standard at the time … strongly and fiercely. Piero didn't have great orientation at the time, or even afterwards. He did what gave him pleasure.

Roberto Girometti.

I met him on *The Dirty Outlaws*, where he was an assistant operator. After that he worked with me as a cinematographer. I have to confess that I have always had the tendency of having a soft spot for second row people … if you know what I mean. This is not really a nice aspect of myself to be honest. Girometti worked well although I was quite disappointed when he deserted me. I called him for a film, I think it was *That Movement* and he gave me an excuse that he had to rush to India to get his brother, who was a wreck, a drug addict. He had to bail him out … I don't remember the details. I was forced to find someone else and we never worked again after that.

Again, who is Franco Rossetti?

One who tried to … someone … someone who tried, first of all, to be worthy of his father and that managed very little to do so. Maybe sometimes, in some fleeting moments he managed to rise to the occasion but for the most part he wasn't able to. Rossetti is a character that isn't dying particularly satisfied. Though, it could have gone worse … a lot worse.

Rome, 2016

1967 Destruction in Slow Motion
The Cinema of Enzo G. Castellari

"I work for nobody. I don't care about the Manhattan Corporation! I don't care about the girl, I don't care about politics, I don't care about anything! I believe in nothing. I'm Hammer—the Exterminator!" —Vic Morrow in *1990: The Bronx Warriors*, 1982

Introduction by Gian Giacomo Petrone

The opening of *Vado ... l'ammazzo e torno* (*Any Gun Can Play*, 1967), the second Western directed by Enzo G. Castellari (born 29 July 1938, Rome), sees the gunman, enigmatically called the Stranger (George Hilton), cross paths with three banditos. Despite having generic Hispanic-sounding names, the three are characterized by faces and clothing that strikingly bring to mind three great actors/characters of the Italian West: Franco Nero from Sergio Corbucci's *Django* alongside two of Leone's icons, Lee Van Cleef—Colonel Mortimer/Angel Eyes and Clint Eastwood—Joe/Monco/Blondie. The Stranger, with a few accurate gunshots, eliminates the triptych of "body doubles." Beyond the parodic intent of the sequence in the mocking dissociation from (and tribute to) the two directors who more than anyone else represented the undisputed model of spaghetti Westerns, it highlights two significant elements: firstly, that the heroes of Leone and Corbucci had already become part of the Myth and were ready to become caricatures despite the genre, which was chronologically, nonetheless, relatively fresh and still going strong; secondly, the depiction of the characters, within the genre, is described perceptively by Castellari who reveals few relevant features that are not related to the facial characteristics of the actors, but with the presence of some rather schematic outward signs which suggest an identikit rather than an identity. The clothing, together with the Spartan aesthetic charm and charisma, creates the gunman and the type of character that lurks beneath. Besides, in just a few minutes Castellari manages to create a representative, symbolic and linguistic synthesis of the major and recurrent traits of Italian Westerns, ranging from the hovering closeness of death (the protagonist is presented to us riding a chariot with three coffins), to the ironic transformation into comic book stylizations; the details and close-ups of eyes and faces cutting to long shots that depict the desolate atmosphere of the village as a backdrop to the event create a continuous, rhythmic change in the calibration of the exterior; the blowing wind, the soundtrack punctuated by the use of the whole arsenal of effective choirs, percussions, trumpets and harmonicas; by the laconic and sententious verbal duels, to the rapid and fatal ones with guns; and finally, the diegetic context that is only outlined. In conclusion, in a sequence we find some of Castellari's peculiar technical and linguistic skills, expertly blended with some of the specific and recurrent characteristics of spaghetti Westerns in general, exposed and symbolically represented with intuitive subtlety. Not definable as a master of the West or a true forefather—his best work, *Keoma* (1976), will germinate well after the twilight of Italian Westerns—Castellari can still boast ten endeavors within the genre making him at times a more than decent representative. It should also be noted that the substantial continuity between Westerns and Italian police thrillers—from the frontier of sand and rock to the one of asphalt—relocates Castellari in the middle of the confrontation between these two unique turning points of popular Italian cinema. He will transfer to his gangster/cop films the same tinges and imagery, both aesthetical and thematic, that are present in his westerns, managing to multiply and perfect them thanks to an acquired stylistic maturity. This makes Castellari one of the icons of Italian genre and exploitation cinema of the seventies. The primum movens of Castellari's imagery is the Body in relation to Space, linked to the laws of gravity, together with the cinematic possibility of violating that law, of hovering almost weightlessly in the air, of overcoming any physical obstacle thanks to agility and balance; hence the inevitable choice to build the cast around actors able to move with ease in any spatial context and especially putting them beside acrobats able to fulfill any movement that nature permits. The ineptitude of acting can also be corrected, in the vision of the director, perhaps with dubbing, with editing, with the right shot, even with silence—in short, with all the artifices that this form of expression offers; physical ineptitude, however, is never excused and does not have alternative solutions. That is why Castellari's favorite actors are people like Franco Nero, Fabio Testi, Fred Williamson and

Enzo G. Castellari lines up the shot (courtesy Nocturno Cinema).

Giancarlo Prete, alongside with a plethora of stunt performers promoted to supporting actors: their dexterity allows them to move, run, jump and roll without difficulty, indeed often with the ease of circus performers.

From these considerations emerges the second and most important aspect of Castellari's aesthetics: cinema is movement and action, the rest is snobby uselessness, which is boring to the viewer and also to the person behind the camera. Even the lyricism of slow motion, the acceleration of overlapping frames, the music, the architecture of the set, the optical and color effects are elements of exploitation of the kinetic moment, the apotropaic rite of motion that exorcises the doldrums, the sacredness of the action that gives meaning and unity to the unformed visual material. The fact is that Castellari is not only an action director, but also and above all a man of action and this makes him suitable to be at the heart of the action, to experience it from the inside, not to just scrutinize it from afar. When he merely films the maneuvers of others, he is sometimes indecisive, because the action is on the other side of the camera, he is not a part of it but is simply describing what happens. The camera seems to come to life when it is an integral part of that action. When he explores the outside, Castellari believes exclusively in saturating the screen with events and actions so as to have that "fullness" capable of resolving any situation. The main films of the seventies directed by Castellari are often absolute cinematographic machines, thanks to a different topographical structure and environmental dynamics dissimilar to the Western, because the metropolitan settings will present a proliferation of architectural elements, complex geometries and incumbent, restricted areas bristling with obstacles. These will allow Castellari to have full control of the space inside, and his shooting techniques to merge with the places and characters in an often perfect symphony.

When a man with the camera comes across an urban environment overflowing with architectural elements laden with composite geometries, that environment will be his visual prey, especially if the man in question is Castellari. He concocted an urban trilogy between 1973 and 1976, with his three main films of the decade: *La polizia incrimina la legge assolve* (*High Crime*, 1973), *Il cittadino si ribella* (*Street Law*, 1974), *Il grande racket* (*The Big Racket*, 1976), followed later by the less incisive appendices, *La via della droga* (*The Heroin Busters*, 1977) and *Il giorno del cobra* (*Day of the Cobra*, 1980). This triptych opens and closes Castellari's intense season of Italian police thrillers. If before 1973 the genre was still looking for a strong and lasting identity, in 1976–77 it was already full and ready to fire its last and mostly harmless cartridges before drifting into the parodic. *High Crime*—although debtor in spirit to works like *The French Connection* (1971) by William Friedkin, *Bullitt* (1968) by Peter Yates and *Dirty Harry* (1971) by Don Siegel—is a real progenitor/archetype for most Italian police thrillers that will follow, much more than the admittedly important *La polizia ringrazia* (*Execution Squad*, 1972) by Stefano Vanzina, in which political and sociological hints will be later set aside. *High Crime* serves as a forerunner both thematically and "morally" for the most brutal and vicious examples of the genre, when the lawless Western frontier gets transferred to modern metropolitan areas, almost exclusively national, and where this simple/simplistic assumption predominates: if crime is savage and without rules, civil society should be the same, both in its public dimension (the police) and in its private one (ordinary citizens). The latter aspect, concerning the ordinary man's reaction, is elaborated in the following two titles of the trilogy: *Street Law* and *The Big Racket*. Beyond the dubious morality of such hasty axioms, depicting a darkly reactionary and repressive horizon, it should be noted that the Italian genre, in its predominant subject lines, does nothing but tickle the latent anxieties of a widespread discontent though perhaps not quite polished in understanding the sociopolitical dynamics that triggered it. There's one point that has to be clarified: the police thriller/action films filled theaters as much as, for example, the politicized Westerns of the late sixties, while adhering to completely different ideologies; this simply means that both the first and the second genre worked well from rhythmic and dramaturgical viewpoints, resulting in excellent entertainment machines. And that is perhaps the key point: the political-sociological justification is nothing but a pretext, at least in many cases, to create the most spectacular product possible, with the main purpose of attracting the audience with the skill and professionalism of the filmmakers. Ultimately, we are talking about genre and action films, that cannot indulge in psychological-anthropological subtleties and need shrewd and vigorous synthetic conditions. Moreover, it is far simpler to be politically correct in a context such as that of the Wild West, where the only rule is that of the gun, rather than in a historical framework, more modern and marked by civilization, by law and by legal guarantors.

The police trilogy in question can be conceived as a symphony in three parts or as a single, giant, gargantuan progressive rock suite transferred to action films, in which from one title to the next, from one city to another, there is the crumbling of a realism lacking recognizable environmental connotations, slipping increasingly into formal abstraction, in relentless experimentation with changing rhythms and visual solutions that become more and more extreme. *High Crime* has even moments of introspection and suspension, due to the presence of Fernando Rey and a certain tinge the director manages to give his character, or the idyllic moments of commissioner Belli (Franco Nero) with partner Mirella (Delia Boccardo) and daughter Anita (played by the director's daughter, Stefania Girolami, credited as Stefania G. Castellari), as well as a reflection coating the conflict between old and new crime. *Street Law,* with its rhythmic editing, daring multiple angles and futuristic shots, the frenzied movement of bodies and vehicles and the acting of the protagonist (again Nero), is even more paroxysmal and "hysterical" than *High Crime.* After all, not surprisingly, we talked of progressive rock and *Street Law* is in the central part of this suite, with its peak in the final battle in the enormous industrial warehouse, where there is a triumph of reverberating sound effects, the echo of voices, the sound of gunfire amplified by the architectural shape of the place, with the image that focuses on fragments and totals, flat, horizontal drain pipes, vertical, oblique, from top to bottom and from bottom to top, while objects and bodies circle rhythmically with the whistling of bullets. An audiovisual riot capable of rendering literal the harmony of violence and conflict. *The Big Racket* ups the stakes even further, intensifying the already savory ingredients of the previous films and reaching a high impact finale, which looks like the industrial version of *The Wild Bunch* (1969) by Sam Peckinpah, an ending that functions, in fact, as a final tombstone not only for the genre, but also for the creative pathway of Castellari, who from then on, no longer had the ability to outdo himself, except maybe with that very personal project that responds to the title of *Keoma*. In fact, the next two thrillers, *The Heroin Busters* and *The Day of the Cobra*, seem animated by a kind of "inferiority complex" with respect to previous titles, almost afraid of exposing themselves, of facing an uneven confrontation. The first attempt plays an unlikely sociological card linked to trafficking and drug use, with specious, socio-political notations, smoky and strangely verbose scenes, although there are more than worthy action sequences, where among other things, the two protagonists, Fabio Testi and David Hemmings, often do not use stand-ins. Definitely better is *The Day of the Cobra*, the most balanced in determining the love for pure action with the melancholy of a genre not only in its twilight, but probably also out of time.

Between the first police triptych and the next diptych, we find an anomalous piece of work, which is probably the director's most personal and heartfelt film: *Keoma*. The intentions in atmosphere and use of space and time make it a kind of closing swan song of the genre that had seen the birth of Castellari, first as a spectator, then as a director. In fact, it is a pure concentration of style and experimentation, as well as the completion of an evolution, within the genre, that the director felt he had not yet reached. In the film we perceive the converging of all the technical obsessions, themes, culture, visual angles, sound, climate, environment, in what can be called a summa of his love for cinema. More than a baroque film one could speak of a Rococo one, seeing the constant chisel blows, inlays, decorations, embellishments, audio-visual nuances. Almost inevitable is the suggestion of Old Testament, rather than evangelical, themes, despite the attempt to make the protagonist, the half-breed Indian Keoma (Franco Nero once again), a Christological figure, he recalls more the image of an angel exterminator from the Old Testament, in an innovative Gomorrah; it is Lisa (Olga Karlatos), the young pregnant woman who holds a new life within her womb, who is able to give rise to an assonance with the figure of the Madonna. References to the Homeric epic abound (Keoma reminds us of Ulysses' homecoming) so do those to Shakespearean tragedy, with clear references to *Julius Caesar* and *King Lear*. Also quite prevalent are iconographic and chromatic links with the cinema of Mario Bava, Hammer, Roger Corman, in an overall atmosphere that refers to those already present in other "gothic" Westerns such as *Se sei vivo spara* (*Django Kill … If You Live,*

Castellari (left) instructs Fabio Testi on how to uncover *The Big Racket,* in 1976 (courtesy Nocturno Cinema).

Shoot! a.k.a. *Django Kill!* 1967) by Giulio Questi or *E Dio disse a Caino* (*And God Said to Cain*, 1970) by Antonio Margheriti. The overall result is possibly discontinuous, but by some strange alchemy it works perfectly, thanks to the overwhelming and restless music, the countless and sometimes ingenious directorial solutions and sound effects, while the location of a small, murky Western village in ruins gives the story a hyper-realistic feel.

One last important period, at least from a historic point of view, in the filmography of Castellari is the post-apocalyptic trilogy that the director will create between 1982 and 1983, and that includes *1990: I guerrieri del Bronx* (*1990: The Bronx Warriors*, a.k.a. *Bronx Warriors*, 1982), *I nuovi barbari* (*Warriors of the Wasteland*, a.k.a. *The New Barbarians*, 1983) and *Fuga dal Bronx* (*Escape from the Bronx*, a.k.a. *Bronx Warriors 2*, 1983). The era of implementation, together with the technical and aesthetic outcomes, reveals a now subservient Italian industry. It is no longer its own master and no longer controls its once dazzling, innovative and often archetypal creativity, but pays servile and gregarious respect to the foreign market. This is just after the last rattling and ultra-violent backlash of the cannibalistic subgenre: the death of a giant is always angry, loud, bombastic, before the final fall. The post-apocalyptic Italian matrix is located a few seconds before that fall. This current adds nothing and takes nothing away from its unattainable Anglophone reference points like *The Warriors* (1979), *Escape from New York* (1981), or *Mad Max* (1979), which are its raison d'être, and is located in a productive environment in which, by now, it is not important what you show and how you show it, but simply to build, in the wake of successful films at the box office, iconographic scenarios that are derivative and subordinate. Directors, therefore, become the mere manpower of a cinema that tolerates them and uses them up while it's still possible. The fact that Castellari, in this context, and despite everything, manages to assemble some convincing products, in which at times his taste and peculiar staging of action emerge, does not change one iota of this overall consideration. The goal is to fill the shelves of what is now a filmic emporium of products, at times low budget and almost always low-key, to place next to more valuable and better packaged works, so that all the spectators can have their "pound of flesh" to quench their hunger. It is no longer a genuinely popular cinema, free creator of new models, of visual or narrative solutions, but a grimly crass cinema, which offers the indistinct and amorphous.

Let's start by talking about your father. I'd be interested in having your personal portrayal of Marino Girolami.
My father begins as a European boxing champion, an activity he interrupted early, when he was twenty. Afterwards he got a degree as a physical therapist and opened a gym, which also specialized in therapeutic massages. This was, for the time, an incredibly innovative idea and in fact not long after he began being sought by actors and celebrities. Among the people that asked for my father's expertise was Anna Magnani, who took her son Luca to him. That was the beginning of a close friendship between Magnani and my father. Before continuing, you must know that my dad also wrote short stories, poems, ideas and scripts … he had a fervid imagination. The fairy tales he would tell us when we were children, were incredible. He gave her the script of *Campo de' fiori* (*The Peddler and the Lady*, 1943) that she loved and passed on to Aldo Fabrizi. The story was rewritten by my father, together with Federico Fellini and the film was directed by Mario Bonnard, who asked him to be a volunteer assistant director. After that, he started working steadily in films. He got noticed and more and more directors wanted him by their side. Consider

that my dad was one of the only ADs that spoke four languages, because during the war my parents harbored a Jewish woman, to whom my father would perform massage treatment. He was in her villa when soldiers broke in to take her away. He knocked down ten of them and brought her home to safety, where she stayed for roughly a year. She was very cultured and taught him a few languages. So the Americans would often ask for him, when they came to Italy. But he considered his master Mario Soldati, with whom he worked numerous times. My father was ravenous for life, he always wanted to learn more and was particularly fascinated by cinema. If I had to choose a word to describe him, I'd chose dynamic. He was resilient both physically and mentally. I learned everything from him.

How was your relationship with him on set? How would he behave with you?

He behaved with me in the same way he behaved with every other crew member. My father loved telling jokes. Between takes he would stop everything to tell a story or crack a joke. Actors would feel relaxed with him because he would create a very joyous atmosphere. I'd do everything on his films: catch a chair, make coffee, play a bit part, do a stunt or, because of my architectural studies, I'd also work on the set design. Later, when I became a 1st AD, I started editing his films as well. The most vivid memory of my childhood is joining my father in the editing suite after school. When I was a student, my favorite holidays were spent with my father on a film set. If anyone asked, "Who'll get that chair?" the answer was always, "I will!"; "Who'll get the coffee?" "I will"; "Who'll stand in for the actor?" "I will!"; "Who'll jump out of the window?" "I will!" Cinema became my passion, my life, my everything…

What do you remember the most about that long period working on other directors' sets?

I must say that being on a set as an AD, an extra, a stuntman or an actor was not very different to being on a set as a director. As long as I am on a set I'm happy. The reason is that I breathed cinema since birth. My father often used to pick me up at school and take me to the editing room where he'd be working on one of his films. I was fascinated, in fact for me the editing of a film is an extraordinary process and my greatest passion. Today I teach my students that understanding editing is fundamental for a director. Without this knowledge you cannot envision how the different shots can be put together. There are directors who detest editing, who find it a waste of time and this clearly reflects on the way they shoot. A director has to know how to obtain what he has created in his mind and in order to do this effectively he must be extremely familiar with the process of editing.

Particularly in your more action-based films it is evident that editing has a fundamental role.

I have mentioned this in the past, but my "relationship" with editing became even stronger after having seen *The Appaloosa* [1966] with Marlon Brando and John Saxon, I was flabbergasted. At the time I was filming *7 winchester per un massacro* [*Renegade Riders*, a.k.a. *Seven Winchesters for a Massacre*, a.k.a. *Blake's Marauders*, a.k.a. *Payment in Blood*, 1967] and Sidney J. Furie's shots stunned and surprised me. His film is in Cinemascope so if there's a close-up, let's say, of you talking to me … it gets lost from whichever way you look at it, so Furie placed a huge sombrero on the actor who is speaking, covering three quarters of the screen thus guiding the spectators' eyes to the actor's face. I made this method my own. I learned from Furie how to shoot close-ups and value the background when doing it. I was also helped by my studies in architecture and the fine arts. These kinds of studies forge your aesthetic understanding, and in fact what inspires me is the setting. As you know, in all my films, there's at least one scene set in an abandoned factory where I have the possibility of finding interesting perspectives. The arrangement of the shot is of great importance to me … every detail must be in place. I paint when I shoot. All my shots are extremely natural and my layouts blend perfectly with the surrounding.

You have often said, when interviewed, that you consider yourself first and foremost a Western director. When did your love for this genre begin?

I used to love watching Westerns as a kid and I never missed one: the great classics, the low-budget ones, all of them, no matter what kind. The onset and invasion of Italian Westerns gave 1st ADs the possibility of trying their hand at directing. I was lucky and I started my career as a director thanks to this phenomenon. Ah! You know what film really struck me? *The Seven Samurai* [1954] and in particular the death scenes. Kurosawa shot the death of each samurai normally but just when they were about to hit the ground it would be in slow-motion: the dust that rises, the body that bounces slightly before settling… And then came Sam Peckinpah, who is my absolute master.

Your cinema is incredibly masculine and hyperbolic. Your settings are generally exaggerated, linked more to a legendary and virile kind of imagery rather than anything founded on reality.

Let's start by saying that I wrote all my films. Initially with Tito Carpi, who was my father's writer for many years, and subsequently by myself, alone. A director should always be the writer, or co-writer of his films and in my case even more so because being a super-expert editor—I even married an editor—I knew exactly what was important to have in a script and what wasn't. As far as my personal imagery goes, I've always been convinced of the fact that cinema is supposed to be larger than life, the emotions have to be real but the action doesn't have to be. I would often have animated conversations with Alberto De Martino about this because he would look for some kind of reality, but nobody wants real life when they sit in front of a screen.

It is a well-known fact that you are the real director of Pochi dollari per Django **[A Few Dollars for Django, a.k.a. Some Dollars for Django, 1966]. Tell me about your relationship with Klimovsky.**

With Klimovsky, well … not so much my relationship as my father's relationship since he produced the film you just mentioned. I met him when my father sent me on the set of *A Few Dollars for Django*, with Anthony Steffen and Frank Wolff. He was an extremely kind, little old man, a musician. I think he was a doctor … anyway a really sweet, timid man. He starts filming the first scene, "Motor! Acciòn! Corte, positiva!" The first take was always good. I go up to him, "Excuse me, Leon…" "No, no, don't worry, it'll be all right." "But what will you do when you have to edit? There's nothing we can work with…" I realized he didn't understand. He was subject to the Spanish producer, an ambiguous, odious fellow who was always on the set … Rafael Marina I think his name was. I informed my father of the situation and he came, saw the rushes and announced, "As from tomorrow, Enzo will be directing this film. I'm the producer, I decide." Klimovsky stayed on set but didn't actually do any directing. I'm also, to use your words, the real director of *A Ghentar si muore facile* [translation: *At Ghentar It's Easy to Die*, 1967].

You met Alberto De Martino during your time in Spain.

Yes, the first film I worked on as an AD was directed by José Louis Madrid. Unlike Klimovsky, he spoke a lot but was equally incompetent. I didn't care because I had no real stake in the film so I went along with the "Corta, Positiva!" We were in Barcelona for this film and I was staying at a hotel owned by the Balcazan brothers. They had created a Western village nearby. It was a terrible place built on a kind of mosquito-infested hill. All their low budget films were shot there, not in Almeria. It was there that I met Alberto De Martino who was filming Ringo, Django, Bingo or whatever, which turned out to be a huge success.[1] His first AD was Giorgio Ubaldi, a stunt coordinator. We became friends. I spent the evenings with Alberto, an intelligent, cultured man. I recently met him at a film festival in France and he's still a charming person. Back in Rome after Spain, I worked for my father while De Martino directed *Upperseven, l'uomo da uccidere* [*The Spy with Ten Faces*, a.k.a. *The Man of a Thousand Masks*, a.k.a. *Upperseven, the Man to Kill*, 1966] produced by Emo Bistolfi. When Bistolfi realized that De Martino's first AD was Ubaldi the stunt coordinator, he was completely pissed off. He said a first AD had to be intelligent and well-educated, not a stableman. "I could ask Marino Girolami's son…" "Is he an AD?" "Yes, I met him in Spain." That is how I started working with Alberto and his was also the first film in which I worked as a stunt coordinator.

How was your relationship with De Martino?

One of great respect. We hit it off talking about music, because he was a great jazz expert and musician. He was always very prepared on set. Technically he hasn't received the recognition he deserves. He was particularly clever in the creation of elaborate, long tracking shots, which were conceived in such a way as to always have the important lines in close-up. Though we would sometimes discuss because I would find his choices not sufficiently dynamic, but he was a very good director.

For how long did you work as first AD in films produced by Amati?

A couple of years, roughly. After I'd finished working on Klimovsky's second film, *A Few Dollars for Django*, co-produced by my father, Sbarigia, the head of Fono Roma,[2] saw the film and said, "I didn't know Kilmovsky worked so well…" to which my father replied, "My son directed it." "Well then, why don't you ask him to bring me a screenplay?" So Tito Carpi and I wrote a script, showed it to him and to my father and Sbarigia produced *Renegade Riders*. After this, Edmondo Amati called me to be De Martino's first AD. "But I've already worked as a director, I can't go back to being an AD." "OK, bring me a script and you can direct." My uncle Romolo Girolami [Guerrieri] had a good script. Tito Carpi and I worked on it and then I returned to Amati. Amati always wanted people to narrate the stories and I'm an excellent storyteller. I improvise, invent, use sound effects, music … and I can immediately tell if the other person is captivated and Amati was. He had a perfect title for this film, *Vado… l'ammazzo e torno* [*Any Gun Can Play*, 1967] which is what Eli Wallach says in *Il buono, il brutto e il cattivo* [*The Good, the Bad and the Ugly*, 1966]. The film was a tremendous hit because it was funny without being a hoax or a parody. In the last scene there's a duel in an abandoned church with an incredible organ. For this scene I chose Bach and gunshots in the finale…. Who gets killed? Nobody. The bullets hit the pipes of the organ and like a slot machine, the money comes pouring out. Inventing action scenes was never a problem for me, I loved it. Of course it wasn't easy for the script supervisor and the AD because I decided there and then. When they asked me, "Who fires?" "I don't know," was my reply. I did what I felt was right, nothing was planned. What was crystal clear in my head was the final result. On *Keoma* I shot the ending on the second day and we didn't even have a script. Both Franco and I didn't like the one we had so we threw it out. I invented everything day by day and Joshua Sinclair translated the dialogue into English for the actors. I would arrive and say, "When we shoot the scene of the father's death, I want a monologue like Marlon Brando's over the dead body of Caesar in Mankiewicz's film. I want a tracking shot of him talking about his dead father as if he were talking to Caesar…" or else I'd say to Joshua that I wanted Keoma's encounter with Death to be like the chess game in Bergman's *The Seventh Seal* [1957]. Many actors who worked on *Keoma* were chosen without even knowing what they would be doing. I remember asking Manolo Bolognini to get me Woody Strode. "But what will he do?" "I don't know. Sign him up and we will think of something."

The very first outline was written by Luigi Montefiori.
Yes, the initial storyline was wonderful…. But we started shooting without a script. On the first day I shot what I knew would have never been chucked out: riding scenes, action stuff. In the evening the script arrives and we all sit down and read it … I nearly threw up. I call Bolognini and tell him, "This is utter fucking rubbish. They ruined everything that was good about Montefiori's story. I will do it my way." The actors and the producer trusted me completely. Sometimes they'd ask, "What will you do next?" and I'd answer, "I don't know." "No problem," was the reply.

Why didn't you follow the writing of the script?
I was editing *Il grande racket* [*The Big Racket*, 1976] and Franco Nero was filming *21 Hours at Munich* [1976], so neither of us had time to follow the writing process. The only thing we had read was Gigi Montefiori's storyline and we trusted that something good would have come out of it.

Let's go back to the sixties. So, after years as an AD you directed, uncredited, the Klimovsky films and then directed your first real film, **Renegade Riders,** ***followed by*** **Any Gun Can Play.** ***What happened next?***
I was contacted by all the producers. Everyone was talking about my innovative way of shooting, and when the film was being edited at the Safa Paladino, my sister-in-law Tatiana Morigi, who had edited all of Alberto Sordi's films, told me how people kept walking into the cutting suite trying to catch a glimpse of something. When the film was released, it was a stunning success. It was clear that I was the most sought-after film director. Next, I read Sergio Corbucci's script, *Johnny Hamlet*, which I liked very much. The producers called me to direct it. Filming a Western version of Hamlet seemed absurd; the action was limited compared to my other films, but I was up for the challenge. Andrea Giordana, a very popular TV actor at the time, having just finished *Il conte di Montecristo* [*The Count of Montecristo*, 1966] was perfect for Hamlet. If you've seen this film, you'll understand my enthusiasm despite that shitty title they decided to give it, *Quella sporca storia nel west* [translation: *That Dirty Story in the West*]. What was wrong with *Johnny Hamlet*?! I think some of my most beautiful shots are to be found in this film. Changing the title was a mistake. Nobody went to see it. If they'd kept *Johnny Hamlet*, the response of the public would have been different.

Franco Rossetti told me that since Corbucci was unable to direct it, he was called, considering the success of El desperado *[The Dirty Outlaws, 1967] which he had directed, also starring Giordana.*

Not true. I don't think I have ever heard of this Rossetti. The script passed from Corbucci's hands to mine.

What do you remember about **I tre che sconvolsero il west—Vado, vedo e sparo *[One Dollar Too Many, a.k.a.* I Came, I Saw, I Shot, *1968]?***

It was a true slapstick with an abundance of stuntmen, exaggerated action and three important actors: John Saxon, who I finally got to meet, Frank Wolff and Antonio Sabato. It was produced by Dario Sabatello. By the way, speaking of Sabatello, you must know how irreverent Corbucci was, right? He had nicknames for everyone. I was "the intelligent muscle" and Dario Sabatello was "the only stupid Jew." The problem with that film was that the leading female role was given to Sabatello's lover—Flori, I think her name was. One evening at a restaurant there was a terrible argument between Sabato and ... yes, Agata Flori: "You can't bust my balls because you're fucking the producer!" She started screaming. I took advantage of the situation and ate all the "perceves," the delicious seafood they had all stopped eating.

What was John Saxon like?

When we were younger we looked like twins, we were virtually identical. We got along wonderfully from the start because we both love art. He had attended the Accademia delle Belle Arti [Academy of Fine Arts] in Rome, where I got my diploma so we discovered we had similar tastes.

Humor is an important ingredient of your Westerns.

Yes, irony is nearly always present. I was the first director to introduce this in Italian Westerns, so much so that I was supposed to direct the *Trinity* film produced by Italo Zingarelli. We're talking about the early seventies. It wasn't exactly that story but it was supposed to be a Western-comedy with Terence Hill [Mario Girotti] and Bud Spencer [Carlo Pedersoli] but Hill was called for another film and was replaced with Antonio Sabato, with whom I had already worked. We were set to go but then the project collapsed due to production reasons, lack of funds ... I don't know exactly.

Tell me about Frank Wolff.

I met him on Klimovsky's set where he played the part of the bad guy. He was rather coarse but a good actor and always prompt ... but you couldn't eat with him.... The noises he made, the things he did... I was a witness to the terrible tragedy he experienced during *Gli occhi freddi della paura* [*Cold Eyes of Fear*, 1971]. Tito Carpi and I wrote it and Wolff's wife translated it into English. She was British and he was extremely attached to her. Frank had to play the part of a fragile man who slowly goes mad. Frank's wife had left him and although it was terrible for Frank, the film benefited. Frank was living this personal drama as we were shooting and you could see how this had an effect on the character he was playing; he too, was going through this difficult psychological trauma. It was terrible to watch.... He killed himself while working on the following film. He was incredible but seeing him fall apart when the woman he loved left him was awful.

After a prolific period in which you worked nearly exclusively in Westerns, you directed **La battaglia d'Inghilterra *[Eagles Over London, a.k.a.* Battle Command, *1969]. *Is it true De Martino was supposed to direct it?**

Yes, I was called by Amati. Alberto was working on *Dalle Ardenne all'inferno* [*Dirty Heroes*, 1967] but production took longer than what it was supposed to and so I was asked to take his place. I loved the title but the script was terrible, a kind of soap opera. I turned it into a proper war story. Originally there was supposed to be very little action. There were legal problems tied to that film, because during that period the British were preparing a film with the same title [*Battle of Britain*, 1969, by Guy Hamilton]. A legal battle that Amati won because it was a ridiculous charge, you can't have rights on the name of a historical event. What is funny is that because they shared the same title the British film came out with a completely different title in Italy and vice versa our film was renamed for the foreign market. A simple translation would have been the most logical thing but they tried not to make them compete, though my film ended up winning. I wasn't interested in historical accuracy and that is why mine did better at the box office, it was more cinematographic. The British film had great actors but it's practically a documentary.

You also used the split-screen in that film.

Yes! I had just seen *The Boston Strangler* [1968] with Tony Curtis and I was really impressed by the use of the split-screen so I decided to try this technique for the very first time, specifically in the opening credits but studying it first, choosing each perspective carefully. Remember I was one of the only directors in Italy, if not the only one, to use storyboards. I prepared meticulously for those scenes.

How does **Cold Eyes of Fear** *come about?*

I liked the idea of shooting a film entirely in interiors, but it was very challenging for me. *Wait Until Dark* [1967] with Audrey Hepburn had been released not long before, entirely shot inside a house and I adore Audrey Hepburn…. Tito Carpi and I wrote the story and creating the set at the studio was no problem. Unfortunately, when we had almost finished shooting, the distribution collapsed and I didn't even know if the film was ever going to be released.

The film is quite strong, sexually I mean.

We called Karin Schubert for those scenes. She used to come on the set with her boyfriend, a stuntman, who never took his eyes off her. I asked for Karin because she was known for being the one to call for tougher scenes. She didn't have any problems with nudity. There was also a Spanish actor I liked, Julian Mateus and then of course the great Fernando Rey, a true gentleman in every way. Gianni Garko was also very good, not to mention the beautiful Giovanna Ralli.

The music is by Ennio Morricone but the composer you are most associated to is Francesco De Masi.

I have to edit with music, it's one of the most important elements of a film and a fundamental editing tool. I would add the music I thought would work best. While working on *Keoma*, that has a soundtrack by Guido e Maurizio De Angelis, I would use songs by Leonard Cohen for example. I played the music directly on the set to immerse the actors in the right atmosphere. On *Johnny Hamlet* I often used "Misa Flamenca" while editing. Francesco created a sound starting from that and the result is incredible. I think that it is the best soundtrack he composed for me.

Another strange film in your filmography is **Ettore lo fusto** *[Hector the Mighty, 1972], which had an incredible cast.*

Yes, Giancarlo Giannini was perfect to play "Ulysses" in this modern version of the Iliad and it was his first comedic role. Only later I discovered that he had asked director Pasquale Squitieri to help him master the Neapolitan accent. A funny thing happened on that film. Rosanna Schiaffino came, on her first day on set, with a newly corrected and rewritten script. I got it and threw it in the air. "This is crazy! An actress dictating changes to the story!" I called Amati right away and he begged me to go along with this charade. I didn't know what he had in mind but I did what he asked. We would shoot the scenes added by Schiaffino's writers with no film in the camera. All the others actors were in on it.

What about Sensività *[The House by the Edge of the Lake, a.k.a.* The Last House Near the Lake, *1979]?*
The film is absolute trash! I didn't shoot that shit. It all started when I tried to help a friend of a friend, Josè Sanchez. He was young and inexperienced but promising and I helped him. He wrote this story and I offered to direct it under another name. Then the production ran out of money and the film was interrupted and I returned to Rome from the Costa Brava. The producer then contacted me and told me that if I acknowledged the film they would find the money to finish it. So, I decided to finish the film and sign it on condition I did things my way to which they agreed. As soon as I started editing, we were again interrupted, definitively this time. Later Putignani and Curti, the distributor and producer respectively, completed the editing in their own manner but the film was released with my name. They shot some new scenes, I think, directed by Alfonso Brescia.

Did you cast it?
Leonora Fani had already been selected. I chose Patricia Adriani, Vincent Gardenia and Wolfango Soldati. Fani was very sweet, a lovely person and well-mannered. This was also the second time working with Vincent Gardenia. He was an amazing man. I was fortunate enough to have him on this film after having worked with him on *The Big Racket* ... extraordinary. Spoke Neapolitan really well. He was also a very good cook and he cooked for the whole crew.

Speaking of actors, I read somewhere that you didn't get along with David Hess.
That was on *Johnathan degli orsi* [*Johnathan of the Bears*, 1994]. Franco Nero was the lead and he wanted some of his friends to be in it. There was this Hess guy, but it should have been Ass not Hess ... a presumptuous prick! Jack Palance had a terrible reputation but he was a cultured man, loved art and was very courteous. He loved talking about boxing; Muhammad Ali was a friend of his. Then there was Erik Estrada and he too was supposed to be a difficult person, but we got on extremely well. Lou Ferrigno was born deaf and dumb but thanks to his enormous willpower he learned to communicate. In the past he had had negative experiences with the stuntmen he worked with. They always spoke in Roman slang and he couldn't understand them. When he met me he finally met a director who understood him. My son suffered from the same condition so he felt at ease and protected. Furthermore, he was happy to have the opportunity of interpreting a comic role. When you get to know an actor it often turns out that he's exactly the opposite of what you expect.

In an old interview I remember you saying that you would tease Glenn Saxon.
Yes, he couldn't get on a horse. "Come on, fat ass!" He always needed to be helped. He was a good-looking fool. I hold De Martino responsible because he initially wanted

Giuliano Gemma as the lead actor so Amati organized a meeting. At a certain point De Martino said, "Yes, but this is a De Martino film not a Giuliano Gemma film!" Giuliano stood up and said, "Very well then, go ahead without me," and left. Alberto was convinced that a talented director didn't need a famous star. "I don't need any big names, wait and see!" He chose Glenn Saxon: good-looking, blond, blue eyes, but a useless fat ass. Generally I got along with all the foreign actors I worked with. Edd Byrnes and Guy Madison were in the first film. Edd Byrnes was extremely popular having just finished filming the very successful serial *77 Sunset Strip*. I wanted Robert Redford whom I had met a month before in LA. He had recently finished *The Chase* [1966] with Marlon Brando. "Who is he?" the producer asked me. "When *The Chase* is released, you'll see … a young Brando and remarkably handsome!" Redford wanted between 25,000 and 30,000 dollars. Edd Byrnes happened to be in Rome at the time and the producer said, "Look, we've got this guy here now! Anyway, who the hell is this Robert Redford? Nobody's heard of him!" That's why I made the film with Byrnes; he was agreeable and fairly athletic. And then there was Guy Madison, a typical American and a real cowboy. He had his own gun belt and pistol. The problem with him was that he drank too much and there was no real understanding between us. In *Any Gun Can Play* I had Gilbert Roland. "Who is he? Oh yes, the one with the little moustache … yes, yes I like him," said Amati. I'll never forget Gilbert's arrival at Cinecittà. I was in my second or third week of filming. I was having lunch with the organizer, Mario Mariani, when he walked in; white jacket, open shirt, a big chain around his neck, dark, dark, with his little moustache, athletic…. Then there was Horst Frank. I have great memories of him in *Johnny Hamlet*, a splendid actor who had problems communicating. He was very reserved. However, we talked about his part and he had some brilliant ideas. I was very fond of him, a good actor but I never saw him again after that film.

I know you've told this story many times, but please could you tell me again about your encounter with Charles Bronson?

Around 1970 I was in touch with Jacques Bar, an important French producer. I had asked for Bronson for *Any Gun Can Play*. "Who is this Bronson?" Amati didn't know him so I made him watch *The Magnificent Seven* [1960]. "Look, he's the woodcutter with the kids." "He'll never have a lead role with that face" … and so that is how George Hilton got the part. Anyhow, Jacques Bar showed me a book called *Arizona Justice* by Gordon Shirreffs, a writer specialized on novels set in the Far West. I read the book but the screenplay they had also handed me was dreadful. That summer Tito Carpi and I started rewriting it from scratch. Every evening the pages we had written were first translated into English and then sent to Gordon Shirreffs who adapted it to the Western slang. We sent the script to Charles Bronson who was filming on the French Riviera with Terence Young.[3] Jacques Bar and I went to Cannes to meet him. We waited two weeks before he finally decided to see us. He walked into the room: shorts, flip-flops, vest … and a pipe, without so much as a "Nice to meet you." We asked him whether he had read the script and whether he liked it. He kept nodding and pumping the muscle of his arm. "Look at this guy," I thought. "Here's a chance for him to work on an extraordinary film and there he is examining his muscles instead of listening to the producer." I took off my jacket, rolled up my sleeve and started flexing my muscle. Bronson looked at my arm and then at his. Finally he said he wasn't interested. He didn't like the ending. He wanted to kill everyone, bang, bang, bang, whereas the whole point was to focus on the enigmatic character of the protagonist. "OK," I said, "that's it!" I challenged him to an arm-wrestling contest. He couldn't refuse and I won without a problem. Fuck Charles Bronson!

After your more rigorous Westerns of the sixties, in the following decade you go back to the genre, and with the exception of Keoma, the tone has undoubtedly changed. Buffooneries have taken the place of irony. Let's begin with Tedeum [Sting of the West, a.k.a. Father Jackleg, a.k.a. Con Men, 1972].

I enjoyed writing the screenplay with Tito Carpi and I also enjoyed changing things around a bit when we were dubbing, but the actual filming was not quite what I wanted even though I had an excellent understanding with Giancarlo Prete and Jack Palance, also with Renzo Palmer and Lionel Stander. But I felt there was something missing.

Do you have similar feelings about Cipolla Colt [Cry, Onion! a.k.a. The Smell of Onion, 1975]?

No, I like that one. I saw it again with my students and they thought it was hilarious. It's a slapstick comedy with Franco Nero in a chaplinesque role. I enjoyed making that film. Plus, to direct Sterling Hayden was one of my dreams. Every director has a list in his mind of actors he would love to direct and Hayden was in mine so you can imagine my joy. I had seen him, not long before, in *The Long Goodbye* [1973] by Robert Altman. When I proposed his name to Carlo Ponti and he agreed, I was overjoyed! I've always been a big fan, after having seen him in *The Killing* [1956] by Kubrick.

Right at the beginning of this interview you spoke about the importance of editing. It shouldn't surprise anybody to know that you have worked, for most of your career, with the same editor, Gianfranco Amicucci.

I met Amicucci when I was working on *Eagles Over London*. I had to edit every evening and I needed someone to help me so we called Vincenzo Tomassi who brought his assistant Gianfranco Amicucci. During all those months in Spain I got to know Gianfranco. Vincenzo and Gianfranco worked on my next film, after which I asked Gianfranco if he'd like to edit *Il cittadino si ribella* [*Street Law*, 1974] and from then on he was my editor.

La polizia incrimina la legge assolve [High Crime, 1973] marks the beginning of your collaboration and friendship with Franco Nero.

My film was made, as many were, following the success of *La polizia ringrazia* [*Execution Squad*, a.k.a. *The Executioners*, 1972] by Stefano Vanzina but his was more of a political film whereas me and Amati wanted to make a more spectacular cop thriller. To be more precise I wanted to fuse together the story of *Bullitt* [1968], the action of *The Getaway* [1972] and the gritty realism of *The French Connection* [1971]. "Who shall we get?" I wanted somebody with a convincing face, an actor that would be credible but that had the physique and charisma of an action star. It wasn't easy to get to him. Franco was a big international star, known for being very picky with his projects. I remember talking to his agent, "What has this young director done?" "Westerns." "I don't know ... my client is into more artistic projects now. He is working with Elio Petri..." Fuck off. I managed to get to him through his personal hairdresser, who had worked on a number of my father's films. I called her up, "Where are you shooting?" "At the Elios Studios, with Anthony Quinn." "Could you set up a meeting with Nero?" Our first encounter wasn't great. A five-minute chat during lunch break. I honestly didn't think anything would have come out of it. I left asking him to read the script ... and he did! He called me up and that was the beginning of a wonderful relationship. Franco is a great spectator and he really loves cinema, intensely. He wasn't a great speaker, Franco, but he had wonderful ideas and I always understood what he meant and wanted.

Is it true that the producer wanted you to make a sequel to **High Crime?**

Yes, he wanted me and Franco Nero, but nothing came of it because Amati did not agree to a higher cachet. There was also a script, which was changed and later directed by my father. I'm talking about *Roma violenta* [*Violent Rome*, a.k.a. *Street Killers*, a.k.a. *Violent City*, 1975]. Maurizio Merli owes his entire career to this, because he was picked to replace Franco. If Amati had accepted our fees maybe he would have never become a star. He was cast primarily because he looked like Franco Nero.

You never worked with Merli…

Why work with the copy? I had the original. Plus, Merli had a great physique but not the acting skills.

So what happens after **High Crime?**

Cecchi Gori then called us to work on *Street Law*. I liked the story written by De Rita and Mauri and accepted. I wanted to change the beginning but this was ruled out because what I had in mind would have cost too much. I came to an agreement with the stuntmen, who worked for free, and with Rocco Lerro…. We shot those short little scenes a bit every day … I'm talking about the footage we see in the credits at the beginning of the movie. Those are all stolen sequences, made with no permits.

Let's talk about the sequence in **The Big Racket** *when Fabio Testi gets thrown down a hill in his car.*

Everyone has asked me how I shot that, even other directors. When I didn't want to disclose my secret, I used to invent crazy things. We were shooting in an abandoned factory which once produced spare parts for tracked vehicles and noticed these huge iron hoops: I asked my special effects man to weld together two of them so as to create one enormous wheel and in the middle to weld the passenger compartment of the car to the hoops, removing the engine and the boot. There was a large field in front of the factory where we placed this contraption which we could then turn manually. I placed a camera in the front, on Fabio Testi and another on the window at the side. When we made the wheel turn you could see Fabio's head going around and the contents of the car flying all over the place. It looked real.

After two films with Nero, why Testi?

Like in the case of Andrea Giordana for *Johnny Hamlet,* he came with the package. The producers wanted a film with Fabio Testi. I got on wonderfully with him. Fabio is golden: a kind, generous man, cultured but most of all well-mannered. At that time, I think it's safe to say, he was the most handsome actor in the business.

Le avventure e gli amori di Scaramouche *[The Loves and Times of Scaramouche, a.k.a.* **Scaramouche,** *1976] is a film you've never talked much about. You directed it in the period you were mostly active in police thrillers.*

I got off to a good start because the idea was amusing but the choice of the actor was not right. I liked Michael Sarrazin, particularly after watching *They Shoot Horses, Don't They?* [1969] directed by Sidney Pollack, so when they proposed him I accepted willingly but he wasn't the Scaramouche I had in mind. I had great fun with Aldo Mac-

Castellari (hat and sunglasses) with his favorite actor Franco Nero (looming over Castellari's shoulder) and a giant wind machine on the set of *Keoma*, 1976 (courtesy Nocturno Cinema).

cione who played the part of Napoleon. In some of my films you can tell I feel a great connection to surrealism, to a ridiculous comicality, for me *Hellzapoppin'* [1941] is the greatest film ever made. For example, in *Scaramouche*, Ursula Andress comes out of the water like in *Dr. No* [1962]. I liked putting these kind of references in my films.

What about Quel maledetto treno blindato [The Inglorious Bastards, 1978]?

It was an entertaining film and I enjoyed making it but I don't understand Quentin Tarantino's predilection for it. He liked the title *Inglorious Bastards*, which he modified slightly. The title is mine, my idea, and it was great but then the producers insisted on calling it *Quel maledetto treno blindato* [literal translation: That Damned Armored Train]. Thank God they left my title for the foreign releases. I was talking to the writer of the film and I said "bastards without glory" to describe the characters and Fred Williamson went, "Hey man! That's cool! You should use that as the title!"

What kind of person was Fred Williamson?

Fred knew everything, and I mean everything, about cinema! He is an actor, director, editor, producer … he could do everything. Plus he had an incredible athletic instinct—he was an American football champion—which made the understanding we had flawless. We would talk about the characters and the story on a physical level. He did all his own stunts. In the scene in which the protagonists exit the building using the rope, Fred did it on his own. So Bo Svenson came to me and said he wanted to do it on his own as well

Michael Pergolani and Enzo G. Castellari on the set of *The Inglorious Bastards*, 1978 (courtesy Nocturno Cinema).

but he wanted a special rig with a hidden rope around his waist while Fred did it with no help.

Let's jump to the eighties:* Tuareg, il guerriero del deserto *[Tuareg, the Desert Warrior, 1984].

Unfortunately the distribution was a mess on that. It was an idea of Giuseppe Bertolucci's or rather, the first person who had the idea was a Spanish producer who was also a director ... I forget his name. Anyway, this guy had bought the rights of the book and had contacted Bertolucci who then called me. I met ... Vincente Escriva ... that's his name, and I told him I'd read the book, in fact I'd read all of Figueroa's books. He had also written the screenplay but authors just don't know how to do that, so Tito Carpi and I rewrote it. For the casting I went to L.A. I used to go to the United States for the casting of my films. It was a tremendous opportunity to meet famous actors. I used to make a list of the people I wanted to meet and every time it was a fantastic experience.

***It is said that for* Il cacciatore di squali *[Guardians of the Deep, a.k.a.* The Shark Hunter, *1979] you didn't have a script.*

Well, Franco Nero called me from Mexico City and told me about a film that a Mexican producer wanted to shoot in the Caribbean. It was a co-production: Mexico, Spain and Italy. I went over immediately and I started looking for the locations and actors. Enzo Doria was the Italian producer. The script, which had been written in Spain, was due to arrive with Eduardo Fajardo but at the airport in New York all his luggage was stolen, so we had no script. I said, "What do we need a script for?" We started shooting and I invented the story as we went along, day by day. Ramon Bravo, an underwater cameraman and writer, filmed all the sequences with the sharks. That was the best part!

On this set you come up with the idea of* L'ultimo squalo *[Great White, a.k.a.* The Last Shark, *1981], right?

Yes, because as we were working on *Guardians of the Deep*, Bravo handed me a little script he had written years back. Me and Vincenzo Mannino developed his idea but the producers ignored the fact that Ramon Bravo had written the first outline, something for which he received no compensation and there were huge consequences for this.... The film was released in L.A. and was a stunning success! It was unbelievable! Universal Films were getting ready to shoot a third *Jaws* film and felt threatened by this little Italian film. They accused us of plagiarism and took legal action. Sure enough our film was suspended. Had the producers taken the trouble to stipulate a contract and pay Ramon, none of this would have happened and we would all be millionaires because Ramon had written his story long before Spielberg's film.

What about* Zombi 2 *[Zombie Flesh Eaters, 1979]? You were asked to direct it.

Yes, but horror is not my thing and then Lucio Fulci was contacted. In fact, I suggested his name to the producer. I was glad he ended up being chosen because he hadn't been working for some time and I knew he would be perfect. I had met Fulci many years before because he had worked with my father.

In the States you are also very well known for your three post-apocalyptic films.

The first one, *1990 I guerrieri del Bronx* [*1990: The Bronx Warriors*, a.k.a. *Bronx Warriors*, 1982] was a fantastic experience. It was a huge success and gained the fifth position on the *Variety* chart of the fifty best blockbusters. When we were shooting in the Bronx, the whole neighborhood participated. There was this one guy who, whenever I shouted, "Action!" would echo, "Action!" I went up to him and yelled, "You see this knife? If you don't fucking shut up, I'll scratch your eyes out!" Then I got him to follow me, sat him down in my chair and made him shout, "Action!" every time. The problem was solved.

Mark Gregory. Who is he and when and where did you find him?

Marco Di Gregorio would go to the same gym I used to go to. I took notice of him after some time. He would always be in a corner, in silence, doing weights. He had long hair and a sad look on his face but he was handsome. A really good-looking seventeen-year-old. As time went by I saw him really evolve from a physical point of view, so when Fabrizio De Angelis called me for *Bronx Warriors* and told me I had to come up with a lead, I said, "It's done! I've got him down at my gym." I brought him to the production offices and it was a deal. He was the brooding, silent type. Strange kid, Marco, but perfect for the role. After my post-apocalyptic films I lost track of him. Maybe if I'd stayed by his side he would have stuck around longer. I don't know what happened to him. We were supposed to do a whole series of films together, produced by Fabrizio but I was called for *Tuareg*. Fabrizio decided to direct them himself but I don't know how their relationship was on the set and after that, Marco gave up films.

You are referring to* Thunder *[1983] and its sequels, aren't you?

Yes. I was supposed to direct those. I participated in the pre-production of the first one but I didn't work on it. I visited the set of the first sequel. Fabrizio invited me and my brother to Arizona. "Come over! We'll have fun." I never saw the films. Fabrizio wasn't a great director but he was clever ... clever and sly.

Castellari (left) next to an unidentified motorcyclist on the set of his first post-apocalyptic flick, *1990: The Bronx Warriors*, 1982 (courtesy Nocturno Cinema).

In the 1980s you made some minor but interesting action movies in the States. Let's start with* Il giorno del cobra *[Day of the Cobra, 1980].

I like that film. The idea of bringing Philip Marlowe to life was, for Franco Nero and me, terrific. We started filming in San Francisco with Marlowe following a woman who had betrayed her husband with another woman. We invented that scene there and then. There were a number of scenes we invented on the spot. Same goes for *Colpi di luce* [*Light Blast*, 1985], though I don't remember that one very well. I do remember the enjoyment I had shooting in San Francisco, with Erik Estrada in the leading role.

Then there is* Hammer *[Hammerhead, 1987].

I'd need to see it again. I edited it but when producers disappear for whatever reason, you have no idea what happens to the film. I did it before *Striker* [1987] which I know had been offered to Umberto Lenzi first. In fact, the idea for the films was his. The film was going to be shot in Santo Domingo so when the producer offered it to me I accepted but refused to acknowledge it.

What can you tell me about the leads of these two films, Frank Zagarino and Daniel Greene?

Zagarino didn't have a large range of expressions but had a great physique. Greene was such a charming person. First he appeared in *Striker* and after that I wanted him for *Hammer*. Only a few months separate these two films.

Around this time you also worked on Cobra Mission *[*Cobra Commando, *a.k.a.* Operation Nam, *1986]* ***by Fabrizio De Angelis.***

Yes, I play an army official and I also filmed some sequences.

Detective Extralarge *[1991–1992]* was the first thing you did for television.

Yes, it was my first experience working for TV. I insisted on changing the script. It was absolute shit. There were six stories. Pedersoli [Bud Spencer] wrote the first one which was fine and I rewrote four others. The last one, *Magia nera* [*Black Magic*] with Dionne Warwick, was written by Gianni Romoli. At that time Bud Spencer was a hero for kids. He was playing the part of the gentle giant but in the *Miami Killer* episode he deals with a dirty cop with a dual personality who kills little girls. I got along wonderfully with Bud Spencer. His only problems were his weight and his age. He was not as agile as I would have liked, but I found the perfect stand-in, a wrestler. He resembled Bud in every way and he was intelligent. He observed Bud in silence, the way he walked, the way he moved and imitated him to perfection.

Your director of photography was Roberto Girometti, with whom you had worked many times previously.

But in my earlier films he had been an operator. The experience with him on *Extralarge* was not good…

You didn't get along?

Mamma mia! For goodness sake … no comment! You would explain the scene and he would go "yes, yes, yes" and then did nothing of what you had asked. "Go fuck yourself!" I had a shitty crew on that series. I resisted five, six months and with my teeth and nails I managed to get what I needed.

Going back to cinema, after quite a few years of silence you go back to directing with Caribbean Bastards *[2010]*. A strange film…

OK, when they call me to go and speak in schools or universities I run because I learn more than the students. I had just ended a master class at a university in Latina when I received a call from a producer. "Hi Enzo, there's a film we would like you to make." "Yeah, right … where?" "Isla Margherita." "In the Caribbean?" "Yes." "I'll do it." "The story…" "I don't care … I said I'll do it." Later on I discovered that the story was inspired by *A Clockwork Orange* [1971] and of course by Tarantino. My interest in the story was quite relative…

Is there anything you would have liked to do but wasn't able to?

Yes, of course, a film written by Oliver Stone, *Cover-up*. Stone had just received an Oscar for the screenplay of *Midnight Express* [1978] but he had hardly done anything as a director. Fernando Ghia was in the U.S. and was producing for Cristaldi. He had commissioned Stone to write this screenplay. It was an excellent story about the kidnapping of the president's daughter by a group of terrorists. The screenplay was in English and only a handful of our producers could read English, therefore it was translated into Italian, losing a lot of its appeal. It was only later, when Stone had finished filming *Platoon* [1986], that everyone wanted that story. I wanted to buy the rights but my lawyer said we could obtain it without spending anything. At that time I was working on the action unit of *Il segreto del Sahara* [*The Secret of the Sahara*, 1988], directed by Alberto Negrin, so I was unable to follow the matter and when I returned, Stone was no longer willing to sell. That was a tremendous disappointment.

Going back to the late eighties, I would like to ask you one last question: when in the States, you worked incognito, on a series of action films, didn't you?

Yes. In the States my name had become well-known, especially thanks to *1990: The Bronx Warriors*. So when I went to visit my daughter, Stefania, who was then in North Carolina working on a film as an AD, people would come up to me and say, "You directed *Bronx Warriors*! Would you consider directing the second unit?" I accepted and filmed sequence after sequence. It was easy for me, like being on holiday. I couldn't appear in the credits because of union problems, but I didn't care. I had no trouble giving my sequences to another director. What do I get out of it? The tremendous fun of directing stuntmen, special effects, fistfights, shootings, chases, with the advantage of not having to worry about the film being good or bad, as long as my work was excellent. I did the same thing also in Italy. I already mentioned *The Secret of the Sahara*, for example…

When did you realize that Italian cinema was beginning to go through a crisis?

In the late seventies … by the number of scripts. Before, every year I would receive six or seven scripts and you had to refuse a number of them. Then all of sudden you started getting only a couple a year until one day none arrived … one script every two years, if you were lucky. This was a collateral effect of the crisis: there were no producers, no distributors…. For me it was traumatic because I was never one that had to really struggle much to get a film off the ground. In the nineties you found yourself having to deal with television … fuck.

Keoma Rises, any chance this project will ever see the light of day?

Absolutely! It will be a German production and they are working steadily. Next week we have a meeting to discuss the funding and there's also another project that's up-and-coming: "Roma città violenta" [translation: "Rome Violent City"]. It will be made up of various episodes, each one directed by a different director: me, Umberto Lenzi, Ruggero Deodato, Sergio Martino and my uncle Romolo Guerrieri. This too will be a German production. Each segment will be a quarter of an hour long and each of us will have a week to shoot it. Rome is still a violent city, with a different kind of criminality but still very dangerous. As long as there is violence, there is the need of directors like myself!

Rome, 2016

From Uruguay with Love: Interview with George Hilton

Jorge Hill Acosta y Lara, real name of George Hilton (born 15 July 1934, Montevideo), was one of the leading men of his generation. Characterized by a certain athleticism and a sometimes overused brooding look, Hilton, unlike Franco Nero, Tomas Milian, Giuliano Gemma and other contemporary stars, remained rooted in genre cinema, never managing (or wanting) to deviate into more politically or socially committed arthouse ventures, the only exception being his uncredited role in Marco Ferreri's *L'harem* (*Her Harem*,

1967). When talking about him, Castellari defined him "a lover of the sweet life": "George liked women, sunshine and laughing. He was like James Bond but without all the action parts." Lucio Fulci not only directs Hilton in his first Western, in 1966, but gives him the opportunity to successfully jump-start the Italian part of his career after many years working in his native Uruguay. "Before landing my first speaking and credited role, I participated in a large number of films in bit parts. This was before starting my theater career, which later helped my attempts with cinema. As a young theater actor I interpreted authors like Bernard Shaw, Chekhov and even Shakespeare. When I left Uruguay I was a well-known face but in the theater world I was quite famous."

In Westerns Hilton will be directed by Castellari, Giorgio Capitani, Nando Cicero and Giuliano Carnimeo. His willingness to change registry, will bring him to more morose territories under the inspired direction of Romolo Guerrieri first and then Sergio Martino but also Tonino Valerii. Unlike Westerns, to which Hilton will be introduced when the genre is already going strong, with gialli, he is there from the start, but in the sixties and seventies we can find a wide range of other types of films: war movies, adventure films, comedies, police and action thrillers. Gianni Martucci, who directed him in *Milano ... difendersi o morire* (*Blazing Flowers*, 1978), summarized Hilton as follows: "He was a good actor but he could have become a great actor if he hadn't listened to that part of his brain asking him to start drinking martinis and go look for swimming pools."

Your first film was Los tallos amargos [The Bitter Stems, 1956]. Correct?
Yes, by Fernando Ayala, which was filmed in Argentina in the mid-fifties; but that for me was what in Argentina is called a "bolito" ... a kind of ... well not even a cameo, because I wasn't known. It was a very small part. I think I played a journalist.

Hilton in Lucio Fulci's first western, *The Brute and the Beast*, 1966 (courtesy Nocturno Cinema).

How does this first film come about? How do you discover cinema?

Let's start by saying that I was artistically born in Uruguayan theater. This is my origin, the Uruguayan theater. Before that, I used to write. My grandfather was an important South American writer, my maternal grandfather, Manuel Acosta y Lara and I, like him, wrote poems, novels and short stories. Then, I became a part of what was called the "teatro indipendiente," the amateur theater, let's say. At that point I was asked to work in Uruguayan radio. Keep in mind that there was no television yet. I remember I had a program dedicated to poetry. Anyway, I was doing radio and theater, but there was no way to earn real money or get recognized, and therefore I decided to drop everything and leave. My wallet and career would have never flourished if I'd stayed there. It was all small and a little provincial. At the time, taking the leap meant crossing the Rio de la Plata and going to Buenos Aires, where I arrived in '55. At that point I knew I wanted to be an actor and there I really tried to get started, tried to connect with the right people. After a while, I managed to get some work on Argentinian television, Channel 7. I auditioned, they liked me, I must say, almost immediately and gave me some pretty nice things. Meanwhile, my agent gave me this, let's call it, special figuration in *Los tallos amargos*, which for me wasn't a big deal … maybe just a little push in the right direction. But I got to work with Gianni Ferrio's wife, Alba Arnova. Oh no … that's not the film. Arnova I met on *Una viuda difícil* [translation: *A Difficult Widow*, 1957], the following year.

All this happened in the heart of the fifties.

Yes, between 1955 and 1957. There had been the fall of Peron, and the revolution was still going strong. The political and social situation was terrible. You could hear gunfire at all hours of the day. Going out for dinner—I was in a hotel—was quite an endeavor. A mess, really. Anyway, I was fortunate enough, after these initial experiences, to be introduced to Catrano Catrani, an Italian director, who cast me as, what is called there, the "galan" … in other words, the young actor, the promising star to launch, to promote. This was my first real film as a protagonist. *Alto Paraná* [1958], was filmed at Iguazù, near the waterfalls. Enchanting! The film was a box-office hit and got my career started.

You become quite prolific, something you will continue being throughout most of your career.

Yes, everything was put into motion from that moment onwards: I got a nice role in *La procesión* [translation: *The Procession*, 1960], we won a prize at the Mar del Plata Festival with *El bote, el río y la gente* [translation: *The Boat, the River and the People*, 1960] and then I made *Los que verán a Dios* [translation: *Those Who Will See God*, 1963] and there something unbelievable happened … you see, I firmly believe in destiny. I wasn't able to go with the rest of the cast and crew to the film's premiere and … well … they all died…. The production had rented a coach. There was an accident and nobody survived. All dead, from my co-stars to the producers and director. It was a true miracle [I survived].

As your career in cinema started taking shape, you continued doing theater, am I right?

Absolutely, so much so that I managed to put together my own company after some time. The culmination of my theater activity arrived when I reached the Odeon, which was the biggest and most prestigious stage in Buenos Aires, where Vittorio Gassman would go when he performed there, where all the great actors would go. I put on a show with my company, which included Beatriz Tai and Gloria Guzman. We would go on long tours around South America. I became quite appreciated and well-known at an early age.

What was your perception of Italy, film-wise? Did you like Italian cinema? What and who were you aware of?

Yes, I liked it a lot. For example, Silvana Pampanini was an idol for me. I remember seeing her at a festival and being able to speak to her was a great honor for me. *Un marito per Anna Zaccheo* [*A Husband for Anna*, 1953], I remember was a big success in my country. I was just a kid and all of us would go, "Just think of what women they have in Italy!" The cinema! Italian films were held in great consideration. Now, Italian cinema isn't even distributed in South America. It doesn't exist. When I started out, you could really feel the Italian presence abroad, not only in Latin American countries. Westerns, gialli, horror films were big hits all over the place. Nowadays, who knows what goes on in Italy? Who sees Italian films?

What circumstances bring you to Italy?

For, let's say … passionate reasons. There was this woman, how can I say … she created a big problem for me, and I decided that I had to leave, leave Argentina. I had to escape. She was a woman who was trying to involve me in what could have become a scandal. She was pregnant, and stated that the child was mine, which I knew to be false. So I ran away, went to the airport of Sesia, and bought the first ticket available with the little money I had managed to scrape together in a hurry. "There's a plane at midnight that goes to Milan." "OK." I did not know a word of Italian, nothing, but I was in a hurry to leave and I got on that plane. I arrived in Milan on July 16th, the day of my birthday. It was terribly hot. Keep in mind that in Buenos Aires it was the middle of winter and I was wearing a sweater, winter stuff. On the plane I met a lady who kindly helped me and took me to buy some summer clothes. I stayed in a hotel near the station, but I had no money. Milan was completely deserted and assaulted by truly asphyxiating heat. The hotel manager asked me, "What are you doing here? Go to the sea, to the coast, to Genoa." I took the cheapest bus and went. I still remember my arrival at Stazione Principe. It was 1962, and while I was walking around, I got stopped by a girl, blonde, beautiful, who recognized me. "But aren't you Jorge Hilton?" At the time people called me Jorge. "I was in Mendoza with my family and we saw you at the theater, in a show, 'Mrs. Minister.' What are you doing here?" I explained everything to her, that I had just arrived and was urgently looking for a place to stay. "But you cannot go to a hotel, they are very expensive here. Wait … let me call my mother." So she invites me to stay at their home: they were in Boccadasse, a beautiful place. That was the beginning of a love affair with this girl, who was a very famous pianist. But after a while, I began to wonder, "What am I doing here? I fell from the frying pan into the fire. I cannot stay here, with this woman. I have to get away." I invented a story, lied about having to go to Cannes to see relatives, but actually went down to Rome. But once in Rome, I didn't know anyone or where to go. I had very little money, but instinct has always led me to the best places. I went to Via Bocca di Leone, Hotel d'Inghilterra, a stunning five-star hotel. I talked to the manager, "I'm a Uruguayan actor, I just got here, I don't know what to do…" "But this is a very expensive hotel." "Is there something you can do to help me?" He must have liked me, "Look, one of our waiters is on vacation for a month … you can stay in his garret." He asked for virtually no money, and naturally I accepted his offer. One of the first things I did, was to go and visit Via Veneto. I started talking to a bunch of people who asked me if I was Latin American—at the time I had my hair gelled back which was the fashion in my country—and I was invited to their table. A table full of people: Lea Massari, Antonio Cifariello, whom I had already met in Argentina when I was awarded a special prize for *El bote, el río y la gente*, Fausto Tozzi, Nino Persello. They were all wondering what I was doing there. Some people said, "Look, winter in Rome is very difficult, you have to have some sort of plan." It was Nino Persello, who rescued me, "Look, I have to go to Yugoslavia shortly, to shoot a cloak-and-dagger film. You can stay in my apartment. Just pay half the rent." The rent was twenty thousand lire a month for a beautiful apartment. He even gave me the name of an agent who spoke Spanish … I can't remember her name … Di Leo, maybe.

What was the first film you got picked for?

This agent called me to audition for an adventure epic, another cloak-and-dagger flick. *L'uomo mascherato contro i pirati* [*The Masked Man Against the Pirates*, a.k.a. *The Black Pirate*, 1964]. I go to the Titanus offices to meet with the director, I still remember his name, Vertunnio De Angelis. I don't know what happened to him. The moment he sees me he goes, "But this is not what I asked for … he isn't any good. We want a Steve Reeves type and you bring me this Latin Gary Cooper! Not good!" Just then, the door opens and the producer enters. A fat man, a Sicilian. I think his name was Pino Addario. He looks at me carefully, "Ah, you seem an interesting guy. Where are you from?" "I am Uruguayan." "Are you known in South America?" "Well enough. I won some prizes." "You'll do… Do you know how to fence?" "Yes, yes, of course." It wasn't at all true. Never fenced in my life. "I used to fence when I was kid." Ah! Grazia Di Leo was the agent's name! She called me a few days later. "You got the part. They'll give you a million lira." It was great, I paid twenty thousand lira for the rent, and I even bought myself a FIAT 500. I bought everything. Consider that I had left everything, every single thing, house, clothes … everything to this woman in Buenos Aires. Oh well, I made this film which was awful, something despicable. Then, there were problems with payments, even for us actors. So much so that at one point I took the floor and said, "If you don't pay us, I'm leaving." For one day I didn't work, I stayed locked in my dressing room. "I'm not coming unless you slip the money you owe under the door." However, the movie came out and they made me sign another contract, again for a million lira, for a film of the same genre. I do not know if it was ever released or what happened to it. It was called something like, "The Masked Man on Treasure Island," or something along those lines. Meanwhile, while on vacation at the sea, I met a woman who shortly after became my wife. After seeing the things I had done, she advised me to look for a more important agent. By this time, I had also started doing a lot of publicity and photo-stories, and was earning quite well. I was taken to an agency owned by Nando Basile, Amleto Adami and Gino Malerba, who dealt with people like Johnny Dorelli, Massimo Ranieri and later on even Carmen Russo…

Was this choice the turning point you were hoping for?

Yes, exactly. Through this agency I got the chance of auditioning for Lucio Fulci, an important film with Franco Nero and Nino Castelnuovo: *Le colt cantarono la morte e fu … tempo di massacro* [*The Brute and the Beast*, a.k.a. *Massacre Time*, 1966]. They chose me out of over 500 candidates, despite the fact that I looked totally different to the character I was supposed to represent: a drunkard and a lecher. I made my hair and beard grow and prepared thoroughly for the part. The film was a big success and I was well praised. Even Michelangelo Antonioni asked to meet me. I have to say, it was one of my best portrayals and the one I'm the most proud of. My career really began with this film.

How was your relationship with Lucio Fulci?

Not very good. Fulci was a great director but as a person he was completely lunatic. I am too and we had our fair share of fights on set. But if I have to be completely honest, I have to admit that I owe him everything: if I hadn't made his film, I wouldn't be giving this interview about my career now.

You had a very "old Hollywood" presence at the time, a seductive, slightly ambiguous charisma, with a sort of silky Clark Gable quality, atypical compared to most Italian leading men of that period.

Yes, many people would tell me this. Personally, I wasn't aware of it. But one thing is for sure, if I'd had the same career in Hollywood, now I would still be working a lot. Here, they forget about you. John Wayne made films until he died. If he hadn't been able to get on his horse, they would have put him on it with a crane but rest assured, he would have continued working. In Italy … they have a short memory.

Going back to your films. Before working with Fulci, you took parts in two Franco Franchi and Ciccio Ingrassia comedies.

Before? Ah yes, previously I had worked on *Due mafiosi contro Goldginger* [*The Amazing Doctor G*, a.k.a. *Goldginger*, a.k.a. *The Two Crazy Secret Agents*, 1965]. That project came to me because Franchi and Ingrassia had my same agent. Amleto Adami offered me the role. I was supposed to play a kind of pseudo Sean Connery. It was a cameo. Then after came *I 2 figli di Ringo* [*Two Sons of Ringo*, 1966]. In both films I played the more serious roles but it was fun to be part of comedic mechanisms.

How was it working with them?

Working with them was wonderful. No problems. I was particularly happy working with Franco Franchi, who was great fun. Ingrassia was a more brooding kind of person, quiet, he kept to himself. But however, with both of them things went more than smoothly. Two good people, and very professional. After *The Brute and the Beast* they asked me to do *The Two Sons of Ringo* as I said before. I wasn't really craving, after a big success, to play a small part, but they paid me very well, and it was a pleasure working with them. Both of these films were directed by Giorgio Simonelli, who was a very easy director to please.

Westerns are one of the two genres you are most remembered for.

I never liked Westerns. Even now, I don't go to the cinema to see them. I've never been interested in the genre at all, but I was a very good horseback rider. Back in Uruguay, my family owned some farms and we would often go horseback without a saddle, bareback. Then, as a youngster, I was a boxer, so I was very athletic. In fact, many directors I worked with were amazed, because unlike some actors who worked in Westerns, I wasn't a stuntman. I was an actor who knew how to do certain things. I acted and had a well-toned physique. I think this was the reason for my success in the genre.

Which is your favorite Western, between the ones you made?

Surely *The Brute and the Beast* takes the podium, but I also have a close bond with *Los Desperados* [*A Bullet for Sandoval*, a.k.a. *Those Desperate Men Who Smell of Dirt and Death*, 1969] with Ernest Borgnine. I like the movie very much, first of all because Borgnine was in it, a wonderful actor who had won an Oscar for *Marty* [1955], a film I had loved. There was also an actor friend of mine—I was able to place many friends in the film—Alberto de Mendoza, but also George Rigaud and Julio Buchs, a director with whom I had a wonderful relationship. We shot the whole thing in Almeria, and I have marvelous memories of this movie. I think *Ognuno per sé* [*The Ruthless Four*, 1968] by Giorgio Capitani is also one of the best Westerns I've worked in. It is also in the archives of the Cinematheque Francais because it is considered amongst the best Italian Westerns ever made. It was unusual because it was a kind of remake of *The Treasure of the Sierra Madre* [1948] with Humphrey Bogart.

Among the other leading men of the Italian West, which is the one you admired the most?

The greatest was Tomas Milian. We were friends and had many things in common. He is Cuban, I'm Uruguayan, we both spoke Spanish. He was very handsome. We used to talk a lot, plus we both began our career in the same period. I know he isn't well. I guess he is now paying the price for his excesses.

Speaking of your colleagues active in the genre, each one had his own specific "character." Milian was the peon, often with revolution in his heart, Nero was the melancholic and mystical figure, Gemma the lovable idealist. How would you define your Western persona?

I represented the light-heartedness of the West, thanks to characters like Alleluja, Tresette…. Edmondo Amati, after having seen me in Fulci's film, decided I was perfect for more ironic Westerns. In fact, my second film in the genre was *Vado … l'ammazzo e torno* [*Any Gun Can Play*, 1967] by Castellari.

The two directors that, through irony, helped you shape your Western persona were Castellari and Giuliano Carnimeo. How was your relationship with them?

Very good, with both of them. The one I see and hear the most is Enzo, who is still a very good friend of mine. Carnimeo[4] instead, I haven't had any news in years but he was someone who always had a lot of ideas. A talented director. Another one who doesn't get enough credit for his work is Nando Cicero, with whom I made *Professionisti per un massacro* [*Professionals for a Massacre*, 1967], a hardboiled Western with an uncommon amount of violence. But these films owed a lot also to the stuntmen, people like Attilio Severini or Romano Puppo. They would work with all these directors I've mentioned and this would help me feel I was always part of the same family, or community.

Before passing onto your other main genre, giallo, tell me something about your experience on L'harem *[Her Harem, 1967] by Marco Ferreri.*

Ah yes, *Her Harem* … they cut everything. As I was shooting *Any Gun Can Play*, my agent calls me and tells me: "Marco Ferreri wants you for his next film and he wants to couple you with Carroll Baker." A mess to manage and get the proper permits, wrap up before schedule on Enzo's film and leave for Yugoslavia, Dubrovnik, where they were shooting. Anyway I was glad to work with Ferreri, who was a raving lunatic, a strange man. A month later they call me to tell me that my scenes had been cut. They paid me of course, but I practically don't appear in the film. In the end I didn't lose anything, I got paid well and the film was a flop so from my perspective, things went quite well.

So you do Ferreri's film, starring Carroll Baker, and then, shortly after you find her again on the set of Il dolce corpo di Deborah *[The Sweet Body of Deborah, a.k.a. The Body, a.k.a. Married to Kill, 1968], your first giallo. First of all, what kind of person was Baker?*

I did that with her and then *Il diavolo a sette facce* [*The Devil with Seven Faces*, 1971]. A fine actress and a great one for me. You know, I've worked with many American actors and I can tell you, they were impeccably prepared. Having made films with Van Heflin, Borgnine, Baker, Stephen Boyd I have to say they cannot be beaten. They arrived on set always on time, they would be quiet in their dressing rooms, and when they were called, they were always ready and never got a line wrong. Even when they had problems, like Van Heflin, who was always drunk, when it was showtime, he was impeccable. I also worked with great Italian actors: Salvo Randone on *Mio caro assassino* [*My Dear Killer*, 1972], and Enrico Maria Salerno, a great friend who taught me a lot, for example.

Last question regarding Westerns: when did you realize the genre was dying out?
At one point producers started exaggerating and made loads of them, 90 percent of which were bad, Z movies. People got fed up, they realized they were being ripped off and stopped watching them. Then, well … I didn't like them, it was hard work, making them was really ball-busting. The heat, no night life. I did them, but without much joy. But that is a genre that was murdered.

With the rise of gialli, your face changes and irony leaves space to a strong sexual ambiguity.
Yes, there was quite a radical change. My characters became darker and shadier. They used to describe me as "brooding and mysterious." I consider myself quite eclectic. I've done dramas, action films, comedies. This is because I had a solid background, theater is an incredible school. I loved the giallo genre immensely, I fit perfectly in it. Except the first one, the one I consider the first, *Lo strano vizio della signora Wardh* [*The Strange Vice of Mrs. Wardh*, a.k.a. *Blade of the Ripper*, 1971] in which I just didn't see myself. The next one was far better, *La coda dello scorpione* [*The Case of the Scorpion's Tail*, a.k.a. *Scorpion's Tail*, 1971], in which I deliver one of my best performances. In *Mrs. Wardh* I'm not convincing, maybe because it's my first real attempt, I don't know, but something doesn't quite work. The film was very successful but I'm not satisfied. My favorite gialli are *My Dear Killer* and *Scorpion's Tail*.

Tutti i colori del buio [All the Colors of the Dark, 1972]?
Less, a lot less. It's a solid piece of work but if I have to judge my performance I can't say I'm completely satisfied. The only film I'm really happy with is the Fulci Western. Everything that came later … well, I never really prepared so much for a role as I did on that film. Maybe I didn't take things as seriously as I was supposed to. I was too sure of myself.

Speaking again about the main directors of your career, a special mention has to go to Sergio Martino.
I never had a single problem with Sergio, a serious professional. Generally I made a lot of films with them, the Martino brothers I mean. I was very sorry to hear about Luciano's death. I had an excellent rapport with him. I introduced him to Edwige Fenech,[5] and his last wife, Olga Bisera.

I didn't know. How and when exactly did you meet Fenech?
I can tell you precisely when I met her. It happened in Tirrenia, where I was shooting *Il dito nella piaga* [*The Liberators*, 1969] with Klaus Kinski, at the same time that she was

The Italian poster of *The Killer Must Kill Again*, 1975.

there to make a film … I do not remember the title,[6] a movie with an actress who had the greatest body you can imagine, Rosalba Neri! She had an ass worthy of a stardom of its own. We were in the same hotel, Hotel Continental, and we crossed each other in the lobby one evening. We started talking and … let's say it was friendship at first sight, one that continued once we were back in Italy. We went out several times. Luciano Martino had already noticed her and had lost his mind, he was completely under her spell. One day he asked me to introduce her to him. "We can do a film with both of you. You can pick the role you prefer for yourself." That is how everything began.

In the first half of the seventies your filmography was dominated by gialli, however, you returned to Westerns from time to time. For example, what do you remember about Ah sì? E io lo dico a Zzzzorro! [Mark of Zorro, a.k.a. Who's Afraid of Zorro, 1975]?

With Lionel Stander, right? Another great American actor. That film was a massive flop … it made nearly nothing. I did it because I liked the idea of making a comic Zorro, an over the top parodic version. The director was Franco Lo Cascio, a nice enough man. I never met him again after that film. I knew his mother, who was the assistant director of Vittorio De Sica, whom I had met.

Did you meet De Sica socially or professionally?

No, no … for a film! He asked to see me for a role in *Il giardino dei Finzi Contini* [*The Garden of the Finzi-Continis*, 1970] but he ended choosing Fabio Testi, and did well. Fabio was more suitable for the part.

Let's jump to another exception in your giallo-dominated period: **Sette ore di violenza per una soluzione imprevista [7 Hours of Violence, 1973], Michele Massimo Tarantini's first film as a director.**

Tarantini was my brother-in-law, the brother of my ex-wife, which is the reason he managed to work. I'd get him on board, working on films by Carnimeo or Sergio. When he was ready to make his directorial debut, he asked me to be the protagonist and I accepted. It's a strange film but quite well made, it has its moments.

When I interviewed Gianni Martucci, who directed you in Milano: **difendersi o morire [Blazing Flowers, 1978], he told me that at that time you were more interested in comedic roles.**

Yes, I wanted to become a comedian. In films such as *Teste di cuoio* [translation: *Leather Heads*, 1981] by Giorgio Capitani, I played a mad Turkish terrorist, or something like that … people laughed. Yes, I felt more like a comedy actor. Not in the same vein of Lino Banfi, something a little more sophisticated. I definitely felt more comfortable in roles of this type than in films such as *7 Hours of Violence*, which I felt had nothing to do with me. The character did karate, smashed things, shouted. However, I wanted to give my brother-in-law a hand so I did it, without problems, but I wasn't made for those roles.

What has your relationship with the public been over the years?

Very good, I've always had many fans, not only in Italy, but all over the world. I used to receive letters, especially in my Western phase from everywhere: from Vietnam, from the United States. But not just me, actors like Franco Nero, Fabio Testi, Gianni Garko, Tomas Milian. We were, and are, followed by people around the world. Now an Italian actor isn't known anywhere outside the country … if he goes to Lugano, at the Swiss border, he'd be a complete stranger. Now I don't work much, but many people still seek me out, especially on Facebook. I get an incredible number of messages every day, letters of people who discover or rediscover my films, some who see them for the first time. Only this morning I received a request for an interview by an Austrian newspaper. These are films that have a cult following that none of us would have ever expected.

And with critics?

Eh, they've never been very generous. Abroad things would be a little better. I received some good reviews in South America for example, but in Italy we were perceived, actors like myself, as ruthless mercenaries that would do anything for a buck.

For directors there was a strong division between genre and committed cinema associated with a preconception that the two couldn't mix. Was it the same for actors?

Officially no, but I think there was. There was a, how can I put it … well, some actors wouldn't be picked because they were connected to a cinema that wasn't perceived as socially or politically committed. Sometimes a major director would call you. Monicelli, for example, asked to see me but in my opinion, many producers were opposed to mixing these two realities.

Regrets? If you could go back, would you do everything the same way?

No, I think I was wrong in trying to grab too much at once. I had agents that made me sign one contract after the other, and year after year my schedule was always full, but they didn't take the quality of the projects and scripts into consideration. "Look, here they give you more, this pays well…." I accepted everything they put under my nose, to make money, and in fact financially I can't complain. Sure, I was very lucky, I arrived in Italy when it was making thousands of films and had an industry which was one of the strongest in the world. As I always say, I discovered America in Italy, in the sense that I found a reality that really took care of me and my well-being. They paid very well at the time. What I asked they gave me. Like when I did the "Splendid" coffee ad, I was given a sum of money which is unthinkable these days. Perhaps now I'd try to pick better films and more important directors. This, however, doesn't necessarily mean that I'd have a longer career or that I'd become more famous. There have been many actors who made more sophisticated films, who have disappeared completely and no one remembers.

Not many people know that you were also a producer and distributor at one point.

Yes, I had a company called 3G International, because my associates were Giorgio Stefanutti, Giancarlo Ferrando, the director of photography and then there was me, George Hilton. Three Gs.

This happened in the mid-seventies, right?

Yes, but I don't remember exactly. It didn't last long. It worked like this: I went to MIFED,[7] I always went at the time, I'd buy films, the ones that cost less, then I'd get them distributed regionally. All done with promissory notes. None of the films turned out to be hits and only one was of quality, to which I gave the title *Marika degli inferni* [*Mariken van Nieumeghen*, 1974]. A Dutch film by a great director, Joss Stelling, which had a strange title. This is the only one that did pretty well, in the sense that we didn't lose money. Generally, our main problem was that we couldn't get them screened in the best theaters. The only good theaters we managed to get were Tiffany and the Rouge et Noir in Rome and that was only because we had an erotic film, I can't think of the title, something like "The sins of my wife" … something like that. That is another one that did OK.

You only distributed?

No, we also produced for television. Precisely, the opening credits for some shows, definitely one for Pier Francesco Pingitore. When I realized the company wasn't going anywhere, I sold my share to our sales manager and never looked back. I didn't want to know anything more about it.

Rome, 2015

1968 The Serious Caress of Frivolousness
The Cinema of Vittorio Sindoni

E va bene, ragazzi. Fatela pure questa rivoluzione, ma per l'ora di cena tutti a casa!—Italiani! È severamente proibito servirsi della toilette durante le fermate. [Fine, kids. Go and have your revolution but be home by dinner time!—tagline for *Italians! It Is Severely Prohibited to Use the Toilet During Stops*, 1969]

In 1953 Giorgio Capitani was directing his first film, schooled, as he was by Vittorio Cottafavi, Mario Bonnard and other barons of fascist-era celluloid while Romolo Guerrieri was still Girolami and learning the ropes on his very first sets, waiting and hoping to unfetter himself one day from his older brother Marino. In the first half of the fifties, Giulio Petroni was back in Italy looking to continue his successful streak of documentaries, reinvigorated after his long stay in the exotic lands of Southeast Asia while Alberto De Martino's years observing his father at work on the hair and make-up of divas, were long gone as he starts passing from set to set, accumulating experience and shaking hands with other struggling members of a new generation of filmmakers, like Sergio Leone and Sergio Sollima. When in 1956, Franco Rossetti and Umberto Lenzi approach the market after having both received their diplomas from the CSC, Mario Caiano had already started putting together a substantial filmography as an AD and Petroni had put behind him his experience as a "directing collaborator" for Giuseppe De Santis, who will later call Guerrieri for the same role. In the heart of the decade, Capitani continues to direct, looking for a hit that would make a difference in his career but finding only mild reactions, remaining still very far from the success that awaits him in the future. Umberto Lenzi, in 1958, travels to Greece full of expectations for what should have been his big debut but will only draw a blank, whereas things will go better for Petroni who the following year will officially become a film director. Towards the end of the fifties, Enzo G. Castellari takes his uncle's place alongside his father, starting out as a volunteer assistant. Alberto De Martino will manage to direct his first feature not long after, in 1961, the same year in which Lenzi gets his strongly craved second chance. Rossetti, in the meantime, abandons his activity as an AD preferring the one of a writer under the wing of Ennio De Concini. The subsequent year Caiano, in Spain, directs his first feature-length film while Guerrieri's long apprenticeship reaches a new evolutionary stage as he helms his first second unit. Shoulders brush throughout the many folds and frenetic concatenations that mark the fifties, as the paths of these directors, together with the ones of hundreds of others, cross, overlap and in some cases tightly intertwine and by the start of the sixties all of the above mentioned had begun, or were on the brink of, initiating their directing careers. Vittorio Sindoni (born 21 April 1939, Capo d'Orlando) is the first director in this book to take his first steps in cinema in a brand new decade:

> I'm a son of the sixties, culturally and artistically speaking, but I was lucky enough to start out in cinema enveloped in the comforting hold of the previous decade. The so-called "Hollywood on the Tiber" years were over so I never lived through the glorious reconstruction of Cinecittà, the arrival of the Americans, the golden age of mythological epics. I witnessed all that from afar but in the early sixties you could still feel that similar kind of electricity, that vibrant atmosphere. There were still many Americans working here and everything that had been built over the fifties was still standing strong.

Sindoni's first role on a set, as a volunteer assistant to be precise, is for a rather mediocre historic adventure epic directed by Siro Marcellini *Il colpo segreto di d'Artagnan* (*The Secret Mark of D'Artagnan*, 1962) with George Nader in the lead role. The kind of medium-budget film that followed the teachings and trends of adventure epics of the previous decade.

The early sixties is a period of assessment: the Westerns being made were still very much molded by the American perspective; peplums were still around and going strong but the more we dig our way to the heart of the decade the more we can easily notice how, year after year, the genre was being saturated by cheap, derivative products often characterized by increasingly comedic or self-parodic elements, a sort of rehearsal, on a

Vittorio Sindoni, with Sophia Loren on the set of his TV movie *La mia casa è piena di specchi* (*My House Is Full of Mirrors*), 2010 (courtesy Vittorio Sindoni).

smaller scale, for what will happen later on to Westerns. "When I started working, cinema was going through a small crisis, maybe not straight away but shortly after having begun my experience as an assistant director. Not a big one, nothing like what will happen in the eighties and nineties but there was some concern related to the departure of the Americans. Producers and directors struggled to try and figure out what the public wanted, they strived to search for new genres." These are the words of Sindoni which help describe what was a very scrabbled period in which the audience's needs and tastes were changing and shifting as rapidly as the country's social customs and the technological evolution that had begun at the start of the previous decade, the biggest event being the rising power of television. From the fifties, the spread of TV grew at an astounding pace, as had previously happened in the U.S. market. In those years a television set was a luxury item that very few Italians could afford, so bars and cafes became grouping points in which to share the very first and extremely popular Italian game shows. Towards the end of the decade, the first news broadcasts were aired and particularly relevant in 1957 was the advent of Caroselli[1] (translation: carousel), a famous part of the TV schedule where the advertising message had to adhere to strict stylistic and narrative regulations. Then in 1962, the first satellite link between Italy and the United States marked the beginning of interplanetary communication, allowing global events to be shared by everyone, almost simultaneously, like the landing of the first man on the moon in 1969 which drew about 500 million spectators in front of the screen. These first years of the sixties, as already mentioned elsewhere, see the Italian economy reaching its moment of maximum expansion, in what is known as the "economic miracle." This massive growth, that from 1956 had a major propelling force in export, is characterized by an important new stability in prices and a total absence of imbalance in payments. Naturally this is not an exclusively Italian phenomenon but what makes Italy's situation different is the anomalous increase in the gross domestic product, which has been quite rightly compared to a "miracle."

The novelty of the small screen has repercussions on the film world and from 1960 to 1964 the number of spectators, though still remaining high compared to the statistics of previous years, was declining; this marked the beginning of a slight but constant decrease in audience numbers, which from 1966 onwards will accelerate in pace. "The combination of a lack of direction in the film industry together with the advent of television had created a certain extent of chaos but to be honest I didn't really fully understand it until some years later. To me, as a 20-year-old, the world of cinema was something wonderfully absurd. A film set was like this crazy, super-populated train ride screeching through the sky at breakneck speed." Despite a crucial and indispensable apprenticeship in films, Vittorio Sindoni will find his big chance to stand out in the theater world, directing the company "Il collettivo" (translation: The Collective) in Rome, a role that will consequentially bring him to work for some years as author of several cultural programs for RAI, that will then help him close the circle and turn back to cinema by the late sixties. Specifically, Sindoni's debut arrives in 1968 with a film that ironically will represent the biggest anomaly of his career: the giallo *L'assassino ha le mani pulite* (*Deadly Inheritance*, 1968). With Femi Benussi and Tom Drake in the lead roles, the film in question shares some narrative traits with the French-inspired, pre–Argento gialli of the late sixties like the films of Umberto Lenzi or Romolo Guerrieri: the motive for the string of murders in this pop-colored, funky-sounding world is tied to logical and material dynamics and to financial motives, with none of the psycho-sexual traumas that will animate the serial killers of the seventies, and the setting is that of a fractured family.

That film gave me the opportunity of experimenting with the medium. It was a perfect project and genre with which to do this, because a mystery thriller really puts you in the position of making original and unlikely visual choices. As far as the whole look of the film is concerned, that was dictated, primarily, by the fact I wanted to make a film for young people, I wanted to capture the youthful exuberance of the time. Of course, it's all over the top but *Deadly Inheritance* had a very young crew. Most of the people had just come out of the CSC. Apart from some key elements, everybody was new to the business. I was not even thirty when I directed it. I wasn't really into those kind of films. I certainly wasn't aware of what was being done in Italy, though I had seen some Mario Bava films.

After *Deadly Inheritance,* Sindoni makes a controversial diversion into the bittersweet 1968 parable, *Italiani! È severamente proibito servirsi della toilette durante le fermate* (translation: *Italians! It Is Severely Prohibited to Use the Toilet During Stops*, 1969), which is also deserving of mention for having given Silvia Dionisio her first major role after a string of bit parts. From 1973 onwards, the Sicilian director will dedicate his entire career to comedies, making his debut his best-known film abroad, and the following year he created a significant and fruitful partnership with Walter Chiari (8 March 1924, Verona–20 December 1991, Milan), thus saving an artist who had been one of the greatest showmen Italy has ever known, from an incomprehensible exile. He had been the star of such films as *Falstaff—Chimes at Midnight* (1965), *Bonjour Tristesse* (1958) and *The Little Hut* (1957), where he met and started a relationship with Ava Gardner, who, although still formally married to Frank Sinatra, was estranged from him. With Chiari, Sindoni creates a very delicate and warm type of comedy, set in the northern provinces and with stories that rotate around married couples, the fear of aging and the difficulties between parents and their offspring. Chiari is part of a close team of actors put together by Sindoni which includes Luciano Salce, Macha Meril and Gino Bramieri.

> It wasn't quite like anything that was being done at the time. It had none of the characteristics of the sex comedies that were becoming increasingly popular, despite there being some sexual elements in the stories, but there was hardly any nudity—I mean, you could see more of Femi Benussi under the shower in *Deadly Inheritance*—and especially there was no gratuitous vulgarity. The only other director I feel was trying to do something similar was Giorgio Capitani, who is somebody I've always had great admiration for. His approach was different; my films were more Italian, while his had more of a French touch. Capitani and I had a chance of working in very close contact because, after having both abandoned cinema for television, we founded, with other colleagues, a sort of syndicate of Italian TV directors. He was the president and I was his vice.

Sindoni is the first of the two to turn to television, becoming in the eighties and especially in the nineties, one of the barons of the small screen, directing the highest profile TV movies and series.

> Undoubtedly, the transition from film to digital has changed the pace of work: once, to see if one take was good or not, you had to wait days, in some cases even a week. Now you just press "play" to see what went wrong, what you can improve, there and then ... on the spot. I'm the kind of person who wants to share the set with my actors and I like to show them what I'm trying to achieve and to know what they think of a certain scene. From an operational point of view, however, I can say that I haven't noticed that many differences because I use the same crew and have been for over thirty years and with whom I have a great relationship, not only professional but also and above all, human.

How did your adventure in films begin?

In 1959, I saw this poster publicizing courses for cinema and television at the International University Pro Deo. I come from a small Sicilian town so I got on a train with a third class ticket and some money given me by the a local grocer who wanted to help me, and went to Rome. But after fifteen days I realized this course was a waste of time. So I went around looking for work. The person who gave me my first job was Siro Marcellini. I was a volunteer assistant on his film *Il colpo segreto di d'Artagnan* [*The Secret Mark of D'Artagnan*, 1962]. They hardly gave me anything to eat, I would have to wake up at five in the morning to hitch a ride with one of the grips but it was an important experience. Then he called me again for *L'eroe di Babilonia* [*The Beast of Babylon Against the Son of Hercules*, a.k.a. *Hero of Babylon*, a.k.a. *Goliath, King of Slaves*, 1963]. My first film as a 1st AD was *Maciste nelle miniere di Re Salomone* [*Maciste in King Solomon's Mines*, 1964] by Piero Regnoli. I think that was also the first time I got credited. But this phase overlapped with my activity in theater and in fact I progressively let cinema go and dedicated myself to theater more and more.

If you had to choose one anecdote, one image that describes being an AD at that time, which would it be?

In these adventure films and peplums there would be big crowd sequences with battles, armies, horses and so on. I directed one of these scenes and thought I did a good job. It was probably a second unit, it might have been *The Beast of Babylon Against the Son of Hercules* ... anyhow it was one of my first films as an AD. Directors or producers would, at times, let assistant directors who showed talent, direct some scenes if they were behindhand with the schedule. Anyway, as I said I believed I had proved that I was competent but the next day I get called by the producer who started going, "Do you know what you did?!" I was shocked and didn't know what to answer. He was angry and I just couldn't understand why. "You shot the actors' faces!" "So?" "How can I sell it now?!" Because I didn't know at the time, that producers would sell these battle scenes to smaller productions that would then recycle them for their own films. If you think about it, it's genius, producers at the time had incredible creativity. On *Maciste in King Solomon's Mines*, for example, since we'd finished using the sets, they would be sold to another production for another film. It was a continuous cycle and nothing went to waste. One set could be used a multitude of times. We used to make more than four hundred films a year and do you know why? It was all possible thanks to promissory notes. If you had the necessary money to buy the first promissory note, you could go and deal with the regional distributors. Films would be released immediately, make money and then you could pay off all the pyramid of debts. Plus, people would all go to the cinema. They would say, "let's go and see a film" and not "let's see this or that film." The focus was on the social event and not on specific titles. People would go out and head to the cinema without even knowing what was being shown.

You are one of the few Italian directors to have come from the theater.

Yes, I attended the CUT, the Centro Universitario Teatrale [University Theater Center] in Rome and immediately after I started as a theater assistant director. I was an assistant, together with Mario Prosperi,[2] on *L'assedio di Romanzia* [translation: *The Siege of Romanzia*]. The company was going through a bit of a crisis and seeing I had contacts with the Greek amphitheater of Tindari, near where I come from, they decided on having the premiere there. Due to budget issues and various problems, the director wasn't able to move from Rome, or didn't want to, so the choice was between me and Prosperi. I was chosen because they said I knew the language, and by that they meant Sicilian. This event got things going and I started my career as a director of summer plays. Subsequently I became the head of a company because I saved the Eleonora Duse Foundation. They were closing when I intervened and by involving new, young actors, I managed to turn things round. Within this new generation of theater actors, there were people like Nando Gazzolo and Gabriele Lavia who would be placed beside big names, like Paola Borboni for example. Things were going very well but then I started working for RAI—at the time there was only one channel—specifically for a program entitled *Cronache del cinema e del teatro* [translation: *Chronicles of Cinema and Theater*].

In what years was all this taking place?
I started working for television in 1965/66 and my life in theater began roughly five years earlier, in 1961. Initially, while working in the editorial staff of this program with RAI, I would only deal with the theatrical aspects of things but slowly I started talking more and more about cinema.

So, by the late sixties you had accumulated a lot of experience both in cinema and theater. How did these two worlds integrate and help shape your subsequent career?
Well, those years as an AD taught me everything, technically speaking. Because all those directors—Siro Marcellini, Piero Regnoli—weren't great directors but they were formidable technicians. Theater instead, taught me the art of acting, how to talk to actors and getting the best out of them.

What was the experience that turned things around and got you back into films?
The first big experience was when I was called as a second unit director on a film that was set in Vietnam. Well, not exactly. The story took place in Vietnam but the scenes were actually shot near Rome, at the park of Manziana.[3] The film was *LSD—Inferno per pochi dollari* [*LSD—Flesh of the Devil*, 1967] by Massimo Mida. I shot everything that you see during the opening credits and then a sequence with American soldiers hiding in the jungle … the Italian-Vietnamese jungle. But this film was the trampoline towards my debut as a director with the giallo, *Omicidio per vocazione* [translation: *Murder by Vocation*].

The film is better known as L'assassino ha le mani pulite *[*Deadly Inheritance*, translation:* The Killer's Hands Are Clean, 1968*].*
Yes, but I discovered many years later that the title had been changed and the film distributed again with it, and with a new poster. It was a very unlucky film and very hard to make. Most of the crew was made up of greenhorns from the CSC. The money finished after one week. In fact, initially we were supposed to go and shoot the film at Marseille but we ended up doing all the exterior scenes at Anguillara,[4] changing the story slightly. It had a solid cast though: Femi Benussi, the American actor Tom Drake, Valeria Ciangottini, Ivo Garrani.

What do you remember of Tom Drake? And were you aware of what was being done in Italy, in the same genre?
I had some problems with him. He was very full of himself and wouldn't lose a chance to eulogize his career and go into raptures over his past. "I've worked with Liz Taylor…" or, "In Hollywood, we…" You know, stuff like that. As far as the story is concerned, the idea came from Romano Migliorini and we then developed the script together. I can't say I was particularly knowledgeable about the genre or aware of similar films in that same period, but I liked the story we wrote. Though *Deadly Inheritance* started off being very ambitious, it had to be scaled down and modified as we went along when we

became aware that there wasn't enough money. But nonetheless, the film turned out fine, I think, and if it had been made with a real production company and had been distributed normally, it would have done well. The producer, from Turin—I don't remember his name—didn't really care about it. He only produced it because he was infatuated with Femi Benussi. This is the only reason the film was made. It was quite funny, in retrospect. The producer would come on set, ignore me and head directly towards Benussi … or when I tried to talk to him about how production was going, he would interrupt me to ask, "How is Femi doing?" Sometimes he would close himself in the dressing room with her and you could hear him say, "Honeypot, don't be angry! What's wrong, my little sugar?" Drake tried to fuck Femi but didn't succeed. Well everybody tried to get into her panties, she was very exuberant. Reason why the producer would always have a stink-eye with every man that hovered round her.

The production company had further problems even after the film was finished.
Yes, it failed shortly after and in fact at the time, the film didn't have a real distribution. It was produced by Semafilm, which was not the most stable of companies to start with, but it had problems when the promissory note of the foley artist was turned down by the bank. Tonino Cacciottolo was one the biggest special sound effect technicians working at the time and the production owed him money and I don't think he was the only one not to have been paid for the film. It's important to understand that back then, all, and I mean all, Italian cinema was based on promissory notes. Anyway, even if the film wasn't seen much, it got some attention by colleagues and producers and I got called by Stefano Canzio[5]—who was the curator of the film column I had worked on when in RAI—and by CineRiz. They asked me to direct a film on the students' protest that was taking place in those years. *Italiani! È severamente proibito servirsi della toilette durante le fermate* [translation: *Italians! It is Severely Prohibited to Use the Toilet During Stops*, 1969].

It's a film that had some problems with censorship, didn't it?
Huge problems. I put my foot down and didn't want to cut a single frame. They had a specific problem with a castration scene. It was a surreal situation, because we were in the screening room with the producer on his knees in front of the committee. "Please, save me from this maniac, he doesn't want to listen. If the film isn't released, I'm ruined!" The film did get cut and I can't say the version that came out reflects the film I wanted to make. It became inoffensive, which is what they wanted.

How was the castration scene shot?
It's a little trashy. This woman, disappointed by the intellectual decadence of this fake revolutionary she was in love with, decides to castrate him by tying his testicles with a guitar cord, which was connected to a massive pile of books placed precariously on the door of an open wardrobe, which was also tied to the telephone receiver. She leaves, calls, he answers the phone and there you go, the books fall and so does the rest. It was something that was supposed to be more symbolic than anything else. This is the scene that shook people up and one of the reasons I chose to produce my next film, *… e se per caso, una mattina* [translation: *… And If by Chance, One Morning*, 1972]. A small budget and most of it was spent on the film's star, Pamela Tiffin.

That film has kind of disappeared from the radar.
Yes. It had no success when it was released but again, like in the case of my previous

films, it was well seen by insiders and this time, also by critics. The general public talked more about the soundtrack then they did about the film. The music is by the Roman group Gruppo di improvvisazione Canzonanza,[6] which included people like Ennio Morricone, Daniele Paris and Egisto Macchi. But the film got the attention of an important production company like P.A.C. "If you have a more commercial film in mind, we'd like to know about it." "You are like a young Fellini…"—producers loved to pump up directors' egos—"…but you have to start thinking more about the public."

What was the first film you directed with them?

A film with a strange and misleading title but actually it was a very light and refined comedy, *La signora è stata violentata!* [translation: *The Lady Was Raped!*, 1973]. The title was suggested by writer Roberto Mazzucco. This was also my biggest cast to date: Enrico Montesano, Pamela Tiffin, who by that time was stably living in Italy, Carlo Giuffrè, Ninetto Davoli. It was my biggest financial success, too.

After this film your career becomes tied completely to that of Walter Chiari. How did you meet him?

At the start of the seventies, alongside cinema, I started working for television again. I would direct plays for RAI, like *Anfitrione* [*Amphitryon*] by Plautus, for example. At one point I was in Naples directing one of these plays, *Il sistema Ribadier* [*The Ribadier System*], with Montesano and Isabella Biagini. We were staying in a famous hotel in the historical center of the city. But at night there was a hellish racket … music, guitars, shouting, singing, coming from the room next to mine. After one sleepless night, I stormed out into the corridor and knocked at the door. The man who opened was Tony Renis.[7] This seemingly insignificant event changed my life and career forever, because the following evening, at the hotel, he invited me to his table for dinner … you know, to be forgiven. He was in the company of Walter Chiari. This happened just after the scandal which had seen him arrested for drugs. The story is known: Walter was found with a certain amount of cocaine on him. He was tried for consumption and trafficking, which was ridiculous

Macha Meril and Walter Chiari in *The Roses Have Bloomed Again,* 1975 (courtesy Nocturno Cinema).

of course. It's a terrible story. He passed seventy days in jail and wasn't even let out for the birth of his son. He discovered his wife had had a baby boy through a prison guard. Even if Italy was going through a revolution, under the surface it was still a very primitive country. His career was completely destroyed and he became an outcast. Nobody would give him work or even want to be associated to him. Walter was a big, international star at the time and from one day to the next he had become a leper. Anyway, he was in Naples for a musical show, I think he was there as a presenter. Small stuff, but he needed work. I was preparing a comedy, something to follow the success of *The Lady Was Raped!* and by the end of the evening I told him I would have liked to have him in it. "A cameo?" he asked. "No, I want you as the protagonist." "I don't believe you." He genuinely couldn't believe anyone would want him as a lead in a film. How sad is that? The first film we did together was *Amore mio, non farmi male* [*Don't Hurt Me, My Love*, 1974].

But wasn't it difficult to convince P.A.C. to accept Chiari?

Yes ... well not that difficult because they trusted me. Let's say they weren't overjoyed by my choice but I had given them one of their biggest hits so I guess they decided to give me a chance and didn't regret it. The film was a massive success, two billion lira at the box office. In total we made six films together. The first three I'm very proud of, the others I did with little passion, if any. Those are the only films for which I used pseudonyms.

Another recurrent name in your films of the seventies is Luciano Salce.

Yes, Luciano was a friend and loved acting in films directed by others. He would say, "I get paid well for a small amount of work. Plus I have no responsibilities." Maybe those years working in theater made me want to create a sort of company of actors in films as well. Chiari and Salce were part of a group that I would call as often as possible. Other actors I would revert to were Macha Meril and Valentina Cortese, for example.

The comedies you direct in this period with these actors are very different to what was being done in the genre. The films you and Giorgio Capitani were making had nothing in common with the "commedia all'italiana" and even less with the sex comedies that were becoming increasingly successful.

Probably, if I had been more of a vagabond I would perhaps have ended up compromising a lot more but I've always been a little sentimental in my choices. I decided to stick, for most of my film career, with P.A.C. They gave me my first big push, they were the first to really trust me, so I remained faithful to them. By doing this, we established a relationship and channel of communication which permitted me to choose the projects I wanted, very freely. The producers of the so-called barons of the "commedia all'italiana"—Gassman, Sordi, Manfredi—tried to seduce and lure me towards them. Well, consider that for the films they produced, 400,000 lira of the budget would go just to pay the lead, when my films would cost overall 200,000 lira and would make billions. So I did receive offers and a certain degree of pressure. Angeletti and De Micheli, who were the producers of Ettore Scola and Mario Monicelli, would say, "We are a family, we can help you grow." Luigi De Laurentiis once sent his son, Aurelio, to talk me into making a film with them. Papi and Colombo, who had been the most important producers of Westerns, put a check for five million lira on my desk, which was supposed to be the advance payment for a film they wanted to make starring Massimo Ranieri. I refused them all. P.A.C. had trusted me and had given me certain privileges I would have never had with other companies. I had a good percentage on the proceeds of the films. I was 50 percent producer of the films I made. But another reason, and this brings me back to your question, was the lack of compromise I had with P.A.C. Other producers wanted me to direct their films but I wanted to make my films.

From 1973 onwards you only direct comedies. Why? Ever wanted to go back to other genres, maybe try a giallo again?

I have always considered myself an artisan of cinema and by that I mean that I would do what the market wanted from me. I was perceived as a comedy director so that is what I directed. Then I would inject the films with my own sensibility and I would direct them with a certain tone and atmosphere but the market came first. Each director has a role and once I was given mine, I stuck to it. I know what I am and what I'm capable of doing. But I like to think that in my comedies you can find elements of interest. Many were very light, maybe even frivolous but I would try and put some substance into them: my vision on the evolution of the Italian family, some of my political ideals…

Another interesting characteristic, which is recurrent in your films, is the role of women. I would even go so far as defining your cinema matriarchal. Especially in Don't Hurt Me, My Love, *1974,* Son tornate a fiorire le rose *[translation:* The Roses Have Bloomed Again, *1975] and* Per amore di Cesarina *[translation:* For the Love of Cesarina, *1976].*

Yes, it's true. In the first film you mention we have a mother, played by Macha Meril, who is responsible for her daughter's sex life and is aware of what is going on much more so than the husband. There is a scene in which she tells her daughter how her first sexual intercourse should be. Women in my films are strong, intelligent and most importantly manage to stand their ground with men without using sex or the promise of sex.

You interrupt this sort of trilogy to direct a bittersweet comedy on immigration, a subject matter close to you, Perdutamente tuo … mi firmo Macaluso Carmelo fu Giuseppe *[translation:* Desperately Yours … I Sign Macaluso Carmelo, Son of the Late Giuseppe, *1976]. The protagonist is Stefano Satta Flores. What do you remember about him?*

Stefano was fantastic, a real actor, full of passion. He would be doing stuff all the time, without ever stopping. Jumping from one set to another, embracing simultaneously as many projects as possible. He would live 24 hours a day. Tumultuous love affairs, some of which I witnessed in all their craziness and drama … traveling all over Italy … shows, theater… He would never stop and managed to do everything well. We were like brothers and for a long period we would always be together. When he was diagnosed with leukemia, he didn't tell me, he kept it hidden. I discovered it only towards the end when they attempted a transplant using his brother as a donor. I lost a dear, special friend when he died. He should be remembered more but unfortunately in Italy we tend to forget our actors and artists and the few times we do celebrate them, it's only after they have passed away.

Like Giuliano Gemma, with whom you worked.

Giuliano is another person that is deeply missed, not so much for his acting abilities but because he was a good person and a friend. I worked with him in television and he really suffered being continuously compared to Terence Hill. When, in the nineties, Hill started becoming successful again in television, Giuliano tried to rival him but without tangible results. Gabriele Ferzetti is another actor, and a great one for that matter, who was totally ignored in the last period of his life. He once told me, "Maybe when I die, people will start taking about me again." It's not like this in other countries. French actors are treated like royalty even when they're ninety.

In For the Love of Cesarina *you give the titular role to a young Cinzia Monreale, who later becomes very active in genre cinema, and more importantly an icon of horror, especially thanks to the films she makes with Lucio Fulci.*

Cinzia was a very sweet and generous girl. Walter fell in love with her and they had a very fiery and passionate affair throughout the making of that film. Walter really chased her down, right from the start. He was one of the most women-hungry people I've ever known. He also had an affair on *Don't Hurt Me, My Love* with Leonora Fani. A strange girl, very shy who was always under the pathologically attentive eye of her mother. Chiari went after her like a hawk. Monreale, instead, was very happy to have his attentions but Fani had that perverse Lolita quality to her.

The progression from the seventies to the eighties: What are your thoughts?

Everything degenerated from a certain moment onwards. Let's take comedy for example, the sex farces we mentioned earlier had a reason to exist because people could go and see naked women and joke about sexual customs and it was a social valve in a way. But once the sexual revolution was finished, the great season of Italian comedy had died out, the market was saturated by products that didn't have a real direction, a real purpose, especially with the advent of porn. Many cinemas switch from regular films to pornographic ones. Television all of a sudden offered a product that had characteristics similar to those pertaining to cinema and was accessible to everyone.

Was this the reason you abandoned cinema for television?

Giorgio Capitani and I were the first to realize that television was the future and one of the few ways to survive the crises. But when television came knocking, I had no willpower to continue working. I was making films as if I were on an assembly line, without even using my name.[8] I lost my son, my only son, in an accident. When I was thirty-five I felt the world was at my feet and all of a sudden I was a mere shadow. I started making television because it was a safe way of working. In cinema it's a struggle, you spend more time looking for your next project than actually working on one and I didn't have the energy to continue that kind of life. Television meant stable work and money. If I hadn't been hit by this terrible tragedy maybe I would have made different choices, I don't know. [Only then my suspicions are confirmed. That smiling young man portrayed in all those photos behind him, on the wall and in picture frames on the desk in front of him, are of his son.]

Rome, 2016

1968 Real Cannibals
The Cinema of Ruggero Deodato

> *"It's beautiful!"*—Carl Gabriel Yorke, while watching a burning hut full of frightened natives in *Cannibal Holocaust*, 1980
>
> *"FATTY! Who you calling fatty, moose head?"*—David Paul in *The Barbarians*, 1987

Mythological adventure films and peplums, starting from *Le fatiche di Ercole* (*Hercules*, 1958) onwards, will use the anamorphic lens of Cinemascope, vivid colors and a panoramic screen in the attempt to amplify the limits of the increasingly popular television monitor. The film directed by Pietro Francisci is not only one of the biggest and most successful examples of the genre—making Steve Reeves an international star and effectively characterizing and shaping dozens of peplums to come—but is an important cornerstone for all of Italian genre cinema. The Reeves epic emerges in that invisible borderline that delimits the end of the "Hollywood on the Tiber" era and was the most ambitious Italian effort, both economically and visually, within the genre since the end of the war.

As already emphasized elsewhere, the need to make up for small or inadequate budgets brings forth a creativity and resourcefulness which will give these products a charm and immediacy that most of the American films, films that originated the genre, did not have. These films managed to tap into the customs and tastes of the public more rapidly and effectively than one could have ever imagined, not only nationally but worldwide. American producer Joseph E. Levine acquired the U.S. rights for Francisci's epic, simplified the title and released an outstanding 600 copies (175 in the New York City area alone) anticipated by a perfectly conceived promotional campaign, with the use of effective television and radio commercials. This was an unheard of number of prints for a U.S. release of a foreign film, considering of course that we are talking about the days of full-size movie theaters and not the multiplexes we know today. Levine spent more to distribute and publicize the film than the Italian producers actually spent to make the Mario Bava–photographed mythological fantasy. Dell Publishing put into production a comic book inspired by the film, with an initial order for 500,000 copies. This unprecedented success created a widespread euphoria in the Italian film industry which increased the production of similar epics: veteran directors such as Vittorio Cottafavi, Carlo Campogalliani and Mario Bonnard are asked to tackle the newly strengthened genre, while new blood rises through the ranks to help satisfy the increase in demand. Many directors of photography, assistant directors and screenwriters have a chance to make their debut, giving newcomers wanting to work in films the opportunity to step into the industry. Basically what is put into motion is a wonderful recycling of names and roles for directors, technicians and actors.

The "Hollywood on the Tiber" era had left a rich heritage and know-how which the Italian industry will put to good use, creating an exportable yet perfectly recognizable product which will help forge, push forward or sometimes create the careers of such names as Sergio Corbucci, Duccio Tessari, Bava and Leone but also, as we've had a chance to analyze previously, Umberto Lenzi, Mario Caiano, Giorgio Capitani, Franco Rossetti and Alberto De Martino. If the Italian press tended to underline the poorer aspects of this prolific genre (between 1960 and 1965 more than 100 titles are put into production, representing 10 percent of the Italian film industry of the period)—the involuntarily humorous acting of some of the bodybuilders-turned-actors, the lack of effective special effects and the liberties taken with history and mythology—the French examined the "Situation du cinéma italien" concerning mythological epics with great interest, dedicating numerous pages on the prestigious *Cahiers du cinema* discussing the audacious color schemes, hyper-stylizations and comic-book appeal of the best examples directed by Cottafavi, Freda and Bava. If these products are conceived for the unsophisticated appetite of the masses, the phenomenon does not pass unnoticed by the "upper echelons" of cinema: in his episode, *Le tentazioni del dottor Antonio* (translation: *The Temptations of Doctor Antonio*) in the anthology film *Boccaccio '70* (1962), Federico Fellini imagines, for a scene, the making of a peplum with Giuliano Gemma, in the developing outskirts of a deserted Rome; while in a crucial sequence of *Risate di gioia* (*The Passionate Thief*, 1960) by Mario Monicelli, we find Anna Magnani involved in the making of a peplum, which is described as chaotic and filled with actors and manpower willing to do anything for a buck and directors that manage, despite everything, to insert in these films moments of genuine creativity and intuition.

Although some directors were passionate about the genre—Gianfranco Parolini, Michele Lupo and Mario Caiano have often spoken very warmly about their experiences—for most it was simply the perfect container to put into practice what had been learned during their long apprenticeships as ADs and second unit directors. Both Leone and Corbucci, in separate interviews, revealed that while making *Il colosso di Rodi* (*The Colossus of Rhodes*, 1961) and *Il figlio di Spartacus* (*The Slave*, a.k.a. *The Son of Spartacus*, 1962) respectively, they were already "thinking about Westerns." Alberto De Martino, who directed some notable examples within the genre, describes the attitude like this:

> Peplums were fun but hard work—complicated sets, elaborate costumes, special effects, hundreds of extras—but it was the best school in the world, because of all those problems! Even for the smallest of those films you had a big crew and a lot of actors to deal with and they gave you the opportunity to test yourself from all points of view: action sequences, dialogue, effects, drama and even comedic timing. Beside this, I don't think many directors really loved the genre. Personally, I enjoyed myself but these were films that were difficult to impress with a more personal viewpoint. One thing was certain, if you made peplums you were seen, as a genre director, in the worst possible way. If Westerns would later be reviewed and perceived negatively by critics, with peplums things were far worse.

This ties perfectly with the words of another contemporary, Giulio Petroni, who started directing right in the period in which these "sandaloni" were going strong:

> I don't remember if I was offered peplums at that time.... I don't think so, but I would never have accepted anyway, because if I had, I would have been labeled forever. If you directed those kind of

films, there was no going back ... producers would offer you nothing except purely exploitation or genre products. In the late fifties/early sixties I preferred sticking to comedy because a "comedy director" wasn't such a restrictive label. Westerns on the other hand, were a different matter ... they weren't loved by critics but there was greater leniency and could function as a "gateway genre." Plus, they were films you could adapt and shape to your needs. In fact, there were loads of different currents within Westerns: comedy Westerns, romantic ones, others violent or gothic and even strongly political examples, whereas with peplums it was just a continuous adaption of the same trite story.

In the first half of the sixties, as Steve Reeves, Dan Vadis, Kirk Morris and Richard Harrison flexed their muscles in bubbly and opulently baroque ancient Greek and Roman fantasies, throwing down cardboard columns and slaying evil witches and giants, Westerns pulsated under the surface, waiting for Leone to jumpstart the genre into film history. But these aren't the only elements to have characterized Italian genre cinema of the sixties. By the end of the previous decade, comedy, with its new templates and protagonists, became crucial even in the production of films of a musical nature. Grand opera lost its dominant role in the public's taste while "light music" went through a reinvigorating evolution and thanks to the worldwide phenomenon of rock 'n' roll, the Italian music scene was divided between old school and young voices, which elaborated new impulses claiming the need to break away from the past. If in the United States the rise of the "rock 'n' roll movie" was the manifestation of a clear generational distinction, in Italy things were a little more fizzled. Though a writer/director like Lucio Fulci managed to see the bigger picture; in 1959 his *Urlatori alla sbarra* (*Howlers of the Dock*) was released, anticipating many of the anxieties and tribulations that would mature during the course of the following decade. Despite being a light-hearted, fun-loving musical comedy, Fulci's film clearly tells the story of a dying music industry and of what is taking its place.

During the sixties the further change in music binds itself to new images, ways of dressing and expressing oneself, that capture and amplify the much more serious rebelliousness still to come; even more so than with the advent of rock 'n' roll, youngsters configure themselves as foreign bodies within society, with their own language and heroes, the Beatles being at the top of the list. However, the Italian record labels tended to sugarcoat and attenuate the load of the phenomenon, transforming it into reassuring consumer products. Genre cinema as usual, proves to be particularly receptive but in a nonunivocal way. The films, known in Italy as "musicarelli," can be divided in two macrocategories: if some titles manage to channel the increasingly evolving counterculture movement, though more ichnographically—in the use of clothing, hairdos and youthful lingo—than in its political or social content, most of this current is fairly innocuous, inspired in tone more by Frankie Avalon "beach movies" than anything else. The genre will have its reference points in specialized directors such as Domenico Paolella, Piero Vivarelli, Ferdinando Baldi and Ettore Maria Fizzarotti, the latter being the most productive within the genre, having directed 13 films. By the beginning of the seventies, the genre will wear out, the 1968 student revolt, an increasingly tense political atmosphere together with international events such as the Vietnam war, leave little space for such naivety. One of the last directors to have gotten on board the genre is Ruggero Deodato (born 7 May 1939, Potenza), Monsieur Cannibal himself. Deodato not only participates in the success of the "musicarelli," directing two Little Tony[1] movies in 1968, but lives through, mostly as an AD, all of the major changes and turning points of the sixties, and really begins his career the same year of Francisci's *Hercules* and in the wake of the great peplum phenomenon. The future director of some of the most savage Italian horror films

Ruggero Deodato as he directs his most important film, the savage and seminal *Cannibal Holocaust*, in 1980 (courtesy Nocturno Cinema).

ever made, like Romolo Guerrieri, has one of the longest careers as an assistant and second unit director.

Ruggero Deodato moves to Rome at the age of 14, from Potenza, in Basilicata, more precisely he moves to Parioli, an upper-class area of the capital, which will have a crucial influence in his work. He begins in films at a very young age, as an actor, usually in small roles or bit parts. "I participated in the early to mid-fifties in a handful of films and I was even called by Federico Fellini to audition for a role, I don't remember for which film, but in the meantime I had gone through puberty and I had lost my boyish charm, I wore glasses, had bad skin, and was discarded immediately. That was my very last attempt at acting, but the experience had fully convinced me that cinema was the way for me. I knew I was going to make films … just that it had to be behind the camera, and not in front of it!" During his teenage years, his parents will become increasingly close to the Rossellini family and Deodato will build a lasting friendship with Renzo Rossellini, son of the famous father of neorealism, Roberto, and actress Ingrid Bergman. It is thanks to this fruitful and deep intertwining of families that a still young Deodato has a chance to really start working in cinema. Throughout the sixties, once unhinged from the Rossellinis, Deodato becomes omnivorous, participating in the most varied projects, without any kind of distinction: "I was famished for cinema. I would do anything that gave me the possibility of moving around, being on a set, meeting new people. Having worked with Roberto, I had built a solid reputation for myself in just a few years, so finding work wasn't difficult. I was aware of the differences between the films I started out with and the following ones I worked on, but I didn't really care. I was good and I liked the idea of shining on sets that some people would've considered beneath me." Between 1960 and 1966 Deodato works side by side with many of the leading genre directors in circulation, with whom he will, more often than not, maintain a long-term collaboration, touching all the most popular genres: science fiction, gothic horrors and peplums with Antonio Margheriti; Westerns, among which is the cult classic *Django* (1966), with Sergio Corbucci; *Romeo e Giulietta* (*Romeo and Juliet*, 1964) with Riccardo Freda; comedies with Mario Amendola and Bruno Corbucci; a peplum and a war movie with Carlo Ludovico Bragaglia; and *Wanted* (1967) with Giorgio Ferroni. Apart from the ones with Roberto Rossellini, which also includes *Anima nera* (translation: *Black Soul*, 1962), Deodato collaborates with another of Italy's leading auteurs, Mauro Bolognini. "Rossellini and Bolognini are my two masters. Roberto taught me about the truth, how to look for it, while from the latter I got the elegance, the smoothness of the image, the softness of camera movements. The poetry of truth and beauty are the essence of these two masters. But I was lucky enough to have been exposed to many different directors and each one of them has been essential to my growth: Margheriti taught me a lot about special effects, while from Sergio Corbucci I inherited a certain taste for violence and brutality."

Cinema is, yes, an art form, entertainment for masses and niches, a game, a safety valve, a big technical-visual experiment in progressive and continuous evolution, a historical archive in constant update, a collection of snapshots inserted in the photo album of our lives, a time machine, our collective memory, but in being all these things, it also generates ghosts. Celluloid flesh forced to continue moving in an obsessive rituality, a container of ghosts caught on film, destined to repeat forever the same gestures, the same mistakes, the same pain, to reach the same fate, sad or joyful again and again and yet again; and our expectations, our sorrows, our eyes actually drive these virtual purgatories, this repetition of gestures on which we project ourselves, because when we watch a film, we are witnessing a spectacle of ghosts and with them experiencing all that has been projected into it. Film is as much a solitary passion, made of dark rooms and theaters, as it is a silent exchange of betrayed expectations and dreams. In the end, moving along with those ghosts reduced to puppets, there is us, with our irrational fears and drooling desires. "People call me a horror director but actually I have only directed a couple of horror films and I'm not referring to the usual titles of mine I'm associated with. *Cannibal Holocaust* is not a horror film, it's just a depiction of reality. It's not my fault the world we live in is so violent and dark."

If in their period of decline, "serious" genres like peplums and westerns tended to the parodic, it is equally true that, conversely, some of the lighter ones drifted towards the grotesque and monstrous, locating themselves on the thin border between the tragic and the weird. So it was, in its small way, for the Italian adventure film, which in the late seventies and early eighties originated a subgenre, the cannibal one. A possible reference model of this subgenre can be traced in the so-called "mondo movies" of the sixties and its various subsidiaries, at least at the level of the (im)moral thematic setting, the ridiculous ostentation of quibbling, socio-anthropological cogitations and an unhealthy erratic look upon the world. But it must also be said that the architectural narrative, the rhythm and the dynamics that bind the characters together are typical of the adventure stories told by Italian cinema over the previous decades. In the case of this cannibalistic current, one enters the heart of darkness of adventure, and the wonderful becomes repellent, the fantastic discolors into the obscene, the imaginative vulgarizes itself, touching turpitude. Umberto Lenzi, who has never pulled back in the face of a challenge, will also compete with this ferocious branch of horror, also being able to boast a kind of birthright, with *Il paese del sesso selvaggio* (*Deep River Savages*, a.k.a. *The Man from the Deep River*, 1972), conceived as an adventure movie, spiced with documentary elements, erotic inserts, some rare moments of shock, and with more than a passing reference to *A Man Called Horse* (1970) by Elliot Silverstein. Yet, it is *Ultimo mondo cannibale* (*Last Cannibal World*, a.k.a. *Jungle Holocaust*, a.k.a. *The Last Survivor*, 1977) to have the title of first real cannibal movie, considering that in Lenzi's trailblazer, the cannibalistic aspect is marginal, reduced to a single scene.

Last Cannibal World outlined the blueprint to which all the films belonging to the genre will adhere: the use of animals and the actual killing of them, a taste for "reportage" in the look of the film, graphic violent scenes in which we see hungry cannibals in action, and the manipulation of these indigenous tribes for the purpose of social denouncement with an ensuing conclusive moral lesson. If you look at the best and most successful films of Ruggero Deodato, *Last Cannibal World* is certainly one of these that confirms him as a "gut oriented" director: few but well-executed ideas combined with strong technical expertise. A cinema of images, in which words are often troublesome because they are redundant with respect to what you see. Originally the film was to be directed by Lenzi, fresh from the success of the aforementioned 1972 exotic adventure film, so it is no surprise that we find the same two actors, Ivan Rassimov and Me Me Lay. But if Lenzi approached this current, both with this first film and with his subsequent efforts, as well as horror films as a whole, with great detachment, Deodato on the contrary, finds himself in a genre perfectly congenial to him. The characteristics given by the scenic context and the type of story permit the director to make films where technique becomes storytelling, allowing him to stage wild as well as essential films. The heritage of "mondo movies" is blatant in the savageries of the cannibal current, apparent not only in the exotic locations and related tribal contexts, but especially in the continuous exchange between reality and fiction, though with a difference in intentions: while directors such as Jacopetti and Prosperi fused fictional elements with documentary footage in a perverse distortion of reality, Deodato, in his most famous film, which is also the highest point reached within the subgenre, *Cannibal Holocaust*, inserts in the diegetic a true "film within a film," creating a short-circuit. In fact, *Cannibal Holocaust* can be read both as a condemnation and a homage to the "fathers of mondo." In so doing, he creates one of the most influential films of the last forty years. Deodato has rarely written the scripts of his films and like all of his colleagues, he had to bend to the demands of the market, dwelling with the most varied genres: from comedy to post-atomic flicks, from erotic thrillers to slashers. But Deodato has always pursued his own particular aesthetic of violence. His cinema is not dripping with blood, it is not populated by ancestral screams, but is animated by human lamentations, by the sadism of humans on other humans. "Pariolini" (a term well known by the director, that derives from the aforementioned area of Rome and is used to describe people that in money and the ostentation of it, find the meaning of their existence), violent proletariats who become unwitting tools of the cruelty of the middle class, cynical and dissolute, anesthetized couples in search of diversions and ready to do anything for them, journalists whose ambition becomes a cancer that devours them. In the best of Deodato's films, there is no excuse, no salvation, making his ghosts slaves of a ritual even more painful to watch.

What was your first experience on a set?

As an actor, in *Destinazione Piovarolo* [*Destination Piovarolo*, 1955] by Domenico Paolella. I was fifteen years old and I was a good friend of Paolella's daughter, Gabriella. One evening I joined them for dinner, I was wearing jeans and had long hair, I looked like an Italian James Dean. He took a look and asked me if I wanted to have a small role in his film. Then after that, I did a number of bit parts in various films but acting wasn't for me. It didn't take long to realize that I was more interested in what was happening behind the camera.

I once heard you say that your love for cinema grew at the same pace as your love for women.

True, in those years in which I was trying to get acting gigs and I would pass entire afternoons watching films getting shot all over Rome, I was discovering other joys as well. My first contact with the other sex was with the maids that worked in our household. Usually the older ones but the first time was with the daughter of one of these maids ... we were both fifteen.

Your first love?

No, no! My first love arrived when I was eighteen, a British girl who used to give English lessons to Sandra Milo. Her name is Jenny Fletcher. I left my parents' house to go and live with her. After two or three years, once our love had fizzled out, I went back home but my father told me, "We don't have a bed for you here anymore."

Let's jump forward. You were one of the most prolific ADs in the industry for a long time. Tell me how you started.

The first real job as an assistant director was on Roberto Rossellini's *Era notte a Roma* [*Escape by Night*, 1960], where I also had a cameo role. Cineriz made me sign my first proper contract. We started shooting at Ceri, a small town that lived off the land, made of desolation and poor farmers. The first actresses I met were Laura Betti and Giovanna Ralli. I remember I got my chance to shine when we were shooting in the square of Tor di Nona, where we had 300 extras. Most of the scene was supposed to take place under a building that was the property of the Santo Spirito Bank. They stopped us from filming because we didn't have the necessary permits. I rushed to the Ministry of Health, where my father was the general manager. He picked up the phone and in the matter of a couple of hours I had the permit in my hands. When I reached the set, I was greeted like a hero. Rossellini, on that occasion taught me one of my first lessons. "When there's a problem rush to fix it, but don't return if you don't." From that moment onwards, he considered me a valuable asset and would give me more and bigger things to do. I played the part of a priest and then I was Enrico Maria Salerno's double in the wide shots. Rossellini was irritated by Salerno because he would bring him this script and would always ask him to take a look at it.

Do you remember what the script was?

I think it was *Eutanasia di un amore* [translation: *Euthanasia of a Love*] which Salerno later directed himself [*Break Up*, 1978].

When making Escape by Night, *you had practically no experience.*

Well, there was a long preparation period in which I was taught many things and I was given very specific instructions. The other AD on the film was Renzo Rossellini, who was a workaholic. My main job on set was choosing the background actors. Rossellini gave me a great piece of advice, "Once the person you've chosen puts on his costume, he is the character. If you take a man with the face of a bastard and dress him like a good guy, he becomes good!" I realized he was right, especially with popes ... you get a guy with an anonymous face and dress him like a pope, believe me he becomes a credible pope.

You are credited in* Nella città l'inferno *[Behind Closed Shutters, 1958] by Renato Castellani.

Romolo Guerrieri was the 1st AD on that. I just helped during the pre-production.

With Rossellini you worked again on* Viva l'Italia! *[Garibaldi, 1961].

I went wild on that film! I really put a lot of energy into it. In fact, a very proud moment was when Angelo Rizzoli came on set and Rossellini went, "I could have never done it without the help of Ruggerino!" He used to call me Ruggerino. It was a difficult film to make because we had a lot of problems. We travelled up and down the whole of Italy to film it. When we reached Naples for a crucial sequence of the film, we discovered that all the extras didn't know they had to ride a horse ... plus the horses they had given us were the ones used for funeral carriages, not for riding. I can't tell you what happened! Paolo Stoppa was suffering from hemorrhoids so they put a donut on the horse. The horse got mad and threw him off its back. It was a disaster! Rossellini was furious and returned to Rome, for a month and a half. We were left there, all expenses paid. It was one of the best periods of my entire life. I had a hotel room all to myself, I'd go around with the production's car, I had a drop-dead gorgeous girlfriend, I'd have breakfast on the island of San Martino and then off for a swim at Ischia...

You also worked with Carlo Ludovico Bragaglia.

On *Vanina Vanini* [*The Betrayer*, 1961], the third film I did with Rossellini, I had finally became a 1st AD. When Ingrid Bergman was in town, Rossellini would find excuses to leave the set and sometimes I would be left to direct some scenes. On that set I met my first love, Jenny Fletcher—the girl I mentioned before. She was giving Sandra Milo, who had an important role in the film, English lessons. Rossellini knew about my little love story and helped me out with it. Immediately after *The Betrayer*, he was supposed to direct *Kapò*, which Gillo Pontecorvo ended up directing. Everything was on standby when Walter Benelli called me to go to Libya for *Pastasciutta nel deserto* [*Desert Furlough*, 1961] to replace Mario Caiano who was getting ready for his debut as a director. I was quite scared by the prospect so I talked to the Rossellini family and they told me, "Are you mad? Roberto is preparing *Kapò*!" but Jenny insisted I should leave, "You can't stay glued to the Rossellinis forever. You need to break away and get your name known." I went and it was the right thing to do. Bragaglia taught me everything, from A to Z, more so than Rossellini, because Rossellini directed only in his own particular way. He would do a lot of tracking shots. I'm not saying they are easy, you need talent and special expertise to be able to do them well, but you lose the sense and importance of editing.

What kind of person was he, Bragaglia?

He always had his coat and hat on, always very gentleman-like. Despite he was more than 70 years old, when he was working he was quick ... as soon as he went, "Cut!" he would jump from his chair and start preparing the next shot. He would decide what I had to eat, he had a specific diet I had to follow throughout production. I had to have breakfast with a steak and one egg and that was it until dinner, which had to be light. He was a formidable man and I became very attached to him.

With Bragaglia you also worked on Ursus nella valle dei leoni *[Ursus in the Valley of the Lions,* a.k.a. *Valley of the Lions,* 1962].

Yes, I managed to get Jenny in it, as a dialogue coach. This film allowed me to meet Sergio Corbucci and soon after I made *Il figlio di Spartacus* [*The Slave*, a.k.a. *The Son of Spartacus*, 1962] directed by Sergio. Though after *Ursus* I got into a mess ... Bragaglia invited me to stay at his villa in Capri after the film wrapped up. Jenny was there as well because apart from working as an interpreter in films, she would also help rent villas in Capri to rich Americans on vacation during the summer season. So I would divide my time between Bragaglia's house and one of Jenny's unrented villas. But at the same time I was compelled to sleep with a woman.

Ah yes, I read about this story once...

She was the wife of an important producer and daughter of a famous actor. She said, "If you don't have sex with me, that means you're a faggot." I ended up in bed with her, actually on the roof, seeing she had to check if her husband was on his way. I cannot reveal her name. I was crazy about Jenny but at the same time I was in this woman's clutches. Anyway, I ended up confessing everything and she packed her bags and left for London. I was distraught. I kept calling her until she agreed I could go and visit her for the New Year. I drove there with my FIAT Seicento which took forever. When I got there, during a blizzard, I was greeted by her parents, very nice people, but she didn't want to fuck and I was conking out. Plus, on the first day of the year she went to work ... things were difficult. I'm the kind of guy that when he realizes a situation makes him suffer, runs ... as fast as he can. So I called my sister Elisabetta and joined her in Munich where she lived. While there, I got a call from Franco Rossellini: "Ruggero, you have to come to Rome and leave for Cairo." Once I'd managed to reach Rome, everybody had already left for Egypt. Franco Palaggi made me sign a contract with Titanus. The first person I met was Nori Corbucci and I liked her but at first all the crew thought I was Franco Rossellini's boyfriend, because I was cute and well-mannered and he was the one who wanted me on the film. I noticed they would look at me and giggle or eye each other every time I talked with Franco. So I told myself, "OK, I have to do what I do best." Instead of staying at the hotel, I got an attic overlooking the Nile, with production designer Franco Dominici. The place was amazing: it had a grand piano, colored fitted carpet, silk sheets on the bed.... I bought myself a Torpedo convertible, a bunch of linen shirts and every night I would go dancing at the "Laila," a disco-boat on the river. There were beautiful women, French Muslims, coming in from Lebanon. On weekends we would organize big parties at our place, where there was a belly dancer who would perform topless. Once Piero Piccioni came to visit and said, "Ah Ruggero you get more action here than I do back in Rome!" Sergio Corbucci liked me straight away, and so did Franco Giraldi, who was the second unit director.

What was Steve Reeves like?

Dumb. He thought he was a real actor and would demand changes to the script, and add dialogue. Sergio would go, "Yes, yes, no problem, Steve, no problem..." but then he would shoot all his monologues without any film in the camera. Of all these musclemen, the only bright one was Gordon Scott.

What kind of person was Sergio Corbucci?

A born comedian. When things got boring on set he would always find a way to uplift the morale. He was frenetic, spoke fluent English and always had a smile ready in his pocket. I had to be on set at seven in the morning though he arrived in the afternoon. He would never work in the morning. A great director, he could really dominate a set. Nori, his wife, was very much integrated in the jet-set scene and helped him with his career, got him to go to the right parties and mix with the right people.

You worked with him a lot. What do you remember of **Johnny Oro** *[a.k.a.* **Ringo and His Golden Pistol***, 1966]?*

Johnny Oro wasn't a good film. To be honest, as far as Westerns go, I preferred Duccio Tessari. He would take care of the details, be more elegant, plus there was greater irony in his films which is something I appreciate in the genre. Corbucci was more violent, brutal but not very refined in his approach.

What are your memories of **I crudeli** *[The Hellbenders, 1967]?*

We filmed that in Spain. The first thing that comes to mind was Joseph Cotten who after two attempts at getting on a horse shouted, "Double!" and walked off. It was a very relaxed set, unlike *Navajo Joe* [1966] where I told Burt Reynolds he could go fuck himself. He was very handsome, he looked like a young Marlon Brando, but he was an arrogant prick. Every time I would go to pick him up to take him to the set he would grumble and waste everybody's time. Once I got to his trailer and he started complaining under his breath, as if he was annoyed. I exploded. "You know what? Go fuck yourself!" But I never saw Sergio fight with him. Sergio wouldn't fight with anybody … ever! Antonio Margheriti was another very calm director, but when he did get mad … wow! Instead Sergio would arrive and calmly go, "You're wrong," and leave before you could answer back.

How did you meet Margheriti?

When I was doing *The Slave* with Sergio, Antonio was making *La freccia d'oro* [*The Golden Arrow*, 1962] also for Titanus. We met a few times on that occasion but sometime after, Giovanni Addessi commissioned a film to Sergio, that had some footage that had to be recycled: *Danza macabra* [*Castle of Blood*, 1964]. He wasn't able to accept and the project was passed on to Margheriti. I'd already been signed on, so I remained and did the film. They wanted Barbara Steele but she had just made *8½* [1963] by Fellini and was trying to stay away from horror. I was sent to change her mind, because we were friends. I had met her the first time at Demofilo Fidani's house, who had been a set designer for Mauro Parenti. Demofilo was very cultured, he always had a crowd following him around, and Barbara was part of it. She was incredible and so much fun. I remember that when I went to visit, or to return the cats she had left with me before leaving, and Fellini was passing to check on his actresses, she would hide me under the bed.

Another gothic horror film you worked on was **La vergine di Norimberga** *[Horror Castle, a.k.a.* **The Virgin of Nuremberg***, a.k.a.* **Terror Castle***, 1963].*

I don't remember a fucking thing about that film. It's one of those films that I've completely removed from my memory. Another one is *Il terzo occhio* [*The Third Eye*, 1966] by Mino Guerrini. Actually, I remember that Guerrini was peculiar … well really, he was crazy like a fucking horse! I was dating the script supervisor and we went to pick him up to bring him on the set. First he asked us to wait at the door and then told us to enter. When we did, we found him naked. On another occasion we were shooting a scene with Franco Nero and Erika Blanc in the bathroom of Villa Parisi, at Frascati, when he dropped his pants and took a shit in front of the actors and the whole crew. When he made a mistake and I pointed it out, he would go, "I do what the fuck I want!" but he was talented, very talented.

Going back to Margheriti, you also worked on his sci-fi films.

Yes. Those were very well-organized productions. The company was Mercury Films and there was even some American money involved. I remember there was this beautiful actress, Rocky Roberts' former girlfriend. In a scene we did we had painted her gold. I invited her to my place so she could have a shower ... she was Swedish. That is when I met Franco Nero. He had just arrived in Rome and I helped financially. You know I was the one who made him do *Django* [1966] instead of Mark Damon. Corbucci was set on Mark but I asked him to check Franco out. When Nori saw him, she started insisting as well and Sergio convinced himself.

Who wrote the script of Django? *Many names were involved but who actually wrote it?*

As far as I know the main person responsible for the script of *Django* is Franco Rossetti but when I came on board the people still working on it were Piero Vivarelli and Bruno Corbucci.

You worked with both the Corbucci brothers. How did Bruno and Sergio differ?

I liked Bruno, he was funny but he didn't have the talent or the inventiveness of his brother. He wasn't really a director. When I worked with Bruno, I became the director. He would sit down and look at me. "OK Ruggero, make me laugh. Let's see what you can do!" It was just a way of laying around and having someone else do all the work.

What about Giorgio Ferroni? You made Wanted *[1967] with him.*

Ferroni was as deaf as a bell. I thought we had built a solid working relationship but when he fell sick, during the making, he didn't want me to complete the film. I was very offended by this decision. Giorgio Stegnani was called to take his place. I became friends with Stegnani and in fact called him to write some of the dialogue for *Cannibal Holocaust* [1980]. On *Wanted* I also met Sergio D'Offizi, a serious man. I liked his seriousness, that's why he became my most trusted DOP.

It was Margheriti who made you transit from AD to director on the set of Ursus, il terrore dei kirghisi *[Hercules, Prisoner of Evil, a.k.a.* Ursus, Terror of the Kirghiz, *1964].*

Two weeks into production, Margheriti comes to me and tells me the film he was supposed to do after this one had been anticipated and that the producer was pressuring him. "You finish it." "I what...?" "Ruggero, you're good. I'll convince the producers." I directed the following five weeks but I still got paid as an AD. That same year I worked also with Riccardo Freda. He was a genius. I did *Romeo e Giulietta* [*Romeo and Juliet*, 1964] and learned a lot from him. He was incredibly cultured and a bit of a bastard on set. He would treat the crew terribly and in the scenes with horses, he wouldn't hesitate to lame the horses to get what he wanted. Marcello Avallone was his personal assistant. I remember he was his shadow on and off the set. But he invented things that were incredible, stuff I wouldn't have ever thought of. I remember going to see him in the editing suite, surrounded by kilometers of film and he was so quick. He had the whole film in his head.

We can consider **Gungala la pantera nuda *[Gungala, The Naked Panther, a.k.a.* Gungala, The Black Panther Woman, *1968] your first real film as a director.***

Yes, I was called by a production manager called Luciano Cattania. "Can you come here to the De Paolis studios? We are shooting a film and the director is having problems with a quicksand scene." I went and did the scene. The director, Romano Ferrara, just sat in a corner and when I finished, sat up and applauded. "Bravo ... bravo!" They gave me a million lira cash and I walked off. That same evening Cattania called me again. "Can you come in tomorrow as well and do another scene?" I did and bang, another million but this time they asked me to continue on as the director of the film. For the first few days Ferrara continued sitting in his corner, applauding and going "Bravo!" until I went to the producers and said, "Either me or him." Never saw Ferrara again on set. You can say that the film is mine, even because the few things Ferrara had done were unusable. When I went to see the rough footage, the editor went, "Ruggero, I have to warn you, it's a real mess..." In three weeks, this guy had done practically nothing. So, I rewrote the film and even changed the characters. For example the villain played by Angelo Infanti became the protagonist and I reduced Jeff Tangen's character drastically. He was terrible anyway. We went to Kenya for twenty days and I saved the film. But even if I had years of experience behind me, I was still very nervous. Before leaving I called Margheriti to get some last-minute advice and be reassured. The best thing about the film is Kitty Swan, the protagonist. She was beautiful, with a perfect body and a sweet little boyfriend. After my film, she did another adventure film and something went wrong with the special effects and she was set on fire.[2] She had severe burns on 80 percent of her body and her career was destroyed but I was told that she married that sweet kid she was with.

Then comes* Fenomenal e il tesoro di Tutankamen *[Fenomenal and the Treasure of Tutankamen, 1968].

People expected my debut to be like the ones of Bellocchio or Faenza, with an auteurish, high-profile film. But I was very young, twenty-three years old, and I decided to make a film like *Fenomenal*. I didn't want to wait two or three years to make a film. I was hungry for work, so I decided I was going to accept everything I was offered.

What do you remember of the film?

Paolo Poeti[3] was my 1st AD, a nice man. He even plays a policeman in one of the very first scenes of the film. The producer was Mauro Parenti for I.C.A.R., who also plays the main role. Lucretia Love was his woman and she was in it as well, and then there was Carla Romanelli, who I chose. She was my girlfriend at the time. I met her when she was with Franco Nero. Franco and I were good friends, we would often be together, then one day he goes off to make *Camelot* [1967] and tells me, "Take care of Carla ... keep an eye on her!" She was extremely jealous and would call him at all hours. He wouldn't answer but would call me and go, "Are you taking care of her?" After a while she would look for me more and more and ended up falling in love. He called me and said, "Ruggero, how could you fuck with Carlina?" He was pissed off and stopped talking to me! He was a puritan and for him it was a scandalous matter even if he had really left her and in fact soon after started his relationship with Vanessa Redgrave. Carla was an intelligent and diplomatic woman. She even helped me financially when I decided to become a director. Our story ended when I met Silvia Dionisio.

So you consider this your first real film as a director? Tell me more about **Fenomenal**. *How did this film come to be?*

We shot the film in Paris. I'm in a scene, at the beginning, the guy who falls off the bike, but simply because we hadn't enough money to afford extras. Rex Harrison is in it as well, but by pure chance. I was shooting a scene of the crowd cheering during the parade for Charles De Gaulle and he was there. After, I went up to him and asked if I could use the footage and he kindly said yes. Mauro Parenti had made, as a producer and actor, this serious film called *Tempo di credere* [translation: *Time to Believe*, 1962] by Antonio Racioppi. It was shot in Spoleto, and on that occasion me and Renzo Rossellini had met him and even took the piss out of him because he was very full of himself, very cocky. When, years later, he called me for *Fenomenal,* I discovered he was really a rather pleasant person though as far as acting went he was a dog … terrible. I must admit I treated him like shit on set but he called me again for *Zenabel* [1969]. He was fixated on action and adventure films. Before mine, he had produced a spy-story set in Istanbul.[4] He was very good at finding private investors, who were mostly squalid figures: hotel owners, small industrialists, who would accept in exchange for small roles either for themselves or their lovers. I don't exactly know how, but the news that I was good had spread. Maybe they discovered that I had saved *Gungala*. Parenti was also a womanizer. His office was always full of whores and he would ask all the actresses that passed through there for an audition, to strip naked. I would go, "Why naked? We don't need it for the film." "Don't worry about it, it's for something else." Poor thing, he died young. I met him at a cinema and he was completely bald. "What's wrong?" "I have cancer," he answered laughing. He would be always laughing, even before death. He was dating one of these sexy actresses … who was … Paola Senatore! Yes, Senatore.

Maurizio Merli appears briefly in the film.

Actually, his part was supposed to be bigger but one day he didn't come on set and we received a telephone call. "This is the police. We are calling to inform you that Mr. Merli has been arrested." An old woman had seen him on TV and recognized him as the man who had bag-snatched her. They kept him four months in jail. I don't know why. I directed him again many years later in something for television and I also met him a few days before he died. He was trying to convince me to make another police thriller, like the ones he had made in the seventies. A heart attack playing tennis… It's a shame, he wasn't a bad person … a bit of an asshole but not a bad person.

After these adventure films, you move to a completely new territory. You direct two musical comedies with Little Tony, both produced by the Amati clan. What kind of person was Edmondo Amati?

Edmondo Amati was incredible. A good producer who would always come up with a more than adequate budget for his films and would have good ideas that would actually help you in your work. His son, Maurizio, came to a private screening of *Fenomenal*, immediately after it had been completed and they asked me to direct *Donne, botte e bersaglieri* [*A Man Only Cries for Love*, 1968]. After I'd finished it, Amati went crazy. He'd show it to everybody, even to Dino Risi, who was working on a film for him. "Look, look what inventions Ruggero has come up with." To understand if Amati liked a film you had to watch his leg. If he started moving it, that meant he wasn't happy. The first time I'd met him was on the set of *Peggio per me … meglio per te!* [translation: *Worse for Me … Better for You!*, 1967] by Bruno Corbucci, in London. On that occasion, he already liked the way I worked because I had directed practically everything. He wanted me to be the 1st AD on *La feldmarescialla* [*The Crazy Kids of the War*, 1967] which Steno was going to direct. But Steno didn't want me because I wore baggy shirts and had long hair so Amati went, "OK, I'll sign you on for two films as a director." One was *A Man Only Cries for Love* and the other was *Vacanze sulla Costa Smeralda* [*Vacation on the Emerald Coast*, 1968]. But the second was a lot more toned down. The problem with that film was that Amati had managed to get financing thanks to a hotel, Baja Sardonia, which had just opened. So basically the film had to be a long advertisement. Me and Riccardo Pazzaglia started working on a script but we had trouble coming up with a story, all set in a hotel, that would work. Then the usual duo Bruno Corbucci–Mario Amendola were called, but this time even they weren't able to invent anything really exciting.

Let's talk about the cast of A Man Only Cries for Love.

Little Tony was a nice kid. He was a bit shy and ashamed of being an actor but we had fun together. He sings a few very good songs in the film. Then there was Ira Hagen, who was still fresh from the success of *Funeral in Berlin* [1966]. She drove me crazy, though. I auditioned her in London and she was pretty and sweet but then when I saw her on the set, I realized she had a massive chin, plus she came with this terrible back-combed hairdo ... but it wasn't only this, she just wasn't suitable for the part. What really worked in the film was the comedic aspect, especially the scenes with Ferruccio Amendola, who had good timing. Songs and a few laughs, that's what people expected from the film anyway. Janet Agren was also in it. There was a certain feeling between Janet and myself but I was still in a relationship with Carla Romanelli. Janet had just got off the plane from Sweden practically, when I stopped her on the street and asked her if she wanted to become an actress. She was as stiff as a board and didn't know the first fucking thing about acting, but she was beautiful.

The films have rich casts of well-known names of the time but really the only one worth mentioning is Silvia Dionisio.

On the first of the two films I did with Little Tony, Amati told me, "Check out this young girl who goes to the same beach resort I go to. She could work like a charm in the film." I'd already chosen Ira Hagen and didn't want to waste time with another audition. But the second time 'round I didn't repeat the same mistake. Silvia had only worked in one film: *Italiani! È severamente proibito servirsi della toilette durante le fermate* [translation: *Italians! It Is Severely Prohibited to Use the Toilet During Stops*, 1969] by Vittorio Sindoni. When I talked to her the first time I thought to myself, "Wow, she's really beautiful. If I'd known, I would have used her for both films." But I never had any intention of hitting on her, she was seventeen and I was still with Carla Romanelli, though me and Carla were growing apart. While I was shooting this film, I think she was in Greece working on another film[5] ... anyhow we were slipping away from each other. Again, I repeat, I had no intention of trying anything funny with Silvia. In the evening, me and Paolo Poeti—who was still my 1st AD at the time—would go dancing and dredge up girls in clubs. But at one point I had to interrupt production to go to Venice, to shoot some footage of Little Tony during a special concert. I had to stay away three days while most of the cast and crew remained in Sardinia. I went up to Silvia, "Hey babe, behave and don't go around late at night." I kissed her on the cheek, she turned red and I realized, there and then, that she was the woman of my life. As soon as I reached Venice, I sent her a telegram. "Wait for me." She did, she had already fallen in love.

After this "musicarello" chapter of your career, you pass on to something that, ideally, was the kind of film you wanted to make. Tell me about the comedy-Western **I quattro del pater noster** *[In the Name of the Father, 1969].*

I wanted to make comedies, I thought I was suitable for them. Not exactly this kind but I felt this film was a step in the right direction ... but the making of it was hell. The protagonists were Lino Toffolo, Enrico Montesano, Paolo Villaggio and Oreste Lionello, all of them on their way up. They hadn't done much, if anything, for cinema but they were all big TV personalities. Can you believe that I never managed to have them all together, if not on very rare occasions? They were distracted by television, especially Montesano and Villaggio, and Toffolo would run back to Venice as soon as he could. Lionello was maybe the only accommodating one. It wasn't because they were stuck up, it was just that they were distracted by television and the success they were having.

How were you on the set? Enrico Montesano told me that you were the distracted one...

I was hard, maybe a little too much so. I was trying to get them to collaborate but they all wanted to overshadow each other. Initially I was excited to get a cast like this because I thought we couldn't lose. The film was produced by Cittadini and Fiorentini, and they believed in the film a lot. I don't remember being distracted though ... did he mean by women? I was very concentrated.... No dramas during that time, that I can recall...

Then, as you said, Mauro Parenti called you again for **Zenabel**.

Yes, I was very intrigued by the film because it was packed with beautiful women. Parenti cut out a part for himself but generally the cast was much richer and more promising than *Fenomenal*.

What do you remember about the cast?

Lucretia Love was the protagonist and she was Parenti's woman. But there was quite an international cast: John Ireland, Lionel Stander ... I have a funny anecdote about Ireland. We shot the film in beautiful places, mostly in Tuscania, in the castle of Bracciano and at Monte Gelato, where we shot the "waterfall of the virgins." Anyway, halfway through production, we had to shoot a big scene in a wonderful square, in the historical center of Tuscania. I had prepared everything. It was the stake scene, when Lucretia Love had to be burned alive. Everything was ready: the extras, the horses and Lucretia was already in position. The only thing missing was the king, John Ireland. Where was he? He was in his room at the Hilton Hotel waiting for a check, seeing the production hadn't paid his last installment. We were on set with more than 400 people to deal with, Lucretia was shouting, "Ruggero untie me!" It was surreal. At half past twelve Ireland arrives. OK, so the shot was very wide, it got the whole square, the crowd and in the distance, the king, who was supposed to raise his hand and get the blaze started. I call out, "Action," but nothing happened. Ireland didn't move. I was too far away to communicate with him so I sent the dialogue coach to see what was going on. In the meantime Lucretia continued screaming her head off. Mickey Knox, the dialogue coach, came back and said, "Ireland wants to know his motivation and his character's state of mind in this scene." Remember, he just had to move his fucking hand ... I got so pissed off. I went up to him, picked up a midget from the crowd and put him in his arms. "You're doing the scene with this midget in your arms." "What a wonderful idea, Ruggero!" He did the whole film with that midget. Ireland was a ballbuster. Lionel Stander was another one who needed something to hold on to … a motivation. He would drop to the ground after every scene, because of the heat and wouldn't want to continue. But seeing he was always yearning for women, I'd send him a half-naked girl to sit on his lap as we set up everything for the next scene.

This film signaled the end of the first phase of your career. In the following years you worked nearly exclusively for television and publicity. Why?

The film did terribly. It came out right after the bomb at Piazza Fontana[6] so nobody went. People were afraid of terrorist attacks. It was a massive flop. And to think my biggest concern was censorship … I was so unlucky.

How were those "caroselli" years, continually moving between Rome and Milan?

Those were pioneering times. There weren't any real scripts, but more of a general outline and the director had complete liberty. I even edited some of the publicities after having directed them. I brought Erico Menczer with me, because my trusted director of photography Riccardo Pallottini was busy on film sets. I would direct roughly 100 caroselli a year. There weren't many directors as active as I was. Usually they would come in, direct a few and go back to films. I remember meeting Giulio Petroni, who was one of those directors who would take a vacation from films and direct TV spots. There were six caroselli to direct for Linetti aftershave and hair gel. I directed three and he did the other three. He was big, bigger than I was at the time. He came from the huge success of *Tepepa* [a.k.a. *Blood and Guns*, 1968]. We used to go out clubbing in the evening. He was fun to have around, very cultured and quite the ladies' man. Anyway, during all that period I missed cinema. Well, not initially because I was working so much and was always travelling, that there wasn't any time to think about anything except work. But one day I receive a phone call from Enzo Barboni, who had been a DOP on many films in which I'd been a 1st AD and when I answered he goes, "Is this Ruggero Deodato, the notorious television director?" He was kidding around but I was a little hurt. That was a wake-up call.

Once you became reconciled to cinema again, things had changed a lot in the industry.

Well, censorship had changed. Actresses were all stripping, Ornella Muti and Eleonora Giorgi, Silvia's main rivals. So she went, "I have to start taking off my clothes, so I'd rather do it with you." Before, she'd always used a double. That's why she decided to work with me on *Ondata di piacere* [*Waves of Lust*, 1975].

Lamberto Bava has stated that his script had started out as a pure giallo and then changed into an erotic film.

Two producers called me, Vincenzo Salviani and Alberto Marras, who remembered me from *Gungala*. It's a film I hated making but coming from such a long period away from cinema I couldn't afford to say no. The erotic aspect of the story didn't quite convince me. If I could have had more decisional power, I would have insisted on developing the giallo aspect more, but then they even changed the title, which wasn't supposed to be *Waves of Lust*. This is the reason why Silvia wanted to make the film. "You're not doing it, unless you do it with me…." "But we already have a protagonist!" The one that had worked on *La nipote* [*The Niece*, 1974], Francesca Muzio, who was quite a morbid presence.

Opposite: Publicity material for Deodato's erotic thriller, *Waves of Lust*, 1975.

The problem was that she had already signed the contract and so the production had to pay her anyway. Add to that the fact that Muzio got eight million to make the film when Silvia's cachet was forty million but she accepted to do it for five, just to be with me. We had a few rows about the matter. "OK, if there is another actress then neither of us can work on the film." "What the hell are you talking about, Silvia. It's been four years since I've done anything and for once they call me and not you, and you want me to refuse?!"

What can you tell me about the cast?

Al Cliver [Pierluigi Conti] had a nickname, "il sercio" [the stone], because he was rigid and as expressive as a rock. A wonderful face but completely unable to act. Though, at the end of the day, he works fine in the film. Who was a wonderful person to discover was John Steiner, with whom I did many things later on in my career. He was a terrific actor and lots of fun. It was a good cast, there was also Elizabeth Turner. She had just made *Chi sei?* [*Beyond the Door*, 1974] by Assonitis. We made the film entirely in Cefalù and it was really weird because there would be the strongest of suns and then all of sudden a hurricane would arrive. We had to bring the yacht back to the port so many times.

After the success of this film, you were back on the map. The same producers offered you Uomini si nasce, poliziotti si muore *[Live Like a Cop, Die Like a Man, 1976]*.

And I gained the power to decide once again. I loved the two protagonists: Marc Porel and Ray Lovelock. I gave roles to Silvia and her sister Sofia. I wanted to do something different from what was being done in Italy … I wanted something closer to the American approach. I knew it was going to be very violent and I would use sweet, melodic ballads to soften the tension. There is a realism in the film that is reminiscent of Rossellini. I was very attentive to details and I especially focused on the balance between the violence and brutal nature of some sequences and the humor and general likability that the leads inspired.

The film is indeed very violent.

Maybe I exaggerated a little with the violence. I had problems with the censorship committee. The film was released together with another nobody believed in, the first "Monezza" film, *Squadra antiscippo* [*The Cop in Blue Jeans*, 1976]. *Live Like a Cop, Die Like a Man* ended up being a little crushed by the film with Tomas Milian.

Let's talk about the action sequences. The film begins with a very long motorcycle chase.

First I shot the film and then I added this sequence, which was not in the script. Initially Remy Julienne was supposed to do it—he was the best among stunt coordinators—but then he backed out a couple of days before. I don't know why, maybe there wasn't enough money. The producer came up with two Italian stuntmen and told me to start editing. There wasn't any need for my presence on the set, I was told. I accepted but when, after a couple of days, I saw the stuff that was being shot, I intervened. It was awful. They got the driver to go at 180 km/h on a street and they put the camera straight on his face. You couldn't see the buildings flying by, the wheels moving … so he might as well have been driving at 10 km/h. I got mad and the producers agreed with me. I took hold of the situation. I did some really crazy stuff … which today would be impossible to pull off. I blocked the traffic at Piazza del Popolo in Rome, without a permit. I have great memories of those days. One day, as we were shooting, a woman sneaked up behind me and put her hands over my eyes. All the crew stopped and just stared, wide-eyed … it was Ingrid Bergman.

Italian poster of *Live Like a Cop, Die Like a Man*, 1976.

Tell me a little more about Porel and Lovelock.

Porel was a nice kid, good looking, but he had a serious problem with drugs and could become an asshole, a dangerous asshole, at times very aggressive. You had to raise your voice to calm him down and put him back in his place. Lovelock, on the contrary, was mild-mannered, very polite, a delight to have around. He was especially patient with Porel. In the first scene, when they are both on the motorcycle, Porel, who was driving, would move in such way as to try and block Ray off.

Ultimo mondo cannibale *[Last Cannibal World, a.k.a.* Jungle Holocaust, *a.k.a.* The Last Survivor, *1977]* is the first real Italian cannibal movie, but before yours, Lenzi had made Il paese del sesso selvaggio *[Deep River Savages, a.k.a.* The Man from the Deep River, *1972].*

Lenzi's film I think was more inspired by *A Man Called Horse* [1970]. I don't understand why they consider it part of the cannibal genre and the first one for that matter. I don't think it has anything to do with me. I have nothing against Lenzi, but I just don't get why it should star as a precursor of my films. The producer, Giorgio Carlo Rossi, had certainly thought of Lenzi for this project, initially. The script went around for some time and was handed to various directors. I think I was chosen for commercial reasons. I'd had a lot of success with *Live Like a Cop, Die Like a Man*, which was distributed by the same company that had distributed *Deep River Savages*. So the script was passed on to me, but I changed it quite a bit, to be honest ... pretty much all of it. I took inspiration from the images from *National Geographic*. Probably Lenzi would have come up with a completely different kind of story.

You have often expressed your appreciation for Gualtiero Jacopetti.

I have always been a lover of *Mondo Cane* [1962] by Jacopetti. In fact, I'm sorry I never had the chance of meeting him in person. *Mondo Cane* was the starting point for me to direct a film on cannibals. The photography of *Mondo Cane*, the music of *Mondo Cane* and the truth of *Mondo Cane* inspired me incredibly. So the idea was to unite a proper story with the roughness, the cruelty and the style of Jacopetti. The imagery of *Mondo Cane*, but with actors. I managed to do this with *Last Cannibal World* but even better with *Cannibal Holocaust*, in which I went free-handedly. And in this case I also used Riz Ortolani's music, which was a decision completely influenced by Jacopetti's films.

Was Last Cannibal World ***a hard film to make, technically and logistically speaking?***

It was incredibly difficult to shoot. I had ex-cannibals that didn't speak any language at all ... I had to use various strategies to be able to get what I needed from them. The jungle was truly impenetrable, the crew had to take a six-hour dugout journey to reach the set and around us there was literally nothing, not a living soul, and every three meters there was the risk of a tree falling, because it is a rainforest ... and the heat was intolerable. After five days, the crew wanted to kill me, but in time we grew fond of this place and climate. On Sundays we would see who had managed to collect more leeches.... We got used to drinking the water from the ginger, which is a kind of artichoke full of water that has an extraordinary taste ... but generally speaking, we had a very hard time. After the success of *Live Like a Cop, Die Like a Man* my qualities as a director were finally recognized. *Last Cannibal World* is a film into which I put all my skills and my experience, more so than on *Cannibal Holocaust*. I did things the proper way, I went on real locations,

I wasn't satisfied with going to the Kuala Lumpur National Park like many colleagues would later do. So I put everything I was able to put into this film, and this repaid me, but as usual after the success of the film, imitators came along with a lazy and trashy approach, indecent stuff like Holocaust ... Zombie[7] ... terrible imitations. All this pisses me off.

What about the animals?

Well, we had quite a few misadventures with animals. Lamberto Bava, who was the 1st AD, got bitten by a snake. There was a scene in which a bunch of snakes came out of a skull. We had a snake handler of course, who had taken out all the venom but there were snakes everywhere so I explained to Lamberto how to pick them up, from the head, carefully.... Everything was going well until he made a mistake picking up a coral snake and got bit. Even if it had no venom, snakes' teeth are like razor-sharp and Lamberto's hand was covered in blood in a matter of seconds. The snake handler, who was a local, started shouting, "No poison! No poison!" ... but Lamberto became white and fainted.

But what about the animals that got killed?

There weren't that many and I would leave during those scenes. I love animals.

What about the actors?

Massimo Foschi I chose because I had seen him in a theatrical transposition of "Orlando furioso," in Spoleto, and he was fantastic. Ivan Rassimov and Me Me Lay were chosen by the producer. They came directly from Lenzi's film, *Deep River Savages*. Rassimov had a small role but he was good and I liked him a lot.... In fact, I used him again for a couple of films. I was really shocked to hear about his death. He was golden, a kind man.

The film was a big hit all over the world.

I'll tell you a fun fact, which is emblematic of Italian film critics. My film was released in the States in the same period as *Travolti da un insolito destino nell'azzurro mare d'agosto* [*Swept Away*, 1974] by Lina Wertmuller. An article came out here in Italy with a headline that read out something like this: "Big Success of an Italian Film in the United States." Of course, Lina Wertmuller's film was only shown in one theater in New York whereas my film was released in eighty-five cinemas. Not a single word on the film.

Your choices, following your first cannibal and horror movie, for that matter, were quite peculiar.

Seeing that both the Japanese and the Germans had appreciated my work on *Last Cannibal World*, they started asking me for another film, any film, and I did something completely different. I made *L'ultimo sapore dell'aria* [*Last Feelings*, 1978]! In Japan they handed out handkerchiefs together with the tickets, to dry the tears. I continued this trend for quite a few years, because I was extremely irritated by what my film had spawned ... the imitators, I mean. If they'd at least made the same effort I'd made... You can't just go to the nearest park or steal scenes from my films. I don't like it. It's not professional...

Why a tearjerker about a young boy?

After my first lighter, more joyful films I had come back to cinema with films charged with violence and sex. I felt I had distorted my idea of cinema. I wanted to break away from what I was doing. I wanted to maintain the realism of *Last Cannibal World* but in a completely different context and tone. That film had given me a great amount of visibility, especially in Japan. They wanted a film by Ruggero Deodato, any film as long as I

Deodato poses with his cannibals, the real stars of *Last Cannibal World*, 1977 (courtesy Nocturno Cinema).

was the director. When I proposed the idea of *Last Feelings*, they really loved it and Japan became the co-producer of the film.

Before **Cannibal Holocaust,** *you made* **Concorde Affaire '79** *[The Concorde Affair, 1979].*

I was called to direct *L'ultimo squalo* [*Great White*, a.k.a. *The Last Shark*, 1981] that was then directed by Enzo G. Castellari. The producer approved me but Fabrizio De Angelis, who was the production coordinator, disapproved. So I did this other film produced by Mino Loy who was really stingy. He would count and check how every dime was spent. If the film had been made with 100 million lira, the result would have been spectacular. *The Concorde Affair* was a difficult film. I was very depressed. My relationship with Silvia was coming to an end and I was crushed by this, plus I had had an accident and my foot was bandaged and I was limping.

It had an international cast...

James Franciscus tried to hinder me. It was his way of putting me to the test but once he understood that I knew what I was doing, he calmed down. After that, the only thing he worried about was jumping on Mimsy Farmer. I don't know why anybody would want to jump on Mimsy Farmer. She was an American who lived in Rome and had a different mentality compared to Franciscus. On the first day, he got drunk and slobbered all over Farmer and I found myself with two protagonists who wouldn't talk to each other. I can't say Mimsy was my kind of person but when an actress is good and works well, I don't care about the rest. Then there was Edmund Purdom who was nice and I had seen him often in Spoleto. He was very passionate about music and had quite a musical culture. All his scenes were done in Rome, together with Joseph Cotten whom I had already met on the set of *The Hellbenders*. He was extraordinary, silent and fascinating. Van Johnson was also very agreeable. Gay, shy and fearful. They had told him I was some kind of beast so at first he kept his distance. When I told him that he was a hero of mine, he loosened up. It was true, I grew up watching his films.

From the sky to the jungle. Cannibal Holocaust *is your most famous film. How did you come up with the idea?*

In that period there was a serious problem with terrorism, and my seven-year-old son would watch the news on TV showing corpses and violence and this infuriated me. When we did our films, they censored them, cut them, and in some cases even wanted to burn the copies, whereas journalists had a free pass on everything. This made me think, and I proposed this film to Gianfranco Clerici: a film with cannibals in which the journalists were the real enemy. Initially I wanted to make a documentary, but then I realized that was Jacopetti's domain, so we embarked on this adventure using real actors. We started off with a vague outline, a general scenario, a series of elements and ideas which I broadened during the making.

The search for a location went on for quite a while, didn't it?

We went to Leticia, which is a small town 100 meters from the Brazilian border and 100 meters from the Peruvian border. It's the extreme point of a triangle that reaches the Amazon River. It's beautiful, with this majestic river and a port that has remained untouched since the 19th century, but it was also full of drug trafficking, so it was quite a dangerous place. Before going there, I went to Cartagena. A producer had told me to check it out, "Go there…. They shot *Queimada* [*Burn!*, 1969] and a lot of Italian films. It's wonderful!" I went and didn't like it at all. There was nothing … yes, there was the Rio Negro but the vegetation was all wrong, there wasn't a real jungle, so I said, "No, we're not going to film it here … I'd rather go back to Malaysia where we did *Last Cannibal World*." We went to Bogotá but due to technical problems with the plane, we were stuck three days at the airport. In addition, Franco Palaggi, the producer, was pissed off because I had rejected Cartagena. Generally, when I find myself in an airport, I always move around and in these three days we were stuck in one, I started talking to people, in particular to a young man with a camera, a Colombian with a rugged look, and he suggested we go to Leticia. "You have to go there, it's only an hour and a half from here!" So I went to the producer, "We're leaving for Leticia." "You're out of your mind! I'm gonna sue you when we get back to Rome! You keep changing everything! You're crazy!" "Come on, they say it's wonderful…" And since he was a true professional, he said, "OK, let's get the tickets for this bloody Leticia!" As soon as I reached Leticia, I loved the atmosphere. It was full of boats, traffic, people and general chaos, small planes landing on the river, it was perfect. Plus I had an obsession with filming these great rivers, because when you put them on film, they transform into thin threads, wonderful torrents surrounded by the jungle. I needed a boat to go scouting. Palaggi went nuts, "I'm not giving you anything! Forget about it!" so I went to a fisherman and arranged the trip. The next morning I reached the river and saw Palaggi arrive on a motorboat. "Come on board!" He was a terrific professional, he was used to working with Sergio Leone, he was grumpy but knew how to work. The problem with the jungle was the high tide, because that's when you're going to find more snakes. With a low tide you can go through the jungle clapping and the snakes would move away. Everything was very simple, the crew was never hostile in any way, everything went wonderfully. I was able to communicate with the Indios as well as with the Spanish-speaking crew because I speak the language. I had rejected the Peruvian and Colombian Indios, preferring the Brazilian ones who lived as actual primitives and were extremely intelligent. They were slim, unlike the Peruvian and the Colombian Indios who had been spoiled by the presence of the white people. They had food and modern medicines whereas the tribes I chose still used natural herbal remedies and they were really intelligent. I used especially this head tribesman, Atunche; he did most of the scenes and was extraordinary...

What about the casting process?
One of the first decisions we made was to film in English, consequently we did the casting in New York. We put ourselves in the hands of an important casting agency that had just worked with Ridley Scott. I asked for unknowns, as long as they were good, so we picked elements from the Actors Studio. In order for the film to be Italian, we needed at least two Italian actors, but luckily at the Actors Studio we found Luca Barbareschi and in Rome I found the girl. That was a stroke of genius. I did some auditions but there was this friend of my sister's, an upper-class girl who liked to play hard to get, but who was also adventurous and curious: "Francesca, would you like to make a film in the Amazon?" and she went, "Yes! Absolutely! When? Where? Why? Immediately!" To all four of these actors we had a clause in their contracts that obligated them not to work on anything else for one year. "The fact is, you're dead and I'm going to present the film as an authentic event."

Robert Kerman/Richard Bolla and his past?
This is something that made me really angry when I was told about it. I wouldn't have chosen a porn actor, but I do have a justification: on *The Concorde Affair* the casting director was the same, and he had provided me with a lot of actors, among which James Franciscus, and as you can see in the film, in the control tower, there's also Kerman, who is one of the characters who moves around the most. I met Kerman many years after the film, at a convention in the States and he seemed irritated by my presence. Maybe it was because he could tell I looked at him differently, knowing he made porn...

What was the atmosphere like on set?
The great thing was that we invented things as we went along. For example, one day I called Antonello Geleng, the production designer, and I said, "Tomorrow we're impaling the girl ... we've already shot the rape scene." "How are we going to do it?" "That's what you have to figure out!" The next morning, at dawn, Geleng knocks at my door, "I have something to show you..." He takes out a pole with a bike seat attached to it and a metal bar welded on the back. "What am I supposed to do with this?" "You stick it in the ground, the girl sits on it and she holds a stick of balsa wood in her mouth, you cover her in blood and you're done!" When I explained this special effect to Tarantino, he asked me, "How much did you spend?" "Ten dollars." "Naaah!" So it was a very stimulating atmosphere.

Tell me about Geleng, an important figure of his time.
When we stopped shooting, everybody would vanish in a matter of minutes. "Where the fuck is everyone?" One day, the DOP and I followed them to the 1st ADs room and found everybody fucked up on drugs. Geleng was in the bathroom, buck naked, standing in front of the mirror, with the script supervisor next to him, kneeling on the ground. He had a hard-on and I could see he was copiously bleeding from one hand. He had smashed the mirror in front of him. "What the fuck happened?" I asked. He doesn't even look at me and goes, "I entered the mirror." The next day the script supervisor came to

Deodato in the hostile Amazon working on *Cannibal Holocaust* (courtesy Nocturno Cinema).

me saying that Geleng had left her. I went to ask him why. I found him lying on the floor, next to his bed. He stared at me. "Because that whore made me go inside the mirror."

Who is the woman during the "adulteress scene"?

We had to use a girl from the costume department because nobody wanted to do it. I had to call her during the trial to prove that she hadn't been killed. They wanted to condemn me to thirty years in jail for having made a snuff movie.

What happened to the infamous "piranha sequence"?

My fans have always asked me about the piranha scene, and I really don't understand where they got this news. We used to eat piranhas, the make-up artist used to fish them and they were very tasty when cooked on the grill. One day I had the idea of using these piranhas for a scene. In *Last Cannibal World* there's a moment in which ants cover and bite a man's arm so I thought we could do something similar in *Cannibal Holocaust*, attaching real piranhas to the costume and immersing the actor in the water. Of course we hadn't brought rubber piranhas from Rome, so we had to use the real thing. We tried the scene various times but the result was pathetic, the fish seemed dead-like, and it was discarded. The set photographer must have sold the photo she took of this moment, and so I imagine this is the origin of all this curiosity.

An incredibly important element of the film is the music.

I knew I wanted very sweet music for the film, and my ambition was to get to Riz Ortolani but I didn't have the prestige yet, but Palaggi did, having worked with Leone, and got him to attend a screening. Ortolani arrived and he was nice, a funny man. I was trembling, imagining what his reaction might be. Once the film was finished, Ortolani turned to me and said, "You're a genius, this is an extraordinary film."

The film was supposed to be called* I figli della luna *[Sons of the Moon].

The "Sons of the Moon" are the cannibals who see the moon through the branches of a tree. In a way, that's their only light source, even more than the sun itself. Gianfranco Clerici didn't like the change in title, which was a choice of the distributors. With Clerici I've always had an excellent relationship. We had written other films for me, there was enough trust for him to leave me quite a lot of freedom. More than a script, it was an outline ... let's say that the outline of *The Blair Witch Project* [1999] was the one we had, and basing myself on that outline, I would add and extend ideas, stimulated also by the producer who would call me from MIFED saying, "Continue to do whatever you're doing, the scenes you've sent me are fantastic, everybody wants a chunk of this film ... tomorrow kill whoever you want." And this gave birth to the impaling scene, the rape... I had a lot of fun and it was a lot less difficult than *Last Cannibal World*. But the main idea was fantastic, you couldn't get it wrong with an idea like that.

Let's talk about the aftermath of the film, once it was released.

I was in Bogotá and there were queues, kilometers long, to see the film. I was at a party, in the city, with a girlfriend of mine. All sorts of journalists and members of the Colombian cultural scene were present. My friend introduced me, "This is the director of *Cannibal Holocaust*." I was pushed and pulled out of the building. Once back in my hotel, I received telephone calls.... I was afraid, so I called my 1st AD, Salvo Basile, who lived in Cartagena and through him I managed to have the protection of a local mobster who brought me to the Island of Rosario. I stayed there in exile for a week and then I left for Miami. I didn't think the reaction would have been so disastrous for the Italian critics and all the legal problems that followed. We made the film in a relatively short time, thinking we were making an entertaining product. I never expected such a reaction. After *Cannibal Holocaust*, I made *La casa seperduta nel parco* [*The House on the Edge of the Park*, 1980] which I considered even tougher, and my worry was, "What are they going to do to me now, condemn me to death?" because in my opinion it was even more violent. After what happened, I started changing genres ... lighter stuff. They called me for *I predatori di Atlantide* [*The Raiders of Atlantis*, a.k.a. *Atlantis Interceptors*, 1983]. I continued doing publicity, documentaries, but I started getting softer and in particular I refused to do any kind of sequel to *Cannibal Holocaust*, which wouldn't have made any sense. I got close to making one when they offered me *Inferno in diretta* [*Cut and Run*, 1985] which was supposed to be directed by Wes Craven, who, maybe at the time, was less of a box office draw than myself. He would later become much bigger than me but at the time my name was a little more appealing to producers. I changed that script very much as well, and then I worked a lot for TV. I changed continuously and I didn't want to fall into the clutches of the board of censors. Basically I did everything to get rid of *Cannibal Holocaust*. Now it might seem like a ludicrous thing to say but believe me, the heritage was very heavy.

But wait, weren't you supposed to direct* Schiave bianche—violenza in Amazzonia *[White Slave, a.k.a.* Amazonia: The Catherine Miles Story, *1985] which was later directed by Mario Gariazzo?

Yes, what happened there was that I asked ninety million lira for the film, which I thought I deserved seeing the box-office results of *Cannibal Holocaust*. The producer answered that I had gone crazy, and success had gone to my head. But when they gave me 120 million for *Cut and Run*, he came to me and said, "...but we could have given you the same amount for our film...." "Yeah, but you didn't." These were bandits who thought directors were interchangeable. After me, they called Castellari but the foreign distributors wanted me as the director, so they cut the budget, let Castellari go and got Gariazzo to do it.

What is, in your mind, the heritage of Cannibal Holocaust?

The heritage can be divided into good and bad: the young directors tried to imitate *Cannibal Holocaust* shooting with a hand-held camera and moving around a lot, but without having a real narrative dimension. I moved around a lot too, but in front of the camera there was a story, and you need the marvel of cinema. Nowadays I see a lot of confusion. It's the same thing with long tracking shots, you have to know when and how to use certain techniques. So this is the negative aspect. I can speak well about a lot of films, like for example *15 Minutes* [2001] with Robert De Niro, with the two killers that shoot everything they see and die in the style of *Cannibal Holocaust*. I don't like seeing monsters … I was disappointed by *Cloverfield* [2008], which seemed like an excellent film but then when I saw the monster appear, my interest dropped; even *[REC]* [2008] disappointed me because of its monsters. So when you start using zombies and creatures, it violates the real nature of my film.

We mentioned this previously but the time has come to talk about the animals that were killed in the film.

The animal problem … I know, it's ascribed to me, but I always say, "I didn't kill those animals, it was the four journalists." The story is about four journalists who shoot the second half of the film … I shot the first. Sergio Leone, when he saw the film, said, "The first half is OK, an adventure film, the second half is a masterpiece. You will get into a lot of trouble." What could I do, kill people? That wasn't possible. So what I did was just wait patiently, maybe like Jacopetti did, to see what I could film. The guide would tell me, "Tomorrow there is an Indio wedding, you can kill a tortoise"; the natives eat rodents, they even burn the forest to catch them and I didn't think a mouse would be scandalous. The piglet … the costume assistant came to me and asked me if we could kill a pig, "We're fed up of eating all this fish, fish, fish…." So there are four elements, and after 30 years the film was screened in Britain, praised as a cult, with a wonderful premiere. Everybody was there, Vanessa Redgrave … and the only thing that remained cut was the mouse. Therefore I don't think there's anything indecent. Alberto Sordi used to go and see horses being slaughtered. I believe that the slaughterhouse is much worse than anything we've shown. All I did was ask what the locals ate.

Let's talk about the zombie movie you never got to make. Many people might not be aware of this but you were supposed to direct the definitive zombie film. Everything was set up and ready. Why wasn't the film ever made?

As you know I made *Cannibal Holocaust* and *The House on the Edge of the Park* practically back to back, not quite but nearly. During all the rumble that came after the release of *Cannibal*, that caused producers to be afraid of approaching me with projects, the only one, or one of the few that did, was Fausto Saraceni. I had met him while I was an AD with Rossellini in the offices of Documento Films. Saraceni, together with a new partner of his, some guy I had once crossed at Cortina, a rich man who owned a jeans factory, started insisting to have me for a film. They brought me this first treatment, which I don't know where they got from or who wrote it, a zombie film. I was not very much aware of what zombies were and I hadn't seen anything Romero had done, or

Fulci—he had already done something with zombies, hadn't he? I'm not a horror fan and I don't consider my films horror but the story intrigued me … it was supposed to be shot in Mexico. You reminded me that Antonello Geleng had started working on some drawings, because I had completely forgotten. I don't remember if we started all the casting process but what I do remember is that I was supposed to leave for South America to scout for locations when my father fell sick. He lived in Spoleto and a week before I was supposed to leave I jumped in my car and went to visit him. When I got there I found my mother, brothers and various relatives there at his bedside. The situation was more serious than what I had thought. I remained there with him for the following days, while the producer would call me and very politely, but worried, ask me if I was going to be ready to leave. I bought time but my father was getting increasingly worse … but wouldn't die. After some time the politeness vanished and the producers starting getting pushy, until one day they told me they would send me their lawyers if I didn't get back to Rome immediately. That's when I told them to fuck themselves. They ended up not being able to leave, not having a director and my father died the day after. I never heard from them again and when I went back to Rome, after the funeral, I received no telephone call. Though, the other day I was thinking back … you know the only thing missing in my filmography is a zombie film. When I meet George Romero at conventions he has massive queues, kilometers of people waiting to meet him and I have many, many fans but not kilometers like he has. Just think if I had made cannibal movies and a zombie film!

Do you remember anything about the storyline?
Absolutely nothing. Well, except what is visible in Geleng's sketches, that they were water zombies. They were soggy and all over the place, humid and soft. But I believe there were various kinds of living dead. But consider that I would invent a lot on set so God knows what would have come out of a film like this one. Now I wouldn't make one though, I mean a zombie film. There is an inflation that is frankly ridiculous. Plus, maybe if I had done a zombie film I would have lost credibility. I'm not a splatter director, I'm a realist. In this I'm very much "Rossellinian."

Let us go back to what you actually did manage to direct. **The House on the Edge of the Park** *overlaps with the making of* **Cannibal Holocaust**…
I was in New York shooting *Cannibal* when I received a telephone call from Clerici saying that he had an idea for a film. "We can get the guy who did *The Last House on the Left*. Shoot some exterior shots of New York, possibly at night. I will send you a first treatment tomorrow." I read it and liked it because it was about the struggle of social classes. I was very stimulated. I was free, no wife, I was completely over Silvia by this time, I had various girlfriends. It was exhilarating to be able to direct two films back to back. The only problems were with David Hess. The production was the same of *Cannibal Holocaust*. We had spent so little on that film that we could afford to shoot another one.

Before getting to Hess, what exactly did you shoot in the States?
Only the exterior shots, the skyline, the streets, Hess in the car. The rape scene at the beginning was shot in Rome. The girl was Hess's wife, but I didn't know that at the time. All the rest: the garage, the villa, the garden, the pool, all that stuff was done in Rome.

Were you aware of Craven's film? Had you seen it?
No, not at all. Clerici had and he took inspiration from it.

What exactly did Hess do that got on your nerves?

He would create problems, get other actors to back him up, he would enjoy building up fights. David was a bit crazy. But like most giants, you slap them around and they calm the fuck down. After the film he continued on in Italy. He did a film with Pasquale Festa Campanile.[8] I called him again for some of my films because at the end of the day I thought he was a good actor and I felt some affection for him. Our relationship got better in more recent times. We would meet at festivals and conventions and he would always smile and give me a hug. He was gentle really, and I was genuinely sorry when he died. I had talked to him on the phone just a few days before.

Tell me about the rest of the cast.

Annie Belle came from the success of some erotic films. I liked her, she was cute. Then there was the black girl that had appeared briefly in *The Concorde Affair*. She was from Martinica and we had had a bit of a flirt so I got her in the film as well. Christian Borromeo and Brigitte Petronio were perfect for their roles, with their clean-cut faces. They hadn't done much. I think Silvia's mother, my mother-in-law, had recommended them to me. The tall, curly guy—I forget his name—died of an overdose shortly after the film. Lorraine De Selle years later became a producer and turned very vengeful towards me. It's typical … these actresses, when they stop acting, they regret their choices, getting naked, and they take it out on the directors. On the other hand, I'm very proud of my choice with Giovanni Lombardo Radice. I think it was his very first film.

How was it directing the stronger sex scenes?

Everybody was telling me to go down hard, to be as hard-hitting as I could. As I said before, from a certain point of view I feel it is even stronger than *Cannibal Holocaust*. For a long time I hated the film. Maybe, at the time, I didn't really get it but now I'm very fond of *The House on the Edge of the Park*. In a way, it paid the price of having been directed by the same guy who had made *Cannibal Holocaust*. If any other person had directed it, it wouldn't have been massacred as much.

After this geyser of violence, you are quarantined.

Nobody wanted to make a film with me. They were all scared shitless. Thank God Edmondo Amati rescued me from limbo. He called me up, said he had a story, I think written by Dardano Sacchetti. He had gotten in contact with the queen of the Philippines, Imelda Marcos. He sent me over there and they greeted me as if I was royalty. *The Raiders of Atlantis* wasn't a film I was interested in but it was the first offer I had in over three years.

What did you do in that period?

Publicity, publicity and more publicity. The problem was that the few producers who would have called me, couldn't. Carlo Rossi had fallen sick. Marras and Salviani were going through a rough period having had a couple of big flops and the new ones wouldn't call me because of the scandal with *Cannibal Holocaust*.

Did production proceed smoothly on **Atlantis**?

Oh, yes. Christopher Connelly was pleasant, professional and would do everything he was asked. He did many of the stunts, like when he throws himself from the helicopter. I had Michele Soavi as an actor, who I liked and was a big fan of mine. He knew all the films I had made. Plus I had a couple of girlfriends in that period, and a good stunt team. I was satisfied. The script was fragile though, very fragile, and had plot holes all over it.

You don't really like the film, do you?

The production was good but the script was just too weak. The cast was OK, but not brilliant. George Hilton had a role as well. Not a good actor but perfect for these light, minor roles. It went well and in a way, I'm fond of the film because it got me back on the market.

Something tells me you feel more warmly about Cut and Run…

Alessandro Fracassi called me for it. He had a script that Wes Craven was supposed to direct. He was already location hunting in Colombia. I took time because in the meantime I was contacted, once again, by the producers of *Cannibal Holocaust*, Franco Pallaggi and Di Nunzio, who asked me to direct a sequel to our film. Once it was clear to me that there was nothing really tangible in their offer, I went back to Fracassi. *Cut and Run* began as a big thing, a massive production. Not satisfied with the story, Luciano Vincenzoni and I closed ourselves in his house for a month and a half. Unfortunately Fracassi wasn't satisfied and he involved people like Sacchetti who I think impoverished our story a little. Anyway, once we were ready to shoot there was nothing left of the previous Craven script.

Why was Craven put aside?

Because in that precise moment I was simply a bigger box-office draw than he was. I was the director of *Cannibal Holocaust*, which by that time was making good money. But mind you, I didn't want to make another film like that. Yes, there are some elements in the film that might link it to *Cannibal Holocaust*—the indigenous tribe and the television crew—but the themes and plot were very different. Sometimes Fracassi would try and push towards that direction but I would resist. I didn't want to repeat that experience. I was just too scared. When Palaggi and I were in talks for the *Cannibal* sequel, I was in serious difficulty because secretly, I didn't want to direct it.

You had cult figures like Richard Lynch and Michael Berryman in the cast.

Richard was famous because he had set himself on fire in front of the White House in protest against the Vietnam war. If you rubbed him the wrong way, he would become fucking crazy. I got along with him, even if my English has always been lacking. I would explain things moving around and gesturing with my hands and he would understand immediately. Berryman was nice, he had problems with his skin so he couldn't stay under the sun for too long. He told me he lived with five wolves. I never discovered if it was true or not. Everybody thinks I chose him because of *The Hills Have Eyes* [1977] but actually it was because of *One Flew Over the Cuckoo's Nest* [1975]. But most of all I was happy because I was madly in love with Valentina Forte…. We were going strong as a couple.

This film was the start of your "American phase." Your films get made exclusively for the foreign market. In fact, you get called by Cannon for The Barbarians & Co. [The Barbarians, a.k.a. The Barbarian Brothers, 1987].

Golan and Globus were calling all Italian directors for their films: Luigi Cozzi, Enzo G. Castellari…. They had a man in Rome called John Thompson who would help choose the directors. Initially the film was going to be directed by an American. He was sent away during pre-production and I got picked. We shot the whole film in Italy, to be precise at Campo Imperatore, where we had all the elements we were looking for: the waterfall, the mountains…

Did you participate in the script?

No. the only thing I did was change the tone of the film. They wanted a serious Conan-like film and I turned it into something more comical.

Deodato (front, right) and Michael Berryman on the set of *Cut and Run*, 1985 (courtesy Nocturno Cinema).

What do you remember of the two protagonists, Peter and David Paul?

These guys were supposed to be bad-asses but actually they were just two fuckers. They would always be bickering from dawn to dusk. Then, when they weren't fighting, they would be kidding around like teenagers. They would pull down their pants and moon people on the highway, stuff like that. When I realized how they really were, I was even happier that I had changed the tone of the story. Thompson was terrified when we had the screening for Golan and Globus because he knew I had changed everything but they loved it and decided to distribute it in 3,500 copies. Anyway, about the brothers, what was funny was that they had big muscles but small bones so they would break easily.

Before this film, you had made a slasher, Camping del terrore *[Body Count, 1986], probably your most American-like film. Who wrote it?*

I never knew who wrote that film, possibly Alessandro Capone with the help of Dardano Sacchetti. Sometimes it was hard to know who the real author of the script was. It was given to you by the producer, who wouldn't even introduce the writers. You would read it and then another bunch of writers were called in, chosen again by producers or this time by the director himself.

I know you are not fond of the film, are you?

The film had problems. Production was interrupted because of a snow blizzard. Once we had wrapped and left the locations, Fracassi wanted me to add some scenes and a new murder. That's when John Steiner and Ivan Rassimov were called for cameos but all this extra stuff, you can tell, is jammed in the film, badly placed. It was a film more suited for Fulci or Lamberto Bava.

You are not very fond of* Un delitto poco comune *[Phantom of Death, 1988] either.

I absolutely loved the story, I was very enthusiastic about the whole concept, but then they imposed Edwige Fenech and my excitement crumbled. It's not that she isn't a nice person, she is, but she was completely unsuitable for the role. I brought Mapi Galan on the film because she was my woman by that time. The relationship with Valentina Forte was over, it had finished shortly after *Body Count*, where she had a small role—even if I had wanted her as the protagonist.

The producers of* Phantom of Death *were the writers Clerici and Mannino.

They chose me because they had a lot of respect for my style and work, especially Clerici with whom I had done so much ... but our relationship went sour during the making. As I said, I liked the story and, except for the imposition of Fenech, I was happy to make it but there were things in the script that just didn't work. The dialogues were tedious and pretentious and then there was all that long explanation at the end. I hate it when things have to be explained. We fought because in post-production I wanted to cut stuff out. I wasn't happy with the result and I couldn't get over the imposed presence of Edwige. Consider that Kelly Le Brock was supposed to be in it...

Who forced her on you?

Luciano Martino, who was the distributor of the film, and the associate producer was Innocenzi, who was Martino's close collaborator. I think I'm one of the few directors that has never been produced by Luciano Martino. I don't think he liked me. He didn't like me. Maybe I was too costly or maybe he thought I was an asshole. I was seen as a dangerous man because they were worried I would steal their women but I have never made off with anybody's woman.

In between* Body Count *and* Phantom of Death, *you direct a film that is pretty much forgotten:* Lone Runner—lo scrigno dei mille diamanti *[The Lone Runner, 1986].

It was a film that had nothing, not a story, nothing at all. It only had this Miles O'Keefe guy. I entrusted everything to John Steiner, who was the only real actor of the film. Assonitis wanted me to direct and I guess that was the main reason I decided to do it. He was famous because he had chased off every director he had ever had. I told myself, "I will survive Assonitis." The producers were Assonitis and Maggi. Maggi used to tell me, "Fall sick so the insurance can pay." Then, I actually did fall sick, when we moved from Marrakesh to Agadir in a caravan. For a series of deviations we ended up lost in the desert. When we reached a well, I got some water with a can and tasted it, only with a finger, but it was enough to spend the next days vomiting. Maggi would call and go, "Stay in bed another day, just another day or the insurance won't pay!" Miles O'Keefe instead didn't know how to do a thing, like all these musclemen, he just stood around. He had an old wife. He was some kind of toy-boy.

Italian cinema, by this time, was in a deep crisis. You slowly started going back to television. Among your last films for the big screen, we find* Minaccia d'amore *[Dial: Help, 1988] and* Vortice mortale *[The Washing Machine, 1993].

I very much enjoyed making *Dial: Help*. I chose the actress, Charlotte Lewis, through agencies in America. I didn't know who to pick between her and a Puerto Rican model who had made a James Bond film. Very beautiful but not as good as Lewis. It's funny, she was young and a bit of a brat, very spoiled. She was Charlie Sheen's girlfriend. But when she came to Italy, she liked everybody ... on set, all the crew tried to pick her up, even Luca Barbareschi would come by just to hit on her. She was very flirty with me. When she had to do a scene, she would go, "Ruggero, I will do it only if you buy me a pair of silk panties and a bra I saw in the shop window yesterday...." Giovanni Bertolucci and Galliano Juso produced the film. Bertolucci is one of the people I love the most from the film world, after Rossellini. Ah ... I have a fun anecdote about the period of *Dial: Help*. As I was shooting the film, I met this young actress who was making a film in Rome, with Enrico Maria Salerno. She had been Alain Delon's girlfriend. I had an affair with her, but when I dumped her she threatened to have me called by him. "He protects me!" We had been together in Paris, me and her, for a few days but she was a ballbuster ... young and beautiful but a ball breaker. So I left France and joined a friend in Ponza and while we were there, I actually got a call from Alain Delon. My friend Riccardo answered, we had a few laughs and it ended there.

How would you convince actresses to get naked for a scene?
By being professional and more importantly by staying serious. With women I'm never aggressive. I like respecting the various stages of seduction and in filmmaking it's the same. I take things gradually. Anyway, going back to your first question ... yes, cinema was changing in our country. For me, the moment I realized things would never be the same again was when Assonitis told me Carlo Rossi was dying of cancer. I think I even cried.... There was less money. For example, for *The Washing Machine,* I was given the rights for Italy because the producers didn't have enough money to pay my usual cachet.

That film wasn't even released in Italy.
No, it was made precariously, without a distribution signed up. It's a shame because it's an interesting crossover of genres. An erotic-giallo, with a horror tinge to it, and a *Rashomon*-theme throughout. The events that change as the point of view shifts from one character to the other.

What has become clear by now is that you were quite the womanizer, did this create any frictions or problems when working?
Well, I was supposed to make a film with Pippo Franco who refused me as a director because he said I had a bad reputation and was jealous of his wife. Another super-possessive guy was Al Bano. Somebody had told him I was some kind of unscrupulous womanizer. You know, once Italo Zingarelli called me to his office and asked me, "How the fuck do you always have so many women?!" [He laughs.] I looked at him. "Italo, look at you!" [Deodato spreads his arms out wide.] He was enormous. "Yes, but you must have a method." "Since I was a kid I have always been lucky with women. I talk to them, I listen, I make them laugh and I know when to ignore them." But yes, I missed a few opportunities. Luciano Martino was always worried that someone was going to steal Edwige Fenech from him, and someone did in the end. Ray Lovelock kept her away from Luciano for quite some time. But I never-ever stole another man's woman. In fact, I often did the exact contrary, like with Ottaviano Dell'Acqua. We were doing a film and on the first day of shooting I went up to him, took him aside and told him, "Listen, Ottaviano, the lead actress is the producer's fiancé. Just leave her alone, OK? Ignore this one. Pick some other girl." "No worries Ruggero! I won't even look at her!" He fucked her that same night. Ottaviano would fuck me over every time. I think he got some kick out of fucking the producer's women. It happened three times with him.

Now we make a two-decade jump to your next film. In fact, in a few months Ballad in Blood *[2016] should be released.*

Yes, we chose this title because the film is pieced together a little bit like a symphony, a concert of violence, with this angel of death that pulls the strings of the story like an orchestra conductor would. The foreign buyers liked the title immediately and hopefully I will be able to maintain it even for its Italian release. The story is inspired by the murder of Meredith Kercher which took place in Perugia, the night of Halloween, in 2007. That was a story that tickled my imagination: this beautiful girl, Amanda Knox, who you could … you can just tell she had done it … with her cold, distant eyes. Then the fact that a black man had been accused of the murder because she thought all black people shared the same DNA. There were a lot of interesting elements … like this strange boyfriend that has an unclear role in the whole matter.

Did you do any research for the film?

I interviewed young men and women about their experiences during Erasmus. I was told incredible things on orgies and sex parties. This was the premise of the story, the dark side of youth also because I wasn't interested in making a film about the Knox case, a reportage film.

Can you tell us a bit more about the story?

The story, written by myself with Jacopo Mazzuoli and Angelo Orlando, is about three students who, the morning following Halloween, after a night of drugs and alcohol, find the body of a roommate, Lenka, with her throat slit. Actually the body falls from the ceiling, where it was tied to a chandelier. First they have to understand what had happened, because their memory is completely fogged up by a night of excesses and dissipation. From this moment onwards, they enter a spiral of violence. I won't reveal more but I can say that, like in *Cannibal Holocaust,* the violence and consequent truth will be revealed through found footage.

Death has always played a major role in your films, are you afraid of it? Do you ever think about your mortality?

Not really. I lived my life to the fullest and as much as I sometimes complain I don't have a lot of regrets. Only one thought makes me sad at times. I have a very young daughter, she is in her very early teens and the idea I will never see her as a grown woman, I will never see her married or with children … that I guess is my price to pay. The toll of my mortality.

Rome, 2015, 2016

Italy's Whipping Boy: Interview with Giovanni Lombardo Radice

Ruggero Deodato says about Radice: "What I like about Giovanni is the ambiguity he brings to his characters, both sexual and moral. Both me and David Hess, who had already been chosen, knew immediately we had found our actor as we were casting the role of Ricky for *The House on the Edge of the Park*. I wasn't surprised when other directors, like Fulci or Margheriti, started calling him. Those were years, the early eighties, where it was more difficult to find good actors you could trust and Giovanni was one of those few."

You are an icon of the eighties and turned up on the scene at a time of great change, when the first signs of a crisis within the Italian film industry was underway. Let me start by asking about your relationship with cinema during the previous decade and if you felt a change taking place?

The first film I worked in was in the second half of 1979, *La casa sperduta nel parco* [*The House on the Edge of the Park*, 1980] by Deodato. So I started with pure exploitation films, and only after did I do other stuff such as television dramas, for example. Regarding the crisis, I lived through the transition very closely and in my opinion, it all depended on the massive introduction of commercial television. In the sense that when I started, there were still real producers who risked their money exposing themselves in first person and then gradually not a meter of film was used unless there was a television network financial back-up, be it Mediaset or RAI Cinema, but at that point these kind of investments were never granted to genre cinema, because priority was given to family stuff or to auteurs, but certainly not to genre cinema. The decline started from there, with the rise of modern television.

Giovanni Lombardo Radice (photo courtesy Nocturno Cinema).

Do you remember a film, a set, a project where you had, for the first time, the feeling, "OK ... things are changing"?

No, I can't say that there was a specific episode. I believe that the phenomenon took place massively farther on, in the nineties, after Soavi's films, or those directed by Argento, which fell, however, in an independent reality, free. Then after, I devoted myself mainly to television. It was when I approached the film world again that I realized things had really changed, that the production system which had shouldered me, no longer existed. It had been entirely dismantled.

As a stage actor, how was your transition to cinema where, to be honest, actors were somewhat abandoned to themselves?

In this sense the theater was my salvation ... the fact of being an actor but also of having been a director, since I had my own company. The moment I started working in movies, I realized it was a "do-it-yourself" world. The majority of directors could not distinguish an actor from a nightstand, so it was appreciated when you were able to fend for yourself. Of all the directors I've worked with, the only one who I can say knew how to direct actors was Luigi Magni. As for the others, honestly … nothing. So yes, I had to get by alone, but not only that, sometimes I had to come to the rescue. On more than one set I found myself becoming a coach for other so-called actors. Sometimes you found yourself working with people that were everything except actors. Then often we would shoot in English and there wasn't a soul who knew how to speak the language … so in the end I helped. For some producers it was a small miracle to have an actor who not only didn't break the director's balls with questions but could also help out other actors.

Before working with some of these directors were you aware of their work? Were you familiar with the previous films of Deodato or Fulci, for example?

No, zero. I never appreciated these kind of films. I don't like to be scared. The last film I saw was Argento's *Profondo rosso* [*Deep Red*, 1975] and then *Alien* [1979] and I asked myself: why do I have to hurt myself? Did the doctor order this stuff? I stopped watching films that could frighten or upset me. So no, I'd never seen anything of theirs except the films I made, and not even all of them, for that matter. For those films where I had smaller roles, I just saw my scenes during dubbing. Like the one I did with Bava, *Body Puzzle—Misteria* [*Body Puzzle*, 1992] or previously the one by Deodato *Un delitto poco comune* [*Phantom of Death*, 1988]. Even *La setta* [*The Devil's Daughter*, a.k.a. *The Sect*, 1991], I've never seen.

So, no fear in approaching a, let's say, scandalous director like Deodato after years dedicated exclusively to the theater?

In the case of *Cannibal Holocaust* I knew something about Deodato before meeting him through Luca Barbareschi with whom I had been a friend ever since we were boys. But no, no … no fear. Then look, I thought only of work, I had a tremendous need for money because theater had completely depleted me so, sincerely, I was interested only in earning. Then, having said that, I didn't put any less effort in my work. I've always tried to do my best, to go in depth with the characters, develop them as much as possible. Sometimes the role was more interesting than the film itself and I tried to give everything I could to it. Those films … I made as if I was doing *Hamlet*.

Let's go back to The House on the Edge of the Park. *I don't think I'm the first person to ask, but I've always felt that Ricky, your character, had a kind of homo-erotic attraction towards David Hess, in the film. Would you agree?*

No, no … this question has been asked numerous times, so much so that David and I, with whom I was good friends until his tragic and recent death, often joked about it. Once we were in Scotland, at a horror convention, and when we were asked this question, we answered, "Yes, we can finally say it, we can shout it to the world! We have been lovers all our lives and we're going to get married in Barcelona next year!" … and we joked about who would be dressing as the bride…. However, responding seriously to your question, we can say that in every great male friendship there is a homo-erotic component and in that particular case, there was almost a father-son relationship. Ricky was a drifter, left to himself who sees almost a father figure in Alex. This substrate is definitely present, but if you ask me if Alex and Ricky had sex, then no.

Remaining for a moment on this issue, I would like to understand how you outline and build your characters. For example, almost all the roles you've played have a very strong

Radice shares a scene in *The House on the Edge of the Park* (1980) with French actress Lorraine De Selle. The two will also star together in *Cannibal Ferox* (1981) by Umberto Lenzi (courtesy Nocturno Cinema).

sexual component. With very few exceptions, yours are carnal figures in which there seems to be a non-explicit eroticism.

Sexuality aside, I'm a very physical person and I think that I have conveyed this into many of my characters. For example, in *Phantom of Death*, I was completely run over by Michael York, not that I was attracted to him or that I wanted to sleep with him, it was like an electric shockwave. As soon as he touched me I was pierced by a thousand volt shock! In fact, I didn't remember anything, I wasn't aware of what I was saying as I was delivering my lines! Things happen over which you have absolutely no control. One could say that my physical personality comes out, it is transmitted to my characters, whether I like it or not.

What about improvisation? Was it a common practice on these films?

Common enough. I'm a great lover of improvisation. It's a technique that I've studied a lot. It is rare for me to say exactly what's written in the script. Let's say that I tend to store the concept rather than the exact sequence of words. Sometimes I was explicitly asked to do so, like in *The Omen* [2006], where among other things, I fully improvised a scene with Liev Schrieber, which remained in the final cut of the film.

We have mentioned David Hess … Ruggero Deodato has repeatedly talked about a difficult relationship between the two.

Ruggero and David have always had this cat and dog relationship, but between animals living in the same house so everything actually turned into a game. You know, David was "larger than life," full of energy, always moving, talking, commenting, suggesting, asking. Deodato has a very passionate personality, and had no time to shoot, three weeks in all, so he would tell people to fuck off with great ease. Theirs was an adversarial rapport but in a theatrical manner, a bit as if they were masks from the "commedia dell'arte," but in fact they were very fond of each other. Ruggero cast him later for other things and they would talk regularly on Skype. He remained devastated by David's death, and unfortunately I was the one who had to break the news to him.

After The House on the Edge of the Park *comes Lucio Fulci's* Paura nella città dei morti viventi *[City of the Living Dead, a.k.a.* The Gates of Hell, *1980].*

I always confuse the dates and I tend to remember the year of principal photography and not of the year it is released. That was a very hectic period. *City of the Living Dead* and the next, *Apocalypse domani* [*Cannibal Apocalypse*, a.k.a. *Cannibals in the Street*, 1980], came very close together. In fact, I returned to Italy and left again right away. We filmed them both in Georgia, in the States.

This is another characteristic of yours, Italian films but always with an international imprint.

Well, I'm trilingual, in addition to Italian I speak both English and French fluently, though I've never used French. My career has been based on the fact I know and speak English well.

How was your experience with Fulci?

I had already met Lucio Fulci socially before working with him. Duccio Tessari and his wife, Lorella De Luca, were close friends of mine. They had this Renaissance-like living room which was open to everybody. Every evening in the Tessari household, you could meet all kinds of people from the film world, from Antonioni to Paolo Villaggio, from Fulci to Zeudi Araya, who were there to chat, play board games or debate. Duccio was extremely attentive to young people, he kept his eyes open for new recruits, went to the theater and it was there he met Tonino Pulci, with whom I had done a stage version of *Little Women*. I ended up in these evening get-togethers thanks to my friendship with Pulci. I then continued going to Tessari's home for years. So I had bumped into Fulci there. We didn't speak much, as there were fifty people every night, but I was aware of the rumors that surrounded him, that he was someone who treated his actors terribly, was rude and cranky, and so on. With me though, I must say, he has always been exquisite, he respected me. To begin with, he was an educated man and valued culture, which has always surrounded me thanks to my family and he had a great regard for the theater. In *City of the Living Dead*, my character had a hump but I didn't want to wear it. I looked like Marty Feldman. I decided to go to Fulci, maybe he'd tell me to fuck off, but I thought it was worth a try. "Sorry, but isn't it possible to find an alternative, maybe a strange way of holding up my shoulder…?" "Show me." I do this little impromptu thing, making one of my shoulders seem crooked…. At the time I was studying *Richard III* and Fulci observed me muttering to himself, "All right, that's fine." This was the first approach. Then, as I said, with me he was impeccable. I was the only actor who went to dinner with him. On the first day on the set I saw him make a colossal scene and then, that same evening, he explained this approach. "On the first day of filming you have to make a crazy scene on anything … any pretext will do—this fucking fork stinks!—and make demonic screams. I keep them all on their toes and this brings out the best in them." So he certainly put on an act, but with me he was always kind and civil. He was definitely a somber, tormented man who had also had many tragedies in his family, but I never found any fault in his behavior.

With other actors?

With the actress who plays Venantino Venantini's daughter. I don't remember her name. She arrived on set late, the day she had to shoot the few scenes she had, and behaved a bit like a diva. Fulci ripped her open! "Drag this filthy cock-sucking whore off the set!" He exaggerated and the whole thing was pretty brutal, but he was right to be angry.

On Fulci's film you met Michele Soavi, in a period when he was very prolific as an assistant director and actor.

I had swiped the role of Ricky from Michele in *The House on the Edge of the Park*. He was mostly known as an actor, and was also good and had a nice face. He had been Deodato's first choice and then I also snitched his part in *City of the Living Dead*. Michele was supposed to have the part of Bob but then he was given a smaller role. However, he couldn't care less about acting. In fact, when I met him he said to me, "Ah well, you're that big son of a bitch who's stealing all my roles," and laughed. That was the start of a crazy friendship and we became inseparable. Michele was a force of nature. He still is! No less than three years ago, I visited him in the production offices where he was working and all of a sudden he appeared from an upstairs window on the first floor and when he saw me he threw himself down. [He laughs.] At the time he was a bit of a James Dean, even in looks, driving sports cars like crazy. He had a lot of ideas, wanted to do a lot of things and as I said, for years we were really inseparable. We also wrote things together, mostly for Aristide Massaccesi. When he became a director, he obviously called me. Our relationship was unique. We were like brothers, Michele and I.

Since you mentioned Aristide Massaccesi, a.k.a. Joe D'Amato, what was your impression of him?

I met him on *Deliria* [*Stage Fright*, 1987]. Michele's directorial debut was produced by Massaccesi. I thought he was extremely prepared on a technical level. Then ... well ... he was a kind person, polite.... It's not as if we had much in common.

Do you remember disputes or misunderstandings between Massaccesi and Soavi on the set of Stage Fright?

No, not that ... I remember that halfway through the film, production was suspended. I don't remember why, maybe for money issues, and when we began again the camera operator had been replaced by Massaccesi who, from that moment also supervised the photography. But fights ... no ... there were none.

On many websites, you appear credited in Eleven Days, Eleven Nights [1987] by D'Amato, but you never had anything to do with it, right?

No, I don't even know what the fucking thing is about. [He laughs.] I appear, because Massaccesi, having produced *Stage Fright*, held all the rights and used some scenes for this erotic film, but I haven't seen it, I know nothing about it.

Talking about personalities related to Stage Fright, what do you remember about Luigi Montefiori who wrote the film?

I didn't meet him on that occasion. I got to know Luigi much later, when we were both part of the same organization, S.A.C.T.—Scrittori Associati di Cinema e Televisione Italiani [translation: Association of Screenwriters for Cinema and Television].

How was your experience making the film?

I think the movie was cleverly put together considering the fact that there was hardly any money, so there was a single location and it was all shot in interiors. A little like *The House on the Edge of the Park*. The atmosphere of *Stage Fright* was very galvanizing thanks to the presence of Michele. He has always had an edge over others, even over good directors that I very much respected, like Deodato or Margheriti, who I loved as a father. But they were people who had made all kinds of films, they were real craftsmen of cinema who took care of the market's needs whereas Michele had a real passion for horror, he's a Lovecraft scholar, painted with this surrealist taste, and knew all the movies by heart. In short, he had a real love for the genre and filled his set with it. There was never that kind of feeling which implied, "Let's get it done and go home." So this was a real incentive to do your best. On the other side, it must be said, that the cast was pretty mediocre. There was Barbara Cupisti who … oh well … she was pretty and at the time was Soavi's girlfriend and we got along. I also got to see her outside of work. I made some friends, like Mary Sellers, who was doing theater like I was. Amongst other things I looked over the dialogues. Michele always asked me to take a look at scripts and all those "bitchy bitchy" exchanges between the characters are mostly my doing. Coming from theater I knew how insufferable actors can be.

In fact, there is a strong satirical vein connected with theater and the relationship between actors. But you were saying you found the cast mediocre…

Yes, yes, because there were a lot of dickheads working on that film. There was, for example, someone called Gligorov, a kind of model that I would have gladly thrown against a brick wall. Then there was David Brandon who, let's just say, wasn't the most pleasant of people but at least he was a competent enough actor, but there was a gang of whores and musclemen that were quite fastidious.

We spoke of The House on the Edge of the Park *and* City of the Living Dead, *but we left out another big cult movie of the early eighties:* Cannibal Apocalypse. *How was your relationship with John Saxon?*

[He laughs.] Ehhh … nonexistent. Saxon has the human empathy of a piece of marble in January, very professional, mind you, I can't say anything as far as that is concerned. He was also very good in the movie, but outside of the set he was a dead man. He would never hang out, he would never join us for dinner. He's just made that way. We met at a convention, some time ago and … for example, when I saw Bo Svenson again, we had a laugh, pats on the back, jokes but with Saxon … nothing. He just shook my hand with the expression of a constipated cod. I've always thought that he never really felt like making that film. There was just one moment of collaboration between us: I had become friends with May Heatherly, who's a nurse in the film; an American, cultured and witty, who lived in Spain. She was part of the Spanish quota, when we shot one week in Madrid. Among other things she was the girlfriend of the son of the Spanish ambassador at the Holy See. In short, May had to do a scene of a cannibal blowjob. Her character has an affair with a doctor and is supposed to bite and rip off his penis during oral sex after that a disease had turned her into a cannibal. She, poor thing, didn't want to do it and came to me and to Saxon for help. We went to Margheriti who immediately said, "You're right." So, in the end, the tongue substituted the penis and that was the only moment of real communication with Saxon.

You said earlier that you had a great time with Margheriti.

Margheriti was Olympic, so graceful in everything he did, such a gentleman and he never seemed to have problems on the set, despite it wasn't an easy film. There was a mixed crew, half American, half Italian so with two completely different mindsets. For

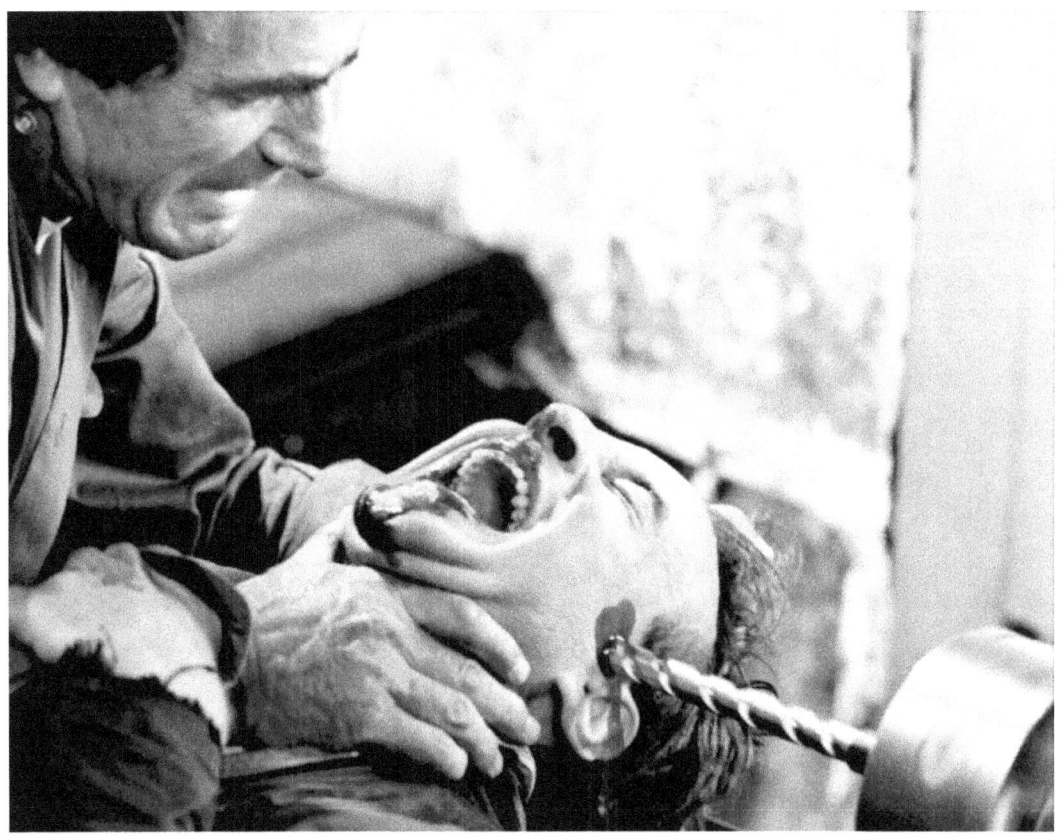

Radice gets his head drilled by Venantino Venantini in *City of the Living Dead,* 1980 (courtesy Nocturno Cinema).

example, a special effect was needed? The Americans went, "Sure, no problem … in a week. We have to organize and prepare." Then came Bombardone [Gino de Rossi]: "A week?! Give me five minutes. OK, let's get some scotch-tape and string…" [He laughs.] The script had, I think, been written by the producer, one of the Amati associates or else the idea was his. A terrifying nimrod. In fact, when I read the script I liked the character a lot but the story seemed to me like a colossal piece of shit. Seen in retrospect however, it has something metaphorical. Well, now this concept that war, the violence of war, is like a virus that creates monsters is interesting but then some time after the film's release, reports regarding AIDS burst out, so the film became unintentionally prophetic. However, Margheriti was very respectful of the actors, he was one of the few who imposed silence on the set when one tried to focus or when he was preparing for a complicated scene. In Italy this is a problem, you know, not just when you're rehearsing but also when you shoot. You're in the scene, and there is a seamstress who goes, "I haven't taken a shit in days." Margheriti was always professional and respectful. After, we had another experience together, *L'isola del tesoro* [*Treasure Island*, 1987]. There Antonio was crushed by the figure of Anthony Quinn who, may he rest in peace, was a monster, a person of unspeakable evil: he stamped his feet, he would try and make you slip during your scene. Then, one evening, Quinn rewrote the entire dialogue and came the next morning on set with this pile of papers in his hand, "This is the dialogue for today." You had twenty minutes to learn everything. An inconvenient presence, so Margheriti was really dominated in that situation. It was painful to watch.

In Italy these films were reviewed terribly, but you came into contact with other realities, such as the American one. Did you notice differences in approach?

I never followed the lives of the films I made. Moreover, at that time we didn't have the media we have today. I realized much later that these films had a long-term potential. If I'd realized this before, I'd have moved differently but for all I knew these were films that got released in second category theaters, remained there a few weeks and then disappeared forever. The newspapers came out with a short article in which they spoke very badly about them even though I must say that sometimes they would save me. "The film is worthless but Lombardo Radice is very good." But really, I had no way of knowing that on the contrary, outside of Italy, there was this growing cult following. From time to time over the years, some friends returning from abroad, perhaps from Germany or the United States, would say, "You know, I've seen a lot of posters with your face, there's also a cinema that projects this and that…." But I didn't really take much notice at the time.

Having made a considerable number of religious television series and films, I would like to ask about your relationship with religion and faith.

I'm pretty religious. I am deeply Christian, deeply linked to Jesus Christ and to the Christian doctrine. I believe in the great revolution of the Christian message, as compared to other religions: the centrality of man, the importance of doing, the importance of giving. I have always tried to volunteer and to maintain a proactive attitude towards the ills of the world. Then, with how Christianity channeled into Catholicism and then to the institution of religion, I have a troubled relationship. Against the church, the pope and the monstrous shit that gets said by clerical powers, with these things I have problems. But I would define myself a Christian, yes.

Returning to your filmography, let's talk about Impatto mortale [Deadly Impact, a.k.a. Giant Killer, 1984] by Fabrizio De Angelis. Now, if I've understood a little about your parameters, De Angelis can't have been a director you felt comfortable with…

No, in fact, working with him was hell. Let's start by saying that the movie comes after a long pause in which I had worked on other things and I hadn't made that kind of film. I had finally detoxified myself of my ongoing addiction to cocaine. Here on this table there could be a mountain and I would throw it out without the slightest hesitation. So I was out of that trip. Now, another premise … the stunts in all these films, for certain physical qualities, were always done by me, but when I got to *Deadly Impact*, I had lost my hand a bit. Jesus, when I think about the things I did on that movie! Bo Svenson and Fred Williamson had dummies … even if they had to get into a car, they had dummies. In the movie, I was a crime boss and during all the chases I was the one in the passenger's seat while my right-hand man was at the wheel. During the chase sequences, the stunt driver was a certain Alan … I don't remember the name now, a famous French stuntman. He was nice but always philosophizing about death. I was with him doing these crazy things, no seatbelt, no nothing. I ask, "Any chance of a dummy?" Fabrizio De Angelis, "Are we making a fucking Muppet film?" But this was nothing. There was a scene where the villain's car I was in, ended in an impasse. The one who was driving escaped up the fire stairs, but I had to get out, jump onto the hood, load the shotgun, shoot and climb up the stairs a second before the police car hits ours, destroying it. If I just stumbled or got the timing wrong, I wouldn't be here to tell you about it. In all this, De Angelis was both director and producer and so you couldn't complain to anyone. On the last week, it was in mid–December, we were shooting in Las Vegas. Apart from the fact that if hell exists, it must look like Las Vegas, a place where whatever you touch you risk an electric shock for all the electricity there is, but then De Angelis decided to shoot round the clock, with two units. I was alienated, I did not know what time it was. A nightmare.

How did you get on with Svenson and Williamson?
Williamson was kind, placid and quiet, always with a cigar in his mouth. But, for narrative reasons, I had more to do with Bo Svenson, who was a little "heavy." Years later, when we met at conventions or festivals, it was all fun and games but at the time, during the making of the film, he drank a lot and therefore was often aggressive, difficult to manage and he was jealous of me. I have no idea why. Remember that he was a big man, two meters tall and would at times hurt me during some scenes but I realized he wasn't bad or malicious and I tried to be civil about the matter. Then, when we returned to Italy to shoot some things at the De Paolis studios, maybe because he was confused, did not know the language, he opened up a lot, invited me to his dressing room, began to talk about his family, his wife… In fact, I have good memories of him let's say, but then and there, he was involuntarily aggressive with me.

After Eleven Days, Eleven Nights, *let's dispel another myth. According to many sources you appear credited in* La sposa americana *[The American Bride, 1986] by Giovanni Soldati. But you've never worked on this film, have you?*
No, never. I have no idea why it's there. I believe there's another actor that has a similar name to mine.

After Deadly Impact *comes a very strange film, in which for the first time, you disentangle yourself from pure genre films, appearing in a cameo in* I soliti ignoti vent'anni dopo *[Big Deal After Twenty Years, 1985]. How did you end up in this film?*
That participation stems from the fact that during my entire life, I've been a close friend of the D'Amico family, with Suso but especially her daughters. The film was produced by Silvia D'Amico who gave me a part. Then it has to be said that within the intelligentsia, in the spheres of theater for example, they didn't even know I was doing these movies and if they'd known, they would have thought it was a game, an eccentricity not to be taken seriously. At the time I was doing theater, so for them, that is what counted. Plus, I knew Marcello Mastroianni well, seeing he was a great friend of my father-in-law, Paolo Panelli.

Finally, from your filmography of the eighties, we are just missing Soavi's La Chiesa *[The Church, 1989]. What do you remember of the film?*
Aesthetically it is pure Soavi with its dreamlike quality, a very visual piece of work. Michele paints and has this very personal taste in the staging. His films are like paintings. However, it's a film that doesn't give the slightest importance to logic. Having, as I said before, also written things with him, I often found myself having to come to terms with the fact that Michele doesn't even know how logic is spelled whereas to me the lack of logic is a problem. In this sense, with *The Church* I had an initial struggle, then … oh well … one understands the game and I continued without problems. That's a whole visionary film. Inside there's Bosch's surrealism, love of the grotesque … Michele directed it with a lot of passion.

Again, emphasizing intersections and links between actors: on this film you met Tomas Arana, whom you would meet again on **Body Puzzle**...

I can't say I didn't get along with Arana, but he was a little stuck up. Maybe if I'd had his attitude, I would have gotten more done, I don't know, but I have too much love for "understatement." That said, I've never liked those who behave as if they shit daisies. On that movie, *The Church,* the character that was insane was the old Feodor Chaliapin. You have no idea what that man was! He couldn't remember shit. There were prompters everywhere, under tables, in the confessionals, behind the curtains…. Noooothingg… He couldn't get one fucking line right. He was off his rocker! Once he went to pee and came back on set with his cock hanging out and no one knew what to do. He walked around the set with these massive old man balls bouncing around. Chaliapin was just crazy.

You then worked again with Soavi on **The Devil's Daughter,** *but not on his last horror:* **Dellamorte, Dellamore** *[Cemetery Man, 1994].*

Unfortunately no. He called me, "You are my lucky charm. I want you in the movie but I don't know what role to give you." In fact, what role could I have played? Michele had also, for a moment, speculated that I could play the assistant of Rupert Everett's character but I was not suitable, there were constraints related to the book. In short … there wasn't a role. The movie is lovely and I'm really sorry I couldn't be in it.

What do you remember of **Body Puzzle?**

I don't know why, but I remember very little of that film. I think I was working simultaneously on a theater play. I remember playing a fag and that I was an antiques dealer. Bava was very professional. I remember, yes, his great professionalism and he could really hold the set in his hands.

At this point, in the early nineties, genre cinema was really falling apart. Except for Soavi who was gearing up in those years, or Argento, who continued making his films, the others faced an incredible crisis. Among the directors you had worked with, Fulci was very sick and had entered a decadent phase, Lenzi had problems working and Deodato was returning to television. Do you think that the formation of the "film commission" which placed the film administration in the hands of the state was responsible for the final blow?

Yes, absolutely. But there is also a cultural culpability. In Italy there has always been a gloomy intelligentsia, that has always made a distinction between noble and ignoble cinema, something that has never happened in America or in other countries. There are art films to be put on a pedestal and then the vile products for the masses. This attitude has ossified everything, so the so-called art films have never tried to be commercial, in the good sense of the term, and genre cinema has remained ghettoized. The health of a film industry is in its ability to produce everything. This outlook belongs to Benedetto Croce.[9] We Italians are "Crociani": low and high. Our aesthetic is that of Croce who, for example, had a biased attitude towards comedy which he considered low. We are the country that spat on Totò until he was dead and buried. Except for some directors, like Tornatore or Muccino, no one seems to have realized that films cannot be made only for Italy and that a foreign distribution is just as important. Now, for example, I'm in talks for a movie, a horror with beautiful aspirations. I practically compelled them to shoot in English. They were unsure about what language to use and I said, "Guys, you'll give yourselves a pickaxe on the balls if you shoot it in Italian."

What is your approach to the world of conventions?
Initially, only the idea of getting paid for an autograph seemed to me tremendously boorish, and I had all my ancestors turning in their graves. Then I realized that everyone else was doing it and it was a common practice. What the fuck, let's try! I first went to Manchester and I was fine. It was funny, with lots of friendly, unassuming people. Then I went on a tour of America for about three months to four, five different conventions. It was crazy! For them it's a normal thing, they're happy to give away twenty dollars for an autograph. I'm friendly, I like to chat with people, spend time with them, I'm curious to know what they have to say. The thing that amazed me, apart from the enormity of these events is the variety of people. On the one side, the people you'd expect, full of piercings and tattoos and freaks of various kinds, but then you can also find the businessman, old women, mothers with prams. I enjoy it very much anyway, I like going to conventions.

A curiosity: what are the films that you are most remembered for in these contexts?
Cannibal Ferox[10] and I'd say *City of the Living Dead* for the drilling scene.

What happened to the project of The House on the Edge of the Park Part 2?
It went as follows: Deodato and I never lost touch, we continued talking, sometimes working together. Now, one day he calls me and tells me, "They've called me from Britain with an idea for a sequel to *The House on the Edge of the Park*. It seems like shit to me but I speak very little English … look it over…." He gives me this treatment and it's horrendous, an absolute waste of time. Absurdity and violence. I called Ruggero. "All right," he says, "I'll tell them to fuck off." "No wait! Tell them we are interested but we want to rewrite the script." That film could have a sequel, because it is one of the few in which I don't die. Then Ruggero and I started writing like crazy, in an exciting brainstorming, like two kids. Reviewing old movies, walking up and down, talking and eating. After four days of madness, we came out with a very strong story.

Broadly speaking, what is it about?
I go to prison, well Ricky does, after the events of the first film, but I'm unjustly held for more time than I deserve, due to a ruthless prison guard who humiliates me, sodomizes me, pisses in my face. Finally I get out, lost and confused, and I go back to the garage, the one we see at the beginning of the first film where I meet a young man, who reminds me of Alex and I begin another story with this madman, this sadist. Yes, I follow him on his rounds but I also try to stop him in a class-related violence that originates from the relationship that the young man has with this rich lady who uses him as a toy for her sexual perversions and then abandons him. I try to foil the final massacre, without, of course, succeeding. It was a story that had some very strong elements. We wrote a very detailed treatment. This English guy said it was fine and we'd written a good script. The money didn't arrive and he starts saying that we have to do a remake before a sequel. Yes, you can do a remake but then, do you use the original actors or the ones of the remake for the sequel? We realized that this English guy, who was mostly a writer and an improvised producer, was full of bullshit so we got tired and broke the deal off … though he still continues to claim rights on the script, without ever having paid us. So, I guess we will never see a sequel to the film. It's unlikely, at least.

Going back to your reputation abroad, who gave you the name of "sacrificial victim of Italian genre cinema"?
In times when even I didn't understand the phenomenon that had taken place elsewhere, a monographic book about me written by British film critic, John Martin, came

in which he analyzes the kind of characters I portrayed and their fate. In doing so, he defined me "Italian cinema's whipping boy." They even made T-shirts. Also, some time ago, a university professor called Patricia McCormack was writing a book on Italian genre cinema and wanted to meet me. Now, one thinks of a university professor as an austere type, a severe or at least serious looking person. She was a punk, her hair was dyed with seven different colors, needles stuck everywhere ... [he laughs] and she started talking about my career pulling out names like Lacan and Freud.

But there is something almost mystical in your characters, a tragic mysticism. Extreme and perverse, weak and erotic, that live between guilt and violence, redemption and social exclusion.

Yes, indeed. You know, referring to a question you asked me earlier, I'm bisexual. As a young man I represented, well, an attractive but ambiguous beauty and in my opinion, I may have, in the midst of all those musclemen and heroic virile types, unknowingly embodied the latent homosexuality of my directors. As long as I was young and handsome I collected more heterosexuals than Jennifer Lopez. I managed to seduce very well-known personalities, who of course I cannot mention in an interview. So I think at that time I had something that breached into the hearts of certain heterosexuals. The element of sadism perhaps stems from this. Repressed homosexuality and sadism. Then you know, a man has a way of treating women and a way of treating other men, which is often a locker room way. Since this clearly didn't work with me, they had an approach which was almost seductive, in a sense. The fact is that they were not sure how to go about it so this created a short circuit.

According to you, what is magnetism in an actor?

Magnetism is the ability to communicate with one's body. An actor I detest is Steven Seagal because there's nothing, just emptiness. An actor, even if not equipped with an immense talent, must always be able to enter into the folds of a character, to move. Take Jeremy Irons; he will captivate you completely by just reading the phone book. Who taught me a lot about film acting was not an actor, nor a director but a cinematographer, Sergio Salvati, on the set of *City of the Living Dead*. He had a little "artistic crush" for me. Photographers and DOPs will fall in love with faces. I am very grateful to Salvati for teaching me how to have a healthy relationship with the camera, the carnality of the relationship between actor and lens, which is not an object but a sensual being. This, I feel very strongly.

Is there room for ambiguity and sexuality in current Italian cinema?

No, from a certain point on, we started to chase the stereotypes from ... below. The sex bomb is the sex bomb, the macho is the macho, the queer is the queer. I've played queens, the one in *Stage Fright* was a fag, for example. But I'm not like that, that's not my nature. In this country today, if things aren't spelled out and aren't reassuring, there's no room for them.

Rome, 2015

1969 Of Films and Horses
The Cinema of Marcello Avallone

"Summoned or non-summoned, evil will come."—Cyrus Elias in *Maya*, 1989

If you go down to the tombs today you're in for a nasty surprise.—Tagline for the British VHS of *Specters*, 1987

In the early sixties American cinema was going through a creative and productive crisis. This pushes Italian producers to start tackling genres not typical of Italian culture, in an attempt to satisfy international requests, in a way not dissimilar to the rise of the mythological adventure epic during the course of the previous decade, which then split in various directions. Science fiction and horror are injected with new life thanks to the efforts of Hammer Films and the unpredictable success of *The Quatermass Xperiment* (1955) by Val Guest and *The Curse of Frankenstein* (1957) and *Dracula* (1958), both by Terence Fisher. From then onwards the British company manages to relaunch in color, the mythos of creatures made famous by Universal Studios during the thirties. The first in Italy to take on the challenge, contemporarily to the rise of Hammer, is Riccardo Freda (24 February 1909, Alexandria–20 December 2000, Rome) with *I vampiri* (*The Vampires*, a.k.a. *The Devil's Commandment*, a.k.a. *Evil's Commandment*, 1957). The film didn't have the commercial success that was hoped for, being received with great skepticism by an audience in a country that lacked a horror tradition in its cinema. Throughout the sixties, the success of Italian horror nationally will be a relative one, receiving most of its consensus abroad, exactly in the same way as peplums, finding appraisal among French critics and distribution in the States through independent companies such as Arkoff's and Nicholson's AIP. Freda, and primarily Mario Bava, don't only satisfy the broader drive-in public but also the more curious and attentive filmgoers—Francis Ford Coppola, Joe Dante, John Landis and Martin Scorsese will all declare, in later, more recent years, their love for this cinema and the influence it had on their taste and art. Similarly and even more so than in the peplum genre that overlapped it, the evolution of Italian horror is tied linguistically to budget and logistical limits, which in one way or another characterized all of the various currents of genre cinema in post war years: the capacity of inserting within the macro-structure of the genre, similar in all these kinds of films, Italian or otherwise, elements ascribable to the literary culture of the countries; a strong ironic vibe which winks at the public as if aware of the incredulity the stories encompass; and finally the tendency of exaggerating the visual stylings and the narrative elements, highlighting the directorial work and stylizations and the perverse psychologies of the characters to compensate for the presence of plot holes and sometimes the absence of adequate or sufficiently rich set designs. Like elsewhere, the genre is infused with a strong melodramatic flavor which is visible in the characterization of the female roles, the harsh photographic contrasts and the sweeping emotions and villainy of the characters. One of the greatest protagonists of this chapter of Italian genre cinema is without the slightest doubt its initiator, Freda, who with films like *L'orribile segreto del Dr. Hichcock* (*The Horrible Dr. Hichcock*, a.k.a. *The Horrible Secret of Dr. Hichcock*, 1962) and *Lo spettro* (*The Ghost*, a.k.a. *The Specter*, 1963) has found a permanent spot in the hearts of fans of the Italian gothic everywhere. Both these films are filled with themes untouched for their time, such as necrophilia and other psycho-sexual deviations that make them very different to other contemporary examples. Freda conceives horror as a claustrophobic nightmare which has no metaphysical component within it but is ascribable to the perverseness of human nature. Most of his efforts are set in enclosed spaces, in precise architectural structures which turn into disassembling labyrinths which alienate and confuse, becoming the physical manifestation of the characters' corporal and mental diseases and deviances. The uncontested star of the genre is Barbara Steele, made famous thanks to Mario Bava's 1960 classic *La maschera del demonio* (*Black Sunday*, a.k.a. *The Mask of Satan*, a.k.a. *Revenge of the Vampire*). Bava's official debut, after having completed or co-directed, uncredited, various films, is very baroque, virtuoso and full of special effects, in other words different compared to Freda's approach but both have one binding element: women represent the narrative motor of the films, they are at the center of the action, the object of abysmal and hidden desires that give most of these films a latent "sinful" eroticism that tickled the curiosities of the public. Under this aspect, Bava is the ancestral and Freda the terrain, the earthly. Bava is the expressionistic light and Freda the crypto-psychological darkness. "Freda wasn't a grim man but he had an accentuated cynicism that could easily border into dark places. Believe me, you haven't met anybody as cynical as Riccardo was. He would call his horror films d'épouvantes, which in French means 'horrors' simply because, as he would say, it gave this stuff a little nobility." These are the words of Marcello Avallone (born 26 August 1938, Rome) which together with those of Ruggero Deodato, Freda's AD on *Romeo e Giulietta* (*Romeo and Juliet*, 1964), paint a vitriolic portrait of the director: "You had the impression that he didn't give a fuck about anybody. He would step over your dead body if you were blocking his way, even if only a few seconds earlier you had been talking and joking around with him." And yet, Avallone can boast an exclusive relationship with Freda: "I wouldn't have entered the film world without Riccardo and for a long period of my life I would pass more time with him than with my father. I've said it in the past, he was in many ways a second father. You know like in American cop movies: bad father, good father. I'm joking ... Riccardo was not only one of the most cultured men you could come across but he was also a formidable technician. He knew the art of filmmaking inside out. It was second nature to him. I had the best teacher I could have possibly hoped for. It was a hard school which began with picking up his dogs' shit. He loved those dogs more than he loved any other human being."

Marcello Avallone has been for the most part wrapped up in television, directing documentaries, reportages and TV shows but also found time to make seven feature length films in a career spanning over almost 40 years. "Like Freda and most of that generation of directors, I considered myself a professional, and by that I mean my profession, my job was to convey my visual sense to what was needed, whether it be something for

A portrait of Marcello Avallone by Eugenio Ercolani, made during the documentary directed by him, and for which Avallone was interviewed: *Banned Alive! The Rise and Fall of Italian Cannibal Movies*, 2015 (author's collection).

television, a documentary, publicity or a film." In a career clearly less thriving but nonetheless very similar to the one of his contemporary Deodato, Avallone has shown undoubted technical abilities, a knack for survival—in the nineties when popular cinema was on the brink of disappearing completely, Avallone was granted budgets only an extremely limited number of genre directors had access to—and both of them, after brief stints as actors, went through long apprenticeships as ADs, in the case of Avallone not only for Freda but also for Lucio Fulci and Giovanni Fago. With only seven films, Avallone managed to touch the most varied areas of the industry: starting with Luciano Martino and ending with producer Italo Zingarelli in a career as long as it is contradictory, in which, just like in the case of Freda and the director of *Cannibal Holocaust* (1980), the biggest mark is present in horror. "Il cinema dell'orrore," according to Avallone, unravels itself in three films. The first was a thriller, *Un gioco per Eveline* (*A Game for Eveline*, 1971) followed by two purer examples of the genre at the end of the following decade: *Spettri* (*Specters*, 1987) and *Maya* (1989). *A Game for Eveline* (written exactly like this, without a "y"), Avallone's second film as director, is an elegant (para)psychological giallo starring Erna Schurer (stage name of actress Emma Costantino) and Marco Guglielmi. Due to its atypical structure and look, the film is a notable effort among the first experiments within the genre in the early seventies. The presence of a close-knit family nucleus, with all their secrets and subtle morbidities, may bring to mind the French-influenced gialli of the late sixties, that find in Umberto Lenzi their main cantor. On the other hand, the geographical setting and paranormal nuances make this a standalone among the giallo genre, anticipating some of the elements that will become increasingly crucial during the following Dario Argento–dominated years. The film rotates around two couples in a house by the sea, one host and the other hosting. The husband and wife that own the isolated villa are going through a deep crisis due to the disappearance of their young daughter. The wife secretly suspects that her spouse is keeping her segregated somewhere, and their relationship has become a tense tapestry of accusations and resentments. Then one night, little Eveline appears before the incredulous eyes of their guests, holding a white ball and then again a second time playing an old violin. Her apparitions are particularly effective, often followed by feeble, disquieting laughs and a rarefied and uncomfortable atmosphere which many find ascribable to Mario Bava's gothic tonalities. "I was well aware of what had been done and expressed in the horror genre by the old masters ... by Riccardo Freda of course but also by Bava. Those visual-based directors of Italian cinema have always accompanied me in my career, they are part of my DNA, both as a movie freak and as a professional. I don't remember if the iconographic element of the white ball Eveline holds in her hands is something I got from Bava, but I wouldn't be surprised, maybe on an unconscious level I did." Are the nighttime manifestations of the girl part of a devious plot aimed at making people insane? Are they hallucinations? Is she a ghost? The final twist trespasses into the metaphysical, leaving the spectator to his own inevitably surreal interpretation. Despite above average intuitions, the film did not have the success the director was hoping for and was put aside over the years by fans of the genre. Avallone attributes this to two factors, the first being the cast:

> What the film is missing is a strong figure within the cast. The film had a mixed bag of names, some of which worked and others not at all but this wouldn't have been such a massive fault, most Italian films had this trait, if it hadn't been for the fact that there wasn't a big name that tied everything together. When I say "big," I mean both commercially and as far as charisma and talent are concerned. Let's be honest, in *A Game for Eveline* there were quite a few awful actors. Anyway, that is my favorite film, maybe because it wasn't fully appreciated or understood or perhaps because it had one of the best scripts I have ever come across. It had problems but great potential. If I were now in the position of directing a film again and if I could choose my project, I wouldn't hesitate ... it would be a remake of *Eveline*. I strongly believe that story has as much relevance today as it did 40 years ago. With more money and a better cast, it would still have a reason to exist. Though another thing I would modify, which is the film's second flaw, is the ending. I like its ambiguous quality but it's too rushed.

A little less than two decades later, Avallone will return to the horrific with the duo *Specters* and *Maya*, profoundly different from the sunbathed Sicilian psychodrama of the 1971 chapter of his career but very similar to each other. If *Eveline* had a taste and look indissolubly tied to its decade—the swinging music by Marcello Giombini being an emblematic example—these two films are exemplary fruits of the eighties, both linguistically and narratively. Television was taking over cinema from every perspective, introducing a certain "polished" photography, welcoming cinema directors while contemporarily invading films with new actors bred and raised within the small screen compounds. So it shouldn't come as a surprise that both films produced by Maurizio Tedesco made between 1987 and 1989, were realized under the umbrella of Reteitalia. The company was founded in 1979 with the initial intent of buying television programs and formats to be transmitted on the rising Fininvest networks, now known as Mediaset. However during the eighties, Reteitalia changed its agenda becoming an increasingly important and prolific film production and distribution company. With an archive that includes more than 200 titles for the big screen but also TV movies, series, shows and even cartoons, inexorably the company became a tentacular force, impossible to reckon with, having behind it a multifaceted empire built by Silvio Berlusconi. The Fininvest creature could afford to flop and invest with an ease that was unthinkable for any other production company and in fact many projects produced by Reteitalia, especially in its first phase, remained undistributed for years or often recycled for the direct-to-video market. During the most successful years, it became the main branch of Silvio Berlusconi Communications, managing to establish important partnerships with major American companies of the caliber of Paramount, CBS and Metro-Goldwyn-Mayer. Reteitalia didn't seem to have a precise policy when it came to choosing the projects to which to apply its name as Avallone himself confirms: "They were all over the place and would put money into everything and anything. Of course they attempted to cling on to what they felt were the trends of the moment. They made no distinction between genre cinema or any other kind. They behaved like a multinational or if you like, with all the necessary distinctions, like a big Hollywood studio." Cinema and television, out of their two progenies, only one seemed to be overfeeding off Reteitalia's enormous reservoir tit, though during the eighties and early nineties the company produced or participated in the production of Tornatore's directorial debut and Umberto Lenzi's last film, in Sergio Corbucci comedies and in a couple of Damiano Damiani dramas but it also tried to introduce a certain kind of cinematic horror to the small screen, and it did so by involving some of the main directors of the genre: specialists like Lucio Fulci, the aforementioned Lenzi and Lamberto Bava. The first two will direct the four "damned houses" films while the latter will helm the two series/containers *Brivido giallo* and *Alta tensione* each made out of four TV movies. Nonetheless, most of these projects were never aired because, like in a perfect short circuit, they didn't attain to the rules of television. Even Avallone's films were designed, in an initial stage, for the small screen: "Yes, when Tedesco and myself proposed the idea for a horror film to them, they first asked if we were willing to think of it for television, which was something I didn't want. I knew it was going to be a small budget film but I wanted it to have a cinema vibe to it. They were still, despite the flops they had had, convinced they could bring horror to television but in doing so they only made cinema more television-like."

Describe yourself in one sentence.
I was lucky enough to have grown up with a mother who taught me to waltz and with maids willing to teach me to tango.

The genre you are more associated with is horror, even if you only directed two.
Yes. Well, my interest in making a horror film arrived late. The idea came to me when I found myself in the U.S. making a documentary about New American cinema…

What year are we speaking of?
The eighties … I can give you the exact year … it was … it was 1980, exactly. I was there because Francis Ford Coppola's Zoetrope, together with Marina Cervi's production company, Splendida Films, which represented RAI, financed a series of documentaries on new directors and the phenomenon of American cinema. Interviews with George Lucas, Spielberg, Woody Allen, Scorsese and so on. While directing it, I became really engrossed in the atmosphere there and I realized, among other things, how much this horror cinema was becoming mainstream; though I don't know if we can really call some of these films horror. For some people they were, for others they were something a little

different ... we call it "the cinema of fear." Anyway, I understood that this cinema was having an unprecedented impact on the American public. Horror films were becoming a mainstream attraction. It was like the revenge of the B-movies ... even if in the States "B-movie" is not used in a derogatory sense. It's a term that identifies films made on small, sometimes shoestring budgets, for a certain type of circuit, with a certain type of distribution. Well, I realized that suddenly B-movies had invaded the A-movie circuit and made A-movie money. So, I returned to Italy with the desire of making a horror, aimed at the American market. Some time passed before I found myself submitting an idea to Maurizio Tedesco. "We can give it a shot." I said. He agreed so Andrea Purgatori and I began writing the script of *Spettri* [*Specters*, 1987]. We were fortunate enough to cross paths with the rising Fininvest, which was conquering the market. The film was very successful, and thus soon after I made another one, *Maya* [1989], which did pretty well too but not as well as *Specters*, also because those were the last years of Italian genre cinema. The peak of horror films was long gone and everything was dying out.

You are recognized as a horror director but what was your relationship with the genre previously, as a spectator?

I loved and love—but now much less—American cinema. Their films are the ones I grew up with. Mind you, they are genre films ... even if they have titles like, say *Cape Fear*, they remain genre films. They don't have, you know, hierarchies and pseudo-intellectual distinctions of what is high-art and low-craftsmanship, they don't have this terrible disease we have always suffered from. Italian cinema has been heavily influenced by literature, ours, which has always had a strong realist matrix, which was then amplified by war, famine, poverty, and the subsequent rebirth. So critics have always had this criteria in judging films. My stuff of the eighties—but the same goes for the masters of the past like Bava or Freda—was perceived as a distraction from real problematics, from reality ... which of course they were, but in Italy we have never given the right importance to fairy tales. And what are horror films if not exactly this? So, as a spectator I can tell you I have always loved fairy tales, dark fairy tales.

It seems that the critical intelligentsia tried, at one point, to apply the rules and lessons of the Cahiers du Cinéma without having really understood them.

Let's not even go there! I had some big discussions with Callisto Cosulich on the matter. I have always accused him, in a friendly fashion, of not having done anything to help cinema of pure entertainment. One of the problems was that the criteria in judging a film has always been the same, the same state of mind, the same pen, the same standards. It is as if I used the same basis of comparison to judge a book by Umberto Eco and one by Danielle Steele. To talk about better and worse is stupid. They are simply different things and a film should be judged by its objectives and nothing more.

Don't you think that those directors who made films of a political or social nature, regardless of the actual outcome of the film, had almost a union-like protection?

Absolutely! And the money made from those films would end up in the safes of left-wing political parties. We were left to ourselves! Absolutely! Clubbed as the village idiots.... Then, some of us were actual idiots, but there were as many on the other side. Have you ever noticed that, except in very rare cases, the so-called top directors—and we aren't talking about Visconti or Fellini of course, but the invisible mass of baby wannabe auteurs—have never ventured into genre cinema? They were always forced to look for what was once called "the message," because they were protected by politicized journalists and critics. America is not like this ... the skill of a director is not determined by what kind of story a director chooses to impart or by the genre he prefers.

Now, back to your career ... but right from the beginning. You start as an actor...
Oh yes, but I didn't do much...

You take part in an important film like Poveri ma belli [Poor But Beautiful, 1957] by Dino Risi. How did you end up, so young, on the set of this film? And then, how many films did you make as an actor?
I don't even know. The only one that is worth mentioning is *Poor But Beautiful*. These things happened by chance. I was eighteen, summer was at the door and it was a way of making a little easy money. I lived in Rome in an area called Flaminio, very close to the huge offices of Titanus.[1] My friends and I, like all the kids in the neighborhood, would hang out in the park nearby and so sometimes they'd pick a few of us to participate in some scenes. Seeing we were kind of rich kids, they usually dressed us in white and put champagne glasses in our hands for elitist, snob party scenes. For that film, Risi was looking for interesting faces and he chose me and another four/five kids from my area. But from the start, I was more interested in what was going on behind the camera. I wanted to be an operator, a script supervisor ... stuff like that. And here something that has nothing to do with cinema takes over and plays an important role in my cinematic evolution: the world of horses. My father was the owner of a big racing stable and I grew up surrounded by horses, smelling horse shit from morning to evening, right from the day I was born and well into my adolescence. At that time—I think things have changed radically now—the film business and the world of horses were connected, they evolved in unison. Many producers, De Laurentiis for example—not Dino, but his brother—many technicians, distributors and a great number of actors were very passionate, sometimes obsessed, by horses and racing. There was a real passion, at that time, for this sort of thing. In this galaxy of horse lovers, there was a director who was good friends with my father. His name was Riccardo Freda. One day my father goes, "Why don't you take Marcello along with you?" I was a kid and Riccardo was this imposing figure, who looked ancient to me. "OK, I think I can teach him a few things." He was a son of a bitch, eh.... Seeing I knew how to ride very well and he had this beautiful mare called Zimbala ... it's incredible, I still remember its name ... he immediately went, "But you have to ride Zimbala every day for an hour, because she is a horse that needs to run and requires a delicate touch. You do this and I will bring you on set."

What kind of person was Freda? They say he was very cynical about his work.
He was, yes. We are only talking about profoundly cynical people. Dino Risi was an incredible cynic, Freda as well, Monicelli ... cold, detached men ... but maybe you had to be, so as not to become the victim of your own work. You had to keep a distance. Freda was, maybe, the biggest cynic of them all. He liked accentuating other aspects of his life: gambling, horses ... he was a gran viveur. Then, yeah, he burnt out and gambled everything he had.

On what films were you his assistant?
Let's see, I was an AD on *Maciste all'inferno* [*The Witch's Curse*, a.k.a. *Maciste in Hell*, 1962], *Le sette spade del vendicatore* [*The Seventh Sword*, a.k.a. *Seven Swords for the King*, 1962] and then we did ... fuck ... that one we shot also at Bracciano ... *L'orribile*

Riccardo Freda, friend and mentor of Avallone, on the set of one his last films (courtesy Nocturno Cinema).

segreto del Dr. Hichcock [*The Horrible Dr. Hichcock*, a.k.a. *The Horrible Secret of Dr. Hichcock*, 1962]. When I was in the States, doing that documentary we were talking about and I told people I had worked with him, they went crazy. I had never realized how big a cult figure he had become.

What do you remember about **Dr. Hichcock?**

Many things. Just think ... that production lasted three weeks! Nothing, eh? Incredible. We shot the whole thing in a villa called Villa Perucchetti, in Rome, in Via Monti Parioli. Now it's a school run by nuns. I was the 2nd assistant and I think the main AD on that film was Giovanni Fago but at one point we split into three units, the main one helmed by Freda and then two smaller ones and I got a chance to direct a few things here and there. Mostly details and small connecting scenes. Freda was brilliant and extremely prepared, but he couldn't give a fuck about actors.

Speaking of actors, what do you remember of Barbara Steele?

During the whole film, she would never be on time. One day, during the umpteenth fight about being late, the producer slapped her right in the face. She screamed, cried and stormed off the set. Riccardo, who agreed with the producer—she was talented, fascinating and at times also funny, but she was also a huge ballbuster—went, "OK, we are shooting the next scene without her." "What do you mean, without her?" I said. "I mean that you will play her." At the time I was very thin, I didn't have a beard, so they dressed me up with her attire and I did the scene, with Freda shouting indications as I walked around like a fairy ... a long shot naturally, in a corridor. So just think how many fucks

Riccardo gave about actors. But at the same time, think how talented you had to be to pull off something like that. I'll give you another example. Today it's easier to move a camera around, because technology has changed, everything is more manageable but at that time it was much more difficult, for example, to move the lighting equipment around. Lamps were massive and weighed tons, cameras were huge. On *The Horrible Dr. Hichcock* instead of moving all this material, he preferred to move the background scenery, the furniture and objects, to be able to get a reverse shot. It's easily said but to be able to do this, and with his results, you needed an incredible ability. Anyway, I met Barbara Steele twenty years later, in the States, when she was just starting out as a producer and I got the feeling she didn't have great memories of that film.

In the mid-sixties, soon after these experiences with Freda, you started directing your first documentaries, didn't you?

By that time you could sense the beginning of a crisis that would last till the end of the eighties. Because now there is no crisis. In order to assert the existence of a crisis, there has to be a pulse and we are dead. Everybody identifies the beginning of the end, in the late seventies but in reality it started long before. Anyway, by the sixties, television was taking off. Premise: I have always been a massive sports fan and still am, any sport. If two mice are racing each other in some godforsaken field somewhere, I'm there watching them. OK, that said, there was a very popular sports program called *Sprint* by Maurizio Barendson and Antonio Ghirelli so I started going to have my coffees at the bar inside the RAI studios. Now to enter you need five passes and a unicorn hoof but at the time you could enter, chat with anybody and leave without any problems. One day, Barendson asked me, "Guagliò"—he was a veracious Neapolitan—"what the fuck are you doing here all the time?" "Looking for work." "What can you do?" "I'm an AD for cinema." "Bring me an idea." I knew it had to be something to do with horses—it was the thing I knew the most about—so I went to Riccardo, "What can I propose to these people?" He came up with an idea: the shoeing of race horses. Something nobody knows a fuck about but is actually fundamental. The work of these farriers and blacksmiths is like that of watchmakers and it's something truly beautiful. They loved the idea and I directed it. At first in a more journalistic fashion … but this is how my work as a documentarian began. This is an activity I retained until a couple of years ago because cinema has come and gone but I've always continued making documentaries.

Exactly what year are we talking about?

Beginning of 1966.

You seem to be one of the few figures, active in that decade, that didn't cross paths with the Western genre.

Actually, few people know this, but I was a 1st AD on a Western directed by Giovanni Fago,[2] called *Per 100.000 dollari t'ammazzo* [*Vengeance Is Mine*, a.k.a. *$100,000 for a Killing*, 1968] with Gianni Garko and Claudio Camaso. That was my very last film as an AD.

You directed your first film for cinema in 1969. A "mondo-movie," L'altra faccia del peccato [The Queer … The Erotic].

It was released in '69 and made the previous year. Yes, it was my debut and it happened by chance. I had made an investigative reportage on the state of Italian hospitals and subsequently Luciano Martino called me. I knew him because we used to go to the same secondary school. We weren't in the same class, because he was older than me, but I was friends with his brother, Sergio. So anyway, Luciano called me, after having seen this documentary I had made for RAI and told me he liked it and needed a similar touch for something he was preparing. Not long before, there had been a film by Luigi Scattini which had done very well[3] and before that film there had been another similar German film which was complete bullshit but even that had had an incredible success, all of which proved that people were curious about titillating matters. Luciano handed me a book by Altavilla on the vices and virtues of Europeans and goes, "Want to do it?" "Of course." Drawing from the book, Giacinto Ciaccio and I selected the phenomena we thought were more interesting. We shot the film completely with a handheld camera and I would give the operator very few indications. I would throw in the scene two/three people trying to create explosive or tense situations. The narrator of the English language version was Edmund Purdom, who I never met, but in the original version, the narrator was the same of the films by Gualtiero Jacopetti, who was brilliant, Stefano Sibaldi. I met Jacopetti and I can tell you he was a genius, a real one, but everything you see in his films is constructed and prepared. Everything. Don't believe anybody who says otherwise.

How did the film fare at the box office?
Very well, so much so that Martino asked me to make another one immediately after. There was already a title: *America cosi nuda ... cosi violenta* [translation: *America So Naked ... So Violent*] but I turned down the offer. I wanted to do other things. Sergio Martino ended up making his directorial debut with that film [*Naked and Violent*, 1969].

After, what happened?
I wanted to make a different kind of cinema compared to what was circulating at the time. I wrote a noir, which is a genre pretty much ignored in Italy, called *Un gioco per Eveline* [*A Game for Eveline*, 1971]. You could make a film on the making of this film. Anyway, it was produced but nobody believed in it. Some forward-looking critics wrote beautiful things about it but the film did terribly. If I have to be a little self-critical, maybe the script wasn't as rich as the story deserved and a chunk of the cast was below par.

Erna Schurer was an interesting figure of that period.
Yes, I chose her because she was a commercial actress who was doing well. I met her through Carlo Maietto, who was a typical character of that period. A Neapolitan who wasn't a real producer. I mean, he was, but he didn't act like one. He was more of a go-between, an elusive middleman, somebody who would find money, get people laid, organize parties. I had an option for three films with him at one point in the early seventies. Films that of course were never made because you couldn't trust him. Maietto sometimes also did business with Luciano Martino, who was the one who introduced me to him, but Luciano, being a much bigger son of bitch, knew how to deal with him. He was over-the-top and fun but when it came down to money, he had no scruples. He ended up having to leave Italy with his wife, Janet Agren, because everybody was after him. But before all this, before Agren, Martino or Miami—that is where he went into hiding—Carlo Maietto met Emma Costantino, that's Erna Schurer's real name, and convinced her to get into films. He produced her first big hit, *Le salamandre* [translation: *The Salamanders*, 1969] by Alberto Cavallone. I don't really know what the nature of their relationship was but I can tell you that I lost touch with him when I started an affair with Emma during the making of *A Game for Eveline,* or shortly after.

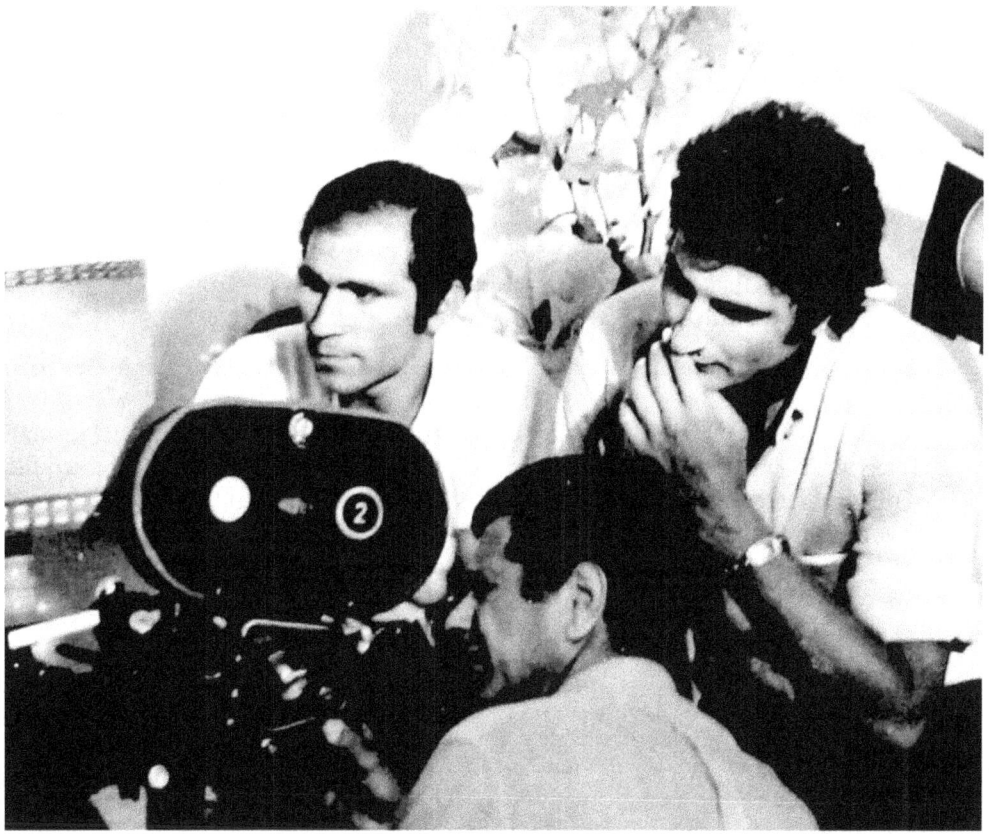

Avallone (right) at work in Sicily on his second feature film, *A Game for Eveline*, 1971 (courtesy Marcello Avallone).

I didn't know you and Schurer were a couple.

She was, and still is, a very intelligent and adventurous woman but I thought that once her career finished, she'd become one of those actresses that sits at home, gaining weight and living in the past but she became a brilliant entrepreneur. Maybe that was one of the things that ended our story. I underestimated her. But we still talk on the phone and I have great affection for Emma.

Did you only direct her in Eveline?

Actually no. She appears in *Specters* in a cameo role. I think she plays one of the tourist guides that you can see in the catacombs. She had already abandoned cinema ... I believe her last film was in 1979. If I'm right nearly ten years had passed. Of course, she did it out of friendship, I'm not even sure she was paid.

Before, you said that one could make a whole film on the making of Eveline. *What did you mean by that?*

I can't tell, I just can't, maybe one day I will, but ... behind the film there were powers, financial powers, you can't possibly imagine. It was an incredible adventure that only naivety made possible. We were very naïve—both me and my 1st AD Sergio Nasca[4]—and looking back, it's quite incredible to think we were involved in something like that. Let's just say that it wasn't a coincidence the film was made in Sicily...

What about the rest of the cast, your choices again?

Yes, my choices. There was Marco Guglielmi, who had worked in very respectable films. He had also participated in some films with Alberto Sordi, then there was Adriana Bogdan and a German, a certain Wolfgang Hillinger who had played a small part in a film by Luchino Visconti. Anyway, after watching the film bomb at the box office, I was so sorry and disappointed that I decided to divorce from cinema and I returned to television's embracing arms. This is the reason behind the big gap in my career. In those years of inactivity it wasn't that I went around looking for work, projects, calling producers … I couldn't give a fuck … I didn't do anything. I earned well with television and I enjoyed the process of directing documentaries.

Until 1976, the year in which you directed **Cugine mie** *[translation:* **My Female Cousins,** *1977].*

I received a call from Amati, the producer. "I have to make a film in a hurry, small stuff. Interested? Three weeks, not a day more." I thought about it for a bit … I liked the idea of directing another film. Plus, I always liked doing different things. In that period I was involved in some pretty heavy stuff with documentaries and the idea of something light was particularly appealing. It was a bullshit gig but I told myself, "Hey, worst case scenario, I won't sign it with my real name." All this without abandoning television. It was like taking a vacation for a few weeks.

The film went well.

It went incredibly well! It made a lot of money but the film is a pile of shit.

One of the few films in which you didn't participate in the writing process.

No, no! I didn't write a single word. I think it was all Roberto Gianviti's doing, who could hardly write, anyway.

What do you remember of the making?

That film was like a ticking bomb, a race against time to get it done. I didn't even have a minute to go to the bathroom. The cast was nearly all female, there were three actresses. One was the producer's wife with whom I had to take special care; another was Carlo Vanzina's wife, who was a friend and colleague, and so she needed special attention as well; the third was Franca Gonnella, who was the star of the film, because she came from some big success, and she required and demanded my special consideration. I went crazy!

And then horror arrives…

Yes, shortly after *My Female Cousins* I went to the States where I lived for a year and in this timeframe I directed that documentary about American cinema.

How did the story of **Specters** *take form?*

Everything began with long conversations with producer Maurizio Tedesco on where the film should take place. I knew I wanted to shoot the film in Rome or in Naples. Naples would have been perfect, because it's a city that has a double face. On the surface the serenades, pizza and the Vesuvius, and underneath you find strange and obscure realities. Even Rome, in this sense is perfect. Above, the small churches, the suggestive alleys but then, underneath, there are kilometers of unexplored catacombs and tunnels. The shadow of what Rome had once been which no longer exists but where you can still find traces of its blood-soaked heritage. Once we'd settled for Rome, I called up Andrea Purgatori, a journalist of *Corriere della sera*, who was interested in the same things I was.

How long did it take to shoot?

If I'm not mistaken, nine weeks. It was filmed in English, also because *Specters* was a film conceived mainly for the foreign market where it fared very well. Consider, the film made two billion lira worldwide.

What do you think of it?

When I see some scenes I cringe in shame and if I could go back I would do many things differently, though this is perfectly normal. As a whole, I think it's respectable and enjoyable, it's not badly directed. I had a very American approach: focus on details, a lot of cuts, fast editing. The special effects seem to pass the test of time, considering they were all done on set, with no CGI and a restrictive budget. It's not easy but I had a lot of fun making these films, inventing tricks. It tickled the childish side of me.

Narratively, Maya, *is a much more ambitious film.*

Yes, and we had a lot more money to play around with. But you know what the real problem with that film is? The setting. The whole idea of the Maya. It doesn't have the right fantastical elements.

Avallone in "one of the few cameos of my life. I played Nosferatu's shadow in a scene of *Specters*" (courtesy Marcello Avallone).

But that is the main reason the film is still remembered.

I know … I know. It's probably me but I feel it doesn't quite work as it should.

A strange cast…

In *Maya* there was also Antonello Fassari,[5] who was a friend. He was mainly a comedian and was doing only that sort of stuff, but I asked him, "Do you feel like doing something a bit different?" Actors like mixing things around. The protagonist was Peter Phelps, an Australian who had just made a beautiful film called *Starlight Hotel* [1987]. I fell in love with him, thought he was fantastic and insisted on having him in the film. Then there was Mariella Valentini as the female lead. William Berger also had a role. He was nice, a sad figure. You could tell, just be looking at him, that he was elsewhere with his mind. Berger didn't have an easy life but he was a true professional and when it was time to work he would give 100 percent. He had practically retired when I called him, living a little like a recluse. But most of the supporting cast was picked there, in Venezuela, from locals.

This is your last horror film.

Each art form has to be put in a position to mature in time. It can't remain a cold star that shines forever. It's like the invention of the car: it has to change, even if this doesn't mean improvement, because it's what the audience wants. And so, as American films started getting more refined, abandoning old techniques and archetypes, becoming more ambitious, we continued—I won't mention names—to make films based on the killer, the stabbing, the heart ripped out.... We remained in our teens while the Americans became adults.

In the nineties, when most directors of your generation were ending their careers, you were making ambitious genre films, with medium to high budgets.

After *Maya*, I received a call from Italo Zingarelli, a big producer, who had liked what I had done with these horror films and asked me to revive the kind of films he had made many years before. I'm talking about *Panama Sugar* [1990]. I didn't believe in the film much but the contract was very good. The budget was surprisingly high for that period. The script wasn't bad but it was dated, out of touch with its time. It went terribly but people seem to have enjoyed it, at least the few that have actually seen the film. I still receive calls and fan mail for that film. I guess it took a while but it managed, over the years, to find its niche, its public. It was the attempt of an old producer, in the twilight of his career, to relive, even if for just a fleeting moment, a golden age, long gone.

Who was this Scott Plank, and how did you choose him?

Plank was chosen by Zingarelli out of a number of actors I selected. He had to choose, or at least approve, the protagonist and the titles of the films he produced. It was a rule with him. I went to the States and picked Plank through agencies. Zingarelli wanted a face that was reminiscent of Terence Hill. Anyway, he was right for the role and a nice, cordial person. I believe he attended the Actor's Studio. I had no problems with him, not one.

Let's talk about Ultimo taglio *[Last Cut, 1997]. How was it having to deal with John Savage, an actor that was known for...*

...I wanted to kill him. Once I nearly did. If they hadn't pulled me away I would have killed him with my bare hands. I swear. He was very infantile ... when he had his fits, he was exactly like a spoiled kid. Ask yourself why he isn't working even in the States. Alcohol burnt his brain. Even if he must have always been rather strange. He would dig his heels for the most absurd things.

An example?

We had built a cemetery on the beach, on the foreshore, with tombstones being slowly sucked away by the undertow, as if the sea was slowly eating them up. It was very evocative, visually and symbolically it underlined the undercurrent theme of the film. In the scene, he had to throw his gun towards this poetically decadent scenery, as a gesture of envoy from revenge. The camera was positioned quite high above him, on a crane, for the wide shot. I had already shot a frontal close-up on him looking at the gun and then throwing it into an off-camera basket. For the reverse high-angle shot we couldn't use the real gun because you could see everything, the sea, the horizon so there was nowhere the prop-man with the basket could hide. I asked the key grip to put together something that could pass for a gun from a distance. With such a long shot, a 32 mm lens, we could have used any fucking thing we wanted. John Savage arrived, I gave him this piece of metal he had to throw, he looked at it and went, "I'm not doing it with this." I invited him to look in the camera and get an idea of the shot. "But I know it's fake." When actors behave like this it means they are jerking you around, or because they're assholes. "What do you mean you can't throw it because you know it's fake? Act, or aren't you capable?" "It doesn't weigh like a real gun." "No problem, we can make it heavier." Nothing. He wouldn't reason. "I'm not doing it with this, in fact I think I'll leave." "OK, fuck off. You are useless. Actually you can consider yourself free. Leave and go to hell." He got into the car and went off. It was one of the last days of production. He came back an hour later—without saying he was sorry—and did the scene. He was a real shithead. What is funny, is that I didn't even want him in the film! It was Ridley Scott's wife who convinced me. Savage had just made *White Squall* [1997] and she spoke very highly of him. "We can call him, immediately," and she passes the phone to me. She told me he had stopped drinking, that he had cleaned up his act. Only later, when it was too late, I realized she was trying to help him, at my expense.

You worked with a lot of American and international stars, both fading and rising.

Mostly fading. If they were crazy, I worked with them. In *Panama Sugar* I had Oliver Reed. There isn't a hotel in Rome that hasn't had a room destroyed by Reed. From the Excelsior to the Grand Hotel. But I had a pleasant relationship with him. Then I had Helmut Berger, with Savage, on the set of *Last Cut,* so on that film I had two raging maniacs. Thank God for Donald Pleasence in *Specters,* he was delightful, a sweet, nice, old-school gentleman. Always punctual, always professional and you could tell he was a man who had done everything in his life, both on and off set. He was a pleasure to have around and also Reed, who drank like a son of a gun.

Avallone (left) and cinematographer Roberto Girometti on the set of *Last Cut,* 1997 (courtesy Roberto Girometti).

Your choice?

Mine, mine. They had told me he was crazy but I get along with crazy people. I like them, except for John Savage, because he was cold and would never show any humanity. These over the top nutcases are usually very sensitive, sometimes too much so, they are receptive. But Savage was detached, cold and would just look at you with spiteful, empty eyes. It was like talking to an autistic person. Even Fulci had a lot of problems with him and Fulci was a good director. I should know, I worked with him.

What about Helmut Berger?

Once we were walking together—I think my 1st AD was with us as well—down a busy shopping street, in a town close to where we were shooting and he notices a pair of red shoes. Sparkling, bright red women's shoes. He turns towards me and asks me to buy them for him. I laugh and we proceed with our stroll. My assistant leans in and whispers, "Was he serious?" "Naaah." Next day Helmut arrives on set barefoot and won't begin shooting until somebody goes and buys him those damn shoes. "Marcello, he was serious." "Don't say a word and go get him his fucking shoes." Two hours later he was prancing around the set with his trousers rolled up to show everybody my present.

On what film did you work on with Fulci?

A Franco Franchi and Ciccio Ingrassia film … *002 Operazione luna* [translation: *002 Operation Moon*, 1965]. Fulci wouldn't fight with actors like Riccardo would. Yes, he was ill-tempered and crabby but a sweetheart compared to Freda. Freda would stop talking to you. Generally speaking, Freda didn't give a fuck about anything. You know what he worried about? If his dogs shat properly.… Before becoming an AD and starting to actually participate in the making of the films, I would follow him and do everything, like sort of a personal assistant. Among my daily tasks, there was bringing his beloved hunting dogs for long walks. I remember one of his setters fell sick and I had to give him enemas every fucking day. That is cinema too. Waiting for Riccardo Freda's dog to shit and memorize the color, is cinema. Believe me, it is.

Rome, 2016

1969 Strange Vices in Locked Rooms
The Cinema of Sergio Martino

"I'll cut you up so bad you'll wish that mirrors weren't invented."—(Luc Merenda in *The Violent Professionals*, 1973)

Enter … if you dare the bizarre world of a psychosexual mind.—Tagline for the American poster of *Torso*, 1973

Introduction by Gian Giacomo Petrone

It is probable that if Dario Argento had never appeared on the scene, the morphology of the Italian thriller/giallo would have been significantly less articulated and its time-frame much shorter. It is not a coincidence that the debut of the Roman director within the genre has become the symbolic divide between the before and the after, starting from 19 February 1970, the release date of *L'uccello dalle piume di cristallo* (*The Bird with the Crystal Plumage*), a point of no return for the Italian thriller genre. Before that date, the Italian giallo generally looked at the darker realms and narrative structures pertaining to French and American cinema, and privileged the narration rather than the visuals, the whodunit structure, the motives of the characters, their psychologies and the internal logic of the events, as well as some concessions to an often glossy and decorative eroticism; with Argento, on the contrary, a sort of Copernican revolution begins to be outlined which will bring the genre to rethink its structure deeply. A sort of wild and anarchic messiah, Argento—together with only a few other genial creators of celluloid nightmares, including Mario Bava and Lucio Fulci—"purifies" the genre from any rational motivation, making the light of insanity break through, gradually destroying the coordinates of logic of the traditional giallo. After Argento's first successes, there is an exasperated attempt by producers and directors to develop films aimed at exploiting the achievements of the Roman master but the fact of the matter is that Argento's cinema is not easily replicable, except in its most blatant and obvious visual aspects, first and foremost the very expressionistic use of color schemes.

Fortunately, despite many pale imitations, there are as many films and filmmakers able to look elsewhere, taking on perhaps more traditional or less innovative stratagems but succeeding, nonetheless, in making a personal and propitious contribution to the genre. In the latter category it is possible to include the first four of the five giallo films

Sergio Martino, in the Dania offices in Rome, photographed by Eugenio Ercolani in 2015 (author's collection).

made by Sergio Martino (born 19 July 1938, Rome) between 1971 and 1973, in particular when taking into account their substantial thematic homogeneity and narrative (due also to the contribution of Ernesto Gastaldi, who signed all of Martino's thriller scripts in the 1970s). On the other hand, the fifth film, *I corpi presentano tracce di violenza carnale* (*Torso*, 1973), has to be analyzed separately, being definitely more articulated, especially as far as filmic language is concerned. In the four titles under consideration, the elements of the main plots are almost always the same, though their dispositions lead to different outcomes, to intriguing overturns of perspective, as well as some, albeit rare, false steps such as in *La coda dello scorpione* (*The Case of the Scorpion's Tail*, a.k.a. *Scorpion's Tail*, 1971). The second giallo made by Martino after *Lo strano vizio della signora Wardh* (*The Strange Vice of Mrs. Wardh*, a.k.a. *Blade of the Ripper*, 1971), is in fact the most unresolved and uncertain among the director's thrillers because it is overly hybridized, with the light tones of a comedy and with a female protagonist (played by Anita Strindberg) paradoxically too sure of herself and laid back compared to the darker and gloomier aspects of the narrative. So, despite a solid cast (worth mentioning, besides Strindberg, are also Luigi Pistilli and George Hilton), the film appears constantly off axis and disharmonic, failing to find the right calibration between the brighter and more sinister sides of the story. It suffers from a fairly predictable plot, a mild environmental nod and no references to the Regime of the Colonels, present in Greece at the time the film was being made and where the story is set, and a finale that is unable to capture attention, despite the usual technical expertise of the director. The incapacity to compensate the lack of morbidity, rhythm, narrative tenure and pathos is evident compared to Martino's other efforts within the genre. *The Strange Vice of Mrs. Wardh*, *Tutti i colori del buio* (*All the Colors of the Dark*, 1972) and *Il tuo vizio è una stanza chiusa e solo io ne ho la chiave* (*Your Vice Is a Locked Room and Only I Have the Key*, 1972) are, instead, well-articulated works that can be considered a sort of trilogy.

In all three titles, there is the shadow of a conspiracy in which the designated victim is (or seems to be) a woman: a story structure that once again, to a great extent, must be attributed to Gastaldi. Both in *The Strange Vice* and the *All the Colors of the Dark*, the plotting against the female lead (in both cases played by Edwige Fenech) is effective, though taking on quite different values in the two films. In *The Strange Vice* it is, in fact, only about the bourgeois scheming for pecuniary reasons, even if it is concealed almost to the end by the presence of a murderous maniac. The narrative score already looks towards the slasher (which will find full realization in *Torso*) and even finds the way of paying homage, albeit marginally, to Alfred Hitchcock's masterpiece, *Strangers on a Train* (1951). In *All the Colors of the Dark*, there is a similar motive but the esoteric-satanic matrix of intrigue takes over and envelops the protagonist in the spire of a tale strongly marked by the influence of Polanski—but there seem to be also echoes from Aldo Lado's *La corta notte delle bambole di vetro* (*Short Night of Glass Dolls*, 1971) as well as one of the progenitors of all "demonic" films, Mark Robson's *The Seventh Victim* (1943)—pervading the film with a sulphurous and hallucinatory atmosphere, which pushes Martino towards evocative stylistic artifices, elsewhere absent. We can find a proliferation of unusual shots, theatrical wide angles, extreme close-ups and details of faces and objects, as well as various assorted psychedelics, which enrich the film with a sophisticated, experimental nuance. *Your Vice Is a Locked Room*, for its part, gently wraps up the coordinates of the other two titles in question, placing Irene (Strindberg), the apparent and potential victim of masculine scheming—in the specific case of the sadistic husband Oliviero Rouvigny (Luigi Pistilli)—in the actual position of a praying mantis. The perverse mind of the woman is the motor behind six different homicides (sometimes committed by her lover, played by Ivan Rassimov), whereas her final defeat will be due to the diabolical black cat of her late husband, ready to avenge his master in a finale that is an explicit reference to Poe's "The Black Cat." Sergio Martino shows his capacity to re-elaborate and make his own the atmospheres of Corman's adaptions of Poe, in particular *Tales of Terror* (1962) and *The Masque of the Red Death* (1964) and even anticipates a crucial sequence of Stanley Kubrick's *The Shining* (1980).[1]

With *Torso*, Martino's last significant contribution to the genre, there is a consistent change of pace, especially as regards to the structure of the narration and its deployment in relation to the spectator. Martino orchestrates a score of pure suspense (in the authentically Hitchcockian sense of the term) changing also, with respect to his previous gialli, the coordinates of the meaning on which the narrative is developed. There are two elements that can be directly attributed to Dario Argento and even, in part, to the omnipresent spirit of the master of masters, Mario Bava: if the motive of the killer is a psychic trauma, in the typical Argento vein (although the primary matrix is, of course, Hitchcock's *Psycho*), the apparent ubiquity, omniscience and audacity of the murderer, along with some distinctive traits of his criminality, find their primary source in *Sei donne per l'assassino* (*Blood and Black Lace*, 1964). Martino moves with original clarity, creating a small gem of tension and technical-narrative skill, which will find many enthusiasts abroad, especially in the U.S. The true added value of the film lies, however, in the intelligent and complex buildup of tension in the last segment of the story. After leaving

Perugia, following the threat of a serial killer, Jane (Suzy Kendall) finds shelter at the elegant and isolated villa owned by the uncle of one of the three friends she is with. The killer is on their tracks, unaware that Jane is with them. From the moment the killer appears inside in the villa in the last half hour of the film, Martino displays a great mastery in the articulation of the filmic language. First of all, the murders of Jane's three friends occur off-camera, through an ellipsis that skips the narration from the killer's appearance before the three girls at night, to the awakening of an unknowing Jane the following morning. The spectator follows Jane's footsteps in the silent house and discovers the bodies of the three girls killed the previous night, while the murderer seems to have vanished, only to reappear once again. The game, skillful and extremely composite, involves the so-called "focus of the story," namely the circulation of information towards the various characters and towards the spectator. First of all, it is to be noted that, in this context, the killer loses his panoramic knowledge, which in turn benefits the spectator and, to a lesser extent, Jane. In this segment, the character who knows the least is the killer, as he is still unaware of Jane's presence, even though his continuous exiting and entering the house persists to the girl's dismay, since his ultimate goal is not the girls' deaths, but the dissection of their corpses. There is a continuous shift from an "external focus" (the tale proceeds in such a way that the viewer receives a greater flow of information than the individual characters) to an "internal focus" (the viewer's information coincides with a single character: in this case, Jane), with a continuous shift from one to the other, to multiply the anxiety. The only piece of information kept from the spectator and Jane, for obvious reasons of narrative tenure, is the identity of the killer. In this beautifully conducted game, it is possible to identify two of Hitchcock's poetic features: the first is the limited movements of the characters, an obstacle that increases their perceptive capacity, decreasing their reactivity. The second consists in Martino's ability to construct the suspense, which creates and dilutes expectations instead of suddenly breaking out into violence, thus leading the spectator towards a continuous and progressive emotional involvement, just as Hitchcock teaches. So, if the final resolution of the affair is routine, with the most traditional of interventions by an external deus ex machina (the physician played by Luc Merenda), the multiplication of events that will bring the story to it is genially conceived by the Roman director. With *Torso* Martino masterfully captures every single aspect of anxiety and orchestrates a magnificent suite of claustrophobic tension, which is probably also one of the highest examples of his cinema. The success of the giallo genre, and specifically the one generated by Dario Argento's debut, influences many film currents and subgenres and can also be noticed pulsing under the surface in what is the stronghold of police thrillers, *La polizia ringrazia* (*Execution Squad*, 1972) by Stefano Vanzina. The political conspiracy theme, found in Vanzina's film and many subsequent examples, can also be regarded as an ideal continuation of the classic giallo/thriller, certainly with other technical-linguistic resources and other thematic purposes, but with corresponding narrative modes, which find the meeting point in the homologous whodunit structure. Moreover, there is also "undeclared" and more specific contamination between police and giallo genres, as in the case, for example of *La polizia chiede aiuto* (*What Have They Done to Your Daughters?*, 1975) by Massimo Dallamano, *...a tutte le auto della polizia...* (*Calling All Police Cars*, a.k.a. *Without Trace*, a.k.a. *The Maniac Responsible*, 1975) by Mario Caiano, and *Morte sospetta di una minorenne* (*The Suspicious Death of a Minor*, 1975) by Martino.

Among the four films made by Martino between 1973 and 1975, and ascribable to the police thriller/action genre, only *Milano trema: la polizia vuole giustizia* (*The Violent Professionals*, 1973) and *La polizia accusa: il servizio segreto uccide* (*Silent Action*, 1975) can be considered pure examples whereas *La città gioca d'azzardo* (*Gambling City*, 1975) and the aforementioned *The Suspicious Death of a Minor* are films that trespass into different territories and genres. *The Violent Professionals* was made in a period of consolidation and codification of the police genre, so much so that Martino's film finds itself between the "vigilantism" approach and that of the "investigative" political conspiracy. Together with *La polizia incrimina: la legge assolve* (*High Crime*, 1973) by Castellari, released the same year, *The Violent Professionals* can be identified as one of the true archetypes of Italian crime films, with the appearance of the first formulations of what will become recurring trappings and distinctive features, with inspector Giorgio Canepari (Luc Merenda) young and dynamic (like that played by Franco Nero in Castellari's film), ready to send the most mature and reflexive cops like Enrico Maria Salerno into retirement, opening the way for Leonard Mann, Franco Gasparri, Maurizio Merli and Fabio Testi. The gangster/Western subtext, with the protagonist infiltrated in a criminal gang (exactly like the characters played by Clint Eastwood in the first two Leone Westerns) devoted to bank robberies and above all maneuvered from above with an anti-democratic, subversive purpose, is at the center of the narration for almost the entire duration of a film which is a concentration of pure action, with a fair amount of chases, shootouts, physical clashes, and violent deaths. The picture is complemented by a functional melodramatic feel, with a faceted and melancholic female figure (Martine Brochard), probably the result of the inspired pen of Ernesto Gastaldi, together with an overall sense of defeat and anxiety.

In April 1975 *Silent Action* is released, which only appears to be following the footsteps of *The Violent Professionals*. Both refer to a plan of destabilization of Italian society by supra-state or para-state entities, with the support of members of politics and high finance, or deflected members of law enforcement. However, in the first of these two films, this grand design is only sketched, mostly evoked in absentia, and the direction focuses on the malevolent milieu that acts as the armored arm of the mandates, that remain, in fact, mostly invisible. Whereas in *Silent Action*, it almost seems as though Martino directs after having come from a sort of immersive search in court proceedings, journalistic investigations, research hypotheses. The director disseminates the film of events that appear to originate directly from the plumbean reality of the time: "excellent cadavers," eliminated witnesses, red herrings, internal diatribes between the various authorities involved in the investigations, conflicts of power, while profiling the silhouette of a reactionary coup. In these elements lies the will to create an ideal bridge between the requirements of spectacularity and those of adherence to the chronicles of the time, while the filter between fiction and reality is entrusted, as usual, to the character of a tough, no-shit cop (still Merenda) and his conflict with the hidden powers that hinder the investigation. The search for truth, the dark atmosphere of threat and the dystopian horizon, leads the story to the insidious and disturbing territories of the spy thriller, moving away from those, perhaps truculent but nevertheless cathartic, of purely action police dramas. The shootout of the pre-finale between the police and the coup militia fills the film with the bitter taste of organized subversion maneuvered from above, even if it is resolved (momentarily) in favor of the police. It is the actual finale, however, to reserve the true message—not quite original, but effective—with the assassination of the protagonist and his main antagonist, Captain Sperlì of the Secret Service (an elegant and sententious Tomas Milian). The open end cannot but be a prelude to new disturbing scenarios, which in real life will materialize on 2 August 1980 with the terrorist attack at the Bologna train station: 85 dead and more than 200 wounded.

Martino, with *The Violent Professionals* and *Silent Action*, exhibits his eclecticism, managing with these two titles to leave a lasting sign on both the main currents of Italian police genres and to outline, in a sort of ideal synthesis, almost all the coordinates of the genre's main themes. This eclecticism will find further confirmation, albeit not always with happy results, in his other two works: *Gambling City* and *The Suspicious Death of a Minor*. The former is a real distillate of heterogeneous influences, from French polar (though with an eye more to Jacques Deray or Georges Lautner rather than to Melville) to spaghetti Westerns, from the risk takings of Newman and Redford in *The Sting* (1973) by George Roy Hill, to the American drama of Shakespearean ancestry like *House of Strangers* (1949) by Joseph L. Mankiewicz or *Broken Lance* (1954) by Edward Dmytryk. There is a lot going on in *Gambling City*, perhaps too much. If the trickster-swindler interpreted by Merenda is impressed with the shrewdness of the French actor's presence, who steal the show are the two great theatrical gangsters played by Enrico Maria Salerno and Corrado Pani, respectively father-master and son-heir of a dynasty forced to eclipse because of the ambition and the envy of the psychopathic and weak progeny towards the parent. The harsh and sharp dialogues between the characters of Pani and Salerno are undoubtedly among the happiest moments of the film. The presence of the two actors, together with the tonal conflict between their interpretations is surely the added value of the film, while the stone faces of the various character actors contribute to liven up the vicious milieu of the story. Even the Western imprint of the gambling house, poker table, physical clashes, duels of gazes, even the impairment to the hands inflicted on Merenda by Pani's henchmen (a direct reference to Corbucci's *Django*), give the film a retro, out-of-time quality. On the contrary, despite the presence of the beautiful Dayle Haddon, what convinces less is the melodramatic side of the story, which develops around the triangle between the femme fatale, the clever card player portrayed by Merenda and Pani's cruel gangster. Perhaps it is the perennial sulky expression of Merenda, perhaps the indecisiveness of Martino in the moments of tenderness, which make *Gambling City* sappy and "soap-operish." *The Suspicious Death of a Minor* is an even better example of crossover between genres and sub-genres, but with the added specter of the comic farce. The plot revolves around the investigation conducted by another infiltrated cop (Claudio Cassinelli) in the underbelly of the small Milanese criminality, although the altars, once discovered, will lead to outline an affair of billions in the upper-class realms of the city: drugs, child prostitution, homicides, kidnapping and money laundering. Despite there being at least three action sequences worthy of note (the one on the rollercoaster, the one at the old Milanese Jolly cinema, demolished in the 1980s which is screening *Your Vice Is a Locked Room and Only I Have the Key*, and the finale), the tone of the story almost never manages to find the right calibration between seriousness and playfulness. There are unoriginal slapstick gags and awkward attempts to hint at a lunar comedic ancestry, similar to that of Keaton or Chaplin—also through the use of a comedic duo (Cassinelli and Adolfo Caruso), all in all ill-assorted and almost never funny—with Argento-like murders (which are not helped by a soundtrack, by Luciano Michelini, which appears to be a coarse copy of the Goblin scores) and typical action-packed moments which lack synthesis thus leading to an even greater imbalance in tone and the loss of a proper thematic fil rouge. In this mingling of comedy and action Lenzi will reach better results the following year with *Il trucido e lo sbirro* (*Free Hand for a Tough Cop*, 1976), while Martino, free of the most serious constraints of the police genre, now on the wane, while continuing to diversify, will showcase his ability with lighter and more farcical tones at the end of the 1970s and early 1980s, with a series of highly successful comedies.

The Martino brothers are synonymous of Italian genre cinema.
I know you mean this as a compliment but my reaction, when I hear this sort of comment, is still to be defensive because for so long I've heard it said in a derogatory way. Personally I have always directed films that were strongly influenced by the demands of the market but our company, Dania, and more specifically my brother, have spread out into so called art-house films. Labeling is a national sport here in Italy and getting rid of them is very difficult. You end up having to live with them your whole life. For example, when I hear my comedies from the seventies and eighties defined as "sexy" or "soft-core," I shudder. I was accused of being vulgar, when in all honesty I don't find anything vulgar in those films. Sure, of course, sometimes I might have given in to some easy or even crass solutions or jokes, but as a whole I don't think you can find anything that can really be defined as vulgar in my body of work. Especially if you compare what I and some of my colleagues did to what is being peddled to viewers now. Anyway, what I'm saying goes for all genres: "poliziotteschi," "spaghetti Westerns," "sexy comedies." Labels … easy labels, aimed at belittling the films and genres we were making.

How did things work within Dania? Would you participate in the choice of the films to produce or would you act as a consultant on other directors' projects? In other words: what was the modus operandi within the Dania structure?
First of all, let's begin by saying that when we started out—actually, I'm now mostly referring to my brother who preceded me in cinema, together with Mino Loy, with whom he founded Dania—there was a formula: to make imitational films on the basis of what the Americans were doing. In fact, one of the genres we started out with were pseudo-007 spy films in the early sixties, but whatever the genre, the important thing was that the films had to have an international appeal. This is what always moved Dania forward: the willingness to offer a more affordable product on the international market that would be as similar as possible to what the Americans were doing. At that time it was possible to be very competitive, derivative of course, but ten times less expensive. A distributor who would come to Italy to buy, for example, a Western, or a giallo or a horror; at the same price with which in the U.S. he would have bought one film, here he was able to buy three. In fact, Dania was born on the tail of the glorious era of peplums, thanks to which Italian cinema was catapulted into a whole new ball game. The genre films that had been made previously, in the early fifties and forties were a bit of a mixed bag … some were sold on the foreign market, others weren't, but it was more a film-by-film scenario. With the advent of peplums, that we called "sandaloni" [big sandals], we became a full-blown industry, which confronted itself internationally. One of our very first films was *I giganti di Roma* [*Giants of Rome*, 1964] that was born with the idea of structuring the story in a way that would remind audiences of *The Guns of Navarone* [1961], my brother's idea. But prior to Dania, Luciano had founded another company called Vox Films, together with screenwriter Federico Magnaghi, and had made a small film called *Il demonio* [*The Demon*, 1963] by Brunello Rondi, which went to the Venice Film Festival.

I was an assistant director on that and on the set I remember, when we hadn't even finished the first week of shooting, the director of photography said to me: "You will be a director soon. I've seen people come and go and you're staying." That struck me. Maybe I was already showing a little bit of talent, or maybe his evaluation was influenced by my family. I was born with cinema in my blood, both me and Luciano. Our grandfather Gennaro Righelli had been a very successful director, who from a certain point of view started creating the rules of what many years later became known as "commedia all'italiana." *Abbasso la miseria* [*Down with Misery*, 1945] and *Abbasso la ricchezza* [*Peddlin' in Society*, 1946] were films that had great casts—De Sica, Magnani, Riento—and were extremely successful and very well considered. My brother and I were sometimes brought on the set, I was just a child, but I mostly remember the trips to the dubbing studios. Dubbing and sound mixing at that time, was something epic. As the actors were dubbing themselves, the Foley artist would have to, in perfect synchronization, replicate all the noises and sound effects. One particularly strong image was seeing Anna Magnani saying her line, then one guy would reproduce the sound of her footsteps, another one would do the window opening and a bunch at the end would recreate the crackling noise of wood burning. It was quite incredible to watch. Sorry, I have been wandering with my reminiscing. Anyway, going back to your question.... This was what we were trying to do: be competitive. *The Giants of Rome*, *The Demon*, the 007 films were all made and contained gimmicks that would satisfy the big, worldwide appetite for an entertaining cinema at a lower cost. We never invented a genre, we would follow the big American successes. Never first but always a solid second place. As far as participating in other directors' projects ... no. Luciano was the producer and he would handle matters. Dania regulars didn't need my consultation. Umberto Lenzi, Mariano Laurenti, Nando Cicero, Michele Massimo Tarantini were all directors who knew what they were doing. I would intervene but on other kinds of films and with different kinds of directors. Especially in more recent years, I've found myself in the situation of having to re-do, add or extend scenes in numerous Dania productions because new directors had problems with tight budgets. One of the last examples I can give you is of a film—I won't say the title—where there was a car chase in which one of the two vehicles hits a fruit cart ... your typical action cliché. The director had shot the scene with a wide angle and there were only two watermelons on the cart! So I went back and made sure more fruit was bought. The problem is that while my generation was forged on sets, big ones, newer generations are all theory and no practice. For example, to be able to make a Western, you need to have experienced the smell of fresh horse dung, you need to have touched the leather of a saddle and finish the day covered in dust.

Among the first directors you worked with we can find Mario Bava...

I was just going to mention him! I worked with Bava, not as an AD, but as a production coordinator. The film was *La frusta e il corpo* [*The Whip and the Body*, 1963] with Christopher Lee and Daliah Lavi. He, for example, was very attentive to the needs and restrictions of the production and would always make sure not to go in overtime. At 7 p.m. sharp he would stop and send everybody home. I have a perfect anecdote to explain what I mean: there was this scene with an Italian actor, who didn't speak English, in which he had to give this long monologue. It was quite late in the afternoon and Bava realized that he wouldn't have managed to shoot it with a classic close-up of the actor. We would have certainly gone into overtime. So he did the scene like this: at the beginning of the monologue he starts on the actor's face, "I have something to say..." then he pans around the room revealing the furniture, flowers, details ... does a full circle and goes back on the actor's face "...that is all I had to say!" The gap was then later filled in the dubbing studio. He would shoot only what he needed, also to save on film, which had an elevated cost. This is the reason why most of his films are never longer than ninety minutes. Plus, at the time technology was different, or should I say nonexistent, at least for some professions. Take script supervisors for example, they didn't even have the aid of a polaroid camera in the sixties while now with monitors everywhere they can re-watch a scene, on set, as many times as they want.

What was Mario Bava like as a person?

Very nice and very kind. A real gentleman. He would always be very well dressed, impeccably so. It was impossible to see him dressed shaggily or disorderly. He loved his dogs and would bring them everywhere, not on set but in pre-production meetings they would always be at his feet. When I see Lamberto I always tell him how incredibly funny and warm his father was. He was just a child when I was working with his father.

What do you remember about Christopher Lee on that film?

I would pick him up, with my Seicento, to bring him on the set. He was constantly worried he wouldn't receive his daily expense pay and was very attentive when it came to time schedules but he was a true professional, like most of these American and British actors who would migrate to Italy. You know, Italy was the elephant graveyard. Needless to say, I'm oversimplifying but it's true that a big percentage of the international names that would come here were aging stars, sometimes downright old, who had problems getting hired in their own countries. It wasn't Lee's case, because he was still relatively young and going strong with Hammer films but other actors I've worked with, like Joseph Cotten and Richard Conte, came here to inject new life into their fading careers. It was a win-win situation for all: they got paid quite well for just a few days' work and we had the possibility of making our films even more sellable and internationally attractive. Some actors even managed to revitalize their careers: having a hit here made them interesting back in their

Daliah Lavi and Sergio Martino on the set of *The Whip and the Body,* 1963. Martino was a production coordinator on the Mario Bava-directed horror (courtesy Sergio Martino).

country. What was funny was seeing these actors adapt to a completely new system and a totally different way of conceiving a set. Sound, for example. Most, if not all, films at that time were dubbed—we didn't use on-set recording, also because sometimes on a film, there would be actors talking in English, others in Italian, maybe some in French or Spanish… It was a very frustrating age for the sound department because often they weren't even called in to work. *Lo strano vizio della signora Wardh* [*The Strange Vice of Mrs. Wardh*, a.k.a. *Blade of the Ripper*, 1971] and *La coda dello scorpione* [*The Case of the Scorpion's Tail*, a.k.a. *Scorpion's Tail*, 1971] were filmed mute. The reason was also financial, especially when shooting abroad: a person less to take with you. When I watch those films I realize that what I felt was of no importance, actually was. The depth of a live on-set sound recording is something that I wish my films had. Now I would do things differently. But the fascination of the "work in progress" that characterized the films of my generation of directors is something that doesn't exist nowadays. To watch your films slowly being assembled is something directors now will never experience: you couldn't see exactly what the camera operator was doing so even that was a surprise when you sat down and watched the rushes; then the dubbing process; the adding of sound effects and also the coloring of the film, because we shot in black and white. It really was like watching your child growing up and assuming adult features. That I miss.

When one talks about your cinema, inevitably the name of Edwige Fenech will come up.

Edwige was a natural choice being part of the family, my family. She was practically my sister-in-law. So, I made many films with her but at the time producers, my brother included, would choose their women, girlfriends, wives, special friends or lovers much more wisely. And more importantly, they were aware of what they were able to do and what their limits were. Now you have your little corporate manager who thinks his girlfriend can become Sophia Loren and in my later television years I've had to put up with these pretty nothings put in leading or important roles. Edwige had charisma, professionalism and was perfect in the films she did, in the roles she had. Particularly in comedies, in the ones she did with me I find her brilliant. *Giovannona Coscialunga disonorata con onore* [*Giovannona Long-Thigh*, 1973] would be a perfect example of her comedic timing. Many remember her in my gialli as well, but to be honest, I've always thought she wasn't the best of choices for those films. She is good in them and she holds up but probably she is too joyful-looking for that genre, too rubenesque and full of life. A darker, moodier kind of woman would have been more suitable. For my comedies I wouldn't ask her to strip naked very often. There is much more nudity in my gialli.

You've just anticipated my next question: indeed, your gialli are filled with a stronger dose of morbidity compared to your comedies. Your so-called "sexy comedies" aren't "keyhole-based" like the ones of your colleagues. Would you agree?

Yes, this is due probably to my personal sense of humor and the fact that I have always been inspired by a more innocent kind of comedy, a lighter touch. The other reason is because I would—but this was common practice at the time—do a longer version of the film knowing that it would be cut. Certain scenes were shot, edited, sound-mixed and shown to the censorship committee already knowing that they would be cut. The committee would always ask you to cut something so it was never wise to show them exactly what you wanted in the film, so by exaggerating you had the possibility of sneaking in a lot more. In *The Strange Vice of Mrs. Wardh* there are some vulgar moments, or perhaps I should say sloppy shots which I usually filmed at the end of the day. There is a scene I hate in that film where Edwige and George Hilton are on the sofa and I shot them from above ... void of any eroticism. It's flat and made no sense but I did it with my left hand knowing that it wouldn't survive the final cut and it didn't: the version that was released did not have that moment. These cuts though, survived because they weren't done on the original negative so when, years later, they were shown on television or distributed on DVD or VHS people had a chance to watch them. Your generation knows these films and discovered them with those scenes, but they were never screened in cinemas at the time of their release. This mechanism definitely occurred on *Mrs. Wardh* and *Il tuo vizio è una stanza chiusa e solo io ne ho la chiave* [*Your Vice Is a Locked Room and Only I Have the Key*, 1972]. I don't remember if it was also done with *The Scorpion's Tail*.... There wasn't much eroticism there, mainly because Edwige wasn't in it.

There is a topless Anita Strindberg.
Which maybe shouldn't be in the film, seeing how fake her tits look. I must admit that in my career I've had one major defect, I was too accommodating with producers and distributors. I should have put my foot down and not accepted so many compromises when it came to adding certain scenes and re-managing stories. I should have complied a little less with the orders from above, but I think I managed to pull things off with relative good taste. Plus gialli, horror and adventure films were very much exported so we had to satisfy different markets, some of which wanted stronger scenes of sex and violence.

You make your debut within a very exploitative genre: the "mondo movies."
Mino Loy, my brother's associate and business partner, had specialized in a certain kind of "sexy mondo," also known as "mondo di notte" [mondo by night]. He did loads of them, all of which were hugely successful. Mino likes to say that he went around the world twice to make them. He would travel for a month or two then go to Paris, where thanks to the help of a woman called Carmen Bajeau, who would organize these adult Pigalle shows, he'd stay there a week or so, film these erotic exhibitions which he then used to separate and give rhythm to the footage. Then came Luigi Scattini who made *Svezia: inferno e paradiso* [*Sweden: Heaven and Hell*, 1968] that pushed things even further. So I began with Marcello Avallone following this wave. He directed the first, which was called *L'altra faccia del peccato* [*The Queer ... The Erotic*, 1969] and I directed *Mille peccati ... nessuna virtù* [*Wages of Sin*, a.k.a. *Mondo Sex*, 1969] and then *America così nuda, così violenta* [*Naked and Violent*, 1969].

Avallone told me he was also supposed to direct Naked and Violent *and that you directed it after his refusal*.
I don't remember it like that. Anyway, *Naked and Violent* is one of the best memories I have...

How come?
Well, first of all, it was my first time in the States. I was twenty-seven, twenty-eight, and America was going through a period of great revolts and changes. It was very stimulating to be able to witness what was happening there: the Vietnam veterans, the protests in the streets, the music. We were there roughly two months. I went to a Rolling Stones concert ... stuff that, at the time, for a European and even more so for an Italian was particularly special. This reminds me of when, in the sixties, I was an AD on the film *Le fate* [*The Queens*, 1966] and we shot a part of the film in France. As soon as the crew landed

in Paris they all dashed to the newspaper stand to buy *Playboy*, because in Italy it was still banned. Remember that the success of many films was due to the fact they showed something for the first time: a lesbian kiss, a naked woman, a woman giving birth, etc. That experience in the States was extraordinary and very formative for me.

You participated, in the late sixties, in two gialli: Così dolce ... così perversa *[So Sweet ... So Perverse, 1969] by Umberto Lenzi and* Il dolce corpo di Deborah *[The Sweet Body of Deborah, 1968] by Romolo Guerrieri.*

My gialli are the natural evolution of those films. In the sense that, of course, there was an escalation in what you could show in terms of violence and sex, so my films reflect the more permissive decade they are part of. In between, there had been *The Bird with the Crystal Plumage* which was more transgressive and raised the bar as far as what you could put on screen. Not so much sex-wise but definitely as far as blood is concerned.

And also stronger themes and undercurrent symbolisms...

In fact, I changed Ernesto Gastaldi's script of *Mrs. Wardh* quite radically. Gastaldi who, by the way, had written the other films you mentioned, wrote a story which was much more classical: a murder, an investigation, a love triangle. It was very much a sixties film. It is basically a remake of Guerrieri's film, so I changed it trying to fill it up with darker and more esoteric, or should I say surreal, elements. The serial killer at the beginning of the film, the one that the two men use to cover up their murders, was not present in the script. That is my doing, and by adding that element I was able to have more

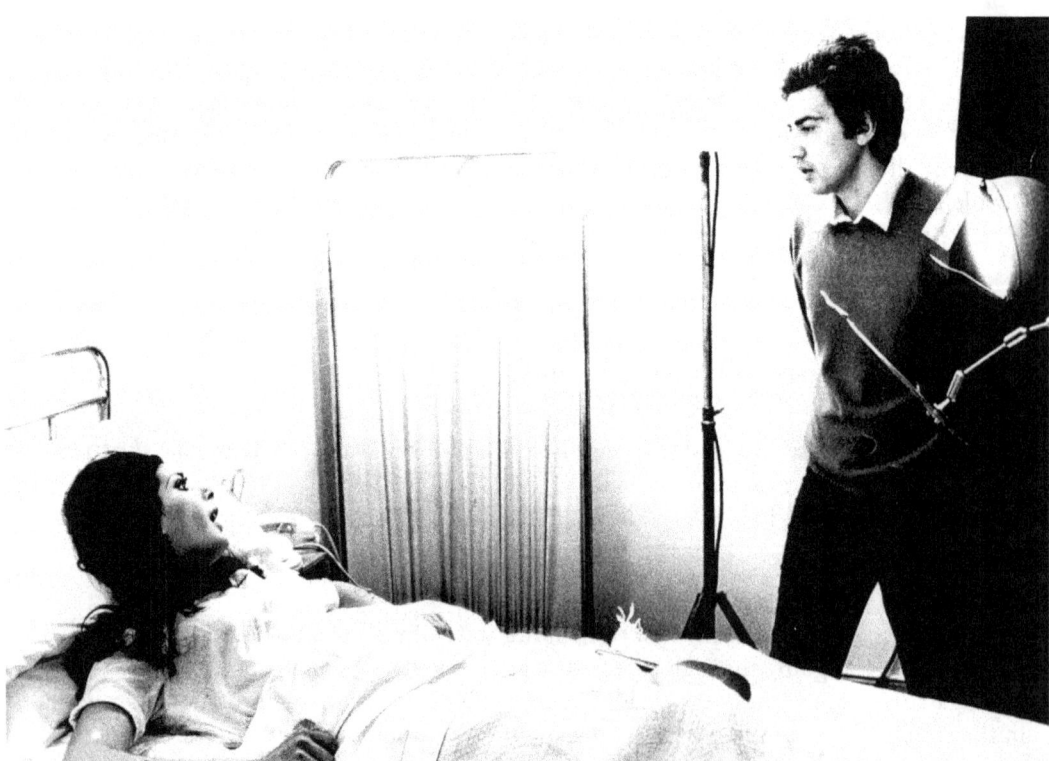

Edwige Fenech and Martino on the set of *All the Colors of the Dark*, 1972 (courtesy Nocturno Cinema).

murder pieces, more action. I left out a lot of dialogue and the figure of the investigator, which was reminiscent of Maigret, to make it more dynamic. The Clouzot/Agatha Christie dialogue-based investigation thriller was dead. What worked was the tension of single mechanisms. For example, the scene of the key and lock in *I corpi presentano tracce di violenza carnale* [*Torso*, 1973]—Suzy Kendall, locked in a room, trying to get to the key, not knowing that on the other side of the door there's the killer. People were glued to their seats during all that. People wanted that more than the contorted story and the detective trying to find out what really happened.

If here in Italy your most famous contribution to the genre is Mrs. Wardh, elsewhere it would have to be Torso.

It would have gone better in Italian cinemas if it hadn't come out in the same period of *Ultimo tango a Parigi* [*Last Tango in Paris*, 1972]. Carlo Ponti, the producer, wanted to make a film that was as international as possible. It was his idea to set it at the University of Perugia, which was a brilliant idea because it gave us the pretext to fill it with American and foreign characters, including a black actress which wasn't very common in Italian cinema at that time.

I will just give you this input: feminism.

Well, I don't know if my gialli can be defined as feminist ... probably not, but I can definitely say that while directing them I was aware of what was going on with the role of women in modern society. My female characters, whether played by Fenech or Strindberg, are strong, capable women, very relaxed and at ease with their sexuality. By the early seventies, things were starting to change and I think that my films incorporate, on some level, that change. I mentioned *Torso* just now ... well, in that film the woman manages to save herself. There isn't a man riding in to protect her. They were in line with a certain attitude. Don't get me wrong, I never set out to direct a feminist manifesto but I did like strong female characters. You can tell even by the choice of actresses: Edwige would never be suitable to play a quivering, frightened little woman. She can't play weak. On the other hand, Carroll Baker, who was the queen of the sixties giallo, was much more fragile looking. Between Baker and Fenech, things had changed.

You seem to have a very lucid and objective attitude towards your work. What do you think of your films, remaining, for the moment, in this genre?

The least dated would have to be *Torso*, for the action-thriller scenes, because the erotic ones are directed quite shabbily. It's definitively less dated than *The Strange Vice of Mrs. Wardh*, which is old. I can tell by audiences' reaction even now. Not too many years ago I was invited to a screening, which was held at the University of Perugia and all the students, young people, were cheering and screaming. *Torso* is also my last giallo. I think I reached my peak with that. Later I did *Morte sospetta di una minorenne* [*The Suspicious Death of a Minor*, 1975] which has elements of a giallo but is too much of a hybrid to be considered a pure example of the genre. I like that as well, though. I think the irony and humor still holds up. My evaluations are based mostly on pace and editing. *Mrs. Wardh* is very slow and has long parts which are redundant. *Torso* is much more essential and fast-moving, making it more contemporary.

Let's talk a little bit further about the casting process.

You got an old American fossil and put it next to some young rising star. That was the winning formula. The first part was easy, the second not so much. Luc Merenda was my discovery. I had seen him in a Western, possibly *Così sia* [*They Called Him Amen*, a.k.a. *Therefore It Is*, a.k.a. *Man Called Amen*, 1972] and gave him the role of the doctor in *Torso*. That was a way of testing him: I liked him, Carlo Ponti was convinced, so we cast him also in the film that ultimately launched him: *Milano Trema: la polizia vuole giustizia* [*The Violent Professionals*, 1973].

Your most important cop thriller. Talk to me about it.

The *Violent Professionals* was born initially following the box-office hit of *Dirty Harry* [1971], but also thanks to the equal, but more surprising, success of *La polizia ringrazia* [*Execution Squad*, 1972]. Stefano Vanzina controverted something that people took for granted, which was that the Italian police were not credible in a thriller or action-based context. This was probably due to comedies ... you know, the Sicilian carabiniere with the unibrow and the mustache who would always mess things up and couldn't conjugate verbs properly. The same goes for gialli and in fact this is one of the reasons why films like *Mrs. Wardh* and *Scorpion's Tail* took place in foreign countries like Vienna and Spain because certain stories and characters were perceived as more credible if set elsewhere. Dario Argento was the one who changed things around from this point of view. My police thrillers have always been made and set in Italy thanks to Steno and his film. In addition, the political and social upheaval that the entire country was going through have to be considered: Brigate Rosse,[2] terrorist attacks, massive strikes. Our films had this terrible pool from which to pick. It was a great resource of inputs for our films. *The Violent Professionals* in particular incorporated a lot of what was happening at that time. Ernesto Gastaldi wrote the story but we worked extensively on it together. A different story compared to *La polizia accusa: il servizio segreto uccide* [*Silent Action*, 1975], which is a story I inherited from another director. I don't remember who was supposed to helm the film but basically there were problems so my brother came into the project, fired the director and it was passed onto me. Come to think of it, I think the distribution had mentioned my name. The script was changed radically. Initially the film was much more political, which was probably why the distribution wasn't happy. I made it more spectacular but the political aspect survived and that too is a film strongly influenced by its time.

Luigi Pistilli and a statuesque Edwige Fenech in *Your Vice Is a Locked Room and Only I Have the Key,* 1972 (courtesy Nocturno Cinema).

Is it true that initially Enrico Maria Salerno was supposed to have a role in **The Violent Professionals?**

Yes, he was supposed to play Merenda's partner who gets killed at the beginning of the film. The part was then given to Chris Avram. I told Ponti: "Instead of paying twenty, thirty million lira to Salerno, let's use that money to get Remy Julienne to do the car stunts." I'm happy I won because the film has some great chase sequences. One specific car crash was used on a half a dozen films afterwards. You can see it also in *Milano odia: la polizia non può sparare* [*Almost Human*, 1974], which I was supposed to do and that was later passed onto Lenzi.

Wasn't there an accident on the set?

Yes. It was a Friday and we were supposed to shoot the scene in which the car explodes. I don't remember for what reason but we decided to postpone it to the next day and it's a good thing we did because when the explosives went off, the blast was much more powerful than what it should have been: the windows of a nearby building were shattered and a group of men who were working on the railroad were injured, minor injuries but still…. Thank God it was Saturday and the office building was empty. We were very irresponsible in a way. Now, making films like that would not be possible and at my age I would feel like a criminal.

You mentioned **Silent Action.** *How was Tomas Milian?*

He was and is, without a doubt, a very capable actor but he was very closed, introspective and was trying to hide himself. Especially in later years, the seventies and eighties, he was completely warped by the idea of hiding behind make-up, glasses, wigs … I believe even the character of "Monnezza" originated from this need. I don't want to play psychiatrist but I think this stemmed from some kind of defense mechanism. He didn't like himself, he would compare himself to other actors, always in need of approval and reassurance. He had a wife who was much older—I don't think she's with us anymore—who was very maternal with him. It was a little morbid to watch them. I know he had a difficult childhood but he maintained a very childish attitude. In this sense he would hold grudges and be very vengeful. One episode I recall is when we were in Romagna shooting his episode of my comedy *40 gradi all'ombra del lenzuolo* [*Sex with a Smile*, 1976]. We were having dinner at a restaurant, Milian, the camera operator and myself and he wanted to play "the tower game." Basically the game consisted in choosing who you would push from the tower between two given names. He went: "Who would you throw from the tower between me and Edwige Fenech?" "I've known Edwige for many, many years and she is my brother's woman. I feel greatly embarrassed … I wouldn't be able to choose." I saved myself with this answer. The operator, on the other hand, went, "Fenech is hot. I would push you!" We all laughed, also Tomas and we continued playing. That same night, at five in the morning Tomas calls me on the phone—we were staying at the same hotel: "I want that man off the set." For him, the idea of not being liked and appreciated was unbearable. I can mention another emblematic episode, which again occurred on that film. In the episode he plays a censor—for which he wore a wig, fake teeth and thick glasses—living in this small town, and despite trying to keep his impulses under control, falls for Edwige's character, the town beauty, married to a cheating husband. The scene we were shooting was set in a barbershop. Tomas enters and from the shop window sees her pass by with her husband and faints. Falling, he was supposed to hit his head against the sink. It was a complicated shot and we ended up doing it like six or seven times.

Tomas had refused to cover the sink with foam to protect his head. "I was trained at the actor's studio. I need the pain. It's what my character is feeling so I need to experience it as well." By the time we got what we needed, his forehead was blue and purple. I had to cut the scene once in the editing room and when he discovered this, he smiled jokingly and said, "You know we will never work together again?" I just laughed but in hindsight, he might have been serious seeing that was the last time we worked together. On *Silent Action*, the main problem was his jealousy: Luc Merenda had more screen time and he considered him to be more handsome. Luc wasn't necessarily a bigger star but he was definitely much more of a sex symbol.

The biggest anomaly of the seventies in your filmography is La bellissima estate *[Summer to Remember, 1974]*.

I had been wanting to make a sentimental drama for some time and I got my chance thanks to the success of *L'ultima neve di primavera* [*The Last Snows of Spring*, 1973]. I wrote the script with my brother, who elaborated the main plot, together with Sauro Scavolini. I directed it quite deftly, with a delicate touch. There isn't an obsessive search for tear-jerking moments. The only thing that doesn't really work is the choice of the kid, his face isn't quite right. Often these sort of films would border on a soap-opera-like atmosphere but I like to think I managed to stay away from that approach. *Summer to Remember* was made as a sort of double-bill, if you will, with *Cugini carnali* [*Loving Cousins*, a.k.a. *Hot and Bothered*, a.k.a. *High School Girl*, 1974]. I come from a middle-class family, of Neapolitan origin, you know … "grandmother's pasta sauce is the best," so I guess *Summer to Remember* also stems from my upbringing. Not the story in itself but the urge to direct that kind of film: a sentimental, family-friendly film. Plus, for me a director has to be able to direct every kind of film. I have never been interested in having a career like Dario Argento's, which is made up 97 percent of gialli and horror. I have always wanted to tackle as many genres as possible. I did all sorts of films, maybe all of them badly … as one critic once wrote, "Sergio Martino can be described perfectly with the title of his first film *Mille peccati … nessuna virtù* (a thousand sins and no virtues)."

La montagna del Dio cannibale *[The Mountain of the Cannibal God, 1978]* is the first installment of the "adventure trilogy" you directed. Had you seen Ultimo mondo cannibale *[Last Cannibal World, a.k.a.* Jungle Holocaust*, a.k.a.* The Last Survivor, 1977]*?

It was a moment in which a director was able to have a wide range of genres to choose from. What made it possible for certain types of directors to pass from one genre to the other was the capability of the foreign market to absorb these films: apart from comedies, Westerns, and police thrillers we also managed to do adventure films. I had seen *Last Cannibal World* but after I had started working on *The Mountain of the Cannibal God*. The film that inspired me was an American one called *King Solomon's Mines* [1950], which was the story of a widow who goes to Africa among the indigenous tribes to look for her husband who has mysteriously vanished. The idea of a classical adventure story got contaminated with the vision of Deodato's film, that pushed me to add a certain aggressive note to the scenes of cannibalism. An element which is not part of my nature but that I put in anyway to satisfy the requests of the market.

How did the production of the film go?

It was a wonderful experience, especially having to climb every day 500 meters to reach the caves, with temperatures of 40°C and 100 percent humidity. [He laughs.] We all lost a lot of weight and when I see the set photos of that film I can't help but notice how fit I looked. I always say, to be able to make that kind of cinema you need the physique, and I wasn't even among those who had to carry all the heavy equipment! I mean I had to carry the weight of responsibility, but nothing that can be calculated in kilos. In Sri Lanka the people were fantastic and warm. I have very fond memories of that period and the places we were able to see. Like Deodato had done months before, we shot the final part of the film in the caves in Malaysia. Though his story is completely different, it's about a man kept prisoner by a group of cannibals.

What can you tell me about the cast?

Claudio Cassinelli was an actor I shared a lot of experiences with. He starred in my last police thriller, *The Suspicious Death of a Minor*. Then there was Stacy Keach, who was a very successful actor at the time. He was very satisfied with the quality of the final product. It's a film I shot with a lot of attention to realism, in real places though some may not know that a huge chunk of the jungle scenes were shot in the botanical gardens of Kandy, where we had bathrooms, an accessible road, an exit nearby... So 80 percent of what seems like a wild and impenetrable jungle was in fact shot with every kind of comfort. The real effort was to shoot in the Malaysian caves. Going back to Keach, he was enthusiastic about the film. We also spent New Year together in Sri Lanka. The only thing he was disappointed about was to see that one of his favorite scenes had been cut from the final montage. But I found it was unnecessary to the story and I've always tried, in my cinema, to give great rhythm to the images.

Martino and Barbara Bach during the time they were at work on *Screamers,* **1978 (courtesy Sergio Martino).**

You mentioned Cassinelli. I would like you to talk about him and, if you feel like it, about his tragic death.

First of all, I want to say that he was a very gentle person and a humble one. Many actors I've met were very competitive, jealous about colleagues, vindictive and resentful. Claudio never enjoyed a great success, he didn't become a star, even if he had some of the qualities of one but he was a good professional and a nice person. I never heard him speak badly about someone or be unfair towards a colleague. A gentleman and a reliable person. An example: I remember on our last film, *Vendetta dal futuro* [*Hands of Steel*, 1986] we were shooting in a place called Page, in Arizona. We were a staying at a hotel, completely isolated in the Rocky Mountains, not too far from the bridge where he lost his life. Each room was actually a small chalet, each crew member had his own—we had booked the whole hotel—and practically one wall of the bedroom was a huge windowpane that looked onto the forest. Well, I distinctly remember noticing that Claudio was the only one who would never raise his eyes to look into people's rooms. Most of us didn't draw the curtains and he would never give a peek. He was a profoundly respectful human being. He ended up being cast in that film because he had asked me for work. He was going through a difficult period. He wasn't working much and I was happy to help him out. He was amused at the idea of playing a villain. You know, Claudio was used to playing intellectuals and usually positive characters. Even when he played cops and detectives he was never the Maurizio Merli–like hero but a more reflective one. Maybe introspective is too big a word, but you know what I mean…. Anyhow, soon after the beginning of production he was offered a role in a French film. He asked me to release him from *Hands of Steel* as soon as possible. If I hadn't re-done the schedule and changed the dates of those stunt scenes, he would still be alive. The helicopter pilot who came was not the one that we had met in pre-production and who had already shot some sequences. He was a new pilot, an older one. Only later, after the investigation, we discovered that he had had, that very morning, a violent discussion with his wife. In the scene, the helicopter was supposed to go under the bridge. Claudio asked me to let him do it and not to use a double. He told me he had promised his son Giovanni that he would do it himself. For nearly twenty years I stopped going on choppers, something I used to do quite often for work or fun. Five years ago I was near Las Vegas and I decided to try again. I didn't go near that location, even if it was very close by, but I finally managed to overcome this block. But going back to the film … on the Colorado River there are some big variations in temperature: the water is very cold but the temperature is hot so turbulences are common. But the pilot was behaving strangely: he had already passed under the bridge but he repeated the scene for some reason and the second time round the chopper struck a steel span under the bridge and fell, in several large parts, 540 feet into the Colorado River. The main rotor had struck the bridge 29 feet below the level of the roadway and approximately 75 feet west of the center of the bridge. I fainted. It was a terrible experience: having to continue production, to come up with solutions to fill in the plot holes…. We invented the character of his double/alter ego and called Roberto Bisacco to play him. But everything was painful after the accident. I felt guilty for many years for having permitted him to do that scene. Actors ask you that sort of stuff but a director should say no…

***You once mentioned that you directed two versions of* The Mountain of the Cannibal God.**

Yes, I even did a version that I didn't think would reach the general public. Sometimes at that time, films would be edited so as to be lengthier knowing that the censorship

The Italian poster of *The Mountain of the Cannibal God*, 1978.

board would shorten some scenes, but though these versions were never released at cinemas in Italy, they were sometimes used for TV and home video releases, so these more complete versions reached newer generations as well as being distributed in other countries. For example, when I met the Dutch distributor in Rome, he kept stroking my arm as he told me that my film had been more successful than the latest James Bond movie. In the Netherlands these films are particularly appreciated, even because my films were always rooted in a strong narrative.

The film is very much remembered for the infamous "monkey-python scene."

Yes, the scene in which a python devours a monkey, which we shot on our last day before flying to Kuala Lumpur and then back to Italy. It wasn't our intention to kill the poor monkey: this python which was always very lethargic—I don't know, maybe it was hungry that day—managed to catch this animal and killed it. I wasn't able to say "stop," so this scene remained and it is undoubtedly heartbreaking. Animalists have criticized me for this choice, but years later I continue to say that my intent was that of showing a monkey being able to escape from the aggression of the python.

In the early nineties, for a short but intense period, you became a director of erotic films.

Yes, but those are films I don't like. There is not much of me in them. I made them very mechanically. For the most part I think that sex scenes in films are quite ridiculous. Directing them is awkward and embarrassing. Most of the actors just go through the movements, like in my film *Graffiante desiderio* [*Craving Desire*, 1993] which, first of all, had some bad choices in the casting department. Vittoria Belvedere was not suitable for that role. Initially Raul Bova was supposed to star as the lead. He was very excited to be in it but I found he was too young. Plus, he had just done his national service and his hair was too short. That is the one occasion I was dead wrong but at the time I thought that a more romantic looking lead was better. The film took off after the release of *Bitter Moon* [1992] by Polanski but I was not able to infuse that kind of morbid decadent eroticism into my film. *Spiando Marina* [*The Smile of the Fox*, a.k.a. *Foxy Lady*, 1992] is another film that was made … how can I put it … in my free time, but at least for that we went to Argentina, which is a place I still carry in my heart. Recently I have been invited to a Festival in Brazil. I would love to go but I would go only because it might be the last chance I have to see some places again. I don't know … Luigi Cozzi is trying to convince me, but I don't know. I'm afraid I would just be nostalgic if I went. Anyway, going back to your question, you have to consider that by the nineties we were all pulling at straws. Umberto Lenzi retired around that time. I was saved by television. What makes me smile is my use of pseudonyms: one more masculine, American-sounding and virile for action films which was Martin Dolman, and one more latino for erotic films, George Raminto!

Now, I won't ask you a question about this. I will just give you an input: the death of Italian genre cinema.

I have a very specific theory about all this. When I started working in cinema, I remember I collaborated with director Franco Rossi on *Le bambole* [*The Dolls*, 1965] with producer Gianni Hecht Lucari and he told me, "Are you crazy to want to become a director? Cinema is dead." But those were years in which they used to do around 300 films per year, thanks to directors who now are not even remembered, and cinema managed to flourish. Directors like Pietro Francisci or Franco Rossi. So Italian cinema has always had a way to regenerate itself. By the seventies, we were doing 350–400 films per year. The real crisis arrived at the end of the decade, because bad politics didn't help renovate ourselves technologically. Before, we would use the same special effects Americans did. For example, if cars had to explode in *Dirty Harry,* five brand new Mercedes would explode … when I did a cop thriller, four old Cinquecento would be destroyed, but the final effect was very similar. Some of the car chases I shot in my thrillers were accomplished by Rémy Julienne, the same person who was doing American films. In fact, sometimes our sequences were even more stunning, seeing they were often done in real traffic, without proper permits. By the late seventies, even the special effects we did in sci-fi films for example, were still good enough to be distributed worldwide. But in the eighties, with the advent of more sophisticated techniques and the new era of digital FX, the gap became too big, and we were not able to fill it. This was a political decision, I shouldn't mention names but I will: politicians like Bettino Craxi and Giulio Andreotti,[3] instead of putting us in the position to better ourselves technologically, deliberately blocked everything. When I went to see American films at the cinema, I was stunned with what they were doing, "How did they do that?" Of course in time I learned the techniques adopted, and it's much more simple and a lot less fascinating then what one might think. None of what you see is true, it's all green screen. When the alien says, "I love you," you know there's nothing there and I feel this takes away pathos. So genre cinema started its deep crisis exactly in this period, primarily because of a lack of a technological evolution. Right until the nineties I continued making films, but selling them on the international market got more and more difficult. *Casablanca Express* [1989] for example, was probably one of the last films that I managed to sell. Now I might still be able to shoot a solid action film, but our market does not have that kind of money. To make a film like that in Italy now, would be economically prohibitive. So we continue doing the same things over and over. I am particularly critical of the way things are being done nowadays: films that get screened only in a certain small niche and are gratified by that.

If in the seventies the comedies you directed were few, in the eighties the genre takes control of your career.

Yes, I become for the most part a comedy director. Probably in ten/twenty years people will remember me mostly for my comedies, at least in Italy. I realize this also because of my medical examinations. I have never been visited by a doctor who didn't spend more time repeating jokes from my films than visiting me. *Occhio, malocchio, prezzemolo e finocchio* [translation: *Eye, Evil Eye, Parsley and Fennel,* 1983] with Lino Banfi and Johnny Dorelli has an average of 35 percent share every time it's shown on television. I participated on all the scripts for my films but on comedies even more so. First of all, I would make them much more action-based, which is something that caused a few diversions with some writers. Raimondo Vianello, who together with Sandro Continenza, wrote *Spogliamoci così senza pudor* [*Sex with a Smile II,* 1976] discovered I had added stuff and got mad. He was a great comedian and a very bright man but he was very irritable, and was prone to have tantrums and fire up in a matter of minutes. On the other hand, Tonino Guerra, one of Fellini's closest collaborators, who wrote *Sex with a Smile,* wasn't at all possessive about his work. When he viewed it at its first screening, he complimented me, "I like the changes." "Really?" "Well, you heard me laugh, didn't you?" Another thing I liked to put into my comedies were actors one wouldn't expect to see. Daniele Vargas acted in many of them but before that he was the villain in adventure movies.

How was it to direct a sequel of one of your more successful comedies, L'allenatore nel pallone *[Trainer on the Beach, 1984]?*

Good but *L'allenatore nel pallone 2* [translation: *A Coach Falling to Pieces 2*, 2008] wasn't what we hoped it would be. Lino Banfi doesn't have the reputation he used to have in the eighties: now he has more of the sweet old grandfather aura. Plus, he probably didn't have the age and energy to reprise that sort of role. I know he said in interviews that we didn't spend enough money but that is ridiculous. As if ten more extras would have made a difference. Probably we didn't begin with the best of scripts: maybe not having Pier Francesco Pingitore on board, who wrote the first film with us, didn't help. Maybe me and Romolo Guerrieri just don't have it anymore. When we wrote the first film we were younger and probably more in touch with what the public expected from that sort of film.

Your favorite appearance in one of your films? Your favorite cameo?

I'm terrible in all of them but I guess it would have to be the nurse in *The Violent Professionals*. Practically a deer in headlights. There were two nurses: I was one and the other was Giancarlo Ferrando, the director of photography.

Explain to me the genesis of Assassinio al cimitero etrusco *[The Scorpion with Two Tails, 1982].*

There was a company wanted by FIAT and Montezemolo who decided to create a television channel and wanted to create a library of films. They commissioned Dania to make this series, a long mini-series, seven or eight episodes, each one thirty minutes long. With Gastaldi we conceived the script in such a way that the story could be adapted to a film, a normal feature-length film. I've read articles that say that the idea of re-editing it was a subsequent idea but it's false. Right from the beginning we decided to make something that was re-adaptable. I took six months to direct the whole series and we managed to hand it over on time and within the budget that had been decided. A year passes by and nothing seemed to happen. We were then told that this new channel, wanted and sponsored by the Agnelli family—probably in opposition to the rise of Berlusconi—was not going to materialize. The episodes as they were conceived have never been used and the negatives have deteriorated a little bit, confirming the legend that the Etruscans bring bad luck. I know that the series was bought by Fininvest that asked to re-edit it from seven or eight episodes down to four ... I know they played around with it for some time, but I never participated in this phase. I never even watched the new versions. I know it was shown on television at one point. I can tell you though, for a fact, that the original version has never been screened anywhere, it has never been shown. Mino Loy might know what happened to it but as far as I know that version is very much ruined, due to bad handling and incorrect maintenance. In the Dania archives I believe we still have the shorter versions.

What do you think of the film?

It wasn't a cheap film, on the contrary there was quite a big capital invested in the project. I think the strongest element is the production design: Antonello Geleng is an extraordinary artist and his work on the film is impressive. The locations and set pieces I would say are the best qualities the film can boast. The cast is a little weak, or should I say a bit of a mixed bag. Claudio Cassinelli is in it and Elvire Audray, who years later committed suicide. She was sweet but pathologically obsessed with being at the center of attention. She would ask me, plead with me, to have more close-ups.

Towards the end of the eighties you continue to be quite prolific.

In the first years of Mediaset they commissioned a lot of projects for the foreign market. The budgets weren't particularly high but I think the results were satisfactory and they are all films that were sold everywhere, all over the world. In Italy they were pretty much ignored but elsewhere they would make decent money. Italian cinema was already in deep crises.

From that whole stock of films, a particularly strange title is **American risciò** *[***American Tiger,** *a.k.a.* **American Rickshaw,** *1990].*

It had an anonymous protagonist and just a few little-known Italian actors but nobody particularly important. Plus, the Americans had, by then, resources we could only dream of. I made the film in Miami, which is a location I would often use for my films in that period. Shooting in August there is an infernal experience because of the dreadful heat ... though this goes for most of the States, like in Arizona where if you put your hand on the hood of the car you would get a severe burn.... With Donald Pleasence, apart from this, I also did *Casablanca Express*. I can tell you an anecdote. The Americans, despite their resources, don't have a strong improvisational spirit. Specifically Pleasence, who in the film had some sort of supernatural powers, in a scene we shot in a theater was supposed to generate this strong wind. On the day we were going to shoot this scene, with the support of an American crew, we find out that the two machines that were going to create this terrible wind which would make everything fly all over the place, couldn't fit in the theater. The American production coordinator came to me and said, "We've

Massimo Antonello Geleng's original post-production sketch for Martino's *American Tiger*, 1990 (courtesy Massimo Antonello Geleng).

lost a day's work." I am a director who has always had to worry about the production aspect of things and have always found a way to get the daily plan done. Losing a day means a catastrophe and American crews aren't cheap. So I had the idea of changing the scene. The character, instead of doing what was in the script, starts grunting deeply and menacingly like an animal. The final result might be comical but it works. For Americans, this attitude is incomprehensible. After having finished the daily schedule early, I would ask to continue shooting but they looked at me, incredulous. It's a way of working they can't conceive. I don't know if things have changed, but when I was working there and I did many films with them, maybe with small budgets, but with American crews. The production department's logic was "you do what's in the daily schedule and nothing more." When working there you also had to be careful with the unions, especially with actors. If you had an extra and you gave him a line, then his fee would go from $50 to $300 because he moves to a new category. You had to be careful with that sort of stuff. When I did films there, I lived a great conflict. I had my Italian approach which had to adapt to their way of thinking.

What kind of person was Pleasence?

Donald Pleasence, like all American actors, was extraordinary. Sure, he was British, but this goes for all Anglo-Saxons. They respect the directors' wishes ... even great names like Glenn Ford, who once asked, "Can I change this line?" An Italian actor would have done it without even telling you. They were extremely respectful. This goes for actors I've worked with like Joseph Cotten and Ford, who are two legends for me. In Italy this isn't as common because the director is seen as the factotum of the set. In the States what the director says is law. If he says the scene has to be finished within the day, the scene has to be finished within the day. Though, if he manages to finish early, then he has to go home! [He laughs.]

You are the only Italian to have directed Nicole Kidman.

Yes, for *Un'australiana a Roma* [translation: *An Australian in Rome*, 1987], a TV movie which was commissioned by RAI. She was extraordinary. Remember she was incredibly young when I met her but she was already primed like a consummate professional and technically she was perfect. She was nineteen but she knew all the lenses, she knew how to calibrate her expressions on the basis of what type of shot I was going to do. I remember that we were shooting a scene in which she had to get up from a chair and run towards her boyfriend, played by Massimo Ciavarro, and without telling her anything, she had already timed the sequence and knew when she had to slow down the action to give the focus puller the time to change the focalization. I've worked with big names, both American and Italian, with decades of experience who weren't as prepared as she was at nineteen. Another incredibly able actress was Annie Girardot, who was already suffering from Alzheimer's when I worked with her. She was wonderful and I feel very close to her condition.... My wife suffers from the same disease. It was an incredible experience to discover this. A tragic one, but incredible nonetheless. It has drawn me very close to her. To feel that kind of fragility in someone you have shared your life with is something shattering.

How is she now? Stable?

The illness is degenerating but I've been told, that compared to other cases, she is holding up quite well. I made the mistake of reading too many books on the subject.

Anyway, she is still at home and until I can, she will stay there. I hope I don't have to put her in a clinic. That, more than anything, would be terrible for me. She was a very bright and intelligent woman, she would help me in many aspects of my life, including my work. She spoke languages, she was very fluent in English, definitely more than me. I never imagined we would spend the last part of our lives like this. I envisioned ourselves travelling the world together ... not this. Being oblivious, my wife will forget how to swallow properly, because that happens as well. This is one of the reasons why I'm not interested in directing anymore.

Are you ever offered any work?

Yes, but crumbs. I'm not interested in directing vague shadows of what was. To be honest, I'm not interested in nostalgic projects that don't have a market. It doesn't make any sense to me.

Rome, 2016

Designing Mayhem: Interview with Massimo Antonello Geleng

Dania Film S.r.l., headed by Luciano Martino and Mino Loy, was much more than a production company, it was a well-calibrated, perfectly functioning war machine which managed to control a conspicuous part of the market for at least two decades, spewing out an incredible number of films every year, without neglecting any of the most popular genres. Though, in a way, Dania worked a lot like a factory, with a solid string of directors that would alternate themselves with the bigger names of the industry (both Lenzi and Fulci worked various times within Dania) such as Nando Cicero, Giuliano Carnimeo, Mariano Laurenti and Michele Massimo Tarantini, most of whom could adapt to the needs and fashions of each period. Needless to say, Sergio Martino was the spearhead of this factory and would, for obvious reasons, have a special treatment when it came to budget and casting. "I was particularly demanding when it came to choosing technicians and collaborators. One of the ones I would always ask for was the director of photography Giancarlo Ferrando and the other one was Massimo Antonello Geleng," Geleng (born 26 June 1946, Milan), a regular of Dania productions, owes a lot to Martino. "I can only define my relationship with Sergio Martino as extraordinary, even because he was the first to hire me as a production and costume designer on *La montagna del Dio cannibale* [*The Mountain of the Cannibal God*, 1978] and incredibly also the last, because he called me for a TV movie entitled *Il paese delle piccole piogge* [translation: *The Country of the Small Rains*, 2012], which is going to remain my last film. So, my career as a production designer, excluding my first experiences with Fellini and a short collaboration with Silvano Agosti, exists thanks to Martino. I think he involved me in at least fifteen projects, both for cinema and television. Though some I'm credited without having done much. Apart from adventure films, with him I did comedies, a genre I don't think I'm suitable for, and also an important series called *Assassinio al cimitero etrusco* [*The Scorpion with Two Tails*, 1982] which was complicated to do because we had to create a whole Etruscan world."

Let's talk about the early stages of your career.

I began my career as a painter, specializing, in the seventies, in avant-garde pictorial techniques. My father, who was Federico Fellini's friend, was asked by him to create a series of paintings for the film *Roma* [1972], so, as a painter I, together with my brother, helped my father paint the portraits of the Cardinals that appear in the defilè. Therefore I started working in cinema as a painter, and I had never dealt with production designing. I worked on this film for quite a while—Fellini's films were known for being very long in the making—a year or even more, and I fell in love with this world. Again with Fellini, immediately after, I had the chance of working briefly on *I Clowns* [1970], on *Amarcord* [1973] as an assistant production designer with Danilo Donati, and on *Il Casanova* [1976], a film in which again I had to deal with difficult pictorial creations. *Il Casanova* had a very specific and evocative aesthetic and in fact, Donati won an Oscar for the costumes. For the film I did a number of things: frescos and paintings of all sorts and as time went by, I fell more and more in love with this job. So after finishing *Il Casanova*, when I was called by De Laurentiis to do some sketches for *King Kong* [1976], I understood that the time had come for me to create original material rather than work on other people's projects and this is how I started a whole new chapter in my career, first as Mario Chiari's assistant and then Mario Garbugli's, until I was called to make my debut as a full-blown production designer thanks to the imprudent courage of Sergio Martino, who decided to involve me in *La montagna del Dio cannibale* [*The Mountain of the Cannibal God*, 1978].

Geleng proudly holding the eye he created for one of the dream sequences of Lamberto Bava's *Delirium*, in his studio in Rome (author's collection).

Were you aware of Deodato's previous cannibal film, **Ultimo mondo cannibale** *[***Last Cannibal World***, a.k.a.* **Jungle Holocaust***, a.k.a.* **The Last Survivor***, 1977]?*

Yes, the main reference for *Mountain of the Cannibal God* was Deodato's *Last Cannibal World*, even though the stories were very different. The main trait d'union between these two films is easily explained: Deodato shot his film in the caves of Kuala Lumpur in Malaysia and the production coordinator, Nino Masini, worked on both films so he was the one to show us where we could shoot, he knew these places very well by then. He had been there months before and knew the pros and cons and the possible difficulties we would incur in. Before going to Malaysia, though, we shot some scenes in Ceylon. The production of the film can be divided into two parts: the first part in Ceylon, between Colombo and the jungle of Kandy, and the second part in the caves in Malaysia. In Malaysia we had to build all the constructions ourselves, and the caves were underground, but you could only enter them by climbing part of a mountain hundreds of meters high, and only then could you begin to descend underground. Nearby there were also some sacred Batu Caves. We had problems because of them, seeing that every night they would destroy the wooden ladders we'd built to access the location. You see, we were not well looked upon by the locals, since our film did not coincide with the moral principles of Malaysia at the time. For narrative purposes the extras had to be practically naked or covered only by small loincloths and the women were topless and wore thongs that were virtually invisible. This said, there was a huge difference in temperature. I mean, outside it was really hot, and inside the caves it could get pretty cold, and all the extras had to be covered with this whitish mud, as you can see in the film, and this mud obviously had to be wet in order to be rubbed onto their bodies. They suffered the cold a lot. Most of the crew ended up getting sick with either dysentery or high fevers. I myself got pharyngitis. This second part of the film was indeed very hard but it was an interesting experience. The film had a strong cast and with some of them I created a lasting relationship, like Claudio Cassinelli, who became a close friend of mine, or Antonio Marsina... Working in certain contexts and sharing this kind of experience inevitably creates a strong bond.

This was your first experience as a production designer. Were there any complications initially?

I found myself working with a very compact group. For example Giancarlo Ferrando and all his staff were Sergio Martino's close collaborators so it was a very solid group of professionals. I had no difficulty in finding my place, first because Martino had put his trust in me and secondly I found the film to be close to my taste. In Ceylon especially we had a great time, because there is a vacation-like atmosphere there, plus we were there during the summer ... when we shot in Italy it was the middle of winter but there it was summer and we had the opportunity of seeing some idyllic places. We stayed at the magnificent Galle Face Hotel, a colonial building by the sea which we also used for some scenes of the film. For the jungle scenes, we didn't go deep into the jungle like I would do later on with *Cannibal Holocaust* [1980]. We managed to find everything we needed in the gardens of Kandy, where in the space of a few square meters we had a luscious vegetation, majestic trees and a wonderful river. Everything went smoothly, and it was particularly enjoyable.

What do you remember of the terrible python scene?

Ah yes, the cruel scene of the snake eating the monkey... It was shot at the zoo, where snakes need to be regularly fed live animals. This is what happens in most zoos, because snakes—most or all of them—cannot be fed dead animals, so the fault, if we can call it that, was to have put a cruel but documentary-style detail in the film. I don't think the scene was ever in the script.

Soon after Martino you worked with Deodato. What were the differences between the two?

As far as the relationship I had with Deodato and Martino, I must say that they were different although in a way similar, taking into account the importance of the dialogue between a director and his production designer. I have to recognize Martino's courage in choosing me on my first solo experience for a film abroad. It's one thing to experiment with a new production designer at home, where he can be replaced easily, a whole other thing is to drag him into the middle of the jungle, 24 hours away from Rome, so I'm very grateful to Martino for giving me this opportunity. Deodato, on the other hand, signed me on when I had already accumulated some experience in these kind of adventure films. The difference between Sergio Martino's film and *Cannibal Holocaust* is very evident: in the first film we were in leisurely locations, whereas with Deodato's film we were in the wilderness, in an uninviting natural context, with a surreal climate, piranhas that would follow our canoes, insects all around us, spiders that would crawl on us … it was a fascinating experience but with a considerable dose of risk.

In **Cannibal Holocaust** *you were responsible for the costumes, like you were in Martino's film.*

I don't think I invented anything. For the creation of the costumes I based myself on local consultants. In fact, manufacturing the various costumes was easy, because who can know these things better than they do? The clothing was made out of leaves which after being pressed and treated became ductile, like fabric. The result, I feel, is credible, even because the cannibals on which Clerici based his script actually exist; the Yanumano and the Yakumo are real tribes that use similar clothing. So more than inventing, I simply proposed the truth, recreating costumes actually used by Amazon tribes. In *Cannibal Holocaust*, the main aspect to follow was that everything had to be authentic, so all materials of the film had to seem as real and rough as possible. This limited my creativity, because priority was given to the crudeness of reality, especially for the images stolen by the lens of the camera, of people who were not quite professional, and from this point of view one has to recognize the miracle achieved by the operator, Roberto Forges Davanzati.

What do you think of the heritage of the film?

Cannibal Holocaust, from a technical standpoint, is perfect because it is based on three columns which are the directorial artistry of Ruggero Deodato, the extraordinary skills of Sergio D'Offizi, who managed—in a context of extreme difficulty and with very little technical support—to beautifully use tricks and strategies that enabled him to resourcefully play with natural light. Take in consideration also the fact that we were not able to see dailies, because those were sent to Italy once a week and watched days later, so if there had been any mistakes we would not have been able to shoot the scene again, and lastly the camera operator, Forges Davanzati, who managed to give credibility to the long found-footage sequences. Having said this, one has to praise the genius of Gianfranco Clerici because without his intuition *Cannibal Holocaust* wouldn't exist. To identify the importance and the heritage of the film is not easy. Let's remember that the first reaction once released in Italy was the banning of the film. After only a few weeks the film was seized and didn't become available again for a long time…. Even in Colombia, Deodato, the producers and some of the most important members of the crew were considered personae non gratae.

Now I'm going to ask you something slightly personal. When interviewed, Deodato told me about an episode in which you are the protagonist. He said he once found you naked in front of a broken mirror, let's say in an altered emotional and psychological state…

[Geleng smiles, both embarrassed and amused.] Did he say I had a gun in my hand?

Actually, no…
What did he say, precisely?

That you were talking about having been thrown into the mirror … having entered it. That your hand was bleeding profusely and that you were in the company of the script supervisor.
[Geleng's embarrassed expression turns into a pensive smirk as he slowly rubs his neck. His eyes, after having gazed around his studio, lock onto mine.] I don't remember a fucking thing about the making of that film. [He speaks slowly, the smirk still fixed on his mouth.] It's all just one big blur. I think that answers your question, doesn't it?

Yes, I think it does. You even worked on Lenzi's* Mangiati vivi *[Eaten Alive!, 1980].
[Geleng, I can tell, is still wrapped up in his memories, his eyes, now disengaged from mine, stare nostalgically into space. I feel almost guilty to interrupt his musings.] Yes, when Lenzi filmed *Eaten Alive!* in 1980 he was an affirmed director, he was very famous and known internationally. He'd had great notoriety with police thrillers and had done big-scale war films, with important actors. I don't think he really desired to make a cannibal movie of this kind…

You mean he was detached?
I mean he couldn't give a flying fuck about the film and wasn't shy about showing his feelings. He believed this sort of project was beneath him and maybe in a way he was right. He had the same attitude also on *Ironmaster—La guerra del ferro* [*Iron Master*, 1983] which I worked on as well.

Tell me your thoughts on the animal aspect of the cannibal genre, the actual killing of them.
As far as the animals are concerned, personally I'm an animalist and my role allowed me to leave. I wasn't obligated to stay on the set as the DOP, the operator and the electricians were. There was a contributory negligence, but as a partial justification I can say

Geleng's conceptual design for *The Great Alligator*, 1979 (courtesy Massimo Antonello Geleng).

that, for example, tortoises killed in *Cannibal Holocaust* are normally eaten in that area. Not only this, but they're considered quite a dish. For example, when the president inaugurated a new broadcasting station during the days we were shooting, the gala dinner consisted of tortoises and rice boiled in their broth. The only way of killing a tortoise is to cut it, so if on the one hand these scenes are incredibly gruesome, on the other the result would have been the same if we had replaced it with the slaughtering of an ox, or the killing of a lamb before eating it for Easter. There wasn't any sadistic gratification, but only the use of local habits. They're documentary moments which are there only to make the story more credible, rather than self-gratification of unnecessary atrocities.

Talk to me a little about your thoughts on Sergio Martino as a director.

I consider Sergio Martino a very versatile artist. There are two types of directors: the auteur, who works on himself and tends to build strongly autobiographical films. Great auteurs are strongly autobiographical even when they confront different kinds of films and themes. One example for all is Federico Fellini who talks about himself even in films like *Casanova* or *Satyricon*, so without using the specific structure of the autobiography he elaborates and analyses himself through the various characters. Then there are versatile directors that manage to tackle various genres independently from themselves and one of these is Sergio Martino, who could be placed in the "Kubrick current." Kubrick has proved himself to be very, very versatile. Maybe more than an auteur he is a great orchestral conductor. He manages to excel in the most varied types of films: from *Spartacus* to *Lolita*, from *2001: A Space Odyssey* to *Dr. Strangelove*. Nobody better than him can be used as the highest example of a director capable of passing from one genre to another without losing his interpretive cognitions and linguistic skills. In front of a masterpiece like *Barry Lyndon*, one can say anything except that there isn't emotion, pathos, culture and depth. Sergio Martino is a part of those directors completely in control of the medium who can pass from adventure films to comedies, to dramas and so on. Lucio Fulci would be another director that is part of this category, though Fulci was more obsessed with certain themes and iconography than Martino.

A lot of things are said about Fulci: that he could be extremely mean, especially with actors, that he would lack in personal hygiene and that generally speaking he could be very difficult to work with.

I didn't work much with him. Our main collaboration was on *Paura nella città dei morti viventi* [*City of the Living Dead*, a.k.a. *The Gates of Hell*, 1980]. Everything they say about Fulci responds to truth but like all truths there are shades of grey. Certainly he was rough and grouchy but he was sustained by success when I worked with him and that brought him to the fore, both commercially and as far his reputation was concerned … because he was always considered a good, a very good director. All directors, except few exceptions, have to be determined in their positions. Actors, in my opinion, need … I have never really been interested enough to dig into the relationship between directors and actors, I was more interested in satisfying the director, trying to interpret what his stylistic approach was, from a visual point of view. But on set I noticed that often directors, to get what they want, have to switch from kindness to determination, and sometimes brutality. They work on psychology. There aren't any rules. If the director manages to get what he wants, the end justifies the means. I don't feel in the position to define a director "bad" simply because he reprimands an actor. What is important is that everything, from a dramaturgical standpoint, fits the global vision of the director. Fulci, like many directors I've met, had a profound figurative culture. Rarely a director without a figurative culture manages to obtain from his collaborators—production designers, costume designers, DOPs—appreciable results. Because cinema is an art based on images and the feeling and sensations cinema offers pass through a figurative knowledge. Fulci had a way of transfiguring emotion through images that was never casual. It was studied and the result of a profound knowledge, of images accumulated and digested during his lifetime. I'm referring to details that can pass unnoticed. He understood how to puncture the emotions of the spectators with the use of certain colors or a crack in the wall that he transforms into a painting by Burri. There was never randomness in his choices and what he wanted to achieve. It was a pleasure working with him and ours was a fruitful collaboration. He had crystal clear ideas on what he wanted.

What else do you remember of him?
What I remember of him is that in his extravagance he was also quite ironic and even had a pinch of maliciousness, but it was the malice of a caricaturist. It's unusual that a caricaturist will underline the positive aspects of a person. He was able to understand the people around him and was able to pinpoint the buttons he could push. By doing so there was also the will to put his "victim" in a situation of difficulty or psychological subjection. To dominate his collaborators he would sometimes tease them ... but he did so with great elegance and sharpness. His vulgarity was only apparent because his culture would make this approach sometimes amusing or anyway, acceptable. When he teased me there was definitely maliciousness, sometimes even real cruelty, especially at the beginning when he didn't like me for reasons I don't want to explain. But we managed to get along and in fact we worked together once more. Though not on a film, but on a TV movie called *La dolce casa degli orrori* [*The Sweet House of Horrors*, 1989].

Does the fact you only worked with him twice have anything to do with him not liking you?
For *City of the Living Dead* I was called by the production, by Luciano Martino and Mino Loy. I had been working for Dania productions, mainly on Sergio Martino's films for some time and I guess they trusted me. Fulci though, had expressly asked for his own production designer, so he hated me before even meeting me. Things got even worse. OK, how can I put this... He thought, deluding himself, that actresses would sleep with him simply because he was the director. In his youth he had managed to get Gloria Paul, a real looker, in the sack, and believed that was the beginning of a long string of successes. Of course it wasn't. On the first film we did, he had a massive crush on Catriona MacColl, who was dating ... yes, me! So, he hated my guts. It took him six/seven years to get over it and then the same thing happened on *The Sweet House of Horrors*. I was going out with the casting director, a beautiful British blonde whom he had noticed and started to circumnavigate. Poor thing, he was truly unpleasant to look at and did nothing to help himself. His clothes were always full of stains, he would smell and clean his mouth using his shirt sleeve.

Going back to Martino ... earlier you said you have been credited without having done much. What do you mean?
Many of Sergio's films, especially during the eighties, were shot abroad. For the most part in the States. I'm talking about the adventure films, the sci-fi and horror ones.

Especially towards the end of the decade, taking me with them was just too costly for the production. So I would plan everything beforehand, draw out the design, make the models if the film required them and then on set Sergio would be assisted by local production designers. For example, he asked me to do some drawings for *American risciò* [*American Tiger*, a.k.a. *American Rickshaw*, 1990], but I didn't do anything else because that film was completely shot in the States. I have the puppet here, by the way ... that kind of ... piglet ...

Can I see it?

Yes. Now, they are nearly toothless. [I follow Geleng around his small but functional studio. A woman-mannequin, with a cigarette in her mouth and a panama hat resting on her white bald, plastic head, guards the threshold of a narrow corridor and gazes blankly towards a lifetime of paintings, canvases resting against the walls, rows of them. On the shelves among sculptures and props I notice also the wooden phalluses designed for Lenzi's cannibal movies and the giant eye from *Le foto di Gioia* (*Delirium*, 1987). He picks up a small object, not much bigger than a fist: something made to look like an ancient artifact, a stylized boar-like creature.] These are the remains of the work I did for the film. I also designed a special medallion. This was made with gypsum which time has deteriorated. One of the tusks has fallen off. These are kind of Chinese boars, a mix between a boar and a dragon. The characters transform into these creatures, according to the script I read. I have actually never seen the film. There were supposed to be these mutations but I never got to see how they ended up making them because I only worked on the pre-production. The same goes for other films, like *Monster Dog* [1984] by Claudio Fragasso. There my conceptual drawing of the canine creature was reused, completely copied, by Enzo Sciotti, for the film's poster.

Rome, 2015

The Origins of EX: Interview with Martine Brochard

Martine Brochard (born 2 April 1944, Paris) hardly needs an introduction, as she is the quintessential French actress of Italian genre cinema, passing from leading roles to small cameos with great ease. She has gone through every genre that composes popular Italian cinema and has collected an impressive number of cult directors: Umberto Lenzi, Tinto Brass, Gianni Grimaldi, Franco Rossetti, Brunello Rondi, Vittorio Salerno and Riccardo Freda. "Freda was mean, he could be very hurtful with actors. When I did *Follia omicida* [*Murder Obsession*, 1981] there was a French actor[4] that he disliked. Well, Freda, who spoke French quite well, would speak to him only in Italian, knowing that he couldn't understand a thing and would shout at him for not understanding. So yes, he was pretty bad but I wasn't one to back down. I would answer accordingly and this paid off." If one had to outline Brochard's on-screen persona, the first words that come to mind are sexual and melancholic. Brochard's delicate frame and pale complexion has often been the canvas on which to paint promiscuous, conniving women, often ambiguous in their sexual orientation: "I became very popular as the protagonist of *La governante*

[*The Governess*, 1974] by Gianni Grimaldi from Brancati's novel. That gave my screen persona a tinge of chic lesbianism. I had already played a lesbian in a previous 'nun film' directed by Domenico Paolella, and I played others in subsequent years." Despite not being her biggest role, the one she portrays in *Milano trema: la polizia vuole giustizia* [*The Violent Professionals*, 1973] is definitely a memorable one: a simple, but effective, compendium of all the characteristics that we are used to associate with the most cynical and destructive fringes of the counterculture of the early seventies. Maria (then Maria Ex after her meeting with Luc Merenda's cop) is intelligent, disillusioned, self-destructive, an idealist, a drug addict, innocent yet seductive. "I liked that role. I wasn't a femme fatale, though in a way I was dangerous. She is sweet. She is a character very much tied to her generation but she transcends it as well. Maria Ex could easily exist today."

Martine Brochard, photographed by Angelo Frontoni, 1970 (courtesy Nocturno Cinema).

How did you find yourself with Sergio Martino?

Martino was very calm on set. He wouldn't talk too much with us actors and when he did, he would be quick and precise. If he didn't say anything, that meant you were doing well. I worked again with Sergio on *Mannaja* [*A Man Called Blade*, 1977] but we never really got close. It was always very professional. I haven't seen Sergio in ages but I did meet Luciano Martino not too many years ago and I told him he was much nicer as an old man. I love it how age softens up some people.

What brought you to Italy in the first place?

When I left France … I had done ballet school there, I had taken acting classes, in other words I went through a long preparation. I have always been a believer in studying as the main means to achieve one's goals. Anyway, I started working in films and television in the sixties, then I did a film called *L'amour* [1970] by Richard Balducci, who was Italian. Previously I had worked on *Le Socrate* [*Socrates*, 1968] which received a prize at the Cannes Film Festival. Around this time Pietro Germi, from Italy, was looking for a French girl to star in a co-production, *I giovedì della signora Giulia* [translation: *The Thursdays of Mrs. Julie*, 1970]. Germi was the producer and to be precise it wasn't a film but a TV series. He chose me and that was my very first Italian project. That is what brought me here, but the idea was always to go back to France as soon as my work was done. I absolutely didn't want to stay in Italy afterwards.

What made you stay on?

I married my first husband around that time. The marriage was a disaster, but anyway I ended up staying. I liked the idea of an adventure, starting everything from scratch. I had just lost my mother as well and I needed something new. I didn't speak a word of Italian, so I really threw myself into this experience. Of course my agent, back in France, was pissed off: "What the hell are you going to do there?" "I don't know yet." My father too thought I was crazy. I mean, I didn't really have a reason to change country, but evidently I needed to shake things up. So I started working here and the very first thing was that television drama for which Germi had chosen me, directed by Paolo Nuzzi I think.[5]

What do you most recall of that first Italian experience?

I remember Germi. I believe initially he was supposed to be the director but switched to producer because he was already sick. At the beginning of production he told me, "You will have a career." I remember thinking, well, if he says so, maybe ... and he was right. I worked a lot afterwards.

What was your first impression of the Italian film industry and what did you find were the main differences between the approach here and the French way of doing things?

I didn't really understand what was going on, I was too young probably, but I could tell there was work. I got chosen because I was pretty, and I was good as well, because I knew how to act. And there was a lot going on. Also in France, but here everything was a little less organized, more crazy, and things haven't changed that much.

I mean, now there's a lot less work. But in France, everything is prepared beforehand in detail, when instead here you have technicians, people resolving and inventing stuff on the spot. For example, in France if a line has to be changed, the actor goes haywire. That didn't happen here. I mean, I liked this. I did a lot of things, like dubbing for example, before starting to do cinema full-time.

Which film do you consider your breakthrough?

That would have to be *Armiamoci e partite!* [translation: *Let's All Take Up Arms and You Leave for War!*, 1971]. I remember my agent told me, "There's a film with two Italian comedians, very well-known, good." So I went to see one of their films not knowing Italian yet and I was a little perplexed ... but I did it anyway and I'm very happy I got a chance to meet them. I remember Franco Franchi was a very nice person. It's a film that went to Cannes because there was also a well-known French singer in it. I also remember that on one occasion, in more recent years, they were awarding prizes in Florence and I mentioned that one of my first Italian films was with Franco Franchi and Ciccio Ingrassia, and later Franco came up to me and said, "Thank you, because nobody ever likes mentioning that they've worked with us." I thought that was crazy, and if you see how things developed.... As my late husband[6] always said, in this country to become important you have to die.

One of the directors that helped forge your career was Domenico Paolella.

Yes, I met Paolella during the first part of my career, and he was a very nice person. People spoke well of him. I did two films with him: *Le monache di Sant'Arcangelo* [*The Nun and the Devil*, a.k.a. *The Nuns of Saint Archangel*, 1973] and *Storia di una monaca di clausura* [*Diary of a Cloistered Nun*, a.k.a. *Unholy Convent*, 1973]. I remember working with him on the part, and I liked his approach. When I first did the audition, I had just given birth to my son and I had to do a very emotionally tense scene. I had to cry, and

Italian lobby card of Umberto Lenzi's giallo, *Eyeball*. Lenzi says, "I picked Brochard and was happy with my choice, though she was way too thin. She had been sick or something.... In the film she is practically anorexic. Remember the shower scene? There is very little eroticism in her, in that film. But she was a real actress and I was happy with her" (courtesy Nocturno Cinema).

I was very tired, and it came really well. So I did this test and there was Tonino Cervi, who was a producer, and he too liked me and so they gave me the part. During the whole making of that film, I had a good relationship with everybody, even with Anne Heywood, although she was very closed. She would go to her dressing room, prepare and then go directly on the set. With Paolella I also had a good relationship away from the set. I would meet him and his wife on various occasions. He came to see me at the theater on a couple of occasions. More than this, I cannot say, because I really wasn't aware of what his life had been previously. I liked him especially because we would work on my role, which is something that now nobody does. I have really nice memories of those two films. Even with difficult scenes of nudity, Paolella would take his time to explain to me how they'd be shooting them, the angle he'd pick, where he'd put the camera. He would reassure me. With directors of his generation there would be a certain distance ... I don't know if it depended on the age or other differences, it's hard to say after so many years. But I do remember that if I had a question or something to say, they would listen. I would always go and speak my mind, because I wanted to feel comfortable with myself, which is what I've taught my son, who is a theater director now. You never have to keep things to yourself. Always go and say whatever is on your mind. Anyway, that was a really great period for us, when there was a lot of work, when we all knew each other, when you were really stimulated and happy to be on a set.

But then things changed...

Yes, then everything changed, and when there was less money, a lot of actors disappeared. Luc [Merenda] is an antiquarian now for example, but for me, quitting was not an option. I continued, I met my husband and still did cinema but less and less. Plus, now we mostly do TV series here in Italy. Not much cinema, and anyway not with that same spirit we used to have at the time. Maybe now people are understanding how fruitful that period actually was.

Rome, 2015

Chapter Notes

1953 *A Touch of Class*

1. ANICA (Associazione nazionale industrie cinematografiche audiovisive e multimediali) is an associazione that deals with and represents Italian cinema-related industries and organizations, in relation to political institutions and in labor negotiations. Established in 1944, ANICA is divided into three sections: producers, distributors and technical industries.

2. The National Liberation Committee (Comitato di Liberazione Nazionale) was a political umbrella organization and the main representative of the Italian partisans fighting against the German occupation of Italy. It was a multi-party entity, whose members were united by a strong sentiment of anti-fascism. It was formed on 9 September 1943, following Italy's surrender to the Allies and Germany's invasion of the country. The member parties were the Italian Communist Party, the Italian Socialist Party, the Partito d'Azione (another liberal socialist party), the Christian Democracy, the Labour Democratic Party, and the Italian Liberal Party. With the backing of the Royal government and the Allied powers, the Committee gained official recognition as the representative of the Italian resistance movement, and had several leaders operating underground in German-occupied Italy.

3. Commedia all'italiana (literally, comedy the Italian way) is a film current which was born in the fifties and proliferated until the mid-seventies. Rather than a specific genre, the term indicates films tied together by a certain style and more importantly by a common approach to similar issues. Some of the traits that characterize these films are: a satire of manners, farcical and grotesque overtones, a strong focus on social issues of the time (sexuality, divorce, contraception, the economic rise of the country and its various consequences, the traditional religious influence of the Catholic Church) and a prevailing middle-class setting. Another fundamental element strongly associated with the films of this current is a very strong layer of sadness and social criticism that often dilutes, and in some cases completely annihilates, the comedic contents.

4. Peplum, also known as sword-and-sandal, is a genre of largely Italian-made historical or biblical epics that dominated the Italian film industry from the early mid-fifties right up to the mid-sixties. Often with an American or international cast, the genre has sometimes been contaminated by horrific and fantastical elements.

5. Paolo Villaggio (30 December 1932, Genoa–3 July 2017, Rome) was an Italian actor and comedian. His roles are characterized by cartoonish and extremely grotesque overtones. He is mostly known for having created the obsequious and meek accountant Ugo Fantozzi, protagonist of ten films, a role that gave him an incredible amount of notoriety in Italy.

1958 *Armed to the Teeth*

1. Callisto Cosulich (7 July 1922, Trieste–6 June 2015, Rome) was a film critic and journalist. Cosulich collaborated as a film critic with a large number of publications, and curated for RAI television several monographic film cycles on Japanese cinema, New Hollywood, Billy Wilder, Josef von Sternberg, Yasujirō Ozu and sports films. He was also active as a screenwriter for a number of films, notably Mario Bava's *Terrore nello spazio* (*Planet of the Vampires*, 1965).

2. Kaufman & Lerner was one of the biggest agencies working in Italy in the fifties and sixties. Founded by Hank Kaufmann and Gene Lerner, the agency became, from 1953, protagonists of the "Hollywood on the Tiber" era, having under contract many big American stars of the time. They were involved in numerous co-productions and were particularly known for peplums.

3. Optalidon is a medicine which is generally used for the symptomatic treatment of painful conditions such as headache, joint and muscular rheumatism, toothache, menstrual cramps and pains in general. Considered dangerous when used for extended periods because of it can create an addiction caused by the high presence of barbiturates and caffeine that in some cases provoke hyper-excitability. Considered particularly dangerous when taken with alcohol.

4. Umberto Lenzi created the literary figure of Bruno Astolfi, an antifascist private detective active in the forties who moves in and around the world of cinema in an attempt to solve intricate and violent crimes. Lenzi's novels mix real wartime events with the glossy reconstruction of Italian cinema. The character is the protagonist, among others, of the novels

Delitti a Cinecittà (*Crimes in Cinecittà*, 2008), *Terrore a Harlem* (*Terror in Harlem*, 2009), which takes place on the set of Carmine Gallone's *Harlem* in 1943, *Morte al Cinevillaggio* (*Death at the Cinema-village*, 2010) and *Il Clan dei Miserabili* (*The Clan of Les Miserables*, 2014), precisely set during the making of *Les Miserables* by Riccardo Freda in 1948.

5. Editoriale Corno was an Italian comics publisher, famous for having introduced and made popular in Italy the characters of Marvel Comics and for creating original characters such as Kriminal, Satanik and Alan Ford. It was founded by Andrea Corno and Luciano Secchi (better known as Max Bunker) in 1962 and went bankrupt and closed in 1984. The character of Kriminal, generated by the success of Diabolik, was created in 1964, drawn by Magnus (Roberto Raviola) following stories created by Bunker. The same duo, in that same year, create Satanik as well.

6. Dania Film was founded by Luciano Martino, brother of Sergio, and Mino Loy in 1972. In the course of its intense activity it produced and distributed more than 350 films. Specialized mainly in genre cinema, it went through every phase: from police thrillers to gialli, from sex comedies to cannibal movies. Dania is responsible for having launched the careers of numerous actors and actresses, among which are Edwige Fenech (the long-term companion of Luciano Martino), Luc Merenda and Gloria Guida. Michele Massimo Tarantini, Nando Cicero, Umberto Lenzi, Sergio Martino, of course, and Mariano Laurenti are just some of the directors who have made films produced by Dania.

7. Irpinia is a region of the Apennine Mountains around Avellino, a town in Campania, Southern Italy, about 40 km east of Naples. On 23 November 1980 there was an earthquake which affected both Basilicata and Campania. It was characterized by a seismic magnitude of 6.9 (6.5 Richter scale). About 2,914 people lost their lives.

8. *L'europeo* (The European) was a popular weekly topical magazine, published between 1945 and 1995. An attempt was made in 2001 to resuscitate the popular magazine but it ended up closing again in 2013.

9. The film by Damiano Damiani that Laura Trotter had just finished was surely *L'avvertimento* (*The Warning*, 1980) with Giuliano Gemma and Martin Balsam.

10. Mediaset S.p.A., known as Gruppo Mediaset, is a mass media company which is the largest commercial broadcaster in the country. Founded in the 1970s by former Italian prime minister Silvio Berlusconi and still controlled today with a 38.6% stake by his family holding company, Fininvest, the group competes primarily against the public broadcaster RAI.

11. Trinity is the character portrayed by Terence Hill (real name Mario Girotti), protagonist of the hugely successful Western comedy *Lo chiamavano Trinità* (*They Call Me Trinity*, 1970) and its sequel ... *continuavano a chiamarlo Trinità* (*They Still Call Me Trinity*, 1971), both directed by Enzo Barboni, under the pseudonym E.B. Clucher, and with Bud Spencer (Carlo Pedersoli) as the co-star.

12. Luigi De Rossi, better known as Gino, is not to be mistaken with special make-up designer Giannetto De Rossi. Luigi De Rossi is a special effects technician and supervisor active since the mid-seventies. He has worked various times with Lucio Fulci and in a number of American-Italian co-productions. Legend has it that his nickname "Bombardone" (literally, big bomb) was given to him for the massive and particularly destructive bombs he would use in films.

1959 *Melancholy and Revolution*

1. "Western rivoluzionario" (revolutionary Westerns), also known as "tortilla Westerns," is a specific subgenre. The films of this particularly successful branch are about the Mexican revolution that took place between 1910 and 1929. *Quien sabe?* (*A Bullet for the General*, 1967) and *Tepepa* are the forefathers. Other titles include *Il mercenario* (*The Mercenary*, a.k.a. *A Professional Gun*, 1968) and *Vamos a matar companeros* (*Companeros*, 1970) both by Sergio Corbucci and *Giù la testa* (*Duck You Sucker*, a.k.a. *A Fistful of Dynamite*, 1971) by Sergio Leone. Even if set elsewhere, these films were metaphors for what was happening in Italy by the late sixties.

2. La settimana Incom ("The Weekly Incom") was a newsreel distributed weekly in cinemas between 1946 and 1965. The episodes, each lasting about 10 minutes, were projected in cinemas before the beginning of the film. The reports would largely focus on the need for reconstruction of a country steeped in the wartime aftermath. In 1967 the Istituto Luce acquired the complete archive of INCOM.

3. The contribution of Antonio Margheriti is a hypothesis brought forward by Marco Giusti in the review presented in his dictionary on Italian Westerns: *Dizionario del Western all'italiana*, edited by Mondadori in 2007.

4. Luigi Pistilli (19 July 1929, Grosseto–21 April 1996, Milan) committed suicide by hanging himself in his house in Milan, hours before he was supposed to be on stage for the final performance of Terence Rattigan's *Tosca*. In the note he left he asked for forgiveness to singer Milva, with whom he had just finished a long and tormented relationship, for the harsh words he had used during an interview. Pistilli was suffering from depression. He is buried next to his son, who had died in a car accident in 1989, at the age of 24.

5. Luciano Salce (25 September 1922, Rome–17 December 1989, Rome) was mainly a film director and writer, particularly active in comedy. He directed the hit *Fantozzi* (1975) as well as a number of successful comedies starring the likes of Alberto Sordi, Vittorio Gassman and Ugo Tognazzi. He was also a prolific actor, often in small but incisive roles.

1961 *Jazzing from the Background*

1. Lilia Silvi (23 December 1922, Rome–27 December 2013, Nettuno) was an actress who gained enormous popularity during the thirties and forties. She appeared with Amedeo Nazzari, the most famous star of the era, in five films.

2. Probably the film version De Martino is referring to, is the one directed by Mario Camerini in 1941, with Gino Cervi.

3. Interviewed for this book, both De Martino and Giorgio Capitani state to have worked on *The Minotaur* as a second unit director. The possibility one of them is mistaken, or confused this with another similar film of the same period is unlikely, seeing both of them remember Silvio Amadio coming in to replace Mario Bonnard. The possibility there was a third unit is equally improbable so the only other option is that they were called at different moments of the long and complicated production.

4. As confirmed by Giorgio Capitani, the director Silvio Amadio was replaced by Mario Bonnard.

5. Franco Rossi's first attempt to direct his adaption of *The Odyssey* fell short and he only managed to bring the project to life in 1968.

6. Sergio Sollima (1 April 1921, Rome–1 July 2015, Rome), passed away after this interview was conducted.

7. Walter Chiari (8 March 1924, Verona–20 December 1991, Milan) was a hugely popular actor, comedian and showman in the fifties. He achieved a certain degree of international success in films such as *The Little Hut* (1957), *Bonjour Tristesse* (1958), *Chimes at Midnight* (1966), and *The Valachi Papers* (1972). He appeared opposite Anna Magnani in Luchino Visconti's film *Bellissima* (1951). In the late 1950s and '60s he was one of the main protagonists of the "Dolce Vita," the glitzy and glamorous Italian jet-set, centered in Rome and especially focused on the booming cinema industry in which he was so at ease. During the making of *The Little Hut* he met Ava Gardner (still formally married to Frank Sinatra but already estranged from him), and started a passionate and tumultuous relationship with the American superstar. Unlike many Italian actors of the time, he had a full and fluent command of English that he put to good use in his Broadway spell, which in 1961 saw him performing in *The Gay Life* for 113 shows.

8. *The Seven Gladiators* was made in 1962 and directed by Spanish director Pedro Lazaga. The concept of the film described by De Martino was resumed in a singular and peculiar attempt to revitalize the peplum genre. In 1983 Bruno Mattei and Claudio Fragasso helmed *I sette magnifici gladiatori* (*The Seven Magnificent Gladiators*) with Lou Ferrigno. The film is part of a string of Cannon-produced fantasy epics, of which *Hercules* (1983), by Luigi Cozzi, is probably the most notable title of the lot.

9. In 2007, during the 61st edition of the Venice Film Festival, an extensive retrospective on spaghetti Westerns was organized. More than thirty films were screened. Quentin Tarantino was one of the presenters and organizers of the event that included a number of discussion panels and meetings with the directors of the films screened.

10. Probably the film De Martino is trying to recall is *The Night of the Generals* (1967) by Anatole Litvak.

11. The same year Cassavetes also starred in Giuliano Montaldo's *Gli intoccabili* (*Machine Gun McCain*) with Gena Rowlands and Peter Falk.

12. Palmolive is the brand name of a soap and shampoo (dishwashing liquid for the U.S. market) produced by the Colgate-Palmolive Company. Palmolive is particularly sold in certain countries, among which is Italy.

13. Gian Luigi Rondi (10 December 1921, Tirano–22 September 2016, Rome) was an extremely well-known film critic in Italy. Among other things, between 1993 and 1997, he was president of the Venice Film Festival. He is the older brother of director and writer Brunello Rondi.

1961 The Bitter and the Sweet

1. Claudio Volontè (12 January 1934, Rome–16 September 1977, Rome), also known as Claudio Camaso, was the brother of the better known Gian Maria and an actor with a curious and troubled life story. He committed suicide in prison, after having caused the death of set electrician Vincenzo Mazza, who was trying to calm a fight between Volontè and his wife, Verena Baer.

2. Among the films made during the seventies worth mentioning we also find *Sono stato un agente C.I.A* (*Covert Action*, 1978), which despite laudable intentions of critical analysis regarding U.S. intelligence agencies during the Cold War, is almost immediately transformed into a spy adventure, definitely well made, but where the political dimension is watered down and becomes harmless; however, what stands out is the performance of a beautifully confused David Janssen, in the role of a former secret agent. Guerrieri's best productions are now behind us.

3. Marino Girolami (1 February 1914, Rome–20 February 1994, Rome) was one of the most prolific directors of his generation, being responsible for nearly eighty titles. He specialized for the most part in comedies, although some films made in the seventies and eighties made him a popular name internationally: crime action films, often starring Maurizio Merli; *Roma violenta* (*Violent Rome*, 1975) being the best example. Another well-known film directed by Marino Girolami is the exploitation horror-splatter *Zombi Holocaust* (*Doctor Butcher M.D.*, a.k.a. *Zombie Holocaust*, a.k.a. *Zombie 3*, 1980). This film, like others, was signed by Girolami as Frank Martin. Another pseudonym often used by the director is Franco Martinelli.

4. Another director who worked as an "associate director" for Giuseppe De Santis was Giulio Petroni on the film *Un marito per Anna Zaccheo* (*A Husband for Anna*, 1953).

5. Peter Falk's wife, when working on *Italiani brava gente*, was Alyce Mayo. The two got married on the 17th of April 1960 and divorced on the 28th of May in 1976. They had two children together.

6. Giorgio Capitani directed Vittorio Gassman in 1969, a year before Guerrieri, in the satirical comedy *L'arcangelo* (*The Archangel*), also produced by Mario Cecchi Gori, with whom Gassman was under contract.

7. "The Circeo massacre," which occurred in 1975, is considered one of the most heinous crimes in contemporary Italian history. Donatella Colasanti

(1958–2005), seventeen, and nineteen-year-old Rosaria Lopez (1956–1975), two friends living in Rome, were invited to a party by Gianni Guido, Angelo Izzo and Andrea Ghirra, wealthy members of the capital's upper class. The party was supposed to take place at Villa Moresca, owned by the family of the latter and located on the promontory of Circeo. The two girls were drugged, tortured and repeatedly raped. Lopez was savagely killed, Colasanti was dumped and thought dead. The brutality, the misogynistic violence and social stature of the three criminals have made this one of the most covered and followed cases in recent history, becoming common knowledge and influencing popular culture. Numerous films have taken inspiration from the tragic facts surrounding what has gone down in history as "the Circeo massacre."

8. Diego Abatantuono (born 20 May 1955, Milan) is a famous actor and comedian. Artistically born in the Milanese theater world and nightclubs as a stand-up comedian, Abatantuono became increasingly popular in the role of the "terrunciello" (a southerner trying to integrate in the northern Milan), creating a specific lingo and mannerisms. After a series of extremely successful comedies he broke away both from the genre and the character that made him a household name. He is often found in the films of Pupi Avati and Gabriele Salvatores. With the latter he starred, among other films, in the Academy Award winning *Mediterraneo* (1991).

9. "Er Monnezza" is the nickname of fictional character Sergio Marazzi created by actor Tomas Milian, screenwriter Dardano Sacchetti and director Umberto Lenzi for the film *Il trucido e lo sbirro* (*Tough Cop*, a.k.a. *Free Hand for a Tough Cop*, a.k.a. *The Numbskull and the Cop*, 1976). A role that he later played several more times, in Lenzi's *La banda del gobbo* (*Brothers Till We Die*, 1978) which is sort of a sequel to *Tough Cop* and *La banda del trucido* (*Destruction Force*, 1977) by Stelvio Massi. The character is still famous in Italy and is the role most associated to Milian.

10. Elena Silvia Petroni (11 October 1947, Colombo, Sri Lanka) was a prolific script supervisor between 1967 and 1978. She collaborated often with directors Fernando Di Leo, Luciano Emmer and her father Giulio Petroni.

1962 Lovable Slobs

1. Caiano might be referring to Romeo Assonitis, a well-known distributor of the time, father of director/producer Ovidio G. Assonitis.

1967 Call Me François

1. Ennio De Concini (9 December 1923, Rome– 17 November 2008, Rome) was an Italian screenwriter, internationally known for receiving a Best Original Screenplay Oscar nomination in 1962 for *Divorzio all'italiana* (*Divorce, Italian Style*) by Pietro Germi. He was extremely prolific throughout his career, working on more than 150 films, both Italian and American. Among the directors he wrote for: Sergio Leone, Tinto Brass, King Vidor, Lucio Fulci, Damiano Damiani and Monte Hellman. He also directed, the most significant title being *Gli ultimi 10 giorni di Hitler* (*Hitler: The Last Ten Days*, 1973) with Alec Guinness and Simon Ward.

2. SIAE—Società italiana degli autori ed editori (Italian Society of Authors and Publishers) is the Italian copyright collecting agency. Founded in 1882, it is the monopolist intermediary between authors, directors, musicians, writers and screenwriters and the consumers, managing the economic aspects and the distribution of money from royalties of Italian-copyrighted products to authors and on their behalf.

3. Probably the reason for the misunderstanding that has tied Rossetti's name to *Zabriskie Point* is a case of mistaken identity. Rossetti used the pseudonym Fred Gardner for his controversial *Emanuelle and Joanna*; this happened to be the name of one of the screenwriters of Antonioni's seminal classic *Zabriskie Point*.

4. The term "decamerotico" (decamerotic) is commonly used to group and describe movies of a highly sexual nature, set mainly in late medieval Italy and narrating the raunchy escapades of both peasants and clergymen. The subgenre is made up of about fifty films made between 1972 and 1976; the apex was in 1972, when more than 30 films found distribution. The "decamerotici" are considered among the main precursors of the "commedia sexy" (sex comedies) and were generated in the wake of the success of the first two films by Pasolini, the so-called "Trilogy of Life": *Il Decameron* (*The Decameron*, 1971) and *I racconti di Canterbury* (*The Canterbury Tales*, 1972).

5. Marina Hedman Bellis (born 29 September 1944, Goteborg) was one of the first Italian porn stars. After working in the 1960s as an airline stewardess, she married journalist Paolo Frajese, with whom she had two children. She began her career as a model in the early seventies and slowly moved to supporting roles in mainstream cinema. Subsequent experiences saw her engaged in erotic films and in 1976 she starred in a hardcore sequence shot for *Emanuelle in America* by Joe D'Amato, aimed at the foreign market. Again for D'Amato, in 1979, on the set of *Immagini di un convento* (*Images in a Convent*), with Enzo Fisichella, she is the protagonist of what is believed to be the first pornographic scene made for the Italian market. The film achieved success, also powered by the scandal of being enacted by the ex-wife of one of the best-known television journalists of RAI. Initially, in fact, she used the name of Marina Frajese, then after a civil suit initiated by her former husband, she assumed the pseudonym of Marina Lotar and Marina Hadman, among others. The scenes she did for Rossetti's *Emanuelle and Joanna* (1979) were used exclusively for the foreign market and were never screened in Italy. She continued working in the porn industry throughout the eighties and into the nineties. In 1991 she seemed to disappear completely and has never been interviewed.

6. Carlo Verdone (born 17 November 1950, Rome) is one of the most popular Italian comedy directors and actors of his generation. He has worked on more than forty films, twenty-nine of which he

was the director. A role he managed to obtain thanks to Sergio Leone who believed in him and produced his first films.

1967 Destruction in Slow Motion

1. The film Castellari is referring to is *100,000 dollari per Ringo* ($100,000 for Ringo, 1965), directed by Alberto De Martino and co-starring Richard Harrison and Fernando Sancho.
2. The Fono Roma was founded in 1931 and was the first company that managed to industrialize dubbing in Italy. It is one of the most prestigious complex of dubbing studios for the film and television industry and its constant technological renovation has allowed the company to compete on the international market.
3. The film Charles Bronson was working on, directed by Terence Young, was the French-Italian-Belgian co-production *De la part des copains* (*Cold Sweat*, 1970), also starring James Mason, Jill Ireland, Luigi Pistilli and Michel Constantin.
4. Director Giuliano Carnimeo (born 4 July 1932, Bari), often active with the pseudonym Anthony Scott, passed away after the interview with Hilton took place. Carnimeo died in Rome from natural causes (10 September 2016).
5. Edwige Fenech (born Edwige Sfenek, 24 December 1948, in Bone, French Algeria, now Annaba) was romantically tied to producer Luciano Martino for roughly 11 years, eight of which were as husband and wife, from 1971 to 1979. Luciano Martino (born 22 December 1933, Rome) died in his house in Malindi, Kenya, from pulmonary edema, a condition he had been struggling with for some years (14 August 2013).
6. The film Hilton is referring to is *Top Sensation* (*The Seducers*, a.k.a. *Swinging Young Seductress*, 1969) by Ottavio Alessi.
7. The MIFED was the Mercato Internazionale del Film e del Documentario (The International Market of Film and Documentary) and it was one of the biggest film markets in Europe. It was held every year in Milan.

1968 The Serious Caress of Frivolousness

1. *Carosello* was a television show broadcast by RAI from 1957 to 1977. The show was made up of a number of elaborate shorts and sketches, of various nature, that would double as advertisements for a wide range of products. At its peak, *Carosello* had an audience of twenty million people. Numerous directors and stars would guest in these shorts, simply known as caroselli.
2. Mario Prosperi (9 August 1940, Rome–19 November 2014, Rome) was an important playwright, director and actor. In 1966 he was in charge of the script for *The Odyssey* which RAI entrusted to Franco Rossi to direct. Prosperi wrote the pilot and was a consultant during the making and editing. Again for Franco Rossi he wrote, with others, the script of *The Aeneid* in 1970.

3. Manziana is a comune (municipality) in the Province of Rome in the region of Latium, located about forty kilometers (25 miles) northwest of Rome. Many small-budget Westerns were shot in the national park there.
4. Anguillara Sabazia is a town in the Province of Rome, around thirty kilometers (19 miles) northwest of the capital. It nestles on a small cape on the coast of the Bracciano Lake.
5. Stefano Canzio (28 November 1915, Catanzaro–1 June 1991, Morlupo) was a journalist, screenwriter, director and television author. Among the films he worked on we can cite Alberto De Martino's *O.K. Connery* (1966).
6. Gruppo di Improvvisazione di Nuova Consonanza (translation: The Improvisational Group New Consonance), also known by the acronym GINC or in some American reprints as "Group" or "The Group," was a musical ensemble specialized in improvisation. It was founded by Franco Evangelisti in 1964 and is considered the first collective of its kind. They published nine albums and participated in the composition of soundtracks. It has had twelve members, among which are Ennio Morricone and Ivan Vandor.
7. Tony Renis (born 13 May 1938, Milan) is the stage name of Elio Cesari. Singer, composer, songwriter, music producer and actor, Renis gained international success in 1962 with the song "Quando, quando, quando."
8. Between 1977 and 1978 Sindoni uses the pseudonym Marco Aleandri.

1968 Real Cannibals

1. Little Tony (real name Antonio Ciacci, 9 February 1941, Tivoli–27 May 2013, Rome) was a rockabilly and pop singer who achieved great success in the sixties. He also acted in numerous "musicarelli" directed, among others, by Mario Amendola, Ruggero Deodato, Bruno Corbucci and Mario Mattoli.
2. In 1972, in the Philippines, during the filming of the Italian-Spanish co-production of *Tarzán y el arco iris* (*Tarzan and the Brown Prince*), Kitty Swan and Steve Hawkes were victims of an accident involving vitriol which caused severe burns. Both actors remained in the hospital under observation for several months. Shortly after, the Danish actress withdrew from the film scene.
3. Paolo Poeti (born 4 September 1940, Recanati), after many years as a 1st AD and then as a documentarian, made his debut under the pseudonym Paul Prince, with *Inhibition* (1976). He later tied his career nearly exclusively to television.
4. The film, produced by Mauro Parenti, Deodato is referring to is *K.O. va e uccidi* (translation: *K.O. Go and Kill*, 1966) by Carlo Ferrero with Parenti, Lucretia Love and Paul Muller.
5. The film Carla Romanelli was working on in Greece was *Lesbo* (1969) by Edoardo Mulargia.
6. The bombing of Piazza Fontana was a terrorist attack that took place on December 12, 1969. The bomb exploded at the headquarters of the National Agrarian Bank (Banca Nazionale dell'Agricoltura) in

Milan. Fifteen people were killed and 88 were wounded. That same afternoon three more bombs were detonated in other areas of Milan and in Rome, and a fourth bomb was found unexploded. The attack was initially attributed to anarchists. After over eighty arrests were made, Giuseppe Pinelli, an anarchist rail worker and main suspect, died after falling from the fourth floor window of a police station where he was being held. The official police account stated that Pinelli committed suicide by leaping from the window during a routine interrogation session. After two long trials and numerous theories it is still unclear who really was responsible for the massacre. The event created panic among the general population.

7. The film Deodato is referring to is *Zombi Holocaust* (*Zombie Holocaust*, a.k.a. *Doctor Butcher MD*, 1980), directed by Marino Girolami. Deodato states that the film Girolami signed as Frank Martin took inspiration from *Last Cannibal World*, but most likely it tried to ride the success of *Cannibal Holocaust*.

8. The film directed by Pasquale Festa Campanile starring David Hess is *Autostop rosso sangue* (*Hitch Hike*, 1977) and was made three years prior to Deodato's film.

9. Benedetto Croce (25 February 1866–20 November 1952) was an Italian idealist philosopher, historian and occasionally also politician. He wrote on numerous topics, including philosophy, history, historiography and aesthetics. Many of his writings and books concentrate on the terms and rules of criticism.

10. Radice talks in depth about his experience on *Cannibal Ferox* in the chapter dedicated to Umberto Lenzi, the director of that film.

1969 Of Films and Horses

1. Titanus is a film company, founded in 1904 by Gustavo Lombardo, which gained great notoriety and prestige in the years following the war. The flop of the Robert Aldrich film *Sodom and Gomorrah* (1963), was one of the main reasons for film production slowing down by 1964. After a hiatus of approximately ten years, Titanus reorganized and resumed film production on a smaller scale. The company seemed to be back on its feet by the late 1980s, though, now, most of its work is being done for television.

2. *Vengeance Is Mine* is Giovanni Fago's debut as a director. It is also the first of the three Westerns he directs between 1968 and 1970. The other two being *Uno di più all'inferno* (*To Hell and Back*, 1968) with George Hilton and *O'Cangaceiro* (*Viva Cangaceiro*, a.k.a. *The Magnificent Bandits*, 1970) with Tomas Milian.

3. The film Avallone is referring to is most likely Luigi Scattini's *Svezia: inferno e paradiso* (*Sweden: Heaven and Hell*, 1968).

4. Sergio Nasca (1 August 1937, Rome–14 August 1989, Rome) would become a director in his own right. His first film is *Il saprofita* (*The Profiteer*, 1974), an erotic drama with Valeria Moriconi and Al Cliver (Pier Luigi Conti). He directed six feature length films, the last one in 1988.

5. Antonello Fassari (born 4 October 1952, Rome) is a well-known comedian, actor and television personality. Not quite reaching national fame or a leading man status, Fassari has gained, nonetheless, a lot of popularity thanks to some high-profile films such as *Romanzo Criminale* (2005) by Michele Placido and the TV series *I Cesaroni* (2006–2014).

1969 Strange Vices in Locked Rooms

1. This is the sequence in which the character played by Luigi Pistilli, a failed writer, fills whole sheets of paper with the phrase "kill and wall in the cellar," obsessively repeated in all possible graphic formats.

2. Brigate Rosse (translation: Red Brigade) was an Italian left-wing paramilitary terrorist organization, born presumably in 1970, responsible for numerous assassinations, kidnappings, illegal weapon trafficking, bombings and other subversive acts. This underground organization sought to create a revolutionary state through armed struggle and to remove Italy from the North Atlantic Treaty. Inspirational models were the Latin American urban guerilla movements. Throughout the "anni di piombo" (years of lead) that began in the early seventies and ended in the early to mid-eighties, the terrorist group attempted to destabilize the nation with murders and bombings. The events surrounding their activities have been at the center of numerous books and films, both Italian and foreign.

3. Benedetto "Bettino" Craxi (24 February 1934–19 January 2000, Hammamet) was the leader of the Italian Socialist Party from 1976 to 1993 and prime minister of Italy from 1983 to 1987. He was the first member of the PSI (ISP) to hold the office and the third prime minister from a socialist group. Craxi was involved in investigations conducted by "Mani Pulite" (Clean Hands) judges in Milan and was eventually convicted for corruption and illicit financing of the Socialist Party. He always rejected the charges of corruption, while admitting to the illegal funding which permitted costly political activity, the PSI being less financially powerful than the two larger parties, Christian Democrats and the Communists. He died in exile at Hammamet, in Tunisia. Giulio Andreotti (14 January 1919–6 May 2013, Rome) was the 41st prime minister of Italy and leader of the Christian Democratic party. Andreotti achieved cabinet rank at a young age and occupied all the major offices of state over the course of a forty-year political career, being seen as a reassuring figure by the civil society, business community and the Vatican. In foreign policy, he guided Italy's European Union integration, and established closer relations with the Arab world. Admirers of Andreotti considered him as having mediated political and social contradictions, enabling the transformation of a substantially rural country into the fifth biggest economy in the world. Critics say he did nothing against a system of patronage that had led to pervasive corruption. At the height of his prestige as a statesman, Andreotti was subjected to damaging criminal prosecutions.

4. Actually the actor Brochard is referring to is the

Belgian actor Henri Garcin (born 11 April 1929, Antwerp).

5. The five-episode television production, *I giovedì della signora Giulia*, was directed by Paolo Nuzzi, together with Massimo Scaglione and starred, alongside Brochard, actors Claudio Gora and Tom Ponti.

6. Brochard is referring to actor/writer/director Franco Molè (born 1939, Terni-Umbria) known mostly for having directed two films: *L'ebreo fascista* (*The Fascist Jew*, 1980) and *La stanza delle parole* (*The Room of Words*, 1990). He died in 2006 from an incurable disease.

Index

Numbers in *bold italics* indicate pages with illustrations

002 Operation Moon 260; see also *002 Operazione luna*
002 Operazione luna 260; see also *002 Operation Moon*
7 Hours of Violence 185; see also *Sette ore di violenza per una soluzione imprevista*
7 magnifiche pistole 116; see also *Seven Guns for Timothy*; *Seven Magnificent Guns*
7 winchester per un massacro 161; see also *Blake's Marauders*; *Payment in Blood*; *Renegade Riders*; *Seven Winchesters for a Massacre*
8 1/2 39, 208
15 Minutes 225
24 mila baci 30
40 gradi all'ombra del lenzuolo 42, 275; see also *Sex with a Smile*
La 100 chilometri 67, 72; see also *The One Hundred Kilometers*
1990 I guerrieri del Bronx 160, 173; see also *Bronx Warriors*; *1990: The Bronx Warriors*
1990: The Bronx Warriors 155, 160, 173, *174*, 176; see also *1990 I guerrieri del Bronx*
2001: A Space Odyssey 290
$10,000 Blood Money 109; see also *10.000 dollari per un massacro*
10,000 Dollars for a Massacre 109, 117; see also *10.000 dollari per un massacro*
10.000 dollari per un massacre 109, 117; see also *$10,000 Blood Money*; *10,000 Dollars for a Massacre*; *Guns of Violence*
$100,000 for a Killing 253; see also *Per 100.000 dollari t'ammazzo*

$100,000 for Ringo 89, 98, 103, 163, 301; see also *100.000 dollari per Ringo*
100.000 dollari per Ringo 89, 98, 301; see also *$100,000 for Ringo*

A Ghentar si muore facile 163; see also *At Ghentar It's Easy to Die*
A tutte le auto della polizia... 132, 264; see also *Calling All Police Cars*; *The Maniac Responsible*; *Without Trace*
Abatantuono, Diego 121, 300
Abbasso la miseria 268; see also *Down with Misery*
Abbasso la ricchezza 268; see also *Peddlin' in Society*
Academy Awards 53, 136, 175, 181, 286, 300
Acapulco 38
Accademia delle Belle Arti (Academy of Fine Arts) 165
Acosta y Lara, Jorge Hill see Hilton, George
Acosta y Lara, Manuel 178
Adami, Amleto 180, 181
Addario, Pino 180
Addessi, Giovanni 208
Adorf, Mario 68, 69, *77*, 78, 79
Adriani, Patricia 167
adventure films 21, 30, 34, 36, 50, 89, 126, 127, 130, 136, 137, 177, 180, 189, 191, 192, 199, 203, 204, 210, 211, 225, 245, 271, 276, 281, 285, 288, 290, 291, 299
Adventures in Last Paradise 62; see also *Incontro nell'ultimo paradiso*
Aeroporto internazionale 62; see also *International Airport*
Africa 92, 276
Afrodite, dea dell'amore 114; see

also *Aphrodite, Goddess of Love*; *Slave Women of Corinth*
Agadir 230
AGIS 48
Agnelli family 282
Agosti, Silvano 285
Agren, Janet 51, 69, 84, 212, 254
Aguilar, Carlos 68
Ah si? E io lo dico a Zzzzorro 185; see also *Mark of Zorro*; *Who's Afraid of Zorro*
Aida 7
Al limite cioè ... non glielo dico 151; see also *Well Then, I Mean ... I Won't Tell Her*
Alabiso, Salvatore 55
Albuquerque 103
Aldrich, Robert 302
Aleandri, Marco see Sindoni, Vittorio
Alessi, Ottavio 301
Algeria 301
Alì, Mohammed 167
Alien 234
All Out 21; see also *Tutto per tutto*
All the Colors of the Dark 183, 263, *272*; see also *Tutti i colori del buio*
Allen, Woody 249
L'allenatore nel pallone 282; see also *A Coach Falling to Pieces 2*; *Trainer on the Beach*
Almeria 53, 84, 163, 182
Almost Human 25, 32, 35, 42, 43, *44*, 46, 48, 49, 275; see also *Milano odia: la polizia non può sparare*
Alonso, Chelo 81, 83
Alta tensione 249; see also *High Tension*
Altman, Robert 169
Alto Parana' 178
L'altra faccia del peccato 253, 271; see also *The Queer...The Erotic*

305

Index

Álvarez, Ángel 135
Always on Sunday 67, **73**; see also *Una domenica d'estate*
Amadio, Silvio 11, 93, 299
Amanti D'oltretomba 130; see also *Lovers from Beyond the Tomb*; *Nightmare Castle*
Amarcord 286
Amati, Edmondo 98, 100, 103, 105, 106, 117, 163, 166, 167, 168, 169, 170, 182, 211, 212, 227, 239, 256
The Amazing Doctor G 181; see also *Due Mafiosi contro Goldginger*
Amazon 51, 52, 57, 59, 221, 222, 223, 224 288
Amazonia: The Catherine Miles Story 224; see also *Schiave bianche—violenza in Amazzonia*
Amendola, Ferruccio 25, 212
Amendola, Mario 203, 301
America cosi nuda ... cosi violenta 254; see also *America So Naked ... So Violent*
America So Naked ... So Violent 254; see also *America cosi nuda ... cosi violenta*
The American Bride 241; see also *La sposa americana*
American Rickshaw 283, 292; see also *American risciò*
American risciò 283, 292; see also *American Rickshaw*; *American Tiger*
American Tiger **283**, 292; see also *American risciò*
Amicucci, Gianfranco 169
Amore mio, non farmi male 196, 197, 198; see also *Don't Hurt Me, My Love*
L'amour 293
Amphitryon 195; see also *Anfitrione*
Anchoriz, Leo 101
And for a Roof a Sky Full of Stars 67; see also *... e per tetto un cielo di stelle*
And God Said to Cain 68, 160; see also *E Dio disse a Caino*
And If by Chance, One Morning 194; see also *E se per caso una mattina...*
Andreotti, Giulio (politician) 281, 302
Andress, Ursula 171
Anfitrione 195; see also *Amphitryon*
Angeletti, Pio 196
Angeli, Siro 11
Anguillara Sabazia 193, 301
ANICA 7, 297
Anima nera 203; see also *Black Soul*

animal cruelty 52, 53, 59, 60, 225, 280, 289
Annaba 301
The Antichrist 89, 92, 95, 102, **105**, 106; see also *L'anticristo*
L'anticristo 92, 95, 102; see also *The Antichrist*; *The Tempter*
Antonioni, Michelangelo 39, 111, 145, 180, 236, 300
Antwerp 303
Any Gun Can Play 117, 155, 163, 164, 168, 182; see also *Vado ... l'ammazzo e torno*
Apfel, Oscar 7
Aphrodite, Goddess of Love 114; see also *Afrodite, dea dell'amore*
Apocalypse domani 236; see also *Cannibal Apocalypse*; *Cannibals in the Street*
The Appaloosa 161
Aquila nera 126; see also *Black Eagle*
Aragosta a colazione 13; see also *Lobster for Breakfast*
Aran Islands 72
Arana, Tomas 242
Araya, Zeudi 236
L'arcangelo 299; see also *The Archangel*
The Archangel 299; see also *L'arcangelo*
Areal, Alberto 78
Arena, Maurizio 66
Arezzo 150
Argentina 51, 177, 178, 179, 180, 280
Argento, Dario 23, 24, 39, 58, 111, 145, 190, 233, 234, 242, 248, 261, 263, 264, 266, 274, 276
Aristarco, Guido 21
Arizona 173, 278, 283
Arizona Justice (book) 168
Arkoff, Samuel Z. 245
Armiamoci e partite! 294; see also *Let's All Take Up Arms and You Leave for War!*
Arnova, Alba 178
Arsan, Emmanuelle 40
Asia 46, 188
Askew, Luke 65, 69, 81, **83**
Assassinio al cimitero etrusco 62, 282, 285; see also *The Scorpion with Two Tails*
L'assassino è al telefono 103; see also *The Killer Is on the Phone*; *Scenes from a Murder*
L'assassino ha le mani pulite 190–191; see also *Deadly Inheritance*; *The Killer's Hands Are Clean*
Assault on Fort Texan 98; see also *Gli eroi di Fort Worth*
L'assedio di Romanzia 192; see also *The Siege of Romanzia*
Assisi 85

Assonitis, Ovidio G. 216, 230, 231, 300
Assonitis, Romeo 300
Astaire, Fred 12
Asti, Adriana 150, **152**
At Ghentar It's Easy to Die 163; see also *A Ghentar si muore facile*
Atlantis Interceptors 224; see also *I predatori di Atlantide*
Attack and Retreat 115, 299; see also *Italiani brava gente*
Attack on the Big Three 30; see also *Attentato ai tre grandi*
Attentato ai tre grandi 30; see also *Attack on the Big Three*; *Desert Commandos*
Audray, Elvire 282
Aulin, Ewa **110**
Aumont, Jean-Pierre 73
Australia 10, 52, 257, 284
An Australian in Rome 284; see also *Un'australiana a Roma*
Un'australiana a Roma 284; see also *An Australian in Rome*
Autostop rosso sangue 302; see also *Hitch Hike*
Avallone, Marcello 1, 209, 245, 246, **247**, 248, 249, 252, **255**, **257**, **259**, 271, 302
Avalon, Frankie 201
Avati, Pupi 300
Avellino 298
Avram, Chris 88, 275
Le avventure di Mary Read 31; see also *Queen of the Seas*
Le avventure e gli amori di Scaramouche 170; see also *The Loves and Times of Scaramouche*; *Scaramouche*
L'avvertimento 298; see also *The Warning*
Ayala, Fernando 177
Azalea Film 87, 88

Baal, Karin 73
Baby Doll 118
Bach, Barbara **277**
Bach, Johann Sebastian 163
Backy, Don **148**
Baer, Verena 299
Bajeau, Carmen 271
Baker, Carroll 22, 23, 34, 35, **37**, 38, 39, 111, 118, 182, 273
Balcazan brothers 163
Baldi, Ferdinando 4, 138, 141, 144, 145, 153, 201
Balducci, Corrado (Monsignor) 106
Balducci, Richard 293
Baldwin, Peter 66
Ballad in Blood 232
Balsam, Martin 90, 103, 298
Le bambole 280; see also *The Dolls*

La banda del gobbo 26, 49, 300; see also *Brothers Till We Die*
Bandits in Rome 100, 106; see also *Chicago*
Banfi, Lino 185, 281, 282
Banned Alive! The Rise and Fall of Italian Cannibal Movies **247**
Bano, Al 231
Barbareschi, Luca 63, 222, 231, 234
The Barbarian Brothers 199, 228; see also *The Barbarians*; *The Barbarians & Co.*
The Barbarians 199, 228; see also *The Barbarian Brothers*; *The Barbarians & Co.*
The Barbarians & Co. 199, 228; see also *The Barbarian Brothers*; *The Barbarians*
Barboni, Enzo 69, 95, 138, 144, 214, 298
Barefoot in the Park 13
Barendson, Maurizio 253
Bari 151, 301
Barilli, Francesco 24
Barry Lyndon 290
Basile, Nando 180
Basilicata 202, 298
Battaglia, Rik 31
La battaglia di Maratona 136; see also *The Giant of Marathon*
La battaglia d'Inghilterra 165; see also *Battle Command*; *Eagles Over London*
Battle Command 165; see also *La battaglia d'Inghilterra*
Battle Force 33; see also *Il grande attacco*
Battle of the Commandos 35; see also *La legione dei dannati*
Bava, Lamberto 56, 58, 214, 219, 229, 234, 242, 249, 269, 286
Bava, Mario 4, 23, 24, 84, 101, 136, 159, 191, 199, 200, 245, 246, 248, 250, 261, 263, 268, 269, 297
Bazzoni, Luigi 24
The Beast of Babylon Against the Son of Hercules 192; see also *L'eroe di Babilonia*
The Beatles 201
Beauty on the Beach 116; see also *Bellezze sulla spiaggia*
Behind Closed Shutters 206; see also *Nella città l'inferno*
Belle, Annie 227
Bellezze sulla spiaggia 116; see also *Beauty on the Beach*
Belli, Agostina 106
La bellissima estate 42; see also *Summer to Remember*
Bellocchio, Marco 210
Belvedere, Vittoria 280

Ben-Hur 136
Benelli, Sem 143
Benelli, Walter 206
Benussi, Femi 190, 191, 193, 194
Berger, Helmut 4, 259, 260
Berger, William 131, 257
Bergerac, Jacques 73
Bergman, Ingmar 164
Bergman, Ingrid 202, 206, 216
Berlusconi, Silvio (politician) 249, 282, 298
Bernini, Franco 140
Berryman, Michael 228, **229**
Bersaglio mobile 144; see also *Death on the Run*; *Moving Target*
Bertolucci, Giovanni 231
Bertolucci, Giuseppe 172
The Betrayer 206; see also *Vanina Vanini*
The Betrothed 93; see also *I promessi sposi*
Betti, Laura 205
Beyond Darkness 56; see also *La casa 5*
Beyond the Door 216; see also *Chi sei?*
Biagini, Isabella 195
Bianchi, Andrea 38
Bianchi, Daniela 73, 99
Bianchi Montero, Roberto 136
Bianco e nero (magazine) 21
Il bianco, il giallo, il nero 69; *Ring Around the Horse's Tail*; *Shoot First ... Ask Questions Later*; *The White, the Yellow, and the Black*
Big Deal After Twenty Years 241; see also *I soliti ignoti vent'anni dopo*
The Big Racket 157, 158, **159**, 164, 167, 170; see also *Il grande racket*
Big Ripoff 144; see also *El desperado*
Bigotti, Rodolfo 62
The Bird with the Crystal Plumage 261, 272; see also *L'uccello dalle piume di cristallo*
Bisacco, Roberto 278
Bisera, Olga 183
Bistolfi, Emo 19, 85, 95, 163
Bitter Moon 280
The Bitter Stems 177; see also *Los tallos amargos*
Black Demons 56; see also *Demoni 3*
Black Eagle 126; see also *Aquila near*
Black Magic 175; see also *Magia nera*
Black Pirate 180; see also *L'uomo mascherato contro I pirati*

Black Soul 203; see also *Anima nera*
Black Sunday 246; see also *La maschera del demonio*
Blade of the Ripper 183; see also *Lo strano vizio della signora Wardh*
The Blair Witch Project 224
Blake's Marauders 161; see also *7 winchester per un massacro*
Blanc, Erika 209
The Blancheville Monster 101; see also *Horror*
Blasco, Ricardo 128
Blasetti, Alessandro 29, 30, 93
Blazing Flowers 177, 185; see also *Milano...difendersi o morire*
Blazing Magnum 104, 107; see also *Una Magnum special per Tony Saitta*
Blood and Black Lace 263; see also *Sei donne per l'assassino*
Blood and Guns 67, 214; see also *Tepepa*
Blood Link 107; see also *Extrasensorial*
Bloody Payroll 132; see also *Milano violenta*
The Blue Lagoon 62
The Boat, the River and the People 178; see also *El bote, el río y la gente*
Boccaccio, Giovanni 146
Boccaccio '70 200
Boccadasse 179
Boccardo, Delia 158
The Body 22, 182; see also *Il dolce corpo di Deborah*
Body Count 229, 230; see also *Camping del terrore*
Body Puzzle 234, 242; see also *Body Puzzle—Misteria*
Body Puzzle—Misteria 234, 242; see also *Body Puzzle*
Bogart, Humphrey 42, 44, 182
Bogdan, Adriana 256
Bogotá 51, 221, 224
Bolkan, Florinda 111
Bolla, Richard *see* Kerman, Robert
Bologna 266
Bolognini, Manolo 143, 146, 147, 164
Bolognini, Mauro 203
Bolzoni, Adriano 79
Bombardone *see* De Rossi, Gino
Bonjour Tristesse 191, 299
Bonnard, Mario 7, 11, 114, 124, 136, 160, 188, 199, 299
Bonnie and Clyde (film) 49
The Book—The Italian Masters Return 107
Borboni, Paola 193

Borghese, Luigi 148
Borgnine, Ernest 181, 183
Borromeo, Christian 227
Bosch, Hyeronimus 241
Boschero, Dominque 66, 129
The Boston Strangler 166
El bote, el río y la gente 178, 180; see also *The Boat, the River and the People*
Bouchet, Barbara 85, 86, **137**, 146, 147, **148**
Bova, Raul 280
Boyd, Stephen 183
"Boys of Life" 30; see also *Ragazzi di vita*
The Boys of Trastevere 30; see also *Ragazzi di Trastevere*
Bracciano 213, 251, 301
Bracken, Eddie 73
Bragaglia, Carlo Ludovico 203, 206, 207
Brahm, John 27
Bramieri, Gino 191
Brancati, Vitaliano 293
Brando, Marlon 78, 161, 164, 168, 208
Brandon, David 238
Brass, Tinto 292, 300
Brasseur, Claude 18
Bravo, Ramon 173
Brazil 51, 56, 107, 221, 280
Brazzi, Rossano 107
Bread, Butter and Marmalade 13; see also *Che notte, ragazzi!*
Break-Up 205
Brega, Mario 67
Brescia, Alfonso 167
Brice, Pierre **17**
Brivido giallo 249
Brochard, Martine 265, 292, **293**, 295, 303
Broken Lance 266
Bronson, Charles 168, 169, 301
Bronx Warriors 160, 173; see also *1990 I guerrieri del Bronx*
Bronx Warriors 2 150; see also *Fuga dal Bronx*
Brothers Till We Die 26, 33, 49, 300; see also *La banda del gobbo*
Brown, Harry Joe 127
Brutal Justice 43; see also *Roma a mano armata*
The Brute and the Beast **177**, 180, 181; see also *Le colt cantarono la morte e fu ... tempo di massacro*
Buchanan, Sherry 148, 149
Buchs, Julio 182
Buenos Aires 178, 179, 180
A Bullet for Sandoval 181; see also *Los Desperados*
A Bullet for the General 68, 81, 298; see also *Quien Sabe?*
Bullets Don't Argue 127, 128, 132; see also *Le pistole non discutono*
Bullitt 157, 169
Bunker, Max 298
Bunuel, Luis 22, 118
Il buono, il brutto, il cattivo 26, 163; see also *The Good, the Bad and the Ugly*
Burma 40
Burn! 78, 221; see also *Queimada*
Burnett, Don 31, 32
Burri, Alberto 291
Burton, Richard 16
Burton, Tim 49
Buscaglione, Fred 67
Buzzanca, Lando 16, 18
Byrnes, Edd 168

Caccia al ladro l'autore 62; see also *Hunt for the Art Thief*
Caccia allo scorpione d'oro 56; see also *Hunt for the Golden Scorpion*
Il cacciatore di squali 172; see also *Guardians of the Deep*; *The Shark Hunter*
Cacciottolo, Tonino 194
Cairo 207
Cahiers du Cinéma 10, 200, 250
Caiano, Carlo 127, 129
Caiano, Mario 4, 89, 126, 127, **128**, 129, 137, 188, 200, 206, 264, 300
Calling All Police Cars 132, 264; see also *... a tutte le auto della polizia...*
Caltiki—il mostro immortale 136; see also *Caltiki—The Immortal Monster*
Caltiki—The Immortal Monster 136; see also *Caltiki—il mostro immortale*
Camaso, Claudio 110, 253, 299
Camelot (film) 210
Camerini, Mario 299
Cameron, Rod 128, 132
Campania 298
Campari 93
Camping del terrore 229; see also *Body Count*
Campo de' fiori 113, 160; see also *The Peddler and the Lady*
Campogalliani, Carlo 114, 199
Canada 104
Cannes 140, 168, 179, 293, 294
Cannibal Apocalypse 236, 238; see also *Apocalypse domani*
Cannibal Ferox 51, 52, 53, 57, **58**, 59, 60, 62, 63, 235, 302; see also *Make Them Die Slowly!*
Cannibal Holocaust 199, **202**, 203, 204, 209, 218, 220, 221, **223**, 224, 225, 226, 227, 228, 232, 234, 247, 287, 288, 290

cannibalism 40, 42, 49, 50, 51, 52, 53, 54, 57, 58, 59, 60, 61, 62, 63, 64, 199, 201, 202, 203, 204, 209, 218, 219, 220, 221, 223, 224, 225, 226, 227, 228, 232, 234, 235, 236, 238, 243, 247, 276, 278, 285, 286, 287, 288, 289, 290, 292, 298, 302
Cannibals in the Street 236; see also *Apocalypse domani*
Cannon Films 228, 299
The Canterbury Tales 300; see also *I raconti di Canterbury*
Canzio, Stefano 194, 301
La canzone del destino 151; see also *The Song of Destiny*
Cape Fear 250
Capitani, Giorgio 7, **8**, 9, **12**, 13, 14, **17**, **19**, 66, 67, 119, 127, 136, 177, 182, 185, 188, 191, 196, 198, 200, 299
Capo d'Orlando 189
Capone, Alessandro 229
Capra, Frank 12
Capri 207
Capucine 53
Cardinale, Claudia 13
Caribbean 172, 175
Caribbean Bastards 175
Carlini, Carlo 79
Carnal Circuit 101, 104; see also *Femmine insaziabili*
Carnimeo, Giuliano 108, 177, 182, 185, 285, 301
Caroselli 214, 301
Carosio, Margherita 92
Carotenuto, Mario 67
The Carpetbaggers 37
Carpi, Tito 162, 163, 165, 166, 168, 169, 172
Cartagena 221, 224
Caruso, Adolfo 266
La casa 3 56; see also *Ghosthouse*
La casa 4 56; see also *Witchcraft*; *Witchery*
La casa 5 56; see also *Beyond Darkness*
La casa maledetta 107; see also *Formula for a Murder*
La casa sperduta nel parco 59, 224, 233, 236; see also *The House on the Edge of the Park*
Casablanca Express 281, 283
Casamonica, Luciano **80**, 83
Il Casanova 286, 290
Casanova, Fernando 130
The Case of the Scorpion's Tail 183, 262, 270, 271, 274; see also *La coda dello scorpione*
Cassavetes, John 90, 100, 102, 299
Cassel, Jean-Pierre 53
Cassinelli, Claudio 26, 266, 277, 278, 282, 287

Castel, Lou 23, 24, 88
Castellani, Renato 206
Castellano, Franco 84
Castellari, Enzo G. 53, 57, 69, 90, 109, 113, 114, 117, 120, 145, 155, **156**, 157, 158, **159**, 160, 162, **171**, **172**, **174**, 175, 177, 182, 188, 220, 225, 228, 265, 301
Castelnuovo, Nino 180
Castle of Blood 208; see also *Danza macabra*
castration 52, 58, 194
Caterina di Russia 31; see also *Catherine of Russia*
Catherine of Russia 31, 32; see also *Caterina di Russia*
Catrani, Catrano 178
Cattania, Luciano 210
Una cavalla tutta nuda **137**, 146, 147, 148; *A Completely Naked Female Horse*
Cavallone, Alberto 254
Cavicchioli, Divo 83
CBS 249
Cecchi D'Amico, Suso 241
Cecchi Gori, Mario 54, 119, 120, 170, 299
Cefalù 216
Celi, Adolfo 99
Cemetery Man 242; see also *Dellamorte, Dellamore*
La cento chilometri 67; see also *The One Hundred Kilometers*
Cerchio, Fernando 127
Cervi, Gino 299
Cervi, Marina 249
Cervi, Tonino 295
Cesari, Elio *see* Renis, Tony
Ceylon *see* Sri Lanka
Chaliapin, Feodor 242
Chandler, Jeff 31, 32
Chandler, Raymond 111
Chaplin, Charlie 95, 169, 266
Charge of the Seventh Cavalry 98; see also *Gli eroi di Fort Worth*
The Chase 168
Che notte, ragazzi! 12; see also *What a Night!*
Chekhov, Anton 177
Chi sei? 216; see also *Beyond the Door*
Chiari, Mario 286
Chiari, Walter 4, 90, 94, 95, 114, 140, 141, 191, **195**, 196, 198, 299
Chicago 100; see also *Bandits in Rome*; *Rome Like Chicago*
La Chiesa 241; see also *The Church*
China 70
The Chosen see Holocaust 2000
Christie, Agatha 273
Chronicles of Cinema and Theater 193; see also *Cronache del cinema e del teatro*

Chroscicki, Enrico 74, 76
Chuck Moll 138, 144; see also *Ciakmull—L'uomo della vendetta*
The Church 241, 242; see also *La Chiesa*
Ci risiamo vero, provvidenza? 84, 102; see also *Here We Go Again, Eh Providence?*
Ciacci, Antonio *see* Little Tony
Ciaccio, Giacinto 254
Ciakmull—L'uomo della vendetta 138, 144; see also *Chuck Moll*; *The Unholy Four*
Ciangottini, Valeria 193
Ciardi, Francesca 222
Ciavarro, Massimo 284
Cicero, Nando 177, 182, 268, 285, 298
Cifariello, Antonio 180
Cinecittà 35, 53, 78, 109, 126, 135, 168, 189, 298
Cineriz 194, 205
Il cinico, l'infame, il violento 26, 47; see also *The Cynic, the Rat & the Fist*
Cipolla Colt 69; see also *Cry, Onion!*; *The Smell of Onion*
Cipriani, Stelvio 46
Circeo 121, 299, 300
Citizen Kane 31, 79
La città gioca d'azzardo 265; see also *Gambling City*
Cittadini, Franco 213
Il cittadino si ribella 157, 169; see also *Street Law*
City of the Living Dead 52, 236, 237, 238, **239**, 243, 244, 290, 291; see also *Paura nella città dei morti viventi*
City Under Siege 118, 119, 120; see also *Un uomo, una città*
Clair, René 27
Il Clan dei Miserabili 298; see also *The Clan of Les Miserables*
The Clan of Les Miserables 298; see also *Il Clan dei Miserabili*
Clarke, Arthur C. 71
Clementelli, Silvio 8, 12, 19
Clerici, Gianfranco 221, 224, 226, 230, 288
Cliver, Al 216, 302
A Clockwork Orange 175
Clouzot, Henri-Georges 21, 23, 111, 273
Cloverfield 225
Clucher, E.B. *see* Barboni, Enzo
A Coach Falling to Pieces 2 282; see also *L'allenatore nel pallone*
Cobra Commando 175; see also *Cobra Mission*
Cobra Mission 175; see also *Cobra Commando*; *Operation Nam*

cocaine 59, 60, 83, 149, 195, 240
La coda dello scorpione 183, 262, 270; see also *The Case of the Scorpion's Tail*; *Scorpion's Tail*
Coffa, Marina 23
Cohen, Leonard 166
Colasanti, Donatella 299, 300
Cold Eyes of Fear 165, 166; see also *Gli occhi freddi della paura*
Cold Sweat 301; see also *De la part des copains*
Colizzi, Giuseppe 68, 96
Colombia 51, 221, 222, 224, 228, 288
Colombo 287, 300
Colombo, Arrigo 84, 128, 196
Colorado River 278
The Colossus of Rhodes 200
Colpi di luce 174; see also *Light Blast*
Il colpo segreto di d'Artagnan 189, 192; see also *The Secret Mark of D'Artagnan*
Le colt cantarono la morte e fu ... tempo di massacro 180; see also *The Brute and the Beast*; *Massacre Time*
Il coltello di ghiaccio 24, 39; see also *Knife of Ice*
Columbia Pictures 12, 13
Comencini, Luigi 144
Commedia all'italiana 8, 67, 72, 119, 196, 268, 297
Companeros 298
A Completely Naked Female Horse 137, 146, **147**, **148**; see also *Una cavalla tutta nuda*
Con Men 169; see also *Tedeum*
Conan 228
The Concorde Affair, 1979 220, 222, 227; see also *The Concorde Affaire '79*
The Concorde Affaire '79 220, 222, 227; see also *The Concorde Affair, 1979*
Connelly, Christopher 227
Conrad, Joseph 71
Connery, Neil 98, 99, 103
Connery, Sean 98, 99, 181
Il consigliori 33, 92, 102; see also *The Counsellor*; *Counsellor at Crime*
Constantin, Michel 301
Constantine and the Cross 29, 30, 139, 144; see also *Costantino il grande*
Constantine the Great 139; see also *Costantino il grande*
Il conte di Montecristo 164; see also *The Count of Montecristo*
Conti, Pierluigi *see* Cliver, Al
Continenza, Sandro 281
Contro quattro bandiere 33; see also *From Hell to Victory*

La controfigura **110**; see also *The Double*
Cooper, Gary 180
The Cop in Blue Jeans 216; see also *Squadra antiscippo*
Copperface 21; see also *Tutto per tutto*
Corbucci, Bruno 4, 33, 46, 66, 143, 203, 209, 211, 212, 301
Corbucci, Nori 207
Corbucci, Sergio 4, 13, 55, 69, 81, 110, 115, 138, 143, 144, 145, 153, 155, 164, 165, 200, 203, 207, 208, 209, 249, 266, 298
Corey, Isabelle 114
Corman, Roger 101, 159, 263
Cornetti alla crema 124; see also *Cream Horns*; *Cream Puffs*
Corno, Andrea 298
Corno Comics 36, 298
I corpi presentano tracce di violenza carnale 262, 273; see also *Torso*
Corriere della sera 257
La corta notte delle bambole di vetro 263; see also *Short Night of Glass Dolls*
Cortes, Hernan 51
Cortese, Leonardo 12
Cortese, Valentina 196
Cortina 225
Così dolce ... così perversa 22, 39, 272; see also *So Sweet ... So Perverse*
Così sia 274; see also *Man Called Amen*; *Therefore It Is*; *They Called Him Amen*
Cosmos Killer 107; see also *Miami Golem*
Costa, Mario 7, 30, 93, 94
Costa Brava 167
Costantino, Emma *see* Schurer, Erna
Costantino il grande 29, 139; see also *Constantine and the Cross*
Cosulich, Callisto 21, 250, 297
Cottafavi, Vittorio 7, 10, 11, **12**, 138, 144, 188, 199, 200
Cotten, Joseph 44, 208, 220, 269, 284
The Counsellor 33, 92, 102, 103; see also *Il consigliori*
Counsellor at Crime 33; see also *Il consigliori*
The Count of Montecristo 164; *Il conte di Montecristo*
The Country of the Small Rains 285; see also *Il paese delle piccole piogge*
Covert Action 115, 120, 299; see also *Sono stato un agente C.I.A.*
Cozzi, Luigi 228, 280, 299
Craven, Wes 224, 226, 228

Craving Desire 280; see also *Graffiante desiderio*
Craxi, Bettino (politician) 281, 302
The Crazy Kids of the War 212; see also *La feldmarescialla*
Crazy Westerners 138, 145; see also *Little Rita nel West*
Cream Horns 124; see also *Cornetti alla crema*
Cream Puffs 124; see also *Cornetti alla crema*
Crescete e moltiplicatevi 85, **86**, 88; see also *Grow and Multiply*
Crime Boss 92, 103; see also *I familiari delle vittime non saranno avvertiti*
Crimes in Cinecittà 298; see also *Delitti a Cinecittà*
Cristaldi 175
Croce, Benedetto 49, 242, 302
Cronache del cinema e del teatro 193; see also *Chronicles of Cinema and Theater*
I crudeli 208; see also *The Hellbenders*
Cry, Onion! 69, 169; see also *Cipolla Colt*
CSC (Centro Sperimentale di Cinematografia) 27, 29, 30, 137, 139, 188, 191, 193
Cugine mie 256; see also *My Female Cousins*
Cugini carnali 276; see also *High School Girl*; *Hot and Bothered*; *Loving Cousins*
Cukor, George 23
Cuomo, Alfredo 79
Cupisti, Barbara 238
The Curse of Frankenstein 245
Curti, Ermanno 167
Curtis, Tony 166
Cut and Run 224, 228, **229**; see also *Inferno in diretta*
The Cynic, the Rat & the Fist 26, 47, 48, 49; see also *Il cinico, l'infame, il violento*

Da Corleone a Brooklyn 26; see also *From Corleone to Brooklyn*
Da uomo a uomo 67, 73; see also *Death Rides a Horse*
D'Adderio, Letizia 7
Dallamano, Massimo 128, 264
Dalle Ardenne all'inferno 99, 166; see also *Dirty Heroes*
Dalle tenebre al mare **28**; see also *From the Darkness to the Sea*
D'Amato, Joe 56, 58, 103, 150, 237, 300
Damiani, Damiano 24, 54, 68, 81, 95, 249, 298, 300
D'Amico, Silvia 241
Damon, Mark 117, 209

Dania Productions 43, 62, 63, 262, 267, 268, 282, 285, 291, 298
Dante, Joe 34, 49, 245
Danza macabra 208; see also *Castle of Blood*
Darwin, Charles 2
Dassin, Jules 42
Daughter of the Jungle 62; see also *Incontro nell'ultimo paradiso*
Davoli, Ninetto 26, 195
Dawson, Anthony 67, 99; *see also* Margheriti, Antonio
The Day of the Cobra 157, 158, 174; see also *Il giorno del cobra*
De la part des copains 301; see also *Cold Sweat*
Deadly Impact 240, 241; see also *Impatto mortale*
Deadly Inheritance 190, 191, 193; see also *L'assassino ha le mani pulite*
De Agostini, Fabio 130
Dean, James 205, 237
De Angelis, Fabrizio 108, 173, 175, 220, 240, 241
De Angelis, Guido 166
De Angelis, Maurizio 166
De Angelis, Vertunnio 180
Death at the Cinema-village 298; see also *Morte al Cinevillaggio*
Death on the Run 144; see also *Bersaglio mobile*
Death Rides a Horse 65, 67, 69, 73, 74, **75**, 76, 77, 78, 79, 81, 83, 88; see also *Da uomo a uomo*
Il decameron 146, 300; see also *The Decameron*
The Decameron 146, 300; see also *Il decameron*
De Concini, Ennio 101, 116, 139, 140, 141, 146, 188, 300
Deep Red 234; see also *Profondo rosso*
Deep River Savages 40, **41**, 49, 51, 204, 218, 219; see also *Il paese del sesso selvaggio*
The Defeat of Hannibal 92; see also *Scipione l'africano*
De Felice, Lionello 29, 30, 139
De Filippo, Edoardo 31
De Gaulle, Charles 211
De Laurentiis, Aurelio 196
De Laurentiis, Dino 251, 286
De Laurentiis, Luigi 196, 251
Deliria 237; see also *Stage Fright*
Delirium **286**, 292; see also *Le foto di Gioia*
Delitti a Cinecittà 298; see also *Crimes in Cinecittà*
Delitto al circolo del tennis 139, 145; see also *The Rage Within*
Un delitto poco comune 230,

234; see also *Phantom of Death*
Della Mea, Ivan 79
Dell'Acqua, Alberto 79
Dell'Acqua, Ottaviano 231
Dellamorte, Dellamore 242; see also *Cemetery Man*
Delon, Alain 231
Del Santo, Lory 124
De Luca, Lorella 236
Delys, Max 112, 121
De Martino, Alberto 33, 43, 67, 69, 84, 89, **90**, 91, 92, **99**, **102**, 105, 107, 114, 127, 136, 137, 151, 162, 163, 165, 167, 168, 188, 200, 299, 301
De Martino, Romolo 89, 92
De Masi, Francesco 166
de Mendoza, Alberto 182
De Micheli, Adriano 196
The Demon 267, 268
Demoni 3 56; see also *Black Demons*
De Niro, Robert 47, 59, 225
Denis, Maria 11, 12
Dentice, Ludovico 119
Deodato, Ruggero 2, 42, 57, 59, 60, 61, 62, 176, 199, 201, **202**, 203, 204, 214, 219, 220, 223, **229**, 231, 232, 233, 234, 235, 237, 238, 242, 243, 246, 247, 276, 277, 286, 287, 288, 301, 302
De Paolis Studios 210, 241
Deray, Jacques 266
De Rita, Massimo 170
De Rossi, Gino 59, 60, 239, 298
De Santis, Giuseppe 27, 72, 94, 115, 116, 127, 188, 299
Descombes, Colette 23, 24
De Selle, Lorraine 52, 60, 227, **235**
Desert Commandos 30, 36, 53; see also *Attentato ai tre grandi*
Desert Furlough 206; see also *Pastasciutta nel deserto*
De Sica, Vittorio 7, 16, 17, 127, 136, 185, 268
El desperado 144, 165; see also *Big Ripoff*; *The Desperado*; *The Dirty Outlaws*; *King of the West*
The Desperado 144; see also *El desperado*
Los Desperados 181; see also *A Bullet for Sandoval*; *Those Desperate Men Who Smell of Dirt and Death*
Desperately Yours ... I Sign Macaluso Carmelo, Son of the Late Giuseppe 197; see also *Perdutamente tuo...mi firmo Macaluso Carmelo fu Giuseppe*
Destination Piovarolo 205; see also *Destinazione Piovarolo*

Destinazione Piovarolo 205; see also *Destination Piovarolo*
Un detective 111, 119; see also *Detective Belli*; *Ring of Death*
Detective Belli 111; see also *Un detective*
Detective Extralarge 175
De Teffè, Antonio see Steffen, Anthony
The Devil with Seven Faces 183; see also *Il diavolo a sette face*
The Devil's Commandment 245; see also *I vampiri*
The Devil's Daughter 234, 242; see also *La setta*
The Devil's Eye 39; see also *Gatti rossi in un labirinto di vetro*
Diabolik 298
Les Diaboliques 23, 111
Dial: Help 230, 231; see also *Minaccia d'amore*
Diary of a Cloistered Nun 294; see also *Storia di una monaca di clausura*
Il diavolo a sette facce 183; see also *The Devil with Seven Faces*
A Difficult Widow 178; see also *Una viuda difícil*
Di Gregorio, Marco see Gregory, Mark
Di Leo, Fernando 13, 14, 25, 42, 67, 112, 113, 121, 122, 143, 180, 300
Di Leo, Grazia 180
Dionisio, Silvia 191, 210, 212, 214, 216, 220, 226
Dionisio, Sofia 216
Dirty Harry 91, 157, 274, 281
Dirty Heroes 99, 166; see also *Dalle Ardenne all'inferno*
The Dirty Outlaws 135, 144, 145, 146, 147, 153, 165; see also *El desperado*
Dirty Pictures 22; see also *Un posto ideale per uccidere*
Il ditto nella piaga 183; see also *The Liberators*
Di Valmarana, Paolo 62
The Divorce 119; see also *Il divorzio*
Divorce, Italian Style 300; see also *Divorzio all'italiana*
Il divorzio 119; see also *The Divorce*
Divorzio all'italiana 300; see also *Divorce, Italian Style*
Dizionario del Western all'italiana 298
Django 135, 138, 143, 144, 155, 203, 209, 266
Django Kill! 159-160; see also *Se sei vivo spara*
Django Kill...If You Live, Shoot!

159-160; see also *Se sei vivo spara*
Django, Prepare a Coffin 138, 141, **142**, 143; see also *Preparati la bara*
Django Shoots First 99; see also *Django spara per primo*
Django spara per primo 99; see also *Django Shoots First*
Dmytryk, Edward 37, 266
Do Not Commit Impure Acts 85; see also *Non commettere atti impuri*
Doctor and the Healer 151; see also *Il medico e lo stregone*
Doctor Butcher M.D. 299, 302; see also *Zombi Holocaust*
Dr. No 171
Dr. Strangelove 290
Dodsworth 40
D'Offizi, Sergio 209, 288
La dolce casa degli orrori 291; see also *The Sweet House of Horrors*
Il dolce corpo di Deborah 22, 38, 111, 118, 182, 272; see also *The Sweet Body of Deborah*
La dolce vita 39, 93
The Dolls 280; see also *Le bambole*
Dolman, Martin see Martino, Sergio
Una domenica d'estate 67, 73; see also *Always on Sunday*
Dominguez, Joaquin 88
Dominici, Franco 207
Donati, Danilo 286
Donati, Sergio 106
Donne, botte e bersaglieri 211; see also *A Man Only Cries for Love*
Don't Hurt Me, My Love 196, 197; see also *Amore mio, non farmi male*
Dorelli, Johnny 92, 180, 281
Doria, Enzo 172
The Double **110**; see also *La controfigura*
Douglas, Gordon 38
Douglas, Kirk 90, 100, 106
Down with Misery 268; see also *Abbasso la miseria*
Dracula 245
The Dragon Strikes Back 129, 130; see also *Il mio nome è Shanghai Joe*
Dragonwyck 23
Drake, Tom 190, 193, 194
Duck, You Sucker 89, **90**, 96, 298; see also *Giù la testa*
Due contro tutti 90, 94; see also *Terrible Sheriff*; *Two Against All*
Duel at Rio Grande 127; see also *Il segno di Zorro*

Duel in the Sun 44
Duel of Fire 21, 31; see also *Duello nella sila*
Duel of the Titans 138; see also *Romolo e Remo*
Duello nel Texas 128; see also *Gunfight at Red Sands*; *Gunfight in the Red Sands*
Duello nella sila 21, 31, 32; see also *Duel of Fire*
Duperey, Annie 53

E Dio disse a Caino 68, 160; see also *And God Said to Cain*
... e per tetto un cielo di stelle 67; see also *And for a Roof a Sky Full of Stars*; *A Sky Full of Stars for a Roof*
E se per caso una mattina... 194; see also *And If by Chance, One Morning*
Eagles Over London 165, 169; see also *La battaglia d'Inghilterra*
Eastwood, Clint 76, 128, 155, 265
Eaten Alive! 21, 27, 49, **50**, 51, 53, 57, 289; see also *Mangiati vivi*
L'ebreo fascista 303; see also *The Fascist Jew*
Eco, Umberto 250
Edinburgh 71
Edipo Re 30; see also *Oedipus Rex*
Edwards, Blake 8
Egypt 1, 130, 131, 207
Eisenstein, Sergei 27
Ekberg, Anita 31
Eleven Days, Eleven Nights 237, 241
Elisir d'amore 92; see also *The Love Potion*
Emanuelle and Joanna 148, 150, 300; see also *Il mondo porno di due sorelle*
Era notte a Roma 205; see also *Escape by Night*
Ercole, Sandone, maciste e Ursus gli invincibili 10; see also *Samson and His Mighty Challenge*
L'eroe di Babilonia 192; see also *The Beast of Babylon Against the Son of Hercules*; *Goliath, King of Slaves*; *Hero of Babylon*
Gli eroi di Fort Worth 98; see also *Assault on Fort Texan*; *Charge of the Seventh Cavalry*; *Heroes of Fort Worth*
eroticism 23, 38, 87, 88, 101, 104, 118, 132, 135, 145, 150, 187, 204, 214, 227, 231, 235, 237, 244, 246, 253, 261, 271, 273, 280, 295, 300, 302

Escape by Night 205; see also *Era notte a Roma*
Escape from New York 160
Escape from the Bronx 160; see also *Fuga dal Bronx*
Estrada, Erik 167, 174
Ettore lo fusto 166; see also *Hector the Mighty*
Europe 7, 10, 21, 23, 42, 45, 51, 65, 70, 71, 91, 95, 100, 119, 160, 254, 271, 301
The European 298; see also *L'Europeo*
L'Europeo 298; see also *The European*
Eutanasia di un amore 205; see also *Euthanasia of a Love*
Euthanasia of a Love 205; see also *Eutanasia di un amore*
Evangelisti, Franco 301
Everett, Rupert 242
Evil's Commandment 245; see also *I vampiri*
Execution Squad 24, 112, 157, 169, 264, 274; see also *La polizia ringrazia*
Executioners 169, 264; see also *La polizia ringrazia*
The Exorcist 91, 105, 106
Extrasensorial 107; see also *Blood Link*; *The Link*
Eye, Evil Eye, Parsley and Fennel 281; see also *Occhio, malocchio, prezzemolo e finocchio*
Eyeball 39, **295**; see also *Gatti rossi in un labirinto di vetro*

Fabrizi, Aldo 113, 160
The Factotum 140; see also *Il portaborse*
Faenza, Roberto 210
Fago, Giovanni 247, 252, 253, 302
Fajardo, Eduardo 172
Falk, Peter 116, 299
Falk, Rossella 103
Falstaff—Chimes at Midnight 191
I familiari delle vittime non saranno avvertiti 92, 103; see also *Crime Boss*
Fani, Leonora 167, 198
Fantozzi 297, 298
Farmer, Mimsy 220
Fascism 2, 7, 35, 49, 64, 67, 120, 121, 126, 138, 188, 303
The Fascist Jew 303; see also *L'ebreo fascista*
Fassari, Antonello 257, 302
Fassbinder, Rainer W. 23
Father Jackleg 169; see also *Tedeum*
Le fatiche di Ercole 199; see also *Hercules*
Feldman, Marty 236
La feldmarescialla 212; see also *The Crazy Kids of the War*

Felicioni, Felice 151
Felisatti, Massimo 132
Fellini, Federico 39, 78, 160, 195, 200, 202, 208, 250, 281, 285, 286, 290
The Female Bodyguard 124; see also *La gorilla*
Femmine insaziabili 101; see also *Carnal Circuit*
Fenech, Edwige 183, 230, 231, 263, 270, 271, **272**, 273, **274**, 275, 298, 301
Fenomenal and the Treasure of Tutankamen 210, 211, 213; see also *Fenomenal e il tesoro di Tutankamen*
Fenomenal e il tesoro di Tutankamen 210; see also *Fenomenal and the Treasure of Tutankamen*
Ferrando, Giancarlo 186, 282, 285, 287
Ferrara, Romano 210
Ferrer, Mel 45, 54, 55, 90, 106
Ferreri, Marco 38, 176, 182
Ferrero, Carlo 301
Ferrigno, Lou 167, 299
Ferrio, Gianni 178
Ferroni, Giorgio 203, 209
Ferzetti, Gabriele 11, 197
Festa Campanile, Pasquale 66, 67, 72, 148, 227, 302
A Few Dollars for Django 162, 163; see also *Pochi dollari per Django*
La fiamma che non si spegne 11; see also *The Flame That Can't Be Extinguished*
Fidani, Demofilo 208
The Fighting Fists of Shanghai Joe 129, 130; see also *Il mio nome è Shanghai Joe*
I figli della luna 224; see also *Sons of the Moon*
Il figlio di Spartacus 200, 207; see also *The Slave*; *The Son of Spartacus*
Figueroa, Alberto Vazquez 172
Filmirage 56
Fiorentini, Stenio 213
The Final Contract 115, **123**; see also *Due vite, un destino*
The Final Executioner 124; see also *L'ultimo guerriero*
Fininvest see Mediaset
First Blood (book) 43
Fisher, Terence 245
Fisichella, Enzo 300
A Fistful of Dollars 43, 127, 128, 132; see also *Per un pugno di dollari*
Il fiume del grande caimano 50; see also *The Great Alligator*
Fizzarotti, Ettore Maria 201
The Flame That Can't Be Extin-

guished 11; see also *La fiamma che non si spegne*
Flaminio 251
Fletcher, Jenny 205, 206
Florence 294
Flores, Stefano Satta 197
Flori, Agata 165
Flynn, Errol 32, 115, 116
Flynn, Sean 116
Follia omicida 292; see also *Murder Obsession*
Fonda, Henry 34, 45
For a Fistful of Dynamite 89, 96, 298; see also *Giù la testa*
For the Love of Cesarina 197, 198; see also *Per amore di Cesarina*
Ford, Glenn 284
Ford, John 21, 31, 36, 37, 44, 60, 73
Ford Coppola, Francis 91, 245, 249
Forges Davanzati, Roberto 288
Formula for a Murder 107; see also *La casa maledetta*
Forte, Valentina 228, 230
Fortini, Filippo 95
Foschi, Massimo 219
Le foto di Gioia 292; see also *Delirium*
Fox, James 12
Foxy Lady 280; see also *Spiando Marina*
Fracassi, Alessandro 228, 229
Fragasso, Claudio 56, 292, 299
Frajese, Marina 149, 300
Frajese, Paolo 300
France 16, 18, 24, 25, 34, 35, 52, 60, 111, 114, 115, 119, 129, 132, 135, 146, 149, 152, 163, 168, 190, 191, 198, 200, 207, 231, 235, 236, 240, 245, 245, 246, 247, 261, 266, 270, 271, 278, 292, 293, 294, 301
Franchi, Franco 181, 260, 294
Franciolini, Gianni 7, 10
Franciosa, Massimo 66, 72, 88
Francisci, Pietro 95, 199, 201, 280
Franciscus, James 220, 222
Franco, Jésus 88
Franco, Pippo 231
Frank, Horst 168
La freccia d'oro 208; see also *The Golden Arrow*
Freda, Riccardo 4, 126, 136, 138, 144, 153, 200, 203, 209, 245, 246, 247, 248, 250, 251, **252**, 253, 260, 292, 298
Free Hand for a Tough Cop 26, 267, 300; see also *Il trucido e lo sbirro*
The French Connection 21, 91, 157, 169
The Freshman 153

Freud, Sigmund 244
Friedkin, William 21, 157
From Corleone to Brooklyn 26, 33, 35, 46, 48; *Da Corleone a Brooklyn*
From Hell to Victory 34, 46, 53; see also *Contro quattro bandiere*
From the Darkness to the Sea **28**; see also *Dalle tenebre al mare*
Frontoni, Angelo 293
La frusta e il corpo 268, **269**; see also *The Whip and the Body*
Fuga dal Bronx 160; see also *Bronx Warriors 2*; *Escape from the Bronx*
Fulci, Lucio 4, 23, 24, 30, 52, 54, 58, 72, 92, 136, 141, 150, 173, 177, 180, 181, 182, 183, 198, 201, 226, 229, 233, 234, 236, 237, 242, 247, 249, 260, 261, 285, 290, 291, 298, 300
Fuller, Samuel 21, 31
Funeral in Berlin 212
Furie, Sidney J. 161, 162

Gable, Clark 181
Galan, Mapi 230
Galicia, Marìa Luz 130
Galli, Ida *see* Stewart, Evelyn
Gallone, Carmine 30, 92, 298
Gambling City 265, 266; see also *La città gioca d'azzardo*
A Game for Eveline 247, 248, 254, **255**; see also *Un gioco per Eveline*
Games 23
Gang War in Milan 24, 25, 42; see also *Milano rovente*
gangsters 16, 24, 25, 27, 42, 43, 49, 90, 91, 116, 156, 224, 265, 266
Garbugli, Mario 286
Garcin, Henri 303
Garda Lake 30
The Garden of the Finzi-Continis 185; see also *Il giardino dei Finzi Contini*
Gardenia, Vincent 167
Gardner, Ava 191, 299
Gardner, Fred *see* Rossetti, Franco
Garfein, Jack 37
Gariazzo, Mario 224, 225
Garibaldi (film) 206; see also *Viva l'Italia!*
Garko, Gianni 51, 110, 117, 166, 185, 253
Garrani, Ivo 193
Garrone, Riccardo 48, 67
Garroni, Marina 62
Gaslight 23
Gasparri, Franco 265
Gassman, Vittorio 8, 18, 119, 120, 178, 196, 298, 299

Gastaldi, Ernesto 2, 42, 43, 49, 118, 262, 263, 265, 272, 274, 282
Gastoni, Lisa 29, 31, 33, 86, **87**
The Gates of Hell 52, 236, 290; see also *Paura nella città dei morti viventi*
Gatti rossi in un labirinto di vetro 39; see also *The Devil's Eye*; *Eyeball*
Gazzo, Michael 103
Gazzolo, Nando 193
Geleng, Massimo Antonello 222, 223, 226, 282, **283**, 285, **286**, 288, **289**, 292
Gélin, Daniel 112
Gemma, Giuliano 62, 68, 78, 79, 98, 145, 168, 176, 182, 197, 200, 298
General Della Rovere 136; see also *Il generale Della Rovere*
Il generale Della Rovere 136; see also *General Della Rovere*
Genoa 179
ceffa di Brabante 126
Georgia 236
Germany 13, 16, 40, 49, 70, 98, 219, 240, 297
Germi, Pietro 24, 91, 127, 293, 294, 300
Get Rita 16; see also *La Pupa del gangster*
The Getaway 169
Ghia, Fernando 175
Ghirelli, Antonio 253
The Ghost 246; see also *Lo spettro*
Ghosthouse 56; see also *La casa 3*
Giallo films 22, 23, 24, 35, 36, 37, 38, 39, 40, 42, 68, 69, 88, 91, 111, 118, 127, 132, 139, 145, 146, 177, 179, 182, 183, 185, 190, 193, 197, 214, 247, 249, 261, 262, 263, 264, 267, 270, 271, 272, 273, 274, 276, 295, 298
Giannini, Giancarlo 55, 118, 167
Giant Killer 240; see also *Impatto mortale*
The Giant of Marathon 136; see also *La battaglia di Maratona*
Giants of Rome 267, 268
The Giants of Thessaly 144, 153; see also *I gigantic della Tessaglia—Gli Argonauti*
Gianviti, Roberto 256
Il giardino dei Finzi Contini 185; see also *The Garden of the Finzi-Continis*
Gicca Palli, Lorenzo 68, 69, 81
I gigantic della Tessaglia—Gli Argonauti 153; see also *The Giants of Thessaly*
Ginty, Robert 57
Un gioco per Eveline 247, 254,

255; see also *A Game for Eveline*
Giordana, Andrea 138, 145, 164, 165, 170
Giordano, Daniela 131
Giorgelli, Gabriella 85
Giorgi, Eleonora 113, 121, **122**, 214
Il giorno del cobra 157, 174; see also *Day of the Cobra*
Giovannona Coscialunga disonorata con onore 270; see also *Giovannona Long-Thigh*
Giovannona Long-Thigh 270; see also *Giovannona Coscialunga disonorata con onore*
I giovedì della signora Giulia 293, 303; see also *The Thursdays of Mrs. Julie*
Girardot, Annie 284
Girolami, Andrea 113
Girolami, Enio 109, 113, 116
Girolami, Marino 38, 109, 113, 116, 136, 151, 160, 163, 188, 299, 302
Girolami, Stefania 113, 158, 176
Girometti, Roberto **147**, 150, 153, 175, **259**
Girotti, Mario *see* Hill, Terence
Girotti, Massimo 67
Giù la testa 89, 96, 298; see also *Duck, You Sucker*; *For a Fistful of Dynamite*
Giuffré, Aldo 150
Giuffré, Carlo 67, 150, 195
Giusti, Marco 74, 298
Il giustiziere sfida la città 25, 43; see also *Syndicate Sadists*
Il gladiator invincibile 89, 93; see also *The Invincible Gladiator*
Gladiators 7 96; see also *I sette gladiatori*
Globus, Yoram 228, 229
Go for Broke 21; see also *Tutto per tutto*
Goblin 266
The Godfather 42, 91
Golan, Menahem 228, 229
The Golden Arrow 208; see also *La freccia d'oro*
Goldginger 181; see also *Due Mafiosi contro Goldginger*
Goliath Against the Giants 115; see also *Goliath contro i giganti*
Goliath and the Giants 115; see also *Goliath contro i giganti*
Goliath contro i giganti 115; see also *Goliath Against the Giants*; *Goliath and the Giants*
Goliath, King of Slaves 192; see also *L'eroe di Babilonia*
Gonnella, Franca 256
The Good, the Bad and the Ugly 26, 117, 163; see also *Il buono, il brutto, il cattivo*

La gorilla 124; see also *The Female Bodyguard*
Goteborg 300
Gothic horror 23, 79, 101, 130, 159, 201, 203, 208, 246, 248
La governante 292–293; see also *The Governess*
The Governess 292–293; see also *La governante*
Graffiante desiderio 280; see also *Craving Desire*
Il grande attacco 33; see also *Battle Force*; *The Great Battle*; *The Greatest Battle*
La grande guerra 136; see also *The Great War*
La grande illusion 9
Il grande racket 157, 164; see also *The Big Racket*
Gravina, Carla 89, 106
The Great Alligator 50, **289**; see also *Il fiume del grande caimano*
The Great Battle 33, 46, 53, **54**; see also *Il grande attacco*
The Greatest Battle 33, 46, 53, 54; see also *Il grande attacco*
The Great War 136; see also *La grande guerra*
Great White 173, 220; see also *L'ultimo squalo*
Greco, Cosetta 153
Greece 29, 31, 93, 188, 192, 201, 212, 262, 301
Greene, Daniel 174
Gregory, Mark 173
Griffith, David W. 42
Griffith, Hugh 85
Grimaldi, Gianni 55, 292, 293
Guardians of the Deep 172, 173; see also *Il cacciatore di squali*
Guerra, Tonino 281
Guerra, Ugo 145, 146
Guerrieri, Romolo 22, 38, 72, 109, **110**, 111, 112, 113, 115, 122, **123**, 127, 136, 146, 151, 160, 163, 176, 177, 188, 190, 202, 206, 272, 282, 299
Guerrini, Mino 208
Guest, Val 245
Guevara, Ernesto 68
Guglielmi, Marco 247, 256
Guida, Gloria 298
Guida, Wandisa 29
Guglielmo Tell 10; see also *William Tell*
Guinness, Alec 300
A Gun for One Hundred Graves 22; see also *Una pistola per cento bare*
Gun Moll 16; see also *La Pupa del gangster*
Gunfight at Red Sands 128; see also *Duello nel Texas*
Gunfight in the Red Sands 128; see also *Duello nel Texas*

Gungala, la pantera nuda 210; see also *Gungala, the Black Panther Woman*; *Gungala, the Naked Panther*
Gungala, the Black Panther Woman 210; see also *Gungala, la pantera nuda*
Gungala, the Naked Panther 210, 211, 214; see also *Gungala, la pantera nuda*
The Guns of Navarone 31, 267
Guns of the Black Witch 29, 30, 31; see also *Il terrore dei mari*
Guns of Violence 109; see also *10.000 dollari per un massacre*
Guyana 49
Guzman, Gloria 179

Haddon, Dayle 266
Hagen, Ira 212
Hamilton, George 34, 45, 53
Hamilton, Guy 166
Hammamet 302
Hammer 174; see also *Hammerhead*
Hammer Films 159, 245, 269
Hammerhead 174; see also *Hammer*
Hands of Steel 278; see also *Vendetta dal futuro*
L'harem 38, 176–177, 182; see also *Her Harem*
Harlow (film) 37
Harrington, Curtis 23
Harrison, Rex 211
Harrison, Richard 33, 89, 95, 98, 201, 301
Harwood, Ronald 12
A Hatful of Rain 103
Hathaway, Henry 37
Hawkes, Steve 301
Hawks, Howard 36, 44, 49, 74
Hawn, Goldie 13
Hayden, Sterling 169
Hayworth, Rita 80
Hector the Mighty 166; see also *Ettore lo fusto*
Hedman, Marina *see* Frajese, Marina
Heflin, Van 13, 14, 183
The Hellbenders 208, 220; see also *I crudeli*
Hellman, Monte 300
Hellzapoppin' 171
Hepburn, Audrey 45, 166
Her Harem 38, 176–177, 182; see also *L'harem*
Herbert, Martin *see* De Martino, Alberto
Hercules 199, 201; see also *Le fatiche di Ercole*
Hercules (1983) 299
Hercules, Prisoner of Evil 209; see also *Ursus, il terrore dei kirghisi*

Hercules Returns 10
Hercules vs. the Giant Warriors 104; see also *Il trionfo di Ercole*
Here We Go Again, Eh Providence? 84, **102**; see also *Ci risiamo vero, provvidenza?*
Hero of Babylon 192; see also *L'eroe di Babilonia*
Heroes of Fort Worth 98; see also *Gli eroi di Fort Worth*
The Heroin Busters 157, 158; see also *La via della droga*
Herzog, Werner 14
Hess, David 167, 226, 227, 232, 234, 235, 302
Heywood, Anne 295
High Crime 157, 158, 169, 170, 265; see also *La polizia incrimina la legge assolve*
High School Girl 276; see also *Cugini carnali*
Hill, George Roy 266
Hill, Terence 55, 62, 68, 76, 84, 96, 138, 141, 165, 197, 258, 298
Hillinger, Wolfgang 256
The Hills Have Eyes 228
Hilton, George 118, 155, 168, 176, **177**, 179, 186, 228, 262, 271, 301, 302
Hitch Hike 302; see also *Autostop rosso sangue*
Hitchcock, Alfred 27, 28, 32, 44, 101, 263, 264
Hitcher in the Dark 56; see also *Paura nel buio*
Hitchhiking Tourists 94; see also *Turista con il pollice*
Hitler: The Last 10 Days 300; see also *Gli ultimi 10 giorni di Hitler*
Hoffmann, Robert 38
Holloway, George *see* Capitani, Giorgio
Hollywood on the Tiber 89, 126, 136, 189, 199, 200, 297
Holocaust 2000 89, 100, 106
Hornsby e Rodriguez—Sfida criminale 56; see also *Mean Tricks*
The Horrible Dr. Hichcock 246, 252, 253; see also *L'orribile segreto del Dr. Hichcock*
The Horrible Secret of Dr. Hichcock 246, 252; see also *L'orribile segreto del Dr. Hichcock*
Horror 101; see also *The Blancheville Monster*
Horror Castle 208
Hot and Bothered 276; see also *Cugini carnali*
The House by the Edge of the Lake 167; see also *Sensitività*
House by the River 23
House of Cards 19

House of Strangers 266
The House on the Edge of the Park 59, 63, 224, 225, 226, 227, 233, 234, **235**, 236, 237, 238, 243; see also *La casa sperduta nel parco*
Howlers of the Dock 201; see also *Urlatori alla sbarra*
Humpert, Humphrey *see* Lenzi, Umberto
Hunt for the Art Thief 62; see also *Caccia al ladro l'autore*
Hunt for the Golden Scorpion 56; see also *Caccia allo scorpione d'oro*
Hunter, Thomas 36
A Husband for Anna 72, 179, 299; see also *Un marito per Anna Zaccheo*
Huston, John 34, 45, **54**
Huston, Walter 40

I Came, I Saw, I Shot 165; see also *Vado, vedo e sparo*
I Hate Blondes 18
I Kiss ... You Kiss 30; see also *Io bacio ... tu baci*
I quattro del pater noster 213; see also *In the Name of the Father*
An Ideal Place to Kill 22; see also *Un posto ideale per uccidere*
Iguazù (178)
Images in a Convent 300; see also *Immagini di un convento*
Immagini di un convento 300; see also *Images in a Convent*
Impatto mortale 240; see also *Deadly Impact; Giant Killer*
The Important Thing Is Not Being Noticed 124; see also *L'importante è non farsi notare*
L'importante è non farsi notare 124; see also *The Important Thing Is Not Being Noticed*
In the Name of the Father 213; see also *I quattro del pater noster*
INCOM 72, 298
Incontro nell'ultimo paradise 62; see also *Adventures in Last Paradise; Daughter of the Jungle*
Incubo sulla città contaminate 45; see also *City of the Walking Dead; Nightmare City*
Indagine su un cittadino al di sopra di ogni sospetto 24; see also *Investigation of a Citizen Above Suspicion*
India 46, 50, 71, 153
Indonesia 130
Inferno in diretta 224; see also *Cut and Run*

The Inglorious Bastards 171, **172**; see also *Quel maledetto treno blindato*
Inglourious Basterds 53
Ingrao, Pietro 27
Ingrassia, Ciccio 181, 260, 294
Innocenzi, Pietro 230
International Airport 62; see also *Aeroporto internazionale*
Interview with the Brain 94; see also *Intervista con il cervello*
Intervista con il cervello 94; see also *Interview with the Brain*
Gli intoccabili 299; see also *Machine Gun McCain*
Investigation of a Citizen Above Suspicion 24; see also *Indagine su un cittadino al di sopra di ogni sospetto*
The Invincible Gladiator 89, 93, 94, 95, 98; see also *Il gladiator invincibile*
Io bacio ... tu baci 30; see also *I Kiss ... You Kiss*
Ireland 72
Ireland, Jill 301
Ireland, John 90, 213
Irons, Jeremy 244
Irpinia 51, 298
Ischia 206
L'isola del tesoro 239; see also *Treasure Island*
Israel 72
Istanbul 36, 211
Istituto Luce 151, 298
An Italian in Greece 29; see also *Mia Italida stin Ellada*
Italiani brava gente 115, 116, 299; see also *Attack and Retreat*
Italiani! È severamente proibito servirsi della toilette durante le fermate 188, 191, 194, 212; see also *Italians! It Is Severely Prohibited to Use the Toilet During Stops*
Italians! It Is Severely Prohibited to Use the Toilet During Stops 191, 194, 212; see also *Italiani! È severamente proibito servirsi della toilette durante le fermate*
Izzo, Angelo 300
Izzo, Renato 95

Jacobsson, Ulla **73**
Jacopetti, Gualtiero 64, 204, 218, 221, 225, 254
Janssen, David 115, 121, 299
Japan 60, 104, 134, 219, 220 297
Jaws 95, 173
Johnathan of the Bears 167; see also *Johnathan degli orsi*
Johnathan degli orsi 167; see also *Johnathan of the Bears*
Johnny Hamlet 145, 164, 166, 168, 170

Johnny Oro 208; see also *Ringo and His Golden Pistol*
Johnny Yuma 117, 122
Johnson, Van 34, 220
Jones, Jim 49, 50, 51
Julienne, Rémy 216, 275, 281
Julius Caesar 159, 164
Jungle Adventurer 21; see also *La Montagna di luce*
Jungle Holocaust 42, 204, 218, 276, 286; see also *Ultimo mondo cannibale*
Jurgens, Curd 13

Kandy 50, 277, 287
Karlatos, Olga 159
Kaufman & Lerner 32, 38, 297
Kazan, Elia 37, 74, 118
Keach, Stacy 277
Keaton, Buster 266
Kemp, Jeremy 87
Kendall, Suzy 38, 264, 273
Kennedy, Arthur 44, 45, 90, 106, 115, 116
Kenya 210, 301
Keoma 156, 158, 159, 164, 166, 169, **171**, 176
Kercher, Meredith 232
Kerman, Robert 50, 51, 222
Kerowa, Zora 52, 53, 61
Kidman, Nicole 284
The Kids from the Block 62; see also *I ragazzi del muretto*
Kill and Pray 74; see also *Requiescant*
Kill Bill 67, 76
The Killer Is on the Phone 103; see also *L'assassino è al telefono*
The Killer Must Kill Again **184**
The Killer's Hands Are Clean 193; see also *L'assassino ha le mani pulite*
King, Henry 126
King Kong (1976) 286
King of the West 144; see also *El desperado*
King Solomon's Mines 276
Kinski, Klaus 13, 14, 130, 183
Kirkpatrick, Harry 55
Klimovsky, Leon 162, 163, 164, 165
Knef, Hildegard 31
Knife of Ice 24, 39; see also *Il coltello di ghiaccio*
Knox, Amanda 232
Knox, Mickey 213
K.O. Go and Kill 301; see also *K.O. va e uccidi*
K.O. va e uccidi 301; see also *K.O. Go and Kill*
Konopka, Magda 65, 78, 83
Korean War 65
Kriminal 36
Kriminal 298

Kuala Lumpur 219, 280, 286
Kubrick, Stanley 169, 263, 290
Kurosawa, Akira 162

Labbra di lurido blu 29, 85; see also *Lips of Lurid Blue*
Lacan, Jacques 244
Ladd, Alan 98
Lado, Aldo 263
I ladri 136; see also *The Thieves*
The Lady Was Raped! 195; see also *La signora è stata violentata*
Lamas, Fernando 32
Landau, Martin 90
Landis, John 245
Lane, Mike 129
Lane, Sirpa **128**, 131
Lang, Fritz 23
Las Vegas 241, 278
Lassander, Dagmar 104
Last Cannibal World 42, 57, 204, 218, 219, **220**, 221, 223, 224, 276, 286, 302
Last Cut 258, **259**; see also *Ultimo taglio*
The Last Days of Pompeii 136; see also *Gli ultimi giorni di Pompei*
Last Feelings 219, 220; see also *L'ultimo sapore dell'aria*
The Last Gladiator 33; see also *L'ultimo gladiatore*
Last Gunfight 69; see also *Il venditore di morte*
The Last House Near the Lake 167; see also *Sensività*
The Last Shark 173, 220; see also *L'ultimo squalo*
The Last Snows of Spring 46, 276; see also *L'ultima neve di primavera*
The Last Survivor 42, 204, 218, 276, 286; see also *Ultimo mondo cannibale*
Last Tango in Paris 273; see also *Ultimo tango a Parigi*
The Last Warrior 124; see also *L'ultimo guerriero*
Lattuada, Alberto 127
Laura (film) 42
Laurenti, Fabrizio 56
Laurenti, Mariano 78, 268, 285, 298
Lautner, Georges 266
Lavi, Daliah 268, **269**
Lavia, Gabriele 193
Law, John Phillip 67, 69, **75**, 76
Lay, Me Me (Me Me Lai) 40, **41**, 204, 219
Lazaga, Pedro 299
Lebanon 207
Le Brock, Kelly 230
Lee, Bernard 99
Lee, Christopher 268, 269

left-wing 65, 67, 71, 123, 250, 297, 302
The Legion of the Damned 35, 39, 53; see also *La legione dei dannati*
La legione dei dannati 35; see also *Battle of the Commandos*; *Legion of the Damned*
Lembi di Albania in Calabria 72; see also *Pieces of Albania in Calabria*
Lemmon, Jack 20
Lenzi, Umberto 21, **22**, 23, 24, 25, 26, 27, **28**, 30, 31, 34, 35, **37**, 40, **41**, 43, **44**, 45, 46, **47**, **50**, **54**, 57, 58, 59, 60, **61**, 62, 63, 67, 90, 111, 118, 137, 138, 139, 146, 174, 176, 188, 190, 200, 204, 218, 219, 235, 242, 247, 249, 266, 268, 272, 275, 280, 285, 289, 292, **295**, 297, 298, 300, 302
Leone, Sergio 48, 73, 74, 89, **90**, 96, 98, 117, 128, 132, 136, 155, 188, 200, 201, 221, 223, 225, 265, 298, 300, 301
Leopardi, Giacomo 27
Lerner, Gene 32, 38, 297
Leroy, Philippe 12, 24, 42
Lerro, Rocco 170
Leticia 51, 52, 59, 221
Let's All Take Up Arms and You Leave for War! 294; see also *Armiamoci e partite!*
Lev, Benjamin 112, 121
Levi, Carol 12, 100
Levine, Jospeh E. 199
Lewis, Charlotte 230
The Liberators 183; see also *Il ditto nella piaga*
Liberi, armati, pericolosi 112, 121; see also *Young, Violent and Desperate*; *Young, Violent, Dangerous*
Life Is Tough, Eh Providence? 67, 69, 80, 84, 102; *La vita a volte è molto dura vero Provvidenza?*
Light Blast 174; see also *Colpi di luce*
The Link 107; see also *Extrasensorial*
Lionello, Oreste 213
Lips of Lurid Blue 29, 85, 86, **87**, 88; see also *Labbra di lurido blu*
The Little Hut 191, 299
Little Rita nel West 138, 145; see also *Crazy Westerners*; *Rita of the West*
Little Tony 201, 211, 212, 301
Litvak, Anatole 299
Live Like a Cop, Die Like a Man 216, **217**, 218; see also *Uomini si nasce, poliziotti si muore*

Lizzani, Carlo 24, 74, 106
Lloyd, Harold 153
Lo Cascio, Franco 185
Lo chiamavano Trinità 95–96, 298; see also *My Name Is Trinity*; *They Call Me Trinity*
Lo sconosciuto di San Marino 10; see also *The Unknown Men of San Marino*
Lobster for Breakfast 7, 13, 18, **19**
The Lodger 27
Lolita 290
Lombardo, Goffredo 101, 146
Lombardo Radice, Giovanni 52, 53, 57, 58, **61**, 227, 232, **233**, **235**, **239**, 240, 302
London 17, 35, 36, 165, 169, 207, 211, 212
The Lone Runner 230; see also *Lone Runner—lo scrigno dei mille diamanti*
Lone Runner—lo scrigno dei mille diamanti 230; see also *The Lone Runner*
The Long Goodbye 169
Lopez, Jennifer 244
Lopez, Rosaria 300
Lord Jim (book) 68
Loren, Sophia 8, 16, 17, 189, 270
Los que verán Dios 178; see also *Those Who Will See God*
Losey, Joseph 12
Love, Lucretia 201, 213, 301
The Love Potion 92; see also *Elisir d'amore*
Lovelock, Ray 24, 45, 216, 218, 231
Lovers from Beyond the Tomb 130; see also *Amanti D'oltretomba*
The Loves and Times of Scaramouche 170; see also *Le avventure e gli amori di Scaramouche*; *Scaramouche*
Loving Cousins 276; see also *Cugini carnali*
Loy, Mino 49, 62, 63, 220, 267, 271, 282, 285, 291, 298
LSD—Flesh of the Devil 193; see also *LSD—Inferno per pochi dollari*
LSD—Inferno per pochi dollari 193; see also *LSD—Flesh of the Devil*
Lucari, Gianni Hecht 78, 280
Lucas, George 249
Lucchetti, Daniele 140
Lucisano, Fulvio 9
Lupo, Michele 200
Lybia 206
Lynch, Richard 228

Macchi, Egisto 195
Macchie di belletto 119; see also *Stains of Rouge*

Maccione, Aldo **17**, 170
MacColl, Catriona 291
Machine Gun McCain 299; see also *Gli intoccabili*
Maciste all'inferno 251; see also *Maciste in Hell*; *The Witch's Curse*
Maciste in Hell 251; see also *Maciste all'inferno*
Maciste in King Solomon's Mines 192; see also *Maciste nelle miniere di Re Salomone*
Maciste nelle miniere di Re Salomone 192; see also *Maciste in King Solomon's Mines*
MacNeal, Maggie 46
Mad Max 160
Madison, Guy 168
Due Mafiosi contro Goldginger 181; see also *The Amazing Doctor G*; *Goldginger*; *The Two Crazy Secret Agents*
Maggi, Maurizio 230
Magia nera 175; see also *Black Magic*
Magnaghi, Federico 267
Magnani, Anna 7, 113, 114, 160, 200, 268, 299
Magni, Luigi 234
The Magnificent Bandits 302; see also *Viva Cangaceiro*
The Magnificent Seven 96, 168
Una Magnum special per Tony Saitta 104; see also *Blazing Magnum*; *Strange Shadows in a Dark Room*
Magnus 36, 298
Maietto, Carlo 254
Maiuri, Dino 170
Malatesta, Guido 37
Malaysia 21, 221, 277, 286, 287
Malerba, Gino 180
Malice 150; see also *Malizia*
Malicious 150; see also *Malizia*
Malindi 301
Malizia 150; see also *Malice*; *Malicious*
Mallorquì, Josè 130
Man Called Amen 174; see also *Così sia*
A Man Called Blade 293; see also *Mannaja*
A Man Called Horse 40, 204, 218
The Man from the Deep River 40, 218; see also *Il paese del sesso selvaggio*
Man Hunt 43; see also *L'uomo della strada fa giustizia*
Man Hunt in the City 43; see also *L'uomo della strada fa giustizia*
The Man of a Thousand Masks 163; see also *Upperseven—L'uomo da uccidere*

A Man Only Cries for Love 211, 212; see also *Donne, botte e bersaglieri*
The Man Who Laughs 143; see also *L'uomo che ride*
The Man with Icy Eyes 103; see also *L'uomo dagli occhi di ghiaccio*
Manchester 243
Manfredi, Nino 196
Mangiati vivi 49, 57, 289; see also *Eaten Alive!*
The Maniac Responsible 132, 264; see also *a tutte le auto della polizia...*
Mankiewicz, Joseph L. 23, 164, 266
Mann, Leonard 132, 138, 265
Mannaja 293; see also *A Man Called Blade*
Mannino, Vincenzo 43, 105, 173, 230
Manzella, Leonardo see Mann, Leonard
Manziana 193, 301
Manzoni, Alessandro 27
Marcellini, Siro 189, 192, 193
Marchal, Georges 129
Marchetti, Giancarlo 36
Il marchio di Kriminal 36; see also *The Return of Kriminal*
Marconi, Saverio 62
Marcos, Imelda 227
Maremma 31
Margheriti, Antonio 4, 74, 78, 101, 160, 203, 208, 209, 210, 233, 238, 239, 240, 298
Mariani, Mario 168
Marika degli inferni 186; see also *Mariken van Nieumeghen*
Un marito per Anna Zaccheo 72, 179, 299; see also *A Husband for Anna*
Mariken van Nieumeghen 186; see also *Marika degli inferni*
Mark of Zorro 185; see also *Ah si? E io lo dico a Zzzzorro*
Marrakesh 230
Marras, Alberto 214, 227
Married to Kill 22, 182; see also *Il dolce corpo di Deborah*
Marseille 193
Marshall Plan 65, 126
Marsina, Antonio 287
Martin, Dean 28
Martin, Frank see Girolami, Marino
Martin, John 243
Martinelli, Franco see Girolami, Marino
Martinica 227
Martino, Luciano 29, 42, 43, 62, 63, 118, 124, 183, 185, 230, 231, 247, 253, 254, 267, 285, 291, 293, 298, 301

Martino, Sergio 42, 43, 50, 57, 62, 63, 124, 176, 177, 183, 254, 261, *262*, 263, 264, 265, 266, 267, *269*, *272*, 276, *277*, 283, 285, 286, 287, 288, 290, 291, 293, 298
Martucci, Gianni 1, 177, 185
Marty 181
La maschera del demonio 246; see also *Black Sunday*; *The Mask of Satan*; *Revenge of the Vampire*
Masini, Giuseppe 93, 153
Masini, Nino 286
The Mask of Satan 246; see also *La maschera del demonio*
The Masked Man Against the Pirates 180; see also *L'uomo mascherato contro I pirati*
Mason, James 301
The Masque of the Red Death 263
Massa Marittima 21, 28, 53
Massaccesi, Aristide *see* D'Amato, Joe
Massacre Time 180; see also *Le colt cantarono la morte e fu ... tempo di massacro*
Massari, Lea 180
Massi, Stelvio 300
Mastrocinque, Camillo 127
Mastroianni, Marcello 8, 11, 16, *17*, 241
Mattei, Danilo 52, 61
Maxwell, Lois 99
Maya 245, 247, 248, 250, 257, 258
Mayo, Alyce 299
Mazza, Vincenzo 299
Mazzucco, Roberto 195
Mazzuoli, Jacopo 232
McCormack, Patricia 244
Mean Tricks 56, 57; see also *Hornsby e Rodriguez—Sfida criminale*
Mediaset 55, 131, 233, 248, 249, 250, 282, 283, 298
Il medico e lo stregone 151; see also *Doctor and the Healer*
Medusa Against the Son of Hercules 98; see also *Perseo L'invincibile*
Mell, Marisa 12, 25
Melville, Jean-Pierre 111, 266
Menard, Julie 78
Menczer, Erico 214
Mendoza 179
Il mercenario 298; see also *The Mercenary*; *A Professional Gun*
The Mercenary 298; see also *Il mercenario*
Mercury Films 209
Merenda, Luc 261, 264, 265, 266, 273, 275, 276, 293, 296, 298
Meril, Macha 191, *195*, 196, 197

Merli, Maurizio 25, 27, 33, 34, 45, 46, 47, 48, 49, 120, 121, 170, 211, 265, 278, 299
Merlini, Marisa 67
Merola, Mario 27
Messalina 144; see also *Messalina, Venere imperatrice*
Messalina, Venere imperatrice 144; see also *Messalina*
Metro-Goldwyn-Mayer 40, 136, 249
Mexico 19, 39, 54, 68, 81, 96, 172, 226, 298
La mia casa è piena di specchi **189**; see also *My House Is Full of Mirrors*
Miami Golem 107; see also *Cosmos Killer*; *Miami Horror*
Miami Horror 107; see also *Miami Golem*
Micalizzi, Franco 26, 45, 46
Michelini, Luciano 266
Mida, Massimo 193
Midnight Express 175
MIFED 186, 224, 301
Migliorini, Romano 193
Milan 24, 25, 32, 36, 42, 53, 66, 67, 73, 85, 91, 112, 121, 132, 153, 177, 179, 185, 191, 214, 265, 266, 274, 275, 285, 293, 298, 299, 300, 301, 302
Milano...difendersi o morire 177, 185; see also *Blazing Flowers*
Milano odia: la polizia non può sparare 25, 32, 275; see also *Almost Human*
Milano rovente 24, 42; see also *Gang War in Milan*
Milano Trema: La polizia vuole giustizia 42, 265, 293; see also *The Violent Professionals*
Milano violenta 132; see also *Bloody Payroll*
Milford, Penelope 107
Milian, Tomas 21, 25, 26, 32, 33, 34, 36, 42, 43, **44**, 45, 46, **47**, 48, 49, 68, 69, 78, 79, **80**, 81, 83, 84, 85, 88, **102**, 103, 113, 121, 176, 182, 185, 216, 266, 275, 276, 300, 302
Milo, Sandra 205, 206
Milva 298
Minervini, Gianni 81, 83, 150
Minaccia d'amore 230; see also *Dial: Help*
Minnesota Clay 115
The Minotaur, the Wild Beast of Crete 11, 93, 299; see also *Teseo contro il Minotauro*
Mio caro assassin 183; see also *My Dear Killer*
Il mio nome è Shanghai Joe 129, 130; see also *The Dragon Strikes Back*; *The Fighting Fists of Shanghai Joe*;

Il mondo porno di due sorelle 148; see also *Emanuelle and Joanna*; *The Pornographic World of Two Sisters*
My Name Is Shanghai Joe; *To Kill or Die*
Miracco, Renato 62
Misiano, Fortunato 37
Missione Lady Chaplin 98; see also *Special Mission Lady Chaplin*
Mitchell, Cameron 115
Molè, Franco 303
Le monache di Sant'Arcangelo 294; see also *The Nuns and the Devil*; *The Nuns of Saint Archangel*
Mondadori 298
Mondello, Luigi 87, 88
Mondo Cane 218
Mondo-movies 203, 204, 218, 253, 271
Monicelli, Mario 94, 120, 136, 137, 151, 186, 196, 200, 251
Monnezza 26, 275, 300
Monreale, Cinzia 150, 198
La montagna del Dio cannibale 57, 276, 285, 286; see also *The Mountain of the Cannibal God*
La Montagna di luce 21; see also *Temple of a Thousand Lights*
Montaldo, Giuliano 101, 299
Montefiori, Luigi 164, 237
Montenero, Paola 148, 149
Montesano, Enrico 7, 9, 17, 18, **19**, 195, 213
Moravia, Alberto 146
Moretti, Nanni 140
Morghen, John *see* Lombardo Radice, Giovanni
Moriarty, Michael 90, 107
Moriconi, Valeria 302
Morigi, Tatiana 164
Morlupo 301
Morocco 30, 72
Morricone, Ennio 46, 67, 74, 75, 76, 79, 83, 96, 98, 103, 128, 166, 195, 301
Morris, Kirk 201
Morrow, Vic 155
Morte al Cinevillaggio 298; see also *Death at the Cinemavillage*
Morte sospetta di una minorenne 264, 273; see also *The Suspicious Death of a Minor*
The Mountain of the Cannibal God 57, 276, 278, **279**, 285, 286; see also *La montagna del Dio cannibale*
Movie Target 144; see also *Bersaglio mobile*
Muccino, Gabriele 242
Mulargia, Edoardo 301
Muller, Paul 126, 301

Muni, Paul 49
Munich 164, 207
Murawski, Bob 53, 63
Murder by Vocation 193; see also *Omicidio per vocazione*
Murder Obsession 292; see also *Follia omicida*
Murnau, Friedrich Wilhelm 44
Mussolini, Benito 2
Muti, Ornella 24, 214
Muzio, Francesca 214, 216
My Darling Slave 16, 18; see also *La Schiava io ce l'ho e tu no*
My Dear Killer 183; see also *Mio caro assassino*
My Dear Nephews 150, **152**; see also *Nipoti miei diletti*
My Female Cousins 256; see also *Cugine Mie*
My House Is Full of Mirrors **189**; see also *La mia casa è piena di specchi*
My Name Is Shanghai Joe 129, 130; see also *Il mio nome è Shanghai Joe*
My Name Is Trinity 95–96, 298; see also *Lo chiamavano Trinità*
My Trieste 94; see also *Trieste mia!*

Nader, George 189
Naked and Violent 254, 271
Naples 25, 26, 27, 43, 46, 47, 48, 52, 53, 70, 91, 132, 147, 167, 195, 196, 206, 253, 254, 256, 276, 298
Naples Shoots 132; see also *Napoli spara!*
Napoli spara! 132, **133**; see also *Naples Shoots*; *Weapons of Death*
Napoli violenta 25, 43; see also *Violent Naples*
Nasca, Sergio 255, 302
Nazi Love Camp 27 **128**, 131; see also *Svastica nel ventre*
Nazzari, Amedeo 298
Negrin, Alberto 175
Nella città l'inferno 206; see also *Behind Closed Shutters*
Neorealism 126, 127, 202
Neri, Rosalba **86**, 185
Nero, Franco 111, 119, 138, 141, 155, 156, 158, 159, 164, 167, 169, 170, **171**, 172, 174, 176, 180, 185, 209, 210, 265
Nest of Vipers 65, 67, 68, 69, 78, 81, 83; see also *La notte dei serpenti*
Netherlands 280
Nettuno 298
The New Barbarians 160, 199, 228; see also *I nuovi barbari*
Newman, Paul 266

Nicholson, James H. 245
Nicolai, Bruno 98, 103
The Niece 214; see also *La nipote*
The Night Is Made for ... Stealing 12; see also *La notte è fatta per ... rubare*
Night of the Serpent 67; see also *La notte dei serpenti*
Nightmare Beach 55
Nightmare Castle 126, 130, 134; see also *Amanti D'oltretomba*
Nightmare City 45, 53, 54, 55; see also *Incubo sulla città contaminata*
Nile 207
Ninchi, Annibale 92
La nipote 214; see also *The Niece*
Nipoti miei diletti 150; see also *My Dear Nephews*
Noi due soli 114; see also *We Two Alone*
Noir 25, 35, 42, 119, 123, 186, 254
Noiret, Philippe 18
Non commettere atti impuri 85, 88; see also *Don't Commit Impure Acts*
La notte dei serpenti 67, 78; see also *Nest of Vipers*; *Night of the Serpent*
La notte è fatta per...rubare 12; see also *The Night Is Made for ... Stealing*
Nouri, Michael 115
Novak, Kim 28
nudity 34, 38, 51, 86, 101, 104, 118, 129, 137, 146, 147, 148, 166, 191, 198, 209, 210, 211, 222, 227, 231, 270, 272, 287, 288, 295
The Nun and the Devil 294; see also *Le monache di Sant'Arcangelo*
The Nuns of Saint Archangel 294; see also *Le monache di Sant'Arcangelo*
I nuovi barbari 160; see also *The New Barbarians*; *Warriors of the Wasteland*
Nusciak, Loredana 110
Nuzzi, Paolo 294, 303

Oasis of Fear 22, 23; see also *Un posto ideale per uccidere*
Obscene Desire 87, 88; see also *L'osceno desiderio—Le pene nel ventre*
O'Cangaceiro 302; see also *Viva Cangaceiro*
Gli occhi freddi della paura 165; see also *Cold Eyes of Fear*
Occhio, malocchio, prezzemolo e finocchio 281; see also *Eye, Evil Eye, Parsley and Fennel*
Oedipus Rex 30; see also *Edipo Re*

Odio le bionde 18; see also *I Hate Blondes*
L'Odissea 94; see also *The Odyssey*
The Odyssey 94; see also *L'Odissea*
Ognuno per sé 13, 182; see also *The Ruthless Four*
Ok Connery 98; see also *Operation Kid Brother*
O'Keefe, Miles 230
Omaggio, Maria Rosaria 55
Ombre roventi 130; see also *Shadow of Illusion*
The Omen 91
The Omen (2006) 235
Omicidio per vocazione 193; see also *Murder by Vocation*
Ondata di piacere 214, **215**; see also *Waves of Lust*
One Dollar Too Many 165; see also *Vado, vedo e sparo*
One Flew Over the Cuckoo's Nest 228
The One Hundred Kilometers 67, 72; see also *La cento chilometri*
Operation Achse 70
Operation Kid Brother 98, **99**; see also *Ok Connery*
Operation Nam 175; see also *Cobra Mission*
Orgasm 22; see also *Orgasmo*
Orgasmo 22, 33; see also *Orgasm*; *Paranoia*
Orlandi, Nora 117
Orlando, Angelo 232
L'orribile segreto del Dr. Hichcock 246, 251–252; see also *The Horrible Dr. Hichcock*; *The Horrible Secret of Dr. Hichcock*
Ortolani, Riz 74, 83, 218, 223
L'osceno desiderio—Le pene nel ventre 87; see also *Obscene Desire*
Ouarzazate 30

P.A.C. 195, 196, 197
Pacino, Al 47
Il paese del sesso selvaggio 40, 204, 218; see also *Deep River Savages*; *The Man from the Deep River*
Il paese delle piccole piogge 285; see also *The Country of the Small Rains*
Pagliero, Marcello 71
Pagony, Gabor 103
Paisà 44; see also *Paisan*
Paisan 44; see also *Paisà*
Palaggi, Franco 207, 221, 223, 228
Palance, Jack 34, 35, 36, 114, 167, 169
Palermi, Amleto 92

Palermo 27
Pallottini, Riccardo 214
Palmer, Gregg 69, 85, 90, **102**
Palmer, Renzo 150, 169
Pampanini, Silvana 179
Panama Sugar 258, 259
Pane, burro e marmellata 13; see also *Bread, Butter and Marmalade*
Panelli, Paolo 241
Pani, Corrado 14, 86, 266
Paolella, Domenico 29, 30, 31, 201, 205, 293, 294, 295
Paoli, Angelo 27
Paranoia 22, 23, 34, 35; see also *Orgasmo*
Paranoia 22, 34; see also *A Quiet Place to Kill*
Parenti, Mauro 208, 210, 211, 213, 301
Parioli 202, 252
Paris 7, 34, 53, 131, 195, 211, 231, 271, 272, 273, 292
Paris, Daniele 195
Parker, David 10
Parks, Michael 56
Parolini, Gianfranco 200
The Party 8
Pasolini, Pier Paolo 30, 39, 66, 146, 300
The Passionate Thief 200; see also *Risate di gioia*
Pastasciutta nel deserto 206; see also *Desert Furlough*
Pastina, Giorgio 7, 10
Patrizi, Massimo 144
Patrizi, Stefano 112, 121
Paul, David 199, 229
Paul, Gloria 291
Paul, Peter 229
Paura nel buio 56; see also *Hitcher in the Dark*
Paura nella città dei morti viventi 52, 236, 290; see also *City of the Living Dead*; *The Gates of Hell*
Pavone, Rita 138
Payment in Blood 161; see also *7 winchester per un massacro*
Pazzaglia, Riccardo 212
P.E.A. 55
Peck, Gregory 31
Peckinpah, Sam 158, 162
The Peddler and the Lady 113, 160; see also *Campo de' fiori*
Peddlin' in Society 268; *Abbasso la ricchezza*
Pedersoli, Carlo see Spencer, Bud
Peggio per me ... meglio per te! 211; see also *Worse for Me ... Better for You!*
Pehar, Olga **54**
Pellegrin, Raymond 85
Pelligra, Biagio 27
peplum 36, 96, 127, 200, 201, 203, 245, 297, 299
Peppard, George 32, 34, 36, 53
Per amore di Cesarina 197, 198; see also *For the Love of Cesarina*
Per 100.000 dollari t'ammazzo 253; see also *$100,000 for a Killing*; *Vengeance Is Mine*
Per un pugno di dollari 43, 127, 132; see also *A Fistful of Dollars*
Perdutamente tuo...mi firmo Macaluso Carmelo fu Giuseppe 197; see also *Desperately Yours ... I Sign Macaluso Carmelo, Son of the Late Giuseppe*
Pergolani, Michael **172**
Persello, Nino 180
Perseo L'invincibile **96**, 98; see also *Medusa Against the Son of Hercules*; *Perseus Against the Monsters*; *Perseus the Invincible*; *Valley of the Stone Men*
Perseus Against the Monsters 98; see also *Perseo L'invincibile*
Perseus the Invincible **96**, 98; see also *Perseo L'invincibile*
Perugia 232, 264, 273
Petri, Elio 24, 91, 169
Petroni, Giulio 29, 65, **66**, 67, 68, 69, **73**, **75**, **77**, **80**, **82**, **83**, **86**, 87, 102, 127, 135, 136, 188, 200, 214, 299, 300
Petroni, Silvia **80**, 121, 122, 300
Petronio, Brigitte 227
Phantom of Death 230, 234, 235; see also *Un delitto poco comune*
Phelps, Peter 257
Philippines 227, 301
I Piaceri dello scapolo 67, 73; see also *The Pleasures of a Bachelor*
Piccioni, Fabio 131
Piccioni, Piero 207
Pieces of Albania in Calabria 72; see also *Lembi di Albania in Calabria*
Piedmont 70
Pinelli, Giuseppe 302
Pingitore, Pier Francesco 187, 282
The Pirates of the Seven Seas 21; see also *I pirati della Malesia*
I pirati della Malesia 21; see also *The Pirates of the Seven Seas*; *Sandokan: Pirate of Malaysia*
Pirro, Ugo 66
Pistilli, Luigi 67, 76, 83, 118, 262, 263, **274**, 298, 301, 302
Pistol for a Hundred Coffins 22; see also *Una pistola per cento bare*
Una pistola per cento bare 21–22; see also *Pistol for a Hundred Coffins*
Le pistole non discutono 127, 132; see also *Bullets Don't Argue*; *Pistols Don't Argue*
Pistols Don't Argue 127, 132; see also *Le pistole non discutono*
The Pit and the Pendulum 101, 130
Pitagora, Paola 67, 72
Pittorru, Fabio 132
Pizarro, Francisco 51
Pizzuti, Riccardo 79
Placido, Michele 302
Planet of the Vampires 297; see also *Terrore nello spazio*
Plank, Scott 258
Platoon 175
Pleasence, Donald 90, 259, 283, 284
The Pleasures of a Bachelor 67; *I Piaceri dello scapolo*
Pochi dollari per Django 162; see also *A Few Dollars for Django*; *Some Dollars for Django*
Podestà, Rossana 31
Poeti, Paolo 212, 301
Polanski, Roman 263, 280
The Police Serve the Citizens? 109, 111, 112, 120; see also *La polizia è al servizio del cittadino?*
La polizia accusa: il servizio segreto uccide 265, 274; see also *Silent Action*
La polizia chiede aiuto 264; see also *What Have They Done to Your Daughters?*
La polizia è al servizio del cittadino? 120; see also *The Police Serve the Citizens?*
La polizia incrimina la legge assolve 157, 265; see also *High Crime*
La polizia ringrazia 24, 112, 157, 169, 264, 274; see also *Execution Squad*; *The Executioners*
Pollack, Sidney 170
Pontani, Filippo Maria 93
Pontecorvo, Gillo 78, 206
Ponti, Carlo 8, 16, 17, 19, 169, 273, 274, 275
Ponti, Tom 303
Ponza 231
Poopsie & Co. 16; see also *La Pupa del gangster*
Poor But Beautiful 251; see also *Poveri ma belli*
Popova, Anya 116
Porel, Marc 150, **152**, 216, 218
Porno 40, 50, 51, 58, 131, 148, 149, 151, 198, 222, 300
The Pornographic World of Two Sisters 148; see also *Il mondo porno di due sorelle*

Il portaborse 140; see also *The Factotum*
Portrait of Jeannie 44
Un posto ideale per uccidere 22, 77; see also *Dirty Pictures*; *An Ideal Place to Kill*; *Oasis of Fear*
Poveri ma belli 251; see also *Poor But Beautiful*
Powell, Eleanor 35
Power, Romina 101
I predatori di Atlantide 224; see also *Atlantis Interceptors*; *The Raiders of Atlantis*
Preminger, Otto 42
Prentiss, Paula 12
Preparati la bara 138, 141, **142**; see also *Django, Prepare a Coffin*
Prete, Giancarlo 157, 169
Price of Death 69; see also *Il venditore di morte*
Primal Rage 55; see also *Rage— Furia primitive*
The Prince of Foxes 126
The Procession 178
Proclemer, Anna 23, 35
A Professional Gun 298; see also *Il mercenario*
Professionals for a Massacre 182; see also *Professionisti per un massacro*
Professionisti per un massacro 182; see also *Professionals for a Massacre*
The Profiteer 302; see also *Il saprofita*
Profondo rosso 234; see also *Deep Red*
I promessi sposi 93; see also *The Bethrothed*
Prosperi, Franco 204
Prosperi, Mario 192, 301
Una prostituta al servizio del pubblico e in regola con le leggi dello stato 95; see also *Prostitution Italian Style*
Prostitution Italian Style 95; see also *Una prostituta al servizio del pubblico e in regola con le leggi dello stato*
Psycho 56, 263
The Public Enemy 49
Puccini, Gianni 27
Pulci, Tonino 236
The Puma Man 92, 106, 107; see also *L'uomo puma*
La Pupa del gangster 16; see also *Sex Pot*
Puppo, Romano 182
Purdom, Edmund 32, 98, 220, 254
Purgatori, Andrea 250, 256
Puttignani, Rodolfo 167

The Quatermass Xperiment 245
Quayle, Anthony 90
Queen of the Seas 31; see also *Le avventure di Mary Read*
The Queens 271
The Queer ... The Erotic 253, 271; see also *L'altra faccia del peccato*
Queimada 221; see also *Burn!*
Quel maledetto treno blindato 171; see also *The Inglorious Bastards*; *That Damned Armored Train*
Quel movimento che mi piace tanto 150, 151, 153; see also *That Movement That I Like So Much*
Quella sporca storia nel west 145, 164; see also *That Dirty Story in the West*
Quella villa in fondo al parco 108; see also *The Rat Man*
Questi, Giulio 160
Quien sabe? 68, 81, 298; see also *A Bullet for the General*
A Quiet Place to Kill 22, 23, 35, 38; see also *Paranoia*
Quinn, Anthony 169, 239

Rabal, Francisco 54
I raconti di Canterbury 300; see also *The Canterbury Tales*
I ragazzi del muretto 62; see also *The Kids from the Block*
Ragazzi di Trastevere 30; see also *The Boys of Trastevere*
Ragazzi di vita 30; see also "*Boys of Life*"
Rage—Furia primitive 55; see also *Primal Rage*
The Rage Within 139, 145, 146; see also *Delitto al circolo del tennis*
RAI 106, 190, 193, 194, 195, 233, 249, 253, 254, 284, 297, 298, 300, 301
The Raiders of Atlantis 224; see also *I predatori di Atlantide*
Ralli, Giovanna 95, 166, 205
Rambaldi, Carlo 55
Rambaldi, Vittorio 55
Randi, Ermanno 94
Ranieri, Massimo 180, 196
Rassimov, Ivan 21, 40, 51, 204, 219, 229, 263
The Rat Man 108; see also *Quella villa in fondo al parco*
Rattigan, Terence 298
Raviola, Roberto *see* Magnus
Raw Wind in Eden 31, 32
[REC] 225
Recanati 301
Reder, Gigi 67
Redford, Robert 13, 168, 266
Redgrave, Vanessa 210, 225
Reed, Carol 71
Reed, Oliver 259
Reeves, Steve 40, 95, 136, 180, 199, 201, 207
Regnoli, Piero 84, 87, 192, 193
Religion 1, 81, 88, 105, 240, 297
Remy, Hélène 114
Renegade Riders 161, 163, 164; see also *7 winchester per un massacro*
Renis, Tony 195, 301
Renoir, Jean 9, 27
Requiescant 74; see also *Kill and Pray*
The Return 139; see also *Il ritorno*
The Return of Kriminal 36; see also *Il marchio di Kriminal*
Revenge of the Vampire 246; see also *La maschera del demonio*
The Revolt of the Seven 98; see also *La rivolta dei sette*
Rey, Fernando 158, 166
Reynolds, Burt 208
The Ribadier System 195; see also *Il sistema Ribadier*
Richard III 18
Riento, Virgilio 268
Rigaud, George 182
Righelli, Gennaro 268
Ring Around the Horse's Tail 69; see also *Il bianco, il giallo, il nero*
Ring of Death 111, 112, 119, 120, 123; see also *Un detective*
Ringo and His Golden Pistol 208; see also *Johnny Oro*
Risate di gioia 200; see also *The Passionate Thief*
Risi, Dino 120, 211, 251
Rita of the West 138, 145; see also *Little Rita nel West*
Il ritorno 139; see also *The Return*
La rivolta dei sette 98; see also *The Revolt of the Seven*; *The Spartan Gladiator*
Rizzoli, Angelo 206
Robson, Mark 263
Rochefort, Jean 18
Roland, Gilbert 13, 14, 16, 168
Rolling Stones 271
Roma a mano armata 43; see also *Brutal Justice*; *Rome Armed to the Teeth*
Roma città aperta 44, 126; see also *Rome Open City*
Roma città violenta 176; see also *Rome Violent City*
Roma violenta 170, 299; see also *Street Killers*; *Violent City*; *Violent Rome*
Romancing the Stone 56
Romanelli, Carla 210, 212, 301
Romanini, Gaia 29, 138
Rome 9, 21, 25, 26, 34, 36, 43, 44, 45, 46, 47, 48, 49, 50, 53,

54, 57, 58, 59, 62, 63, 64, 65, 70, 71, 72, 88, 89, 91, 100, 104, 106, 108, 109, 114, 116, 118, 124, 125, 126, 127, 134, 135, 136, 138, 139, 151, 154, 155, 163, 165, 167, 168, 170, 176, 179, 180, 186, 187, 190, 192, 193, 198, 200, 202, 204, 205, 206, 207, 209, 214, 216, 220, 221, 222, 223, 226, 228, 231, 232, 244, 245, 246, 251, 252, 256, 259, 260, 262, 267, 268, 280, 284, 285, 286, 288, 292, 296, 297, 298, 299, 300, 301, 302
Rome Armed to the Teeth 25, 26, 43, 44, 45, 46, 47, 48, 49; see also *Roma a mano armata*
Rome Like Chicago 100; see also *Chicago*
Rome Open City 44, 126; see also *Roma città aperta*
Rome Violent City 176; see also *Roma città violenta*
Romeo and Juliet 203, 209, 246 see also *Romeo e Guilietta*
Romeo e Guilietta 203, 209, 246; see also *Romeo and Juliet*
Romero, George A. 54, 225, 226
Romoli, Gianni 175
Romolo e Remo 138; see also *Duel of the Titans*
Rondi, Brunello 267, 292, 299
Rondi, Gian Luigi 102, 299
The Room of Words 303; see also *La stanza delle parole*
The Roses Have Bloomed Again 195, 197; see also *Son tornate a fiorire le rose*
Rosi, Francesco 24
Rosmunda e Alboino 114; see also *Sword of the Conqueror*
Rossellini, Franco 207
Rossellini, Renzo 202, 205, 211
Rossellini, Roberto 44, 71, 126, 127, 136, 202, 203, 205, 206, 216, 225, 226, 231
Rossetti, Franco 1, 29, 135, 136, 137, 138, 139, **147**, 149, 152, 154, 165, 188, 200, 209, 292, 300
Rossi, Carlo 218, 227, 231
Rossi, Franco 93, 138, 151, 280, 301
Rotella, Mimmo 3, 4
Russia 21, 31, 32, 43, 65, 96, 116
Russo, Carmen 180
Rustichelli, Carlo 25
The Ruthless Four 13, 14, **15**, 182; see also *Ognuno per sé*

Sabatello, Dario 165
Sabato, Antonio 24, 42, 165
Sabbatini, Enrico 16, 17
Sacchetti, Dardano 26, 43, 108, 227, 228, 229, 300
Saks, Gene 8

The Salamanders 254; see also *Le salamandre*
Le salamandre 254; see also *The Salamanders*
Salce, Luciano 85, 118, 150, 191, 196, 298
Salerno, Enrico Maria 109, 112, 117, 118, 120, 130, 183, 205, 231, 265, 266, 275
Salerno, Vittorio 292
Salvati, Sergio 244
Salviani, Vincenzo 214, 227
Salvo D'Acquisto (film) 111, 120
Sambrell, Aldo 150
Samperi, Salvatore 67, 150
Samson and His Mighty Challenge 10; see also *Ercole, Sandone, maciste e Ursus gli invincibili*
Samson and the Slave Queen 36; see also *Zorro contro Maciste*
San Remo—La grande sfida 30; see also *San Remo—The Big Challenge*
San Remo—The Big Challenge 30; see also *San Remo—La grande sfida*
Sanchez, Josè 167
Sancho, Fernando 301
Sandokan 21; see also *La Montagna di luce*
Sandokan—La tigre di Mompracem 21; see also *Sandokan the Great*
Sandokan the Great 21, 40, 50; see also *Sandokan—La tigre di Mompracem*
Sandokan: Pirate of Malaysia 21, 50; see also *I pirati della Malesia*
Sansone, Alfonso 74, 76
Il saprofita 302; see also *The Profiteer*
Saraceni, Fausto 225
Sardinia 31, 212
Sarrazin, Michael 170
Satanik 36, 298
Satta Flores, Stefano 197
Satyricon 290
Savage, John 258, 259, 260
Savalas, Telly 90
Saxon, Glenn 167, 168
Saxon, John 49, 56, 90, 161, 165, 238
Sbarigia, Roberto 163
Scaglione, Massimo 303
Scala, Gia 31
Scaramouche 170, 171; see also *Le avventure e gli amori di Scaramouche*
Scarface 49
Scarpelli, Furio 16
Scattini, Luigi 254, 271, 302
Scavolini, Sauro 117, 276
Scenes from a Murder 103; see also *L'assassino è al telefono*

Scerbanenco, Giorgio 112
La Schiava io ce l'ho e tu no 16; see also *My Darling Slave*
Schiave bianche—violenza in Amazzonia 224; see also *Amazonia: The Catherine Miles Story*; *White Slave*
Schrieber, Liev 235
Schubert, Karin 166
Schurer, Erna 247, 254, 255
sci-fi 203, 209, 245, 281, 291
Sciotti, Enzo 292
Scipio Africanus 92; see also *Scipione l'africano*
Scipio the African 92; see also *Scipione l'africano*
Scipione l'africano 92; see also *The Defeat of Hannibal*; *Scipio Africanus*; *Scipio the African*
Scoglio, Giovanna *see* Scala, Gia
Scola, Ettore 196
The Scorpion with Two Tails 62, 282, 285; see also *Assassinio al cimitero etrusco*
Scorpion's Tail 183, 262, 270; see also *La coda dello scorpione*
Scorsese, Martin 245, 249
Scott, Anthony *see* Carnimeo, Giuliano
Scott, Gordon 207
Scott, Ridley 222, 259
Screamers **277**
Se sei vivo spara 159–160; see also *Django Kill!*; *Django Kill...If You Live, Shoot*
Seagal, Steven 244
Secchi, Luciano *see* Bunker, Max
Secret Beyond the Door 23
The Secret Mark of D'Artagnan 189, 192; see also *Il colpo segreto di d'Artagnan*
The Secret of the Sahara 175, 176; see also *Il segreto del Sahara*
The Sect 234; see also *La setta*
Segal, George 13
Il segno del coyote 127, 130; see also *The Sign of the Coyote*
Il segno di Zorro 127; see also *Duel at Rio Grande*; *Sign of Zorro*
Il segreto del Sahara 175; see also *The Secret of the Sahara*
Sei donne per l'assassino 263; see also *Blood and Black Lace*
Sellers, Mary 238
Senanayake, Don Stephen 71
Senatore, Paola 50, 51, 211
Sensività 167; see also *The House by the Edge of the Lake*; *The Last House Near the Lake*
Serato, Massimo 114
The Servant 12

Sesia 179
La setta 234; see also *The Devil's Daughter*; *The Sect*
I sette gladiatori 96; see also *Gladiators 7*; *The Seven Gladiators*
I sette magnifici gladiatori 299; see also *The Seven Magnificent Gladiators Sette orchidee macchiate di rosso* 24, 39; see also *Seven Blood-Stained Orchids*
Sette ore di violenza per una soluzione imprevista 185; see also *7 Hours of Violence*
Le sette spade del vendicatore 251; see also *Seven Swords for the King*; *The Seventh Sword*
Setton, Max 12, 13
Seven Blood-Stained Orchids 24, 39, 55; see also *Sette orchidee macchiate di rosso*
The Seven Gladiators 96; see also *I sette gladiatori*
Seven Guns for Timothy 116; see also *7 magnifiche pistole*
The Seven Magnificent Gladiators 299; see also *I sette magnifici gladiatori*
Seven Magnificent Guns 116; see also *7 magnifiche pistole*
The Seven Samurai 162
Seven Swords for the King 251; see also *Le sette spade del vendicatore*
Seven Winchesters for a Massacre 161; see also *7 winchester per un massacro*
The Seventh Seal 164
The Seventh Sword 251; see also *Le sette spade del vendicatore*
The Seventh Victim 263
Severini, Attilio 182
sex-comedy 67, 78, 85, 104, 150, 191, 196, 198, 298, 300
Sex Pot 16, **17**; see also *La Pupa del gangster*
Sex with a Smile 42, 275, 281; *40 gradi all'ombra del lenzuolo*
Sex with a Smile II 281; see also *Spogliamoci così senza pudor*
Shadow of a Doubt 44
Shadow of Illusion 130; see also *Ombre roventi*
Shakespeare, William 33, 60, 145, 159, 177, 266
Shane 98
Sharif, Omar 99
The Shark Hunter 172; see also *Il cacciatore di squali*
Shaw, George Bernard 177
Sheen, Charlie 230
Shoot First ... Ask Questions Later 69; see also *Il bianco, il giallo, il nero*
Short Night of Glass Dolls 263; see also *La corta notte delle bambole di vetro*
Sibaldi, Stefano 254
The Sicilian Boss 26; see also *Da Corleone a Brooklyn*
Sicily 25, 26, 27, 29, 31, 33, 42, 180, 191, 192, 248, 255, 274
The Siege of Romania 192; see also *L'assedio di Romanzia*
Siegel, Don 21, 157
The Sign of the Coyote 127, 130; see also *Il segno del coyote*
Sign of Zorro 127; see also *Il segno di Zorro*
La signora è stata violentata 195, 196; see also *The Lady Was Raped!*
Silent Action 265, 266, 274, 275, 276; see also *La polizia accusa: il servizio segreto uccide*
Silva, Henry 25
Silverstein, Elliot 204
Silvi, Lilia 92, 298
Simonelli, Giorgio 93, 181
Sinatra, Frank 191, 299
Sinclair, Joshua 164
Sindoni, Vittorio 19, 150, 188, 189, 190, 191, 212
Siodmak, Robert 23, 39
Il sistema Ribadier 195; see also *The Ribadier System*
A Sky Full of Stars for a Roof 67, 68, **77**, 79; see also *... e per tetto un cielo di stelle*
The Slave 16, 18; see also *La Schiava io ce l'ho e tu no*
The Slave 200, 207, 208; see also *Il figlio di Spartacus*
Slave Women of Corinth 114; see also *Afrodite, dea dell'amore*
The Smell of Onion 69, 169; see also *Cipolla Colt*
The Smile of the Fox 280; see also *Spiando Marina*
snakes 50, 53, 219, 221, 287
The Snows of Kilimanjaro 31
So Sweet...So Perverse 22, 23, **37**, 39, 43, 272; see also *Così dolce ... così perversa*
Soavi, Michele 58, 227, 233, 237, 238, 241, 242
Le Socrate 293; see also *Socrates*
Socrates 293; see also *Le Socrate*
Soldati, Giovanni 241
Soldati, Mario 7, 93, 114, 151, 161
Soldati, Wolfango 167
Solinas, Franco 79, 81
I soliti ignoti vent'anni dopo 241; see also *Big Deal After Twenty Years*
I soliti rapinatori a Milano 66, 67, 73, 85; see also *The Usual Thieves from Milan*
Sollima, Sergio 40, 94, 188, 299
Some Dollars for Django 162; see also *Pochi dollari per Django*
Some Like It Hot 20
Sometimes Life Is Hard—Right, Providence? 67; *La vita a volte è molto dura vero Provvidenza?*
The Son of Spartacus 200, 207; see also *Il figlio di Spartacus*
Son tornate a fiorire le rose 195, 197; see also *The Roses Have Bloomed Again*
The Song of Destiny 151; see also *La canzone del destino*
Sono stato un agente C.I.A. 115, 299; see also *Covert Action*
Sons of the Moon 224; see also *I figli della luna*
Sordi, Alberto 140, 196, 225, 256, 298
Sorel, Jean 23, 35, 118
Soviet Union *see* Russia
Spaghetti Westerns 130, 155, 156, 266, 267, 299
Spain 16, 27, 34, 35, 51, 54, 55, 68, 84, 88, 95, 96, 101, 114, 115, 116, 127, 129, 134, 143, 148, 162, 163, 166, 169, 172, 180, 182, 188, 208, 238, 270, 274, 299
Spanish *see* Spain
Spartacus 290
The Spartan Gladiator 98; see also *La rivolta dei sette*
Spasmo 24, 38, 39, 51
Special Mission Lady Chaplin 98; see also *Missione Lady Chaplin*
The Specter 246; see also *Lo spettro*
Specters 245, 247, 248, 250, 255, 256, **257**, 259; see also *Spettri*
Spencer, Bud 55, 62, 68, 84, 96, 165, 175, 298
Spettri 247, 250; see also *Specters*
Lo spettro 246; see also *The Ghost*; *The Specter*
La spiaggia del terrore 55; see also *Welcome to Spring Break*
Spiando Marina 280; see also *Foxy Lady*; *The Smile of the Fox*
Spiderman 2 53
Spielberg, Steven 95, 173, 249
The Spiral Staircase 23, 39
splatter 52, 57, 60, 92, 226
Spogliamoci così senza pudor 281; see also *Sex with a Smile II*
La sposa americana 241; see also *The American Bride*
spy-movies 21, 96, 98, 163, 211, 265, 267, 299
The Spy with Ten Faces 98, 163; see also *Upperseven—L'uomo da uccidere*
Squadra antiscippo 216; see also *The Cop in Blue Jeans*

Squitieri, Pasquale 36, 67, 167
Sri Lanka 50, 65, 69, 70, 71, 72, 287
Stafford, Frederick 90, 100, 103
Stage Fright 237, 244; see also *Deliria*
Stagecoach 31, 73, 98
Stains of Rouge 119; see also *Macchie di belletto*
Stallone, Sage 53, 63
Stallone, Sylvester 43, 53, 63
Stander, Lionel 85, 169, 185, 213
Lo strano vizio della signora Wardh 183, 262, 270; see also *Blade of the Ripper*; *The Strange Vice of Mrs. Wardh*
La stanza delle parole 303; see also *The Room of Words*
Starlight Hotel 257
Steele, Barbara 4, 126, 130, 208, 246, 252, 253
Steele, Danielle 250
Stefanelli, Benito 79
Stefanelli, Simonetta 86
Stefanutti, Giorgio 186
Steffen, Anthony 76, 130, 162
Stegnani, Giorgio 209
Steinbeck, John 78, 79
Steiner, John 68, 81, 216, 229, 230
Stelling, Joss 186
Steno *see* Vanzina, Stefano
Stevens, George 37, 98
Stewart, Evelyn 116
Stiglitz, Hugo 54
The Sting 266
Sting of the West 169; see also *Tedeum*
Stone, Oliver 175
Stoppa, Paolo 206
Storaro, Vittorio 146
Storia di una monaca di clausura 294; see also *Diary of a Cloistered Nun*; *Unholy Convent*
La strada 39
Strange Shadows in a Dark Room 104; see also *Una Magnum special per Tony Saitta*
The Strange Vice of Mrs. Wardh 183, 262, 263, 270, 271, 272, 273, 274; see also *Lo strano vizio della signora Wardh*
Street Killers 170, 299; see also *Roma violenta*
Street Law 157, 158, 169, 170; see also *Il citadino si ribella*
La strega di Colombraro 72; see also *The Witch of Colombraro*
Strehler, Giorgio 86
Striker 174
Strindberg, Anita 262, 263, 271, 273
Strode, Woody 124, 164
suicide 32, 49, 51, 165, 282, 298, 299, 302

A Summer to Remember 42, 276; see also *La bellissima estate*
The Suspicious Death of a Minor 264, 265, 266, 273, 277; see also *Morte sospetta di una minorenne*
Svastica nel ventre 131; see also *Nazi Love Camp 27*
Svenson, Bo 171, 238, 240, 241
Swan, Kitty 210, 301
Svezia: inferno e paradiso 302; see also *Sweden: Heaven and Hell*
Sweden: Heaven and Hell 271, 302
The Sweet Body of Deborah 22, 38, 111, 118, 182, 272; see also *Il dolce corpo di Deborah*
The Sweet House of Horrors 291; see also *La dolce casa degli orrori*
Swept Away 219; see also *Travolti da un insolito destino nell'azzurro mare d'agosto*
sword-and-sandal *see* peplum
Sword of the Conqueror 114; see also *Rosmunda e Alboino*
Syndicate Sadists 25, 43, 44, 46, **47**; see also *Il giustiziere sfida la città*

Tajoli, Luciano 94
Tales of Terror 263
Los tallos amargos 177, 178; see also *The Bitter Stems*
Tangen, Jeff 210
Tarantini, Michele Massimo 56, 185, 268, 285, 298
Tarantino, Quentin 2, 34, 49, 53, 63, 67, 75, 76, 134, 144, 171, 175, 222, 299
Taranto, Carlo 151
Tarquini, Enzo 62
Tartaglia, Simona 9
Tarzan and the Brown Prince 301; see also *Tarzán y el arco iris*
Tarzán y el arco iris 301; see also *Tarzan and the Brown Prince*
Tavernier, Bertrand 35
Taviani brothers 39
Taxi ... Mister? 89; see also *Taxi ... signore?*
Taxi ... signore? 89; see also *Taxi ... Mister?*
Tedeschi, Gianrico 67
Tedesco, Maurizio 248, 249, 250, 256
Tedeum 169; see also *Con Men*; *Father Jackleg*; *Sting of the West*
Temple of a Thousand Lights 21, 50; see also *La Montagna di luce*
Tempo di credere 211; see also *Time to Believe*

The Temptations of Doctor Antonio 200; see also *Le tentazioni del dottor Antonio*
The Tempter 92, 95; see also *L'anticristo*
Tenerife 129
Le tentazioni del dottor Antonio 200; see also *The Temptations of Doctor Antonio*
Teorema 146
Tepepa 29, 67, 68, 69, 79, 81, **82**, 83, 88, 151, 214, 298; see also *Blood and Guns*
Terrible Sheriff 90, 94; see also *Due contro tutti*
Il terrore dei mari 29; see also *Guns of the Black Witch*
Terrore nello spazio 297; see also *Planet of the Vampires*
Il terzo occhio 208; see also *The Third Eye*
Teseo contro il Minotauro 11, 93, 299; see also *The Minotaur, the Wild Beast of Crete*
Tessari, Duccio 98, 144, 147, 200, 208, 236
Testi, Fabio 156, 158, **159**, 170, 185, 265
Thailand 27, 40
That Damned Armored Train 171; see also *Quel maledetto treno blindato*
That Dirty Story in the West 145, 164; see also *Quella sporca storia nel west*
They Call Me Trinity 69, 79, 95, 96, 165, 298; see also *Lo chiamavano Trinità*
They Called Him Amen 274
That Movement That I Like So Much 150; see also *Quel movimento che mi piace tanto*
Therefore It Is 274; see also *Così sia*
They Called Him Amen 274; see also *Così sia*
They Still Call Me Trinity see *They Call Me Trinity*
The Thieves 136; see also *I ladri*
The Third Eye 208; see also *Il terzo occhio*
Thompson, John 228, 229
Those Desperate Men Who Smell of Dirt and Death 181; see also *Los Desperados*
Those Who Will See God 178; see also *Los que verán Dios*
Thunder 173
The Thursdays of Mrs. Julie 293; see also *I giovedì della signora Giulia*
Tiffin, Pamela 194, 195
Time to Believe 211; see also *Tempo di credere*
Tindari 192

Tirrenia 183
Titanus 76, 180, 207, 208, 251, 302
To Hell and Back 302; see also *Uno di più all'inferno*
To Kill or Die 129, 130; see also *Il mio nome è Shanghai Joe*
Toffolo, Lino 213
Tognazzi, Ugo 73, 298
Tomassi, Vincenzo 169
Top Sensation 301
Tornatore, Giuseppe 242, 249
Torres, José 67, **80**
Torso 261, 262, 263, 264, 273, 274; see also *I corpi presentano tracce di violenza carnale*
Tortilla Westerns 29, 67, 68, 69, 79, 81, 83, 88, 89, 90, 96, 151, 214, 298
Tosca 298
Totò 136, 242
Tourneur, Jacques 55, 136
Tozzi, Fausto 180
A Train for Durango 130, 134; *Un treno per Durango*
Trainer on the Beach 282; see also *L'allenatore nel pallone*
Tranquilli, Silvano 86
Travolti da un insolito destino nell'azzurro mare d'agosto 219; see also *Swept Away*
Treasure Island 239; see also *L'isola del tesoro*
The Treasure of the Sierra Madre 13, 182
Un treno per Durango 130; see also *A Train for Durango*
Trieste mia! 94; see also *My Trieste!*
Trintignant, Jean-Louis 23, **37**, 39
Il trionfo di Ercole 104; see also *Hercules vs. the Giant Warriors*; *The Triumph of Hercules*
Il trionfo di Robin Hood 31; see also *The Triumph of Robin Hood*
The Triumph of Hercules 104; see also *Il trionfo di Ercole*
The Triumph of Robin Hood 31; see also *Il trionfo di Robin Hood*
Trotter, Laura 54, 88, 298
Trovajoli, Armando 74
Il trucido e lo sbirro 26, 267, 300; see also *Free Hand for a Tough Cop*
Tuareg 172, 173; see also *Tuareg, il guerriero del deserto*
Tuareg, il guerriero del deserto 172; see also *Tuareg*
Il tuo vizio è una stanza chiusa e solo io ne ho la chiave 263, 271; see also *Your Vice Is a Locked Room and Only I Have the Key*
Turkey 36, 185

Turner, Elizabeth 216
Turista con il police 94; see also *Hitchhiking Tourists*
Tuscania 213
Tuscany 23, 36, 29, 52, 143, 147
Tutti i colori del buio 183, 263; see also *All the Colors of the Dark*
Two Against All 90, 94, 95, 98; see also *Due contro tutti*
The Two Crazy Secret Agents 181; see also *Due Mafiosi contro Goldginger*
Two Sons of Ringo 181

Ubaldi, Giorgio 96, 163
L'uccello dalle piume di cristallo 261; see also *The Bird with the Crystal Plumage*
Ukraine 116
Ulisse contro Ercole 127, 129; see also *Ulysses Against Hercules*; *Ulysses Against the Son of Hercules*
Ulmer, Edgar G. 42, 127
L'ultima neve di primavera 46, 276; see also *The Last Snows of Spring*
Gli ultimi giorni di Pompei 136; see also *The Last Days of Pompeii*
Gli ultimi 10 giorni di Hitler 300; see also *Hitler: The Last Ten Days*
L'ultimo gladiatore 33; see also *The Last Gladiator*
L'ultimo guerriero 124; see also *The Final Executioner*; *The Last Warrior*
Ultimo mondo cannibale 42, 57, 204, 218, **220**, 276, 286; see also *Jungle Holocaust*; *Last Cannibal World*; *The Last Survivor*
L'ultimo sapore dell'aria 219; see also *Last Feelings*
L'ultimo squalo 173, 220; see also *Great White*; *The Last Shark*
Ultimo taglio 258, **259**; see also *Last Cut*
Ultimo tango a Parigi 273; see also *Last Tango in Paris*
Ulysses Against Hercules 127, 129; see also *Ulisse contro Ercole*
Ulysses Against the Son of Hercules 127, 129; see also *Ulisse contro Ercole*
Unholy Convent 294; see also *Storia di una monaca di clausura*
The Unholy Four 138; see also *Ciakmull—L'uomo della vendetta*
Universal Pictures 30, 49, 173, 245
The Unknown Men of San Marino 10

Uno di più all'inferno 302; see also *To Hell and Back*
Uomini si nasce, poliziotti si muore 216, **217**; see also *Live Like a Cop, Die Like a Man*
L'uomo che ride 143; see also *The Man Who Laughs*
L'uomo dagli occhi di ghiaccio 103; see also *The Man with Icy Eyes*
L'uomo della strada fa giustizia 43; see also *Man Hunt*; *Man Hunt in the City*
L'uomo mascherato contro I pirati 180; see also *The Black Pirate*; *The Masked Man Against the Pirates*
L'uomo puma 92, 106; see also *The Puma Man*
Un uomo, una città 118; see also *City Under Siege*
Upperseven—L'uomo da uccidere 98, 163; see also *The Man of a Thousand Masks*; *The Spy with Ten Faces*; *Upperseven, the Man to Kill*
Upperseven, the Man to Kill 163; see also *Upperseven—L'uomo da uccidere*
Urlatori alla sbarra 200; see also *Howlers of the Dock*
Ursus, il terrore dei kirghisi 209; see also *Hercules, Prisoner of Evil*; *Ursus, Terror of the Kirghiz*
Ursus in the Valley of the Lions 207; see also *Ursus nella valle dei leoni*
Ursus nella valle dei leoni 207; see also *Ursus in the Valley of the Lions*; *Valley of the Lions*
Ursus Terror of the Kirghiz 209; see also *Ursus, il terrore dei kirghisi*
Uruguay 176, 177, 178, 179, 180, 181, 182
The Usual Thieves from Milan 66; see also *I Soliti rapinatori a Milano*

Vacanze sulla Costa Smeralda 212; see also *Vacation on the Emerald Coast*
Vacation on the Emerald Coast 212; see also *Vacanze sulla Costa Smeralda*
Vadis, Dan 201
Vado ... l'ammazzo e torno 117, 155, 163, 182; see also *Any Gun Can Play*
Valentini, Mariella 257
Valerii, Tonino 139, 177
Valley of the Lions 207; see also *Ursus nella valle dei leoni*
Valley of the Stone Men 98; see also *Perseo L'invincibile*

The Vampires 245; see also *I vampiri*
I vampiri 245; see also *The Devil's Commandment*; *Evil's Commandment*; *The Vampires*
Van Cleef, Lee 67, 74, 76, 155
Vandor, Ivan 301
Vanina Vanini 206; see also *The Betrayer*
Vanzina, Stefano 24, 94, 112, 137, 151, 157, 169, 212, 264, 274
Vatican 81, 106, 302
Venantini, Venantino 236, **239**
Vendetta dal futuro 278; see also *Hands of Steel*
Il venditore di morte 69; see also *Last Gunfight*; *Price of Death*
Venezuela 257
Vengeance Is Mine 253, 302; see also *Per 100.000 dollari t'ammazzo*
Venturini, Giorgio 36
Verdone, Carlo 150, 300
Vertigo 28
La via della droga 157; see also *The Heroin Busters*
Il viaggio 16; see also *The Voyage*
Vidor, King 300
Vietnam 116, 185, 193, 201, 228, 271
Vietnam War *see* Vietnam
Vighi, Vittorio 88
Villaggio, Paolo 18, 213, 236, 297
Vincenzoni, Luciano 74, 228
Violent City 170, 299; see also *Roma violenta*
Violent Naples 25, 43, 46, 47, 48; see also *Napoli violenta*
Violent Rome 170, 299; see also *Roma violenta*
The Violent Professionals 42, 261, 265, 266, 274, 275, 282, 293; see also *Milano Trema: La polizia vuole giustizia*
Violent Rome 170, 299
Visconti, Luchino 118, 131, 250, 256, 299
La vita a volte è molto dura vero Provvidenza? 67, 80, 102; see also *Life Is Tough, Eh Providence?*; *Sometimes Life Is Hard—Rights, Providence?*
Due vite, un destino 115, **123**; see also *The Final Contract*
I vitelloni 39
Vitti, Monica 16, 39
Una viuda difícil (A Difficult Widow) 178
Viva Cangaceiro 302; see also *The Magnificent Bandits*; *O'Cangaceiro*
Viva l'Italia! 206; see also *Garibaldi*
Viva Zapata! 74

Vivarelli, Piero 30, 36, 143, 144, 153, 201, 209
von Sternberg, Josef 44, 297
Vortice mortale 230; see also *The Washing Machine*
The Voyage 16; see also *Il viaggio*
Vulpiani, Mario **83**
Wages of Sin 271
Wait Until Dark 166
Wallach, Eli 13, 117, 163
Ward, Simon 90, 300
The Warning 298; see also *L'avvertimento*
The Warriors 160
Warriors of the Wasteland 160; see also *I nuovi barbari*
The Washing Machine 230, 231; see also *Vortice mortale*
Waszyński, Michal 10
Waves of Lust 214, **215**; see also *Ondata di piacere*
Wayne, John 98, 131, 181
We Two Alone 114; see also *Noi due soli*
Weapons of Death 132, **133**; see also *Napoli spara!*
Welcome to Spring Break 55; see also *La spiaggia del terrore*
Well Then, I Mean ... I Won't Tell Her 151; see also *Al limite cioè ... non glielo dico*
Welles, Orson 31, 44, 68, 73, 79, 80, 81, **82**
Wertmuller, Lina 219
Wertmuller, Massimo 151
What a Night! 12; see also *Che notte, ragazzi!*
What Have They Done to Your Daughters? 264; see also *La polizia chiede aiuto*
The Whip and the Body 268, **269**; see also *La frusta e il corpo*
White Slave 224; see also *Schiave bianche—violenza in Amazzonia*
White Squall 259
The White, the Yellow, and the Black 69; see also *Il bianco, il giallo, il nero*
Whitman, Stuart 90, 104
Who's Afraid of Zorro 185; see also *Ah si? E io lo dico a Zzzzorro*
The Wild Bunch 158
Wilde, Cornel 29
Wilder, Billy 12, 20, 297
William Morris Agency 12, 14, 100, 116
William Tell (film) 10; see also *Guglielmo Tell*
Williams, Esther 31, 32
Williamson, Fred 156, 171, 172, 240, 241

Wilson, Richard 31
The Witch of Colombraro 72; see also *La strega di Colombraro*
Witchcraft 56; see also *La casa 4*
Witchery 56; see also *La casa 4*
The Witch's Curse 251; see also *Maciste all'inferno*
Without Trace 132, 264; see also *a tutte le auto della polizia...*
Wolff, Frank 162, 165
World War II 2, 3, 7, 10, 11, 12, 21, 31, 33, 35, 45, 46, 49, 53, 65, 69, 70, 71, 83, 90, 99, 100, 126, 127, 128, 131, 161, 166, 177, 199, 203, 212, 245, 250, 289, 294, 302
Worse for Me...Better for You! 211; see also *Peggio per me ... meglio per te!*
Wyler, William 37, 40, 136

Yakumo (Amazon tribe) 288
Yanumano (Amazon tribe) 288
Yates, Peter 157
York, Michael 235
Yorke, Carl Gabriel 199
Young, Terence 168, 301
Young, Violent and Desperate 112; see also *Liberi, armati, pericolosi*
Young, Violent, Dangerous 112, 121, **122**, 123; see also *Liberi, armati, pericolosi*
Your Vice Is a Locked Room and Only I Have the Key 263, 266, 271, **274**; see also *Il tuo vizio è una stanza chiusa e solo io ne ho la chiave*
Yugoslavia 29, 180, 182

Zabriskie Point 145, 300
Zagarino, Frank 174
Zampa, Luigi 91, 94
Zeglio, Primo 126
Zenabel 211, 213
Zingarelli, Italo 4, 57, 95, 96, 117, 165, 231, 247, 258
Zombi Holocaust 299, 302; see also *Doctor Butcher M.D.*; *Zombie Holocaust*; *Zombie 3*
Zombi 2 173; see also *Zombie Flesh Eaters*
Zombie Flesh Eaters 173; see also *Zombi 2*
Zombie Holocaust 299, 302; see also *Zombi Holocaust*
Zombie 3 299, 302; see also *Zombi Holocaust*
zombies 52, 54, 63, 173, 225, 226, 236, 237, 238, 239, 243, 244, 290, 291, 299, 302
Zorro 36, 37, 127, 130, 185
Zorro contro Maciste 36; see also *Samson and the Slave Queen*

www.ingramcontent.com/pod-product-compliance
Lightning Source LLC
Chambersburg PA
CBHW081538300426
44116CB00015B/2673